THE AUTHOR

Rich DiSilvio's broad spectrum of historical knowledge and analytical insights have been well regarded by professors, historians, theologians, and publishers, including John J. LaCorte PhD. of Philosophy, H.W. Brands, Dr. Gilda Rorro Baldassari, and Truby Chiaviello, among others. He attended two colleges and an art academy, being mentored by a protégé of Norman Rockwell.

Throughout his professional life, DiSilvio has engaged several fields, having been an architectural designer/remodeler, artist, illustrator, new media developer, educational software programmer, journalist, and a multi-award-winning author of thrillers/mysteries, historical fiction, Sci-Fi/fantasy and children's books.

Some of DiSilvio's endeavors include pioneering the first interactive CD-ROM for training educators how to teach children with autism. The Autism Academy software premiered in 1999 and appeared in Newsday. He has also worked on projects for historical documentaries, films, and cable TV shows, including James Cameron's *The Lost Tomb of Jesus, Killing Hitler: The True Story of the Valkyrie Plot, The War Zone* series, *Return to Kirkuk, Operation Valkyrie, Monty Python: Almost the Truth, Tracey Ullman's State of the Union* and numerous others.

His work in the music and entertainment industries includes commentaries on the great composers (such as the top-rated Franz Liszt Site), and the Pantheon of Composers porcelain collection, which he conceived and created for the Metropolitan Opera.

Meanwhile, his artwork and new media projects have graced the album covers and animated advertisements for numerous super groups and celebrities, including, Elton John, Cher, Pink Floyd, Yes, The Moody Blues, Madonna, Willie Nelson, Johnny Cash, Miles Davis, Janet Jackson, Alice Cooper, Queen and many more.

Rich lives in New York with his wife Eileen and has four children

THE WINDS of TIME

AN ANALYTICAL STUDY OF THE TITANS WHO SHAPED WESTERN CIVILIZATION

From and For a New American Perspective

MASTER EDITION
Featuring Commentaries & Biographies

RICH DISILVIO

Copyright © 2008 by Rich DiSilvio
All Rights Reserved. No part of this book may be used or
reproduced in any manner whatsoever without written permission,
except in the case of brief quotations embodied in critical articles or reviews.
Published ℗ 2009 by DV Books, an imprint of Digital Vista, Inc.
Printed in the USA.

Cover art, jacket design, and interior book layout by © Rich DiSilvio.
Photographs by Rich DiSilvio, purchased collections or
courtesy of Wikipedia's public domain images.

ISBN-13: 978-0-9817625-2-4

DV Books
Digital Vista, Inc.
New York, USA

www.DVBooks.net

WWW.RICHDISILVIO.COM

CONTENTS

ix. – FOREWORD

13. – 48 BC. PRELUDE: A New Dawn

31. – I. AD 14. AUGUSTUS - The Birth of the Roman Empire

    Intro | Roman Republic vs. Greek Democracy | Transition and Octavian's Rise to Power | The New Age of Augustus | Commentary on the Roman and American Empires | Augustus Reprise

112. – II. AD 73. VESPASIAN & SONS - New Blood

    Intro | Titus *– Masada and Judaism | Polytheism vs. Monotheism* Rome & Religion - Judea & Jesus *|* JESUS *|* St. Paul *|* Irenaeus

188. – III. AD 122. HADRIAN - The Need for Borders

205. – IV. AD 325. CONSTANTINE - Conversion of a Man, an Empire, and Ultimately Western Civilization

    Intro | Christianity: *The Rise and Domination of the Roman Catholic Church | The Interpretation of Scriptures | The Influences of Greek Philosophy and Pagan Traditions | Analyzing Christianity | Constantine Reprise and Final Assessment | Who Truly is God?*

294. – V. PART 1: 1320 – 1600. MIDDLE AGES AND THE AGE OF REBIRTH

    The Spark at Dawn
    Dante *– Morals, the Italian language and literature*
    The Radiant Light
    Da Vinci *– The Renaissance Man*
    Debunking Modern Revisions of the Renaissance
    The Medici: *True Architects of the Renaissance*
    Gutenberg *– Dissemination*

BRUNELLESCHI – *Engineering*
COLUMBUS – *Exploration*
A New World - Its American Name - Its Detractors
KING FERDINAND – *Spanish Empire*
QUEEN ELIZABETH I – *English Empire*
SHAKESPEARE – *English Literature*
GALILEO – *Mathematics & Censorship*

390. – PART 2: 1480. POPES, THE BORGIAS, AND THE MEDICI
NEPOTISM AND CORRUPTION

THE BORGIAS: *The Pernicious Pope and Devious Duke*
Leonardo Da Vinci as Borgia's Military Engineer
NICCOLO MACHIAVELLI: *Pragmatic Political Guru*
MARTIN LUTHER: *Protestant against Catholic Corruption*
THE MEDICI: *In the Crosshairs of the Catholic Church*
SAVONAROLA: *Transient Theocratic Ruler and*
Precursor to Martin Luther

418. – VI. 1492 – 1812. AMERICA: THE NEW WORLD –
THE NEW ROME

Intro | *The Founders:* SAMUEL ADAMS, THOMAS PAINE,
GEORGE WASHINGTON, JOHN ADAMS, THOMAS JEFFERSON,
JAMES MADISON, ALEXANDER HAMILTON AND BEN FRANKLIN

476. – VII. 1800 – 1900. DARWIN, MARX, AND FREUD
EVOLUTION, REVOLUTION, AND PSYCHOLOGICAL SCIENCES

Intro | *Communism:* MARX, LENIN AND STALIN |
Psychological Sciences: SIGMUND FREUD |
Evolution vs. Creation: CHARLES DARWIN

499. – VIII. 1900 – 1937. MARCONI - RADIO AND WIRELESS,
GLOBAL & SPACE COMMUNICATIONS

506. – IX. 1889 – 1945. HITLER - POVERTY, PROPAGANDA,
POWER AND HATRED

The Influences of Art and Music

528. – X. 1933 – 1945. ROOSEVELT & CHURCHILL –
SAVIORS OF WESTERN CIVILIZATION

559. – XI. 1880 – 1955. EDISON & EINSTEIN –
THE ELECTRO-ATOMIC AGE

ELECTRIC: EDISON, VOLTA, BELL, TESLA & WESTINGHOUSE
ATOMIC: FERMI, EINSTEIN & VON BRAUN

583. – XII. 1950 – 2009. KENNEDY & McCARTHY– TO THE PRESENT
THE CHARADE OF CAMELOT | THE CRUSADE AGAINST COMMUNISM
FROM COMMUNISM TO ISLAM

JOHN F. KENNEDY: *Charismatic yet Reckless Leader*
McCARTHY & REAGAN: *Crusaders Against Communism*
AFRICAN AMERICANS: *Slavery and Civil Rights*
MODERN PRESIDENTS: *Strength vs. Weakness*
RICHARD NIXON: *Scandal and the Scapegoat*
JIMMY CARTER: *Given the Reins after a Republican Debacle*
RONALD REAGAN: *Reviver of a Demoralized Nation*
OSAMA BIN LADEN: *Islamic Jihad and American Weakness*
BILL CLINTON: *Dismantler of State Security + Moral Vacuum = Disasters*
GEORGE W. BUSH: *Prejudged by Speech and Academic Grades* |
UNDERSTANDING ISLAM | *Religious Cowboy vs. Religious Fanatics*

THE IMPETUS FOR GREAT LEADERSHIP &
CLOSING COMMENTARY FOR AMERICANS

703. – EPILOGUE

704. – PHOTOS/ILLUSTRATIONS

717. – ACKNOWLEDGEMENTS

719. – BIBLIOGRAPHY

723. – INDEX

FOREWORD

The historical stage of Western civilization is filled with a dazzling cast of megastars. They have all lived their lives full throttle, for good or evil, and have not only changed the ideologies and societies of their own time, but have also laid the framework for shaping future ones. Their stories, therefore, are crucial for all generations to study.

As such, this book was written in hope of appealing to a broader audience, beyond those who already have an appreciation of history and propensity to read about it. It appears that books nowadays face a much harder task of attracting readers, being pitted against countless cable TV channels, the Internet, and numerous other rich forms of media. Therefore, this book was designed to be easily readable, enjoyable and enlightening, yet, be forewarned, it will tackle tough and often taboo topics to give as clear, factual, and unsugarcoated a reporting as possible.

This book primarily consists of informal commentaries that examine and assess various individuals, cultures, and eras. There will be frequent moments of reflection that draw upon previous or future events to illustrate new correlations worthy of consideration, quite often to compare and contrast past events or individuals with those of modern America. Infused within these commentaries will be condensed and more formal biographies of select figures.

Although this book proceeds chronologically, it is not one continuous story; rather it is made up of many different stories linked together, as there are considerable gaps of time between certain outstanding characters in history. However, each chapter ends with a transitional segment that joins the gaps and manifests continuity, whereby the reader experiences a whole sweeping story that is organized, chronological and makes sense of the grand epic of time. Additionally, some chapters do build upon or make references to material from previous chapters; therefore, the ideal method is to proceed from start to finish; however the reader may target specific chapters of interest, like a textbook, if they so desire.

When drawing up the blueprint for this work, certain figures were selected above others for their significant actions that have directly influenced or intrinsically mirrored modern events. Naturally, there have been far too many people and influences to include between the covers of this book, necessitating major extractions from this sweeping tale and focusing on events that were deemed most crucial to our civilization's progress. Likewise, these highlights feature lessons that are the most relevant to modern minds, particularly those of Americans, who are the prime target of this work.

It is critical that Americans learn from history in order to avoid the pitfalls of the past, as well as emulate our forebears' most effective solutions. In essence, many of the difficulties that we face today, to some degree, mirror those of the past, for sadly enough, history does repeat itself.

This book's intent, however, is also to make us pause and reflect upon how real and influential so many characters of history were—brilliance, foibles, and all—for their influence still has the power to motivate us.

It is my belief that the winds of time, which carry both influences and warnings, bear the most crucial aspect of the human story, for without being influenced by someone or something from the past, one cannot be motivated to move forward to build a better tomorrow. Therefore, may the winds begin.

THE WINDS of TIME

48 BC. PRELUDE – A New Dawn

The heavens cracked as primal winds screamed down and mysteriously masticated the earth below. Egypt's southern skies moaned a fateful cry, while heatedly masked in the east, the fiery Sun disc rose.

Echoing this celestial turmoil was the debilitating discord and segregation of mankind below. Across the Mediterranean, on the Roman peninsula, a new world order had emerged five centuries previous. Yet, far greater change was now in the making and upon the distant horizon; for several miles north of this Egyptian sandstorm, stood the Roman general-turned-dictator, Julius Caesar. The year was 48 BC.

Caesar had arrived in Egypt six months earlier in pursuit of his former co-ruler—now his rival—General Pompey. The two had shared an unofficial triumvirate with Crassus, who had died earlier in a vainglorious attempt to imitate his two legendary hero friends. Caesar had previously pulled a bold and daring maneuver by crossing the Rubicon River in order to march his troops toward Rome. This restricted safe zone was in place to ensure that no general would seize the capital city. When the Senate ordered Caesar to stand down so they could prosecute him for prior crimes against the state, Caesar was enraged, as he uttered ominously, *"The die is cast."* With ambition and an ego greater than any living being of his day, Caesar crossed the Rubicon and double-crossed the mighty Roman Republic.

Many of Pompey's soldiers deserted him and fled to Caesar's camp, leaving Pompey no option but to flee his homeland and head east toward Greece to amass troops. He had hoped to secure the allegiance of soldiers in the western provinces of Hispania in order to crush Caesar from both sides, but Caesar beat him to the draw. Eventually Pompey headed south to Alexandria; he sought refuge there but instead received the death sentence. Unbeknownst to him, the Egyptian boy-king, Ptolemy XIII, knew of Caesar's manhunt and terrifying reputation, and opted to appease the legendary Roman. As such, Pompey was brutally beheaded.

No sooner did Caesar's feet touch the sandy African shore, than he was presented with the severed head of his fallen foe. To King Ptolemy's surprise, Caesar was deeply distressed by the gesture. As far as Caesar was concerned, a Roman general, especially one respected by fellow Romans and a former colleague, should not be decapitated by a foreigner, regardless of good intent or political kowtowing.

Caesar's grief and suspicions, however, were magically purged once he laid eyes upon King Ptolemy's sister, Cleopatra. The charming twenty-two-year-old seductress had ruled as queen alongside her eleven-year-old brother, but due to Ptolemy's power politics and civil disputes, Cleopatra had been dethroned. The ruling family was Macedonian: they were implanted in Egypt after Alexander the Great's death, when no successor was selected and Alexander's generals all scuttled to secure conquered territories. Ptolemy's clan settled in Alexandria and even adopted the Egyptian tradition of pharaohs marrying their sisters to keep power in the family.

Nevertheless, her brother and his controlling court ousted Cleopatra. Defiant and crafty, she covertly wrapped herself in a carpet and had a merchant carry her to the shore to meet Caesar—her intent being to secure an ally. The diva's charms worked, for her winning smile and personality, along with her clever ploy, appealed to the Roman leader, who happened to be thirty years her senior. Despite the huge gap in age, the two rulers' ambitions turned mismatched disparity into magnetic clarity.

Confronted with Ptolemy's insolent act of beheading Pompey and Cleopatra's charms, Caesar made a decision based upon an experienced warrior's perception and a promiscuous lover's heart. He brazenly declared his intention to reinstate Cleopatra, and thus he ignited a small civil war. The battle was brief, as Caesar's legendary forces effectively quashed Ptolemy's. In typical, omnipotent fashion, Caesar placed Cleopatra on the throne, only this time with her even younger brother Ptolemy XIV at her side. Caesar's intention was clear; Egypt was to be led by a woman—Caesar's woman.

Despite the attraction, Caesar was not smitten; instead he understood the benefits of a close alliance with a young ambitious woman, especially one whom he could mold. Further fertilizing their union, Caesar's seed had been planted—Cleopatra soon gave birth to their son,

Caeserion. Caesar had now secured for Rome, if not a full-blown conquest, at least a decisive role in managing Egypt's future.

As Caesar stood in the sandy and turbulent cradle of civilization, he turned away from the chaos of the sandstorm, which suddenly began imploding, and glanced perceptively northward over the crystalline Mediterranean. There he could envision his homeland just across the sea. Caesar certainly understood the significance of his actions, and of Rome's new and glorious path, for he was pivotal in spreading Roman influence to the far reaches of the then known world. One thing was very clear. As the fiery Sun disc rose that day, its luminous rays vaporized the hazy clouds of the past and ushered in a new dawn for civilization.

Egypt's long and mysterious past has always been alluring, yet it has always remained nebulous. Its ancient language and customs were buried under centuries of time and sand, most of which have unfortunately been lost forever. For as early as the second century, the author/philosopher Apuleius lamented, "Oh Egypt! Egypt! Only fables will remain of your knowledge…"

Apuleius' astute judgment was painfully accurate, for the Rosetta Stone, which was the key to unlocking the cryptic language of hieroglyphics, was only found in 1799. The arduous task of unraveling the mysteries of Egypt's long past has proceeded slowly ever since; yet Egyptian culture and its major influence upon the world stage remained, in effect, buried and lost to time, as countless centuries and cultures trampled over its sandy expanses and marched stridently onward.

Even Greece, with its spectacular moments of glory, which pioneered or perfected philosophy, literature, mathematics, athletics, art, and architectural practices, would likewise falter and face the pangs of decline. Unlike the Egyptians, however, Greek influence would live on in spirit, and touch many minds and nations throughout the ages.

Greek civilization was a spark of brilliance that bequeathed a broad array of talent in many fields to the world, as Plato, Aristotle, and Homer, among many others, played a crucial role in shaping Western thought.

However that burning spark faded when Athens fell to the Macedonians. The Hellenistic period continued the grand Greek tradition, yet without enough fervor or organization to rise up to become a superpower. Like the Egyptians and other great cultures of antiquity, they had had their day, and they, too, like the Egyptians, would succumb to Roman conquest. For it would be the Romans who would assemble all these various elements, ingeniously add to the mix, and mold a new civilization that would galvanize the progressive winds of time.

A new dawn had indeed arrived—one that was rough-hewn in many respects—but one that would fully blossom over the next several decades into a golden age that would advance human development in a profusion of ways. The transient and speckled cultures that once appeared in this quadrant of the earth would become fixtures of the past, as a new Roman order took the reins and forcefully united and shaped the future. This began with the remarkable Roman Republic, which had grown larger and stronger over five centuries. Where the Egyptians remained confined to their North African borders and never ventured outward and the Greeks ingeniously developed idealized visions of what might be, the Romans, in contrast, proactively and pragmatically created organized and workable solutions, and created what would be. This was due to several unique and quite liberal-minded reasons.

The Romans astutely used the rich diversity of other cultures' achievements—Etruscan, Sabine, Greek, and Egyptian—yet they significantly and ingeniously built upon those ideas. Historians with a penchant for all things Greek have all too often branded Rome as merely imitating Greece, while negating many other sources of Roman influence. More importantly, however, they have falsely classified many achievements of purely Roman invention as being Greek.

As we shall see, the Romans' expertise exceeded mere adoption. If it were mere adoption or effortless imitation, the Romans would have succumbed to the same fate as their predecessors. But the Romans advanced over many centuries; therefore, there was obviously much more to this massive and complex equation than adoption. As such, we will tackle this equation to reveal the true results of Rome's often miscalculated significance and magnitude over the next few chapters.

The Romans exhibited a genius for innovation, coupled with an indomitable determination that would truly define their culture. For Rome's destiny was to secure a well-organized and solid foundation for Western civilization that none of its predecessors had been able to achieve on their own. This foundation had many components; however, we shall begin with Rome's sophisticated advancements in architecture and engineering that were simply breathtaking. To validate this uniqueness, it is necessary to reveal a few intricate details, and these architectural details have nothing at all to do with Greek columns, posts, and lintels, or even gable roofs.

First were the aqueducts, which gracefully premiered a potent architectural art form. The Romans inaugurated and mastered the arch, which was not only aesthetically pleasing, but was also structurally far more complex and much stronger than a post and lintel. Post and lintels were used by almost every previous culture, as even the archaic ruin of Stonehenge, built almost three millennia before Christ, offers a clear visual of a simple post and lintel configuration. This tried and true method was used by Egyptians and Greeks, as well as every other advanced culture, from China to the far Western hemisphere. Roman arches, by contrast, were not only unique but were also able to withstand far greater loads, as well as being economical and versatile, and this new technique would be drafted into our first Roman marvel—the aqueduct.

These towering structures were manmade rivers that—for the first time in history—allowed mankind to build cities wherever they desired. This triumph of ingenuity eliminated the long held necessity of submitting to the geographical restrictions of nature, and marked a major turning point in human development. In addition to the aqueduct's awe-inspiring sequence of grand arches, which supported these waterways, one must also consider the complexity of the entire project. Because water had to be transported over many miles of mountainous terrain, these towering structures could not run unobstructed from point of origin to final destination. As such, the Romans tunneled through large mountains and installed conduits that enabled the water supply to maintain its trajectory. In other words, as these grand architectural structures intersected mountains, pipelines carried the water straight through and out the far side, where the structure continued its course. At the same time, these lengthy waterways had to maintain a perfect pitch, since the gravity-fed water needed to flow at the proper rate; too fast would cause erosion and too slow would impede flow. All these considerations were miraculous feats of engineering for their day, and all were unique.

So, too, was the Roman invention of concrete. The Assyrians and Babylonians used clay-based concrete, while the Egyptians used lime and gypsum, however all these mixtures were extremely soft and pliable, and were simply too weak, dry, or brittle. They were used as filling materials rather than vital structural components. The Romans, however, devised unique blends of quicklime and pozzolanic ash to formulate a material that once set was as hard as stone, and even water-resistant. This incredible chemical mixture is still essential to all phases of construction today in its slightly variant form, known as Portland cement. Its importance is so crucial—yet sadly taken for granted, even by today's structural engineers—that to envision a modern world without it would be simply impossible.

Concrete enabled the Romans to build much larger and far stronger engineering projects, giving rise to a whole series of innovations: the first permanent stone bridges, their all-important world premiere of paved roads, and even immense public wonders, such as the public baths. These huge basilicas, with lofty vaulted ceilings, are still marvelous by today's engineering standards. Their grand design was so impressive that Union Station in Washington D.C., emulated the Baths of Diocletian, as did New York's Grand Central Station.

More impressive still was that these buildings used advanced hot- and cold-water plumbing. In doing so, the Romans pioneered the modern public's propensity for personal hygiene. This daily practice is something that most people nowadays take for granted, or believe people always engaged in, or had available to them. Yet, such was clearly—or cleanly—not the case. What only the heads of state or the nobility enjoyed in the past, the Romans bequeathed to the public.

Although the earliest forms of plumbing and sewage systems were found in Mohenjo-Daro, India, the Romans greatly improved upon them. They cleverly introduced underground furnaces to heat huge air chambers under water basins, and ventilated this hot air up through conduits inside the walls, producing the first radiant heat system in history. Romans were also mavens at controlling large amounts of water, since these gigantic pools needed to be refilled often; decontamination by chlorine did not yet exist. Channeling thousands of gallons of water became an art and a daily activity; fountains flowed and the Colosseum was flooded and drained for mock sea battles. Moreover, it must be noted that all these huge basins could only be achieved by the use of their special watertight concrete.

Another monumental Roman invention was the dome, its stunning complexity and brilliant ingenuity being well preserved in the Pantheon in Rome. This archetype of all future domes, was a first in world history, and it miraculously still stands in all its glory. Along with this groundbreaking edifice is that other architectural masterwork: the Colosseum. The Colosseum featured many breakthroughs in engineering, and its immense size and unique features have made it an iconic template for architects ever since. Both structures bear out astonishing feats of engineering that were milestones in their era, and continue to remain in practice today.

Adding more beauty to these grand structures was another Roman invention known as the vaulted ceiling. All earlier architecture, such as the Egyptian and Greek post and lintel method, simply used a vertical column supporting a horizontal beam to create a flat ceiling. Due to the brittleness of marble, flat ceilings had to be limited in span and supported by many columns. The Romans' barrel- and groin-vaulted ceilings eliminated those restrictions. The towering ceilings that would grace basilicas, temples, arenas, and even gothic cathedrals in the distant future, would all feature curved vaulted ceilings. These marvelous feats of engineering were more sophisticated than those conceived by all other civilizations before Rome, as well as many that came after. Succeeding architects have often ventured back to Rome to study its refined architecture, as it has remained the ultimate university for architects for well over a thousand years.

The Romans' uniquely arched, barrel-vaulted, groin-vaulted, circular, elliptical, and domed edifices—along with their new building materials and an array of tools, cranes, lifts, and bracing and centering devices, that were all required to construct these huge edifices—were engineering breakthroughs not found in Greek or Egyptian architecture. This not only dispels the notion of Roman adoption of Grecian architecture, but illuminates how many scholars have thus characterized Roman architecture, simply because they used fluted columns or sculptural friezes. It likewise elucidates how these historians lacked architectural and engineering expertise, and worse still, how they distorted many people's understanding of history.

Even a quick test by any nonprofessional validates this entire exercise; that is, simply looking at the Romans' most famous building, the Colosseum, and then at the Greek's most famous building, the Parthenon. The instant visual of an oval building with round arches and vaults compared to a rectangular building with columns and gabled roof essentially sums it up. *(See page 705)*

Roman ingenuity did not stop there, however. The Romans also invented the apartment building, which typifies every modern city today. The apartment complex became the most common form of housing in Roman cities. The buildings were all equipped with indoor plumbing, making seemingly modern standards of living in ancient Rome an astounding first in world history. It's all the more impressive when we consider that in early twentieth century America, many people lived in homes without running water. One such person happened to be the future president, Dwight D. Eisenhower. As a young boy growing up in rural Texas and later Kansas, Dwight had the chore of fetching well water for his family. Meanwhile, Roman citizens, from two millennia prior, enjoyed the convenience of this useful utility.

As Roman families moved away from their country dwellings, to seek the riches and excitement of city life, they inevitably first settled into rented apartments. If they managed to procure wealth, they could then buy a *domus*, which was a single-family townhouse. Future urban planners would often look to ancient Roman cities to draw knowledge, inspiration, and plans.

Equally important was Rome's highly skilled army, its diverse trade, its network of roads, its well-organized government, and its pioneering set of laws. These will be discussed in due course, but all would stand the test of time and become hallmarks for all other Western nations to follow.

Whereas most previous cultures were xenophobic, and remained largely isolated by promoting their own culture and shunning others, the Romans embraced and enhanced other cultures, and ultimately engendered a new approach, whereby expanding ethnic, religious, and cognitive horizons. When we observe how long Rome reigned supreme, we must realize that this system could never have maintained itself if it wasn't well-organized, strong, tolerant, and even liberal. Many today will probably find these last two traits incongruous due to erroneous histories taught in schools, or witnessed on Hollywood's silver screen. Rome has often been portrayed as an oppressive empire, and although it certainly experienced periods of corruption, it simultaneously bequeathed to the world some of the most formidable leaders and a stunning culture with incalculable assets.

It is crucial to emphasize that all civilizations, old and new, have engaged in deceitful and even brutal activities, open or clandestine. Yet Rome is judged more harshly, mainly for two reasons. First, Rome was the mightiest and longest lasting multi-national empire in Western history—multinational since Rome was the first and only empire of antiquity to engulf and successfully unite the most diverse group of ethnic peoples. Egyptian civilization may have lasted longer, but it was confined to one single region with a limited range of ethnicity. In contrast, the prime real estate that Rome acquired included scores of different ethnic races with scores of different traits, religions, cults, and customs. The Roman Empire eventually controlled territories from the western tip of modern Portugal and Morocco, all the way east to Germany, Iraq, and Armenia, as well as from the southern reaches of Egypt and Saudi Arabia, up to the cold northern extremities of England and Scotland. The abilities required to conquer and govern such a vast expanse was and remains staggering. Quite simply, there was nothing like the Roman Empire. Consequently, it has become the ultimate target of those eager to find fault with greatness.

In a similar fashion, America today stands as the world's leader, and it, too, is similarly criticized, especially by many foreign countries. America now stands alone at the top, since the Soviet Union no longer exists to provide a balance of power. As such, America endures more condemnation and disrespect than ever before. This is a natural human phenomenon, and one that instinctively and defensively surfaces to resist and tear down any single entity that wields total power. That's because one reigning entity gives the impression of omnipotence, factual or not, of being achieved solely by open or clandestine subjugation. In summation, greatness always generates contempt.

The second reason is that many people judge ancient Rome by modern standards. A people and their culture must be judged according to their place on history's timeline. Their ethos cannot be expected to mirror ours two millennia later. Naturally, Rome had its dark and ugly side, yet progress is by nature an upward climb: from our height of maturity, we should look back with objective understanding, not scorn; with wisdom, not ignorance. It is unreasonable to expect the thoughts of ancient Romans to mirror ours today in every capacity. Otherwise, why didn't the Romans invent the computer or a cure for polio? The answer is simple; knowledge is an upward progression.

Therefore, we must afford the actors of the past their own unique consideration, especially in light of the fact that they existed many centuries ago. We must also remember that backward and barbaric tribes resided outside the empire's borders: in direct contrast, Rome unquestionably shines as the zenith of culture and civility of its time. Moreover, we should look into our own modern mirror before casting stones at the past. After all, moral issues ascribed to ancient Rome, such as murder, deceit, or slavery has prevailed until recent times. Assassinations still occur, power politics still operate covertly, and slavery existed in "highly civilized" America as recently as 1865.

Some historians have belabored the issue of Roman slavery, yet this, too, needs clarification. Admittedly, the Romans used slave labor, but they invented a practice called *peculium*, whereby masters gave their slaves seed money to start businesses. This allowed slaves to learn valuable trades, develop strong work ethics, learn managing skills, and even keep a percentage of the profits. Most importantly, slaves could eventually buy their freedom. This system benefited both masters, by drawing on an additional source of income, and slaves who could earn solid livings and their freedom. As we know, the ugly practice of slavery had always existed, yet too often modern historians expect the Romans to have leapt through the corridors of time to fully embrace modern sensibilities. However, *peculium* was a respectable and progressive step forward, and was something that even early America never offered.

Rome was a unique entity, and the new dawn that would blossom into a golden age would secure its place upon the timeline of history. This would have a great effect on many subsequent nations, but a very pointed and special role to play for America. Naturally, this topic has significant importance to Americans from both modern and historical perspectives. Many today have made the obvious connection that America is the distant heir of Rome; however, the seeds were actually planted at the very outset of the nation's formation. This special inheritance warrants our brief attention.

One of the primary reasons for this heritage is that America's founding fathers, especially George Washington, Thomas Jefferson, James Madison, Alexander Hamilton, and Benjamin Franklin, wove many Roman traits into the new American canvas. When attempting to construct their fledgling government, each gazed back into the annals of history and drew inspiration from a kaleidoscope of sources—some even fashioned their lives upon the actions of noble Romans.

George Washington consciously emulated the Roman general Cincinnatus, whose selfless actions and honesty he deeply admired. The city of Cincinnati, Ohio was named after this great Roman general in 1788 by The Society of Cincinnati. Cincinnatus was honored chiefly because he was the role model of the nation's new leader, George Washington.

We must bear in mind; in 1775 the United States of America did not exist. Therefore, these courageous men had to find a previous model of government to study and emulate. Most deplored the English monarchy, which by overtaxing them and capitalizing on their hard labor and resources had many, including Washington, resentful of being treated no better than their own slaves. A guideline was needed.

The writings of John Locke, Adam Smith, Aristotle, Cicero, Seneca, Montesquieu, and others played a significant role in their decisions. Locke was especially influential, for he philosophized that sovereignty belongs to the people, and if any government fails to secure those rights, the people have the right to overthrow and replace the government. With a little scrutiny, however, we can see that Locke's provocative concept was gleaned from the ancient Roman statesman, Cicero.

"The name of peace is sweet, and the thing itself is beneficial, but there is a great difference between peace and servitude. Peace is freedom in tranquility; servitude is the worst of all evils, to be resisted not only by war, but even by death." — Cicero

Cicero and Locke's idea of resisting servitude by force resonated deeply with many colonists and was even incorporated into Jefferson's *Declaration of Independence*. Washington, Jefferson, and Hamilton, in particular, realized that Rome was perhaps the best governing body to scrutinize, since the eternal city left a long and enduring legacy. The adoption of the Roman Republic will be addressed more fully in the next chapter; however, despite its obvious failings, Rome as a republic or an empire had much to offer.

The founders' new American republic—and much of Western civilization—adopted its core set of laws from the Romans. In fact, the first Roman laws date back to the Twelve Tables in 450 BC when Rome itself was a republic. Naturally, there were earlier precedents, such as the Code of Hammurabi, originating in Mesopotamia, but the Roman set of laws was far more comprehensive, and as it expanded over time, the laws slowly became more just and civil. The Romans even incorporated laws similar to modern day "lemon laws" that protect buyers, or "intent to kill" clauses used in murder cases. Moreover, in AD 534, the Emperor Justinian compiled and distilled all these laws into his epic *Body of Civil Law*. Except for England, which many centuries after Justinian's efforts devised its common laws, Roman law was adopted by all of Europe and America.

The next influence had a much broader application for many nations throughout the world; its basic and almost subliminal aspect is colossal— the Latin language, which underlies the English tongue. The Romans' belief in divine providence (which was firmly etched in Latin) affected America's founders, having a direct and profound correlation to the creation of the United States. In this instance, it brings to mind the popular expression "by Jove!"

This expression, which has endured for well over two millennia, originated in the legal courts of ancient Rome. Jupiter, also known as Jove, was the Romans' supreme god. He was in charge of ultimate justice, and in Roman courts of law, all citizens swore to Jove to preside over their hearings and testimonies. American courts adopted this practice of swearing to a divine being. Well beyond that single expression, the English language, as well as the romance languages, such as Spanish, French, and Portuguese, all have their roots in Latin. For example, the word school comes from the word *schola*, and the word triumph from *triumphus*.

Moreover, despite the influence of the Greek language, which was largely based upon the Phoenician alphabet, we must remember that English and the romance languages use the Roman alphabet. Even the Greek words that form some of the roots in English and romance languages had been transcribed from Greek into Latin in order to be understood. The enhancements that the early Romans made to their alphabet made it become the most widely used alphabet in the world today. Perhaps this explains why when most Americans look at the Greek alphabet, they are apt to say, "That's Greek to me." The fact is: the very words you are reading now are formed from the Roman alphabet. Therefore, the very ability to read, write, and verbally communicate in English is primarily the gift of the Romans.

Beyond using the Latin-rooted English language—which two-thirds of its words have Latin origins—Americans handle a piece of paper, zinc, or copper everyday with pure Latin inscribed on it. These Latin phrases may appear trivial, but they actually have much deeper implications, for they were carefully adopted from the Romans by the founding fathers. On the back of the dollar bill is a floating eye that radiates light above a pyramid. Inscribed above and below it are two Latin quotes: On top is *Annuit Coeptis*, which means "approve our beginnings," or more commonly, "providence favors our endeavors." That quote came from the *Aeneid*, by the famous Roman poet Virgil, who lived during the rule of Augustus. Virgil's full sentence included a citation to Jupiter, so the founding fathers only used the first two words. Below the pyramid is the Latin phrase, *Novus Ordo Seclorum*, meaning "a new order of the ages."

On the opposite side of the dollar bill is the eagle emblem and the phrase *E Pluribus Unum*, meaning, "out of many, one"—which confirms that America is united. The eagle emblem is also a Roman heirloom. It was the symbol of the Roman god Jupiter, and was prominently displayed throughout the empire, taking on special significance when used on talismans during combat, as it was always prudent to have Jupiter's divine favor.

The use of these phrases and symbol highlight the all-important fact that America's founding fathers wanted to emulate Rome's soaring and majestic power and have their new nation guided by divine providence. Many other regimes throughout history have used Rome's mighty eagle, yet not all have adopted the very significant issue of divine providence. This religious issue has recently become a topic of heated debate, as many conservative Christians have rallied around the notion that the founding fathers created America as a purely Christian nation. Upon examination, however, we will see that the evidence indicates otherwise. The founding fathers could have specified Jesus or some particular deity by name, but clearly decided not to. This holds true in the *Declaration of Independence*, as well as on American currency.

The Latin phrases used on American currency came from the time of pagan Rome, as the author Virgil lived before Jesus was born. However, like Virgil and the Roman government, the founding fathers wanted God to watch over their new nation. That no specific deity was mentioned by name was done purposely to avoid offending or excluding any religion. However, their primary thoughts did center on Judeo/Christian beliefs.

On the opposite side of the religious divide, secularists have claimed that the phrase *Novus Ordo Seclorum* has a different meaning. They agree that *Novus* means new, and *Ordo* means order, but they claim that *Seclorum* means secular, hence "New Secular Order." However, *seclorum* means ages, while the word *secularis* means secular. Therefore, the correct translation is "new order of the ages," appropriately neither secular nor religious. The founders had wisely declined favoritism and defused conflict, despite the interpretation of those who feel entitled to incite conflict.

Other factions have recently claimed that the floating eye above the pyramid is a Masonic symbol. Yet it had appeared in ancient Egyptian and even early Christian times, long before the Masons or the American government adopted it. We can only assume from its long history and multiple uses that it relates to the eye of providence, that which looks over and protects its presiding religion.

Beyond these linguistic and divine roots, America also adopted certain trivial Roman customs, which many today unwittingly follow. One actually came from the infamous Rape of the Sabines from early Roman lore. Firstly, the term "rape," at that time meant seize or capture, not the definition we use today. The early Roman settlers needed women, and when refused by the Sabine rulers, they slyly lured women to a feast. In all likelihood, plenty of wine flowed and they romanced the young women; no doubt many were forcefully seized and carried off to the men's bedchambers. How many went with their captors unwillingly is unknown, but the Romans did manage to marry off many young couples, ensuring the growth of the budding nation. The act of young men literally carrying their young brides into their bedrooms started the long tradition of a groom carrying his new bride over the threshold.

However, Roman culture had a far more profound influence on America when the founding fathers opted to emulate Romulus, the founder of Rome. Romulus established his city as an asylum where the dispossessed or downtrodden could find solace, and more importantly, have the opportunity to prosper. This displayed a strikingly innovative and tolerant mindset, especially for those times, as every other nation or tribe had always maintained its own culture and routinely shunned outsiders. Yet this gave the new city a diversity that no other had, as the influx of various peoples, like the Etruscans to the north—who were highly skilled at working with water and sewers—and the Sabines, with their religion and Vestal Virgins, and the Greeks with their artisans and academics all made for a fertile atmosphere of exchange. This openminded acceptance of various peoples, their foreign ideologies, and skill sets contributed significantly to Rome becoming the ultimate superpower of its age; and only one modern nation has truly mirrored that Roman "melting pot" ideology—America.

Other connections between Rome and America will appear throughout this book, but Rome's influence exceeded affecting only America, making it the prime prototype that many nations attempted to emulate. Equally enlightening will be how the Romans, while under the leadership of broad-minded rulers, maintained an open and tolerant policy on religion that allowed many religions and cults to flourish, while also welcoming foreign deities into their own pantheon of gods.

This new dawn also bequeathed a booming economy, where widespread trade and commerce among many different ethnic peoples became another trademark of Roman unity and organization. Simply put, Rome was a miraculous entity on the world stage when Julius Caesar arrived. Throughout the previous seven hundred years, the tiny village of Rome had gradually grown so that it was brimming with even greater potential. Julius Caesar recognized that these new horizons needed to be accurately tracked and recorded in the annals of time, which is why Caesar vowed to take action.

The lack of precision in tracking time affected all ancient cultures. Different calendars arose geographically and therefore were calculated using different methodologies. Some used the seasons, others the cycles of the moon. Over time, the lunar calendar took precedence, but even it failed to account for annual natural events, such as the flooding of the Nile, which were crucial to record to ensure a robust harvest. The ancient Egyptians finally settled on a calendar with 12 months, 30 days each, totaling 360 days per year. They realized afterwards that their calculations did not coincide with the solar year, so they added five extra days at the end of each year. But that, too, proved inaccurate.

Later the early Romans devised a calendar fraught with even more complexities. Due to their superstition against even numbers, they added another month called Mercedonius. This inaccurate calendar prompted Julius Caesar to take action, and in 45 BC, Caesar's new calendar with 12 months, containing 30–31 days each, was established.

The months were named after Roman gods—January from *Janus*, March from *Mars*, June from *Juno*—or Latin numbers: *septem* meaning seven, *decem* meaning ten. July was named after Julius himself, and later when his adopted son, Augustus, became emperor, his name graced the month of August.

Additionally, the days of the week also contain the names of Roman gods, whose names referred to planets—Saturn becoming Saturday; the goddess Luna, or moon, becoming Monday. Centuries later, German names replaced the other days of the week, such as Tuesday, which was originally named after the Roman god of war, Mars, being later named after the Germanic pagan god of war, Tyr. Hence, all the days of the week originate from pagan Rome, in one form or another.

Moreover, Julius decreed that the new year begin on January 1, not as it had previously on the vernal equinox in March. Janus was honored for all sorts of beginnings, such as birth or marriage, as well as for healthy harvests, and so January marked the beginning of the new year. The shifting of months explains why December, meaning ten, became the twelfth month. Therefore the Julian calendar that was bequeathed to the world was aptly named after its organizational architect, Julius Caesar.

In contrast, for centuries, most of the Eastern Arab world used an ancient calendar that had a lunar year of only 354 days, with the result that their religious festivals shifted throughout the seasons of each year. However, the Arab's neighbors, the Greek Eastern Orthodox churches, kept their original Julian calendar, which is still used to this day.

It is interesting that even after Christianity gained control of world affairs and clergymen attempted to slightly manipulate the calendar, the pagan Roman names, numerals, gods, and planets, as well as the names of two pagan Roman leaders, have remained intact. This is all the more remarkable since several emperors attempted to change the names of some of the months based on their own. The megalomaniac, Emperor Commodus, went even further and boldly changed the entire calendar by labeling each month with one of his nicknames. However, since it was a *solar* calendar, Commodus' *lunacy* met with a fatal eclipse. The mad ruler was poisoned and strangled to death, and all his playful, moonstruck names were scratched off the solar calendar. The only names to have stood the test of time are those of Julius and Augustus. Therefore, with great and enduring impact, the essential calendar of Western civilization dawned with Julius Caesar.

Julius Caesar had his own shortcomings. Although he was an unrivalled and greatly admired general, who expanded the Republic with countless triumphs, his excessive ambition and greed dictated his demise.

Caesar selfishly terminated the Roman Republic, and after four years of dictatorship under his rule, the senators conspired for his assassination. On the Ides of March, in 44 BC, Caesar was brutally killed; thus began a decade-long incubation period during which senators, generals, and royal families all feverishly jockeyed for power. These were turbulent times, and a new leader was vitally needed to establish order and create a new and stable form of government.

Rome was at a critical crossroads, and amid a formidable array of powerful warriors and brilliant statesmen, one man rose to give birth to a completely new era. Actually, he was only a teenager when he began his grand and noble quest, yet he prevailed against tremendous odds, and created an amazing enterprise that would profoundly imprint itself upon all future generations. This young man, born Gaius Octavius, and later exalted as Augustus, has been justifiably called "The Father of Western Civilization."

I

AD 14. AUGUSTUS - The Birth of the Roman Empire

Intro | Roman Republic vs. Greek Democracy | Transition and Octavian's Rise to Power | The New Age of Augustus | Commentary on the Roman and American Empires | Augustus Reprise
(Unum, Aries, Asher, Peter, January)

The life-giving gas rapidly expanded his tiny virgin lungs, after a brisk slap on the back. Thus was Gaius Octavius' first breath of life free from the womb. He would soon learn that it would be an endless struggle to maintain this precious gift, and that even though every breath one takes is by one's own effort, a supportive slap on the back is crucial to survival.

The unassuming yet determined country boy had played his cards extremely well. He had learned to buttress his own ambition with solid friendships and a natural ability to politick with a variety of people, from common plebeians to the intelligentsia, and from military rivals to manipulative senators. Now in his twilight years, the great emperor, who had come to be called Augustus, or most exalted as the name implies, found himself in the fortunate position of being able to look back and reflect upon his long and illustrious career.

Augustus' early rise to power was marked by many near-death engagements on the battlefield, as well as in the perfidious political arena. With the lifelong aid of his most trusted general and loyal right-hand man, Marcus Agrippa, he had secured many years of peace to calmly reflect upon and cherish with a ripened grin. Priding himself on his earthy good sense, disdain for the ostentatious, and a paternal persona that would guide and elevate an entire empire, Augustus established what he believed was the only solution to a corrupt and war-ridden Rome. His decisions proved right: he presided over a renewed golden age for over four long decades and had made Rome the wonder of the world. Augustus had much to be proud of. *(Photo page 704)*

However, Augustus was not worry free. The hands of time had stridently clicked, and with each new click came a challenging new obstacle, and with each new glorious triumph came the gnawing sound of his aging mortal clock, which grew irritatingly louder, offering a constant reminder that even titans, with their godlike powers, are destined to die. Hence, the burning question remained, to whom should Augustus entrust his glorious Empire?

With three bloodline heirs prematurely dead, Augustus was forced to consider his wife Livia's austere son, Tiberius, from her former matrimonium. Livia Drusilla was a strong and manipulative mother who wanted nothing more than to see her son take the reins, especially after losing her youngest son, and backup, Drusus. Nevertheless, Augustus had doubts; he knew Tiberius was a competent general—who even won a hard victory in the Pannonia campaign—but beyond his taciturn personality, Tiberius had caused Augustus much embarrassment when he petulantly ran off to Rhodes. Tiberius later explained that his self-imposed exile was predicated on his apprehension to interfere with his younger relatives, who were all chosen contenders for the throne.

Marcellus had been the first groomed for succession, being Augustus' nephew by means of his sister Octavia. However in 23 BC, at age twenty-one, his early death deeply grieved Augustus, who was left searching for a replacement. Marcus Agrippa had been the obvious choice during their early empire-building years, yet as the years passed, Augustus yearned for a bloodline heir. Agrippa had selflessly stepped out of the way, but with Marcellus dead, Augustus proposed a traditional solution. He would honor his good friend and maintain his Caesarian bloodline by offering Agrippa his daughter Julia in marriage.

The couple soon gave birth to Gaius and then Lucius who were immediately adopted by Augustus for proper protection and political grooming. Twenty years transpired and Livia had done her part in bringing up the boys. However, unforeseen events ruined Augustus' clever plans once again, as Lucius died of illness in AD 2, while Gaius died in AD 4 from a battle wound. Despite rumors of foul play, which were never substantiated, Augustus was now left with little choice. Thus Tiberius, by luck and default, would inherit Augustus' massive labor of love—the Roman Empire. With Augustus' tough decision finally made, the emperor, or in reality *princeps*, would resume grooming Tiberius, only this time in earnest, to be his successor.

The term *princeps* (meaning *preeminent* not dictator) was an extremely important one, and one often overlooked or flatly discarded by historians. Although Augustus is universally lauded as the first Roman Emperor, in reality, that title was adamantly rejected, and even deplored, by Augustus. In fact, it was his successor Tiberius that first adopted the title *imperator*, or emperor. Meanwhile, Augustus prudently understood the finer mechanics of how his government and its Senatorial leaders operated, not to mention the important ability to not only gauge the pulse of the people but also serve their needs. As such, these special qualities must be addressed.

Augustus, like all Romans, deeply admired the quality of *virtue*, and the man who perhaps best exemplified that noble quality was the Roman statesman/farmer Cincinnatus. When the early Roman Republic was under siege, they beckoned him out of retirement and appointed him dictator to secure Rome from conquest. Cincinnatus left his plow and fought a winning campaign for the Republic, only to magnanimously decline leadership in its aftermath. This selfless and patriotic gesture resonated deeply with Romans, and the man who most blatantly dishonored that virtuous deed was Julius Caesar, Augustus' great-uncle. Henceforth, Augustus wisely understood the ramifications of a big ego, as did America's first president, George Washington, who, two millennia later, likewise championed the venerable qualities of Cincinnatus.

Therefore, Augustus vowed never to exalt his own ego over the thing he valued most, and that was his beloved city-turned-empire—Rome. This is clearly evident by Augustus' new brand of empire that advocated progress and bestowed grand public works for the betterment of all Roman citizens. This was in stark contrast to the great Egyptian pharaohs. The grand pyramids may have been magnificent, they may have touched the sky, and they certainly consumed a nation's time and resources, but these towering monstrosities only housed one little selfish and shriveling man, who, worse yet, callously neglected the needs of an entire nation so that he alone could be glorified. Meanwhile, Augustus' intention was to share the glories of Rome with the rest of the world, by building grand forums, markets, temples, aqueducts and roads wherever he traveled. These gifts that Augustus bequeathed to all Roman citizens are as impressive as they are crucial for modern readers to understand.

Through instinct and observation, Augustus knew his new empire needed a new frame of mind, as well as initiatives not employed by the Egyptians or any previous regime. Augustus was not what we today would call a well-groomed intellect, however, his innate common sense, extremely organized and analytical mind, along with the ability to learn from his and other's mistakes, made his efforts and achievements beyond brilliant. During Augustus' careful and precarious rise to ultimate power, he had wisely left the Senate and Republican infrastructure intact, albeit with some clever revisions. These policies all had clear objectives.

Firstly, Augustus understood the deep political roots and social-economic pedigree of wealthy patricians. They had held and maintained their positions of power for many decades, with some senators like Brutus having family trees extending back 500 years to the founding of the Republic itself. As such, they and their entrenched network would not easily relinquish power. Caesar had arrogantly underestimated them and it proved fatal.

Henceforth, Augustus needed to purge the Senate of those who plotted against his adoptive father; those who remained needed to be cajoled and placated, which could not be achieved by arm-twisting or arrogantly stripping them of power. Furthermore, the Roman citizens of the day had had enough of civil strife. Over the previous two decades they had been dizzied by having to take sides with one potential usurper after another. Loyalties were strained and national enthusiasm drained. Therefore, it was prudent of Augustus to leave the Senate, and its web of influence, intact to some degree.

Secondly, Augustus knew that more than one person with a handful of cohorts was needed to run a sprawling empire. The bureaucratic infrastructure that worked so well for the Republic would serve him well too, as long as he made continual subtle revisions that would wrest the ultimate and abused power from the aristocracy.

Thirdly, and quite ingeniously, Augustus realized the importance of creating a new cultural identity for his government that he could share with all the Roman provinces. In an act of perceptive statesmanship and benevolence, Augustus bequeathed what was available in the illustrious capital city to the distant provinces. This extensive policy had many cultivating facets.

To Augustus, it meant that all newly acquired provinces would be outfitted with the utilitarian effectiveness and the grandness that Rome itself enjoyed—this would be an integral part of the glue binding a sprawling and diverse populace. Grand forums, public markets, housing with running water, public baths with spectacular saunas, and other cutting edge facilities not only improved the standard of living, but equally important, it elicited pride of community and Roman culture.

This psychologically effective technique was not lost on subsequent leaders, even those well beyond Rome, and would influence many European nations and America in the distant future. Not only did the American founding fathers emulate Roman architecture and city planning, but even today, the construction of shopping malls and familiar franchises sprawling across America is unifying the nation, visually and psychologically. There is a downside to this trend—namely, the decline of uniqueness—but the mission of spreading unity, national identity, and different forms of progress is achieved.

Additionally, to display his admiration for Rome's illustrious past, Augustus decorated his forum with a line of statues, each honoring a famous general or statesman. Without television or other forms of media, a public display was far more than political posturing: it was historically educational and it built admiration and loyalty to Roman tradition and the state. It also displayed Augustus' humility and respect for other great leaders. As time would tell, many other rulers became megalomaniacs and showed their true colors by only erecting statues of themselves; Nero and Saddam Hussein come to mind.

The guiding principles of Roman law also served to instill the rich Roman culture in the new provinces. Written and enforced rules of conduct, ethics, and morals cultivated greater harmony among people who often did not have sense or regard for justice. In tandem with codes of civil law was Rome's comforting yet perfunctory religious tradition, which Augustus took great care in fostering.

As noted, the empire consisted of a diversity of peoples with many ancient traditions and rituals, and these were warmly accepted, with some aspects being infused into the Romans' own broadening tradition. Part of this influx included superstitions from a variety of ancient cultures. Even Augustus relied upon sealskin for luck—a variant of having a rabbit's foot—and examined the flights of birds or dead animals' entrails for omens. However, their elastic model of religious belief would be severely tested in due time, as the monotheist Jews grew more restless and the genesis of a new sect, called the Christians, would make seismic waves.

Like his adoptive father Julius, Augustus realized that a larger and more strongly united brotherhood of Romans was mandatory for survival, since organized forces in greater numbers become dominant and more effective. Without it, their entire culture would risk annihilation or a digressive dissolution. Caesar had conquered Gaul and other smaller territories that enlarged the Republic, and following that tradition, Augustus made twenty-one successful conquests, whereby surpassing Caesar's acquisitions and boldly doubling the size of the Roman Empire. This tremendous feat by Augustus is often overlooked, as most are distracted by the tougher victories won by Julius Caesar, who was not only a superior military leader, but one of the world's best. Nevertheless, the size and influence of the Roman Empire gained its most potency under the Augustan regime.

However, in his latter years, Augustus painfully experienced the ruthless resistance of the Germanic tribes just over the Rhine when they annihilated Publius Varus and three Roman legions. Augustus rightfully understood that these backward tribesmen would not assimilate to Roman life, and in his will, he advised his successors not to pursue conquest in this region, knowing firsthand the threat to security that barbarians posed. Expansion was necessary, but so, too, was prudence and forbearance.

Augustus' motive in building the size and strength of his empire went beyond ambition. Over eighteen hundred years later, Charles Darwin would say, "Hence, the more common forms, in the race for life, will tend to beat and supplant the less common forms." The Romans and particularly Augustus intuitively understood the Darwinian principle of survival of the fittest. Augustus also knew that a standing army was essential for Rome's survival, as he quickly surmised that volunteer armies lacked the skill, dedication and training of an effective war machine. Fifteen hundred years later, Niccolo Machiavelli would commit this military philosophy to paper, and a little over two hundred years after that, Alexander Hamilton would echo the same concerns to a new and vulnerable nation. Like Julius Caesar, however, Augustus stipulated that the military must be under the ruler's sole command as a precaution against external and internal threats. The emphasis on maintaining military control and superiority clearly echoed in Julius Caesar's historic line, *"Veni, vidi, vici"*—"I came, I saw, I conquered!"

As a ruler, Augustus inaugurated many exceptional and unique policies: he had learned a great deal by observing his great-uncle, who provided valuable instruction through his many successes and mistakes. The ghastly slaying of Caesar likewise taught the eighteen-year-old Octavius a very valuable lesson—never should he proclaim himself a dictator. The assassination on the Ides of March made it clear that the Senate was a powerhouse seated in tradition with deep and deadly roots.

At this juncture, we need to address Augustus' many name changes. Though Roman names consisted of several names, we shall limit ourselves to only the first of those for simplicity. He was born Gaius on September 23, 63 BC. In his teens, his great-uncle, Julius Caesar, appointed Gaius to his first public position, thus signaling his adulthood—he was then called Octavius, taking on the name of his deceased father. After Caesar's assassination, Octavius decisively changed his name to Octavian, although at that highly emotional time he actually preferred to be called Caesar. Most historians do not use the confusing Caesar title, and even many senators in his day refused to, so we shall do the same to avoid confusion. After his successful rise to power, Octavian was then honored by the Senate with the reverent name of Augustus.

As a youth, Octavius demonstrated an extraordinarily mature mind for his age. After being emotionally scared by the death of his beloved great-uncle Julius, he conducted his actions with great insight, reserve, and precision. His rise to power was not necessarily meteoric but it was extremely well planned and brilliantly executed. Additionally, beneath his ambitions and the bloody fight for survival, Octavius had a code of ethics and love for his country. This became evident when he was eventually hailed as Augustus. He easily could have been king, yet he deferred the dictatorial honor and instead wore an earthy laurel wreath instead of a glittering crown.

Nevertheless, Octavian had also been plagued by detractors, who upon superficial screening labeled him cold and deceitfully calculating with only personal gain and tyrannical power as his motives. Those charges could have only been rightfully leveled if Augustus became a self-serving dictator who killed aimlessly, suppressed his people, and smothered himself in opulence. In all those crucial instances, however, this was not the case, and each needs a rebuttal.

First, the reprisals that Augustus engaged in while attaining power, which often entailed eliminating deadly rivals, were no different from those used by other leaders of the ancient world. This should not come as a shock; however, some have been horrified by Octavian's cold-heartedness. One such example was when one of the last defenders of the Republic was caught. Being condemned to death, the man merely asked for a proper burial. Octavian's reply was chillingly curt, "That is a matter for the carrion birds to decide."

Taken at face value, this was a frigid statement, but it must be put in context. This was not modern America, where such a statement would ruffle many feathers, not to mention those of the disgruntled carrion birds that would face losing a meal if modern thinking prevailed. Octavian at the time was barely out of his teens, and had suppressed his anger, humiliation, and revulsion regarding his adoptive father's savage butchery by the Senate. Therefore, Octavian's coldhearted reaction not only conforms to the eye-for-an-eye mentality of his times—as even the Jewish God threatened his chosen but disobedient flock with similar words, *"Your corpses shall be food for every bird..."* —but also is underscored by a teenager who held back his wrath for as long as he possibly could. More importantly, his wrath was leveled against those who were involved or associated with Caesar's death. In typical battles—against Mark Antony and others, for example—he generally dealt out traditional responses and often clemency, which he also learned from Caesar.

Secondly, many have preconceived notions of Roman emperors, which instantly summons distaste, as if all of them were evil dictators who oppressed the people. As we shall soon see, many accounts validate that the Roman people rose to defend Augustus and preferred him to any rivals, including the Senate. At one point, the Roman citizenry even wished to elect Augustus as dictator, yet he refused. Moreover, he bestowed many gifts, opportunities and incentives upon the people—financial, political, judicial, and especially cultural. These will be discussed in due course.

Additionally, a person's innate generosity is often revealed even when political motives underlie certain actions. In this regard, his generosity had outmatched his rival Mark Antony's, by far. This became apparent when each man tried to win over new soldiers to his camp. Antony offered each soldier a gift of 400 *sesterces*, while Octavian offered a gift of 2,000 *sesterces* to each, which was twice a soldier's annual income. Equally noteworthy was Antony's brutal response when his soldiers laughed at his relatively paltry offer. He immediately had the main hecklers rounded up and beaten to death in front of the stunned soldiers. Antony's reply was terse, "You will learn to obey orders!"

Thirdly, Augustus unquestionably preferred to live in very modest quarters, ate moderately, and wore moderate attire. This was not a man obsessed with personal wealth or prone to extravagance. Instead, Augustus insisted upon moderation, and for the most part, he practiced what he preached. The words of Suetonius come to mind, as he described the great ruler's house as "remarkable neither for size nor for elegance; the courts being supported by squat columns of peperino stone, and the living-rooms innocent of marble or elaborately tessellated floors."

Beyond those charges and issues, however, it may come as a surprise that during his long reign, Augustus was not a dictator or even an emperor in the modern sense. Augustus worked with the Senate, which remained an active body, as well as with other subdivisions of the Republican system. Many officials were still elected to office by the people, despite Augustus having a hand in selecting the candidates. Therefore, much of the infrastructure remained intact, though subtle revisions were made over a long period of time. Augustus knew that abrupt change, good or otherwise, met with some degree of opposition from the masses, who were often content with the status quo. The only time the citizenry welcomed abrupt change was when they faced a crisis that affected their lives directly, at which time even radical change was embraced.

As many noted later, Augustus cleverly manipulated the Senate and he often preferred his private council's advice; however, the Senate was more than just a puppet assembly. Augustus genuinely sought its members' advice, encouraged involvement, and displayed open respect; at least for those with ability, as the one thing that Augustus despised more than anything was dead wood. Almost every change that Augustus made showed significant signs of improvement, for efficiency and tangible results were paramount. Furthermore, the Senate's input regarding political, legal, economic, and military concerns was vital to running the expansive machine of empire. Despite its somewhat diluted role under the Augustan Empire, this is another reason why the republic system maintained its appealing aura throughout the centuries and influenced many nations.

As mentioned, Augustus preferred the title *princeps*, meaning first citizen, and he did an admirable job fostering this image. In fact, all the emperors from Augustus to Diocletian, some three hundred years later, have been cited as belonging to the Principate period. The years after Diocletian were known as the Dominate period, *dominate* being the Latin word meaning "lord". These rulers have often been depicted on coins wearing imperial crowns or divine sunbursts emanating from their heads. The Dominate period was also the era when monotheism became entwined in state affairs. Quite significantly, Augustus did not wish to be, nor was he ever, called emperor during his entire reign.

As mentioned, at one point, the people of Rome had risen in opposition to the Senate and insisted that Augustus be made dictator. This was after a devastating plague and flood caused widespread death and famine. Here again, a dire situation motivated the Roman people to insist upon drastic changes. Augustus maintained his wits and stormed into the vociferous crowd, scorning the illegal role of dictator and the mob's lapse in judgment. He begged to be slain before accepting such an insulting role, and in Roman fashion, ripped his clothes, thus baring his soul and sincerity. Effectively winning over the crowd, Augustus made rational appointments of capable men to orchestrate his plan for supplying grain to the citizens, for which he paid out of his own pocket in large measure. Augustus had the chance to seize complete dictatorial rule, yet he wisely opted to remain Rome's first citizen instead.

All these noble qualities, however, pertain to the mature Augustus. To better understand Augustus the man and world leader, we need to examine his youth and rise to power, which requires a significant flashback in time. In addition to those crucial years, it is essential to examine the political system that started it all five centuries earlier.

The Roman Republic was a stellar achievement, without precedent in human affairs. This republic was so impressive and influential that it demands our complete attention; first, because it was the world that Octavius was born into and that he had to confront in his own bid for ultimate power, and second, to illuminate the Republic's immense impact, which remains largely unrecognized today.

The following section will break off into several tangents in order to shed light on factors that also pertain to today's state of affairs. In essence, this exploration was deemed necessary to give the reader a better understanding of the Roman political system and culture, its similarities and differences to its Greek counterpart, and the importance it had upon Octavian and has upon modern America.

Sometimes the winds of time have an odd way of burying facts and producing long lasting misconceptions, such as the confusion between Greek democracy and the Roman Republic, or the different social cultures and traditions they both engendered. These errors are evident in both academia and in the minds of the general public. Therefore, we shall clarify all these critical issues in one analytical exposition.

Roman Republic vs. Greek Democracy

Romulus founded Rome in 750 BC. Legend has it that Romulus killed his brother Remus and became Rome's first king. Over two centuries later, in 509 BC, Tarquin the Proud seized power, becoming a tyrant king. In defiance, Lucius Iunius Brutus overthrew the king and became the historically titanic founder of the Roman Republic. Quite interestingly, Lucius Iunius Brutus was a distant relative of Marcus Iunius Brutus, who would orchestrate the assassination of the dictator Julius Caesar. Therefore, the Brutus family not only launched the illustrious Roman Republic, but it also assassinated the man who destroyed it.

During the Republic, Rome grew to a respectable size; however, it would gain the largest territory under the Empire. Despite being one of the most liberal-minded people of their day, early Romans were forced to be tough, ruthless, and uncompromising in order to survive. Their rise to power was beset with agricultural difficulties, internal discord, raids, and near annihilation. Perpetually attacked on all sides, Romans even survived having their capital city sacked by the Gauls. Regrouping with even greater determination, the Romans doggedly won back their city and would have conquered Gaul were it not for the unexpected attack by Pyrrhus, a successor of Alexander the Great's war machine. The fighting never ended, and Rome once again faced a deadly foe and annihilation when Hannibal later terrorized their nation. However, once again, another fearless Roman, Publius Scipio, rose up in arms and defeated the infamous adversary. These successes were due to two main reasons.

First, unlike all other armies of antiquity, the Roman army was the first organized institution with specific policies and well-defined ranks. In addition to the standard infantry, cavalry and archers, the Romans included siege engineers, doctors, carpenters, blacksmiths and cooks. Each soldier carried sixty pounds of equipment that was used to make elaborate encampments each night, but also built endurance. The normal requirement of service was twenty years of complete dedication. All soldiers received daily regiments of exercise to ensure endurance and discipline, as well as special training in tactics and strategy. This yielded a tenacious fighting machine that could outmaneuver and outlast their rivals, even when outnumbered. Furthermore, only the Roman army granted its soldiers property as their reward upon retirement. This benevolent and astute policy is sadly lacking in America, where many soldiers return from war only to be abandoned and forgotten.

The second reason for their successes was simple—the Roman's unyielding and intrepid bravery and near worship of their civilization impelled them to survive. The consequences of Rome failing to survive would have been earth shattering, for without the Roman Republic and its immense influence upon Western history, many modern nations, most notably America, would never have been born.

The Republic was a first in world history. It combined three separate branches of government in a gallant attempt to balance power. The historian Polybius would declare that it was the best form of government known to man. Polybius even took an active role in swaying the Greeks to abandon hope of reviving their own failed attempt at democracy and to embrace the Roman Republic. Built upon a solid constitution that was so exemplary in design that it won the admiration of the founding fathers of America almost two thousand years later, the Republic was nothing short of miraculous.

Interestingly enough, many Americans today erroneously believe that the Roman Republic was a meager copy of an earlier developed Greek democracy. Many also think that the Greeks are the fathers of American democracy, which even politicians and the media claims that we promote worldwide. The term "democracy" was indeed coined in Greece, and the political system shares some similarities with a republic, but the two terms have often been confusingly interchanged and misused. So it is not hard to understand why many Americans believe that they live in a Greek-styled democracy, when in reality it is a Roman-styled republic. However, it is time to dispel these fallacies. Therefore, an explanation why the misconception prevails will be made, first by examining the births of these two highly influential systems.

The Greek democracy first began to form in 508 BC, and developed more fully by 460 BC, when Cleisthenes created the role of the Assembly. The Roman Republic began not later, but quite interestingly a year earlier—in 509 BC. The amazing fact is that these two great cultures were developing innovative reforms in political management simultaneously. Despite the scholarly praise of some historians and teachers, Greek democracy was not that most glorious and solitary light burning amid an archaic world of darkness, for not only was another light burning, but it would outlast the Greek flame by more than three centuries and become far more influential, as the American government attests.

This attempt to colorize history with a broad Greek brush of influence has many intricate roots, but the most important question is did these historians intend to deceive or were they deceived? All indications suggest that in most cases, it was the latter. Most were, and still are, misled by a lifetime of grooming. From grade school right up to college universities, whose faculties are inundated with deep admirers of Greek history, newly created historians many times mirror their mentors. Naturally, many of these new historians either end up working in these institutions, or move on and maintain that thorough conditioning only to reiterate the same story in their own publications. Most teachers, in turn, merely relay these homogenous sources. The crux of this deep adoration, however, centers upon the Greek's impressive contribution to civilization, which we shall now address.

The Greeks were an amazingly industrious people who contributed the fullest and, by many accounts, the most advanced forms of literature, philosophy, and visual arts in the ancient world. However, when we scrutinize Greek philosophy, we see that the precursors of Greek thought were not pure Greeks but Ionians. Ionia was located in modern day Turkey, and the Ionian Islands flanked the Turkish shoreline. This Greek-speaking settlement was at the heart of a heavily trafficked route where Babylonians, from the Near East, and Egyptians from Northern Africa, conducted business and exchanged ideas. Naturally, this profoundly influenced Ionian thinking, which differed greatly from that of the isolated Greek mainland that sat over a hundred miles across the Aegean Sea.

When the Ionians eventually migrated to the Greek mainland, they only settled in the small region of Attica; this rich influx is why Athens later spawned the likes of Socrates, Plato, and Aristotle. However, the man most scholars acknowledge as the true father of philosophy and science was Thales, the Ionian who was born 200 years before Plato in 624 BC, and educated in Egypt. Thales' works influenced Pythagoras, who was also an Ionian, and the cascade of Ionian thought flowed down the centuries to the Athenians, most notably Plato and Aristotle.

Therefore, not only was Greek philosophy the child of foreign influence but the Greeks most certainly did not have a monopoly on all these other areas of endeavor, and in the case of political philosophies the

Roman Republic stands as the most blaring contender and unsung hero. Nevertheless, the many magnificent contributions by the Greeks are indeed worthy of the highest praise, especially in the literary realm. The importance of Homer exceeds colossal and the litany of great Greek poets includes such names as Pindar, Aeschylus, Euripides, Sophocles, Herodotus, Thucydides and many others. Hence, also being men of letters, some historians naturally gravitate to and admire the progenitors of their own profession.

In the middle of the fifteenth century, Greek texts flowed back into the west after being lost for centuries, and renewed an interest in Greek culture. This interest reached a new height by the nineteenth century when many scholars studied the ancient texts of Greece exclusively to form their insightful, if insular, views. They studied the great literary works of Greek masters and were understandably impressed by Greek visual arts; however, they almost completely ignored some profoundly flawed Greek philosophies and concepts of nature that inevitably stagnated progress.

Beyond these philosophical and scientific blunders, many historians throughout history have praised Greek thinkers to the extent that their theories and laws were never challenged. Thus countless generations over many centuries have been misled. Moreover, many Americans today have been schooled and influenced by later historians, who had neither the ability nor the inclination to challenge their heroes. Although their admiration is understandable in many cases, it does not justify a lack of research, the concealment of facts, or the blatant disregard of other truly miraculous developments outside of Greece, namely those of the Roman Republic, which actually had a greater impact on the modern world in general and on America in particular

This intense admiration for Greece is compounded by the fact that when Christianity rose to power the viewpoint of history also changed, and centuries of revisions often made Rome the whipping post for flogging pagans. Rome likewise became the tinseled and unsavory regime that allegedly adopted all its greatness from Greece. These slanderous accusations of plagiarism and creative depravity only added validity to the Greek story; as such, the extensive line of historians and schoolteachers who perpetuated these claims ingrained a notion as false as the Greek concept of an earth-centered universe, which persisted for over a millennium.

This mind-numbing theory was compounded by other flawed scientific laws, such as Aristotle's Law of Gravity. Although we today know this law to be untrue, many rarely contemplate just how crippling it was to human development; for it was like an elevator in the Skyscraper of Knowledge being grounded on the first floor. While the complacent masses laboriously climbed its steep flight of stairs, they never once attempted to scrutinize or understand the elevator, because one brilliant Greek philosopher said it was meant to remain stationary. Only when the masses reached the Renaissance floor did a handful of inquisitive people decide to examine the philosopher's theory. To their amazement, they realized that the elevator did move, and many scientists jumped on board as it climbed upward at an amazing and accelerated pace.

However, some brilliant Romans, such as Cicero, had overpraised the Greeks and this became additional evidence for some historians who blindly repeated the claim. This is not to say that much of Greek thought did not lay very crucial and pioneering foundations in many disciplines, but rather too many Greek philosophers were worshiped as undisputable gods positing undisputable facts. There were true Greek geniuses—Archimedes, Euclid, Aristarchus and others who were indeed innovative and scientifically successful—but blind worship by some Romans and many historians missed the greater dynamic. The Romans who looked up to many Greeks as savants actually helped to ingrain the notion that all Greek philosophers only espoused accurate and unassailable truths about nature and the universe. The unquestioning or complacent historians merely followed suit.

Unfortunately, it would be over a millennium later when many of these truths would be revealed as being severely flawed, with some being ludicrous. It would take the enlightenment of the Renaissance to begin the process of dispelling over sixteen centuries of misguided praise and baseless theories. This was because most Greeks preferred idle observation rather than active experimentation. Hence, by stopping to examine the full course of history, which reveals the huge blunders that stymied mankind, the plain facts all emerge and offer a painful reminder of how people can believe in falsehoods for centuries, simply because of rote learning that never questions its sources. This topic is so important that it will be addressed again in a later chapter.

This brings us back to the long held misconception of Greek democracy being the Roman Republic's precursor, and of being America's primary model. Not only does American government more closely mirror that of the Roman Republic, but these two models, as will be shown, share little with the Greek concept of democracy. Perhaps most telling of all, is that the *United States Constitution* does not even mention the word democracy anywhere in its text, yet, it does state, "The United States shall guarantee to every State in this Union a *Republican* Form of Government..."

The founding fathers words clearly illuminated the truth, yet the word democracy is still used to describe our government, regardless of the fact that even our pledge of allegiance clearly states, "I Pledge Allegiance to the flag and the United States of America and to the *Republic* for which it stands..."

Therefore, it is ironic that so many Americans misuse the term democracy to describe their government, as are most people worldwide that describe any nation like America as being a democracy. Upon closer inspection, the Greek democracy actually displayed features of socialism, while the Roman Republic offered three very "democratic" and influential branches.

Perhaps the most unique branch of the Roman Republic was that of the People. No government in ancient history, even Greece, ever offered such a liberal provision. This massive body voted on issues of war and peace, judged criminals of state, and elected the magistrates; of equal importance, they had their own individual rights and freedom. Proud of this distinct feature, it was celebrated in their popular motto S.P.Q.R.—the Senate and People of Rome.

This branch of government broke new ground, and marked yet another way in which the Republic differed from Greek concept of democracy. The Greek system mandated that every citizen must serve at least one term as an official in government. Most importantly, the Greek citizen did not have individual rights, only those dictated by the collective mass of the system. Therefore, the Greek concept of liberty assumed, or rather dictated, that all its citizens hold a harmonious concept of freedom and rights as put forth by this collective state-run regime.

Even calling Greek democracy a state-run regime needs clarification, for no single executive body oversaw operations. The Greeks were at a disadvantage by being a conglomeration of small villages and communities, each of which held long traditional allegiances to their pasts. As such, Greek or rather Athenian democracy did not pertain to the entire Greek-speaking mainland, just to the small Attica region, which itself was broken into many independent villages.

Therefore, when Cleisthenes initiated Athenian democracy, an extremely complex system was devised to maintain concord among the various communities. *Demes*, or villages, were divided into three large groups, *trittyes*, each of which contained thirty different villages. Those thirty villages in turn were divided into thirds by regions or size, one-third coastal, one-third plains, and one-third cities. Ten administrative bodies or *tribes* were formed by each taking one-third of the regional groupings. The task of dividing these numbers was unnecessarily complex, as were the duties of the huge Assembly or Council of Five Hundred, which also butted heads with the *Areopagus* (council of elders) from the previous regime, which did not wish to relinquish power.

The Greek system was unusually complex, and was much closer to a socialist regime than our current concept of democracy. Furthermore, because every citizen was expected to serve a political term, many high-minded aristocrats and thinkers, like Plato, actively denounced this democratic model. Plato believed that most people lacked the experience or knowledge to make sound political decisions, and as such, would fall prey to either sycophants or demagogues.

Then again, in Plato's famous book, quite oddly named *The Republic*, his concept of an ideal society is at odds with almost every modern-day democratic or republican principle. Plato's utopian society prohibited the arts, which he felt misrepresented nature. This would have eliminated all great sculptures and textile paintings, as well as literary dramas and tragedies, which strangely enough, were paramount in making Greece world famous. Instead, Plato advocated a dictatorial government run by elitist philosophers, such as himself, who he believed were the only ones intelligent enough to handle executive decisions.

However, far surpassing his arrogance, Plato advocated eugenic breeding to produce only perfect human specimens, to eventually terminate the burden of the disabled, handicapped, or those who were simply deemed useless. Quite eerily, Plato's regime would have been a Greek variation of Nazi Germany, the variation being that instead of poorly educated politicians exterminating undesirables, Plato would leave that godly decision up to high-minded philosophers. Therefore, even one of the most intellectual and highly prized of Greek philosophers had what many today would call barbaric notions. In the end, Plato ironically proved that he himself was a demagogue, by appealing to prejudice rather than logic.

However, Plato's crude sensibilities were not unique and were mirrored in other facets of Greek mentality. Despite Greece's reputation of being the ancient world's ultimate society with its famed democracy, the reality is that it was a troubled system that was often criticized by its own citizens, failed to be truly democratic, and lasted only 178 years. In contrast, the Roman Republic lasted almost 500 years and even continued in a broken-down phantom version under the Empire for another 500 years.

An additional facet of the Greek mentality is one often overlooked due to its subtle nature, namely the highly acclaimed art of Greek tragedy. Greek tragedy played a significant role in shaping their world, for it was more than just fictional work from imaginative minds—it reflected the Greek's deep belief in uncontrollable destiny. These literary works often became staged performances, which made their ideological message even more potent. Hence, Greek tragedy, as played out through drama, had a psychological impact on its Greek audiences and society.

In general, the common theme that ran through the tragedies was that the main character was destined to fall victim to a tragic chain of events. Sophocles' *Oedipus Rex* is a prime example. Whereas in Shakespeare's tragic *Hamlet*, the main character knew about his mother and uncle's infidelities, and then plotted to take action against them, in

Oedipus Rex, Oedipus was a pawn of inevitability, for he didn't know he married his mother, Jocasta, so the revelation was pure irresolvable tragedy.

After the Greek Golden Age, which only lasted a hundred years, these plays became almost extinct in the Roman Empire. Perhaps they received some attention in Athens, but by and large the Romans favored their own writers. Not that they were necessarily better—many were not—but fatalistic subject matter was not something that the Roman mind could relate to. They preferred topics that were inspiring, exciting, humorous, or useful—in a word, productive, not self-destructive.

Some modern scholars have criticized the Romans for neglecting these cherished Greek tragedies; yet, such attacks warrant cautious analysis, despite appearing to be justified at first glance. It is understandable that many deeply appreciate the great Greek tragedies, but to affront the Romans as being simpleminded brings forth two obvious issues that negate such biased attacks.

Firstly, these tragic plays went beyond mere entertainment or even intellectual appreciation and into the realm of psychological instruction and conditioning. In an ancient world that offered no cable TV channels, libraries, or bookstores, and where schools were scarce, the Romans were a highly motivated lot who preferred to focus on practical matters and positive motivation, and by doing so they created the most enduring empire in the Western world. Therefore, dwelling upon situations that were unbearable and hopeless offered little to the Romans.

In essence, where the Athenian Greeks developed a national poetry reflecting their pessimistic ideology that celebrated the inevitability of tragedy, the Romans were a dynamic people who were spurred to action by an ideology that demanded practicality, national pride, and most importantly, results. The blunt reality is that their proactive ideology was to have a far more profound effect on world history than the highly polished works of Greek tragedy, regardless of how flawless, admirable, and thought provoking they may have been. It is this crucial point that irritates most intellects who savor and extol the mental eloquence of tragic words more than the pragmatic productivity of the Romans who genuinely shaped our Western world.

Secondly, the Romans revered Virgil's meaningful and uplifting *Aeneid* above all others, which shows they did not only gravitate to flippant comedies of Roman playwrights like Plautus. However, comedy and a sense of humor were important for a healthy mind, as laughter purges pain. We can even recognize how America relies upon comedy where oppressed Muslim states do not. The Romans appreciated a good laugh, however, even the comedies of Plautus were saturated with reverence to the gods, in a civic fashion, for the Romans intended religion to instill national pride and unity. Their priorities had a very real and practical objective, which many scholars today fail to understand. It is crucial to remember that the Romans were building a civilization, not simply reaping the benefits of it.

Beyond these contrasting ideological facts are the crude and even barbaric practices that occurred in Greece, which many textbooks and silver-screen fantasies fail to present. Only recently have some movies, like *300* and *Troy*, attempted to show some of these brutal undertones, despite the latter movie's many historic inaccuracies regarding storyline and military tactics. In fact, *Troy* has the Greeks using the Roman-invented *testudo* formation (shields butted together and held overhead, forming a turtle-shelled shroud) when making their D-Day-type assault on the beach. However, that Roman tactic wasn't invented until centuries later—again, the habit of robbing Rome persists.

Meanwhile, Rome has always been featured as a ruthless regime, with an undying obsession, by authors, directors, and the public, with gladiators and carnage. Naturally, the Romans did invent this blood sport, and even engineered architectural masterpieces to hold these gladiatorial bouts. However, despite the archaic nature of these events the full story has not been told.

The Colosseum held several different games. There were animal versus animal, or man versus animal spectacles, executions of criminals, and gladiatorial fights. The last event has captivated many people's attention for centuries and recreations of these fights, especially in the movies, have habitually distorted the truth.

Gladiators were not aimlessly thrown into the arena to savagely kill one another like two expendable animals in a wild cockfight. Instead, they were well-trained combatants who were instructed only to wound and subdue their opponent. These games were akin to modern-day boxing or kickboxing matches, except gladiators used weapons to inflict nonlethal wounds, thus heightening the awe, as well as risks and fatalities. As in any severe conflict, deaths occurred, however, that was not the intention of the entrepreneurs who orchestrated these brutal, if lucrative, events.

Gladiators were mainly slaves; they were required to have physical examinations and aesthetic inspections (the public, especially women, enjoyed attractive specimens) before being permitted to enter a gladiator school or *ludi*. Their manager, called a *lanista*, would train the athlete in a variety of techniques using different weapons. Naturally, they attempted to groom their gladiators better than their rivals—there were four gladiator schools in Rome alone, and competition was fierce. More importantly, just like for major athletes today, acclaim and rewards were great.

In fact, many gladiators became celebrities in their own right, and often lived long lives, something that is never revealed by Hollywood or understood by the masses. The adulation gladiators received even prompted nonslaves to enter gladiator schools in quest of fame. A handful of jealous emperors, craving the frenzied acclaim won in the arena, actually became combatants themselves, which also attests to the nonlethal aspect of these games.

Perhaps the closest example we have today is professional wrestling, which is wildly popular, and to which spectators flock to watch modern-day gladiators on steroids beat their rivals with metal chairs and hammering blows. Likewise, boxing and kickboxing have maimed and even killed some in the process, yet the need for some to fight and spill blood and the greater need for many to watch remains with us today, even if in a mitigated version.

The majority of deaths in the Roman arena were of convicted criminals, who had the opportunity to fight for survival or face their just punishment. Capital punishment still exists today, and as you read this now, many convicted criminals are being led to extermination chambers to be killed in so-called humane fashion. However, death by a steel needle's injection or a steel sword's cut is still death. Regardless of these moral issues that have people rallying for change, we must admit that ugly practices are a part of reality. Public executions existed throughout history right up to modern times; we cannot ignore that early Americans strung up and hung their condemned in public squares, and the French beheaded their victims with the guillotine right up until 1977.

Therefore, it should not come as too much of a surprise that Rome engaged in brutal practices. The spotlight on Roman gladiators is also in small part due to that towering structure, the Colosseum. Its awe-inspiring size overpowers most observers, including historians, and it unjustly cast a huge shadow of death upon the entire Empire. Although a reminder of sordid activities, the Colosseum is certainly not the summation of Rome. Added to the historians that promulgated their full-blown negative perspectives on Rome are those with a Christian perspective.

Naturally, because many Christian martyrs died in the Colosseum, blame was placed on the pagan infidels who perpetrated the crimes. We must realize that the persecutions of early Christians were rare atrocities enacted by deranged rulers, such as Nero, and they have etched indelible disgust upon all generations of Romans. In a similar vein, we cannot blanket the entire German culture with the heinous sins of Hitler, just because his insidious death camps burned for four years. Religious persecutions in the Colosseum were isolated outbursts by a small handful of offenders, for the intended, routine purpose of the Colosseum was to entertain an audience with gladiatorial bouts (not death matches), present wild animal fights, or execute convicted criminals. These activities are peculiar by today's standards, and unfortunately, the over-hyped and partially misinterpreted events of the Colosseum have unjustly taken the focus away from all the great things that Rome bequeathed to civilization, and in this particular instance, the great Roman Republic.

The dark side of Roman civilization is common knowledge, and as we have seen, distorted to some degree, however, very few know of the bone-chilling oddities of Greece. This seldom-revealed side of the glittering Greek coin shall now be examined as well as contrasted to the Romans.

Unfamiliar to most, Greek tradition required women to give birth to healthy children for the good of the state. The concept of family had no place, as the sole reason for a woman's existence was to supply the state with a human commodity. The state would later take possession of the boys, as Greek society was a male-dominated system, which was far more stringent than the Romans, Egyptians, and practically every other ancient culture. The intensity of the male fraternity was so great that it even encouraged ephebophilia (male adults forming sexual relations with young boys).

Coupled with this obsession of male superiority and dominance, Greek men deprived women of almost every dignity. Oddly enough, however, their praise for women, at least in goddess form, mirrored that of other ancient civilizations. In fact, the Greek statues of goddesses, especially during the Classical period, reach the summit of beauty for many. The *Venus de Milo* statue displayed in the Louvre is a prime example. Dating from the late Hellenistic period, which advocated realism or the veristic style, this beautiful statue is believed to be a copy of an earlier rendition from Classical antiquity, when idealism was in vogue. The Greek concept of idealism has even been the ultimate ideal for many artists, who, over countless centuries, have struggled to attain similar feats of perfection.

Unfortunately, the Greek's vision of beauty and admiration did not translate to the real world, for Greek women were forced to live under harsh and insensitive conditions. In essence, their sole purpose was for breeding and feeding. Quite tellingly, the only Greek women to receive tombstones were those who died in childbirth. This honor was granted only because they died in the line of duty for their country.

Conversely, Roman history is filled with prominent woman, mostly wives of emperors, statesmen, or generals, who eventually wielded significant power and influence within their domain. In fact, the impetus for the creation of the Roman Republic was partly due to a woman named Lucretia, who was the wife of an aristocrat Tarquinius Collatinus. Lucretia had been raped by the king's son, and appealed to her husband and her famous uncle, Lucius Iunius Brutus, to seek revenge. This incident, in all probability, was the last of many indignities, and her uncle Brutus led a valiant revolt to defeat the monarchy and establish the Republic.

Meanwhile, Lucretia became despondent over the repugnant violation, and to defend her honor and that of husband, she committed suicide.

Lucretia even stood as a symbol of Roman virtue. Five hundred years later, the Republic's dignified form of liberalism had evolved into feral liberalism, as greed, corruption, adultery, and divorce rates escalated and childbirth declined. This wanton and degenerative trend (which is also evident in America today) became a central issue for Augustus once he became ruler. In response, Augustus enacted laws to restore morals and a Lucretian sense of family structure and honor back into Roman tradition. Ultimately, liberalism without conservative restraints yields chaos.

Augustus had a deep affection for his wife Livia that also spawned liberating decrees. As Suetonius remarked, "He loved and esteemed her to the end without rival." In this loving regard, Augustus granted Livia the legal right to manage her own financial affairs, an inviolable right or *sacrosancitas* that only men enjoyed. He also bequeathed the title Augusta upon Livia, so that after his death she was known as "Mother of the Emperor." Livia was aiming to enhance that title to "Mother of the Empire," but her son Tiberius, who succeeded Augustus, thwarted this maneuver, fearing his ambitious mother's attempts to share power. However, as the first empress of the Roman Empire, Livia set a precedent that many other first ladies followed, some cultivated and noble, some domineering and scandalous. The pattern of Roman women, of high and low esteem, grooming their sons for higher rank—and even conspiring for it—recurs throughout Roman history. Additionally, all Roman women had the important task of educating their children; daughters remained under their mother's tutelage, sons would eventually attend a private school, thus vindicating the involvement and influence of women in Roman life. This female storyline is sadly almost nonexistent in the ancient Greek narrative.

Additionally, although Roman women had no political rights, their legal rights matured over time. Women were eventually allowed to file for divorce, and they had rights to inheritance that often enabled them to wield respectable influence and power. For example, after the Second Punic War, in 201 BC, Roman soldiers were amassing great wealth by plundering Carthage. They sent it back to their wives for setting up dowries and inheritances for their daughters and sons respectively. Many soldiers died, leaving great wealth to their wives and daughters, who in turn were able to gain a sizable amount of freedom. Sculptures of the time, which act like eternal marble photographs, clearly document that women held professions normally performed by men—one relief features a woman running a pharmacy.

Perhaps more importantly, women became loving partners in Roman society, not simply livestock for breeding. Simple activities that we take for granted—such as allowing women to attend the same parties as their husbands—were banned in Greece, yet permitted in Rome. One Roman biographer of the time, Cornelius Nepos, traveled to Greece and reported his distress at how the Greeks coldly repressed their women. He found it unfathomable that Greek women were kept completely segregated, and that even the most mundane activity, like attending social gatherings, was prohibited. The Greek household was setup so that the wife's living quarters were blocked from the entrance. Women were forbidden to answer the door, for fear of encountering a man. This enslavement mentality and lack of true companionship between Greek men and women explains the historical silence of Greek women's feelings and voices, which must have been left to be expressed amongst themselves.

In direct contrast, even the graffiti on the Colosseum's walls indicate a vociferous bunch of women who spoke quite freely and passionately about their crushes on famous gladiators. Additionally, tender letters by Roman statesmen to their wives, and the love poems of the time, openly expressed the deep sense of love and longing between men and women. Perhaps the most modern-sounding statement uttered about Roman women was not by a current writer, but by the famous Roman statesman Cato. He said, "We may rule the world but our wives rule us." This could have been spoken by any number of men today in the free republic of America, yet this voice from over two millennia ago elicits a warm connection to a very distant, yet familiar past.

However, no such connection can be made with ancient Greece, which has more in common with radical Muslim states, which also sequester their women. Unfortunately, very few women are to be found in

Greek history, and their base status and utilitarian purpose did not afford them the amours, voice, freedom, power, or respect they deserved. As for a rare voice that did resound, namely Sappho with her love poetry, she was born before the Greek democracy on the isle of Lesbos near Turkey, and her poems were of lesbian relationships that did not speak for the vast majority of women.

In general, Greek women were required for three purposes; to be companions (the euphemism for courtesans), prostitutes, and wives. Oddly enough, this peculiar order of preference is historically accurate, as it was posited by the Greek orator, Demosthenes, who said, "We have companions for the sake of pleasure, ordinary prostitutes for daily attention to our physical needs, and wives to bear legitimate children and to be faithful guards inside our households."

That was the Greek way; the men had no sexual restraints and even in marriage were free to engage in adultery. Aside from the courtesans and daily prostitutes, most men were groomed as boys in the academy to be the beloved of their adult male mentor. Although homosexual relations outside the academy setting were frowned upon, these mentor-protégé relationships were an expected ritual. Once the boy reached manhood, he could then pursue sexual relations with women.

Further attesting to a Greek male's sexual freedom, a slave woman could not sexually refuse their master, as no law protected women or prohibited any Greek man. Yet, oddly enough, the men still expected their wives to be faithful guardians of his household. It appears the only reward offered married women was the Thmermospheria festival, which allowed them only three days of freedom from their male masters.

Beyond the callous treatment of Greek women was the horrifying process following childbirth, which was practiced in some other ancient cultures as well. All newborn babies in Greece were immediately examined, and if they had any visible defects, were killed or abandoned in a heap of infant trash, where other babies were left to die. The infant boys that survived the daunting entrance into the Greek world would later face another rite of passage. At the age seven, young boys would be taken from their mother and placed into a training academy, where they focused primarily on combat skills, interspersed with academics. Part of their training was to withstand being severely flogged. Those that did not faint or cry would be viewed as admirable soldiers. Meanwhile, girls were not eligible for education and remained in the household to perform domestic duties, and matured to perform their reproductive function for the state

The Greeks were also driven by a deep impulse to analyze life and espouse judgments based upon logic. As we have seen, their philosophies and scientific theories, although commendable for the successes and attempts, were many times deeply flawed. Moreover, although the Greeks made very sound decisions about art, producing astounding works of beauty and elegance, they quite compulsively carried this obsession for aesthetics into their daily lives. The unfortunate consequence was that their cold calculations about aesthetics not only pertained to cold marble statues but also to warm tender humans. One of the Greek's most bizarre and cruel rituals was to scout for and determine the ugliest looking male citizens. They would then round up their hapless selections, drape them in figs, and heartlessly expel them from the city.

This so-called golden age of Greece was plagued not only by tainted ideologies and traditions, but also by the inability of its democratic political system to unite its separate states. Even though Greece thrived in a very small territorial region, these independent city-states, with Athens and Sparta being the largest two, were constantly engaged in fierce rivalries. The inability to create solidarity led to the fall of Athens to the Macedonians in 322 BC, and with it expired its brief experiment in democracy.

Simply put, the Greek model of democracy was nothing like modern day America or the Roman Republic. The citizen-run, socialist mechanism called upon every citizen to play an active role, as it shunned the idea of any kind of executive, unlike Rome or America. Even personal legal disputes entailed gathering 2,000 citizens to hear cases and then pass judgment. There were no judges, and no set code of written laws.

In contrast, the Roman's judicial court system was based upon a written code of laws, namely the Twelve Tables. Roman defendants were brought before a judge and jury who would hear the case and pass sentencing according to the specific laws broken. If this process sounds familiar, it is because the American court system emulated the Roman model.

Meanwhile, Greek courts operated in a vacuum, having no written laws as a guide. Nor did they have judges presiding over hearings to maintain order or instruct the court with the knowledge of law. The 2,000 citizens presiding over these court hearings were actually required to make up the law pertaining to the specific crime. That entailed long and chaotic deliberations, which then led to a verdict and sentencing. As the saying goes, "too many cooks spoil the broth," so even a minor incident consumed excessive amounts of time to conjure up law, debate law, and then decide sentencing.

The Greek economy was likewise hamstrung by this inept system. The Greeks held open sessions on business matters, which grew to inordinate size as thousands of citizens were required to engage in these riotous discourses. Mediating over the exchanges was the Council of Five Hundred, another colossal body that certainly couldn't have been much help in organization or expediency. The Council's function was to draft legislation and oversee meetings. The members in this large body were required to be thirty years of age or older and would be annually selected by lottery.

In light of the unorganized and chaotic anomalies of the Greek version of democracy, it is no wonder that Plato and many in the aristocracy detested it. One Athenian called their democracy "absolute insanity." Considering the massive councils, the lack of executives or written laws, and the negative verdicts by their own citizens, it is clear why the Greek democracy failed. However, it is not clear why the Greek democracy continues to be lauded and improperly ingrained into our minds when describing America.

This now leaves us with examining the true model of America's political system—the Roman Republic. As mentioned, the Republic was divided into three branches, with the Public branch being the most innovative. This body oversaw and protected the rights and interests of the people, as a whole and individually, while also extending the right to vote. This right crossed social lines, since common plebeians and wealthy patricians alike took active roles in choosing their leaders, engaging in political debate and establishing legislature. Personal grievances were also made through this branch of government and resolved issues in a way that no other ancient system dealt with as fairly or effectively.

The second branch of the Republic was the Senate. Here again, even the name Senate makes it clear where America drew its ideas. This branch, consisting of 300 members, was developed as the advisory board. Since it was comprised of wealthy landowners, it wielded great influence and control. Their powers infiltrated the economy as well as politics. Still maintaining some remnants of its earlier monarchy, the Roman Republic displayed signs of a caste system, as wealth and royal blood offered privileges that are still an unfortunate part of modern republics, like America.

The third and last branch of Roman government contained the magistrates, consisting of several tiers of members, each with specific duties. Two consuls were at the top of the command chain; they were elected annually and acted like dual presidents. These executives held supreme administrative and military control. Since there were two consuls, one could check the other with a veto—another familiar term and function adopted by the American founders.

Another fascinating feature of the Roman government was that even plebeians could rise in rank to achieve the high office of consul. More impressive still is that when the Republic became an Empire, this policy remained intact: Diocletian was the son of a freed slave, and managed to climb up the ranks to become emperor. These unique features clearly validate that the Romans crafted an amazingly liberal and effective political system without precedent in the ancient world. Moreover, it was one that endured.

The Republic also maintained two additional appointees called the censors. The censors were entrusted with maintaining a code of ethics, removing corrupt Senators from office, supervising taxation, and managing construction projects. In a state of emergency, one of the censors would be elected to a temporary position called dictator. The dictator held the position of supreme commander for only a six-month term to squelch any severe military or political threats. However, the term *dictator* took on a whole new meaning after the overly ambitious Julius Caesar seized absolute power and irrevocably altered its meaning. That bold action sounded the death knell of the Roman Republic.

For five hundred years, the illustrious Roman Republic proudly stood as the ancient world's beacon of political ingenuity and its social liberator. Its influence, as noted, was infinitely superior to any of its rivals, yet its existence was destined to endure a digression and a change of hands that would minimize and pulverize certain facets of the glittering gem. However, despite this defacement, a new leader was on the horizon who would polish the remaining edges and create the most durable jewel of the ancient world.

Transition and Octavian's Rise to Power

The transition from Republic to Empire was not instantaneous; rather it evolved over a fourteen-year period. The eminent Republic, even prior to Julius Caesar, had shown signs of decay, as the two main political factions, the *populares*, led by Gaius Marius, and the *optimate*, led by the general Lucius Sulla, had grown more aggressive in their dealings. This was partially due to the many conquests of the expanding Republic, for newly acquired lands were immediately devoured by wealthy landowners, greedy senators, and the aristocracy.

Meanwhile, generals, like Sulla, wanted to reward their soldiers with retirement properties for their dedication and service. But the rich landowners refused to give up land. This tightened the bond between soldier and general, thus creating a new dynamic of loyalty. During 88 BC, Sulla made the first-ever sacrilege in Rome's history by illegally marching his troops on Rome. This bold and egregious strong-arm tactic was immediately condemned by the Senate and all of Rome. However, it did resonate with a young and ambitious boy of about nineteen years of age who grew up to be a famous general himself. That, of course, was Julius Caesar, who following Sulla's precedent, boldly and illegally marched his Thirteenth Legion across the Rubicon and on toward Rome.

In AD 44, Julius Caesar stood as the world's greatest general and the dictator of the greatest civilization of his day. He had already conquered vast territories, including what are now Switzerland, France, Belgium,

Holland, and Germany. In the process, he amassed great wealth for Rome and its avaricious senators. However, Caesar's cunning political tactics, which enabled him to boldly rise to power, ultimately failed him when he neglected to restructure or even eliminate the Roman Senate. Many historians have mistakenly claimed that the Republic died upon Caesar's crossing the Rubicon, but that was not completely true, for it was not a full-scale coup with a complete change of regime personnel. Instead, Caesar unwisely maintained his protocol with the Senate. This led to the Senate's false assumption of sustaining power, and their repugnance of his arrogance.

Then again, Caesar's hands were tied, since the only men he could trust were his loyal subordinates or soldiers. Unfortunately, they were all extremely incompetent at administration, including Mark Antony, so a complete take-over was not an option. Caesar should have considered this crucial factor before he made his insulting demands upon the Senate, which in the end proved that it maintained ultimate power. Moreover, although Caesar had plans for social and economic changes they took a backseat to glory. Caesar simply craved ultimate respect and uncontested rule, something he never could or ever did get from the Senate.

The only place where Caesar would receive love, respect, and even worship was among his devout troops or from the distant yet proud citizens that received news of the general's stellar victories. Hence, being a warrior at heart, Caesar again made plans for a mission of conquest and glory. This time his target was the Parthians to the east. However, this campaign never materialized, as the offended Senate had other plans.

On March 15, the infamous Ides of March, the senators lured Caesar to the Theatre of Pompey under false pretenses. Totally unaware, Caesar was presented with a phony petition, which he opened. As he lowered his head and began reading, Casca came up from behind and struck the first blow. Caesar at first attempted to subdue his assailant, but seeing a unified mass of senators wielding daggers, he submitted to his fate. Sustaining twenty-three stab wounds, Caesar fell to the marble floor in the Curia of the Theatre at the feet of a statue of Pompey. Oddly enough, Caesar would die at the feet of his former triumvirate partner and rival, whose head he received on a platter just four years earlier.

The senators, Brutus and Cassius, had orchestrated the deadly hit; yet the most injurious, emotionally, was the traitorous stab by Brutus, who Julius had cultivated like a son. This bond had been further cemented by Caesar's long-term affair with Brutus' mother, Servilia Caepionis. Regardless of Caesar's political favor and paternal kindness toward him, Brutus was an idealist at heart and longed for the revival of the Republic, which his great ancestor established and Caesar had defiled. Sources indicate that Caesar uttered the famous last line, *"Et tu, Brute"* before pulling his bloody toga over his head to accept the inevitable. Caesar's ill-planned dictatorship lasted less than four years.

Nevertheless, Caesar's many victories and generosity toward his troops and the public had won the intense admiration of the lower and middle classes, which constituted the majority of Rome. As such, the name Caesar captured the imagination of the ancient world so powerfully that not only did Augustus adopt it as the crowning glory for himself and all subsequent Roman emperors, but future leaders also adopted the title in the form of *Czar* in Russian, and *Kaiser* in German.

Even over a millennium later, Dante Alighieri, in his *Divine Comedy*, would condemn Brutus and Cassius, along with Judas, to the lowest and most infernal circle of Hell. Even though it was a religious allegory, we see Julius placed symbolically alongside Jesus—Caesar even gained an edge by having two of the three worst sinners. Although Dante's obvious intent was to address the ultimate betrayals of both the heavenly and earthly realms, this interpretation strongly echoes the sentiments of the Romans and their disdain for the two treacherous traitors who betrayed their lord and master, Julius. Likewise, it continued the long tradition, which elevates and supports the lofty name and rank of Caesar, who, despite his downward dictatorial bent, became the icon of the ultimate ruler on earth. Despite the glaring disparities between Jesus and Julius, both were viewed as ultimate world leaders (one of heaven and one of earth). Furthermore, both were tragically betrayed, and ultimately, both brutally killed.

With the vicious death of Julius Caesar, the vacancy offered the world's ultimate seat of power to many contenders, and particularly to our main character, Octavian. This finally brings us to the story of Octavian's long and arduous rise to power.

Unfortunately, little is known about his early childhood. What we do know is that Gaius was a simple country boy, reared by a very protective mother named Atia and her second husband Philippus. Gaius was only four years old when his father Octavius died. We do know that the senior Octavius was an ambitious man who attempted to raise his family's middle class equestrian station by becoming a politician. That involved many rigorous steps, including military action. His trajectory was fast and promising, yet he died unexpectedly of an ailment contracted on a military campaign. He was highly revered for being ethical, bright, and motivated, however, young Gaius never had the chance to know his fine, yet sadly fleeting, father.

Advancing a decade forward, at the age of fourteen, Gaius became Octavius. His great-uncle Julius had bestowed that rite of passage, thus marking the boy's transition to manhood. Two years prior, Julius was impressed by the eulogy the boy gave for his grandmother Julia, Caesar's sister. The boy's eloquence evidently made an impression upon many prominent Romans in attendance, for the art of oration was taken very seriously. More than simply being articulate, a good orator had the ability to move and sway people, thus it was a prerequisite for any successful leader.

During this time, Octavius befriended two of his schoolmates, who would prove to be crucial assets: Agrippa, a strong physical specimen who would eventually become a brilliant military leader and engineer; and Maecenas, a gentle and colorful intellectual. They provided Octavius with divergent, yet well-balanced input that would prove crucial in the years ahead.

Meanwhile, Octavius' great-uncle Julius had grown wildly popular among Romans and world famous for his unprecedented string of victories. For decades, Caesar had marched his legendary troops across the full breadth of Europe and only rarely returned home. Now that he crossed the Rubicon and Rome was under his sole control, Caesar finally had time to become acquainted with his young relation. Caesar immediately took a liking to his great-nephew. Beyond his respectful manners and good looks, the young Octavius showed signs of astuteness and immense promise, especially now that Caesar was dictator and had no legitimate children of his own to name as his successor.

Unbeknownst to both was that the time they could spend together would be relatively brief, however it was extremely deep and irreversibly binding. Caesar then opted to take Octavius on his military campaign to Spain, but the young neophyte fell ill, as his physical constitution was prone to severe and recurring ailments. Despite his body's weakened health, Octavius doggedly struggled to push himself, though in vain. Caesar was exceedingly compassionate, and took great care to encourage and protect his gifted gem, for he secretly included Octavius as his adopted son in his newly drafted will.

Caesar gave Octavius honorary appointments and official duties, so that the teen could begin learning to broker with influential men and to run various public activities. In these capacities, Octavius demonstrated qualities that pleased not only Caesar but won him many admirers—he was lauded as being lucid, efficient, attentive, cautious, judicious, decisive, and affable. Octavius was riding high on a cloud of euphoria, for even he could not predict that his life would change so drastically over these past four years. Every new step offered new adventures, new opportunities, and new bridges of learning. The journey across the immense span that he knew he needed to traverse was off to a grand start, and the future looked radiant.

The year was 45 BC, and Caesar was now setting his Parthian campaign into motion. This time, however, he would make sure that Octavius was well prepared, both physically and mentally, for the serious undertaking. Octavius and his close friends were sent to the northern Greek province of Apollonia, where they received training in academics and military tactics. Octavius spent several months there and devoured knowledge as fast as he won admiring friends. To those in Apollonia, Octavius demonstrated a clear capacity for critical thinking, ethical behavior, and unassailable courage—even if being a deep personal courage, since he had no experience in the gory conflagrations of battle.

Preparations for war were finally in place, and Octavius beamed at the prospect of his great-uncle's arrival and their next glorious campaign. Unfortunately, dark storms were upon the horizon, as a messenger approached and handed Octavius a letter from his mother. The letter was horrifically blunt—his great-uncle Julius had been murdered. The man he loved as a father, as well as his irreplaceable apprenticeship, had been catastrophically terminated.

White with shock, a whirlwind of emotions surged through his veins. Yet, in the distressing letter, his mother Atia had demonstrated her own strength by doing what all parents dread, and that was to release her loving grip on the boy in order to encourage the man. Nevertheless, Octavius had already set his sights on the future and already knew the vital role he wanted to play.

However, this totally unexpected and devastating tragedy had now drastically changed the playing field, especially his prospects for success. He knew he was not ready to make the huge leap from unripe novice to world leader, but Octavius was likewise plagued by something far more pressing. The fact was, if the assassins had the audacity to kill Caesar in broad daylight, then the Julian family was next, and the first on that hit-list was Octavius.

Being cautious yet proactive, Octavius quickly requested advice from his two trusted friends, Agrippa and Maecenas, along with the academic team at Apollonia. Amid the confusion and anxiety, Octavius remained grounded and pensively weighed his options. Meanwhile, another letter arrived, this one from his stepfather Philippus. His words reeked with fear; his advice was to remain in hiding. Octavius, however, had other plans, as he would shed his parents' protective shell and boldly take action. Now styling himself as Octavian, or actually Caesar, he would return to Rome to face the dangerous lion's den.

Arriving quietly on the outskirts of Rome, Octavian coolly began acting on the plans that consumed and enraged him during his smoldering voyage across the Adriatic. His final decision was to postpone vengeance, in order to methodically plot his long and precarious mission to secure ultimate power. He immediately held a meeting with his great-uncle's main financial backer, Lucius Balbus, and other silent partners. It was agreed that many avenues had to be pursued to raise public awareness, support, and the manpower required to overcome the almost impossible odds.

Octavian's next objective was to ensure that the people of Rome received the generous provision left in Caesar's will, whereby every male citizen would get a considerable sum of money. However, Caesar's estate had already been seized by his second-in-command, Mark Antony, who was recklessly devouring the money for personal gain. To Antony, Caesar's generous public endowment was a ludicrous slip in reasoning that fortunately for him had remained a secret.

However, fortune would not favor Antony for long. Octavian publicly announced Caesar's will, along with his intention to fulfill Julius' behest out of his own pocket, despite Antony's abominable greed. The gesture immediately won Octavian admirers for following through on Caesar's munificent wishes. It likewise bought the allegiance of those sitting on the fence. This maneuver effectively established Octavian as a man of his word, a generous benefactor, and a serious contender for a throne that appeared to many, including the Senate, to be solely Mark Antony's.

Additionally, all of Rome was shocked that Octavian did not engage in a bloodbath by hunting down the murderous senators for revenge. They truly expected the enraged teenager to react in a typically violent and impulsive fashion, more befitting his age. As such Octavian's coolheaded approach was welcomed with much relief. Caesar's death had also prompted another unforeseen event. Upon hearing the tragic news, the public went berserk. An intense national outcry of love and veneration for their fallen leader resounded throughout Rome. This deeply shocked the deadly culprits, including Mark Antony. Unbeknownst to the masses, Antony knew of the senators' murderous machinations and conveniently stood by while the horror ensued. However, none of these murderers or conspirators ever expected a violent backlash, especially against what they perceived to be an unwelcome tyrant.

Evidently, the senators' arrogance was blinding, for they believed that life would continue as usual and that they could calmly restore the comfortable and corrupt Republic. However, their Republican reverie was shattered by the crowd's rebellion and Octavian's unwelcome arrival, not to mention the latter's highly disruptive pep rallies.

Faced with these unwelcome and hazardous circumstances, Brutus and Cassius were forced to flee Rome to gather support and troops. Amid the upheaval, two prospective consuls, Hirtius and Pansa, saw an inroad and began conspiring to wrest control from Antony, who nevertheless brazenly stood his ground. Adding insult to injury, Antony had not only selfishly appropriated Caesar's wealth, but he also granted amnesty to Caesar's murderers. The stage was set and it was now Showtime. Octavian, the unripe teenager, would now enter the very complex and deadly arena of ancient Roman power politics. Henceforth, Octavian bravely demanded a meeting with Mark Antony.

As the slender, nascent country boy faced the masculine and well-seasoned general, he was brutishly rebuffed on every topic. Antony refused to recognize Octavian's claim of being the rightful heir, for according to Antony and state law, Octavian's adoption was not officially ratified. Unfortunately, the law necessary to accomplish this transaction had accompanied Caesar's adoption request, and was indeed not yet official. Additionally, and quite insultingly, Antony adamantly refused to surrender the money he had embezzled from Caesar's estate. Octavian left the meeting empty-handed but certainly not broken.

Antony had been notorious as a party boy who loved his wine and women. He may have been a brave battle ox, but Antony's attempts at administration had previously failed miserably under Caesar's reign. Quite possibly it was Caesar's reprimand and demotion after one of Antony's ham-fisted debacles that made him turn and surreptitiously abandon his friend and master. Nonetheless, Octavian had already been bursting with confidence and this cold and very revealing rebuff only further bolstered his desire to outwit the brazen bull. Octavian would now demonstrate what would be only the first of his many abilities.

Octavian presented Rome with ten days of entertainment and games to celebrate the fallen Caesar. In this regard, Octavian operated out of genuine love and a keen understanding of the public's desires and needs. The gala event was paid for from Octavian's personal inheritance and dormant funds from Caesar's defunct Parthian war campaign. Quite miraculously, however, these honorary events were graced by a celestial wonder. During the last seven days of the event, a comet streaked through the heavens. The astrologers interpreted this as the soul of the divine Caesar giving his blessings to his rightful heir. Octavian seized the heavenly moment by erecting a statue of Caesar in the temple of Venus, quite appropriately with a star above his head. With such a fortuitous event, Octavian was off to a stellar start.

This occurrence demonstrated one of Octavian's special gifts—the ability to seize serendipitous events and turn them to his favor. Even his great-uncle Julius had told him that his own campaigns were often predicated upon luck. However, one has to be observant enough to spot luck and clever enough to harness and implement that luck in order to reap the full benefits of luck. Additionally, Octavian was known for his abilities to accept advice, delegate to others who were more qualified in specific fields, analyze situations with a cool and calculating logic, and perhaps most important, learn from his mistakes. In this regard, the young neophyte quickly matured into a sagacious leader, one who even deceived perhaps the most brilliant mind in Rome—Cicero.

Cicero was Rome's greatest orator and philosopher, and a highly respected statesman. Cicero's impact on Western history is likewise immense, for he influenced a dazzling string of future intellects, including St. Jerome, Petrarca, Queen Elizabeth, as well as America's founding fathers. John Adams in particular prized his special collection of Cicero's books and orations that were often discussed in Boston and Philadelphia. Cicero's impact on America's own republic is testament to his timeless appeal and endurance.

Nevertheless, beside his intellect, Cicero was also an old remnant of the rapidly waning Republic. His distaste for both Julius Caesar and Mark Antony was summed up thus, "The Ides of March was a fine deed, but half done!" Hence, Antony's crass seizure of Caesar's vacant seat posed a continued affront to the Republic and Cicero, not to mention being additionally faced with a brazen teenager from the Julian bloodline.

From Cicero's high perch, he viewed Octavian as a naive and even "unimaginative youth," with little prospect of achieving success. His assessment certainly appeared accurate, especially considering Octavian's skimpy resume and the grisly fact that any ruler seizing power would make sure that Caesar's heir was exterminated. With such odds against

Octavian, Cicero shrewdly decided to use the teenager as a tool to regain his lost stature, and more importantly, to resurrect the dying Republic, both of which were quashed by Mark Antony's tyrannical maneuvers.

Cicero immediately addressed the Senate with a series of orations denouncing Antony and hailing Octavian as the redeemer of the Republic. As noted earlier, many have criticized Octavian for being deceitful, yet this is typical of what he had to contend with, for Cicero's miraculous new opinion of Octavian was that he possessed "godlike intelligence and courage." Cicero's duplicitous yet highly effective speech, hastened the senators' decision to grant Octavian a formal position and more importantly gave him the troops to fight Antony.

As Cicero reveled in his covert plot, envisioning Mark Antony's defeat and his own ascension to renewed power, Octavian took advantage of his new position and fooled the old sage with a sequence of unexpected maneuvers. Over the course of a year in battle against Antony, Octavian had been unhappily saddled with the two consuls mentioned earlier, Hirtius and Pansa, who had taken on the roles of general. Consuls acted as dual presidents with ultimate executive powers. Hence, these men were the Senate's insurance policy against Octavian's budding ambitions. Worse yet, Octavian was demoted to a subordinate role in the campaign. The Senate's objective was to humiliate and use power politics to discourage and defuse the youngster, but Octavian was an unusual breed and was extremely patient and skillfully calculating.

During the chaos of war, both consuls died leaving Octavian in sole command. Much has been made of these deaths and no real account survives to indicate whether foul play or genuine casualties of war caused them; however, the crux of the matter was that their deaths left the two powerful consulships vacant. As such, Octavian boldly sent a message to Rome, requesting to be elected consul, despite being too young and inexperienced for the position. Further still, Octavian called for his relative Pedius to stand as the candidate for the other vacancy. The senators at first flatly refused. However, it wasn't long before they caught wind of the intense allegiance of Octavian's soldiers and their willingness to storm Rome if need be. In frustration, the senators bit their tongues and humbly allowed the election process to commence, as both Caesarians won office.

Octavian and his impotent but trusted relative Pedius were now consuls of Rome.

However, a greater shock waited. Sensing Cicero's intentions, as well as acting in his own best interests, Octavian covertly formed an alliance with his ultimate enemy Mark Antony and Caesar's loyal henchmen, Lepidus, to form a triumvirate. Antony, however, had one nonnegotiable term, and that was the death of the troublesome orator, Cicero. Upon hearing of this alliance, Cicero was dumbfounded. All his assurances to the Senate that Octavian would defend and revive the Republic had become blatant indictments of his extreme misjudgment and irreparable folly. Cicero had severely underestimated Octavian, and many in the Senate were astonished by the teen's rapidly acquired political and military acumen. However, more ominous was that Cicero was now on the hit-list.

Antony's personal vendetta against the old vociferous Republican was well known, and so Cicero fled Rome for one of his opulent villas. He knew, however, that escape was futile. When Antony's soldiers arrived at his seaside retreat, Cicero accepted defeat, and bravely stood to be slain. Meanwhile, Octavian's legal adoption had been made law. He likewise managed to persuade the Senate to decree that all conspirators and accomplices in the Caesar slaughter were guilty of murder. Payday had arrived, and Octavian could finally avenge his adoptive father's murder, as several hundred conspirators were exterminated. His long, humiliating wait was over.

Despite these inroads, Octavian was confronted with other serious problems. The newly formed triumvirate was disturbingly unbalanced, with Octavian receiving the least territory due to his youth and inexperience. As expected, all three partners were suspicious of one another, yet somehow they managed to endure a decade of oscillations, as shrewd power struggles ensued. During their jockeying for power, Antony preferred to stay away from Rome and its hostile senators, while Octavian cleverly managed to gain a larger share of the political pie. This allowed him the opportunity to strengthen existing alliances and build new ones with the aristocratic power lords and senators who were the key operators of Rome.

Added to the mix was Julius Caesar's old flame Cleopatra. The seductive queen had enamored Mark Antony not only with her charms, but also with the viable prospect of their jointly ruling the world. Cleopatra needed Antony's military might, while he needed her wealth and grain supplies. Such a strategic alliance made those aspirations plausible. As a result of their passionate encounters, Cleopatra gave birth to twins, to the dismay of many back at Rome, particularly Antony's intensely devoted and militantly ambitious wife Fulvia. Her place in Roman history is unique in that she raised and instructed troops to undermine Octavian. However, her loyal intentions, despite Antony's adulterous affair, failed.

Troubled by Octavian's rising influence back in Rome Antony decided it was time to make a preemptive strike. However, the troops of both sides refused to engage in another civil war. The stalemate forced the leaders to reluctantly renew the triumvirate. During the course of these smoldering rivalries, Antony's wife Fulvia died. In a diplomatic effort to strengthen their relations, Octavian insisted that Antony marry his sister Octavia. Antony conceded, yet with his own stipulation. He demanded more troops to embark on his new campaign—to fulfill Caesar's quest of conquering the Parthians to the east. Antony and his new bride peacefully moved to Greece. The union yielded a daughter named Antonia, and Octavia soon returned to Rome to raise their child while Antony plotted his attack against the Parthians.

Meanwhile, Octavian was diplomatically united (though not officially married) to Antony's stepdaughter Claudia. However, with other situations brewing in the region, Octavian was advised by his intellectual friend and advisor Maecenas to marry Scribonia as a tactical measure, since she was related to Sextus Pompey, the son of Pompey the Great. Unfortunately, Octavian held no affection for Scribonia. Moreover, the elder Pompey's death at the hand of Caesar caused much stress in this partnership. However, beyond the benefit of merging with a powerful Roman family, Sextus Pompey was wreaking havoc in the Mediterranean, and the alliance appeared to offer a sensible solution.

To the blatant insult of Rome, Sextus was boldly hailing himself as the Son of Neptune, due to his superior naval fleet that habitually pirated grain supplies heading for Roman ports. According to the Senate, next to Mark Antony, Sextus posed the biggest threat of usurping power in Rome. Action was required and Octavian engaged in the marriage with an aim of helping the state. His only true reward was that he fathered his only child, Julia—he divorced Scribonia a year later.

Soon afterward, Octavian fell in love upon meeting Livia Drusilla, who was married to an outspoken opponent of Octavian. Livia's husband had proven to be an oddball who made enemies as fast as he made friends. Evading the authorities, he had dragged Livia, and more recently their infant son Tiberius, all across the empire. Upon returning to Rome, Livia had had enough of being the wife of a perpetual fugitive, and happily welcomed Octavian's advances. This loving marriage would endure for the remainder of their long and eventful lives.

Nevertheless, Octavian's earlier brief marriage to Scribonia had failed to procure accord with Sextus Pompey, who continued his assaults at sea. With Rome still being pilfered and dishonored, Octavian had to make a move, so he borrowed 120 ships from Antony. With his war vessels secured and a sound battle plan, Octavian made his bold naval attack. To his utter dismay, however, this battle proved to be a devastating defeat for Octavian, and he barely escaped with his life. Swimming to the shoreline, Octavian was seriously distraught. Not only was his resolve and self-esteem shattered but it was painfully clear that any respect he had already earned was critically compromised. Worse still, Roman citizens now feared a reprisal from Sextus.

However, rather than submit to misfortune, Octavian summoned his inner strength and rekindled his spirits. With the aid of his feeble third partner Lepidus, they plotted another attack. This time he and Lepidus would make a sweeping land invasion. Landing at Sicily, they marched toward Pompey's base camp. Meanwhile, Octavian's fleet, led by Agrippa, took to the seas for a three-pronged attack. As it happened, Agrippa spotted Sextus at sea and victoriously crushed his malicious Neptune fleet. The threat of Sextus Pompey was finally extinguished. In a moment of opportunistic glory or perhaps underhanded greed, Lepidus rallied Pompey's leaderless troops to his side and ordered Octavian to leave the island. Octavian was faced with a critical decision, either to cave in or charge in.

In typical Octavian fashion, he did neither. Heroically, he took one bodyguard and brazenly walked straight into Lepidus' camp. Ordered to strike down the bold, young leader, some soldiers refused while others hurled their javelins. Amid the halfhearted salvo of spears, Octavian strode forward and snatched the eagle standard from their legion. Lepidus' troops stood in awe, and then jubilantly hailed Octavian as Caesar. Their vote of allegiance was clear, and no blood of their fellow Romans was spilled. Octavian strategically and peacefully had crushed Lepidus in a landslide.

Octavian's resolve and convictions paid off. He had turned defeat and rejection into victory and adulation. Naturally Agrippa was instrumental in the realm of military strategy and tactics, however, Octavian clearly demonstrated a natural gift for instinct, and often eschewed typical or expected responses. Almost two millennia later, Napoleon Bonaparte posited his belief that a leader's ability to tackle situations with pure instinct was far more desirable and admirable than using preplanned and routine methodologies. In this regard, Octavian often surprised his rivals and colleagues with a quicksilver maneuver that more often than not was unexpected and brilliant.

Moreover, Octavian surprised all of Rome by not killing his traitorous co-ruler Lepidus; instead, he bestowed clemency, allowing him to live a full life. Moreover, Octavian even allowed Lepidus to retain his religious title of *pontifex maximus*—the highest priest. Romans had much to celebrate, for Sextus Pompey's terror tactics had finally ended, and Roman blood was saved. However, much still lay ahead.

Back in Greece, Antony's fourth year of marriage effectively ended. His renewed ambitions for glory prompted him to divorce Octavia and reunite with his Egyptian flame. Antony and Cleopatra made a long-dreamt-of rendezvous in Antioch, where they were finally married. Tagging along with the Egyptian queen were their two children, as well as Caesarion, her lovechild from her earlier liaison with Julius Caesar. The young boy was now her co-ruler, as Egypt tradition prohibited a woman from ruling alone.

Impulsive as always, Antony hastily proclaimed his four-year-old children as rulers, and even went a step further by granting eastern territories to them as gifts. These actions conveniently fueled Octavian's already effective propaganda campaigns that accused Antony of treason. Antony's alliance with the Egyptian queen caused many of his close associates and soldiers to grow uneasy about her leadership role in Antony's affairs. King Herod of Jerusalem even suggested that Antony kill her. With growing tensions between Antony and Octavian mounting, many in Antony's camp began to reevaluate their loyalties. If Antony was to attack Rome with an Egyptian at his side, the consequences could be deadly, as no Roman would embrace a foreign leader who would defile the rich Roman pedigree.

As fortune would have it, a defector informed Octavian that Antony had secured his will in the Temple of Vesta, and that it was scandalous in nature. The Vestal Virgins refused to hand it over, but if he were so bold as to defile the sanctity of the Temple, they would not stand in his way. Believing that the will's toxic content would justify his irreverent actions, Octavian boldly entered the Temple and seized Antony's will. This was a gutsy gamble that now awaited a verdict.

Octavian then read aloud to the Senate all of Antony's wild and traitorous propositions. Among other things, Antony's will offered all inheritance of empire to Cleopatra and their children. Worse yet, Antony intended to move the capital from Rome to Alexandria in Egypt. Needless to say, the anger infused by this revelation quickly vaporized Octavian's indiscretion at the Temple and united all of Rome to rally behind him.

The showdown took place in the Ionian Sea, near the Greek province of Actium. Cleopatra played her part by providing her husband with additional ships and a supply line emanating from Egypt. All the prime actors in this conflict were on board, as Octavian and Agrippa sailed the Adriatic to confront Antony and Cleopatra. However, Octavian's fleet shrewdly kept a low profile—it was prudent to make Antony appear to be the aggressor. Octavian and Agrippa separated as Octavian's fleet made landfall in order to scout the rocky shore. Meanwhile, Agrippa sailed his force south of Antony to cut off the crucial lifeline supplied by Cleopatra's Egyptian network.

As Antony's heavier and more sluggish ships made their attack, the smaller and faster vessels designed by Agrippa out-maneuvered them and began inflicting serious damage. As ships sank, Cleopatra became more anxious. With death and defeat looming, she decided to flee the battle and steered her ships toward Egypt. Antony was in the throes of combat when he suddenly turned and saw the sterns of his lover's fleet receding southward. This is when Antony's true allegiance came to the fore, as he impulsively abandoned his Roman compatriots. Commandeering a smaller ship, Antony feverishly chased after his queen, and the two scheming lovers hastily returned to Alexandria.

Antony's abandoned fleet agonizingly lost heart and in utter humiliation, they capitulated to Octavian. Meanwhile, Antony's land forces had been left in the dark about their leader's ignoble actions. Octavian knew that he could not pursue Antony until his legions were confronted and the matter of loyalty was resolved. Weeks passed, however, before Octavian encountered the leaderless soldiers. By this point, the soldiers knew something was amiss and they immediately began negotiations with Octavian to maintain their active commissions rather than face disgrace and decommissioning. After days of haggling, Octavian generously granted their request. With the allegiance of his new soldiers secured Octavian took to the sea once more.

However rather than impetuously hunting down Antony, Octavian had much to mull over, therefore, he opted to take a hiatus on the island of Samos. Octavian now acquired an oversized military force that couldn't be maintained for the rest of the mission. Therefore, Agrippa was ordered back to Rome with thousands of soldiers who were to be decommissioned. They would receive the bad news once they hit shore, as all the older veterans would have to hand in their weapons.

Octavian couldn't be sure where Antony and Cleopatra had fled; perhaps they sought sanctuary in some distant territory outside the known realm of the Mediterranean world or perhaps they sought to enlist the forces of distant provinces of the empire. Octavian prudently waited until he knew that Rome's several client kings, who ruled lands quasi independently, remained loyal to him and Rome rather than Mark Antony, the runaway traitor and rebel. The Armenians and the unconquered Parthians, who Antony had left to confront Octavian, took this unsettled moment to remain defiant. However, they would be dealt with later, as Octavian not only needed to resolve the Antony issue, but was also presented with an urgent message from Agrippa. The disgruntled veterans back in Rome were growing rebellious; they had been discharged without property or financial reward, and as such, faced homelessness and penury.

Octavian returned to the Roman peninsula at the southern port city of Brundisium. He was greeted by all the Senators from Rome, which was very unusual yet impressive. That they would all leave the imperial city to greet Octavian several hundred miles away was a tremendous sign of loyalty, and for some capitulation. In essence, they knew Octavian was Rome's new undisputed leader and they had to pay their respects.

Displaying his skills of leadership, Octavian effectively quelled the disgruntled soldiers, not with tangible compensation, which he did not possess at the time, but with the promise of even greater rewards, once his Egyptian mission was complete. Octavian had long pondered conquering Egypt, for his adoptive father had never fully seized the country, which was rich in grain, exotic spices, golden artifacts, flamboyant jewelry, and royal heirlooms. With this added incentive, Octavian could now begin the last leg of his decade-long mission to secure ultimate power. For the final showdown, however, Octavian would not be accompanied by Agrippa; he would face Antony alone.

Saturated with the sea's misty air and a sense of assuredness, Octavian sailed south and entered the port of Alexandria. Meanwhile, Antony and Cleopatra had lived the past year in excess, knowing the end was near. Antony had fallen into bouts of deep depression, so Cleopatra made sure feasts and wine numbed his dark affliction. With word of Octavian's arrival, Antony quickly dispatched ships to confront his adversary. But after the shameful debacle at Actium, Antony's seamen peacefully deserted and greeted Octavian without drawing swords. With his now enlarged fleet closing off the port, Octavian landed ashore.

Left standing alone and abandoned, Antony flew into a rage and cursed Cleopatra for his men's desertion—he had turned his back on them for her sake, and now they stood defenseless. In a last ditch effort, Antony sent a message to Octavian challenging him to a duel, mano e mano. Octavian shook his head with a grin, and coolly responded that "there were many different ways that Antony can die," and this was certainly not one of them.

Dreading this calamitous moment, Cleopatra locked herself inside her mausoleum. It was stocked not only with countless treasures, but also flammable materials that, if need be, she could ignite. Her immolation would deprive Octavian of her riches and more importantly, her body, which would be used as a token of Octavian's victory, and a symbol of her disgrace. In a state of frenzy, Cleopatra sent a message to Mark Antony stating that she committed suicide. As Antony nervously read the devastating words, his heart cried to be silenced. In anguish, he drew his sword, spun it around, and thrust it into his stomach.

Antony's aim, however, went amiss, and the wound was not fatal. Asking someone to strike the deadly blow, Antony lay slowly dying as those nearby ran away and abandoned the disgraced leader. He then received word that Cleopatra was still alive. Dutifully, the queen's servants carried his limp body to her mausoleum. Fearful of Octavian, Cleopatra refused to unlock the doors, so Antony had to be hoisted up to an opening above the sealed entranceway. Cleopatra feverishly helped to pull him inside, her faced contorted with physical stress and emotional strain. As her lover came within reach, she pulled the limp carcass onto her lap. Drenched in blood and tears, Antony pleaded with her to save her own life, and then died in her arms.

Stricken with grief, the queen sat numb, as the weight of her dead lover in her arms mirrored the weight upon her soul. As she gazed into his lifeless eyes, she realized what is gone is gone, but what remains might not remain. As her tear-filled eyes traveled upward, her mind's eye pictured her innocent children, who having been placed upon the throne at early ages exempted them from clemency according to the rules of war. The deadly folly of Antony and Cleopatra was painfully sobering.

In desperation, Cleopatra knew she had to make a final effort for survival, not only for her children but also for her own lifelong struggle for ultimate power. Wiping her tears, and swallowing a lump of pride mixed with pain, she summoned her servant. With renewed composure, Cleopatra gave her message—the queen was prepared to meet Octavian.

Upon receiving the queen's plea, Octavian honorably allayed the servant's' fears and was escorted to the mausoleum. As the doors unlocked, Octavian assertively entered Cleopatra's chamber. To his amazement, the seductress brazenly attempted to use her charms to lure her third Roman prey. However, Octavian was impervious to her parlor tricks. After a last ditch effort, of pointing the finger of blame on Antony and others, it became painfully clear that her efforts were in vain, and Octavian calmly silenced her and then sat down beside her.

Cleopatra had effectively seduced men more than twice her age, however, this time she was coldly reprimanded point-for-point in a paternal fashion, oddly enough, by a man three years her junior. The conniving and over-ambitious queen was numbed into silence. For the first time, she was powerless to beguile a Roman master of the world. Although Octavian came from the same stock, he was certainly a different breed. In desperation, Cleopatra fell to her knees and begged to be slain.

Cognizant of his newly acquired power, Octavian looked down at her as a deluge of emotions flooded his senses. Suddenly, he felt the shame that Cleopatra brought to his great-uncle Julius and Rome by fathering Caesarion, not to mention the threat to his inheritance. Then he thought of her insulting marriage to Caesar's closest friend Antony, and how Antony in turn traitorously pardoned Caesar's killers and seized his estate. However, most unavoidable was how the seductress rapaciously worked his great-uncle, then Antony, and now even him. A mixture of revulsion and vengeance surged through his veins. But suddenly there was a new emotion—pity.

Octavian stepped back and paused. With another completely unexpected maneuver, Octavian promised to spare her and grant her the right to give Mark Antony full honorable funeral rites. With utter calm, Octavian turned and exited the chamber.

Sitting in solitude, Cleopatra contemplated how shameful it would be to be paraded as a dethroned spectacle in Rome, when two decades earlier she had been paraded as Caesar's glittering queen. Suddenly the traditional Egyptian rite of self-sacrifice seemed most appropriate. Having one of her servants smuggle a poisonous asp hidden in a basket of figs, Cleopatra awaited her final breath.

As the queen sat, visions of the glorious days with Caesar and the more recent escapades with Antony flashed through her mind. Her ambitious path had seemed so full of hope. Meanwhile, the asp slithered up Cleopatra's arm. With a sudden prick, she flinched; her happy memories painfully vanished. Her body fell flaccidly, and a bright vision of Julius embracing Octavian must have flashed before her eyes. As the queen hit the floor, reality jarred her senses, for the reptilian creature now stared her straight in the eye. To her shock, it appeared as if the Caesarian kiss of death had been administered. Her heart jolted as darkness stole her last breath.

Receiving word of her desperate deed, Octavian rushed to her chamber, but, alas, it was too late. Octavian's trophy of victory was destroyed, and all that remained was her letter of instruction—her final request to be buried alongside her husband, Mark Antony.

Being viewed by many as the ultimate strategist, some feel that Octavian may have calculated Cleopatra's demise. However, at this point, all that was left was for the jackal-headed god Anubis to haul her soul into the underworld. As for Antony, very few Romans cared where his tarnished soul would venture.

Octavian took the opportunity to finally seize full control of the Egyptian state. Egypt would remain under his personal supervision, for its rich grain supply was crucial to Rome. As such, it was a vital ace to hold, particularly when playing against the scheming senators back at the Forum's grand casino of power politics. Naturally, having Egypt's royal treasury would also be crucial for paying off his debt to the thousands of soldiers awaiting compensation.

When Octavian finally returned to Rome, he organized an extravaganza that celebrated his triumphs over the course of three days. The ceremonies ended with a procession of rhinoceroses and hippopotamuses, animals the Romans saw for the first time. Also on parade were Cleopatra's and Antony's twins—they had both been spared. However, Caesarion, being a threat to the throne, was not spared. With civil war over, and stability finally restored, the people of Rome rejoiced.

Fifteen years had passed since the murder of Julius Caesar, and after many military and political stratagems, Octavian's aggressive phase of the operation was finally over. Some Romans were still understandably apprehensive, as they had no idea what to expect. Octavian certainly proved to be calculating and ruthless in his military quest for sole authority, but would bloody political reprisals now erupt? Furthermore, although battle-hardened and a quick learner in military strategies, what kind of legislative statesman would this inexperienced young man possibly be?

Once again, Octavian proved unpredictable. The last man standing in a brutal battle for domination, Octavian unexpectedly returned to his humble country boy roots. To the amazement and delight of all, his temperate provincial core had remained intact under his steely armor, where it was forced to lay dormant for fifteen years while the task of securing control was achieved. Thus began his metamorphosis, whereby yielding his new title, Augustus. As Augustus, he began his long tenure of instilling new laws, programs, and morals to form an empire devoted to peace and progress. Hence, the bloodstained hands of Octavian would be cleansed by the peaceful and pious ones of Augustus.

The New Age of Augustus

Octavian soon proved that his competency and effectiveness at administrating war translated well in the political arena. His forte had been gathering intelligence and advice, mainly from Agrippa and Maecenas, analyzing data and supervising his campaigns. Unlike Caesar and other militarily bred men of his time, Octavian only had a crash course to launch his career. Furthermore, he was simply not made of military stock. Although he overcame his initial infirmities and became a somewhat skilled general, he had always had Agrippa at his side, except for the last voyage and final showdown in Egypt. This silent co-partnership was an asset, for many times their strategies relied upon simultaneous attacks by land and sea, thus surrounding and unexpectedly crushing the enemy who was only positioned in one location and led by one commander.

Octavian's innate talent for administration was hardened with practical military experience. In this regard, Octavian would have been better suited to being a modern-day general, where physically engaging the enemy is not required. Oddly enough, Octavian has been ridiculed by some past and present for not being a rough physical specimen in battle, like Julius or Agrippa. However, not only are generals today exempt from physical engagement but this critique also conveys an additional double standard. Ruling women, such as Queen Elizabeth or Catherine the Great were never expected to physically engage battle and their final appraisals never reflect that shortcoming. However, because Octavian was a man and lived in a world where generals were expected to physically lead he was held to a different standard.

Therefore, using today's standards, Octavian's war record should be praised; like Eisenhower during WWII, Octavian oversaw great generals who had more bravado and field experience than he did. Patton and Eisenhower were two different beasts, the first more brutish and seasoned in the battlefield, the latter more refined and calculating. Yet, even these twentieth century generals were not expected to strap on armor, wield a sword, and accompany their men in hand-to-hand combat, regardless of how far back in the ranks they were. Therefore, a double standard exists for evaluating ancient generals. Octavian's "shortcoming" has been one of the major complaints about him from his day until present, which may very well explain why his bold adoptive-father remains more popular to this day.

However, that Octavian managed to secure a long string of victories, even later on, without Agrippa by his side, indicates some command of military strategy and leadership. Furthermore, the overall victories and territories that would be won under his regime exceeded that of Julius Caesar. As the empire's head commander, Octavian deserves this much credit. Agrippa's role is inseparable from the equation, however. Agrippa was not merely full of bravado; his impressive strategic and engineering skills, coupled with his rugged physique clearly made him the more gifted of the two in battle. Furthermore, it was Agrippa, more than anyone else, who cultivated Octavian's skills in warfare.

Nevertheless, Octavian's talents would now be utilized in areas far more suited to his innate temperament and skill sets, these being, the acquisition and analysis of data, conceptualization of both large and small projects, problem solving, and organization. This is where his true talents were finally unleashed and really shone. Likewise, Octavian's ability for diplomacy and engaging the wily senators and high-browed aristocracy was also something that Agrippa lacked. Together, they proved to be the perfect and unrivalled dynamic duo.

After the showdown with Antony, Octavian and Agrippa still only held the seats of high consuls. However, everyone knew that Octavian was the mastermind and that Agrippa was the loyal and powerful right arm. At a Senatorial session, one day, Octavian approached them with two very odd requests that left many shocked and bewildered. First, he asked to be allowed to stand down and relinquish all his power. Second, he would hand over all the territories he had won for Rome.

As we have seen, Octavian was a master at calculation and this maneuver was not pure benevolence and certainly not mindless folly, for he had laid a solid and respectable foundation. During his long tenure as consul, Octavian had befriended many governors and aristocrats throughout the empire. His favors and support would now require a vote of confidence in return. Additionally, after his house-cleaning period, where his adoptive father's assassins were eliminated, Octavian instated new blood in the Senate. Many senators were still of the old Republican stock, however, so Octavian's gesture was also meant to allay their fear that he would follow in his adoptive father's tyrannical footsteps.

Octavian's gesture was brilliant politically: the shocked senators quickly appointed him executive powers, and honored him with the new name Augustus, meaning Revered One. Although Octavian's plan was well calculated, we must also not lose sight of how fair-minded and even noble his actions were. Too often Augustus has been lumped into the stereotypical bin of maniacal emperors or domineering dictators. This is grossly incorrect, for he was viewed by the Senate as the most capable man to lead their government—which he undoubtedly was—and furthermore, Augustus did not wrest control and demand imperial powers. More importantly, Augustus did not dismantle the Senate or

Republican infrastructure. These men were still to be part of the governing process: in the United States today, American senators likewise expect a single executive to run the country while they have their specific duties and influence. Further still, the founding fathers of America did not choose the purely Republican model, but rather the Augustan variant, with one overriding executive who chooses his own counselors or cabinet. Therefore, this new precedent, which occurred on January 13, 27 BC, was monumental in many respects.

Octavian's transition was crucial for other personal reasons as well. As Octavian, he had genuinely fought to defend the honor of his adoptive father, who was his sole ticket to power. As such, he never forgot or ignobly disrespected his loving mentor. Furthermore, Octavian ensured that revenge was properly exacted and that Caesar was honored accordingly. Part of the Caesar legacy is due to Augustus, who kept the name alive for all succeeding emperors to use, and foreigners to adopt. However, Octavian was not a mere shadow of his great-uncle. Octavian had a powerful vision, one that in some ways opposed Caesar's, and it was now *his time* to prove *his mettle*. Therefore, distancing himself from Caesar in terms of dictatorial behavior, and gaining the new name of Augustus were crucial for starting on a clean slate.

Augustus eagerly committed himself to peaceful and industrious endeavors, which must have been a great relief to him. In fact, when Augustus heard of Antony's demise, he reportedly burst into tears. This was certainly not for losing a fellow Roman; instead, the emotional dam had been purged thus releasing over a decade's worth of harbored emotions. In essence, Octavian, the toxic reservoir turned into Augustus, the purified aqueduct.

This became reality, in a figurative sense, when Augustus' huge engineering and construction projects commenced, with Agrippa's technical aid. With new aqueducts, political edifices, libraries, shopping centers, apartment buildings, and temples, not to mention an elaborate network of roads, ancient Rome was transformed into a beacon of imperial splendor. Augustus also turned the local roadways into a marvelous multicontinental superhighway. That vast network, which even exceeds America's present highway system in scope, naturally improved military swiftness yet it also bolstered communications and inevitably enhanced commercial trade.

The importance of roads nowadays seems almost trivial in hindsight: they are taken for granted and most people only focus on their personal advantages. However, economic studies indicates how trade via roadways or river systems has had a direct effect on many nations. President Eisenhower endorsed emulating Rome's highway infrastructure, which has had a tremendous effect on America's growth, lifestyle, and efficiency. Earlier still, turning the Mississippi River into a major trade route caused enormous change along the river, not to mention the migration of people and rise and fall of job markets in the wake of such major enterprises. Similarly, the road system that Augustus bequeathed to all of Europe, and parts of Africa and Asia, had an enormous influence on altering the social, economic, and political dynamics of the ancient world and those of future generations.

Augustus also inaugurated Rome's first official police and firefighting force, called the *Vigiles Urbani* (watchmen of the city), as well as the Praetorian Guards (Secret Service)—all of which were pioneering, vital organizations for public safety and political security. Modern readers may not be able to fathom how society could operate without police or firefighters, however that was the bane of ancient civilizations. These three crucial organizations, despite the neglect of some future leaders to maintain them, have become part of every great nation today.

Augustus' initiatives also included expansion along the empire's borders, including Dalmatia, Egypt, and parts of Germania, Spain, and the Middle East. Conquering these troublesome territories finally closed vulnerable gaps and solidified the empire. However, this expansive area presented Augustus with the difficult task of unifying a staggering diversity of peoples. Even though his new and expanding empire was bound together under a united system of rule, many of its fringe provinces held onto their national traits and customs. This required an innovative approach to maintain political order, public relations, and religious tolerance, and Augustus managed it with aplomb in all regions, except for Germania. The vicious refusal of the German tribes to accept Romanization was akin to the warring Muslims today who despise

Americanization. Augustus prophetically perceived this irreconcilable clash of ideologies, and after a disastrous defeat near the end of his reign, Augustus avoided further confrontation. Centuries later, his worst fears were realized when the barbarians (more so by immigration than invasion) despoiled the greater part of the Romans' rich culture.

Added to Augustus' precarious task of maintaining secure borders and peace was the important issue of economic stability. The Roman economy was based upon a solid coinage system. Although it was initiated during the Roman Republic, Augustus revamped the system and introduced a new set of seven coins. These proved to stabilize the economy during his own administration and lasted for three hundred years (until Diocletian revamped them due to economic pressures). Some later emperors even diluted the precious metal content of their coins and frequently manipulated exchange rates in an effort to achieve financial stability.

This stands in direct contrast to the modern revisionists of history, like sociologist Rodney Stark for one, who assert that Roman emperors totally controlled and suppressed the economy. Many historians, with the aid of archaeologists, have now confirmed what was previously known—the early Roman Empire was primarily an open market of trade and commerce. As with all ancient regimes, Rome had its share of despots, such as Caligula or Nero who manipulated coinage for their own personal greed and to control markets, but during the golden age of Augustus—which lasted over two centuries—many documents and archeological finds reveal a booming economy.

Pompeii is an example of one such thriving city. It supported metalworkers, dyers, bakers, tanners, jewelers, and other prosperous businessmen. Like other major Roman cities, it contained many shops that sold vegetables, ceramics, wine, oil, and fish among many other products. These dynamic venues of commerce, along with lavish housing throughout the city and the villas nearby, all indicate an extremely prosperous society, unhampered by economic suppression.

Interestingly enough, most historians have measured Roman colonization solely upon its huge urban developments, but modern excavations have unearthed expansive villas in rural areas, which were of equal importance. Under Augustus the Romans leveled existing mud shacks and constructed elaborate facilities that enhanced agricultural harvests and enriched the lifestyles of its rural citizens. Moreover, the Roman roads initially built to traffic troops, immediately increased trade significantly and proved beneficial for all sorts of communications.

Commentary on the Roman and American Empires

In recent years, perhaps due to America's involvement in the Middle East and the accusation of America's aggressive imperialism, there has been an increase in the number of books by scholars who have an innate distaste for Rome. Perhaps the three main authors are Rodney Stark, Roger Osborne, and John Dominic Crossan, although there are certainly others. In general, they see Rome as the evil and aggressive conquering empire that many centuries later got what it deserved when it was ransacked by the barbarians. Their views inevitably attempt to compare modern America to Rome in a distorted and even offensive manner. As such, our attention will now shift to analyzing this modern phenomenon along with its ancient roots.

There can be no doubt that many see an obvious connection between Rome and America. But where this author sees a fair balance of good and bad qualities inherited from Rome, these authors often fabricate fiction to support their ideological agendas. Their hatred for the ancient progenitor takes on new heights of condemnation by stripping Rome of every single facet of greatness, thus grinding the famous gem into dirt. This seems to be done with the dual aim of making America look like it, too, has run amok. Like radical Hollywood actors who mindlessly defame America, some scholars trash Rome for its aggressive power (which shall be discussed in turn) and even its creativity, such as building roads.

Criticizing roads may seem trivial, but roads were not only a huge multi-continental project but also a colossal advancement for human activity and productivity. The network of roads in the ancient world is equivalent to the Internet today, for interconnectivity incites progress. Therefore, by trivializing roads, critics debase Roman ingenuity. The sociologist, Rodney Stark, lambastes Rome as being utterly impotent and attacked Roman roads as being not only overrated but also "useless."

Further claiming that the stone construction of roads was substandard and "hard on legs and feet when dry, and very slippery when wet."

With colossal audacity, Stark attacks a vast system of roads that were built and maintained for well over a thousand years. Road construction, repair, and maintenance bills have been found and documented, as well as communications from emperors, public officials, and landowners that reveal the understanding and necessity of maintaining these integral networks. Additionally, a special department was created, headed by the *curatores viarum* (guardians of the roadway), to keep these vast roadways in good condition. The amount of time, resources, money, and labor to not only start this project, but also continue it over many centuries, which spread over the full breadth of Europe and beyond, would have been the most colossally stupid enterprise undertaken by countless rulers and administrators in all of history if it were not useful.

As for the construction of roads themselves, they were not simply stones randomly tossed about; the process was soundly planned and extensive in nature. The roadways were first mapped out and then excavated, which required digging a three-foot trench, which was then filled with various layers of gravel for stability and drainage. Finally, the topmost layer of paving stones were carefully shaped and installed. These stones were not simply laid flat, but were carefully shaped with a slight crown in the middle of the road for drainage. The core methodology of this painstaking process is still used today.

What is true, however, is that roads fell into disrepair from the Dark Ages to the eighteenth century. This included roads in England. With the excessively high rainfall and humidity in England, perhaps it was these roads that Stark referred to as being too slippery to be of use. Nevertheless, road construction and repair ceased during the Dark Ages due to the weak decentralized governments that, unlike Rome, did not understand how vital it was to maintain roads for the unity, efficiency, and security of their nation-states. When Roman government ceased to exist, feudalism and eventually small city-states took hold of the sprawling and splintered territories, none of which desired to invest in external matters, for under the veil of isolationism, both rivalry and indifference increased and unity decreased.

Furthermore, during Augustus' reign, he directed the senators to impress upon the local officials the need to build and maintain roads. Augustus was the first Roman ruler to understand the broader implications and necessities of roadways. Yet his plea fell upon deaf ears: many of the villages were content to remain self-sufficient, and saw no need to break their isolated existence by building or repairing roads. Despite their complacency and refusal to embrace change for the sake of progress, Augustus dug into his own pocket and implemented a full-scale roadway operation. This not only forced interactive trade and the exchange of ideas but was more extensive than any Republican before or emperor after ever attempted to achieve. Moreover, the increase in communication and trade throughout the empire due to this network was incalculable, as its effects extended well beyond its own day and had an immense impact on future generations.

Roman builders received praise over many centuries for devising and constructing this vast network of roads—which later developed into cobblestone streets and eventually asphalt highways—for one obvious reason—progress. Roads made life easier and far more productive. It is also important to note that the cobblestone streets from the sixteenth century, past the Industrial Revolution, and right up to the early twentieth century were not very smooth thoroughfares. These later roads, in fact, showed very little progress beyond their Roman prototype, thus verifying how very few improvements were made in road construction after the Roman precedent. Therefore, for any scholar to claim that the Romans weren't inventive or industrious, especially in light of the many other engineering feats they pioneered, simply defies logic and the huge abundance of tangible evidence that exists.

The Roman commercial shipping industry was also an extensive network that supported international trade. One such example was the huge ceramics industry, which transported pottery, urns, jars, oil, and foodstuffs to all parts of the empire. The infiltration of products, especially those that were transported deep into rural areas, lends further evidence that the villages were not self-sufficient entities operating apart from the mighty empire, but were integral parts of a unified economy; or cogs of a well-oiled and organized machine. Despite extraction of resources from foreign outposts to benefit Roman citizens (which America does likewise), the economy of the empire was based upon open trade and a competitive market of goods that fostered inventiveness and a consumerist spirit.

This is further substantiated by the fact that many archeological excavations have revealed independent shops, like those in Pompeii, as well as shopping malls at sites scattered across the empire that sold foreign goods. Surviving records of taxation and trade, some in the hand of the emperor's own words, which ordered "fair mindedness", along with many large enterprises operated by the landed aristocracy, only proved to bolster the economy. Even without an independent mercantile class, or the compulsory fixed-rate purchases used to feed the army, the Roman state used incentives and adjusted taxes in order to influence traders and boost the economy.

When Nero dishonestly raised taxes to sponsor his ostentatious Golden House in the center of Rome, the citizens openly revolted. Tolerance for Nero's extravagance wore thin and he was faced with assassination. Justice, however, finally prevailed when Nero opted for suicide. Yet these flagrant atrocities burn deeper into the minds of modern readers than do the significant number of stupendous deeds by good and even great emperors. Many of these men made genuine and respectable attempts to improve the empire, and keep the lifeblood of this amazing enterprise, with its long and proud past, flowing well into the future.

People of varying ethnicities from all parts of the sprawling empire contributed different languages, products, and customs that had to be dealt with in order to make this huge political and economic machine work. In this regard, the Romans planted the first seed of international trade laws and economics that grew into the root of our global economy today. Where the Romans traded over their network of roads, today we network over the Internet; where the Romans developed laws to unite a variety of peoples, the United Nations governs with international law; and where the Romans minted a universal coinage system, the Europeans have now minted the euro.

These solid infrastructures of economics, trade, law, coinage, architecture and the military were initially developed during the previous Republic, yet it was Augustus, and his significant alterations, that effected all these policies, which began the long and fruitful rise of an amazing empire that influenced all of Western civilization.

As history shows, Augustus successfully ruled Rome for almost half a century. As a result, all Romans knew that the times had changed for the better, and they willingly embraced this most prosperous and peaceful era—later to be known as The Age of Augustus, or in Augustus' own words, the *Pax Romana* (Roman Peace).

Despite Augustus' successful rise to power being replete with bloody battles, double-dealing, propaganda, and the elimination of his and Julius Caesar's rivals, some critics today forget that all great nations have been born in blood, not anointed oil. Yet, some detractors piously mount their idle podiums and lambaste many ancient rulers and nations for their hostile tactics. However, many factors need to be assessed when analyzing historical figures, their actions, and their nation's actions. Therefore, the issue at hand is that the fight for survival, which includes preemptive tactics, is sometimes an unwelcome necessity. At the heart of that initiative are profound ideologies and beliefs that often trample on ethics. This intense and controversial issue not only applies to Rome but also to its distant heir America, therefore, we shall now address this American issue with its Roman roots.

America was built upon aggression that eventually conquered an indigenous race to achieve what they perceived as the best culture, a culture moreover dedicated to progress and survival. This was perhaps most notably executed by President James Polk *(see pg. 712)*, under the banner of Manifest Destiny. Our forefathers' deep-seated ideology, graced by divine guidance, boldly espoused the cultivation, promulgation, and preservation of their culture as a right, for themselves and for their children's and culture's survival. This vision is simply unimaginable to many in today's politically correct crowd, who only wish to see idyllic harmony, rather than confront cold reality. Yet, here they stand more than two centuries after their nation's birth, not comprehending the realities of its creation or the nation-building process in general.

This lapse in judgment can perhaps best be understood by a psychological analogy. Some children who are born into wealth find it easy to ungratefully criticize or even ignorantly abuse the comfortable privileges that their family struggled to accumulate and secure. It is often these subsequent generations, who are born into a world of luxury, liberty, civility, and stability that fail to appreciate the sacrifices of their forebears who allotted them their peaceful and prosperous station in life. Studies show that these later generations, detached from the pangs and pains of survival, quite often squander and lose their families' wealth.

Nowadays, this attitude no longer afflicts only wealthy families, but many Americans who have been born into a peaceful and secured nation. Their ancestors were the ones who faced peril and fought in the bloody battlefields to secure peace, for the cold wars and terrorism of today still pose little to no direct threat to the vast majority of these fortunate generations that never had to pick up a rifle. Their ability to even understand this vital connection has sadly been severed.

Despite our logical and principled preference for peace, we must understand that our forefathers committed these harsh and unpleasant actions to survive, for without such actions their way of life most assuredly would have faltered or failed. Furthermore, their progeny would have either been subjected to foreign domination or most likely never born at all. Sadly, it is often this satiated and comfortable generation—living in a pristine environment and thinking pristine thoughts—that reaps all the benefits derived from these brave souls that endured immense sacrifice and spilt their blood, sweat, and tears.

What these peace-loving critics overlook is that the birth of any great nation, including our own, is similar to childbirth, for it is inevitably drenched in blood. It is during this bloody and traumatic beginning that leaders fight to either survive and foster progress, or simply fight for greed or prejudice. The latter was not America's intent, despite some anomalies, nor was it always Rome's. Obviously, some Roman emperors destroyed the grand vision by selfishly ignoring the fundamental rules and objectives laid down by Augustus, as well as the many other great rulers before and after him, but the purpose of the Roman mission was most often to secure their way of life.

This can be seen by comparing Roman conquests to those of Alexander the Great. Alexander conquered other nations purely for self-gratification, as he had no economic or political plan for cultivating and assimilating these peoples into a better or more cultured way of life. Alexander was first and foremost a warrior, and the foreign captives in his wake eagerly sought to regain their old nation-states and traditions, which most successfully did once Alexander died. Although the city of Alexandria in Egypt stands as the best remnant of Alexander's exploits, this city, along with a few others, were primarily established by Alexander's generals who were left up to their own devices to create something tangible. However, all would fall to Roman conquest. Hence, Alexander's numerous glorified conquests amounted to very little but personal glory and murder. This type of conquest is impossible to justify.

In contrast, most Roman missions were designed to expand the size of their civilization by uplifting the conquered to a higher standard and winning converts to their cultivated way of life, whereby securing the empire's existence. Strength comes in numbers, which inevitably needs to be buttressed by a larger landmass. This was a guiding principle of survival for the Romans as well as the early Americans.

Thomas Jefferson was a noted pacifist, yet, once he became president, he unconstitutionally acquired the Louisiana territory. As a visionary, Jefferson knew this landmass would help secure his nation's future, however despite the peaceful purchase, Jefferson knew that Americans would still have to confront and battle the Native Americans that inhabited much of that land, and indeed, blood was spilled.

In essence, a motivated group that is willing to sacrifice everything in order to build something new and highly precious is likewise willing to protect that interest at all costs. This explains how and why strong leaders rose in the past who today would face condemnation.

Naturally, we all crave a leader who is perfect, yet such a leader never existed, at least not in the mortal realm. Even George Washington, who is often hailed as the ideal leader, commanded his troops with an iron fist, and those disobeying certain commands would be shot; such a practice would be considered barbaric by today's standards. Similar practices by the Romans were flaunted and heavily condemned, but in George Washington's case, it remained discreetly unmentioned until recently.

Punishments today have softened, but defending cultivated ideologies against barbarism or even tribal mavericks unfortunately requires weapons and blood, not pen and ink. So punishment for deadly rebels or traitors, for example, still requires the harsh life sentence. Every great leader had flaws, and we can only assess them on whether their merits outweighed their demerits, and if their intentions were selfish or selfless. What a leader or nation bestows on the world or posterity is what matters—the key question will remain, did they instill more positive or negative influences? In an imperfect world, this certainly appears to be the way founding leaders and their nations must be judged.

The modern notion that peaceful or civilized negotiations can solve all issues can never apply to nation building. Many today criticize Andrew Jackson *(photo pg. 712)* for his Indian Removal Act, which, we must remember, the Senate passed. This Act instructed Native Americans to relocate to the west with financial assistance from the federal government. Those remaining would be subject to all United States laws and be required to culturally assimilate. From a modern perspective, Jackson's Removal Act certainly was cruel and insensitive, but, in his day, Jackson was a realist, and from *his* perspective, it was done with good intentions. We may scoff at that today, but Jackson had firsthand experience and intelligence of American and Indian relations; as such, he sought to put an end to the slaughters that had already annihilated several tribes, while accomplishing the controversial goal of Manifest Destiny.

Jackson was reared in the military and fought many battles against the Indians, yet had befriended many chiefs along the way. Jackson had even raised an orphaned Indian boy, so some Indians had a modicum of respect for him even as an adversary, while he, with some degree of empathy, understood the Indian peoples, even if he possibly viewed them as an inferior race. Jackson was no modern man, but he clearly saw that the Indians did not wish to intermingle with whites or abandon their cultures. Some may have received an American education, like the Cherokee, but most would not renounce their tribal beliefs and customs. More importantly, they refused to be governed by American laws. This inability to fully assimilate caused an impasse, and Jackson knew this would lead to their annihilation if some sort of peaceful act weren't drafted.

Therefore, Jackson viewed The Indian Removal Act as being a logical and peaceful attempt to remove the Native Americans from a situation that he knew could erupt into bloody warfare. Although many relocated without incident, others took up arms, thus sadly involving bloodshed, yet fortunately not their extinction. Despite the unfortunate injustices that prevailed, and the regrettable Trail of Tears, Andrew Jackson did manage to prevent the Five Civilized Nations of Native Americans from being annihilated. However, what this illustrates is that even with peaceful attempts to achieve nation building, blood will be spilled.

Sadly, modern revisionists, with limited perspectives, have unjustly maligned many American heroes and the American storyline. The unprovoked Indian attacks recorded by Daniel Boone (that killed his sons and friends) and stories of many others bear this out. The Apache and Comanche, for example, even massacred each other, let alone the white man. Moreover, the budding nation had to contend with the Spanish, French, and British who were all vying for and devouring the New World's vast territory, as they *all* (including their native allies and native foes) posed very real threats to the new nation's security. Therefore, not only did this necessitate the need to expand America's borders, but it also demanded that all its new inhabitants were united citizens under one set of laws and customs.

Therefore, none of us today would enjoy our civilized station in life, or sense of security—being heirs of a huge powerful nation—if it were not for these brave souls, such as the early Americans or ancient Romans who boldly took action. The Romans' actions are what raised wayward tribesmen into industrious citizens, and they built villas and cities where mud huts and shacks previously existed, for the Romans fought for what they firmly believed to be progress. The evidence of their progress in many fields of endeavor clearly indicates that the colonial forefathers' preferences aligned with the Romans in this regard. The fruits of their endeavors unquestionably enhanced civilization. Extending that forward, we today have very similar preferences as well.

Americans today would no doubt prefer our modern society to living half-naked in teepees and huddled around a campfire; therefore, the Romans' preference for their lifestyle as compared to the barbarians, who lived in mud huts and huddled around a campfire, is not only comparable to our own predilections, but also helped shape them. If the barbarians prevailed and we were descendents of their way of life, we today might look back upon Roman civilization as too demanding, too materialistic, too grandiose, too complex, or too organized and preferred the more indolent and unstructured lifestyle that our barbarian heritage ingrained in us. It may seem difficult to imagine such an ideology, one that is reticent toward progress, order, and cultivating knowledge, but there are plenty of third world nations today, way beyond America's suburban minimansions or posh metropolitan apartments that do house these backward cultures and do have archaic histories. Their stagnant and broken-down lot in life is the tangible result of forebears with a more indolent ideology. So, should we condemn our forefathers as sinners or praise them as survivors?

Simply put, the Romans were faced with a clear decision of either forging a civilization, as they perceived it, or passively submitting to the prevailing barbarians and their dark concept of life. Although we can make the argument that the Romans lived in a distant past that was not cultivated like ours today, and as such, needs to be factored-in regarding their actions, this issue, in reality, exceeds just time and cultivation. In fact, it even exceeds religious compassion, which some Christian authors say pagans lacked, for that misses the intrinsic point.

First, there is a strange dichotomy when viewing history. On one hand, we see ancient man as barbarous, aggressive, or uneducated, and on the other, we expect them to be more modern than they really were. This last notion is primarily based upon viewing their magnificent achievements, such as their masterful edifices or beautiful artifacts, or even the admiration we have for their timeless words that traversed the ages.

In this last regard, we undeniably share the thoughts of the ancient Roman statesman, Cicero, who said, *"We are obliged to respect, defend, and maintain the common bonds of union and fellowship that exist among all members of the human race."*

Cicero's words sound not only shockingly "modern," but also "Christian," despite the fact that Jesus was not born when Cicero penned those benevolent words. Cicero was not alone, for another pagan Roman,

Seneca, said, *"It is a denial of justice not to stretch out a helping hand to the fallen; that is the common right of humanity."*

These quotes refute contemporary Christian authors who claim that men only began to display true compassion and humanity once Christianity graced mankind. They also underline a very crucial factor; namely, that most ancient people would have preferred peaceful interactions with other people *if it were always possible.*

This brings us to the second vital point. Here, the words of another ancient writer will elucidate how certain human traits simply do not change. Democritus bemoaned the fact that *"there is no device in the present state of society to stop the wrongdoing of officials."*

In this instance, we not only share his timeless and unresolved problem of inventing a perfect political system that would eradicate mankind's propensity for corruption, but it also points out how nation-building is likewise a timeless and unresolved problem, for today we would face the same tough decisions as the Romans or our own American founders if we were presented with the same situations. The fact that we today have been born into a well-established and powerful nation should not make us think for one minute that if we were forced into a deadly game of survival that our actions would be much different.

Moreover, just as Democritus' statement about unethical politicians confirms how certain human traits never change, so, too, have the disparate and irreconcilable beliefs of mankind never changed. Germanic barbarians or American natives held firm and polar beliefs from their foes, and neither side, *in total*, was willing to forfeit those beliefs. It is easy to imagine making peaceful negotiations with peaceful like-minded peoples, but that was simply not always the case. We only need to look at radical Muslims to see that neither they nor we would ever adopt our enemies' beliefs or surrender to live under our foe's sole dominion.

From the very first landing by Columbus, Europeans confronted Native Americans with different beliefs. Some were friendly and wronged by the white man, but others were hostile warriors or even godless savages. The Italian navigator Giovanni da Verrazzano *(photo page 710)* was exploring the Bahamas in 1528 when he landed on an island. He was captured, killed, and eaten by cannibals. Hence, the New World was not

Paradise like the revisionists claim, and not all natives were innocent victims of the white man—irreconcilable differences existed, and conflict was inevitable.

Even Biblical leaders spilt blood, for both Abraham and Moses took up arms and attacked the native Canaanites in attempts to found a nation. More provocative still is that those directives emanated from God himself.

Hence, the Romans' and Americans' actions all fall upon highly unstable moral grounds, for it all boils down to one's own beliefs, and the defense and promulgation of those beliefs. There is no doubt that civilization today would be vastly different if the Romans had not provided the civilization they did, which cultivated and drove mankind to live more productive lives.

As for those who belittle the Romans, it is key to remember that Americans today have the distinct vantage point of assessing primitive societies from their high perch atop the hierarchy of cultivation, of which the Romans were the chief architects who laid more solid tiers of century-long blocks than any other cultural contractor. From the advent of Rome in 750 BC to its official demise in AD 1453, the Romans have laid twenty-two blocks as opposed to America, who only contributed the top two. Such a long and, more importantly, influential existence, commands our attention, understanding, and even respect, not cynicism.

Despite the objections of those today who are fortunate enough to sit in the lap of luxury and espouse passive or pious methods for all human interactions, it is indisputable that their voices were only made possible by the strength and blood of these indomitable forefathers of Western history. And one of the most influential of all those early leaders was Augustus.

Augustus Reprise and Concluding Commentary

Augustus' agenda was clearly one of taking Rome to new heights. Amid the transitional turmoil, from Republic to either some new regime or total collapse, Augustus was in a position to either resign to failure or design a new future. His long-term vision, and ultimate success, all point to one of being resolute upon defending a lifestyle and culture that clearly out performed anything else in its day, as well as advocating and activating the wheels of progress. This was in lieu of acquiescing to a broken Republican system, which might have fallen to the primitive Germanic tribes or Persian kingdoms that encroached dangerously on Rome's borders.

Augustus' ultimate success, however, rested primarily upon one crucial fact, his vision was for Rome and Romanization, not for building an empire to fuel his own ego. Where Caesar looked inward, Augustus looked outward. When we compare Augustus' humble lifestyle as emperor to the grandiose achievements and enormous growth of his majestic empire this point becomes patent.

Beyond the visible grandeur of Rome, Augustus' actions that are more discreet strengthen this assessment. Augustus ordered 80 silver honorary statues of his likeness to be melted down into coins. He then donated large sums of that money to 250,000 civilians and 120,000 veterans. Additionally, he spent 700 million *sesterces* to purchase land for his veterans to settle on, and he practically eliminated the national debt incurred by the long civil war, all of which indicate a selfless man dedicated to the common good.

Augustus' unprecedented long reign of commanding the world stage for forty-four years, and his sense of justice, clemency, and morals, especially as he grew older, are all indications of a new regime that not only worked but also appealed to and inspired the masses. The Republic was missed, but the new order took care of the people's most pressing daily needs. They may have had a voice in government previously, but brokering with the wealthy senators and the Republican bureaucracy had its own flaws, so the trade-off seemed to suit the majority.

Although the Roman Republic was a highly original and extremely impressive system, it eventually succumbed to over-liberalization that stripped Rome of order, decorum, and morals. By 90 BC, lenient laws and enfranchising distant cities (which previously had no voting rights but now saw an opportunity to manipulate government for self-interest), eventually added another destabilizing element to an entrenched ruling class, who were reveling in the excesses of life and blatantly becoming ripe with arrogance, complacency, and greed. This degradation had begun during Caesar's early childhood and became full-blown by the time of Octavian's rise to power. In direct contrast, Augustus' new empire was one of serious industry, perhaps too serious for some, with a clear focus on morals.

Previously, under the Roman Republic, senators were able to appoint lower level administrators for limited terms, and they were generally nepotistic choices that routinely procured unskilled amateurs or incompetents. As such, certain senators gained influence over certain districts of the Republic, depending on their ring of appointees. As a remedy, Augustus appointed well-trained civil servants that had to answer directly to him. This gave Augustus not only control, but also personal insight into all the various districts across the empire. The senators' greedy and leisure-loving cronies were thus replaced with industrious administrators.

Augustus had a gift for organization and a growing concern for regulating behavior. As such, some right-winged Christian historians have recently tried to lambaste Augustus for being overly oppressive, or essentially a despot. Oddly enough, to prove this claim, they cite the austerity of certain features of architecture during the Augustan era as being reflections of its suppressive ruler. Their premise is that although the facades were ornate, the sides and rear were almost void of design. This has been assessed primarily by the two remaining Augustan structures in France, one being the Temple of Augustus and Livia, and the other being the Maison Carrée.

These Augustan buildings had a huge influence upon Thomas Jefferson who adopted this model for governmental buildings, which still stand across America today. However, two factors must be considered. First, only a small handful of Augustan structures remain fully intact, therefore we cannot condemn all Augustan buildings upon two remains. Second, the fact that Jefferson modeled America on this golden age warrants a closer look, despite the personal opinions of these historians. What Jefferson saw were buildings that offered an inspirational decorative façade, but that economically cushioned the government's purse with peripheral simplicity. As with many decisions made by Jefferson, it was a levelheaded compromise, and one that most probably echoed that of its frugal progenitor Augustus.

These right-wing religious historians also criticized some of the sculptural reliefs of human figures during the Augustan era as being too stiff, and thus allegedly indicating tyrannical suppression. However, when we view the extremely stiff cadaver-like statues, which lack any emotion or movement whatsoever, which adorn gothic cathedrals, it becomes incumbent upon them to turn their gaze and criticize their own churches in the same way.

Therefore, their arguments that Augustus was oppressive must be put into context. Both the Augustan and Gothic eras were indeed more conservative and controlling, however, this atmosphere of control was in reaction to the prevailing liberalness or anarchical wantonness that demanded change. This does not prove that either of these eras was suppressed or under complete despotic rule. More conservative or even strict does not always mean oppressive or tyrannical.

Furthermore, one can appreciate the Augustan mindset as being necessary to restore order amid the greed and over-liberalization that diluted the effectiveness of the Republic, as well as to quell the external threats that existed just outside their borders. Since it was Augustus' laws to curtail decadence and promote morals that produced this conservative order, one would think it would elicit Christian praise rather than condemnation. Augustus' regime was certainly not perfect, but a perfect regime on earth never has existed and probably never will.

Augustus did not have a template of a flawless regime from which to work; he was restricted to the contemporary and historic systems available to him. Yet, one must also examine the basic dichotomy of impulses as well. Where the Augustan age boldly confronted its foes to control and secure its destiny, the Gothic era was one of fear and isolationism that sought sanctuary from the chaos surrounding them. The famous gargoyles that were perched atop these cathedrals, in order to ward off evil spirits, attest to this mindset. Therefore, if these religious critics condemn Augustus as being a despot simply because the Augustan Age was characterized by stiff statuary, then what does that say about the religious leaders during the Gothic Age with its extremely stiff, cadaver-like statuary?

Equally important is the accusation that Augustus was immoral simply because he was a non-Christian pagan. However, this is a biased misnomer, and the topic of moral pagans must be addressed, especially Augustus, who has had a significant affect on the virtues of future leaders and nations, including our own.

As mentioned earlier, young Octavian engaged in many tactics to gain control that many today would deem immoral, but nation-building requires unconventional actions that intrinsically conflict with morals. Both pagans and Christians have been forced to make these tough moral decisions. Augustus was well aware of his transgressions (or sins as Christians call them); however, young Octavian was able to transform himself not only into Augustus, the able military and political leader, but also into Augustus, the moral leader. This was a commendable trait that many recognized in his day, and that many today should do likewise.

Many prominent Christians had checkered early lives but managed to convert themselves into better men. Even one with a similar name comes to mind, for St. Augustine was a self-confessed hedonistic youth that transformed his ways, as did many other Christians who had committed far worse sins. Augustus is perhaps the prime pagan model of such a noble transformation. His mission was to instill his virtuous code of conduct into the empire, for Augustus knew government and laws would be better served by a populace that was guided by a shared and sound moral code.

As it was also part of his plan to instill the notion of divine providence, Augustus erected temples throughout the empire as strong and significant visual cues for the public. Once again, this idea struck a chord with Thomas Jefferson and many of the founding fathers; for although church and state were to remain separate, the motto "In God We Trust" was part of the founders' agenda, regardless of their religion.

Many Christians today rally to defend their American leaders as being moral Christian soldiers, yet they never stop to examine the variety of religious beliefs and practices that the founding fathers and some very prominent presidents held. They are wrong to assume that America was forged as a purely Christian nation.

Washington, was a Freemason, in addition to being an Anglican, but held his own personal set of beliefs. Washington never received communion, refused to kneel during prayer, and did not invite the clergy to his deathbed. Liberal-minded Christians may find this inconsequential or even acceptable, but many staunch Christians, who believe in the significance of receiving communion, feel that those who refuse God's host and grace are as good as infidels. Washington's religiosity depends upon the reader's own interpretation of faith, but he would not be called a devout Christian by everyone.

Meanwhile, Lincoln never belonged to any church. Abraham took it upon himself to hold a strictly personal relationship with God, and this earned him much scorn and ridicule from numerous Christian communities. However, Honest Abe's noncommitted form of Christianity is never honestly revealed in school curriculums.

Thomas Jefferson had very personal and highly unconventional views about religion, while Benjamin Franklin made it a practice to make all religious leaders from various denominations feel that he was one of their parishioners. Franklin became a Deist and even wrote pamphlets professing his belief that Jesus was not God, but rather a monumental religious teacher. Franklin later tried to suppress these controversial thoughts, for he knew how important religious beliefs were to the majority, and Franklin, who became famous and very successful by using amicable diplomacy, loathed making waves. Nevertheless, Franklin clearly understood that religious morals played a significant role throughout much of Western history and were crucial for the individual as well as for the stability and survival of the state.

Franklin, Jefferson, and others were prudent enough to see how even the pagan Romans integrated a public form of religion into their empire as a measure to bind its diverse populace. The early Romans also allowed religious freedom, as long as all paid their respects to the state's civic religion, which helped solidify morals and public unity. This commingling of the positive traits of religious and governmental practices, in order to breed solidarity and inspire progress, is what Augustus sought in his pre-Christian regime. It was a formula, which many centuries later was perceptively observed by Niccolo Machiavelli during the Renaissance.

Machiavelli believed that the Romans used religion as an instrument to unite and maintain order, conformity, and decency in their efforts to achieve a civilized state. However, this state religion was not like Judaism or its later offshoot Christianity, for it was more concerned with the well being of the state rather than personal salvation. However, many emperors believed they were destined to rule by a higher power, and this divine providence not only watched over them, but their success in turn would extend down to the people who would share in that success. Therefore, the public's belief and support for a seemingly just leader benefited all. However, the actions of various emperors seem to indicate just how much some may have believed in a higher power, for comparing Augustus to Nero conjures up two very distinct conclusions, namely divine guidance and egocentric omnipotence.

In tandem with religion, the Roman tradition, in general, was one built upon a person's reputation. This reputation earned them respect, and that was achieved by virtuous actions, not simply wealth, which may have been inherited or swindled by ruthless greed. This concept of character and respect came to the fore with men like Cincinnatus, who left the arena of power politics to settle for a simple farm and plough. Likewise, the aforementioned, Seneca, who was only a young boy when Augustus died, would become a noted Roman philosopher and playwright who wrote 124 letters dealing exclusively with morals.

In addition to these noble principles, the Romans inaugurated the Fetial Law, which condemned wars of senseless aggression and thus invented the concept of a just war. This has influenced many future regimes and organizations, such as the Geneva Convention that is entrusted with establishing rules for international conduct and warfare. Naturally, the Romans encountered many flaws in their struggle, as the budding United States had and still encounters today.

The founding fathers, mindful of the Roman precedent, conceded that religion, while having its own inherent flaws, is essential to building morals, responsibility, duty, and affability toward one's fellow citizen, which in turn unites a nation. Benjamin Franklin's America was predominantly a Protestant nation, yet he helped John Carroll become the first American Catholic bishop, even against great odds, since Franklin believed in tolerance and respect for all religions.

With today's heightened climate of religious fervor, many have been overzealous in attaching Christian doctrine to the *Constitution* and *Declaration of Independence*. Beyond the variables in the founding fathers' beliefs was the perhaps shocking fact that many did not believe that Jesus was divine or the Son of God, nor did they believe in the concept of the Holy Trinity. As Thomas Jefferson aptly said, "Ideas must be distinct before reason can act upon them, and no man ever had a distinct idea of the trinity." To many of the founders, Jesus was a great prophet, most notably the greatest, but not divine.

As for Augustus and his new regime, we must remember it took place before Jesus and the Christian era, which once in the hands of the future clergy attempted to claim sole credit for establishing and enforcing morals. However, many moral decrees by Augustus, and others before him, prove that mankind was not a mass of evil and soulless creatures before the Christian era. The Roman Twelve Tables collated secular laws, as well as moral codes of conduct. The Greek philosophers before them also spent much time pondering and analyzing ethics, virtues, and morals in an effort to uncover the eternal truths of moral behavior, and in so doing they arrived at many revelations that mirror religious beliefs. The similarities between pagan and religious morals extend beyond the quest for morals and even mirror some of the main protagonists in some interesting ways. We shall compare two of them here.

Socrates was the preeminent master who was condemned to death, and his able and motivated pupil, Plato and his pupil Aristotle, would carry Socrates words and ideas forward. Jesus Christ was the preeminent master who was condemned to death, and his able and motivated disciples, Peter, Paul, and the four gospel writers, would carry Jesus' words and ideas forward. Neither Socrates nor Jesus ever wrote a single word themselves, but their messages were recollected, interpreted, and carried forward. Both Socrates' philosophical and Jesus' religious beliefs would have wide, deep, and long-lasting influence.

In both instances, their followers were crucial to keeping the message alive, by expounding and expanding their masters' ideas. They did this by passionately establishing academies and churches to teach and preach to future generations, not only their masters' thoughts but also a wealth of newly added material, which was often questionable. Over the centuries, opposition led to the development of new schools of philosophy, as stoics disagreed with Epicureans or later Schopenhauer differed with Hegel, while a plethora of philosophers with differences of opinion arose. Meanwhile, monks like Martin Luther splintered off the Catholic root with his Protestant branch, which rapidly grew and multiplied as Calvin and Evangelicals followed suit. Hence, the parallel paths of secular philosophy and Christianity are strikingly similar.

Nevertheless, there were practices in the ancient world that were viewed as immoral and these would later gain firm opposition from the church. As mentioned earlier, Greek culture was ingrained with ephebophilia among their all-male academies. This practice of elderly scholars mentoring, and often forming sexual relations with their young male protégés was an accepted practice and tradition, which obviously did not break any of their codes of moral conduct. Even Plato spoke highly of it, saying these loving bonds were necessary for men to accomplish excellent things in their lives. Homosexuality was so customary that it was even artistically depicted on Greek kylixes (drinking cups), which featured adult men kissing or even fondling adolescent boys. As the Greek poet Anacreon said, "Are not the beautiful boys gods, too, to us?"

Moreover, the homosexual bonding of Spartan soldiers was credited for their cohesiveness and effectiveness in battle. When soldiers left the military to find wives, primarily to have children to continue their lineage and support the state, most engaged in a bizarre ritual. The soldier's wife would dress as a young boy on their wedding night and then ease her husband into the heterosexual experience.

These practices were exclusive to Greek culture; however, most religions and cults did not comprehend or condone this lifestyle. Augustus, too, distinctly rejected this Greek tradition. Though he knew that some of his associates engaged in homosexual activities, he viewed the practice as immoral. His policies promoted heterosexual relationships for the production of offspring and strong family bonds. Therefore, many viewpoints about truth and morals were indeed expounded upon before

Christianity. Augustus did not operate in a void, and had a broad spectrum of precedents to evaluate and thus form his own code of ethics, which, oddly enough, the church often mirrored.

Furthermore, Augustus' influence on the literary geniuses who sprouted under his paternal regime cannot be underestimated. Augustus was introduced to three emerging poets by his close friend Maecenas, and beyond relishing their talent, he was a strong advocate of the importance of the written word.

The works of Horace show humor, style, and wit, as well as demonstrating serious contemplations of life. Augustus admired Horace's talent and even asked him to be his secretary to handle correspondence. However, that dry and sterile task did not appeal to the gifted poet and he declined. Augustus' response is worthy of note, for he genially replied, "Even if you were so arrogant as to spurn my friendship, I decline to return your scorn!"

While another ruler might have taken offense at the rebuff and acted harshly, Augustus instead left us a pleasant raillery, which is even "Christian" in its benignity, even though Christianity did not yet exist.

Augustus' next favorite poet was the highly influential poet Ovid, who was extremely imaginative. Ovid's *Metamorphoses*, in fifteen volumes, wove ancient Greek and Roman mythology together in order to create a fantastic narrative of the creation and history of the world. The revival of this work during the Middle Ages had an immense impact on subsequent writers, including William Shakespeare, and Ovid's vivid tales even inspired Renaissance visual masters of the arts.

However, Ovid was also prone to being naughty and off-color. For instance, the poet's popular book, *The Art of Love*, was a series of three books that most probably didn't resonate with Augustus. Ovid's advocacy of extramarital love and his intimate revelations were out of tune with the new moral code that Augustus sought to instate. Then again, even Horace wrote off-color poetry. The real reason for Augustus' displeasure with Ovid was that he was associated with the rebel-minded Lucius Paullus, the husband of Augustus' granddaughter Julia. Paullus was sentenced to death for a failed coup, while Ovid was exiled.

The last and greatest poet, however, was Virgil, whose better works reflected Augustus' virtuous set of morals, and the author's majestic epic, the *Aeneid*, became a national heirloom. The *Aeneid* extolled the grand sweeping evolution of Rome, from its first settlement by Aeneas to the advent of Romulus and Remus, rising up through the Republic and into the glorious golden age of Augustus.

Virgil's appeal and eminent literary status remained intact even when Christianity rose to prominence, for not only did Virgil sing praise of the founding of Rome, which had become the new Holy City, but he also alluded to the prophecy of the coming Christ in his Fourth Eclogue. The future poetic titan of the Middle Ages, Dante Alighieri, would honor Virgil in his intense epic, the *Divine Comedy*, making Virgil his astute guide who escorted Dante through Hell and Purgatory.

These three golden voices spoke from a new perspective, in a new empire, which likewise offered the ancient world a new perspective, the chief architect of which was Augustus Caesar. The fact that he not only permitted but actually encouraged freedom of speech, regardless of an author's political affinity, refutes those who maliciously labeled him a tyrant. The first professional historian in Roman history also emerged under Augustus' open-minded administration. In his magnum opus *Ab Urbe Codita* (From the Founding of the City), Titus Livius, known as Livy, offered an account of Rome's long history. Livy's views about his contemporary world were colored with a romantic leaning toward the old Republic; however, Augustus remained secure in his own actions, and by the praise of millions of Romans, and welcomed Livy's liberal views.

Even Virgil expressed a kinship to Cato and other old Republicans, yet unlike the many true despots that had their secret servicemen hunt down and silence dissonant voices, Augustus never shackled the human spirit; instead, he fostered an open atmosphere in which thoughts could buoyantly reign free.

In the ancient world, a common practice among cunning monarchs or tyrants was to control history. This did not necessarily involve revising the histories of predecessors but generally portrayed glowing accounts of their own regime. Only those outside the regime's reach could pass down alternate perspectives, which later proved extremely valuable. As such, the noble precedent by Augustus to welcome criticism or opposing viewpoints was actually quite rare and rightfully impressed many successive rulers throughout the ages.

Augustus devoted much time to touring the empire to ensure that his new reforms were operating efficiently and that the people were satisfied. Despite their limited voice in government, the tradeoff was evident; the rich amenities that Augustus bestowed upon Rome had clearly won the day. The Republic may have been drastically altered, but the majority appreciated the more efficient government that took aggressive steps to eliminate corruption. Beyond reshaping the Republican infrastructure, Augustan laws were passed that prosecuted those taking bribes, and included a strict guideline of duties that made everyone accountable. In essence, Augustus created the first true efficient and honest bureaucratic structure in history.

Despite any forlorn thoughts of the old Republic, Augustus clearly succeeded overall, for he made Romans feel like fortunate shareholders in a new and glorious enterprise that was bursting with vitality, visual splendor, prosperity, and promise. As Augustus proudly said on his deathbed, "I found Rome of clay: I leave it to you of marble."

That statement bears much truth, for Augustus' building programs were broad and extensive and his economic and political reforms showed definite results. The people of Rome could easily see improvements and share in the success. Augustus was a man of his word, and against insurmountable odds, he achieved his dream—a dream of order, decency, prosperity, and peace. That Augustus died an old man in his bed, and was not assassinated during such aggressive times, also testifies to a miraculous man achieving a miraculous achievement.

Unfortunately, Augustus has unfairly remained in the shadow of his great-uncle. Although Julius Caesar was a vibrant personality, who was a military genius, and a maven at rhetoric, it is sadly overlooked that it was his eighteen-year-old great-nephew who single-handedly took the reins of pure chaos, created by greedy and corrupt senators as well as his despotic great-uncle Julius, and patiently, methodically, and calculatingly created a new world order. Where Caesar was Helios—all power, ego, and bravura that burned fervidly like a scorching fireball—Augustus was Prometheus, who harnessed that extreme energy and brought it down to Earth to be used sensibly.

In modern terms, where Caesar was a nuclear explosion, Augustus was nuclear energy. Even in this regard, the raw and uncontrolled power of a nuclear blast remains far more impressive to most people than the utilitarian effectiveness of nuclear energy. Despite this difference, these two volatile leaders are the only two humans in the whole of history to be eternally honored by having their names grace two consecutive months, aptly during the hot and intensely bright summer months.

Hitherto, a far greater number of historians have studied and praised Caesar than have Augustus, but a renewed interest and appreciation for Augustus appears to have finally arrived. This appreciation quickly turns to deep admiration when one considers the immense obstacles that Augustus had to overcome. Born with a slender frame and prone to illness, the young Octavian had to fight his own physical limitations while fearlessly confronting a ruthless world of cutthroat politicians and highly experienced—not to mention deadly—warriors in order to make his way and inevitably make his mark.

After his initial and colossal struggle to wrest ultimate power, which required cunning, resourcefulness, and many precarious battles, Augustus spent the remainder of his long life bettering himself to become the consummate and paternal politician, who carefully administrated and cultivated his precious and prosperous new crop. Along the way, Augustus pioneered many institutions, such as the police and fire departments, took road building to unprecedented heights (which spread knowledge and trade), encourage free speech, inaugurated the branding and franchising of the Roman system (which spread to all corners of the vast Empire), and he instituted many other policies that exist to this day.

Moreover, the titanic skills required for achieving all those amazing goals, especially considering that his provincial education was cut short, thus necessitating a need to devour knowledge, as well as discern the virtues and treachery of human nature whereby he could act decisively and judiciously, remain to this day immeasurably off the charts.

This new breed of leader, which as Suetonius proclaimed "held idealism over egotism in a noble effort to create the best possible government" had not only made a monumental beginning for Rome, but more importantly, one of seismic proportions for Western civilization.

Augustus' long and successful reign finally ended in AD 14. However, the last years of his reign were plagued with the uncomfortable prospect of formulating a political system that would both please the Roman public, by not being an obvious monarchy with a bloodline, as well as being a system that would continue the prosperous and peaceful objectives he worked so hard to implement.

Fortunately, due to the crafty ways in which Augustus shaped his new executive seat—which pleased the citizens, for he was praised as a loyal patriarch rather than an autocrat, and most senators, for they still maintained some powers and respect—the Romans in general welcomed the idea of a bloodline successor.

Naturally, some senators would have liked to revive the Republic, but it was far too risky, for Augustus had cleverly secured control of the military and created the Praetorian Guards to prevent such maneuvers. Tiberius became his successor and the Juilian/Claudian bloodline continued, as Caligula, Claudius, and Nero respectively took the purple.

However, Nero would ultimately disgrace and irrevocably destroy that rich bloodline once and for all, thrusting Rome and Western history into one of its most volatile and event-changing moments. During this turmoil, a small and troubled religious group took shape, for their leader had earlier been crucified, and they now began to chart a new and separate course, separate from their core ancestral roots. From the ashes of Nero's maniacal mayhem, a new Roman family rose up to seize control and restore order. This family would preserve the Empire and renew its mighty surge forward. Thus enters the mighty Flavian family.

II
AD 73. VESPASIAN & SONS - New Blood
Intro | Titus – Masada and Judaism | Polytheism vs. Monotheism
Rome & Religion - Judea & Jesus | Jesus |
St. Paul and Irenaeus

(Duo, Taurus, Benjamin, Andrew, February)

A rancid cloud of war-dust entered the nostrils of a Roman lieutenant—inciting an involuntary gag. With a violent bark, a murky glob of phlegm jettisoned out of his mouth and viscously cemented itself to the ground. Looking down, he saw the slimy blob begin to congeal with the blood-drenched soil. Dead carcasses lay strewn about him in every direction, as he pulled out a swatch of cloth to wipe his soiled lips. Several yards away, squadrons of cavalry and foot soldiers clashed in the midday plume of death. It was a massive and brutal campaign waged by his commander-in-chief, Vespasian, who was now standing at his side in the tumultuous Judean province.

As the battle raged on, Vespasian informed his subordinate that he'd be taking leave to set sail for Alexandria, as more than insurrection plagued the empire. He ordered that a message be sent to his son, Titus, with instructions to execute the final blow, whereby ending the Jewish revolt, while he attended a far greater problem.

Vespasian was a down-to-earth ox of a man. He was a stocky, well-built machine with sharp, black-and-white vision that made him a man of action. After the previous bloody year that spawned the premature suicide of the deranged Emperor Nero, and three emperors currently vying for power, Rome was in grave disorder.

It appeared that the Julio-Claudian bloodline after Augustus had become a rollercoaster of competency. With Tiberius and Claudius riding at, or near, the crests, the valleys plunged from Caligula, who was ridiculously rotten, to the ultimate valley of death, being Nero, who was repulsively rancid. It was time for new blood, and Vespasian knew it was time for him and his Flavian lineage to make their move. He had been blessed with two strapping sons, and they would buttress his every move. However, Vespasian was not alone, as three other men vied for this vacant seat of ultimate power.

This power struggle was known as The Year of the Four Emperors. It was the year AD 69, and two years previously, Nero appointed Vespasian governor of Judaea to silence the Jewish revolts. His progress was steady and assured, but with Nero now dead, along with two unsuccessful usurpers, it left only Vitellius vying for power, hence a decisive move was needed.

Vespasian was now about to embark on a journey to Alexandria in a strategic effort to cut off Egypt's crucial grain supply from reaching Rome. In the meantime, Vitellius, the last of the three *flash-in-the-pan* emperors, was in Rome preparing to execute Vespasian's brother Flavius Sabinus for an ill-fated coup attempt. Vespasian was well liked and commanded many allies back in Rome. Vespasian's entourage made the final assault and literally toppled Vitellius. Once captured, they brutally killed him and threw his half-naked carcass into the Tiber River. Vespasian's younger son, Domitian, who was stationed in Rome during the bloody assault, took part in ruling while his father stayed on in Egypt. Meanwhile, Vespasian was waiting for his eldest son, Titus, to clean up shop at Jerusalem, as a new band of Jewish rebels had emerged in AD 70.

Once emperor, Vespasian became one of Rome's greatest builders. Vespasian's greatest project was the construction of the Flavian Amphitheater, better known as the Colosseum. This huge arena projected the power and might of Rome. Here, Romans not only controlled life and death, while entertaining an audience, but showcased an unrivalled engineering feat…one of profound sophistication, practicality, and beauty of design. With the Roman invention of concrete, and their ultimate mastery of arches and curved walls, the Colosseum boasted seating for 55,000 spectators, eighty portals for easy access and exits, a sub level with elevators to hoist wild animals and gladiators up to the arena floor, and a water-tight basin that, once flooded, could allow for mock sea battles. Additionally, it sported a huge retractable awning that offered shade for its spectators. This grand, oval design remains practically unaltered to this day, as all major sports arenas proudly pay homage to this glorious masterpiece.

Yet, in AD 72, Vespasian was still irritated by the small pocket of Jewish resistance that had risen two years previous to disrupt Roman order. High atop King Herod's defunct mountain fortress of Masada, the last remnants of Jewish rebels hunkered themselves in. Feeling secure, behind the massive walls of this highly perched and historically safe haven, they waited for the Romans to retreat in humiliation. However, the resolute emperor, Vespasian, had ordered his son Titus to extinguish this last trump of resistance. Titus, who was a chip-off-the-old-block, was also unyielding, and retreat was *not* an option.

TITUS - *Masada and Judaism*

Gusty winds screamed through the chiseled chasms, as Roman soldiers scurried about. Although spending several long months in the Masada Valley, Titus and the 10th legion were far from idle. Their mission had taken them into a barren wasteland where only one edifice stood.

Masada was a fortress that sat atop an enormous plateau, which sharply jutted upward out of the valley's rocky floor. Like a towering Valhalla, Masada was an intimidating structure. Just the sight of it made some soldiers faint of heart. In fact, many soldiers had seriously questioned the probability of ever scaling the huge monolith; however, due to their commander's ingenuity, determination, and patience, their long arduous task was finally complete.

The soldiers had been ordered to build a gargantuan ramp of beaten stone and earth that astonishingly rose up from the valley floor right up to the plateau's summit. Two nights previously, the Romans had fashioned battering rams and built huge edifices of interlocking timber, filled with earth, near the fortress' walls. The Romans then rammed the walls, creating large fissures, but the trapped rebels quickly repaired them. In an attempt to smoke out the enemy, Flavius Silva had ordered the timber edifices be lit on fire. A billow of thick black smoke at first headed towards the Romans until a providential change in wind hurled it back toward the fortress. This sign of divine intervention further strengthened the soldiers' resolve.

However, the shock and awe of flames and smoke had died out over the cold night, and the ramp needed mending before sun up. The dawn was now beginning to illuminate the barren valley with golden tones, while pitched in the dirt at the edge of the encampment stood the embroidered eagle vexillum, as it blew in the faint breeze.

Growing anxious, Titus approached his leading commander, Flavius Silva, and instructed him that he could not tolerate any more setbacks. It was now clear that the gods favored a move and he ordered the charge.

Flavius barked out the command, and each soldier immediately strapped on their *lorica segmentata* and then eagerly grabbed their gladius and large protective *scutum*. As Flavius and his squad stormed up the ramp, their clattering armor and stampeding feet echoed throughout the valley. A fine, dry dust arose in the warriors' wake, as their battle cries reverberated among the valley's chiseled chasms.

Approaching the peak, their echoes gradually subsided, giving way to an eerie silence. Like armored beetles, a few soldiers quietly scaled the large, stoned wall. As they reached the crest, they cautiously crawled on their bellies and then peered down one by one. Then turning about, they called out to Flavius to witness the odd sight down below.

Flavius scaled the wall, and with an equal look of shock on his face, he calmly slipped his pristine gladius back into his scabbard. He then signaled for his remaining unit to approach. In bewilderment, he then turned back toward the bloody carnage below. He was fairly sure that the Jewish rebels were prohibited from committing *desperata salus* (noble suicide), but whatever happened, it certainly looked like their one and only God had forsaken them.

Crawling down into the huge stronghold, the Romans slowly walked through mounds of bodies—gazing upon the self-slaughter in disbelief. Over nine hundred carcasses of men, women and children lay strewn about, coldly drenched in their own languid pools of blood. Walking past cadaverous bodies of women and children with fresh lacerations through their chests and slit throats, made some soldiers furious, as others turned in disgust.

Meanwhile, other soldiers rummaged through the storage chambers and spotted piles of ample rations, magazines of weapons and even religious artifacts. As they rummaged about they discovered two Jewish women and five children; they had found refuge in a huge cistern. The women relayed their tale of woe, which was later recorded by the Jewish historian Josephus. The survivors had abstained from committing suicide fearing, or rather faithfully obeying, the Sixth Commandment. However, the tribe's leader, Eleazar, had convincingly brainwashed his fanatical followers. The following was his last words to the almost one thousand rebels who committed suicide.

"God hath convinced us that our hopes were in vain, by bringing such distress upon us in the desperate state we are now in, and which is beyond all our expectations; for the nature of this fortress, which was in itself unconquerable, hath not proved a means of our deliverance; and even while we have still great abundance of food, and a great quantity of arms, and other necessaries more than we want, we are openly deprived by God himself of all hope of deliverance."

Titus shook his head in disbelief upon hearing of this mass suicide. Ever since his father, Vespasian, was a general under Nero, up to his ultimate rise to emperor, of which he would soon follow, his family had been forced to engage the Jews in what he and most Romans viewed as a senseless feud. He found their insurrections extremely hard to fathom, especially since the Romans offered them complete freedom to worship as they chose and the rights to build their temples and prosperous cities. He was likewise irritated that when his father was honored with the title of emperor even foreign nations sent embassies to congratulate him, yet this particular Jewish band of zealots decided to plot a revolt instead.

Titus knew that only a small portion of Rome's many legions were required to manage their limited numbers, moreover, he knew that no other nation would be foolhardy enough to embrace their cause, especially against the might of Rome. The Jewish community was not only an extreme minority but most importantly they shunned all others. This was due to their provocative chosen status that was lauded in their proprietary scriptures. Therefore, many Jews haughtily abhorred the Romans, while the Romans were often perplexed or humiliated by their religious bigotry.

However, many High Priests did manage to deal with the Romans and found the relationship copasetic and highly advantageous. The problem that arose during Titus' lifetime was that the Jewish community was not one unified group, it consisted of smaller sects, some being radicals, such as those at Masada. Furthermore, peace in Judea also depended upon the overlord in charge, and some Roman emperors had done their share of the damage. Nevertheless, from Titus' perspective, all he could see was a radical tribe that for years sabotaged assimilation and wreaked havoc.

Therefore, despite the gruesome self-slaughter by these rebellious fanatics, the Roman troops were relieved; their long battle was finally over. Titus proudly announced that their several-months-long siege and the building of their colossal ramp achieved success and showcased their unflinching determination. Rome, once again, was stabilized and victorious. The troops eagerly rallied together and then lifted their swords and trophies in exultation. Triumphantly they paraded down the ramp, shouting repeatedly, *"Victoria! Victoria!..."*

The Masada event was a significant and well-documented moment in history. Although this conflict has received much attention, it was actually just one historic event amidst a momentous time of change. These other earth-shattering events will be addressed in turn, but first the showdown at Masada did have its own significance. Eleven years later, in AD 84, the triumphant Arch of Titus was erected in the Roman forum. On its surface, detailed carvings recounted the many victories that Titus commanded, including the eventual victory of this Jewish campaign *(See page 705)*, which were all etched into history's eternal memory. The arch still stands today as testament to Rome's unyielding determination and ability to maintain order regardless of the obstacles.

The enormous ramp that they constructed to reach the mountaintop was as a reflection of how the Romans were adept at inventing solutions to overcome seemingly unimaginable odds. About a hundred years earlier, Julius Caesar also shocked and awed the Germanic tribes when he fashioned a bridge out of local timber to cross the Rhine. The engineering of Caesar's bridge, with tree trunk pilings, thirty feet long, each driven deep into the riverbed on angles to support a heavy timber superstructure, was extremely innovative. Just as miraculous, Julius Caesar's men built this bridge in only ten days. Titus and his men would similarly follow the Roman tradition of never accepting failure, and this unyielding determination was the fuel of their empire.

However, along with their determination, the Romans also displayed leniency and tolerance toward other ethnic and religious groups, particularly toward the Jews. This is revealed in the fact that Jews were granted liberties not offered to other religions or cults. Despite this fact, many Jews have slandered the Romans as being intolerant villains, and this makes the incident at Masada become worthy of closer attention.

As mentioned, the Roman Empire was vast. It was a colorful spectrum of different races and sects, and with the Roman invention of paved roads, they actually shrunk the world. This effectively inaugurated trade on a new and robust level. Yet intense conflicts between religions were on the rise, and unfortunately, Vespasian's predecessor, Nero, often added fuel to the fire. However, Vespasian and Titus boldly stepped to the fore, as if valiant firefighters determined to quench the toxic flames, for their mission was to not only regain order, but also to essentially rescue their civilization.

Once Vespasian wrested control of the floundering government, he had to contend with this aberrant Sicarii tribe, which had begun their rampage many years earlier. Therefore, this last pocket of revolt had to be put down and that meant even in the harshest manner if necessary, for to leave these rogues unchecked would have allowed them to regroup and cause greater havoc or, worse yet, set the example that Rome was anemic and open to revolt by any radical faction.

Not too surprisingly, however, is how Jewish historians have often attempted to retell the Masada event as a Jewish victory. Their interpretation is one of religiously defiant Jews taking their own lives rather than submitting to the oppressive Romans. As noble as that may sound, that, too, bears scrutiny.

Firstly, and most importantly, it defies their core religion. It claims that suicide is permissible by allowing mortals to overrule God's Commandment as they see fit. This is clearly against the words of Yahweh, their Lord God. This blasphemy is further backed up in

Deuteronomy 27:26 *"Cursed be everyone who does not abide by all things written in the book of the law, and do them."*

Secondly, the Sicarii tribe's name actually reveals its identity, and anti-religious intent. The word *sica* means stiletto or dagger. Hence, this Jewish tribe acquired its name for killing, not the peaceful worship of Yahweh.

Thirdly, it insinuates that William Travis, Davy Crockett and their cohorts at the Alamo, who were also trapped in a fortress, all gallantly fought to their last dying breath in vain. Namely, that if they took their own lives it would have somehow transformed their plight into victory. Interestingly enough in this scenario, the side that emerged victorious was that of the slain, for it was the Texans' tenacious United States that eventually prevailed. However, such was not the case for these Sicarii rebels. Yet here the notion of dying with valor is demeaned, while fanatical suicide is hailed as noble.

Lastly, there were Christian and Judaic claims that foresaw this event as the glorious fulfillment of a divine prophecy, as foretold in the Old Testament. This fascinating point will be elaborated upon later. Henceforth, considering all these factors, the rationale of these Jewish revisionists can only be deemed flawed. In contrast, most historians today firmly conclude that the Sicarii were a small rebel group of Jews who were extreme radicals, or more appropriately, *zealots*.

This is an interesting and conclusive point. The term *zealot* was actually coined by the writer Josephus during this exact moment in history. Born into a wealthy family of Jewish priests, Josephus was later put in command of forces to repel Vespasian (Vespasian at the time was a Roman general). However, during this battle, which was also Josephus' military premiere, he appealed to reason, and his own sense of morals, and persuaded his rebel guerillas that their mission was futile. Josephus surrendered to Vespasian and spared further bloodshed. He was briefly held in captivity and later released.

Vespasian treated Josephus with clemency, and even granted his freedom, a freedom that enabled him to be a key voice in history. Moreover, Josephus' new term *zealot* defined these fanatical Jewish rebels, which he witnessed firsthand, because they fought zealously for God. And to some extent, these zealots were akin to the religious fanatics of present day Jihad. Their extremist bent on suicide, as being an honorable deed for their maligned concept of faith, resounds with unnerving familiarity.

Historic records elucidate how these religious zealots would slip into a crowded square and silently stab their foe, and then amid the panic, exit the scene. When they were acting as so-called martyrs, they would blatantly commit suicide. From a religious viewpoint, it is one thing for a martyr to be executed by a foe, and another when they defy God's Commandment and commit suicide. This fanatical act clearly illustrates how they truly act upon their own accord, and not that of the true Lord they supposedly represent. As such, Masada cannot be recognized as the ultimate symbol of Jewish martyrdom, but rather a mass of fanatical suicides by infidels of Yahweh.

A contemporary of Josephus, named Yohanan ben Zakkai, likewise abhorred the radical tactics of these zealots, and he, too, surrendered to Vespasian. Zakkai, on the other hand, was granted the freedom to establish a rabbinical academy, and Zakkai's new canonized Bible became the Jews' official text. It is noteworthy that this important contribution to Jewish tradition was made possible by Vespasian's benevolence. Abandoning their old holy war tactics, Zakkai's new Bible advocated peace, love, and harmony, especially with their overlords, the Romans.

Therefore, Josephus and Zakkai were two powerful voices of reason for the Jewish cause that often get overlooked. Both men formulated these views by personally analyzing and witnessing Roman tolerance firsthand. Additionally, it was blaringly apparent that the indomitable victories of Vespasian and Titus offered security that was unrivalled. Yet some Jews prefer to avoid such voices of history, and paint their own picture of Roman suppressive might and Jewish pious resistance.

A little over two hundred years previously, in 164 BC, these holy wars for Yahweh reached a climax when the Jews, led by the fervent Maccabees tribe, defeated the evil King Antiochus in Judea. However, this Jewish conquest was brief. Antiochus was a mad ruler, a remnant of the transient Greek Hellenistic regime, and he reveled in brutally killing and torturing Jews en masse. It is perhaps the first recorded instance of martyrdom in history, as one tale recalled in gruesome detail how a woman watched her seven sons be mutilated, each choosing to die for Yahweh, rather than acquiesce to the mad tyrant, Antiochus. These early Maccabees were true martyrs, unlike the later Sicariis. The horror and gore of these tortures and killings was so heinous that it created a band of Maccabee zealots, who retaliated in a fit of vengeance. Therefore, as the decades passed, certain Jewish sects were increasingly becoming martyrs and zealots.

The Sicarii tribe utilized both tactics of holy war in a final effort to initially attack the Romans with guerilla tactics, and then retreat to become these so-called martyrs at Masada.

The fact remains, that after Masada the Romans, under Titus, seized Jerusalem and the surrounding territories, engaged another uprising with some remaining rebels, whereby destroying the Temple, and in the aftermath, the Romans erected a new city. They continued to enforce Roman law and collect taxes, while extending to the Jews the continued freedom to peacefully practice their religion. Simultaneously, however, this powerful reprimand initiated an exodus, as Jews and the new Christian sect began emigrating to other parts of the empire.

Despite the atrocities by earlier mad emperors, like Caligula and Nero, the Romans had a long history of extending liberal laws to the Jews, laws and exemptions that were more generous than those which were offered to other religious groups. For example, the Jews were exempt from the *Pax Deorum* ritual that was required by all Roman citizens, and they established laws that prohibited non-Jews from entering Jewish Temples. This even included Roman legionnaires that could be executed for illegally trespassing.

When Augustus annexed Egypt, he established laws to keep peace between the Greeks and Jews, particularly in Alexandria, who were showing visible signs of outward contempt and rivalry. The discord between the two sects had earlier roots, as more and more Jews settled in the prosperous region. The social and religious traditions of the pagan Greeks and monotheist Jews intrinsically clashed, and it was the Romans who acted as mediator. In reality, however, the Roman policy of religious tolerance offered more protection to the Jews.

Augustus cleverly offered tax breaks to those who conducted themselves in concord with his new regime, thus gently prodding all to assimilate and conform to his notion of Roman unity. When Caligula's bad policies later inflamed this region, his successor, Claudius, displayed his diplomatic skills by criticizing Caligula's bad policies and restoring full rights to the Jews. However, Claudius demanded mutual toleration, and tactfully warned the Jews not to scorn other religions. This last decree alludes to the distinct possibility that the Jews' verbal antagonisms quite possibly goaded the Greeks to retaliate in open and visible force.

Therefore, the Romans treated the Jews with forbearance and a sincere respect for their religion, far beyond that of other groups. Therefore, when people today hear that the Romans burned the Temple of Jerusalem they quite naturally condemn the Romans as being ruthless barbarians. However, this is primarily due to many later historians and theologians who have not relayed the entire account. Once one reads the historical account from the actual words of those present, such as Josephus, the Jewish historian and eyewitness, or Titus himself, and then processes that information along with the knowledge of modern day Jihad, one suddenly realizes a whole new perspective of this historic event.

Again, this is not to say that the previous regime under Nero, and his corrupt henchmen, like Gessius Florus, did not extort and persecute the Jews, but as we shall see, the Jews did make antagonistic maneuvers. Furthermore, Vespasian's rise to imperator had rescued the Empire from its downward spiral. Not only did he restore order, and the grandeur of Augustus' golden era, but Vespasian was also setting new benchmarks that gave birth to a whole new era of growth and prosperity. It was actually a small renaissance.

When Vespasian's son Titus began his siege of Jerusalem, the city was in turmoil, not only by his legions engaging the rebels, but also by the rivaling Jewish factions that were in bloody combat amongst themselves. Josephus relays in detail how many highly admired Roman warriors were slaughtered right before their eyes. One such soldier slipped and fell to the ground while bravely attacking a group of rebels. As his metal breastplate crashed and clattered to the ground, the retreating rebels suddenly turned and darted back to the fallen warrior. Looking like a helpless turtle, flat on his back with his tank-like armor, the rebels began piercing his metallic shell with their spears, until his crimson oil oozed out of the weep holes, and stained the sandy soil.

Shortly after this painful sight, Titus received recon that the rivaling Jewish rebels were maniacally slaying each other inside the Holy Temple itself. Upon hearing this shocking news, Titus immediately solicited the advice of his commanders as to the best strategy to seize the Temple. Titus judiciously listened as his enraged commanders opted to destroy the Temple. In their minds it was no longer a Temple but rather a chaotic citadel, a madhouse crawling with deranged and bloodthirsty warriors that already defiled its sanctity. Therefore, their assessment was that any destructive actions taken would be after the fact, and no harm to Roman integrity. However, Titus then revealed his wise and final decision, which was not to destroy inanimate objects, especially of a sacred nature, for the culprits were the troublesome humans.

Then Josephus tells of a defining moment by Titus, conveniently suppressed by some theologians, when a zealot rebel from the Temple confronts Titus, which was now in a desecrated state of chaos. Here is Titus' actual reply:

"Have not you, vile wretches that you are, by our permission, put up this partition-wall before your sanctuary? Have not you been allowed to put up the pillars thereto belonging, at due distances, and on it to engrave in Greek, and in your own letters, this prohibition, that no foreigner should go beyond that wall? Have not we given you leave to kill such as anyone who goes beyond it, though he were Roman? And what do you do now, you pernicious villains? Why do you trample upon dead bodies in this temple? And why do you pollute this holy house with the blood of both foreigners and Jews themselves? I appeal to the gods of my own country, and to every god that ever had any regard to this place; (for I do not suppose it to be now regarded by any of them;) I also appeal to my own army, and to those Jews that are now with me, and even to yourselves, that I do not force you to defile this your sanctuary; and if you will but change the place whereon you will fight, no Roman shall either come near your sanctuary, or offer any affront to it; nay, I will endeavor to preserve you your holy house, whether you will or not."

Titus' powerful words speak volumes. Firstly, they validate how the Romans allowed the Jews to construct walls to prohibit entrance into the Temple by foreigners, which likewise attests to the Romans' religious tolerance and leniency.

Secondly, and most importantly, it elucidates how these extremist rebels butchered their own Jewish brethren, along with Roman soldiers inside their own Temple. Here their wanton disregard for human life, once again, unnervingly parallels modern day Jihad terrorists, and the hatred that exists between their own Shiite and Sunni sects.

Lastly, we can hear that Titus' deep sense of morals and logic speaks loudly. His disdain and genuine repulsion over this sacrilegious atrocity summons his appeal to reason, thus offering to take the fight to another location in order to preserve the Temple. Unfortunately, this fell upon deaf ears— ears that were irrevocably connected to malignant minds. For not only did they shun the Romans, but also their own God.

As the battle unfolded, Titus gave the Jews every reasonable opportunity to either surrender or relocate, but the unpredictable nature of war led to a different fate. As Titus was occupied in a nearby tower, he was informed that a Roman soldier disobeyed orders and set a fire to smoke out the rebels. As Titus rushed to the scene, the Temple was ablaze. Amid the unbridled confusion, with screams of vengeance, Titus' order to quench the fire was too late and unheard. Even Josephus describes the accidental destruction of the Temple as mournful, yet somehow destined by fate.

These enlightening documents of history, which are not revisionary religious credo, along with the Jewish perspective of Josephus and Zakkai, who both recognized the benefits of Roman culture and understood their "Lenient Unless Provoked" policy, all validate who the Romans and the Sicarii really were. Furthermore, the words of Titus present a tangible record that validates a mind ruled by logic, and a heart bestowing benevolence.

The prominent and dominant storytellers of history have also colored the rituals performed within these Jewish Temples. Later theologians, anxious to paint a grim picture about the pagans, were quick to denigrate them for performing wild and primitive rituals of sacrifice. However, since the very beginning, Jewish temples engaged in animal sacrifices, mostly lambs, bulls or fowl, which were slaughtered and burned. When one reads how God requested specific sacrificial offerings in the Bible, one is struck by how pagan-like Hebrew tradition is, such as these passages in Leviticus.

1:15 "And the priest shall bring it unto the altar, and wring off his head, and burn it on the altar; and the blood thereof shall be wrung out at the side of the altar: 1:16 And he shall pluck away his crop with his feathers, and cast it beside the altar on the east part, by the place of the ashes: 1:17 And he shall cleave it with the wings thereof, but shall not divide it asunder: and the priest shall burn it upon the altar, upon the wood that is upon the fire: it is a burnt sacrifice, an offering made by fire, of a sweet savour unto the LORD."

Moreover, in regards to larger mammals, such as lambs or goats, the Lord had specific requests. Leviticus 3:3 *"...the fat that covereth the inwards, and all the fat that is upon the inwards, 3:4 And the two kidneys, and the fat that is on them, which is by the flanks, and the caul above the liver, with the kidneys, it shall he take away."*

Upon reading those hallowed words, one immediately sees the word "pagan" flash in their mind's eye. However, when these rituals were officially abolished, by the Romans no less, the Jews and Christians wasted no time in revising history. Hence, the notion that it was only the *godless* pagans who engaged in primitive ritual killings is another fiction espoused by later authors, and believed by the majority in modern society.

Of equal importance is the misnomer that Rome was a purely secular entity. King Numa Pompilius, who succeeded Rome's founder and first king, Romulus, was a religious man who declared that he received advice from the gods. It was Numa who initiated the priesthood of *Fetiales*, and the more popular and enduring Vestal Virgins who Augustus would continue to honor in his new Empire seven hundred years later. Likewise, the *augures* were priests who studied the flight of birds for predicting the will of the gods in terms of their immediate future. Whether going to war, or taking on any major undertaking, the augur, or augures, would be called upon to take what was called the auspices, where they would interpret the divine blessings before engaging any role or action. Although some callous monotheists mock these ancient religions, to the point of calling Rome a purely secular state, we today must realize, contemplate and even respect these ancient peoples' beliefs to truly understand their world and actions.

As for the Holy Temple in Jerusalem, it was the most important in Judaism, and dated back to King Solomon who constructed the First Temple some ten centuries BC. However, the Babylonians, during their conquest, destroyed it in 597 BC. The Second Temple was finally reconstructed under King Herod in 19 BC. The historic battle at Masada and the destruction of the Second Temple decisively ended Jewish revolts, as well as their hopes of ever having a Jewish state for almost two millennia. Titus' historic victories also caused many Jews to migrate, as they began to scatter throughout Europe, Africa, and Asia.

Jerusalem was placid for more than half a century until some Jews, while searching for a new scapegoat, blamed the destruction of the Temple on the Christians. They believed this wayward, new Christian sect only showed signs of increasingly corrupting their sacred Tanakh (Jewish Bible), and being repulsed by the destruction of the Second Holy Temple they inserted a special malediction into scripture. It would even become their central daily prayer, which although slightly revised, is still recited to this day. It reads, "May the apostles have no hope, unless they return to Your Torah, and may the Nazarenes and the Minim disappear in a moment. May they be erased from the book of life, and not be inscribed with the righteous." As the Christians blamed the Jews for Jesus' death, the Jews now cursed the Christians for defiling their religion.

The infuriated Jews' next revolt would occur some sixty years after Masada under the future emperor Hadrian. Hadrian sought assimilation from all quarters of the empire, and upon his erecting a pagan temple to Jupiter in Jerusalem, the Jews revolted. Quite interestingly, a newly hailed Jewish Messiah named Bar Kochbah was attempting to rival Jesus' lofty position by building a Third Temple. This was to fulfill an ancient prophecy, which Jesus failed to accomplish.

However, Hadrian deftly ended the revolt, destroyed the uncompleted Temple, and even renamed parts of the Judea province, creating Syria and Palestine. Hence, with Hadrian, the Jewish state, which in reality had long been a Roman province well before his reign, was effectively terminated and erased off the map. Thereafter, major Jewish revolts were nil. In fact, Jerusalem was razed, and then rebuilt following a typical Roman city plan. It wasn't until some 1800 years later in 1948 that the nation of Israel was finally born, and again, this was not won by holy war, or standard warfare, but granted in a treaty by England and condoned by the United States.

Judaic history has certainly displayed moments of intense revolt, yet there have also been considerable periods of relative nonviolence. This is evidently because the orthodox sects sought strict isolationism, while the latter liberal sects sought assimilation rather than military aggression. This is borne out by centuries of nonviolent slave status under Egyptian rule until the exodus by Moses, the 1800 years of primarily minor conflict after Masada under Roman rule, and the diplomatic granting of the nation of Israel in 1948. Embedded in the middle of a Palestinian hotbed, Israel had and still has, no recourse but to retaliate militarily. Then again, when we look at the long history of the Judea territory, they never held with any certainty their own nation with defined borders to defend.

Before the Romans fully annexed Judaea as a province in AD 6, they instated King Herod to rule as their client king over the Jews. Therefore, even Herod's reign was not one over a sovereign Jewish state, for he, too, had to broker with his Roman overlords. Furthermore, well before Herod, the Greeks controlled this territory, and before them the Persians, and even before them the Babylonians, and further still the Assyrians.

Predating the Assyrians, even the Torah (The five books of Moses) tells of Moses and Joshua being instructed by God to conquer the Canaanites. This was perhaps the world's first exercise in Manifest Destiny. Canaan was a non-Jewish settlement that existed long before Joshua ever stepped foot on this supposedly sacred Jewish soil to annihilate its population. Henceforth, Moses initiated the long warring maneuvers that his successors, primarily Joshua, would carry out to eventually gain control over this territory. This vital territory consisted of modern day Israel, the West Bank, Gaza Strip, as well as parts of Lebanon and Syria.

Furthermore, since its founding, Jerusalem had been conquered some thirty-seven times, and the principal religion of the city changed approximately eleven times. Therefore, in the final analysis, this particular region was not originally settled by the Jews and it had a perpetual turnover rate; hence, the granting of this region to the Jews to form the religious state of Israel inevitably opened a new, and unfortunately bloody chapter in Jewish history.

This new chapter brings us to the point of examining events that are more recent, for many prominent American Jews had significantly orchestrated the state of Israel. During World War II, they convened a meeting at the Biltmore Hotel in New York City. Their intentions were to deal with the recently confirmed news that the Nazis were exterminating European Jews en masse. Their proposal demanded that the gates of Palestine be opened so that they might establish a Jewish Commonwealth. This, they declared, would be the only way to correct the age-old wrongs against the Jewish people.

Even before the group decided upon this religious zone, however, the British had already made inroads of allowing Jews to settle in this region. After World War I, Britain was awarded control of present day Jordan, Israel, and the surrounding West Bank and Gaza Strip by the Treaty of Versailles. This was known as the Mandate of Palestine. Hence, some Jews had already settled in the area, thus appearing to the Biltmore Jewish committee and British government to be the most obvious solution.

However, many liberal and comfortably assimilated American Jews adamantly rallied against the *Biltmore Declaration* when it was first drafted in 1942, including the famous physicist Albert Einstein. They all saw this as a declaration of war against the Arabs that would only incite major conflict, and their predictions have proven to be accurate.

Therefore, the modern religious state of Israel makes for a volatile collision of interests and deep-seated beliefs. Between the strict exclusivity of their religion, which heatedly interfaces with their surrounding neighbors/enemies, and their being granted lands that have ancient histories and religious connotations for many other races and religions, Israel, the religious state, appears destined to cause perpetual unrest and unending violence, unless the intolerance of the opposing religions can be overcome.

An alternate plan had been put forth by Franklin Roosevelt, who believed that rather than granting a Jewish state, a consortium of Jewish, Christian, and Islamic leaders should have administered the Palestinian region. However, his premature death prevented this plan from taking root. But even this solution has its quagmires, as the thought of these three volatile religions operating in unison and accord remains the ultimate dilemma and mission today.

Judaism also suffers from its small size, for even though the Christian and Islamic empires have collided at various times throughout history, the sheer size of these two religions somehow manages to maintain a balance of power. Meanwhile, the minority status of Jews continues to keep them in the perpetual crosshairs of their opponents.

Then again, all monotheist religions, in general, have always caused conflict throughout history, and this raises another issue that is often debated today.

Polytheism vs. Monotheism

The Jews and the latter Christian sect both proved problematic for the Romans while, in contrast, the various pagan religions afforded Rome many centuries of relative peace. Many secular historians today are now blaming these monotheist religions for their intolerance and bloody holy wars that they leveled against the pagan polytheists.

These critics praise polytheism for its tolerance of all other religions, as well as their welcoming of foreign gods into their pantheon, while the monotheist religions have exclusionary Commandments against worshiping other gods or idols. This is a simple concept to grasp, however, although their point is correct, they do overlook one very crucial point, namely, why is this so? The answer delves into the fact that these ancient polytheistic cults were not ingrained as deeply as are Judaism, Christianity, or Islam with their single God.

To begin with, we need to realize that these three monotheist religions are not built upon reason; they are built primarily upon blind faith. This faith centers on the fact that what their ancient forefathers told of Yahweh, Jesus, or Allah is not only the truth, but most importantly, those truths incontestably explain their personal place and purpose for living in the world, as well as what actions are necessary to achieve grace, redemption, and acceptance into their Lord's heavenly kingdom, be that on Earth or in the afterworld. Such profoundly deep and personal beliefs, regarding one's own soul in regards to Heaven and Hell, gave rise to a new dynamic, one that intrinsically arouses a volatile defense mechanism when threatened.

Just as deep political or ideological views cause fiery disputes and violence, so, too, can the Jewish, Christian, and Muslim faiths. The religious beliefs of monotheists, however, are customarily much stronger and deeper than political ideologies. Nevertheless, history has shown that when people with deep political convictions or fervent monotheist beliefs are severely threatened, both have reacted ardently to protect and defend their belief systems. Where one will produce warriors and heroes, the other will produce crusaders and martyrs, hence both will defend their beliefs with their lives.

Conversely, polytheism was not as powerfully rooted in the individual, and was more akin to astrology or other beliefs that many even today engage, yet nowhere near rivaling the intensity of the monotheist religions, and as such, would not be stirred to violence or radical behavior if called into dispute or threatened.

Therefore, these secular historians miss this vital concept simply because they never personally experienced or forgot just how intense these belief systems are. A profound faith that organizes the creation and order of the universe along with one's own soul is significantly different from a leisurely concept of vague gods with frequently changing names, who offered some guidance, comfort, or quasi morals. Nevertheless, their final appraisal stands correct, for polytheists were not as aggressive.

Despite that reality, for many centuries, religious revisionists have portrayed pagans as the aggressive and evil firebrands that also reveled in sacrificial killings. As we have seen earlier, the Judaic tradition was well rooted in animal sacrifices in all their Holy Temples. Even the sacrificial lamb at Passover was symbolically ingrained in the Gospel of John, who maintained that Christ's crucifixion, and the eating of his flesh and blood was in keeping with this intensely Jewish tradition. If any Christian reads accounts of pagans at this time they would realize how the pagans were actually repulsed by this whole concept, especially as it related to eating human flesh, even if symbolic, as it carried with it a cannibalistic connotation.

Naturally, some pagans did fall prey to the propaganda of mad emperors or the earlier pharaohs who rallied the masses to persecute the monotheists. Interestingly enough, both these rulers simultaneously held the position of *Pontif Maximus*, or Divine Ruler, and held full authority over religious and secular affairs. Yet, even their dual stations must be examined.

Egyptian pharaohs fought primarily for their own personal divinity rather than the religion itself, meanwhile, Roman emperors fought solely for the state of Rome and imperial conquest. Therefore, the early emperors were not pursuing religious goals or fighting holy wars. Furthermore, the fact that many Roman polytheists were incensed by the Christian persecutions, especially when raised to fever pitch under Nero or Diocletian, offers valuable testimony that the polytheists themselves were not the aggressors.

Another interesting fact is that Judaism was not the first monotheist religion, but perhaps more importantly, its precursor likewise displayed the aggressive gene of intolerance, which is associated with all monotheist religions. Against popular Judaic belief, the Egyptian pharaoh Akhenaten had created the first monotheist religion known to mankind. Akhenaten had merged separate gods of the Amun religion, such as Ra and Horus, to form Aten, a singular Sun god. Akhenaten's birth name was Amenhotep IV, yet upon assuming the throne he changed it to Akhenaten, adding the Sun god's name to the end of his new name, Akhen-Aten. He shared his throne with the well-known Nefertiti, who would later give birth to their far more popular son, the future King Tut.

However, Akhenaten callously enforced his monotheist religion upon Egypt to the extent that a wave of terror ensued. Inscriptions referring to the names of the old Amun gods were scratched off obelisks, shrines, temple walls and anywhere they appeared. Even small insignificant artifacts used by the common people have been found that mirrored this intolerant religious decree, indicating the fear that prevailed.

After Akhenaten's death, however, his nine-year-old son Tutankhaten rose to power. The pressures of the people most likely caused Tut's senior counselors to not only revert back to the old Amun religion, but Tutankhaten changed his name to Tutankhamun; the Amun appendage reflecting the peaceful return to their traditional polytheist religion. Hence, with this reversion, the aggressive monotheist religion of his father Akhenaten had effectively faded into Egyptian obscurity.

However, beyond the distant realm of ancient Egypt, there are other examples of monotheist aggression much closer in time and far more familiar. The Spanish Inquisition and Crusades are perhaps the most notorious Christian atrocities known to Westerners, and were solely conceived and executed with a monotheist agenda. As mentioned, statistics indicate that the death toll of these lethal pogroms exceeded by far all those committed by the pagan Romans on Christians. Henceforth, despite our desire to uphold a superior sense of civility and benevolence, the pagan world of polytheism was unequivocally less aggressive than monotheism. As such, we should view ancient civilizations with an open and educated eye, for despite our firm faith in a one and only God or his anti idol-worshipping Commandment, the reality was that these polytheist religions *most often* did not instigate conflict.

Polytheism, while under the Roman Empire, would eventually be challenged and attacked by the monotheistic religions for numerous reasons. Beyond the failure to worship the only true God, they also rejected but ultimately capitulated to coercion by one cult, which had been solely endorsed by the Roman state. Those actions sealed the pagan world's destiny. Oddly enough, their new rival had old Jewish roots that, for several millennia, hardly spread. The fact was, polytheism had always reigned supreme, however, their pantheon of the ancient gods was suddenly falling under a new shadow. The great Sun disc would indeed be eclipsed by the stormy heavens, as this new religious order flared up out of the sands of the Judaean province of Rome. This whirlwind of faith would eventually turn and spurn its Jewish ancestor, while burying polytheism in its turbulent wake. Only the pagan art of astrology would survive in the dusty shadow of the new Christian colossus.

ROME & RELIGION - JUDEA & JESUS

Within the walls of the mighty Roman Empire another great influence emerged. Off in the remote Judean village of Bethlehem, some seventy-four years before Masada, a young Jew named Jesus was born. He later began to wield an influence that after his death would eventually mutate in the hands of his followers. As Roman pagans converted to Christianity, the religion itself mutated even further as it adopted many of the hierarchical traits of Rome, thus conquering the religious domain with a very Roman-like political infrastructure.

Therefore, before addressing the life and influence of Jesus, it is essential to touch upon the fact that many centuries of Christian dominance have camouflaged many historical realities that underlie this grand epoch. Many today have been well groomed or color-blinded by the small palette of consecrated colors that the church allowed or trained them to see. Yet, herein, we will equate truth to turpentine, which although may be strong and offensive, will strip away the thick, centuries-old layers of this heavily-varnished Christian canvas to reveal a full spectrum of colors; colors that were hitherto unseen, and in some instances unimaginable to the modern Christian mindset.

One will see how the glorious message of Jesus, which was unmistakably magnificent, spiritually penetrating, and immensely far-reaching, quickly mutated after his death, as the hands of mankind tainted the newly-formed church. This manmade enterprise, once in power, slowly altered and suppressed pagan histories to validate their self-ordained power and even preached about the corruption of their pagan predecessors. However, underneath this pious veneer, they simultaneously adopted many Roman traits that enabled them to claim ultimate dominion over Western history for many centuries, hence leading right up to the sixteenth century when the Christian colossus internally began to fracture.

Contrary to popular belief, this colossal Christian movement never began as a monolithic entity, nor was it an orderly progression in its rise to power. As we examine this long and restless path upward, one cannot overlook Christianity's devastating decline, as approximately 25 percent of Europeans today have become secularists or are non-practicing dropouts.

Many modern day Christians also believe that Christianity conquered Rome by extinguishing pagan Roman influence, and enabling it to craft a purely new Christian world order. However, during Christianity's transition from small cult to state religion, Rome did in fact intrepidly prevail in many ways that may startle the Christian reader. For beyond Rome's influential laws, government, engineering, art, architecture, economy and military that clearly mark every great nation today, Christianity's own success was likewise made possible by key Roman figures, Roman law, and Roman might.

As such, Christianity eventually flourished in ways it never could have attained purely on its own. Its success was a combination of its rich core beliefs, as preached by Jesus, by the many hands of devout followers, benevolent saints, opportunists, and even power-hungry fanatics who joined the religion for that sole purpose. Some of these men were faithful bishops, others were pagan Roman converts, some were pious popes, and naturally others were corrupt or even hellish warriors, such as the Crusaders that turned Pope Innocent III's Muslim attack into a campaign against fellow Christians in 1205, which forever stained the sublime cause.

We shall always keep in mind that during the Dark and Middle Ages we cannot paint the entire Christian canvas black, as many gave themselves wholly and freely to the spiritual attraction of the Jesus message, and they lived very virtuous and influential lives. However, many others would be cruelly forced against their will, for the church amplified the First Commandment from the Hebrew's Old Testament, *"You shall have no other gods before Me"* and even took on the aura of the Jewish God who smote others who did not heed his word. This power was likewise made possible by the great wealth the church accumulated over many centuries, a wealth that will also be explored in Chapter IV.

As mentioned, it is also crucial to note how the Catholic Church once inundated with Gentiles, or more plainly, pagan Roman converts, it soon adopted a more powerful hierarchy that mirrored the Roman Empire. The church's ruling body of bishops soon mirrored Roman senators, deacons and priests mirrored tribunes and governors, and later still, they even created a semi-divine position of immense power, called pope, that not only mirrored Roman emperors but actually rose above them by performing their coronations.

At the peak of their power, popes not only held complete control over the governance of state but also the soul of every person in their vast kingdom. However, this seat, like the imperial throne, soon attracted many power-crazed opportunists. Becoming "Emperors of the Altar" some of these newly-created popes would later win converts by force, and would rigorously eliminate those who didn't bend to their mortally altered creed. The histories of these bad popes read equally as brutal as many of the bad emperors preceding them, yet have rarely, if ever, been told to the broader public.

Unfortunately, many devout Christians today refuse to believe these truths. Despite these dark and ugly moments in Christian history, however, the powerful words of Jesus have shaped and enhanced many great leaders as well as a large portion of the masses, which remain uncontestable truths of a benevolence that penetrated exceedingly deep and spread miraculously worldwide. Hence, there is nothing diabolical about seeking the truths of Christianity's origins and rise, for as Jesus said himself *"Seek, and ye shall find."*

Therefore, the quest herein is certainly not to demean or dismiss God, but to expose human intervention and interference to show how their revisionist history is not something Christians should blindly accept and worship without proper scrutiny and consideration. Many centuries of Christian rule afforded the church the ability to disclose only the histories they deemed appropriate for their flock, namely the corrupt and ruthless affairs of Roman emperors and a soulless empire that still fascinates the public today, yet they conveniently concealed the ugly sins that took place within their own afflicted walls. The purple robe may have been replaced by white, but crimson red still flowed from the hands of both tenants. To man's eternal shame, the true meaning and message of the Christians' savior, Jesus Christ, was irrevocably transformed and blatantly corrupted.

Before we begin, it is important to reiterate that Jesus and his divine message have survived many tumultuous centuries, and for good reason. Many devout Christian followers held firm to their unshakable beliefs and kept the real faith alive. We also know of the many glorious souls who advocated and engendered the positive message of Jesus, to the betterment of the Western world in general. However, herein, we will focus primarily on the more obscured histories that have rarely been told. This is not to paint a one-sided picture, instead, this is because the vast majority of Christians already know the celebrated stories that are routinely reiterated in catechism and church, and many of them rightfully so. As such, the intent herein is to simply reveal a clear, unfiltered and unbiased reading of how Jesus rose to prominence, and how the church, from a purely historical viewpoint, actually grew. Additionally, we shall see how Christianity was not a movement outside, and completely against the Roman Empire, but in fact became intertwined and adopted many of its attributes, both good and bad.

As we know, the Christian recruit is first immersed into the religion by being programmed to simply learn of Jesus' birth, his glorious life and death in Judea, along with key personalities or prayers by rote memory. The Christian student is not truly expected to question or dispute these truths, since they are taught as lectures, not an open forum, and are projected in a manner that insinuates that they were written in stone as if by God himself.

Quite interestingly, few stop to even ponder a most basic question, which is, what is the name of the Christian entity that spawned all others? The answer is simple; everyone knows it was the Roman Catholic Church. However, this, too, we learned by rote, without truly questioning the reason why. If catechism teaches us that the Romans formed the pagan empire, which they also *wrongly* say Jesus denounced, then why or how could this name be the official name that branded the religion? Would that not clearly be an affront to Jesus?

Furthermore, what are we to make of the fact that after Christianity became the Roman Empire's official religion, it miraculously relocated from the Middle Eastern province of Judaea, where its deep Jewish roots formed several millennia earlier, to the distant capital-city of imperial Rome? Herein lies the key, not St. Peter's Key, but the key that will unlock the door to reveal a whole myriad of other truths yet, this title, in and of itself, offers clear evidence of, not only Roman influence, but also Roman domination. One can make no mistake that once this religion solidified the mighty name that branded this monolithic enterprise was appropriately entitled the Roman Catholic Church. It was not the Jerusalem Catholic Church, or the Nazarene Catholic Church, or even the Jesus Catholic Church, no, it was the *Roman* Catholic Church.

In addition to the church's Roman name, and Roman hierarchy, is the fact that the Greek Orthodox offshoot, which was forced to remain in the east, while the Roman Catholic Church gained ultimate dominion in the west, was based upon the ancient Greek ideology of governance by council. Akin to the Greek's socialist version of democracy, the Greek Christians also chose to rule by council. In direct contrast, the Roman Catholic Church was forged by Roman Christians who followed the structure of their Empire, hence why the exalted seat of pope was created, and another reason why the Roman Catholic Church eventually dominated all other religions, just like its former imperial self.

Likewise, Christianity did not even retain its own language, for once the Romans infiltrated the religion, Hebrew, Aramaic, and Greek, were all discarded as Latin dominated the very voice of the religion as well. Latin not only remained the language of this religion until recent memory in America, but most importantly, it still prevails at the highest echelon at the Vatican. Many other facets of the religion—some perhaps trivial and others quite profound—will be explored, but the origin of this spectacular moment in history begins with Jesus.

JESUS: *His Rise, Followers, Detractors, and Demise | God or Messiah? | The Need for Gospels*

Upon discussing Jesus, we shall try to eliminate any miraculous conjecture and simply focus on the factual realities we know and can confirm with some degree of assuredness, as even this historical realm is often hazy. We must also realize that all the existing ancient texts about Jesus, outside the minor pagan contributions, are accounts intended to proselytize, rather than record an accurate historical narrative. Therefore, this, too, shall color our vision as we proceed, but the intent is to unravel truth from fiction.

To begin with, very few people realize that the name Jesus is not his original name; it is the Greek and Latin version of his real name, which was Yeshu. Jesus and his disciples spoke Aramaic, which was a language that later developed from its Hebrew roots, much like how Italian, Spanish and the Romanic languages emerged from their Latin root. Yet, to keep our modern ears in tune with what we've become accustomed to, we will use the name Jesus herein, in lieu of Yeshu.

The beginning of our journey starts with a gaping void, for the historical data regarding Jesus' birth is missing. It was recorded as recollections many decades after his death, and from a purely factual standpoint, the birthplace of Bethlehem is not conclusive nor can it be proven, however, because it conformed to ancient prophecies, it was later recorded as fact. However, no official public records to indicate such a birth were ever found. As such, it is unfortunate, yet historically prudent to leave the birth of Jesus at that, and only say that he was born of Mary.

Mary remains an elusive personality in scripture, yet one deeply loving and devoted to her son. Naturally, her Immaculate Conception delves into the realm of the miraculous, which would be refuted by many in her own day, and many forever after. However, Mary would also develop a passionately strong following many centuries later that persists to the present day. Despite many Christians today believing that this was a one of a kind supernatural event, they must realize that miraculous births by mortal women were nothing new in the ancient world. As such, we will take a brief look at one in particular.

Beyond the many Greek gods that fornicated with mortal women was the account of Augustus being fathered by Apollo. This tale began circulating after Augustus attained ultimate power, and some naturally sought a divine connection. Many different tales arose, but one was that his mother, Atia, had been visited in the night and was impregnated. Her glowing womb was allegedly witnessed by her mortal husband, Octavius, who prophesied that their son would be the *Light of the World*. One cannot avoid the direct similarity to that of Jesus' miraculous birth. Yet again, the majority of these stories emerged well after the main players were dead; hence, the facts remained conveniently unverifiable.

The question of Jesus' father likewise remains a controversial issue, for Joseph is a highly enigmatic figure who either did or did not take part in the mysterious birth of Jesus, or his siblings for that matter, for according to Mark's Gospel, Jesus had many. *"Is not this the carpenter, the son of Mary, the brother of James, and Joses, and of Juda, and Simon?"*

It remains awfully curious that these blood relatives of the most important figure in Christianity would somehow become so insignificant that they almost vanished from history, or at least from the history taught in catechism. Then again, once Jesus was proclaimed God himself, how could his mortal siblings ever be properly explained? Moreover, how could they ever remain in the spotlight, for that matter?

However, Jesus' brother James did receive some very prominent attention, for immediately after his brother's crucifixion, James was said by some to be his most assertive supporter. In fact, most modern Christians will be astonished to learn that James became the bishop, and leader, of the Jerusalem Church after Jesus' death. As such, as Jesus' brother, it was very likely James, not Peter, who led the core Jesus movement along with his family members.

Quite intriguing is that the discarded *Gospel of Thomas* conveyed this leadership role; for the disciples had asked Jesus who would lead them after he departed. *"Jesus said to them, 'Wherever you are, you are to go to James the righteous, for whose sake heaven and earth came into being.'"*

Yet, oddly enough, all the canonical Gospels, which we must remember were hand selected by Irenaeus, hailed Peter as the founder and leader of the church, while omitting James.

However, James was briefly mentioned in Galatians and Acts as being the elder to whom Peter and Paul appealed to for critical input. Yet, because James recruited orthodox Jews in Jerusalem these so-called Pharisaic Christians were very strict observers of the Mosaic Laws, and they didn't appreciate the fact that Peter and Paul catered to the Gentiles. Worse yet, Paul was allowing all Gentile recruits to avoid circumcision and other Jewish customs established by Abraham, according to Moses in Genesis. James initially disapproved of Paul's wayward practices, yet eventually he condoned his liberal policies, for as he opined, even Jesus said that *all* would be able to seek the Lord through him.

This lent credence that induction would no longer be through the long-held Hebrew belief that God favored their race exclusively. This divine birthright was firmly instilled by the covenant made between God and Moses on Mount Sinai. These were provocative and challenging words by Jesus, which Paul fervently endorsed, yet those of strict orthodox faith would fervently not accept.

Therefore, James found himself caught in the middle of trying to appease his Pharisaic congregation, while at the same time appeasing Paul's largely Gentile congregation. James' role as mediator was no easy task, and his final decision, although fair-minded, was anything but decisive, for he believed that the Pharisaic parishioners should keep their Judaic Laws of Moses, while the newly inducted Gentiles could simply circumvent them.

Paul, on the other hand, adamantly believed that the message of Jesus was clearly a new order or covenant that negated the need to follow the Laws of Moses, especially the tedious eating rituals and the physical devotion of circumcision. Here again, the discarded Gospel of Thomas gives evidence that circumcision was no longer a necessary ritual. When asked by his disciples if circumcision was beneficial, Jesus answered, *"If it were beneficial, their father would beget them already circumcised from their mother."* Most importantly, however, Paul believed that salvation could only be attained through Jesus. This is where a huge confrontation between James and Paul erupted, and this is when James and the elders placed Paul under house arrest for not complying with James' dual policy.

What has become increasingly apparent to most scholars is that along with Peter and Paul we now see James as not only being one of the three (four, including Mary) most important figures in the new Jesus movement, but very possibly its senior leader. However, James was not an apostle (apostle literally means missionary, or one that goes out to preach and convert others), for unlike the apostle Paul, James remained fixed at the church in Jerusalem, and again, apparently holding the supreme position of the new Jesus movement. However, within three decades, James would meet a similar fate as his brother when the Jewish High Priest, Ananus, had him brutally killed. This, too, is a telling event, for it was most often the leaders of any rebellious movement that were executed, like Jesus before him, and John the Baptist before that. As we shall see, once both Peter and Paul rose to that lofty position, they, too, would be executed.

Yet it is also crucial to understand the Roman backdrop to all these Judeo/Christian events. Judea was always a troublesome province, and the Roman procurators governing this area often had to make concessions or, when things went awry, rule with an iron fist. One Roman procurator named Felix even married a Jewish princess to ease relations, but this only enraged the vast majority of strict orthodox Jews. Their contempt added fuel to the growing tensions in the region, as Felix grew ever more humiliated by their hostile reaction. The Roman governor's gesture had failed, for the Jews only saw the marriage as a sacrilegious insult. This eventually gave rise to the infamous Sicarii guerillas who rose in fierce opposition. This, in turn, would lead to the Masada event in AD 73, which occurred over a decade after Felix's reign.

However, during his tenure, Felix soon became noted for being merciless, so naturally, revolts and mayhem ensued. This led to Felix's aggressive series of executions, until finally all hell broke loose. However, although history has painted Felix as a ruthless tyrant who obviously did go on a killing spree, we can at least understand his deep-seated humiliation that led to his rage. Just how much humiliation and outbreaks of crime he was forced to endure is anyone's guess, but his rough handling of the situation only further agitated the area.

In AD 60, a new governor named Festus replaced Felix. Festus came into office with a new and open-minded approach. He even assisted Paul with his troubles with the law, which will be addressed later, yet Festus died unexpectedly only two years into office. This death may or may not be suspicious, but this caused a gap in securing a new Roman procurator, and this gap allowed the Jewish High Priest, Ananus, to step in and take matters into his own vengeful hands. Without proper authority, Ananus acted as governor to fulfill the malignant agenda of his Jewish sect, which was to execute the troublesome Jewish/Christian named James.

Once again, history is replete with incidents that point the finger of blame at the Romans when, in reality, the villain craftily resided elsewhere. In this case, it was a matter of Jewish rivalry between a radical traditional sect, and the new liberal breed, later to be called Christians.

During James' thirty years of leadership, however, Peter and Paul had already begun to assert their own positions of power and influence, and as we shall see, Paul became more crucial than even Peter. After James' death, the Jesus family, namely James and all his siblings, would be overshadowed, overruled and significantly overlooked in the pages of Christian scripture, almost to the point of total obscurity.

Yet it is interesting to note that after James' execution, his eminent seat, or *episcopus*, which means "overseer", was not given to Peter, but to James' blood cousin, Symeon. This once again offers further evidence that if James were indeed Jesus' blood brother, as the Gospel of Mark clearly indicates, then that would explain their paramount concern for keeping the family's bloodline in control after the crucifixion of Jesus. However, with the utter turmoil in Jerusalem leading to the destruction of the Holy Temple, this caused the majority of Jews and early Christians to emigrate north and elsewhere. It was during this chaos and fear of impending doom that the Jesus family dissipated as well, along with their influence.

The mysterious evidence that James and his siblings did exist, as canonical scriptures verify, yet the apostolic founders and church have understandably eschewed explanation or further investigation, brings us briefly back to Jesus' earthly biological father, Joseph. Other scriptures, written well after Jesus' death, state that Jesus was the one and only Son of God, or a divine entity, therefore having no paternal connection to his mortal father, Joseph. Either way, after Jesus reached the age of twelve, Joseph was never mentioned in any texts as having any contact with his soon to be famous son. Without any historical evidence to support the actual birth of Jesus, or who his father truly was, we could only put forth these conflicting recollections, and leave that to one's personal beliefs, as we proceed forward.

As a young man, Jesus was said to be a humble carpenter, like his earthling father, Joseph, until he encountered John the Baptist. John was a charismatic preacher who was making a considerable impact on Jews in the outskirts of Judaea. John had revived the teachings of the ancient Jewish prophet Elijah that seemingly attracted many new recruits. This was based upon the notion that a new kingdom of God would come and bring salvation to all, namely all devout Jews. According to Malachi in the Old Testament, Elijah was also expected to return as the messiah to prepare all of mankind before the Last Judgment. *(As an interesting side note, this was why Jesus was later asked if he was Elijah.)*

However, more importantly, John declared that the waters of baptism would wash away and purify the sins of mankind. Since this was a new ritual, it wasn't just newborns that were baptized— as is customary today—for the majority was adults who yearned for purification. Therefore, adults were John's prime candidates for being baptized, and as such, they were expected to repent while performing this sacred ritual. This washing of one's soul, which not only erased sin but also prepared one for the kingdom of God, fascinated Jesus, who offered himself to be baptized by John in the river Jordan.

This incident is very interesting for many reasons, because, according to the Gospel of Mark, Jesus now learns of his divine status. For upon his baptism, Jesus had a vision, where for the first time God spoke to him, saying, *"You are my beloved Son, in whom I am well pleased."*

Firstly, this is rather unusual that God in the form of Jesus did not know himself beforehand. After all, God is supposed to be all-knowing. Moreover, if Jesus were God himself, he must therefore be free from all error and sin. Yet, Jesus conceded to being purified by a mortal preacher. This raises a host of questions that many great thinkers have pondered.

Why would God have a mere mortal cleanse his Son (or in reality himself) of sin if God is sinless? Moreover, was this just a strange act by God, allowing John to perform this mock ritual or, more importantly, did Jesus truly acquire mortal sin while on Earth? If Jesus did acquire sin, and needed John's purification, then how are we to believe everything Jesus said as being the true inerrant word of God?

Furthermore, some scholars believe that Jesus was John's protégé for almost a year before being baptized. Even more peculiar is how the gospels changed the storyline. In the first written gospel, Mark pithily states that John baptized Jesus, however Matthew attempts to clarify this odd occurrence by having John ask Jesus why he should baptize the Lord. John's gospel, being the last in line, ignores this illogical baptism altogether and focuses on John simply declaring Jesus' divinity.

As such, it is understandable why some early Christian Church leaders did not savor this peculiar event. Furthermore, they even tried to bury it, although quite unsuccessfully. John had already become wildly popular, and there was no way to prevent the recollections of his rise and demise from being recorded by his followers and other sects; hence, why the story of John the Baptist survives, and why his role is openly mentioned yet not truly scrutinized.

However, John the Baptist's message of the coming of a new kingdom also attracted the attention of the Judean king named Herod Antipas, son of Herod the Great. Antipas was not particularly enthralled that John's new foretold kingdom would naturally replace his own, so he preemptively arrested John. Tradition tells us that when the king's stepdaughter, Salome, danced for him and his guests during his birthday celebration, he granted her any wish. Salome then requested John's head on a platter, since that was what her mother Herodias suggested. This was because Herodias was King Antipas' niece, and this incestuous marriage had earlier caused John to openly condemn their unnatural union. As such, Herodias was ripe with vengeance. With two crucial strikes against the bold preacher, King Antipas summoned his executioner and John the Baptist was brutally beheaded.

Upon hearing of John's tragic execution, Jesus fled to Galilee. There, Jesus would continue the gospel of his earthly mentor, John the Baptist. Even this act of fleeing causes us pause to ask why or how could Jesus simply run away from this gross atrocity? We know the peaceful nexus of what Jesus preached, but to flee from the brutal and senseless killing of his beloved mentor (from a human perspective), or beloved child (from a divine perspective), seems rather baffling. Hence, as believers, we are left with ignoring this brutal act, to simply say that it was of a divine nature that ignored Jesus' Old Testament Bible, and its eye for an eye policy, for his own new policy of turning the other cheek.

Nevertheless, from the purely historical viewpoint, Jesus refused to retaliate against the vicious Jewish overlords, and moved to Galilee to follow his mentor's lead. This Jesus did by not only continuing the ritual of baptism, but also declaring that the new kingdom of God was not something in the future, but instead was already here. Luke 17:20 *"The kingdom of God cometh not with observation. Neither shall they say, Lo here! or, lo there! for, behold, the kingdom of God is within you."*

Fully adopting and altering John the Baptist's message, Jesus now became a charismatic preacher in his own right, with an even more powerful message. With John the Baptist *"preparing the way for the Lord,"* Jesus quickly rose to prominence in this tiny backwater and soon surpassed his mentor.

Galilee was a rustic, seaside village that lay over a hundred miles north of the Jewish epicenter of Jerusalem, both being Middle Eastern provinces of Rome. Jerusalem was a large city located in infertile desert-like terrain, which boasted the most eminent of Hebrew priests and scholars with an equally good head for business, while Galilee was populated with uncultured fisherman, farmers and laborers in a lush agrarian setting. Even their rural Galilean accents differed from the more sophisticated intellects that roamed the Holy City. This is also perhaps why Jesus spoke in simple layman terms, and why he held strong suspicions and even distaste over the ways of the elite and wealthy. In essence, Jesus' Galilean audience was a different breed from those in Jerusalem, and this humble village is where Jesus influenced what would become his staunch followers.

Simon, later to be known as Peter, would become Jesus' first follower, and remained his closest disciple to the very end, despite some discrepancies, which shall be addressed later. However, even though Peter denied knowing Jesus immediately after his crucifixion (not once but three times), Peter did regain his former state of grace after witnessing the risen Jesus. The scriptures offer two conflicting stories as to how Peter became his loyal disciple, but both have Peter, along with his brother Andrew, as being the first two supporters to enter the fold.

Jesus soon established a devout following with a powerful ministry of peace and goodwill. Although Jesus claimed to be continuing the Hebrew tradition, his profound benevolence was in stark contrast to that found in the ancient Tanakh. The Jewish God was often jealous and revengeful– even to his chosen flock if they disobeyed. *"The LORD shall smite thee with madness, and blindness, and astonishment of heart."* Or *"The LORD will afflict you with the boils of Egypt, with ulcers, scurvy and itch..."*

Meanwhile, Jesus preached, *"Ye have heard that it hath been said, Thou shalt love thy neighbor, and hate thine enemy. But I say unto you, Love your enemies, bless them that curse you, do good to them that hate you, and pray for them which despitefully use you, and persecute you."*

Although the Old Testament contains passages of love and good will it has many others of God smiting his creations. Meanwhile, despite a passage by Jesus in Luke of smiting nonbelievers, his ministry was largely one of good will and forgiveness. Here again we can recall how Jesus peacefully walked away from the brutal murder of John the Baptist without smiting them. This was a radical departure from the aggressive words of Yahweh, and this new benevolent message cannot be understated, as Jesus also said *"Be not overcome of evil, but overcome evil with good,"* as well as *"And unto him that smiteth thee on the one cheek offer also the other..."*

In this instance, we can make some sense of Jesus' lack of retaliation after the beheading of his beloved mentor, for John would find his rightful place in heaven, while his executioners would not. However, John was extracted from the real world while his evil and plotting enemies remained afoot to wreak further havoc.

Nevertheless, Jesus also took John the Baptist's message of the kingdom of God a step further, for not only would those wishing to enter heaven need to renounce worldly temptations and live a loving and moral life, but they could only enter through him.

John 10:9 *"I am the door: by me if any man enter in, he shall be saved, and shall go in and out, and find pasture."*

Even though Jesus clearly stated in his Sermon on the Mount that he was here to fulfill Judaic Law, his actions and words often indicated otherwise, for Jesus also professed that on Judgment Day man stands before God as an individual, and not because of his affiliation to any temple or organization. This is documented in Luke, or more vividly in the later discarded Gospel of Thomas. Consequently, this radical young preacher incensed all the Jewish leaders throughout Judea, which included the Pharisees, Sadducees, and Essenes among other sects. Their suspicions soon turned into contempt and then outright hostility. In certain regards, the Jewish High Priests were no different from emperors, for if they perceived someone to be a threat to their rule, like John the Baptist, they were dealt with severely or brutally executed.

Today, perhaps to ease tensions between Jews and Christians, some Jews now claim that Jesus was only one among many prospective messiahs, and would not have incited the wrath of the ancient Jews to plot his crucifixion. However, it is quite clear that Jesus contained many non-orthodox traits, even exceeding those of John the Baptist which, in total, would have made him more than an impotent Jewish rabbi; instead, Jesus would have been viewed as a genuine threat to everything they held sacred, namely their authoritative and unalterable Tanakh, in both literal and oral form. Likewise, Jesus' views on greed and gross wealth were in sharp contrast to the business-minded Sadducees who fixated on profits and power. This unquestionably was a profound threat.

Jesus eventually decided that he and his devout followers should attend the Passover feast in Jerusalem. As an additional impetus, Herod Antipas wanted this troublesome disciple of John the Baptist out of his domain. Again, from a purely historical viewpoint, this is perhaps why Jesus knew his demise was imminent and the proper time to make influential waves before his parting. From a faithful perspective, it appears to have been part of the divine plan. In either case, Jerusalem at Passover was ideal.

This most holy ritual drew thousands of Jews from all distant quarters, and was the ultimate convention center to market one's beliefs or to make a bold and urgent statement. However, due to the various and intensely rivaling Jewish sects, which at the time numbered over twenty, disturbances were commonplace. As such, the Roman governor, Pontius Pilate, would undoubtedly be present.

Jesus then humbly rode into the hallowed city on a donkey, which apparently fulfilled the ancient Jewish prophecy, which stated that the next King of the Jews would indeed appear in Jerusalem in such a fashion. At least he did so according to Jesus' apostles, who recorded this event several decades after Jesus died. However, the fact remains that there were two such prophecies according to Jewish scripture.

One was of a Davidic king who would radically change the world in his lifetime, build a new Temple, attract all previous exiles, and militantly rule over all peoples. The other Messianic prophecy described a king who would also enter Jerusalem on a donkey; he, too, would rule from sea to sea, yet would bring peace by eliminating warfare. Henceforth, to all devout orthodox Jews, Jesus failed to meet either of these requirements in full, and as such, this incident became a single facet of a myriad of reasons why he was not universally embraced.

However, the spark that would ignite the most cataclysmic religious event was about to occur. Once inside the holy city, and four days prior to the actual Passover Feast, Jesus brazenly stormed the Holy Temple and physically began reprimanding the Jewish Saducee priests for their capitalistic greed. Repulsed by the profane profiteers who were defiling the Temple, Jesus began cutting loose all the animals awaiting sale or sacrifice. Then in a moment of rage, the only one recorded, Jesus physically toppled over the moneychanger's table. In the Gospel of John, Jesus even fashioned a whip to beat the moneychangers out of the Temple.

Passover in Jerusalem brought out the best and worst of the Jews. In one instance, it brought together prominent spiritual leaders and followers deep in the faith, and in another, the holy city was notoriously transformed into a bustling marketplace that peddled almost every commodity and service imaginable. Most symbolic of all, however, was the money used to perform all of these transactions, hence, why it remains the most memorable in scripture.

This is the only mention of Jesus taking such a violent course of action. As such, we must infer that this action angered Jesus more than any other, or perhaps it was a sign of just one major disappointment Jesus had for mankind that would perhaps make the most waves and cause the desired result.

What remains clear, however, is that this provocative outburst is what most pointedly enraged the ruling High Priests. However, to their utter humiliation, they were prevented from making a reprisal for several reasons. Their grand Feast was gearing up to commence and the furthest thing they wanted was a spectacle or a riot that would deter business and jeopardize profits. Then there was the matter of their Roman overlords who demanded order amidst these typically supercharged feasts, as they expected the High Priests to keep the peace. Additionally, when they questioned Jesus about his hostile actions, he cleverly answered them with a question instead, saying, *"John's baptism, did it come from heaven, or from man?"*

If they answered from heaven, it would justify Jesus' similar claim of divine instruction from above, and if they answered man, it would negate John the Baptist's popular ritual, and insult his many followers who were present. Either answer would ensnare the High Priests into Jesus' trap, so the public confrontation was humiliatingly dropped. However, the thought of vengeance would not be dropped. As such, a covert plot was needed to entrap the wily rabbi, who interestingly enough, was being hailed by some as the Messiah.

The whole issue of a messiah is a crucial one, and at this juncture, we need to pause to consider the following: as mentioned, Jesus did not fulfill the ancient Jewish prophecy that clearly stated that the Messiah would destroy the Temple and establish a new kingdom on Earth during his lifetime. Interestingly enough, several decades later, Josephus reported how the emperor Vespasian was hailed for fulfilling this enormous prophecy. This was quite logically put forth because Vespasian squelched the revolt in the Holy Land, destroyed the Temple, and rose to become supreme ruler. However, even though Vespasian certainly rescued the Roman Empire from the treacheries of Nero and brought it back to renewed heights, his failure to fulfill the Jewish requirements, basically not being a Jew, obviously prevented Vespasian from taking root in Jewish tradition.

However, what has not been considered by most historians or theologians is that regardless of the Jews or Christians who tried to lambaste the Roman Empire, this vote to name Vespasian the Messiah clearly underscores a crucial point, namely, how the Romans, at least while under good rulers, were not ruthless savages, but rather respectable men. In essence, they represented a regime that could even produce a spiritual leader, if he was of the chosen faith. Furthermore, this additionally underscores Vespasian's dedication to restoring the more tolerant ways of Augustus, which yielded a renewed golden age.

Additionally, and of equal importance, is the fact that the Roman historian Suetonius gives a different account of this prophecy from the pagans' perspective. In his great work, *The Twelve Caesars*, Suetonius informs us that the pagans had a prophecy that proclaimed a new ruler would emerge from the Judaean province. Yet the Jews infused their own ancient prophecy into this pagan prediction, and aiming to make it manifest with a Jewish champion, they murdered their Roman governor, and then forced the Roman governor of Syria to flee when he attempted to restore order. The rebels even stole the eagle talisman as a souvenir, which was a serious insult to Rome. These riotous actions were what prompted Nero to assign Vespasian to put down the revolt.

Henceforth, from this historical yet religiously silenced viewpoint, the initial spark of all these hostilities in the region was not solely by Nero, or his corrupt governors, but by some Jewish guerillas who were attempting to control the fate of their prophecy, with the hopes of uncovering their new messiah. However, the radical rabbi named Jesus was clearly not their idea of the chosen one. This interesting record from pagan history sheds an entirely different light on this intense moment in history, which traditionally has done well in portraying the Judaic/Christian perspective as angelically clear and focused, while blurring and demonizing what very well could have been the truth.

Most important are the facts that the Jews did murder the Roman governor, and the Jewish High Priest Ananus did illegally seize the governorship's vacancy to execute his evil plans and execute Jesus' brother, James. Furthermore, the beheading of St. John the Baptist by King Antipas only added more evidential fuel to a scorching-hot Jewish flame. Hence, much plotting was afoot among the Jewish high command, which evidently ignited all these catastrophes.

Returning to our Jesus narrative, another critical fact to ingest is that Jesus himself had the opportunity to scorn the Roman Empire as evil, which at that point was under the reign of Tiberius, yet Jesus never did.

When the doubting Jewish Pharisees questioned Jesus whether or not they should pay taxes, Jesus said, *"Render to Caesar the things that are Caesar's, and to God the things that are God's."*

Many Christians have misread this remark. Jesus here clearly instructs people to comply with Caesar's regime in offering them things that are temporal, whereas offering things of the spirit to God. He did not say anything remotely derogative or firmly against Caesar or the Roman Empire, nor does he anywhere else in the four Gospels. Yet many have misinterpreted this passage to mean that Jesus was against Caesar, organized government, and even against money. The words of Jesus in the Gospels, however, do not posit such a meaning.

History has proven that Christianity had every opportunity to create the kingdom of God that Jesus spoke of during the many centuries leading up to, during, and even after the Middle Ages. The church had ultimate power, however, the theocracy of Christendom faltered just like the temporal empires and transient governments on Earth, in fact during the Dark Ages it even subjected the masses to the worst living conditions it ever had to endure. From a religious or even historical perspective, we can only conclude that Jesus did not intend his kingdom to replace earthly kingdoms but, instead, to work in unison or at least in parallel with them.

This aptly brings to mind the story of when Jesus was asked to pay his own taxes. The tax collector had approached Peter and asked him if his master pays taxes. Peter replied, *"Yes,"* and then proceeded into a house to summon Jesus. Jesus tells Peter not to offend them and to collect a gold coin from the mouth of a fish and then pay the tax collector. This odd story has been interpreted in different ways, with some claiming this was a refusal by Jesus to pay taxes, however, this interpretation fails on three major points.

First, when asked if Jesus pays his taxes Peter told the collectors, *"Yes."* As the closest right-hand man to Jesus, he knew his master's habits and replied accordingly. Second, Jesus' statement that the tax collector, or government, takes money from strangers, and not their own children, has led many to believe that people should not pay taxes, yet this deviates from the story and misses the point. For Jesus also said, *"Lest we should offend them,"* and then proceeds with his fish story in order to find the money which Peter was to *"give unto them for me and thee."* Hence, Jesus did not wish to offend them, and he instructs Peter to gather the coin that will serve as payment for them both.

Lastly, we face the interpretation of Peter gathering the gold coin from the fish, which could be viewed as a miraculous act of Jesus, or a symbolic one; we must recall that Jesus taught Peter and his brother Andrew to be *"fishers of men."* Therefore, his catch was not literally fish, but men that were converted to the Jesus movement, who in turn became their children. Hence, this indicates a collection from a new member of their family, which was acceptable, as opposed to taking money from strangers. As for the oddity of getting gold from the fish's mouth, that has been explained by the fact that many villagers lacked money, so newcomers to the religion would give up their gold teeth. Hence, gathering this payment from a new member's mouth, rather than a fish's mouth, is not only plausible, but most probable.

Most importantly, Jesus and Peter did not refuse paying their taxes, and this act likewise gave credence to the future church that made collections an integral part of their own institution. In fact, during the Renaissance this scene was painted by Massacio on a chapel wall with the intent of stating publicly that the church also pays their taxes. This was because many wars demanded that the Florentines pay taxes for defense and survival. As Cosimo de Medici said, *"No price is too high for our liberty."*

In a similar vein, the avoidance of paying taxes proved devastating to the Byzantines, as seen when the Muslim Sultan Mehmet II conquered Constantinople. After the Muslims plundered the houses of the fallen Byzantines, Mehmet realized that many citizens avoided taxes and selfishly hoarded their money and treasures. The Sultan questioned them, "What was this wealth for?" The hoarders stared in silence. Then glaring down at the hidden treasures, he poignantly added, and "What good are they now?" Although many still balk about paying taxes, its use, when not misdirected, is essential for many crucial reasons.

In the final analysis, although perhaps not completely at ease with the outside world of strangers, and in this case government and taxation, Jesus always did pay his taxes, which again was verified by Peter's initial response. Furthermore, this tale clearly indicates that Jesus paid his taxes once again, regardless of its miraculously divine or symbolically mortal interpretation.

Therefore, according to the scriptures, Jesus did not say that government, or the Roman Empire, should be terminated. If Christianity and all theocracies throughout history have proven to be fallible in their own attempts to govern, then we can only logically conclude that God did not intend mankind to establish his kingdom on Earth, for as Jesus even said, his kingdom was not of this world.

Henceforth, in that crucial moment in the Bible when Jesus flipped over the moneychangers' table where, again, Jesus said nothing derogatory against Rome, we must note that before and during this momentous event, Jesus did lambaste the inquiring Jews for being wicked hypocrites. Furthermore, we must recall that God the Father had no compunctions about scolding Egypt when Moses began the Exodus, and he even employed his own hand in physically smiting Egypt. Yet, no damning words, or vengeful actions did Jesus or his Father level against the Roman Empire or Caesar.

Later Christians have also wrongly interpreted Jesus' words and actions by accusing the Romans of being sinful because of their Roman coinage and capitalistic wealth. Although the Romans played a role in promulgating trade, commerce, and basic capitalistic practices in general, it was explicitly clear that Jesus was solely targeting the money-hungry Sadducean Jews, who desecrated the Temple by turning it into an unsightly marketplace. Jesus even scolded them for defiling *"my Father's house."*

As noted above, Jesus evidently had no qualms with rendering to Caesar things that are Caesar's, but this sacrilege by the Jews prompted him to aggressively react like he never had done before, and this was the message that was lost on so many Christians, to their own misfortune, as well as that of the maligned Romans.

If Rome, with its coinage, or government in general, were the focus of Jesus, he would have openly condemned not only Rome, but also every ruling body at that time, or *of any time* for that matter. However, as the canonical Gospels clearly indicate, Jesus did not. His verbal and physical hostilities were leveled against those who turned the Holy Temple into a commercial mockery.

This aptly shifts our focus onto the real transgressors, and a very interesting fact about the special coinage that Jews used. Because the Second Commandment prohibited graven images, the Jews could not use Roman coins. Therefore, they minted their own imageless coins so that Jews entering the city could buy them in exchange for their Roman coins. Naturally, this transaction was performed for an additional profit. This likewise added fuel to Jesus' aggressive outburst, for their attention was blatantly on money and wealth rather than on Passover and God. This fact also sheds light on how mistaken people are to condemn Rome and its coinage in this crucial moment, for Roman coinage was not even being used, it was Jewish currency.

It is also clear from the scriptures that Jesus had an overriding aversion to wealth and the affluent, as he once said to a rich man, *"How hardly shall they that have riches enter into the kingdom of God! For it is easier for a camel to go through a needle's eye, than for a rich man to enter into the kingdom of God."* Jesus further instructs this rich man to confer all his money to the poor, so that he may then follow Jesus on the correct path.

The powerful and sublime words of Jesus have stood the test of time and influenced billions, yet in this pivotal instance, Jesus' dissatisfaction with the evils of money, wealth, or materialistic greed did not stand the test of time, as coinage and the capitalist system would stridently prevail along with avarice. Not only did money and the desire for wealth consume the early empire, and all succeeding eras right up to our own, but it would also eventually become embedded in the future Christian Church and witness some of the worst abuses of wealth imaginable. Hence, the corruptive power of money not only knows no bounds in the secular world, but also in the spiritual realm.

However, the other side of this ugly and wretched coin does sparkle, as the church and secular enterprises have funded some of the most munificent and magnificent enterprises in history. Hence, the question of money and wealth is an ongoing phenomenon with no signs of ever fading from human affairs.

What remains ironic, and perhaps blasphemous to some, is that the inscription "In God We Trust" is plainly etched on American coins and bills. This is something that Theodore Roosevelt adamantly tried to eradicate, yet quite unsuccessfully. It is likewise something that Jesus himself would have most likely found repugnant or at least paradoxical.

Nevertheless, with Jesus' bold and damaging maneuver in the Holy Temple, and his followers hailing him as the *"Son of God"* or even the *"King of the Jews"*, Jesus had caught, not just the attention, but also the ire of the High Priests. The Gospel of John would later relate, *"After these things Jesus walked in Galilee: for he would not walk in Jewry, because the Jews sought to kill him."*

At this point in our narrative, it is almost anti-climactic that the notorious story of Judas Iscariot enters the fold, because, by all accounts, Jesus had already established his enemies. Yet, we are told that it is Judas, the apostle, who is the treasurer for Jesus and his disciples, who clandestinely decides to betray his master. The story put forth was that Judas' betrayal was for monetary compensation, for Satan entered his soul and compelled his greed and disloyalty. However, Judas' consumption by evil, or at least the moment it actually took over his soul, is not clearly defined. One verse claims Judas had already been taken in by Satan, and was a thief who habitually stole money from their purse, while another verse tells that it was at the Last Supper that Judas was overcome with Satan, that is, once Jesus handed him a piece of bread that designated him as the betrayer.

Nevertheless, after the Last Supper, Jesus traveled over the Kidron Valley to the Garden of Gethsemane. While away, Judas conspired with the Jewish chief priests to hand over Jesus for the healthy sum of thirty pieces of silver (Thirty pieces of silver perhaps being symbolic of Jesus' age rather than the actual amount). As such, it was decided that the man whom Judas would kiss would identify the blasphemous messiah. When Judas finally arrived with the High Priests and their entourage, he walked over and gave Jesus the infamous kiss of death. However, John's Gospel differs in that he mentions no kiss at all, instead his version has someone ask who among them was Jesus of Nazareth, and Jesus answered, *"It is I."* Regardless of minor discrepancies, this treacherous incident would have an immense impact on the new religion and its future. Judas was inscribed into scripture as the man who betrayed his master, or more pointedly God, and became *the* icon of evil.

However, the four decades following Jesus' death marked a growing separation between the budding Jesus movement and its Jewish orthodox roots. Moments of intense rivalry mounted, so that by the time of the authorship of the gospels the two sects were diametrically opposed. With this in mind, it remains curious how this betrayer of Jesus, named Judas, would have a name that is synonymous with Judaism. The coincidence is unavoidable. Was Judas a predestined pawn in the Jesus plan to have that fitting name, which simultaneously labeled the Jews as betrayers? On the other hand, did these early Christians, who were growing more resentful of their Jewish brethren, tag the betrayer with the nickname "Judas" during their long oral tradition, between incident and induction into scripture? Did they attempt to kill two birds with one stone? Even though this is highly hypothetical, and would require all the various Christian sects involved to share the same mindset, we do know symbolism was an important aspect of Judaic and Christian traditions. Hence, changing the betrayer's name, whoever he might have been, to Judas is an interesting possibility to consider, for even a slight name change from Jonas to Judas, or even a label given to the offender to mark him may not be too far-fetched, especially when we consider the following.

We know in the famous Cain and Abel story that both of their names were merely representational of their professions and not their actual names. Many attempts to reconstruct their actual names have been made, since the original Hebrew *Havel* differs from Tiberian Hebrew *Habel*, as well as the English translation *Abel*. Abel, however, means herdsman and Cain means agriculturist or farmer. Many names of antiquity derive from their place of birth, profession, ancestors or their deeds. Therefore, during oral traditions, translations or transliterations many liberties were taken. Hence, the notion of early vengeful Christians using the name Judas as a universal indictment against not only the betrayer, but also the entire Jewish community, stares us in the face.

Adding weight to this hypothesis is the fact that there is only scant mention of Judas in regards to this most heinous act, as only a mere few lines detail his treacherous actions. More interesting still is that only some gospels mention the demise of this most evil man, for John's Gospel ignores it completely. How could such an integral and loathsome man's just punishment be eliminated from any apostle's account?

Although the name Judas was rather common during that era, the notion of symbolism remains open, for even his last name, Iscariot, has no meaning in Aramaic, Greek or Hebrew, hence, no true translation can be rendered. What was also the rule of the day was that last names referred to a family's town, profession, ancestors, or other obvious designation, yet Iscariot remains oddly unique, and out of sync with standard tradition. In the end, these issues remain open to speculation and remain speculation.

Henceforth, that returns us to our narrative. After Judas unfaithfully betrayed and pointed out Jesus, the High Priest Caiaphas immediately placed Jesus under arrest. Caiaphas was intent on taking swift action, as his huge business network was placed in jeopardy by Jesus' hostile actions earlier at the Temple. However, Caiaphas needed to silence this troublemaker in a discrete fashion, since his situation was compounded by the fact that the Roman governor, Pontius Pilate, was currently in town for the Passover stint, therefore his own neck rested on quelling the disturbance.

Pilate was appointed by the Emperor Tiberius, and Pilate soon became known for being harsh and even unsympathetic. Caiaphas, on the other hand, was from a long line of Jewish Saducean High Priests who brokered with the Roman authorities. The Sadducees managed all the commercial enterprises that operated within the Temple itself, which included moneychangers, animal slaughterers, metal workers, stokers, stone masons and a full array of marketers selling their wares and services. The Passover Feast was a huge, profit-generating gala, and Caiaphas would be vigilant in keeping his well-oiled, moneymaking machine in order. As such, with Jesus poking his bad-tempered two-cents into the crankshaft, Caiaphas quickly set the wheels in motion to eliminate this annoying glitch.

Caiaphas' clever entrapment will be discussed more fully in due turn, but at the moment another simultaneous event unfolded. A Jewish leader named Barabbas had recently been incarcerated for robbery and was scheduled for execution. Under Roman law, Pontius Pilate was allowed to pardon one criminal at these annual Passover Feasts, which habitually generated mischief and various crimes. Caiaphas seized this opportunity by shrewdly ensnaring Jesus in a ploy that would force Pilate's hand to, if not convict and crucify Jesus, then at least defer him back to Caiaphas for sentencing. As such, the wily High Priest effectively began prodding the Jewish populace to crucify Jesus with his words, *"It is better for one man to die for the people."*

The fact that Jesus arrived from a minor village, and was only known by a mere one percent of the entire Jewish population, would certainly not have generated an outpouring of love or sympathy, especially from this resolutely orthodox crowd, regardless if some had come specifically to hear Jesus' message of peace. It is quite evident that the variegated mass that was present at this quasi-legal public hearing consisted of a majority of Sadducees, and their influence ruled, as the crowd quickly sided with their High Priest, Caiaphas, to demand the pardon of Barabbas. That more Jews knew Barabbas also aided Caiaphas' plan, and unremittingly they demanded that Jesus be crucified, who in essence would become the sacrificial lamb.

As such, Pontius Pilate, whose only concern was to maintain order, symbolically washed his hands, thus deferring to the ruling Jews to pass sentence. Pilate clearly wanted no part in the lynching, as he declared, *"Take him yourselves and crucify him; I find no case against him."*

As we shall soon see, there was much debate between Pilate and Caiaphas over Jesus' guilt, yet the die was cast. The relatively unknown and blasphemous Messiah named Jesus was brought to the hilltop named Golgotha, which means "skull", and was crucified. *(See page 706)*

Many misconceptions have prevailed since this monumentally tragic event, which raises some issues that need clarification. First, the invention and tradition of crucifixion has for long been falsely linked to the Romans. The fact remains that the black art of crucifixion originated in Persia. This device was even incorporated into early Jewish tradition, for those labeled with *blasphemy* by the Jews would be stoned and then crucified, ala the Jesus manner.

Likewise, many Christians today still condemn the Romans for being evil executioners who reveled in unbridled crucifixions. However, this technique of execution was utilized specifically for capital punishment against the most dangerous in society, and was not used for citizens who committed high crimes. Although wrongly condemned, Jesus was made to look guilty by his conspirators; therefore, the unknowing public and Roman soldiers believed Jesus warranted crucifixion.

Furthermore, all ancient regimes, tribes, or kingdoms engaged in harsh and ugly forms of capital punishment. This included beheading, stoning to death, crucifixion, or a combination of techniques, such as those used by the Jewish High Priests who executed Jesus' brother, James. These particular priests threw James off the Temple's parapet to fatally cripple him, and then they viciously stoned and clubbed him to death.

In addition, we must not forget how even the later death machine, the guillotine, was used in France right up until September 10, 1977. Henceforth, we cannot deride all French people throughout history as being barbarians. However, those wielding the biased brush of brutality have always found the Roman Empire to be a broad canvas to smear.

Another misconception is the excessively cruel torture that the Roman soldiers allegedly inflicted upon the condemned Jesus. These terrifying tales, however, have all been supplements to the canon, and written not by eyewitnesses, or even contemporaries of Jesus, but by later zealots of the cloth who have clouded reality with their fanciful, yet macabre mist, a bloody mist that reads like a Steven King novel, or worse yet has been painstakingly recreated by Mel Gibson in his blockbuster film *The Passion of Christ*.

To begin with, we need to realize that Pontius Pilate repeatedly refused to find fault with Jesus, while the Sadducean High Priest, Caiaphas, orchestrated Jesus' arrest, mock trial and execution. Caiaphas, with Judas Iscariot's assistance, managed to arrest Jesus, as mentioned. This covert operation occurred at night, and due to the nocturnal arrest, Jesus was ushered not to a judicial courthouse, but to Caiaphas' house. This highly shady arrest, or lynching, was not so much for interrogation but rather *in-terror-gation*. Assisting Caiaphas was his fellow High Priest, and father-in-law, Annas. More prominently, however, were the High

Priests' henchmen who antagonized and roughed Jesus up, for according to the Gospel of Matthew 26:67 *"They spat in his face and hit him with their fists; others said as they struck him, 'Prophecy to us, Christ! Who hit you then?'"*

It is clear to see that these Jewish High Priests had a personal vendetta against this troublemaker who threatened their powerful Mafia-like organization, which controlled the Holy city. Moreover, like the Mafia, they had connections and pull with the Roman authorities. As such, Caiaphas decided to make his appeal to Pilate the next morning to execute Jesus, knowing that his Godfather-like image and business would suffer greatly if his own hands were stained with the blood of an innocent rabbi, especially one who rightfully pointed out the mockery they committed at the Temple.

To Caiaphas' surprise and dismay, however, Pilate did not wish to kill this innocent man. Evidently, Pilate's earlier insensitivities toward the Jews had prompted the Emperor Tiberius to reprimand Pilate, so he, too, needed to be cautious, and could not be too rash and unjust toward Jesus. After Pilate's repeated refusals to convict Jesus, Caiaphas' only recourse, as we shall see, was to deceitfully conjure false testimony to blackmail Pilate into action.

The Gospel of John states that Pilate concluded after a brief interview that Jesus committed no wrongdoing, and as such wanted the Jews to take Jesus and judge him according to their own law. The Jews, in response, demanded his crucifixion. However, during Pilate's interrogation, he had questioned Jesus about claims that hailed him as being the King of the Jews, and Jesus responded, *"Thou sayest it."*

It is significant to realize that during their discussions, Jesus never once admitted being the King of the Jews, and all the gospels patently reflect this. This indicates, firstly, that Pilate was fed this information, which obviously was supplied by Caiaphas, and secondly, that Jesus had no intentions of insulting or infringing upon those who ruled the earthly kingdom, namely Rome. During Pilate's further inquiries, Jesus finally stated *"My kingdom is not of this world,"* and as far as Pilate was concerned, this, too, posed no threat. Hence, Pilate, once again, tells Caiaphas and his hostile clan *"I find in him no fault at all."* The events that followed are perhaps best stated by John's Gospel:

"The Jews answered him, we have a law, and by our law he ought to die, because he made himself the Son of God. Pilate sought to release him: but the Jews cried out, saying, If thou let this man go, thou art not Caesar's friend: whosoever maketh himself a king speaketh against Caesar. ...and he (Pilate) saith unto the Jews, Behold your King! But they cried out, Away with him, away with him, crucify him. Pilate saith unto them, Shall I crucify your King? The chief priests answered, we have no king but Caesar. Then (Pilate) delivered him therefore unto them to be crucified. And they took Jesus, and led him away. And he bearing his cross went forth into a place called the place of a skull, which is called in the Hebrew Golgotha: Where they crucified him, and two other with him, on either side one, and Jesus in the midst."

We see here how Caiaphas deceitfully manipulated the situation to his favor by twisting Jesus' words, thus making him appear like an earthly king that threatened the kingdom of Caesar. However, Jesus pointedly replied that he was not a threat to the kingdom on Earth; hence, neither was he a threat to Pilate or Caesar. But Caiaphas strategically forced Pilate's hand, whose next move would be crucial, for if word reached Tiberius that someone spoke against Caesar and claimed himself to be a king, Pilate's own head would roll.

It is also interesting to note that the Jews had also accused Jesus of not giving tribute to Caesar, yet as we have seen, Pilate continually finds no wrong in Jesus, hence this charge of not paying tribute must have been trumped-up, or unsubstantiated, because this would not be something Pilate or Tiberius would tolerate. This is further reinforced by the fact that even after Pilate handed him over to the Sadducee Jews, Pilate still maintained that Jesus was innocent.

This also explains the fact that when Pilate inscribed the conviction notice, which would be displayed on the cross in Latin, Greek and Hebrew, it simply read 'Jesus the Nazarene, King of the Jews'. This wording annoyed the Jewish High Priests who asked that it be changed to read that Jesus *claimed* to be King of the Jews, yet Pilate answered, *"What I have written, I have written."* This was an intentional and prudent maneuver by Pilate to justify the execution, for a bogus or unsubstantiated claim would have caused suspicion and doubt in both Jews and Romans alike. Knowing that Jesus never admitted to being a threat to the kingdom of

Caesar, Pilate needed to appease the mob and protect himself from any possible backlash. Therefore, to our knowledge, Jesus never broke any Roman laws, and he harbored no malice against Rome, except perhaps indifference. Meanwhile, Pilate was goaded into carrying out the will of Caiaphas and his Jewish mob, while literally and symbolically washing his hands of the whole mess.

We now come to the inflammatory issue of scourging, which in Mel Gibson's movie, *The Passion of Christ*, is unquestionably the most blisteringly memorable and appallingly bloody. Most Christians who were interviewed after Gibson's movie were horrified by the intense brutality, yet all believed wholeheartedly that Christ suffered such a fate; after all, that Jesus suffered and died for their sins is the cornerstone of Christian belief.

However, when we look at how the gospels describe this event, Luke makes no mention of scourging at all! This is simply astounding, and quite revealing in its silence. Meanwhile, Mark, Matthew and John only say the single word "scourged". The only extra detail that Mark relates was that a reed was used to smite his head, and again, nothing more. Hence, offering no long and gruesome depictions of severe torture or skin-tearing tools as those fabricated in Mel Gibson's excessively gory horror flick. The reason for this is simple, rather than using the New Testament, Gibson faithfully used the imaginary account written by a nineteenth-century German nun; her name was Anne Catherine Emmerich.

Emmerich was a mystic, with a literary flair for the horrific, who set about recreating and inventing tools of torture, such as metal rods with thorns, and iron chains with sharp hooks that Gibson visually recreated in gruesome detail. Sadly, Gibson did so as if she were an authentic primary source, yet Anne lived some eighteen hundred years after the real passion of Christ. The standard practice of Roman scourging has been recorded in historic documents, and actual scourging whips, which were leather not metal, did sometimes have round metal pellets at the end. However, they were not the razor-sharp metal rods or skin-piercing iron chains that Emmerich envisioned, for scourging was not meant to kill the criminal, which Emmerich's and Gibson's torture tools surely would have done. Although this pre-execution process of scourging was certainly not pretty or even humane, it served to punish and subdue the criminal for the next painful step of crucifixion, and was not the excessive and "lethal" depiction discharged on the silver screen by *Lethal Weapon* star, Mel Gibson. After all, the crucifixion itself was horrific enough.

This is not to say that those in power or their executioners didn't sometimes treat convicted criminals poorly or pitilessly, which we must remember Jesus was, even if unfairly condemned, but the point is twofold. Firstly, Jesus was painted as a criminal to the public and his executioners, and capital punishment used against such criminals generated few sympathetic hearts, as even today spectators attend death row executions, quite content or even happy to see criminals expire.

Therefore, if soldiers spit at or hit a convict this would have been natural, but this brings us to our second point, namely, we have no descriptions other than "scourged", and those vivid scenes and tools later invented by Emmerich were not in any way typical or based on historical evidence. Moreover, if the beatings were abnormally harsh and wicked in nature, the Gospel writers would have certainly expounded upon it in detail, but they did not, and again, Luke interestingly makes no mention of any scourging whatsoever, from Pilate's handing of Jesus over to the Jews for crucifixion (23:24) to Jesus' last breath (23:46). Moreover, this unusual and intense torture would have been self-defeating and lethal. Yet Gibson's blow by blow recreation of a German nun's macabre and fictitious nightmare has been indelibly seared into the hearts and minds of millions with this theatrical branding iron, as if the inherent truth.

What may also come as a drastic surprise is that the famous fourteen "Stations of the Cross" are also fictitious, at least partially. Most stations, such as #3 the first fall, #4 Jesus meets his mother, #6 Veronica wipes Jesus' face with her veil, #7 the second fall, and #9 the third fall are all merely literary inventions by Franciscan monks during the medieval period. These literary depictions have been embedded in catechism and visually displayed on church walls, again, as if fact.

Yet, there is not one shred of canonical scripture to prove any of these stations mentioned above, or any of those excessive and vivid scenes of lethal scourging. All these falsehoods, which have been continually ingrained into the Christian faith, have likewise been adopted upon blind faith, not historical fact.

As for their descriptions of Christ lugging the entire cross on his back, this, too, defies what historical information exists of crucifixion. The *patibulum,* or horizontal crossbeam, was generally secured to the criminal and then lifted and placed atop the *stipes,* or vertical member, which most probably had a mortise and tenon joint to lock it in place. That a special cross would have been fashioned exclusively for Jesus seems highly unlikely, since not a single religious or pagan source states such a novel device. The scriptures that mention Jesus carrying the cross must therefore refer to the horizontal *patibulum.*

Therefore, most of *The Passion of Christ*'s visual imagery of the Stations of the Cross, including Gibson's own heart-wrenching, cinematic addition when the mounted cross accidentally drops, smashing Jesus' face into the ground, have all been pathetically fabricated. Likewise, Mel Gibson's entire ten-minute long, drawn out spectacle of scourging and horrific torture was purely sadistic, artistic license and morbid self-gratification. Gibson's intent was naturally to instill profound sympathy, which is understandable even if grossly exaggerated, yet more invectively it was to incite intense hatred for the antagonists, who mercilessly beat and tortured Jesus, thus further instilling the false notion that all Romans were cold-hearted barbarians and all Jews evil conspirators.

This last point against the Jews was cemented further by Gibson also using Matthew's famous verse *"Let his blood be on us and on our children."* This verse has been cited by many radical Christians with an agenda to blanket the entire Jewish community as evil, yet this statement was voiced by a crowd that was predominantly Sadducees, certainly not the entire Jewish community. Finally, this statement may have been overstated to insinuate a *crowd,* when it could have been only a *few,* or even less.

However, as we saw earlier, Jesus' indictment, covert arrest, mock trial and conviction were craftily staged by one man, the one man who did more than even Judas to crucify Jesus, and that man was Caiaphas. In light of the scriptural evidence, the true villain in this story is Caiaphas, along with his likeminded Jewish followers, including Judas, who were all motivated by greed, power, intolerance and hate. As a result, a number of Romans were most likely guilty by association with these Jewish mobsters, while those who flogged and crucified Jesus most likely didn't know of

Jesus' innocence, and those who did find out, did so after the fact. However, the brush used in this tale often paints both Romans and Jews in total as being evil, and this is clearly not supported in any way, nor could such a broad and all-inclusive indictment ever be factual. Therefore, logic and evidence both indicate that a less radical and less religiously motivated view must prevail.

Caiaphas had done so well in remaining clandestine and removed from the spotlight that it took countless centuries for historians to realize the grand role as architect that he played. The pawns that he maneuvered into place, from his henchmen guards, to his scapegoat Judas, to the humiliated Pilate, all show how Caiaphas cleverly forced the grandest of all kings into checkmate, and then tragically secured his crucifixion.

And although most Christians will rally for the ultimate architect being God, who maneuvered all these earthly pawns, we are still left with the blaring fact that even the name "Caiaphas" has remained in the shadows and virtually unknown to the vast majority of Christians for two millennia. And as the pivotal villain, more so than even Judas, who actually pulled all the strings to get Christ crucified, his escape from the limelight and just punishment of this ultimate of all crimes, only engenders curiosity, regret, and even contempt.

Oddly enough, because of the immense nature of this event as well as Jesus' immense influence that persists to this day, Christians have a vision of Jesus and his crucifixion as being earth-shattering news in his day. However, the shocking news is that Jesus never managed to gain much attention outside of Judea's small religious community. In fact, quite remarkably, not a single contemporary historian mentioned Christ, only later ones, and each only allotting one short paragraph to Jesus, with only Josephus, who was born centuries after Jesus, allotting two paragraphs.

More amazing still, Philo of Alexandria wrote a lengthy biography of Pontius Pilate, and Jesus was not even mentioned once! Philo had no love for Pilate and even labeled him merciless, insensitive and obstinate, so he certainly would not whitewash Pilate's record. So, if the extraordinary attention to this "King of Jews", and his horrific scourging were so out of the ordinary and brutally cruel, wouldn't this have merited at least a word or two from Philo?

One must question why did these preeminent historic voices of their day fail to document this messiah, or his death? And why did later ones fail to recognize his extreme importance or catastrophic death? Was his crucifixion a high profile spectacle, like Mel Gibson's movie, or a commonplace execution? On a more profound note, was the divine message of Jesus for all mankind or just for a chosen few? And we must recall that these chosen few, at that time, were a small handful in respect to the world's population. Many have also queried, was Jesus actually God or just another messiah? After all, there were many others in Jesus' day who claimed to be messiahs, so why would Jesus be any different?

After all, Muhammad was a messiah who, centuries later, also inaugurated a colossal religion, namely Islam, and he was mortal. In fact, the Muslims have always believed that Jesus was mortal, for the Koran states, *"The Christ, son of Mary, was but an apostle, and many apostles had come and gone before him."*

So, was Jesus just a highly influential mortal? Or does Jesus' divine plan simply exceed human logic? Then again, why give humans the ability to reason if they cannot use it? One thing, however, is certain: such questions have and will continue to keep many busy, quite possibly for many more centuries.

In reviewing Jesus' rise and role as a preacher, it is astonishing to consider that Jesus' entire ministry, from his premiere to his crucifixion lasted only one year. Due to discrepancies in dating, some scholars believe longer, yet in all cases it was exceedingly brief. It is generally believed that Jesus was about twenty-nine when he met John the Baptist, and within a year, Jesus himself would meet a similar demise. However, the death of Jesus had a deeply demoralizing effect on his core followers, as even they remained, in a written sense, mute for many decades. During this incubation period, they remained a small Jewish offshoot with variegated viewpoints, and remained just one of many cults throughout the highly diversified empire.

Oddly enough, forty years elapsed after Jesus' death before his devout disciples finally tried to record the higher meaning of what transpired. They were profoundly baffled that their Messiah was dead, and that his highly proclaimed apocalypse, or new kingdom, never materialized in their lifetimes. This was even stated by Jesus in Mark's Gospel, despite Luke or Thomas, for example, indicating that Jesus referred to his kingdom as not being tangible. As such, their everlasting hope forced them to interpret and record these amazing events in an effort to make sense of the chaos left in Jesus' wake. For to do nothing would clearly make their Lord pass into oblivion, since no contemporary historians documented Jesus' life or execution, thus being completely unknown by all others throughout the expansive empire. Hence, Jesus could have remained just a small footnote in history.

The exact date of Jesus' death is not known, but has been established as AD 30, and the chain of events that followed in the Roman Empire played a significant role in motivating these scripturally mute disciples to speak. The Roman Empire would shift into one of its most ugly periods, as Nero took the purple in AD 54. His rule actually began quite moderately, and even somewhat promising, but slowly escalated into blatant madness by AD 68, the last year of his reign. Nero's brutality is legendary, yet his persecutions were far from being limited to early Christians who, as we know, were wrongfully blamed and then crucified for burning Rome, for it was Nero who initiated the rigorous campaign to silence that other troublesome group, the Jews.

Nero abolished the liberal and tolerant policies of Augustus and demanded full conformity to Rome in both legal and religious matters. This caused the Jews to revolt, thus prompting Nero to appoint Vespasian to put down the insurrection. However, it was during this massive campaign that Nero's luck finally expired back in Rome, as the Romans finally had enough of his madness. Being confronted with assassination, the nefarious emperor Nero opted for suicide.

It was during this crucial moment in world history that Vespasian and son entered the fold. Vespasian secured the reins of the empire, had his son, Titus, finalize the mission, and thus ended Nero's reign of madness. As we have seen, Titus made clear that the aberration under Nero was over, and that he and his father ruled firmly, yet tolerantly. Nonetheless, with the complete victory at Masada and the destruction of Jerusalem, unfortunately including the Holy Temple, the Jewish world was now completely shattered.

Many early Christians foresaw this cataclysmic event as the divine wrath of God, namely to punish those who crucified Jesus. Likewise, this once again explains why Vespasian was temporarily hailed as the new Messiah. But most importantly, this offered another incentive for Jesus' disciples to finally commit words to scripture; for the Jews had been problematic not only to the Christians, but also, quite foolishly, to the Romans, and had now suffered from the wrath of Rome, or God, according to the revelations of some clergymen. With the might of Rome and or God reprimanding their Jewish rivals, this prompted early Christians to speak more freely, and in a manner more diametrically opposed to their older kin. Now that the Jews had become the primary targets, whose Holy city and Temple were strikingly razed, it was prudent for the Christians to finally sever the umbilical chord, and thus free themselves from the Jewish womb, whereby they could finally stand up on their own.

The exact dates of Peter's or Paul's death are not known, but anywhere from AD 67 – 69 have been estimated, and this coincides roughly with the duration of the Masada incident, and one to three years prior to the destruction of the Second Temple by Titus. With their lives and voices gone, except for the epistles, the necessity to tell the story and mission of Jesus became more pressing, and once again, the destruction of Jerusalem not only served as an impetus to record past events, but also compelled them to abandon the holy city of Jerusalem once and for all. For as mentioned, the central hub of the religion would eventually shift from Judea in the Middle East, to a transitory post in Antioch, Syria, and then eventually across the Adriatic Sea where it settled on the Italian peninsula, right in the heart of the empire's capital city of Rome.

This shift of the religion's most supreme and sacred nucleus cannot be overlooked or dismissed as inconsequential, for even the city's claim of having the remains of Peter is one that has never proven that possession or title. Saint Peter's basilica was supposedly built over Peter's grave site, yet no evidence of his remains have ever been authenticated or even properly displayed, as some speculate that Peter's remains are still somewhere in the Judean region. In any case, the eventual seat of not only St. Peter, but of Christendom itself, would now be located in the former pagan city of

Rome, clearly indicating the takeover that occurred by these early Roman Christians who supplanted their Judaic, Greek, and North African Christian brethren. This shift of power was not immediate but rather it evolved over the period of two centuries. However, the religious turmoil after Jesus' death and the political turmoil of the region caused these early followers of the Jesus movement to commit their story to a written format. This would secure their faith in the event that they, too, should prematurely perish, hence, the need for gospels.

It is crucial to note that the gospels were not written at the same time; for Mark's Gospel appeared first about AD 70, those of Matthew and Luke about AD 85, and John's a decade later, about AD 95. Therefore, it wasn't an instantaneous recording of events by all four apostles, nor was it so for all the other apostles, whose gospels and religious texts were later discarded. Instead, many voices vied for supremacy in a slow and evolutionary process.

Furthermore, this process was not a harmonious recollection of a singular oral tradition, but rather a discordant debate with many conflicting viewpoints. Even among the four accepted gospels it is clear that an evolutionary process shaped them as well, as very significant and different material was introduced into later gospels, especially John's Gospel which, we must remember, was written a decade after both Matthew and Luke, and over two decades after Mark. It becomes unmistakably evident that the more time given to reflection gave rise to a more miraculous and divine adoration of Jesus.

Some today believe that the oral tradition leading up to the four gospels, many decades later, would retain a very clear and linear path or focus on Jesus' life and activities. They contend that oral tradition, even as practiced today, proves that key elements of authenticity and truth remain intact. However, although that is possible in some instances, the Jesus story cannot fully hold to this line of thought.

For example, if one were to ask World War II veterans to recollect a sergeant of theirs from forty to fifty years ago, their views would probably coincide on many physical activities that took place, however there would be some discrepancies about the personal character of the man. Some might say he was too pigheaded and harsh, while others might hail him as being perceptive and heroic. Moreover, as for recording direct quotes of what their sergeant said, it would certainly be limited in scope, probably contradictory in certain instances and definitely prone to vague paraphrases, rather than direct quotes, hence leaving room for error. Yet, even this little scenario is only describing a sergeant that was not very significant or controversial in the grand scheme of world history. Let's see what happens when we recollect a highly controversial figure like John F. Kennedy, for example.

Kennedy is viewed by some today as one of the greatest presidents. Senator Lloyd Bentson is a prime example of those smitten with admiration. During the 1988 vice-presidential debate, Lloyd Bentson sarcastically retorted to Dan Quayle, "Senator, you're no Jack Kennedy."

Kennedy has even generated a cult-like following of admirers who romanticize on his utopian visions of Camelot. However, there are those who viewed John Kennedy, along with his brother Robert, as reckless adulterers, as well as ruthless and arrogant racketeers, and this hatred of John Kennedy even led to his assassination, as well as his brother's.

Jesus, we must confess, was similarly highly controversial, and even though some regarded him with the utmost admiration and love, we must not forget that he was hated by others who viciously plotted and secured his death. Therefore, such controversial figures always generate a plethora of perspectives that always include the most polar of views.

Yet most worshipers of Christ can never even contemplate such a negative and intense hatred against their God, and in so doing, they fail to see how oral traditions can be degenerative, different, colored or even flawed. There are many gospels that were intentionally discarded, gospels with very conflicting viewpoints about Jesus, and this must lead us, with a modicum of sense, to realize that some errors in judgment were made on both sides, and that some errors could be significant. After all, none of these gospels was given to mankind by God himself; rather these were all conceived, written, and heatedly debated, as well as even censored by fallible humans. Therefore, some aspects of Jesus' life, as well as his true divine or mortal nature remained in the hands, and written words of his devout followers, each with different perspectives and agendas, and all were unequivocally vying for supremacy.

Even among his most devout followers, Jesus was not understood by all in the same way, hence, the fact remains that regardless of the many scriptures that were later discarded or labeled blasphemous they do relay the firmly held beliefs and perspectives of other eyewitnesses. These include Thomas, Philip, Mary and even Judas, in addition to many others from other generations of oral tradition. Therefore, the oral tradition of Jesus, with its kaleidoscope of perspectives, and opposing interpretations does not form a monolithic pillar of thought, or a basic unified belief shared by all. Just as modern day Evangelists differ from Catholics, and they in turn differ from Protestants, and so on, there is much that is contradictory and up for serious debate. Some of these conflicts shall be examined as we proceed.

Unfortunately, many Christians today are unversed in the details of theology, and as such, they believe that not only were these gospels all written at the same time, but that they were done so independently of one another. Hence, when Matthew's Gospel merely reiterates the majority of Mark's verses, some word for word, it gives the illusion of unquestionably being the true inerrant word of Jesus. However, the next author in line did have time to access the previous scripts to merely reiterate them if necessary. Yet, most importantly, and as will be seen, some of the later material is in direct opposition to earlier texts.

Likewise, many believe Jesus' disciples wrote the four canonical gospels. Yet none of them mentioned the author, as the names were added almost a century later. But as for these problematically named gospels, only Matthew was a direct disciple of Jesus. Mark was a disciple of Peter, and Luke a disciple of Paul, henceforth, extending the line of oral tradition down another generation before finally being committed to scripture. Meanwhile, the Gospel of John, which was the last written gospel, has caused much controversy, as some scholars attribute its composition to three different authors. The author of this most provocative gospel, likewise, never mentions himself by name, and is believed, by some, to be the mysterious "Beloved Disciple" that is only mentioned in this canonical gospel.

One very noticeable development over the course of these gospels appearances was the divinity of Jesus. John's is the only gospel to blatantly define Jesus as being one and the same as God above, whereas all his companions before him believed that Jesus was the gifted Messiah, or Christos. Christos in Greek means anointed one, hence, he who was made Lord by his father. The term messiah, as understood by Jews and Jesus' followers, who were all still Jews at the time, was used to describe a descendant of King David who would come to rebuild Israel, end war, restore the Davidic kingdom and judge the living and the dead. This messiah was to be a mortal, akin to Moses, certainly not God. Therefore, this lack of clarity in other gospels in defining Jesus as the one and only God, but only as a messiah, is highly significant and not to be dismissed with a clerical slight of hand.

John, however, clearly establishes this at the very opening of his Gospel by saying, *"In the beginning was the Word, and the Word was with God, and the Word was God,"* or more pointedly, *"I and my Father are one."* Meanwhile, Luke, some decade or two before John, clearly stated that Jesus was not the same as God Almighty, for upon his crucifixion he states *"God has made Him both Lord and messiah"*.

God, as we know it, exists for all eternity, with no beginning and no end, and therefore cannot be made, yet Luke clearly stated otherwise in referring to Jesus being *made* Lord.

Additionally, it is only John's Gospel that mentions how Jesus raised Lazarus from the dead shortly before his own crucifixion. This John states to claim that it wasn't that Jesus incensed the High Priests by overturning their moneychanger's table, thus condemning their greed and positions of power and wealth, but that they feared his miraculous godly, or rather ungodly, powers; and for this reason they rallied to have him crucified.

Again, this is a very different interpretation of a core piece of scripture, yet few give it much attention or even realize the significance of the different storyline and message being told. The first highlights a mortal prophet named Jesus and his reaction to mankind's greed and irreverence in an earthly fashion, while the latter portrays Jesus as some sort of a warlock, being feared by his enemies who seek his destruction.

As we have seen, after Jesus' horrific death the disciples and their followers searched the Torah for prophetic answers, and during this quest they made many bold assertions with the hopes of fitting the baffling pieces of the Jesus puzzle together. Yet, as they began documenting their recollections, viewpoints clashed. As mentioned, Matthew was the only direct disciple of Jesus whose Gospel was selected for the official canon, as his peers, Thomas, Philip and others had clashing views that would eventually be labeled blasphemous. It is crucial to keep in mind that all these other gospels were not merely viewed as being unmoving or simply inadequate, but rather as being vile distortions and grossly sacrilegious, which warranted extermination.

In unveiling all of the heated opposition between these disciples one cannot help but recall Jesus' words at the Last Supper, *"A new commandment I give unto you, that ye love one another; as I have loved you. By this shall all men know that ye are my disciples, if ye have love one to another."*

Most people mistakenly believe that the disciples heeded Jesus' words, and then lovingly and orderly carried Jesus' message forward in solidarity; however, this is unfortunately not the case. Right from the very start, Jesus' words were flatly ignored by his closest followers. As their views and rivalry escalated an intense schism erupted; one that lasted for well over two centuries until only four gospels, among a sprawling sea of scriptures, were finally selected as definitive.

Surprisingly, even the four accepted gospels were riddled with inconsistencies, for not only could the Jesus puzzle not be completely reconstructed on its own accord, as internal disputes between core followers prevailed, but it also did not fit properly into Jewish tradition. That tradition was outlined in the Torah, which was uncompromisingly protected by its strictly orthodox guardians. Even though the Torah itself abounds with many vagaries, its stalwart defenders saw otherwise with regard to these apostles, and as such, they grew increasingly irritated as these story-wielding upstarts made startling declarations.

That Matthew began his narrative stating that Jesus was a descendant of King David, and was the Davidic Messiah of prophecy, immediately aroused suspicion and much contradiction. Matthew's Gospel opens with, *"The book of the generation of Jesus Christ, the son of David, the son of Abraham."*

Matthew tried to establish a firm connection with this most holy ancient Jewish bloodline, yet quite clearly in vain. In one breath, Matthew hails Jesus as David's genealogical descendant, which he ironically traces via Jesus' uninvolved stepfather Joseph, which instantly severs the bloodline, unless of course Joseph was his real biological father. In another breath, Matthew states how Jesus was conceived of Mary (herself being an Immaculate Conception) via the Holy Spirit, once again, without any intervention by Joseph, or Joseph's highly touted bloodline. It becomes very evident that Matthew's desperate attempt to link Jesus to David's sacred bloodline was severed by the uncertainty of Jesus' true birth.

Theologians and devout Christians may attempt to explain this away as a simple human foible or that Matthew sought to understand something beyond his meager comprehension. However, that is far too simplistic in light of the many facts. Here we have the only disciple to write one of the accepted gospels that was actually a member of Jesus' core entourage, yet forty years later he still had no idea of Jesus' birth. Not only is this extremely odd, but if Matthew didn't fully know this, how could the other gospel writers, who were removed to the point of having no physical contact with Jesus at all, possibly know this? This leaves the credibility of Jesus' divine birth, or even his earthly birth with its hallowed bloodline, profoundly in doubt, and this is doubt by the most intimate of canonical sources. That other gospel writers also expressed doubt about Jesus' true birth only confirms this integral and unresolved issue even further.

Likewise, Matthew clearly stated that Jesus preached to his followers that they must adhere to the Laws of the Judaic Old Testament in order to attain salvation. Meanwhile, Paul stated that one only needs to believe in the death and resurrection of Jesus, for only through Jesus can one attain salvation. This dichotomy of another core principle of the faith would likewise cause much debate and intense rivalry.

This brings us back to the mysterious problem of James and other siblings of Jesus. While some scriptures hailed James as the blood brother of Jesus, born of Mary and Joseph, this posed a problem to others who realized this mortal bloodline destroyed Mary's virginity and the divinely Immaculate Conception that was now becoming crucial to their maturing religion.

Then, as mentioned, appearing in the Gospel of John is the mysterious "Beloved Disciple", or *"the disciple whom Jesus loved"* that is mentioned numerous times, yet his identity is never revealed. This Beloved Disciple is the one that asks Jesus at the Last Supper who is it that will betray him, yet other gospels indicate that it was Peter who asked this question. Likewise, John's Gospel tells that this Beloved Disciple ran with Peter to the tomb, even reaching the tomb first, even though Peter was allowed to enter first. Yet, this mysteriously unnamed disciple is not mentioned in any of the other three synoptic gospels. This becomes even more baffling because this glorious distinction sheds a strange and hallowed light upon this individual, and in so doing, it simultaneously casts a dimmer light upon the rest of Jesus' disciples, who we must assume Jesus loved less, since they did not receive this emphatically passionate title. One would almost think that this disciple could have been a woman, like Mary Magdalene, yet the disciple is clearly referred to in the masculine form, hence one can only assume it is John himself.

However, it is interesting to note that the discarded Gospels of Mary Magdalene, Thomas, and even the recently discovered Gospel of Judas Iscariot, each mention a beloved disciple, yet each of them openly refer to that special disciple as being none other than themselves. Hence, only John's beloved disciple remains a mystery, much like his other miraculous verses that find no mention in the other gospels.

Many such contradictions abound in the various gospels, even the accepted ones, which comprise the canon of Christianity. In their effort to indoctrinate self-styled links with religious tradition, which many Gentiles unacquainted with scripture readily believed, the apostles and their followers failed to win over the orthodox Jews, whose scrupulous and unwavering eyes guarded their ancient texts.

The apostles' original intentions were to simply append their texts to the long Judaic tradition, but the Jewish High Priests were like senior editors, and they flatly rejected all of them. Small provincial villages of farmers or fisherman were one thing, but Jerusalem was another. Their erudite sense of the Tanakh was unshakeable, and this neophyte sect, with their newly-created scriptures, would never alter their beliefs. Moreover, since the orthodox Jews were the entrenched majority, especially in Jerusalem, this posed a serious obstacle.

One main roadblock for orthodox Jews was the fact that their God was one God, and could not be divided in any fashion whatsoever. During the first three centuries AD, the Christians themselves could not agree upon Christ's nature, but eventually conceived the Holy Trinity, which further bewildered and exasperated the Jews. They could not understand how this division could possibly work to make all three pieces, of a singular whole, each obtain and share equal divine power. For to say one division had less would indicate it was not an equal piece, but subservient to the Master piece, hence destroying the One God known in the Old Testament.

Regardless, the Christians' scriptures indicated otherwise, as Jesus himself said, *"I seek not my own will, but the will of Him who sent me."* Here Jesus clearly states his subservient status to carry out the will of his Father's master plan. Likewise, appearing in the Gospel of Mark, Jesus said, *"Why callest thou me good? There is none good but one, that is, God."* Here, once again, Jesus himself makes the separation of Father and Son very clear.

However, the most revealing and chilling statement of all was when Jesus was nailed to the cross, he cried, *"My God, my God, why hast thou forsaken me?"*

There is no clearer statement in scripture to confirm a subservient Son, not only questioning, but actually pleading to his all-powerful Father, who omnipotently pulls all the strings.

Therefore, the Trinity, with its uneven distribution of power, indicated that the Hebrew God was being subdivided by these new revisionary Christians, and in a fashion that not only didn't make sense, but Jesus' own words could not validate. This only caused a deeper rift between the budding new Christians and their firmly-planted Jewish roots. This deluge of rivalry caused crashing waves that would eventually sever them from their thorny Jewish roots and carry their sect-saving scriptures out into a sprawling sea of Gentiles. The man most responsible for carrying this new branch beyond the confines of Jerusalem was the self-proclaimed apostle named Paul. This would occur some twenty years after Jesus' death.

ST. PAUL: *Headstrong Leader, Religious Reformer and Doorman for the Pagan Masses*

Originally known as Saul of Tarsus, Paul was a Jewish rabbi from Caesarea who was a fierce opponent of the Jesus movement. However, one day on his way to Damascus, Paul claimed he saw a vision of Christ. This is when the passionate Pharisaic Jew suddenly converted, and Saul became Paul. Fervently adopting his new religion, Paul took it upon himself to elevate his rank to the equivalent of the twelve apostles. (There were still twelve, because at this point Peter had indoctrinated Matthias to replace Judas Iscariot).

Most curious is the fact that Paul never even attempted to make contact with the founding apostles during the first three years of his ministry. Furthermore, when Paul finally decided to give Peter a visit, he only made contact with James, the controversial blood brother of Jesus. Even more fascinating, Paul set out once again, this time for a staggering fourteen years, to continue preaching his own version of the Christian message. Perhaps not surprisingly, once Paul did make full contact with Peter, they had a distinct difference of opinion. Paul would later record some of their differences in his *Letter to the Galatians*.

Evidently, Peter was more of a mediator than a leader, as he attempted to bridge the gap between James, who maintained strict orthodox, Jewish traditions, and Paul, who now being a Jewish defector, began rejecting more aspects of his former religion. Jewish tradition had long held the dietary regulations of eating only certain foods and never eating with Gentiles. When Paul traveled to the Syrian city of Antioch he noticed Peter eating with Gentiles, yet to his surprise, when a follower of James arrived, Peter abruptly and quite callously rebuffed all the Gentiles. This duplicity angered Paul, who openly reprimanded Peter, *"God is not to be fooled: a man reaps what he sows."*

Here, Peter bent to the will of James and conformed to a position strongly opposed by Paul. Paul had spent over fourteen years of his life preaching and converting Gentiles, thus being an integral part of his ministry. As such, Paul made it quite clear that anyone who interpreted the message of the Lord differently than he did, was in grave danger, even if it was Peter, Jesus' first disciple and the supposed heir and leader of the church.

Peter and Paul were like oil and vinegar, and where Peter opted to side with James by maintaining their rigid, Jewish orthodox roots, Paul saw the necessity to break free. Paul's bold outward steps were a radical departure from Judaic tradition as well as from the new Jesus movement. Essentially, Paul found more in common with pagan Romans with their liberal beliefs than with his conservative apostle friends.

As the religious historian, Eusebius, rightfully made clear, the ease by which Paul could travel the empire to spread the gospel was due to the roads and unity established by Augustus. Paul's travels and his evangelical mission would have been significantly curtailed if these thruways did not exist. Henceforth, Paul became the traveling doorman who literally opened the gates of Christianity to pagan Romans. This would have a profound impact on the religion, especially in the centuries that followed. However, of even greater and immediate importance was that Paul revised the religion itself.

Paul's provocative revisions included abandoning the need to learn the colossal Jewish Tanakh, forsaking circumcision, waiving the need to abstain from eating certain foods during Holy week, and discarding a myriad of other oral traditions ingrained in Judaism.

The sacred act of circumcision dated back to roughly 1312 BC, and was part of the covenant that God bestowed upon his chosen Jewish flock at Mount Sinai. According to Genesis, it was instilled earlier by Abraham as a form of sacrifice to Yahweh—a physical sign of devotion. To break this one tradition alone was unthinkable to any devout Jew. The Jews also had compulsory dietary restrictions, which accentuated their chosen status above the base pig-eating pagans. Therefore, this naturally caused problems for most newly converted pagans as well as for the early Jewish Christians who faithfully maintained their orthodox traditions. Regardless, Paul waived all of these sacred requirements, thus making conversion seamless for Roman Gentiles, despite the fact that it simultaneously incensed the Jewish-born Christians.

Furthermore, the fact that Paul was but a recent convert who once denounced the Christians, never even met Jesus, or surprisingly maintained only a vague knowledge of Jesus' life, deeply irritated the founding members who actually sat and broke bread with their Lord, not to mention the pain and suffering they endured over his cataclysmic death. Therefore, to have their religion revamped by a rookie who was a converted outsider, and didn't even stop to converse with them before starting his fourteen-year-long ministry, naturally caused a great deal of friction. Furthermore, Paul's inclusion of his fellow pagan Romans, which infringed upon the sacred Jewishness of their long-standing religion, was a terrible affront. By all accounts, Paul was viewed by his fellow founders as an irksome and meddlesome outsider.

Conversely, the orthodox Jews viewed Paul as an aberrant insider - a defecting traitor - who was abandoning their highly sacred pacts with God and contaminating them with his subversive and sacrilegious modifications. Hence, Paul was an extremely provocative figure who made enemies on all sides.

Even the strict Ebionites, who also followed Christ, took their shots by claiming that Paul was actually a Greek, with little knowledge of the Torah. In his younger days, they claimed that Paul entered Jerusalem and came across a beautiful Jewish woman. Filled with passion, he opted to be circumcised to win her over. However, when he failed to obtain her hand in marriage he became enraged, thus initiating his long and biting agenda of denouncing Moses' Torah and its laws. Whether factual or not, Paul certainly had a very selective regard for the apparently outdated Torah, and it wasn't long before he realized the dead end the entrenched leaders presented. Therefore, outward Paul ventured, for the old orthodox Jews would not swallow his new Christian host.

However, although Paul's new religious order was far less demanding, it was far more inclusive. This was also because Paul followed Jesus' footsteps, whereby permitting women to take part in his administration. This was clearly against the entrenched Jewish custom, and the majority of Paul's fellow apostles maintained that exclusionary bylaw. In the Gospel of Thomas, Peter's intense disdain for Mary Magdalene and women in total is revealingly recounted, *"Let Mary leave us, for women are not worthy of life."* However, Jesus informs Peter that he will make sure that women will have the ability to achieve a state of equality with men, and thus have access to the kingdom of heaven.

Regardless, Peter and his brother, Andrew, maintained their sexist views, for after Jesus' crucifixion, both disciples adamantly rejected Mary's claim that Jesus imparted words of wisdom to her, believing he would not have entrusted such information with a woman. Levi was present, and rebuked Peter, saying, *"Peter, you have always been hot-tempered. Now I see you contending against the woman like the adversaries. But if the Savior made her worthy, who are you indeed to reject her?"*

In essence, the disciples and Jews had all clung to the sacred words put forth in Genesis, that Eve was easily corrupted by the devil, and in turn doomed all of mankind by offering Adam the tainted apple. As such, they all advocated limiting or, in reality, eliminating women from any significant role in their religions.

However, in time the new Christian sect would reject Paul's unisex policy whereby implementing the controversial decree of celibacy for all male clerics. Abstinence was suddenly proclaimed to be necessary for full devotion to Christ, yet a dual and much camouflaged reason was to effectively eliminate women from influencing or manipulating their male counterparts or, worse yet, gaining access to key positions of power.

Even the Roman historian, Tacitus, relayed in his *Annals* how a Roman senator named Caecina proposed that governors should not take their wives with them when moving to a province to serve their term. The senator made his point even more pressing by stating that when women infiltrated the army they caused all sorts of havoc. Caecina pointedly said: "A female entourage stimulates extravagance in peacetime and timidity in war... Relax control, and they become ferocious, ambitious schemers, circulating among the soldiers, ordering company-commanders about... Remember that whenever officials are tried for extortion most of the charges are against their wives."

This speech, Tacitus tells us, was rebutted by another senator, who while defending the rights of women to accompany men in the army at certain times, agreed that women can be schemers and corrupt, just like their male counterparts. Hence, the threat of women gaining too much control and power concerned both pagan and religious councils alike.

Celibacy would also be a point of contention in the very distant future when the Lutheran Reformation tore away from the Catholic Church. The Protestants argued against Saint Matthew's controversial verse that prompted early Catholics to inaugurate celibacy.

Matthew 19:12 *"For there are some eunuchs, which were so born from their mother's womb: and there are some eunuchs, which were made eunuchs of men: and there be eunuchs, which have made themselves eunuchs for the kingdom of heaven's sake. He that is able to receive it, let him receive it."*

That verse does not emphatically state that each and every devotee of the kingdom of heaven must be celibate, but simply that he who is able to receive it, can receive it. The issue of celibacy has recently reared its head once again with the significant number of Catholic priests exposed as pedophiles. Hence, this divisive issue still prevails.

Paul also foretold the apocalyptic end of the world. This impelled his subjects to become penitent parishioners, for Judgment Day was "coming soon" and their alternative was damnation in hell. His fiery words proved very effective until many began questioning when this day would arrive. Paul clearly stated that they would all witness Jesus' second coming and receive entry into God's kingdom. But Judgment Day or Jesus never arrived; hence, negating Paul's veracity while also afflicting all successive generations with the fear of Armageddon.

Paul's radical ideas coupled with his abrasive personality, which even he himself admitted, invariably made Peter only too happy to see Paul leave Judea to recruit Gentiles. Subsequently, Paul would head westward and utilize the vast Roman network of roads to tour present day Turkey, Greece, and other provinces of the Roman Empire with the intent of winning converts. As Gentiles flocked to his newly styled ministry, many Jews became enraged with jealousy and hatred. After all, the Jewish God himself was one of immense jealousy, as he declared, *"...for I am the Lord, your God - a jealous God."* Moreover, as the Lord would smite his own creations who did not love him as he commanded to be loved, the angered Jews would eventually incite a depraved emperor to smite Paul.

Being accused of bringing Gentiles into Temple who did not follow the Laws of Moses, Paul was placed under house arrest by the Jews in Caesarea. The mob's anger swayed the governor, Felix, to imprison Paul in chains for two years. When a new governor, Festus, attempted to resolve Paul's religious dilemma with a trial in Jerusalem, the astute apostle, recalling the fate of Jesus in the Holy City, chose to make his appeal to the pagan Caesar instead. Traveling to Rome, Paul was acquitted upon the favorable testimony of Governor Festus and a Roman Centurion. He remained in Rome for two years, and then began his travels once more.

Sometime later, after repeated conflicts with the Jews, Paul was once again brought up on charges that unfortunately brought him under the wrath of the Emperor Nero. The repeat offender, as one of the new Jesus movement's prime leaders, was beheaded in AD 67. Because Paul had acquired Roman citizenship, he was spared crucifixion.

Paul's widespread missionary work, and most importantly his radical modifications, which included opening the sect's doors to pagans and eliminating rigid and demanding traditional rituals, played a monumental role in reshaping the new religion and altering its future.

However, despite Paul's huge efforts, the sect was still a minority over a hundred years after his death; furthermore, much discord prevailed among those who recorded their recollections of Jesus and the Jesus story. Just like America's founding fathers, harmony soon faded into opposition. However, unlike the founders who came to resolutions that reached a common ground, the disciples, with their divided sects and conflicting scripts, battled it out for a winner. Losers would be expunged.

IRENAEUS: *Judge and Jury*

Irenaeus was an immensely influential bishop from the distant city of Lyon, Gaul. In fact, without his input it is uncertain what kind of creed would have prevailed. Many of Jesus' apostles were at odds, and there was a raging sea of conflicting scripts. As such, Irenaeus appointed himself Captain Editor, who sailed through this stormy sea to find truth. The result was that Irenaeus only preserved four gospels; all the rest would be tossed overboard and left to sink in his massive wake.

However, his final decision and the grueling task of enforcement would not be easy or appreciated. Irenaeus fought unwaveringly to eliminate what he believed were false prophets, sects, beliefs, and scriptures. This included the Gospels of Mary, Thomas, Philip, Judas, and other religious texts, which he determined were both inaccurate and blasphemous. Irenaeus was also the first to champion the mystical and unique Gospel of John—despite his mentors not even knowing of this gospel—and incorporate it into what became the New Testament.

As previously mentioned, the Gospel of John claimed that Jesus was the divine Almighty God, while others saw him as a mortal messiah or earthly Lord granted special powers from God the Father above. John also professed that salvation could only be attained via the church. Meanwhile, others had professed that salvation and the kingdom of God were personal matters. This had immense ramifications for those wielding power, such as Irenaeus and his fellow bishops, as their intermediary services would be rendered useless.

As cited earlier, Luke made it clear that Jesus said, "...*behold, the kingdom of God is within you.*" More pointedly, the deliberately silenced Gospel of Thomas claimed that Jesus was a mortal messenger, and that an intimate one-on-one basis with God was in keeping with the true message of Jesus. Where Luke merely mentioned Jesus' words without giving them much import, Thomas and other disciples made them a crucial part of their doctrine and ministries. This infuriated Irenaeus, but his unyielding efforts to silence these threatening authors and their creeds evidently paid off. Thomas' Gospel, along with all those of like mind by his fellow disciples, would be so effectively expunged that they were lost to time for countless centuries, until they were finally discovered in 1945 in the town of Nag Hammadi, Egypt.

Naturally, Irenaeus also flatly rejected the Gospel of Judas. This gospel's name alone caused Irenaeus to most likely never even read it, for his denunciation of this text offers open condemnation without making any singular reference to any details within. The recent discovery of the Gospel of Judas, which actually surfaced in the late 1970s and was improperly stored for some twenty-five years, has shed an interesting light on early scripture. Naturally, the Christian community at large will continue to refute its authenticity or intent, just as Irenaeus did, yet carbon dating places this codex at a slightly later period than the New Testament gospels themselves. Moreover, even if this script is a piece of highly provocative propaganda, its appearance and alternative viewpoint are interesting nonetheless, and worthy of a brief examination.

The reason for this worthiness is that since AD 200, when Irenaeus condemned all these texts as heretical, they have been completely lost. This only offered one side of the story regarding Christianity for well over a millennium and a half. Not that this one piece of scripture will overturn the foundation of Christianity, but hearing the story of Judas and Jesus from another perspective is fascinating, for it clearly offers us a broader sampling of the various mindsets of the period. And what the Judas Gospel does posit is a completely different view of this religiously and historically-maligned apostle. Here Judas is the beloved disciple, the one Jesus confides in regarding his predestined plan, and asks Judas to *"sacrifice the man that clothes me."* Judas accepts the infamous role of betraying his master, and becomes not the ultimate traitor, but the ultimate tragic hero.

What is fascinating is that this codex is scientifically dated, so this is not some recent forgery meant to disrupt the Christian Church, instead it is the voice of someone from the past who had seen and known this tale from another perspective. Whether that view is tainted and false or even true remains a mystery, but it unequivocally documents that not every Christian was on the same page; in fact, they were at polar ends of the spectrum. Likewise, it validates the fact that opposing interpretations did exist and that even the accepted gospels must contain some human errors in judgment, be they minor or even major in scope.

It is equally interesting how the Gnostic gospels (those rejected by Irenaeus) are all much more heavily infused with pagan astrological overtones. For here, Jesus tells Judas *"Lift up your eyes and look at the cloud and the light within it and the stars surrounding it. The star that leads the way is your star."* Jesus then tells Judas that he shall become the sublime thirteenth star, yet his sacrificial role will have to endure intense scorn. *"You will become the thirteenth, and you will be cursed by the others, because you reign over them."*

This new revelation, if true, would in fact have an immense impact on Christianity. Yet even though the document's age is authentic, by placing its authorship within the third century AD, it is a work by a Coptic (an ancient Egyptian language) copyist, who transcribed this from an original Greek source. However, we must also realize another astounding fact: the New Testament scriptures that have survived, and that Christians base all their hopes and faith upon, are all copies. None of the original canonical gospels exists. One of the earliest complete New Testament Bibles only dates from about AD 350, several hundred years after the originals were written. The oldest, known, surviving gospel fragment, which is also a copy, dates to about AD 125, and comes as close as we can to the originals.

Therefore, as for this new codex of Judas, in the final analysis it undeniably offers some insights into ancient thought from a different perspective, but cannot stand as solid irrefutable fact, at least not until other documents are discovered that can prove the Judas codex authentic. Moreover, even if it was authenticated as being authored by Judas, we still are faced with the very real possibility that he deceptively wrote his gospel to clear his name.

However, how is it that we believe the canonical gospels as being authentic without demanding similar irrefutable proof? Rather blindly, all modern Christians have placed total faith, not in Jesus or the gospel writers per se, but on some later bishops who deemed these codexes (which were chosen and possibly edited by Irenaeus), as the inerrant truth. This is a huge degree of trust and blind faith to place in a handful of human bishops, especially once we reveal the many follies they made during this long Christian story. This will be discussed in Chapter IV.

Nonetheless, in addition to the many gospels and countless scriptures that Irenaeus boldly rejected, there were many sects, such as the Valentinians and Marcionites, who held sizeable congregations of opposition. These bishops and their large groups of followers all lost the battle of documenting the Christian story, a crucial story that would go on to groom and condition countless millions.

The Marcionites, for example, denounced the Torah, declaring the Old Testament's God a demiurge (a lesser God) and stating that although he created the world, he was jealous, judgmental, and wrathful. They likewise believed that Christ, not Jesus the man but rather his spiritual entity, was the new God, one who was loving, forgiving, and merciful.

They saw Jesus' good news as deliverance from the bad news, which was the strict Law of the Old Testament.

This sect, along with all the others that Irenaeus loathed, fell under the umbrella of Gnosticism and were all declared heretics, and effectively expunged. As such, Irenaeus was pivotal in collating the gospels of Matthew, Luke and Mark, known as the synoptic gospels, along with John's, into what would become the New Testament. Over a hundred years of severe protest followed, but eventually these splintered factions were somewhat unified by yet another huge step of influence.

In a sharp and historic turn of events, a Roman Emperor would rally behind this small cult and adopt it as the official religion of the Roman Empire. His imperial decree firmly secured Christianity's legal protection, funding, proliferation and ultimate rise to power. Hence, even the destiny and influence of Christianity were significantly due to outside Roman intervention. Yet this great story would unfold over two centuries later, and as such, is preceded by another windy chapter of time.

As we have seen, the actions of Nero, Vespasian, and Titus produced both positive and negative conditions that profoundly influenced the new direction of the small and growing Christian sect, while rigorously and effectively subduing the Jewish community. Likewise, we have seen how Vespasian's firm control brought stability back to Rome and thus began a renewed golden era. And this golden era was not one that smothered him in golden opulence. In fact, Vespasian razed Nero's enormous Golden House, which was a blatant eyesore of just how egocentric Nero had become, and he filled in Nero's palatial lake to build the Colosseum for the pleasure of his Roman citizens.

Furthermore, although Vespasian was rough hewn, and not particularly enamored by the arts, he *was* a staunch advocate of education. Quintilian was one of several talented scholars entrusted with bolstering Roman education. His farsighted theories included the prospect that a child's father *and mother* should be well educated in addition to being mentored by well-trained teachers. Essentially, a fully immersive and positive environment was vital for cultivating talent and effective leaders.

Pliny the Younger was a prominent student of Quintilian, and possibly Tacitus, all three being important educators/historians that flourished under the auspices of Vespasian or his son Titus. Pliny the Elder (uncle to Pliny the Younger) likewise wrote several important works during this time, including his historic encyclopedia, *Naturalis Historia*. Pliny the Elder witnessed the cataclysmic Mount Vesuvius as it erupted, and heroically died attempting to rescue his fellow Romans at Pompeii. Titus, being emperor at this time, once again demonstrated his good graces by extending much aid to the devastated city. Nevertheless, this revitalized era eventually led to the celebratory rule of Trajan.

Trajan ruled from AD 98 to AD 117, and the Senate and people of Rome hailed him as one of the greatest emperors of all time. In fact, a popular expression for wishing someone good luck went, "May you be more fortunate than Augustus and better than Trajan."

However, although Trajan brought greater strength and prosperity to the empire, along with making logical and honorable legal decrees, Trajan was primarily a conqueror. Trajan impressively expanded the empire to its largest extent; however, greater size brought greater threats, chiefly upon the outer extremities. Outside the safe haven of the empire existed many barbaric factions that all posed a new and very real threat. As such, this threat demanded some kind of a solution, and that task would fall upon Trajan's eminent successor, Hadrian.

III
AD 122. HADRIAN - The Need for Borders
(Tria, Gemini, Dan, Bartholomew, March)

Dark clouds billowed as a moist gale blew icy droplets into the surrounding trenches. Nearby, mossy bogs became sodden, as dank odors emanated into the damp air. The dreary landscape, lined with gnarled trees and knobby hills, made a foreboding impression. In the midst of this desolate place, muddy mules and oxen dutifully labored alongside their human counterparts in their grueling task. Standing nearby—in his saturated purple toga, with rain droplets cascading down his face and off his curly beard—was the great emperor, Publius Aelius Hadrianus; better known as simply Hadrian.

The mighty Caesar was visiting the work site at Vindolanda in Briton (current day Chesterholme, Britain). Hadrian was the first and only emperor to physically visit every province of the vast empire. This was another golden age in the Roman Empire and Hadrian did much to elevate it further. As such, the villagers from all sectors routinely showed their appreciation.

Hadrian made many routine inspections, often having to walk through fields of drenched grass and rolling hills that characterized this alien land. With its frigid climate and excessively high amount of rainfall, most Romans found Briton uncomfortable. Nevertheless, the scope of Hadrian's latest endeavor was immense. Despite the wall not featuring the sublime attributes of other projects built during his reign, Hadrian's Wall had its own splendor, and most importantly a very crucial function.

The wall was built to ward off malignant immigration and hostile invasion. It traversed an eighty-milliarium stretch (73.5 miles) that cut the British island clear across, extending from the west coast of the Irish Sea to the east coast of the North Sea. Due to Briton's hilly terrain the wall twisted and winded along various crests and valleys, making the project all the more difficult and remarkable.

This well-planned project included milecastles (large fortresses) that were built at every Roman mile along the wall. Fortified with rations and several dozen troops, sentinels were stationed atop these milecastles as well as atop turrets that were evenly spaced between each milecastle. Therefore, a sentinel spotting trouble could easily signal to the next turret or milecastle to mount a quick and well-organized defense. Moreover, a ditch, which ran parallel along the entire wall, ensured further protection. In essence, Hadrian had taken all measures into account to construct an efficient and intimidating barrier to protect his precious empire.

In this instance, we can literally cite Hadrian for not only being the originator of this immense project but also for taking an active role in its design. Hadrian was an outstanding architect himself, for recent scholars are accrediting him with more than superficial authorizations, but actual structural, engineering and design considerations. While touring the empire Hadrian's photographic memory captured and analyzed a wealth of architectural data that he later used to produce some of the empire's most impressive structures. But, for Hadrian, now standing in this damp and desolate land, this was no place to create wonders of aesthetic or even religious perfection. He had serious threats to contend with, and these threats were further ingrained in the Romans' memories by the warring campaign of Boudica some sixty-years previously.

Boudica was the queen of the Iceni tribe (modern day Norfolk) that led vicious attacks against the Romans while under Nero's rule. Nero's avaricious bent for over-taxation, and his refusal to recognize her ascension to power after her father's death, forced Boudica to rally local tribes to mount an assault. During her killing spree she slaughtered a few thousand Romans. Stirred with shock and vengeance, Nero supplied the Roman governor with new legions that annihilated the insurgents at the Battle of Watling Street, despite being outnumbered almost 20 to 1. The Britons' devastating losses were estimated at 80,000. This impressive victory renewed Nero's interest in maintaining Briton as a province.

Julius Caesar was the first Roman to ever attempt the conquest of Briton, as it sat only twenty-two miles across the sea, and must have piqued his curiosity. When his mission failed, Caesar rightfully complained that the population was larger than expected, thus the reason why his limited forces couldn't accomplish the task. Some later historians claimed that Caesar was simply trying to make excuses in order to maintain his perfect record, yet recent discoveries have validated Caesar's claims, as the population was much larger than most historians realized.

However, under the rule of Emperor Claudius, a renewed attempt of conquest was made in AD 43, and after several decades, all of lower Briton fell under Roman rule. With Nero succeeding Claudius, it was under Nero's regime that the continued attacks mounted to complete the task. However, once Briton was conquered, Nero's greed and lack of public relations only instilled resentment and eventually vengeance. Unfortunately, as we have seen earlier, anything Nero's sulfuric hands touched exploded into volatile flames, be it his dealings with the Jews, the Christians or the Britons. Nero's bloody fourteen-year rule was burningly brutal, but transient. Although he caused a great deal of havoc and significant shifts in world history, Nero has also procured a tidal wave of bias that some historians wish to use to drown the entire empire.

However, after Nero's death, Vespasian ordered the admired general Agricola to handle Briton. *(Agricola also happened to be the father-in-law of Tacitus, the leading Roman historian of the age.)* Agricola conquered almost all of Briton yet was stopped from completing the task by the then reigning emperor—Domitian, Vespasian's second son. Agricola was also a superb peacetime administrator and was highly influential in Romanizing Briton. This not only included building roads, houses, villas, and temples, but Agricola also ensured that all the sons of prominent Britons were educated in the liberal arts. This was the foundation of ingraining Latin into Briton and why the future English language has Latin as its root.

Nevertheless, the times and treatment of Britons had changed, particularly under Hadrian who took a personal interest in every region throughout the empire. Hadrian authorized many projects during his vast travels, including urban developments in Libya, Athens, or even his timber blockade along the troublesome Germanic border; his architectural signature is to be found in almost every province. Along with these ventures came new knowledge and progress, as carpenters living in timber and mud villages slowly learned stone and mortar construction. Additionally, hydro technologies were adopted along with architectural and agricultural tools and apparatus, which were either invented or improved upon by the Romans.

However, as always, a select few still attempt to deny these facts. Here again, Rodney Stark comes to mind. Stark simply reiterated the claims of J.G. Landels, who in 1978 stated that Roman vehicle designs and technology were unsophisticated. From this tenuous statement, Stark drew his conclusion that there was no such thing as Roman invention, only stagnation. However, in this specific instance, much of Stark's evidence was based upon Landels' study of carts and chariots. Unfortunately, Landels dispensed with examining the real artifacts, and instead examined depictions of them that were carved by stonemasons into triumphal arches and monuments.

Upon his examination, Landels saw primitive contraptions that almost appeared to be unusable, and rightly so, because these stonecutters were not industrial draftsmen, but superficial visual artists. However, archaeologists have unearthed both Roman passenger and labor carts with pivoting steering assemblies and suspension systems that clearly reveal what, in fact, did exist in Roman times. These discoveries positively validate that these stonecutting artisans did not depict these vehicles accurately, be it for simplifying their laborious task, artistic license, or simply lacking the technical knowledge of cart construction. However, it was from these artistic sculptures that both men, either directly or second-handedly, drew their conclusions.

As would be expected, carved depictions of naval vessels also lacked specific details, which once again gave these two authors the same false impression that Roman ships were simplistic vessels. However, a detailed sketch of a ship does exist from ancient Pompeii, along with an actual Roman ship discovered off the southern coast of France. Hence, both of these artifacts clearly elucidate the errors of both men, for they have based their harsh criticisms on mere assumptions, and relied solely upon viewing artistic renditions rather than going to the source, namely the architect's drawings or the actual artifacts themselves.

The Landels/Stark process of examining antiquity is like a future historian two thousand years from now saying that twentieth century people played primitive musical instruments based upon finding Picasso's famous painting "The Three Musicians", rather than looking for a technical drawing or an actual instrument. Taking this process an amusing step further would be if an alien (having no idea of what humans looked like) drew its conclusion about the visual form of humans solely upon finding a typical Picasso portrait. The alien would think that a humanoid had two eyes on one side of its head.

Therefore, Rodney Stark's elaborate and vexing indictment against the Romans, whereby accusing them of stagnating thought, invention, and progress, is based upon flawed methodologies and fallacious assumptions that are likewise *alien* to the standard and proven practice of dealing with facts. However, where Landels simply made a false assumption on feeble evidence, Stark was motivated by an agenda, which is to lambaste and strip all pagan civilizations, especially the Roman Empire, and shift all their efforts, advancements and inventions into the lap of the Catholic Church. Unfortunately, Stark is not alone, as other right wing Christian authors, such as Richard Horsley have also engaged in grossly distorting history. Naturally, the Catholic Church played a role in advancing civilization, but Stark and company's pathetic attempt to strip pagan history of its rightful claims never does him or the church any justice, instead it only elicits shame. The truth is, no single regime or religion can claim exclusivity over innovation and progress.

However, Stark had much more to criticize. He lauded how the British developed a much superior cart than the Romans, which featured a suspension system and a pivoting steering mechanism. However, the British developed their cart many centuries after the Romans had already occupied and later deserted their country.

Rome's crucial, albeit transient, occupation was likewise dispelled by Stark as being a suppressive conquest that did not instill anything useful, and as far as he was concerned, they even retarded progress. This vaporous assumption, once again, negates the tangible proof that abounds, for archeological evidence clearly shows that the British merely copied these technologies from Stark's archenemy, the Romans.

As for Roman cart construction, this technology would not become fully developed in England until many centuries later; the reason being that the Romans opted to abandon their northern British province, hence, along with their withdrawal went their advanced knowledge. Amid the warring indigenous tribes who eventually prevailed, some Roman proficiency may have marginally lingered in the hands of the few Britons who learned Roman technologies and the few Romans who remained. However, the majority of Roman technology vanished. Only many generations later did some Britons find and emulate old Roman carts, whereby producing their own models with Roman features. Further evidence of decline in Briton after the Roman evacuation was that the processes of quarrying for stone and manufacturing building materials, such as brick, mortar or tiles likewise disappeared. Hence, after the destructive Celtic raids, most Roman advances were lost for centuries.

Rodney Stark's attack also included the blank statement that the Romans' "carts and wagons were so primitive that seldom was anything of substantial weight moved very far overland." Evidently, Stark failed to notice the towering Egyptian obelisks that still adorn many public piazzas throughout Rome. These colossal monoliths were transported to Rome by several Roman emperors, with some weighing well over 220 tons. The process was enormously difficult and very sophisticated, as these massive obelisks were miraculously taken down in one piece, carted overland to the Egyptian shoreline, placed on barges that sailed across the Mediterranean Sea, and, once again, were carted many miles overland to their new location, where they were carefully erected and mounted on a plinth. How the Romans achieved this amazing feat still baffles modern engineers, not to mention how the Romans managed to transport these monoliths such great distances over land, sand, mountains, and sea without fracturing the brittle stone.

Stark also criticized the Romans for using oxen and donkeys for labor rather than swift horses, like those used in England centuries later. Yet he overlooked the fact that the climate and soaring mountainous terrain of Rome and Europe made these other animals more efficient and, as a result, they lived longer and more productive lives. The low, rolling hills and pastures in England presented a far different environment than the craggy, Alpine terrain in central Europe, thus requiring a different solution. This is why donkeys and mules are still used today in the Grand Canyon rather than horses, or why camels are preferred in Arabian deserts, simply because they are better animals for the terrain and climate. Once again, a simple-minded charge can be rebutted with a simple answer.

On a final note, Rodney Stark's claim that the British inherited nothing from the Romans once again meets with a simple fact. In 1725, the engineer, Ralph Wood, was faced with the dilemma of building the world's first bridge for the newly invented steam engine. Unable to find any contemporary models to emulate, the engineer was left with no recourse but to examine ancient Roman bridges. The result was the Causey Arch in Durham County with its 100-foot "Roman styled" stone arch. The blaring fact remains that after two thousand years, engineers (including English ones) were still harkening back to the Romans for guidance.

Beyond Rome's influence on England, however, the Roman Empire controlled the full breadth of the Mediterranean coastline, with its countless shipping ports, as well as the larger part of all Europe and parts of Africa and Asia. Their shipping and land-based modes of transport for a variety of goods defy any claim of Rome being a stagnant or suppressive regime. Recent archeology has further enhanced our understanding of the rich and booming trade network that the Romans created. After decades of studying Roman archeological evidence, Kevin Greene had this to say: "These means of transport were of a quality which at the least equaled, and in most cases exceeded, that of their medieval counterparts. Indeed, many of their features would not be matched again until the eighteenth century AD..."

Henceforth, after Rome's decline, the world did lie in a state of quasi-stagnation until the Middle Ages and Renaissance, and in some instances, as noted, even later during the early Industrial Revolution of the eighteenth century.

Moreover, accompanying the Romans' valuable influence was their goodwill toward all peoples. Too often, this trait gets lost in the Roman storyline. However, this, too, remains visibly evident, for etched right on Hadrian's Wall, the soldiers used a quote from the famous Roman poet Virgil to express their intent and success. It succinctly summed up Rome:

"You created one homeland for the differing peoples. Those without justice benefited from your rule; by allowing the vanquished to share in your own laws you made a city out of what was once the world."

Hadrian continued the noble intentions of his virtuous predecessors, and being a highly educated man, Hadrian affected positive change in many fields, including law. Before Hadrian's legislation, a father could sell his unwanted or misbehaved children into slavery, or even kill a slave or an adulterous wife, yet these laws were repealed. Hadrian issued new laws, revamped others, and he supported the use of making state money available as loans to individuals who paid interest to their local communities. This money revitalized their local economy, and in a show of pagan benevolence, it also went toward supporting local orphans.

Hadrian also kept alive the building programs established by Augustus, which were followed by Claudius, Vespasian, and others. Beyond the clear advantages of aqueducts, roads, and innovative facilities, which greatly enhanced living conditions, was the fact that all these endeavors blatantly projected Roman might, ingenuity, and in a word, superiority. This had an immense psychological effect, not only on Romans, but also on all others who aspired to become Romans. Hence, in this regard, Hadrian played his part brilliantly.

Hadrian was a master builder, as his architectural hand has created some of the most influential and impressive structures in history. Hadrian's projects stretched across the entire breadth of the empire, as the historian Augusta said, "In almost every city he constructed some building and gave public games."

Despite all these edifices, Hadrian's grandest masterpiece was unquestionably the Pantheon in Rome. The Pantheon is an awe-inspiring structure donning the first and largest dome of antiquity. Measuring 142 feet in diameter, the sophistication of its engineering, as well as the majestic perfection of the entire building's interior, stuns even the modern viewer, especially when one bears in mind that this masterpiece was built in AD 116. Its broad foundation was solid stone and marble, while the dome was cleverly constructed of pumice.

The Pantheon is also the only dome to have an oculus at the apex. Measuring thirty feet in diameter, this round opening allows light to bathe its divine interior. A ring of voussoires supports the oculus, while eight barrel vaults, which are concealed inside its thick drum walls, support the downward thrust of the dome. The immense thickness of the dome tapers from an amazing twenty-one feet thick at its base to four feet around the oculus. The Romans built things to last, and this ancient relic has done just that. The inside of the dome is decorated with rows of square coffers, which in addition to reducing the weight of the cement dome, also gives the illusion of being airy and almost weightless.

The Romans' choice of materials was also revolutionary, for as mentioned, they had used pumice stone to construct the Pantheon's massive dome. Pumice is a lava-based rock that contains tiny air pockets, thus significantly reducing its density, yet maintaining structural integrity. Hadrian and his fellow Romans' cleverly understood this when devising their solution, however, their secret mixture of concrete to mold this dome remains a mystery to this day. It has been analyzed that modern Portland cement would never be able to support the 5,000-ton load, as its tensile strength is insufficient to maintain the expanse. Hence, Hadrian and his master architects had technological secrets that still baffle engineers today.

Unfortunately, the highly advanced yet esoteric knowledge used to construct this dome was lost during the Dark Ages. The Middle Ages showed a reawakening by utilizing Roman architectural principles, yet it veered off into new directions, as gothic cathedrals remain prime examples. However, at the dawn of the Renaissance, the great dome of the Florence Cathedral marked a full-scale revival in Roman engineering, and that enormous enterprise was executed by the great architect Filippo Brunelleschi. His success was singularly due to his intricate studies of the Pantheon. The splendid dome of St. Peter's by Bramante, Michelangelo and Dela Porta had followed, along with all others throughout Europe and western Asia, and all are indebted to Hadrian's architectural masterpiece.

This influence eventually spread to the New World. Thomas Jefferson is credited with introducing the dome to America, as his design at Monticello was fashioned after the Pantheon. Many colleges have followed this example, yet no one can ignore that the U.S. Capitol Building, as well as the vast majority of state capitol buildings throughout America have all followed the domed motif. It was only fitting that later in the twentieth century, John Russell Pope fashioned the Jefferson Memorial after the Pantheon, for this was in homage to both Jefferson and his admiration for this sublime structure.

Beyond the impressive fact that the Pantheon inspired all domed buildings throughout the Western world is the miraculous feat that this grand structure still stands today. Few prototypes from antiquity remain in full form, as the Colosseum or Parthenon in their ruined states come to mind, yet the Pantheon's huge dome remains intact, its interior almost pristine, while its weathered exterior, despite being intentionally stripped of its marble and bronze, remains solid, and oddly divine. *(Photo page 705)*

In addition to the Pantheon, was Hadrian's huge mausoleum, which centuries later was renamed Castel Sant'Angelo once the Romans became Christianized. The Christians not only changed buildings' names, but also plundered them or revised them. The Pantheon was stripped of its rich ornamentation, while the bronze statue of Trajan that sat majestically atop the Trajan Column *(See page 705)* was replaced with a statue of St. Peter. Oddly enough, the triumphal column depicts many imperial scenes of Trajan's military campaign to conquer Dacia, yet the Christian apostle, without much forethought by Pope Sixtus V, crowns a memorial dedicated to the warring victories of a pagan emperor.

Nevertheless, even more magnificent, is Hadrian's Villa at Tivoli, which is located fifteen miles outside Rome. Hadrian's Villa features a broad array of styles infused with his own inventiveness, and was an influential resource for many future architects throughout Europe. This grand complex sported pavilions, porticos, ponds, statues, and manicured gardens, which are not only striking, but served as the template for most of the imperial gardens of the later French, German, and English monarchs.

Furthermore, Hadrian was the first emperor to incorporate symbols from the various provinces onto the back of Roman coinage. This minting of specifically tailored coins allowed them to maintain their personal cultural identity, while still riding on the back of the massive Roman Empire. There was an anomaly, namely with Britannia, for Boudica would certainly not be honored on the back of Roman coinage, thus the female goddess Britannia, devised by Hadrian to personify the province of

Britannia, did appear on coins. Oddly enough, many British subjects, even today, proudly denounce any sort of Roman influence on Britain, yet what cannot be avoided is that even the very name Britain was coined by the Romans, not to mention the Latin root of their language or the many other facets of Roman influence. Even their beloved Queen Victoria's name is from the Latin word *victoria*, meaning victory. Nevertheless, Hadrian's new goddess, Britannia, would honor the British, be minted on his unique Roman coins, and be graced with a shrine that he built in York.

Interestingly enough, the United States Treasury has recently copied Hadrian's clever idea, as the back of new quarters each feature a specific symbol honoring one of the fifty states. As such, beyond Hadrian's dome on the Pantheon that inspired all other domes or his villa and gardens that inspired all other imperial gardens, even Hadrian's small but gracious contribution to coinage has been resurrected.

Hadrian was regarded as being not only extremely intelligent but also a polymath. He was raised in the military, well-educated, well-cultured, and often showed moderation and justice, as well as having great insight into administering and unifying the empire's many distinct provinces. However, Hadrian also despised rebellion and nonconformity. His renewed reprimands upon the unruly Judaic community were harsh and unrelenting.

Despite some heavy casualties, Hadrian not only managed to subdue the mayhem in Jerusalem, but enacted laws to prohibit Judaic practices, such as circumcision. Additionally, he took every opportunity to demolish the Holy City and turn it into a pagan metropolis. As mentioned in the previous chapter, these campaigns caused the Christians to migrate, commit their story to scripture, and escape the authoritative hand of Titus as well as the terminal temper of Hadrian several decades later.

The Jews, under the leadership of Bar Kochbah, had incensed Hadrian like no other rebels, thus unleashing his uncompromising and quite deadly military upbringing. Hadrian had done so well in suppressing this aspect of himself while engaging many noble endeavors. However, this single facet of Hadrian has been the most disputed; as Jews naturally label Hadrian as an intolerant monster while others deem him a godsend. The answer, obviously, must lie somewhere in-between.

When Hadrian first visited the province, he was dismayed by the destruction caused by the first revolt, which had occurred several decades earlier, and was harshly put down by Vespasian and Titus. Hadrian initially had sincere intentions of rebuilding Jerusalem, yet he clearly had no idea of the Judaic community or their intense faith, which was built upon their long and proud history. When Hadrian attempted to rebuild the city with temples and statues of imperial Rome, the Jews naturally revolted. Hadrian's lack of homework into the history of his foreign subjects quickly escalated into a showdown of strength. As such, Hadrian had no choice but to rise up and demolish the territory, whereby he established both Syria and Palestine, which still stand today.

After Hadrian's reign, the volatile epicenter of Jerusalem did eventually restore itself to its religious Judaic origins. However, the Holy Temple never regained its place in Judaic history, for the Muslims conquered Jerusalem in the seventh century, and they defiantly built their golden Dome of the Rock over the Jews' sacred spot, where it still stands today.

Hadrian's twenty-one years of rule, however, had many lasting impacts upon the world, beyond the names of these enduring nation states in the Middle East, to many endeavors with much less controversy and far more positive attributes, as mentioned earlier. A key endeavor has been Hadrian's Wall, for during the early- to mid-second century, the empire was in a prosperous and healthy position, and Hadrian was at the helm to secure it at all costs, even if that meant subduing internal dissidence or building a wall to ward off foreign incursions. Hadrian's Wall thus becomes even more crucial and worthy of re-examination with today's border crisis in America.

As tensions flare over illegal immigrants crossing the borders, America now faces a similar situation. At certain times, the integrity of great nations requires unexpected or even unwanted remedies, such as walls, and they have proven very effective as temporary solutions. Here, temporary means a century or many more, depending upon the wall in question. Border walls have fulfilled their objectives as long as the defending nation maintains its ground. Hadrian's Wall, we must note, only became useless after the Romans abandoned the British Isles.

Some may cite the Berlin Wall as a failure; however, the Berlin Wall divided a once unified nation in half between two foreign and opposing political ideologies. This explains why it only lasted approximately four decades; for it was inevitable, that once communism fell, so, too, would the wall. Therefore, a unified nation that builds walls to ward off foreign invasion or infection remains an entirely different matter.

In this regard, America must protect its own culture from the illegal invasion of aliens that refuse to assimilate. Unlike the legal immigrants of yesteryear—who eagerly sought American citizenship and proudly fought in WWII to preserve their new nation—illegal aliens of today are forcing Americans to adopt their culture, while they reject the duty and honor of becoming an American. This submissive mentality of allowing foreigners to infiltrate and manipulate a country was also prevalent during the fourth to sixth centuries in the Roman Empire. This we know from the personal letters of clergymen and dignitaries who made the mistake of passively watching while foreign immigrants recklessly bucked assimilation and caused Roman culture to deteriorate. Everything the Romans thought important, such as laws, engineering, commerce, morals, speaking Latin, and the patriotic duty and pride of being Roman slowly eroded.

America faces a similar situation, as well over twelve million illegal dissidents reject assimilation and demand that their English-speaking hosts speak Spanish. As such, the elite politicians, corporate lobbyists, and multicultural appeasers that cater to their whims for the sake of cheap labor and ethnic harmony, while propagating their foreign culture (to the detriment of American culture and sovereignty) are just as criminal as these illegal aliens, with the added offense of being treasonous. It may seem odd that illegal aliens reject America's superior culture since that is what drew them to America in the first place, but the allure is purely monetary.

Illegal aliens damage the economy by stealing millions of blue-collar jobs from Americans, and by costing respectable taxpayers money due to their illegal use of medical, educational, social, and other benefits. Latino criminals and gangs also wreak havoc and further burden ICE agents and prison resources, not to mention putting the lives of innocent Americans in grave danger. Alarmingly, this concern also extends to fanatical Muslims who are dedicated to Jihad, and obsessed with vengeance.

The Mexican border has been porous for decades. This expansive southern border has been the primary gateway for the majority of illegals who currently maintain unlawful shelter and illegal employment in America. However, emanating even farther south of Mexico are the newer immigrants of Central and South America. Some are radical Muslims who established deadly training camps for their Jihadist movement. Debunking hype or fiction, these camps have been documented by U.S. Intelligence and have even appeared on film. Their mission to destroy the infidels, with America being the head of the satanical snake, is all too real and very deadly. Moreover, infiltrating America, via the Mexican border, is so easy it's embarrassing. Preserving America's rich culture from internal sabotage and ideological decline is a top priority, and here is where Hadrian's solution offers us the answer.

Americans should welcome immigrants that desire and respect citizenship, but not illegal invaders with foreign objectives. Americans should pressure their legislators to take aggressive action. Amnesty must be repealed, all illegals deported yet allowed proper legal access, employers of illegals penalized, since they are the magnets, sea ports seriously screened, and effective identification systems implemented. However, until legal remedies or even hi-tech virtual borders are available a physical solution is required to prevent this massive influx.

Hadrian's Wall was an impressive barrier that effectively repelled militant invasions, as such, it serves as a prime model for eliminating the pedestrian influx that America encounters. As mentioned, all walls eventually lose their import due to a variety of reasons, but mankind has never built an eternal solution for any problem. Meanwhile, Hadrian's solution lasted for three long centuries until the Romans withdrew from Britain *(See page 705)*. Hence, Hadrian's Wall unequivocally served its purpose, and a wall would likewise prove effective for America.

Hadrian's long and successful reign ended in AD 138, however, before his death, Hadrian prepared very wise and admirable plans for the empire. His successor was Antoninus Pius, who was a capable man who ruled for over twenty years, yet Hadrian had peered even further into the future, for he stipulated that Pius must adopt two very young and promising youths, namely Lucius Verus and Marcus Aurelius.

This careful selection ensured a line of two more emperors, each proving to be good and brilliant emperors in turn, with Marcus Aurelius being hailed as the greatest philosopher of his day. Aurelius' literary work *Meditations* offers us a glimpse into his logical and moral mindset amid his endless campaigns to secure Rome's borders. Unfortunately, unlike Hadrian, Aurelius failed to ponder the gravity of succession, for he handed over his rule to his reckless and maniacal son, Commodus.

As mentioned in the Prelude, Commodus was a megalomaniac who changed every name of the calendar to one of his ridiculous nicknames. He was also prone to wearing animal skins as he took on the persona of Hercules, and even engaged gladiatorial battles in the Colosseum for sport and adulation. However, these bouts were actually more of a spectacle, since no one dared harm the emperor. After Commodus' odd and degrading twelve-year reign, he was succeeded by two inept emperors until Septimius Severus took the purple.

Severus proved to be a much-needed breath of fresh air, as he temporarily restored order and was noted for his leniency with the Christians. However, he was succeeded by Caracalla, another brutal emperor whose huge thermal Baths of Caracalla in Rome remain his greatest positive legacy. Caracalla is credited with offering Roman citizenship to all freemen of the empire, which naturally offered greater rewards and security for these people, but it likewise added immensely to the taxes imposed and collected, hence the motive appears to be one of generosity to satisfy greed.

Caracalla was merciless. He murdered his brother, Geta, who initially shared the throne, as well as his own wife and father-in-law. Caracalla only remained in power for two years, yet he was a sign of the times. Rome was in a fallen state of mismanagement, as it was run by emperors of outright brutality or simply of mediocre stock. With the rise of Maximinus Thrax, who was charged with being a barbarian himself, the era known as the Crisis of the Third Century truly began.

This critical period, from AD 235 – 284, saw Rome's near collapse, as political and military turmoil coincided with devastating pandemics that shook Rome to its knees. Quite remarkably, the ancient historian, Cassius Dio, had reported nearly 2,000 deaths per day in Rome due to the plague, and revised estimates now place the total death toll at a staggering five million. Even the highly revered emperor, Claudius Gothicus, died from the plague, yet he and his successor, Aurelian, were vital to Rome's survival.

In response to the barbarians' vicious attacks, Aurelian even emulated Hadrian by building the Aurelian Wall. However, this wall encircled a portion of Rome and was twelve miles long and twenty-six feet high. This remedy likewise proved effective, warding off invaders for centuries.

These critical centuries, however, had a number of infectious dynamics working in unison, which would inevitably cripple the Western Empire. Beyond the pandemics and political corruption was the evolutionary decay of the Roman army. As the wealthy empire grew, many Romans sought the comforts of prosperity, and as such, no longer desired military life. Therefore, recruits were drafted from newly conquered territories. Additionally, the new Christian community, which preferred the peaceful ways of their Lord, Jesus Christ, likewise had no desire to take up arms. Naturally, this would change in time, however, the current result of this evolution was a weakened army that no longer trained as diligently, and had far less impetus to fight as relentlessly. Therefore, barbarian raids became more effective and these collective disruptions all caused economic instabilities across the empire.

Moreover, as barbarians infiltrated the Roman army they likewise reaped the superior benefits of Roman life. Many future Germanic leaders, such as the famous Visigoth, named Alaric, were initially Roman soldiers. They were well trained in Roman tactics, spoke Latin, and some were even Christians. Alaric's raid in AD 410 was not truly an invasion, for Germanic-Roman soldiers opened the Salarian Gates to allow him access. Moreover, against popular belief, and according to several sources—including a protégé of St. Augustine, named Orosius—Alaric clearly intended to restore the glory and dignity of Rome, and did not wish to be remembered as a usurper. Hence, the notion of barbarians sacking and conquering Rome has been embellished, for Rome was consumed primarily from the inside as well as from without.

Nevertheless, the previous period, known as the Crisis of the Third Century, eventually led to the rise of the emperor Diocletian in AD 284 *(See page 705)*. Realizing the unmanageability of a vast and deeply demoralized empire, Diocletian formed a Tetrarchy, and sliced the empire into quadrants with a ruler governing each section. This was an attempt to better organize Rome's defensive posture and protect its distant borders. This he miraculously managed to achieve, however, even though Diocletian restored order, his successors would not share his liberal concept of dividing power, nor did some of them appreciate the renewed persecution of Christians under his rule.

One of those successors would take firm action and face down his rivals to ultimately rise to prominence. Once in control, he would make vital changes of such immense proportions that Western Civilization would be dramatically changed forever. That man was Constantine, and those bold actions would earn him the name Constantine the Great.

IV

AD 325. CONSTANTINE: Conversion of a Man, an Empire, and Ultimately Western Civilization

Intro | CHRISTIANITY: The Rise and Domination of the Roman Catholic Church | The Interpretation of Scriptures | The Influences of Greek Philosophy and Pagan Traditions | Analyzing Christianity | Constantine Reprise and Final Assessment | Who Truly is God?

(Quattuor, Cancer, Gad, John, April)

Under a thick blanket of gray clouds, the air was moist and motionless. Suddenly a mysterious turbulence split the clouds as a celestial beam of light pierced through the cumulus mist like a divine rapier. Riding in full battle regalia was Constantine, one of the three remaining rulers of Diocletian's crumbling tetrarchy that had turned into a triumvirate. The year was AD 312, and Constantine, along with his legions, was approaching the Milvian Bridge just outside Rome. It was at this precise moment that the pagan ruler witnessed an apparition that would not only alter his beliefs but also miraculously change world history forever.

As the clouds parted, Constantine beheld a startling vision—a cross of light in the sky that beckoned, *By this sign you will be victorious*. That night, Constantine had a dream in which Christ appeared and instructed him to use the sign of the X and P in the form of a cross on all his battle standards, X and P being the first two letters of the name Christ in Greek. (Greek had become the chosen language of the new believers of Christ, who upon infiltrating the faith dispensed with its Jewish-rooted languages. However, that would all change, for once Constantine fully seized the religion, Latin was firmly implanted as the religion's official tongue.)

The next day, Constantine inaugurated this symbolic cross, or *labarum*, by ordering his men to use ash from burned sticks to inscribe the iconograph on their shields and helmets. Equipped with this divine symbol, Constantine engaged with and effectively dominated his rival and former co-emperor, Maxentius. It was a victory of prophetic proportions, only the first of many heaven- and earth-shattering changes that would soon follow.

Although this colorful tale is riddled with divine drama, for Constantine's close bishop friend and author, Eusebius, penned it into history many years later, the essence of Constantine's physical action was historically profound. First, Constantine's use of the cross as a divine symbol to motivate and unite his Roman troops was strikingly new, for not only was his army mainly pagan, but the cross had only been associated with horrific torture and suffering. Even though Saint Paul made the initial attempt to portray Jesus' suffering as redemption, Christianity itself was still based upon and branded by the peaceful waters of baptism, which soothingly welcomed newcomers into its congregation.

Prior to Constantine, icons of Jesus had portrayed the Messiah as a young peaceful shepherd *(see page 706)*; however, after Constantine, Jesus became the ultimate martyr, nailed to the cross with a golden halo illuminating his divinity, or sitting in a pagan "emperor-like" fashion with a halo. These depictions were all adopted from Roman and even earlier pagan cultures, for the Jewish tradition, which the early Christians still adhered to, shunned graven images or idolatry. This long tradition dated back to Moses and the Ten Commandments, which directly referred to the strange and bizarre idols worshiped in Egypt at that time.

With the advent of Constantine, all of this effectively changed, and quite remarkably, his victories established the cross not only as Christianity's new and ultimate icon, but one that was eagerly embraced and admired by pagans as well. As for the spiritual emphasis of the religion, it permanently switched over to the suffering and resurrection of Jesus who died for the sins of mankind.

Overcoming adversity in order to prevail was fast becoming the new order of the day. As a result, the intrinsic character of the religion, and the mindset of its followers, began shifting from one of the passive lamb to the aggressive lion. However, a crucial point to note is that Constantine never used the cross to coerce conquered peoples or his own empire's religiously diverse constituency; that mutation would occur at the hands of future leaders.

It reached a new height of corruption seven hundred years later when Pope Urban II notoriously organized the First Crusade in 1099. Urban's original mission was to recapture the Holy Land, but the mighty symbol of the cross blossomed into a war machine to win converts by force. Knights were assured a place in heaven for their lofty deeds by earthly popes who only sought world conformity and Christian dominance. Along their bloody trail, they forced Jews and Gentiles to the baptismal font by sword, to either convert or die. Reaching its zenith, the bloody Fourth Crusade even attacked, raped, and pillaged its own Greek Orthodox Christian brethren when it sacked Constantinople in 1199. All of Europe and beyond would at that time come under the maligned influence of the mighty cross, a cross that Constantine first branded on the religion, a cross that served both wicked and divine purposes.

The second important facet of the miracle at Milvian was that Constantine's amazing epiphany, as mentioned, was written about many years after the event. Therefore, both the author and emperor had the opportunity to carefully reconstruct the miraculous event. What many cannot avoid is that although Constantine was obviously deeply moved by the new religion, it also happened to coincide with his political agenda.

Constantine at that moment was faced with an immediate threat. He had just suffered a defeat by his rebellious co-emperor, Maxentius, therefore, a victory at the Milvian Bridge was crucial. Constantine's ultimate goal was to unite the sprawling empire that many decades earlier had suffered under a string of transient emperors, and in turn was eventually cut up into quarters under Diocletian to ease the strain of administration. This quartering, although effective at subduing foreign onslaughts, caused a breakdown of the empire's internal unity, which impeded concord and productivity. Naturally, personal ambition added to the elusive quest for order. As such, any methodologies Constantine could use to achieve his goal of reunification were certainly thoroughly researched and carefully considered.

Unlike in modern times, visions and divine apparitions were common occurrences in antiquity and they became effective tools that savvy leaders used to sway and control a largely uneducated populace. We must also acknowledge that some people today, particularly from Evangelical congregations, resolutely believe in divine revelations and miracles—people being cured of terminal diseases, blind people regaining eyesight, or crippled people regaining the ability to walk. Therefore, what seems blatantly fabricated and absurd by the majority of people today, was in most instances, readily accepted in Constantine's day. This hard-to-fathom mentality makes sifting fact from fiction all the more difficult for some modern readers.

Yet it appears that Constantine, along with Eusebius, did well in modeling his actions along those of previously successful prophets. One correlation has been made between Constantine and Moses. Since Moses was the savior who freed the Jews from the Egyptian Pharaoh, Constantine likewise became the savior who freed the Christians from the pagan Diocletian.

One must be mindful that even some of the actions and events of Jesus were later retrofitted with ancient prophecies. So these visionary tales by Eusebius were not outlandish in their day, instead they were commonplace and readily acceptable. We must also remember that Paul claimed that the Lord transported him up into heaven, but he said these divine visions could not be humanly expressed. John, who differed in opinion, did tell of his amazing journey in heaven, what became famously known as the Book of Revelation. Therefore, Constantine's divine vision of the cross, followed by a visit from God later that night, fit well into the mindset of the day.

Such ancient stories only further complicate modern interpretation, which sometimes fails to acknowledge the pious intent lying beneath questionable miracles. Some modern historians completely rule out spiritual analogies as being pure fiction, which they feel was often motivated by selfish ambition. This especially holds true of Constantine, who today is viewed by some as a ruthless secular leader who fabricated a spiritual persona. This judgment largely began in 1853 with the Swiss writer Jacob Burckhardt, who upon reading the spiritual connotations waved his hand over the full breadth of Constantine's endeavors, dismissing them as political maneuvers by a selfish megalomaniac.

But as a young man, Constantine was clearly motivated by a sense of higher purpose. His actions and letters attest that he was driven by a divine mission, for Constantine firmly believed that he was divinely chosen to rule. There are later accounts that confirm that he intensely studied the Christian scriptures daily, from the first day of his conversion right up until his final breath. Even if this were exaggerated, his engaging personality certainly would have made him peruse these scriptures, or at least consult clerics periodically.

Granted his belief was in a higher divine power that was never clearly defined, yet to condemn him as a charlatan or godless man is also unfounded. The actual divinity and nature of Christ at this time was not even fully understood by the religion's core leaders, so it is wrong to condemn Constantine for his unsettled curiosity about the true Lord God, or his overall religious beliefs.

Religious freedom was part of Roman culture, as many people intermingled Persian, Greek, and Egyptian gods and goddesses to create their own ideal. Therefore, Constantine was simply a man of his times. Whether his was a secularist's search for a ploy to control the Christians, or he came to truly believe his ploy's God over time, or even believed in this God from the very start, we will never know. Yet his actions can be assessed.

Even though Constantine rallied behind the mismanaged and small Christian faith, albeit possibly for the sake of political gain, he still had to contend with a predominantly pagan constituency and a completely pagan army that put him at grave risk. Such a gamble only seems viable for a believer to take, and if Constantine was not a full-blooded Christian believer, he at least had faith in a single higher divinity, one that certainly in his mind chose him to be the supreme lord over all men. However, as will be shown, that dominant role would not be solely for personal gain and selfish control but also for the purposeful mission of defending and promoting Christianity.

Much has been made of the fact that Constantine not only embraced Apollo or Sol Invictus, but also proudly portrayed them on imperial coins. However, as mentioned, Constantine most probably did not view the ultimate Lord God as Jesus or Apollo, but rather some indefinable entity that many races and religions for thousands of years had tried to label and own. Therefore, to mint a coin with Jesus on it would have been sending a message to only a small Christian community, which at the time amounted to a mere ten percent of the population. Such advertising would have certainly been deemed useless when attempting to rally unity among a predominantly pagan empire.

Constantine's faith was indeed wavering in certain regards, particularly during his formative years when he embraced several deities. He was searching for the right god—the one that he could truly feel was behind his efforts and guiding his actions. These were not simply mundane daily actions but ambitious ones that would propel him to greatness and secure his beloved empire.

Before Constantine found himself standing at the Milvian Bridge, he had embraced the monotheist religion of Sol Invictus, yet it failed to yield any significant results. As such, Constantine found Christianity a newer and perhaps better vessel. Certainly its followers seemed more resolute than most, and its growing array of bishops, although being at odds with one another, were beginning to wield considerable sway in the community and became valuable contacts for any astute leader who wished to maintain order in the vast empire.

The majority of pagan power lords, who were comfortable with tradition, did not recognize this small sect as anything significant or worthwhile. The small religious cult presented Constantine with either promise or ruinous results, yet he wholeheartedly embraced it. Therefore we must even consider additional factors that influenced his decision.

Constantine's father had demonstrated that he was at least an active sympathizer for the Christians. For when he was a Caesar under Diocletian's tetrarchy, he stood firmly against the supreme ruler's persecution of Christians, which had risen to fever pitch. Years later, when Constantine faced his pivotal dilemma at the Milvian Bridge, the recollection of his father's good fortune from honoring this single God strengthened his resolve to embrace Christianity, and thus became a new source of divine confidence to confront Maxentius.

Even Constantine's mother Helena was a devout Christian. Helena claimed to have found an actual piece of the cross that was used to crucify

Jesus. It was later enshrined in the Church of the Holy Sepulchre that Constantine dedicated to his beloved mother, and which still stands today within the Old City of Jerusalem.

So Constantine's parents played some role in influencing their son, and certainly lent moral support to his later decisions. Moreover, the importance of the cross was burnt into Constantine's mind, spirit, and even his battle standards, which would eventually become the ultimate symbol for Christianity itself.

The Roman Empire was at a critical crossroads. It had suffered many years of ineffective and corrupt rulership, economic breakdowns, and religious conflict. There were various religions vying for power—mainly the pagan cults of Sol Invictus, Isis, Mithras, and Dionysus, as well as Judaism and the upcoming Christian sects. All of these factors produced grave unrest and divisiveness.

The emperor Diocletian had previously established Rome's first tetrarchy in an effort to maintain order. The expansive empire was becoming a burden to manage as the ability to solidify the masses became more difficult. This is the world in which Constantine was born; therefore, it is important to see how Constantine rose through the ranks, starting with his illegitimate birth.

Constantius was a military tribune who had a brief liaison with a peasant woman, Helena, one night on his military route. Unbeknownst to the traveling soldier, Helena conceived Constantine on that fateful night. Nine years passed, as Constantius rose in affluence, eventually becoming a governor. But he still didn't know he had a son.

Meanwhile, Helena got word of his high-level appointment and immediately sought an audience with him. As proof of their earlier coupling, Helena had kept the cape Constantius left behind nine years earlier. Constantius, however, did not need reminder or proof of their union, and embraced the two as his family.

Being of good stock and a rising star, it wasn't long before Constantius was eyed for higher duty. Unfortunately, political tradition advocated arranged marriages with equal or higher stock, and Constantius conceded. He and Helena were said to have been heartbroken, but they both accepted their fate, realizing the benefits of a better life for their son.

Soon after, Constantius attempted to prearrange a marriage for his son to elevate Constantine's rank, but the headstrong youth refused—thus displaying one of his major attributes, that of being an independent thinker. He was not easily manipulated or influenced, and relied heavily upon his own logic, research, and gut instincts.

It was in AD 293, while Constantine was still in his twenties, that Diocletian established his famous tetrarchy, which included Constantine's father. It consisted of two supreme leaders taking the title Augustus and two subordinate leaders with the title Caesar. These appointees included Maximian, who shared the highest title of Augustus with Diocletian; Constantine's father Constantius, who became Caesar of Briton and Gaul; and Galerius, who became Caesar of the Balkans.

Constantine was immediately ordered into Emperor Diocletian's army as collateral to ensure that Constantius could not develop a dynastic order. Constantine engaged in his new position with gusto, and learned a great deal from Diocletian and his unique brand of ruling.

Diocletian was an able leader who was obsessed with organization. Yet his most unique quality was the ability to share power. The confusion and disorder of the empire irked Diocletian to his fastidious core, and he beckoned for additional hands. Because he shared the reins of ultimate power with three other rulers, the empire was saved from falling to its foes, and the Roman populous rewarded Diocletian with adoration for both amazing feats. This alone was enough to shower Diocletian with eternal honor and respect by Romans and historians. However, Diocletian's obsessive bent for organization and systematic control would not be so successful in other matters.

Diocletian tried to control the economy by establishing a set price for all goods. His intent was to equalize profits so that all businessmen would stand on equal footing, yet this remedy backfired, as black markets instinctively arose. Worse still, Diocletian's fastidious nature would reach its ultimate failure when he attempted to organize religious beliefs.

The Caesar Galerius evidently had a major impact in persuading Diocletian to solidify Romans under one religion, demanding conformity to their prevailing pagan rites. Galerius had a mean streak, and he advocated harsh and aggressive action against the Christians. Diocletian was not as bigoted by nature, and he proceeded with milder and more cautious tactics. His first edict, made in AD 303, targeted the confiscation of Christian property, rather than the Christians themselves. Some bishops capitulated, while those who sternly refused were reprimanded. This further divided an already fragmented religion.

Diocletian's palace at Nicomedia was set on fire, and blame fell upon the Christians. Christian uprisings throughout the empire were causing discord and Diocletian's patience died. A new and unwavering decree was issued—all bishops must sacrifice to the gods of the state or face imprisonment. This incited major revolt, and after repeated denials and incarcerations, the penalty was upgraded to death. Christian persecutions were reestablished on a grand scale, which had been Galerius' intent. However, his evil plot would have colossal repercussions in the coming years.

The first major persecution of Christians occurred under Nero when he looked for scapegoats after the suspicious burning of Rome. Two hundred years later, emperors like Decius and his successor Valerian initiated empire-wide persecutions, but they quickly subsided. Now some three hundred years after Nero, the emperor Diocletian, being prodded by Galerius, rekindled the religious persecution of Christians, which caused a mixture of satisfaction and delight on one side, and hatred, outrage, and even sympathy on the other.

Christians throughout the ages have been quite vociferous in retelling these Roman brutalities, however, the shocking news is that more Christians killed Christians than all of the Roman persecutions combined. The Crusades, Inquisition, and many centuries of Protestants, Catholics and other sects bloody infighting had exterminated far more of their own brethren than had the Romans, and with an equal flare for horrific torture. The historian Will Durant was perhaps the first scholar to put forth this astonishing fact, but it cannot be stressed enough that butchers of the human flesh existed on both sides. In this instance, however, more butchers were Christians than Romans, and this is something that few Christian readers are aware of and that catechism never truthfully reveals.

Despite Diocletian's "anti-Christian" flaw, we must remember that Diocletian was highly regarded by the masses, and he did exhibit some noble intentions. Although the Roman Republic initiated the precedent of consuls relinquishing power to the most capable, and not a blood relative, Diocletian can be applauded for doing this while at the height of power.

Since the dawn of time, mankind has had a fixation on establishing blood regimes, be they temporal or religious. Diocletian's amazing gesture of opposing a dynastic regime preceded George Washington by well over a millennium. Yet, oddly enough, even the United States has fallen prey to minor dynasties with John Adams and John Quincy Adams, James Madison and his second cousin Zachary Taylor, William and Benjamin Harrison, Theodore and Franklin Roosevelt, whose distant cousin happened to be Ulysses S. Grant, and the Bush dynasty.

At any rate, Diocletian was now facing the twilight of his life, and with his acquired wisdom, he believed that more competent men would better serve the empire. He asked with imperial gravity that his fellow Augustus, Maximian, also step down. Although Maximian shared the title of Augustus, he was never truly an equal, for everyone knew Diocletian was the supreme ruler. As such, Maximian stepped down with reservations and hidden desires that would resurface years later.

After Diocletian's retirement, and progressive ill health, the newly appointed Augusti and existing Caesars quickly vied to strengthen their own circle of influence. The innate beast of favoritism and power once again reared its restless head. As such, many of their heirs were placed into prearranged marriages. Constantine's father was no exception, and likewise took the initiative to elevate his son up through the ranks.

After Constantius' premature death, Constantine was appointed Augustus by his father's legions that had witnessed his fearless leadership in battle. Moreover, Constantine's nomination was supported by the civilians in his father's quadrant of the empire who admired Constantius' honorable leadership. But Galerius was still the reigning Augustus in the east, and he refused to authorize this supreme title; therefore, Constantine tactically settled for Caesar.

Subsequently, Constantine initiated his political advertising campaigns to gain further influence. He began to promote his lineage, which he claimed stemmed back to Emperor Claudius Gothicus (briefly mentioned in the previous chapter), who effectively quelled the advances of the Goths for over a century. This enticing bit of propaganda was aimed at conditioning a vast empire, now ruled by four leaders, to support the return to a single hereditary bloodline.

Additionally Constantine wisely adopted Apollo as his god of choice, who had also symbolized the reign of Emperor Claudius Gothicus. At this time, Constantine also embraced the religion of Sol Invictus; its praise of the Sun nicely coincided with the Apollonian legend. As a way to imprint this image into the minds of the Roman citizenry, Constantine minted coinage that depicted him with Apollo, with the invincible Sun's rays divinely radiated out from behind Apollo's head.

Eventually, after much chaos and nepotism, the tetrarchy crumbled and Constantine established a triumvirate, sharing power with two brothers-in-law. His co-emperors were Maxentius, who controlled Italy and North Africa, and Licinius, who controlled the Balkans, Middle East, and Egypt. This left Constantine with Briton, Spain, Gaul, and the Germanies.

Maxentius was the son of the begrudgingly retired emperor Maximian, and was well known as a blithe pleasure-seeker. It was only after hearing of Constantine's rise to Caesar that Maxentius discarded the joys of leisure and plotted for his share. He shrewdly managed to use his father's influence to win support from the Senate in Rome, despite their waning power, and defeat the incumbent, Severus. After achieving this goal, Maxentius quickly turned his back on his father.

Maximian, who still hungered for power, was Constantine's father-in-law. Entering back into the fold with Constantine and his daughter Fausta, Maximian foolishly tried once more to regain power. This time he attempted a coup by trying to kill Constantine with his own hands. The old and delusional former emperor stalked into Constantine's dark bedchamber, but killed a servant by mistake. Quickly captured, Maximian dutifully took his own life with dignity, in accordance with tradition.

Regardless, Constantine and his young rival, Maxentius, were still in a power struggle. This eventually led to Constantine's famous confrontation, which brings us back to the Milvian Bridge. Anticipating a raid, Maxentius had destroyed the bridge and constructed a temporary floating pontoon, which could be dismantled in an emergency. However,

Maxentius' strategy failed when he was forced by Constantine's superior army to retreat. As Maxentius' cavalry frantically galloped back over the flimsy pontoon, it collapsed. Maxentius and his soldiers plummeted to their deaths and drowned in the Tiber River.

In triumph, Constantine immediately ordered his dead brother-in-law dredged out of the Tiber, and had his severed head paraded on a pike through the streets of Rome. This now added Italy and North Africa to Constantine's share, sizably outweighing the share of his remaining co-emperor Licinius.

One can only assume that Constantine's wife Fausta couldn't have been too pleased to hear that her brother was subjected to this gruesome, though customary triumphal display. However, Fausta had previously warned Constantine when her deranged father plotted to assassinate him. So, it seems Fausta had a strong bond with Constantine, or she shrewdly knew which power lord would best protect her own hide, as well as secure her children's ascension to the throne. Fausta may have been right about choosing the most able leader, but she was dead wrong about saving her hide. (That debacle will be addressed in the Constantine Reprise.)

With the victory at the Milvian Bridge validating Constantine's divine apparition, his stature and seemingly blessed invincibility became apparent to all. Constantine effectively attributed all these victories to his new Christian *labarum*. This led to further successes, in which even his remaining partner Licinius used the *labarum* to score major victories.

Soon after, in AD 313, Constantine would author the Edict of Milan. This landmark decree pronounced that religious tolerance, and in particular Christian worship, was every man's right. Although this edict referred to Christianity, Constantine also stated the following, "...we have also conceded to other religions the right of open and free observance of their worship for the sake of the peace of our times, that each one may have the free opportunity to worship as he pleases; this regulation is made that we may not seem to detract from any dignity or any religion."

Constantine's powerful edict preceded John Locke's words about religious freedom, which influenced James Madison and Thomas Jefferson, by over thirteen hundred years. Madison had witnessed the intolerance that marked his Anglican home state of Virginia, and only became exposed to a more tolerant religious attitude when he attended Princeton University. His professor, John Witherspoon, was pivotal in fostering Madison's thirst for knowledge by supplying him with books by John Locke. Meanwhile, Thomas Jefferson had only three epitaphs engraved on his tombstone, one of those being his gift of religious freedom to the new American republic. With the clarity of far greater hindsight, all these great men are indebted to Constantine for being the first in history to pen such rational and benevolent words.

Although religious tolerance had originated in the Roman Republic, it had never been etched in writing, and this allowed later emperors to take their own intolerant and even brutal course, for there was nothing tangible to hold them accountable. By contrast, the result of Constantine's Edict was that it profoundly ended Christian persecution, and afforded both the Christians and Constantine much greater influence. Although Licinius co-signed the edict, he appeared never to have been a staunch defender of Christianity and this made for bad blood.

Stories allege that Licinius became suspicious of many Christians holding high office in his domain, and subsequently began executing those suspected of disloyalty. Such events presented Constantine with sound reason to take action. The battle wouldn't last long. Within a few months, the land battle moved to sea where Constantine and his son Crispus engaged Licinius for the final showdown. Licinius offered to surrender with the condition that his life be spared. Constantine granted his brother-in-law's wish, and peacefully seized all the remaining provinces. A year later, suspicions of intrigue surrounded Licinius, and Constantine had his brother-in-law hanged. Constantine was now sole ruler of a vast and once again united empire.

In the year AD 324, Constantine made a bold maneuver of major historic importance; he established a new capital city, aptly named Constantinople. Having located the capital far off to the east began a long and debilitating process of stripping Rome and the western provinces of power. In fact, it would later become the new eco-political center of the empire. Equally shocking, was that the construction of the new capital city did not follow the typical Roman plan, for Constantinople would feature Christian churches in lieu of pagan temples. During this time, Constantine likewise made some historic rulings; he banned pagan sacrifices of animals, he banned gladiatorial contests, and he outlawed sexual immorality. These were all noteworthy strides in progress, human decency, and morals.

Although Constantine championed the Christians, he was not baptized; furthermore, he did not wish to sever his ties with the pagan worshipers of Sol Invictus. The pagans were still the ruling majority, and Constantine knew to proceed with caution. Yet he astutely realized that many pagans were fed up with Christian abuse, and a spirit of good will permeated the air. This allowed him just enough elbowroom to maneuver.

In his new capital city, Constantine ordered the initial construction of Hagia Sophia (Holy Wisdom) and Hagia Eirene (Holy Peace), while back in Rome the original Saint Peter's made its monumental debut along with Saint John Lateran and countless other churches throughout the Empire. Thus through Constantine's auspices, Christianity was given a solid foundation in the East and West on which to flourish.

The bishops that governed these churches, however, still posed serious problems. Bitter rivalry caused many schismatic factions to form and each fought for dominance. As such, all that existed was chaos. Constantine's solution was to gather all these headstrong bishops and convene a meeting under his supreme leadership. This landmark meeting would become a significant moment in Western history.

❧❋ Constantine's Nicaean Council ❋ℰ

In AD 325, Constantine's Ecumenical Council gathered for their first meeting in Nicaea. The huge chamber slowly filled with over 300 bishops from all parts of the empire. Although there were several adversarial factions in attendance, including the Donatists and Meletians, the two main rivals were Arius and Alexander, both hailing from Alexandria, Egypt. As the bishops sat awaiting the emperor, three of Constantine's relatives entered and took their seats, followed by a few friends of the faith, and, to the bishops' delight, no soldiers. Then the moment arrived; Constantine entered the chamber and all the bishops rose to their feet.

As Bishop Eusebius of Caesarea eloquently recorded, the emperor entered "like some heavenly angel of God, his bright mantle shedding luster like beams of light, shining with the fiery radiance of a purple robe, and decorated with the dazzling brilliance of gold and precious stones."

Constantine was out to impress, and he looked more like a shining apparition than a mere mortal master of ceremonies. The emperor walked powerfully toward the head of the chamber where a fabulously ornate golden chair awaited. Looking like a statuesque relic of Jupiter, Constantine stood majestically while the bishops courteously beckoned him to sit. As the emperor slowly took his seat, the bishops respectfully followed suit.

After a brief introduction by Constantine's friend and Christian advisor, Bishop Eusebius, the emperor proudly scanned the assemblage, and opened the meeting with the following address:

"It was once my chief desire, dearest friends, to enjoy the spectacle of your united presence; and now that this desire is fulfilled, I feel myself bound to render thanks to God the universal King, because, in addition to all his other benefits, he has granted me a blessing higher than all the rest, in permitting me to see you, not only all assembled together, but all united in a common harmony of sentiment."

The rivaling factions of bishops must have silently looked at one another with incredulous eyes—upon hearing the emperor's claim of *being granted a blessing higher than all the rest*—and with somewhat embarrassed hearts, as they knew concord did not prevail among them, nor had it for three long centuries.

A thick and tense atmosphere must have filled the chamber. We can only speculate what actually transpired at this council, as the record left to us by Eusebius is scant. However, we do know what preceded this event, thus causing Constantine to convene this council, as well as what changes occurred as a result of this meeting; the latter having immense implications for the religion and, more importantly, Western civilization.

Roughly twenty-years previously, Constantine had his first encounter with the aggressive Donatist sect, located in Carthage, Africa. Taking its name from its charismatic leader, Donatus Magnus, this sect routinely clashed with other Christian factions, thus giving Constantine a firsthand look at the strife within this volatile religion. At that time Constantine had just won his miraculous victory at the Milvian Bridge, which he proclaimed was due to his new Christian religion that, furthermore, was branded as a cross on his standard. Being a Christian novice at the time, Constantine doubtlessly expected Christian bishops to share the same "easy-going" mindset of pagan priests. However he was in for a rude awakening, as he soon found himself caught within a whirlwind of conflict that divided his newly adopted religion.

Donatus had survived the earlier persecutions under Diocletian and soon after was consecrated Bishop of Carthage in AD 313. With his fiery personality and fervent faith, Donatus ignited a strong and independent following that not only clashed with neighboring Christians but even resulted in his lashing out at Constantine's son and successor many years later, demanding: "What has the church to do with the emperor?"

Evidently Donatus had no clue as to how determined Constantine or his kin were about meddling in religious affairs. Furthermore, as his opening speech indicated, Constantine firmly believed that God endowed him with a special divine blessing, giving him ultimate authority. Moreover, he called himself "a bishop, ordained by God to oversee whatever is external to the church."

In reality, Constantine escalated his authority by not only issuing external imperial laws that favored the church but he also concerned himself with governing and influencing doctrine. Building upon St. Paul's modus operandi of self-elevation, Constantine appointed himself first as a bishop, then head bishop, and ultimately as the thirteenth Apostle. Yet, even here, he later managed to be buried in the middle of twelve empty apostolic sarcophaguses, commanding the all-important center position.

Additionally, we cannot overlook the fact that mosaics, which soon decorated Constantine's Catholic churches, portrayed the emperor sitting very prominently at the center of the congregation with the bishops subordinately flanking him on both sides. In stark contrast, and unbeknownst to Constantine, the immense favoritism and power that he bestowed upon the Christian clergy would overturn this arrangement several centuries later, thus giving rise to popes performing coronations for emperors, as an early painting of Charlemagne's coronation attests.

Nevertheless, Bishop Donatus harbored deep resentment; he was angered by the harsh reprimands sanctioned against him and his sect by Constantine, both before and at the Nicaean Council. Prior to the council the Donatists frequently badgered Constantine to hear their pleas, yet their irrational and petulant ways exasperated the emperor, who once remarked: "I found it evident that they declined to have before their eyes either respect for their own safety or, what is more, the worship of Almighty God."

During the Nicaean Council the Donatists were further outraged when Constantine rebuffed their pleas and focused on issues that would eventually strip them of power. Actually, Constantine sounded the death knell, for within five decades the Donatist sect would become extinct. As Saint Augustine later documented, his home city of Hippo was once dominated by Donatists, yet they all "converted to Catholic unity by the fear of imperial laws." Constantine's imperial wishes had stridently prevailed.

However, Constantine and the other bishops had far greater problems to resolve at the council. And here is where Constantine made the monumental decision to side with Alexander and his secretary Athanasius in direct opposition to Arius. This schism had many components but centered upon a most burning question, was Jesus divine or a mortal prophet? However, along with Constantine's new tidal wave of shocking change, which included his sectarian preference and imperial favoritism, were the vital laws that would soon flow after the council's massive wake. These empire-altering laws will be addressed in due turn, however, the central question of Jesus' divinity was indeed colossal, and Constantine's decision to embrace those who professed Jesus' divinity was, quite obviously, immensely crucial to the religion. We must also take notice of how these rivaling sects continued to clash even after this council, yet, in the end, *all* would lose out to Constantine's preferred and newly created Catholic Church, just like the Donatists. This speaks volumes, as we can only ponder the immense ramifications if Constantine had opted to side with Arius instead. This leads us to the main controversy between the two head bishops from Egypt— Alexander and Arius.

Arius had long argued that according to the synoptic gospels, Jesus was the "Son of God" and a messiah, *not* "God the Father" who resides in heaven. As far as Arius was concerned, Alexander and others interpreted many passages in the Bible incorrectly.

Alexander rose in stern opposition, stating that the three synoptic gospels may be authoritative, but so, too, was the highly regarded Gospel of John. As far as he and his followers were concerned, Irenaeus rightfully placed John's Gospel ahead of the other three. This omission by Arius was viewed as intolerable and dangerous, for John clearly stated that Jesus *was* one and the same as God above.

Arius heatedly countered that God, as they all knew, always existed. That clearly meant beyond the past and beyond the future, in a word *eternal*. However, there *was* a time when Jesus *did not exist*, and that instantly negated his oneness with God the Father, and, quite importantly, negated his divinity.

Alexander's devout secretary, Athanasius—known for his pit bull temper—lunged to his superior's defense, declaring: "There is a Father eternal, a Son eternal, and a Holy Ghost eternal, and yet they are not three eternals, but one!"

Amid their many rousing arguments—before, during, and after the council—Constantine was often driven mad, demanding that they stop bickering and find common ground. It was painfully clear that Constantine wished for them to resolve their differences whereby they could finally standardize the religion. As he said, "My sole desire [for convening the Nicaean Council] was to effect universal concord."

Naturally, this was a major article of faith that needed to be resolved, and it is shocking for most Christians today to hear that Christ's divinity was not even settled among his most devout believers some three hundred years after his death. However, despite the intense conflict that even persisted after the Nicaean Council, it is unavoidable that Constantine's preference for a divine Jesus not only won the day but also all the days henceforth, right to this very day.

Many have placed a great deal of *faith* on the prospect that the *true* religion would have won the day no matter what Constantine did. However, that pious notion apparently falls flat once we consider how both Alexander and Arius commanded strong and sizeable followings (amid many other smaller sects) and neither major combatant would have power-politicked their way to a victory that would have forced all these losing denominations to adopt their single proprietary doctrine. The proceeding three centuries of no resolution among these many sects clearly proves that. Moreover, what cannot be avoided is that Constantine's imperial laws decisively terminated *every competing sect* that stood in his way. The emperor's singularly chosen denomination would become the mighty Roman Catholic Church.

The colossal conflict over the divinity of Jesus remains profoundly intriguing, as well as disturbing, to most Christians. However, Constantine took steps to ensure that the interpretations of his divinity were not only secure but resolved once and for all. At the Nicaean Council he introduced a new word into scripture: homoousios, which means *of similar substance* or more plainly *of one substance*.

Many bishops at the council recoiled in astonishment, especially the Arians (followers of Arius). The word *homoousios* was actually condemned as heretical only fifty-seven years previously in AD 268. As such, they demanded to know if the green-horned emperor knew what he was suggesting. Constantine made clear his lucidity on the matter and informed them that it was not just a suggestion but rather a command; *homoousios* would appear in scripture.

Naturally, Jesus' divine status and composition was a core article of the religion's faith, and Constantine's inclusion of this word would forever be explained to the masses as the elusive *Mystery of the Faith*. The perplexing notion that one being can also be two or more and still be deemed *one* was and remains baffling, hence the mysterious label and the inability to explain it using logic. This issue not only disturbed the bishops in Constantine's day but also millions of others over many centuries. In fact, many of America's founding fathers privately concluded that Jesus was actually mortal and the whole mysterious *Trinity* conjured up by his fanatical followers.

Interestingly enough, many modern day Christians feel as though this divine mystery was unique and therefore all the more special. However, the concept of Jesus being both Son and God had a similar precedent, that being the Egyptian god Horus. Horus had become one and the same as his father Osiris, and he, too, was called *The Light of the World*. Therefore, John's odd and vivid account, which was explained in far greater detail than his fellow gospel writers, did have a precursor, one that originated thousands of years earlier in ancient Egypt. Whether adopted or factual the *Mystery of the Faith* remains just that, and people can thank or condemn Constantine for cementing that idea into doctrine.

Hence, Constantine's ruling passed, even if not completely quashing discord. Arius and two other bishops refused to accept the emperor's ruling. As Constantine had said earlier, namely, how the stubborn Donatists seemed to have little "respect for their own safety," the same applied to Arius and his dissenting followers, as all three were banished and sent into exile.

Dissension tapered off after the council, and, two years later, Arius diplomatically pleaded to have his sentence repealed. He won his freedom by shrewdly kowtowing to Constantine's agenda, yet he quickly resorted to reestablishing his powerbase of opposition. This soon exploded into open conflict over a myriad of issues. Constantine's humiliation with these pigheaded bishops was scaldingly preserved, when he railed:

"Even the barbarians now through me, the true servant of God, know God and have learned to reverence him, while you bishops do nothing but that which encourages discord and hatred, and to speak frankly, which leads to the destruction of the human race."

These are powerful and revealing words from a man that some have called a ruthless pagan. The intense conflict among these different sects would in time be resolved, thus becoming the unified Catholic church, yet, as we know, they would begin bickering anew during the Renaissance, thus splintering into many discordant factions that did engage many large wars (i.e. Spain vs. England) and small pogroms of torturing and burning each other (i.e. Puritans vs. all infidels). Thus Constantine's prophetic words are profoundly worthy of closer attention by all factions today.

Many years followed where Constantine was drawn between siding with Alexander's successor Athanasius or with Arius on additional topics of debate, yet the primary objectives that Constantine sought were already firmly etched into law and were either slowly or rapidly taking shape.

The process of bishops ironing out the fine details of dogma would indeed persist slowly, yet the powers allotted them by Constantine—that even extended into the civic realm of judging cases, whereby he allowed their final decisions to be indisputable—would not only create a new power elite but their influence and control would blossom in the centuries ahead into reshaping the political environment. That was something Constantine never anticipated and naturally would have never advocated. Basically, Constantine graciously handed over the keys of power and influence to the bishops, which some appreciated and used wisely, yet others would abuse, thus seeking greater power and ultimate control.

Constantine also inaugurated a superficial mutation in the religion. The Dominate period (introduced by Constantine's predecessor Diocletian) transformed the Principate period (established by Augustus) from one of down-to-earth practicality and simplicity into one of glittering pomp, as gold crowns and ornate imperial garb marked their reigns. Constantine readily followed Diocletian's precedent and directly influenced his humble bishops, who likewise adorned themselves with more elaborate vestments. Furthermore, Constantine issued clear instructions that his bishops should abandon their once humble houses of worship and construct huge glittering basilicas. This was all due to Constantine's redirection of imperial funds that not only inflated the coffers of his new Catholic Church but also allowed bishops to request whatever they deemed necessary to complete their tasks.

More importantly, Constantine not only began the process of stripping pagan temples of bronze and other precious materials to outfit his new Christian basilicas, but he also took a role in their design, demanding that they be more grand and beautiful than anything yet built in the religious realm. In total, this *was* colossal.

Perhaps in gratitude, portraits of Constantine in religious settings depicted him with a golden halo. This practice was adopted from pagan tradition, where Helios, Ra, or Apollo were likewise adorned with halos. More interesting still, is how Constantine and succeeding emperors were depicted as Roman warriors sporting a radiant halo, and in a similar fashion, portraits of Jesus likewise morphed from simple to gallantly divine. There is a third century wall painting that depicts Jesus as a humble shepherd, meanwhile, in St. Peter's there is an old mosaic (dating sometime afterwards) that depicts Jesus as a Roman-styled, valiant, Apollo warrior with chariot and horses sporting a cruciform halo. *(See page 706)*

Perhaps Constantine's oddest, yet profoundly significant, decree was changing the Catholic religion's holy day of worship. Judaic tradition had firmly established Saturday as being the holy Sabbath, and the Christians followed suit. After all, in Genesis, God himself declared Saturday as being *the* day of rest. Meanwhile, it was well known that pagan tradition worshiped their Sun gods on the day specifically named for them; Sunday. Hence, Constantine's decree not only came as a shock to his bishops but also comes as a shock to most Christians today that have no idea that they worship Christ on the pagan's day of worship, Sunday.

As noted, Constantine still harbored pagan traits and preferences that were either too hard to abandon or were tactfully exploited to show the pagan majority that unlike Judaism Christianity was flexible and open to Roman interests. Constantine never used force to coerce his Christian agenda yet he did use both subtle and barefaced tactics to make pagans—and even Christians who were now deemed heretics—seriously look at his new religion as the only true path. Despite all the turmoil and aggravation, Constantine's grand Christian vision would succeed.

Constantine's ecumenical council at Nicaea was a momentous milestone in Western history. It profoundly organized a diverse group of Christianities into a new and unified Catholic entity. Since Jesus' death, three hundred years earlier, these factions were a hodgepodge of obstinate clerics with their own version of the Jesus message. In addition, even though Irenaeus collated the synoptic gospels—which would remain Christendom's official canon—they were not fully embraced by all sects, thus causing intense conflict. For that reason, Constantine decided to intervene. As a result, he forced these intractable bishops to sit face to face under his mediating eye.

Constantine remained fixed on his objectives and continued to arbitrate internal woes, though not always successfully. Some historians have questioned the effectiveness of Constantine's council for not rectifying some of these disputes. They also cite that the following decade was unstable due to Constantine at first excommunicating Arius and then after continued hostilities, reinstating him. Likewise, there were several other prominent bishops at the council who were ousted in due time, not to mention the brief exile of Athanasius in AD 335. At one point, previous to his exile, Athanasius sent henchmen to ransack a Meletian church. They irreverently toppled the altar and broke the Meletians' sacred chalice, thus being a volatile sign of these early Christian times.

Both Athanasius and Arius were not only fighting to secure their dogmatic beliefs but were also fighting for their sect's very survival. With Constantine's imperial presence and supreme authority looming over their bickering heads the bishops knew only one version of the religion would emerge victorious. Therefore, these setbacks, although many times ugly or even outrageously unacceptable by anyone's moral standards, must at least be understandable and somewhat expected considering the profound changes being demanded. The faith was at a critical crossroad and only one version would prevail. Therefore, both combatants tried their best to finagle favor with their overlord, who by imperial decree was going to pick a winner, one way or another. Henceforth, even though Constantine was unsure about Arius, as well as, at times, about Athanasius, we must contemplate the end result.

The concept of Jesus being the subordinate mortal Son of the supreme and heavenly God the Father was not just the opinion of Arius and his clan; it was a widespread belief held by many Christians for three hundred years. Many scriptures, both in and out of the canon, mention Jesus as being subordinate to his Father, however, after Constantine's council, this viewpoint—favored by Arius—was forever quashed. Hence, Constantine's objective, regardless of oscillations and unrest, ultimately prevailed.

Furthermore, Constantine's ecumenical precedent, whereby emperors chaired religious councils, continued for another five hundred years. This continued right up to the creation of the official seat of pope. Most importantly, many noteworthy rulings at Constantine's first council did stay intact, regardless of these disputes. This becomes very clear once we review the colossal rulings made at the Nicaean Council and beyond, which unequivocally achieved Constantine's desired result.

Aside from establishing ecumenical councils, Constantine passed earth-shattering legislation. This was evident when the headstrong Donatists refused to comply; Constantine ordered them to surrender their churches to the Catholics, while also confiscating their smaller meeting places. Moreover, when noncompliant sects refused to evacuate a church or facility, Constantine did not refrain from using the military to physically implement evictions. Many other legal programs directly empowered Catholic bishops, so that from the first council onward, Christianity would have the exclusive political support of the Roman Empire, support that it utilized to the fullest for many centuries.

Moreover, one cannot overlook the profound and indelible changes that Constantine's Nicaean Council made. On that day, the profession of faith was born, which after centuries of discord finally described God as *homoousios* and unquestionably divine, consisting of three natures: the Father, Son, and Holy Ghost. As noted, the word *homoousios* was not only embedded into Christian scriptures by Constantine, but the word itself had been banned as heretical by Church leaders several decades earlier. Therefore, it was largely due to Constantine's negation of Arius and favor of Alexander and Athanasius that Jesus would eternally be described as "of one substance."

Adding further to this decree was the term that Jesus was *begotten not made*. This put an end to the centuries long debate over whether there was a time that Jesus did not exist. That he was begotten of the Father indicated that he existed before his earthly appearance, and this was vital to ensuring his divinity.

In addition, Constantine's Nicene Creed created the phrase, "God from God, Light from Light, true God from true God", which is still incanted in every Roman Catholic church to this day. Additionally, this council inaugurated the Catholic Church's daily repeated phrase, and firm belief in "one holy, Catholic, and apostolic church."

These were all profound doctrines of Christian ideology and of church identity. That the Roman Catholic Church was now a monolithic enterprise was beyond being important for the religion—it would be colossally instrumental in shaping the future world.

CHRISTIANITY: *The Rise and Domination of the Roman Catholic Church*

Constantine's actions are so intertwined with the official inauguration and eventual rise of the Roman Catholic Church that he will resurface periodically throughout the remaining sections of this chapter. As mentioned previously, Constantine's numerous and profound actions explain why this unsettled multiplicity of Christians finally solidified, and why it became the state religion for the entire empire. Likewise, this explains why it eventually became known as the Roman Catholic Church, for it took the authority of a Roman emperor to end three centuries of conflict and to officially institute this new Roman Catholic regime. Even the comprehensive program of building churches, along with establishing their architectural template by retrofitting Roman governmental basilicas to yield extremely opulent churches, all began with Constantine.

Contrary to what every Christian has been taught, the Catholic Church did not overtake the Roman Empire; instead, a Roman emperor embraced the Jewish-rooted religion and made it a Roman Catholic enterprise. Naturally Saint Paul's revision of opening the gates to Roman pagans was a crucial precursor, for as mentioned, that directly allowed Romans to infiltrate and manipulate the religion over the following three centuries. However, dissension and conflict prevailed among this very small (ten percent) minority. Constantine's intervention ensured the religion's rise, as will be further demonstrated, thus making Constantine the true founder of this new, solidified, Roman Catholic movement.

The Roman dynamic is rarely if ever addressed, as many either fail to notice or intentionally ignore how the Romans, or Gentiles as the Bible refers to them, infiltrated the religion, shaped it, and then dictated its future course. Naturally, the aggressive aspects of this influence all run counter to Jesus' peaceful message, and as such, they chose to obscure this intrinsic trait. However, it explains why Christianity eventually grew into the strongest religion the world had ever known, for it reaped all the constructive benefits and controversial behaviors of both entities. Jesus' message of offering love, good will, compassion, salvation, and morals, when fused with the temporal benefits of Roman pagans, who were highly proficient at organization, commerce, and structuring bureaucratic hierarchies of administration, and of course, possessed the feisty trait of ultimate survival, made for a powerful amalgamation.

Naturally, the Roman contribution was heightened by Constantine, who instilled doctrines, mediated councils, passed favorable legislation and financially aided the Christian cause exclusively. On the downside, the intolerance found in the Bible, which condoned "an eye for an eye" or vehemently condemned all infidels, when combined with the influence of Roman military might would erupt centuries later to inflict the dark stigma of the Crusades and Inquisitions.

For three centuries prior to Constantine, Romans had infiltrated the religion due to Paul's evangelical ministry. During this period, the religion's spoken language changed from Greek to the Romans' native tongue, Latin. If this small sect had remained true to its exclusive Jewish roots it never would have changed its language—like the unwavering Jews with their Hebrew language—nor, most importantly, would it have been given the chance to proliferate, as it would have mirrored the minimal growth of its Jewish ancestor. This all drastically changed with Constantine, as he sealed the fate of even the religion's language, demanding all new Latin Bibles for his one and only Apostolic Church. *(Over a millennium later, Protestant England did likewise with its King James Bible.)*

Furthermore, the earlier influx of pagans had caused discord, as some of these new Latin-speaking Roman members clashed with the original Greek- and Aramaic-speaking members. As mentioned in the second chapter, after Titus destroyed the Temple, Christians and Jews migrated to other locations, particularly to Northern Africa and other Middle Eastern regions. The new dominant Christian centers were then in Egypt and Syria, yet suddenly they were forced to contend with the intervention of Roman-minded bishops and then later with a Roman emperor.

With the influx of converted pagans becoming Christian bishops, the administrative seat broadened, as Roman sensibilities subtly permeated the religion. They had the power to personally control their congregations via potent weekly oratory, which did preach the good word but it was accompanied by severe consequences. The influence of the Gospel of John which presented prophecies of doom caused the system to begin to function increasingly as if it were a well-disciplined military academy—becoming soldiers of Christ was serious business.

The Romans developed the most successful army in ancient history. It was based on a rigid structure of leadership, along with strict rules that ensured loyalty. In essence, it operated on a reward and punishment system. Roman soldiers knew that if they lived an honorable life they would be richly rewarded at retirement; similarly, Christians knew that living a faithful life offered them the ultimate reward of heaven.

Of equal importance, where a Roman soldier was constantly mindful of the threat of execution by his peers for cowardice or desertion, a Christian parishioner feared suffering the fiery flames of Hell for sacrilege or denouncing his faith. This fear of a doomed afterlife, coupled with the bishops' role to maintain leadership and control on an intimate weekly basis, like a general, helped to form a solid network of devout followers beyond the magnetism of the religion itself.

This is another reason why Constantine made a staunch effort to convene and control these upstart bishops, and why he declared himself the chosen one, ordained by God, to lead their glorious effort. It must also be noted that most emperors took on the role of *Pontif Maximus*, yet pagan religion was merely a state tradition that did not carry the religious weight and fervor that Christianity engendered, hence Constantine also stood to gain additional stature and deep ideological control.

Constantine was a skilled orator, who was not only crucial in unifying the conflicting bishops, but also made direct appeals to the plebeians. No other emperor cared to routinely orate face-to-face with the lowest tier, who naturally lacked power or influence. This indicates Constantine's awareness of the bishops' pulpit politics, and the constituency that he, too, could cultivate. However, the emperor's busy schedule limited his effectiveness in this regard, which is why the bishops became his primary target. And any great general, which Constantine surely was, knows how to select the optimum target.

This also elucidates why Arius and his Egyptian rivals, Alexander and Athanasius, all fought to gain favor with Constantine, for he was in essence subtly seizing, if not complete, at least significant control. It is also noteworthy that before the Nicaean council, Constantine contacted two northern bishops, one in Rome and one in Gaul. Both despised the Donatist sect, which was located primarily in Northern Africa. As time and history would soon reveal, the Donatists and those of influence in Northern Africa soon faded, as the capital city of Rome became the new seat of Catholic power.

Likewise, Constantine's new capital in the east, Constantinople, would later become the capital of the Eastern Roman Empire, or Byzantium, and be of major importance in the centuries ahead. Many Greek-speaking people, who clung to their version of the Christian message, lived in this eastern half of the empire. By rejecting Constantine's directives, they began what became known as the Greek Orthodox Church. However, their branch of Christianity was deadlocked in Byzantium, while Constantine's solely endorsed Roman branch became the main trunk of Christianity, which in turn, dominated Western civilization.

Once again, it was Constantine's favoritism and firm requisition that enabled Roman bishops to power politic the Saint Peter legend to make Rome become the new massive root of the religion, a root that soon grew into a towering colossus that would overshadow all of its tiny root hairs in other cities. Therefore, all the different Christian sects scattered about the Middle East and North Africa became subordinate to the imperial Roman Catholic epicenter. By no strange coincidence, the Roman imperial capital housed the command center of the Roman Catholic Church.

Hence, pagan Roman influence was highly significant. For if Christianity truly seized control of the Roman Empire, as most devout Christians have been purposely, yet mistakenly, taught, there would have been one single and united Jesus Catholic Church, one that spoke Hebrew, Aramaic, or possibly Greek. Likewise, it would have been located in Judea—the land of its roots—and far away from the pagan elite, who dominated Rome. Moreover, as to its inherent traits, Christianity would have remained a more peaceful theocratic entity as practiced by Jesus, or even his direct disciples, one prone to having martyrs in times of conflict, not warriors. Yet the shape of the Catholic Church, as we know it, would indicate otherwise.

Additionally, if pure Judaic Christianity eradicated Roman paganism, it would stand to reason that Christians, especially after two millennia, would have eliminated or at least altered the pagan Julian calendar. The names of Jesus and his eleven faithful disciples could have become month-names, thus expunging Julius (July) and Augustus (August). However, the names of these two pagan emperors remain with us today, as do the Latin names of all the other months, with Janus (January) and Mars (March) for example, being most sinfully pagan gods.

History shows that administrators of ancient religions routinely established their own calendars, which have remained decisively fixed and unaltered. The Hebrew calendar and those of other religions often used simple numbers or agricultural elements when naming their months, so even simple numerals could have been an obvious choice for the new ruling Christians; but that never occurred.

Being of pagan birth, Constantine was obviously satisfied with the pagan Roman calendar; however, he did take advantage of his supreme position to make a minor adjustment. Constantine would inaugurate a new date for Easter. This was done to clearly separate the important celebration from the Jewish holiday, Passover. These feasts were celebrated on dates calculated by the lunar calendar, thus explaining why the dates shift on our solar calendar. However, in an effort to clearly separate the once connected religions, the new date for Easter was calculated by a lunar ecclesiastic algorithm. Although future clergymen adjusted this dating system, Constantine's decree served two purposes: one was to distance it from Passover, and the other was to set a firm date that all Christians would worship in unison, since at that time various parts of the Empire calculated and celebrated Easter on different days. Here again, Constantine attempted to put order to chaos.

Another attempt to adjust the calendar for Christian purposes was made in the sixth century. The monk, Dionysius Exiguus, made a huge alteration when he used the birth of Jesus to recalculate the calendar years. Unfortunately, his miscalculations have confounded rather than clarified history, since in setting AD 1 as the year of Jesus' birth (which should have been AD 0), he missed a year. Worse still he completely overlooked scriptures that indicated that Jesus was born during the reign of King

Herod the Great. Herod died in 4 BC; therefore, not only do we have no idea when Jesus was born, but our calendar years are totally meaningless in a spiritual sense as related to Jesus. This once again proves, however, that those in power did attempt to control the calendar. But due to pagan Roman traditions and influence within the Christian religion, the Julian calendar remained primarily untouched.

As for Constantine's attempt to separate Easter from Passover, this was the result of brewing animosity between the two sects. As we know, Constantine advocated freedom of religion, as his Edict of Milan proves, but he was compelled to protect his new state religion from any adversaries, and the Jewish sect posed the most threat. This he clearly stated in a letter written shortly after the Council of Nicaea: "... it appeared an unworthy thing that in the celebration of this most holy feast we should follow the practice of the Jews, who have impiously defiled their hands with enormous sin...Let us then have nothing in common with the detestable Jewish crowd; for we have received from our Savior a different way."

This detestation of Jews was the result of three centuries of conflict, which led to a distinct separation, so that by Constantine's day, disrespect and even hatred filled the hearts of many Christians. Constantine's policy was not to provoke, harm, or expel the Jews; however, he would not tolerate any interference or antagonistic actions from the Jewish community either. Reprisals were swift and stern. Taking precaution a step further, Constantine even outlawed the conversion of Christians to Judaism, with the strict proviso that any Jew found guilty of forcibly attempting to convert a Christian would be executed.

It was clear that Constantine would not persecute other religions, however, Christianity was to be the sole religion aided and protected by the emperor and the mighty Roman Empire. It is also unavoidably clear that Constantine was the primary architect of redesigning the Christian enterprise that was now endorsed and funded by the state.

As Constantine's new precedent matured, changes and unforeseen mutations occurred. One of the key attributes that Constantine bestowed upon the Church was the heightened authority and immense power of the bishops. As the centuries passed, some within this new bishop elite grew overconfident and arrogant, and the need to defend their newfound position of authority became more pressing and far more aggressive.

This aggression even led to murder in AD 363 when Constantine's nephew Julian inherited the purple. Succeeding Constantine's three sons, Julian tried to reverse his great uncle's Christian favoritism by attempting to reinstate pagan polytheism as the Empire's state religion. His short year and a half reign ended when he was fatally shot with an arrow during a battle against the Persians. Julian's assassination was never resolved, but several Christians claimed credit, stating it was a divine order sent to Mercurius to strike down the apostate, or traitor. As such, Julian became known to history as Julian the Apostate. The power, affluence, and influence that Constantine bequeathed to the bishops were now far too great to be obstructed. With Julian and polytheism irrevocably silenced, Christianity continued its charge forward.

Additionally, and more importantly, however, bishops were given the legal power to judge civil cases, and of course, enforce the new Nicene law that they helped establish. Constantine also granted them tax exemptions and donations, and this created a supreme new status for bishops, unheard of before. Their enormous wealth was combined with their unique position to serve their congregations on a weekly basis for a lifelong term, while their secular counterparts—governors and local officials—only served two or three years. This proved vital to the growth and dominance of Christianity amidst its new imperial setting.

Furthermore, and quite effectively, any church that ignored Constantine's Nicaean decree, which established the one and true holy Catholic Apostolic Church, had its taxes increased or was issued mandatory public services. This significantly aided in the disappearance of conflicting Christian sects and their secret proprietary scriptures.

Constantine's imperial decrees proved to be earth-shattering in their immediate and long-term effects. His massive precedent would eventually be followed up by an even more unyielding man, when Emperor Theodosius I took the purple.

Theodosius had become obsessed with his new Christian religion, and as such, in an edict in AD 391, he banned all other religions. He then ordered the destruction of pagan temples, and even extinguished the eternal fire that burned in the Temple of Vesta, a fire that had remain lit since the Golden Age of Augustus. As that golden fire died out, the empire, too, quite symbolically began its decline, for Theodosius would be the last emperor to rule over a single and united Roman Empire. The Eastern capital would thus become the Roman Empire's sole beacon of hope to live on in physical form.

After decades of invasions and pandemics, the Western Roman Empire finally fell in AD 476 to the Ostrogoths, led by King Odoacer. By strange coincidence, the West's last emperor was named Romulus Augustus, being the names of both Rome's founder and first emperor. Odoacer exiled Romulus Augustus, yet we must note that he only ruled this territory as an agent of the Eastern Roman emperor named Zeno. Contrary to popular belief, Odoacer, who some historians labeled a barbarian, was well acquainted with Roman culture, was a Christian, and more importantly was managed by the Eastern capital.

Furthermore, over the centuries the Western Roman army had evolved into a new entity. The mighty army, which began as a unified and well-trained institution of devout Romans, had mutated after centuries of conquest and expansion. Seeking the comforts and riches of the empire, many became complacent and outright negligent. Deferring the duty of fighting to newcomers, the Roman army began recruiting foreign men into the ranks, so that by the fourth to sixth centuries, the army was predominantly comprised of foreign subjects—many being former barbarians. Hence, the zeal for Roman culture seriously diminished.

This trend is sadly evident in America today. Where the soldiers from the Revolutionary War up to the Korean War had a much stronger desire to fight for our nation's survival, the riches of the American Empire offer little incentive for many United States citizens today to leave their cozy houses, classy cars, cable TV, or iPods to pick up arms and fight. Moreover, the American military is now recruiting soldiers from the Philippines as well as planning to offer citizenship to illegal aliens who are willing to serve in the military. Hence, history does repeat itself and it should offer us a stern warning.

Added to the Roman army's foreign mutation was a series of pandemics that took a devastating toll on the Italian peninsula. With millions of deaths weakening morale and the economy, the West was self-imploding when Odoacer stepped in to assume control in AD 476.

However, sixty years later, the Eastern Roman Emperor Justinian recaptured Rome and the western territories in AD 536. This reunification of the Empire would only be fleeting, and the West would soon be retaken after Justinian's death, leaving only the Eastern Roman Empire standing. The West had now permanently fallen, as Christian bishops vied and allied with Germanic tribes and even Byzantine emperors, giving rise to the Holy Roman Empire. The West would never regain the unification or strength it enjoyed under the Roman Empire, and was relegated to a dispersion of isolated villages, monasteries, and small feudal states.

As a sidebar, Justinian's brief recapture of the West had been accomplished after much rape and pillaging by Attila the Hun. The capital city of Rome itself had been saved by the bishop of Rome, Leo I, who when confronting the barbarian foretold of his inevitable doom—all those who attempted to sack Rome previously had failed. Being highly superstitious, Attila opted to retreat. For achieving this miraculous feat, Leo was given the title, Leo the Great. (Although also known as Pope Leo I, the title "pope" signified *father*, not the preeminent seat it later became.)

Emperor Justinian had also ordered the massive reconstruction of the Hagia Sophia Church, initially built by Constantine, which soon became Christianity's crown jewel in Byzantium. This newly designed edifice was an impressive architectural wonder based upon the Pantheon model, yet breaking new barriers in structural virtuosity. In every respect, the church was magnificent. Furthermore, Justinian closed the schools of pagan philosophy in Athens in AD 529, thus reaffirming Constantine's new Christian tradition, yet with more zeal.

Constantine's endorsement of Christianity had also marked another significant change in the religion, as compared to Judaism and all other religions. Because of the immense wealth the Church was able to accrue, it remained a dominant force, even though the Western Roman Empire had fallen. This wealth is what allowed the Church—acting like a huge corporate entity—to fund projects during the Dark and Middle Ages when they wielded a monopoly. During the imperial breakdown, the once robust economy and army, which sustained this impressive civilization, followed in digressive unison. The economy was crushed and without a unified or patriotic army to ward off attacks, the West fell into dire straits.

During Justinian's reign, Saint Benedict established his famed monastery atop Monte Cassino in AD 529, thus beginning the so-called Golden Age of Monasticism. Benedict's missionaries ventured out of Southern Italy to western and northern Europe in order to convert a large rural populace to Christianity, and to escape the dangers of a growingly decadent and hostile world. These chaotic events significantly contributed to the rise of the long, sheltered Dark Ages.

In an effort to reclaim the humble message of Jesus, and rather than deal with savage Vandals, Goths, Huns, and other invading or migrating tribes, monks eagerly sought desolate locations. Their ability to turn seemingly useless terrain into productive communities was indeed miraculous. However, their secluded world evidently reaped the same mixture of benevolence and butchery found outside their protective shell.

Unfortunately, numerous pious activities were matched by cruel practices of religious fanaticism and coercion. Beside their solitary devotion to God, the monks' duties included preaching to local villagers about the damnation of their souls if they lived immoral lives. Additionally, and quite regrettably, monks would serve as God's alleged administers of punishment. Gruesome details were documented of how some monks blinded, tortured, or even burned many nonbelievers as heretics. Their renunciation of all human vices, which often led them to abandon humanity itself, was coupled with self-mortification as repentance, an alien practice that many then and today find barbaric, not to mention unchristian.

However, we cannot disregard the other side of the golden coin, as many good and pious monks made outstanding contributions. Monks offered spiritual guidance, social support, and when necessary, financial assistance to the needy, supplying hope and tangible sustenance to thousands during hard times. When plagues later ran rampant, killing millions, the clergy offered much consolation, and more importantly the will to live. Many monks became notable religious philosophers since they maintained huge libraries and diligently studied the ancient scrolls. Moreover, monks developed into proficient accountants, and contributed significantly to enhancing economic practices, though only within the limited radius of their small domains. Their wealth, which was accrued from loans and other business ventures, helped the monastic network, as well as the papacy, thus making noble attempts at maintaining normalcy amid chaos.

These contributions, however, must be placed in context, for some modern theologians have romanticized the issue. Forgetting how bleak the times were, they have credited these wealthy Christian enterprises as providing sole benevolent leadership that single-handedly fostered, funded, and allowed progress and capitalism to flourish. Additionally, they failed to realize where this immense wealth and power came from, for, quite unwittingly, the other side of their hypothesis chastised the Romans for stagnating progress under the previous imperial regime.

As a wealth of evidence indicates, the progress made by the Romans not only outperformed that of the theocratic Dark Ages, but also supplied all of these later Christian enterprises with their initial wealth. Moreover, the person who planted the seed-money and supplied the resources to nurture and cultivate that rich crop, was Constantine, who many centuries earlier had channeled imperial funds into the church's coffers. These coffers grew so rapidly that within Constantine's lifetime bishops rose to a level of affluence and power easily rivaling that of the aristocratic senators in Rome, as well as other wealthy landowners throughout the Empire.

After the passage of several centuries this wealth grew into the immensely rich Vatican. Its network of monasteries brokered loans with private enterprises, such as textile manufacturers, vineyards, granaries, and other entities under their control. However they were by no means liberal, as they only funded Christians, and then strictly dictated what their constituency was permitted to do or read. Despite the hording of important texts, leniency prevailed, as they established great learning centers. But the later shock of the Reformation finally caused much panic, thus forcing Catholic Church leaders to reevaluate their position.

In retaliation, the Counter Reformation began a strict and radical period of rigidly adhering to and protecting their scriptures, which were essentially being heisted and reinterpreted by Martin Luther, John Calvin, and others, who also took with them the much desired wealth of large populations. This was the uncompromising period during which Galileo was imprisoned for his heretical ideas, and other scientists and layman were condemned to death. Scholars estimate that during the sixteenth century, at least 50,000 people were burned to death or brutally butchered for the bogus charge of witchcraft. Therefore, the bold claim about the church's piously self-made wealth, along with it being the sole reason and impetus for progress can only be viewed as fanciful fiction.

The church's rise to power also included a systematic program to win converts and eradicate rivals. In tandem with its truly generous and pious deeds, it waged countless little holy pogroms. Mithraism had long been one of the main contenders in the struggle for religious dominance, yet due to its strictly male membership, and its Persian undertones, which conflicted with certain Roman traditions, it attracted mostly soldiers, and thus remained a virtually secret brotherhood. However, its influence still ran strong and deep, and was allegedly the key motivation behind the Christian persecutions proposed by Galerius, which were effectively inaugurated by Diocletian.

Quite possibly in retaliation for those persecutions, the Christians later built some of their churches directly over the Mithraea (Mithraic caves of worship) in an attempt to literally bury their rival's existence. This extirpation was rather successful, for Mithraism was buried out of memory for over a millennium until the dawn of the Renaissance.

The church by that time was slowly loosening its oppressive grip, as a new inquisitive secular breed galloped toward enlightenment. What these humanists literally uncovered were hundreds of caverns of worship that were adorned with illuminating iconography. The paintings and statuary revealed not only Mithraic sites of worship, but the relics of other cults as well that were all entombed under the colossal headstone of Christianity.

Beyond burying the holy shrines of their rivals, the church had grown over many centuries to become warriors outright. The Crusades began with justifiable intentions to win back the ancient Holy Land from the Islamic infidels but turned disastrously sour. By this time, popes had amassed the power of emperors and often acted like them, oscillating between noble and notorious, as even fellow Christians were killed. The glaring reality was revealed: power, in most mortals' hands, is intoxicating and deadly. When Pope Boniface VIII issued his *Unam Sanctum* in 1302, which decreed that all men, including secular rulers, were subject to the Roman pontiff, the noose of Catholicism drew even tighter.

Nevertheless, it was during those earlier centuries that the church secured the majority of ancient texts, both religious and secular. However, all these great works were strictly coveted and concealed in the dark vaults of many mountaintop monasteries, only later to be revealed in the mid-fourteenth century. This concealment of knowledge and the bloody Crusades had added two more dark indelible blotches upon the religion that the church was never able to remove, despite all its great work.

Interestingly enough, the Crusaders were using Constantine's cross as their battle standard, yet in ways that were diametrically opposed to Constantine's core beliefs of religious tolerance. Constantine certainly used the cross to aid his political agenda, but he never used it to enforce conversion, or worse yet, kill fellow Christians. This was sadly not the case with the popes that fueled the Crusades. Forsaking Jesus' peaceful lexis, the mortal hand of Christian man altered and desecrated its noble religion.

Equally noteworthy, Constantine's triumphant use of the cross as an icon of strength and success was so strong that it was even maintained centuries later when the Byzantines (Eastern Roman Empire) banned all religious icons. This censorship of religious imagery was enacted in response to the new Islamic threat upon the southern border.

Muhammad's Islamic movement had begun by conquering lands in the region during the seventh century. Successive kings would continue to carry on expansion, so that by AD 726, Muslims occupied the lower portion of the Byzantine Empire—the territories that today make up the Middle East. Because the Muslims were so successful in occupying and maintaining these lower regions, the Byzantine emperor, Leo III, surmised that their success was due to their noniconic religion.

The Islamic religion, like Judaism and early Christianity, prohibited graven images; they did not allow visual depictions of God, prophets, mortal characters of any sort, or even graphic symbols. Therefore, Leo III became the first Byzantine iconoclast, and banned all imagery and icons, as did his son Constantine V. Though all pictorial images and icons were erased or destroyed, Constantine's cross remained as the only single iconic symbol that would valiantly remain on Christian shields.

In essence, the influence of the founder of Constantinople and the Byzantine Empire would still prevail among the hearts, minds, and battle standards of his heirs. In desperation, they clung to reviving Constantine's great successes, to defend their capital city and also possibly to win back lost territories. This they managed to do for almost seven centuries, until Constantinople and the last remnants of the great Byzantine Empire fell to the Muslims.

The concept of worshiping graven images is a thought-provoking and controversial topic. Some modern theologians and historians have lauded Christianity as being the sole reason for inspiring what they deem to be the greatest visual artists who ever lived. It is true that the Renaissance produced among the best works of art ever created and has immeasurably enhanced civilization, but was it truly the Christian faith that was responsible for its artistic genius or something else?

Although many, including myself, have always preferred to believe that God inspired these great Renaissance artists to achieve excellence, technically, we need to examine evidence of a concrete nature—evidence that was literally written in stone. Jews and Christians were strictly forbidden from making graven images of deities, false gods or idols, as well as God. The Ten Commandments, which God himself etched in stone, clearly commanded that mankind never engage in such practices. "Thou shalt not make unto thee any graven image, or any likeness of any thing that is in heaven above, or that is in the earth beneath, or that is in the water under the earth." (*Any thing* includes God, thus explaining why Jews abstained from such practices.)

Therefore, all Christian art defies God's commandment, so faith cannot be the sole reason for these artists' genius. Where these Christian artists learned to visually honor their God, with such splendor and aplomb, is oddly clear—directly from the pagan Romans, the Greeks, Egyptians, and other pagan entities before them.

As noted, Roman influences infiltrated the religion early on, yet it was primarily after Constantine's imperial intervention that Christian iconography began its new and illustrious course. Ancient Roman ruins from Constantine's era reveal frescoes and mosaics that set the standard for future Christian artists who created icons, statuary, and ultimately the great frescoes of the Renaissance. Even portraits of Constantine, who was eventually depicted as a god with halo, would heavily influence the future Gothic era, with its golden divinity discs that adorned Jesus and the saints.

We also cannot overlook the architecture of Christian churches, which were simply Roman basilicas yet lavishly adorned. Moreover, Christian architects later scrutinized the pagan capital, and adopted the Pantheon's dome, which adorned their greatest cathedrals, including the Hagia Sophia and their ultimate masterpiece, Saint Peter's Basilica.

Therefore, the rise of the Catholic Church was profoundly indebted to pagan Roman influence, which at times even disobeyed God's commandments. In the final analysis, the use of graven images, the enormous power allotted the bishops, and the church's immense wealth, were all the results of directives initiated by the mighty pagan Roman emperor, Constantine.

CHRISTIANITY: *The Interpretation of Scriptures | The Influence of Greek Philosophy and Pagan Traditions | Analyzing Christianity*

The Christian religion was marked by another unique feature, which likewise attracted Constantine, and that was its ability to allow newcomers to reshape the religion. Unlike the strict Judaic tradition that prohibited change, the new Christian sect was in constant flux. Greek philosophy and pagan traditions had been infused into the religion over centuries. Oddly enough, many Christians today are unaware of just how much outside influence their religion adopted; therefore this section shall shed light on some of these intriguing as well as vexing influences. During this varied exposé, several disturbing facets of Christianity will be analyzed, thus offering fiery food for thought and even an antacid remedy if possible.

As mentioned earlier, Irenaeus was one such newcomer who was pivotal in reshaping the religion and his interpretations and authoritative doctrines demand our attention once again. This influential clergyman arrived on the historical timeline about one hundred years prior to Constantine.

Irenaeus was born in Turkey, just outside the Judeo-Christian nucleus. From an early age, Irenaeus was influenced by the Greek Logos concept of theology (which is based upon logic), primarily by his mentor Justin Martyr. He would eventually settle in Lyon, in the province of Gaul (modern day France), where he made his impact on Christianity by collating what would become the New Testament.

This consisted of the three synoptic gospels—the ones with synchronized viewpoints, namely those of Mark, Matthew, and Luke—plus John's very dissimilar gospel (which Irenaeus positioned first) to ultimately form the canon of the New Testament. This, we must remember, was after a hundred years of intense conflict.

Irenaeus vehemently silenced all other gospels (including those of Thomas, Philip, Judas, and Mary) and chose the four gospels not only because he believed their content, but also because of the significance of the number four: Greek philosophy proclaimed there were four regions of the universe, four primary winds, and four directions. Therefore, Irenaeus felt that there should be only four gospels. This philosophical platitude, to Irenaeus, was uncontestable, and these four gospels would stand like four pillars of stone to support his concept of the New Testament.

While these particular Greek inclinations certainly did not appear to be remotely logical, and certainly not Christian, Irenaeus did conceive of some very compelling logic; and like the apostles, especially Paul and other Gentile newcomers to the faith, they all used their own sense of logic to mold and reshape the religion right from its inception.

As mentioned, John's Gospel differed greatly from the other three. In fact, John begins it with Jesus attacking the moneychangers and merchants in the Holy Temple, whereas all other accounts have this episode near the end, for the simple reason that they all claimed this act is what prompted the Jews to have Jesus arrested, tried, and then crucified. John's version of this incident is also far more aggressive, for rather than merely pushing over the tables, John tells us that Jesus fashioned a whip out of knotted cords, and then physically beat the moneylenders out of the Temple.

Moreover, John focused on Jesus' miracles, not his death, and only John mentions how Jesus washed the feet of his disciples on the Thursday before his crucifixion. This ritual is still performed every year by the pope upon his cardinals, as well as by the Mormon head president, and even many Baptist and Protestant leaders upon their direct subordinates.

As mentioned, Irenaeus favored the Gospel of John above the others due to John's mystical account of Jesus being one and the same as the Lord God. None of the other apostles made this claim so definitively, as the question of Jesus' mortality baffled most believers. Therefore, the strong-minded views of a few (with the Roman lawyer/Christian leader Tertullian and Irenaeus being the most strident) were enough to elicit support and widespread belief, despite the continued protests.

Irenaeus also loathed the notion that Jesus was the blood brother of James. Interestingly enough, a new piece of evidence recently became known in April 2002. An ossuary (a small limestone vault that houses the bones of a deceased person) was discovered that bore the inscription, "James, son of Joseph, brother of Jesus." It was written in Aramaic, the language used by Jesus and his kin, and it has been scientifically authenticated, at least as being from the correct time period. Many wondered if discovery of this ossuary would drastically change history by offering a tangible piece of evidence, literally written in stone, that links James and Jesus as brothers.

Naturally, theologians and scholars, most of whom never examined the artifact firsthand, instantly ridiculed the inscriptions as forgeries. However, beyond their biased and unprofessional negations are serious concerns, such as the large number of families during that era having similar names, which prevent making this find indisputably conclusive. Nevertheless, if further evidence one day validates that the ossuary's inscriptions are authentic, the results would indeed send shockwaves throughout the Christian world.

This fear of revealing a mortal bloodline also explained why Irenaeus staunchly fought to eliminate the Gospel of Philip. Philip stated that Jesus was the mortal son of Mary and Joseph, and that the later reference to Mary's Immaculate Conception, as well as her mysteriously remaining a virgin, was not to be taken literally. Interestingly enough, it is believed that the apostle Matthew read the Greek transliteration of Isaiah's ancient prophecy in the Hebrew Torah, which proclaimed, *"a virgin shall conceive,"* yet the actual Hebrew word did not mean virgin, but, in fact, only meant a young woman. Therefore, the transliterated sources, which even the apostles drew upon in an attempt to make sense out of mystery, often caused misinterpretation and further mystery.

We have seen how the apostles engaged in trying to retrofit Jesus into ancient prophecies, such as the story of his riding into Jerusalem on a donkey, or Matthew seeking to connect Jesus' bloodline to the ancient Judaic King David, and now added to this we even had transliteration issues, from Hebrew into Greek, which caused many anomalies in the apostles' gospels. This also added to the diversity of viewpoints among these often-contradictory ancient texts.

In this instance, Irenaeus was fundamental in labeling all other Christians who expressed opposing views of the Jesus miracle as heretics. His influence and power politics were so effective that his concept of the canon held unshakably fixed as if written in stone by God himself.

Additionally, and quite importantly, Irenaeus favored and firmly established the notion that the only way to receive access to God was through the Christian church, specifically through its offering of the Eucharist. This had previously been seriously disputed, but Irenaeus made it strict Christian doctrine. This was monumental, because it cemented the church into Christian tradition, and since every person had to attend mass that meant that churches needed to be built in every village, city, and port, for these venues offered the only doorway to salvation. In contrast, other religions required their parishioners to attend sporadically, once a month, once a year, or even once in a lifetime, such as the pilgrimage to Mecca that is required of all Muslims.

Likewise, Irenaeus condemned the Jews, who he said lost God's favor, and as such were no longer the chosen people or God's chosen priests. This was because they failed to recognize Jesus as the Lord, and worse still, because they orchestrated his execution. Irenaeus effectively built upon the Christian tradition of instituting law by analysis and logical conjecture; this provides decisive proof of how effective and influential newcomers to the faith could be.

Irenaeus' interpretations via analytical conjecture went even further. He viewed humanity as a maturing entity that was not fully developed with the initial creations of Adam and Eve. That explained why their fall from grace was inevitable, since just like adolescents they sought instant gratification and ate the forbidden fruit that hung from the *living tree*. Irenaeus then asserted that God sent Jesus as a new paradigm of maturity to aid mankind in overcoming that initial calamity. That ultimately explained why the body of Christ hung upon the symbolically *dead wood* of the cross.

This was a very astute analogy and interpretation of the Old and New Testaments, in which Irenaeus cleverly interwove his own logic to create a new Christian ideal. Naturally, it never attracted the belief or appreciation of devout Jews, who must have been incensed to have their portion of this hypothesis—Adam and Eve—regarded as juvenile, while the new Christian sect claimed the mature aspect of God's divine workings.

Irenaeus also explicated that Judaism was based upon the *fallen from grace* status of Adam and Eve, which essentially doomed them to a hopeless life of helplessly waiting for God's return to be offered salvation. In contrast, Jesus' lesson of *suffering, death, and resurrection* instinctively instructed men to make sound moral decisions to achieve grace in their own lifetime and thus achieve salvation after death.

This is why, in the story "Jonah and the Whale," Irenaeus equates the whale to death, thus forcing Jonah to either turn to God and find salvation or lose God's favor and suffer the consequences. The decision, however, was Jonah's to make. The specter of the whale symbolizing death was later used to great effect by Herman Melville. However, Melville's Captain Ahab disregarded God's will, and he forged a course of revenge and self-destruction, taking down his entire crew, save one.

However, we can see how reinterpreting past or even present events was what differentiated Christianity from other religions. Where the Torah remained unalterable, the New Testament has been continually appended with external interpretations that perpetually reshape Christian dogma. Even today, Evangelical and other sects sprout up nationwide, all preaching the word of Jesus, yet all with a new and distinctly modified philosophy.

Hence, the interpretation and manipulation of the religion by newcomers was very prominently demonstrated by Irenaeus. His actions naturally influenced others, and in particular Constantine.

As we have seen, Constantine, with the astute help of Eusebius, resurrected the Moses legend to ingrain the pagan emperor into the Christian storyline. Constantine's divine vision and visitation had been effective keys for accessing initial passage into Christian ideology, despite their unverifiable authenticity. Breaking into this mindset was no easy task however, as Constantine only needed to look at the Christian martyrs to see how unyielding the sect was.

The martyrs provided Constantine with perhaps the strongest visual evidence of just how unique and resolute this cult really was. These were true martyrs, and not like the Jews at Masada who defied God's word and committed suicide. These Christians stood firm before their executioners and heroically met their deaths, all the while proclaiming the glory of their one true God.

Constantine did manage to infiltrate the religion, however, and made his own monumental set of changes, as previously discussed. His actions in turn finally unified the splintered religion and significantly diminished internal discord. However, the church and many Christian authors today attempt to paint a pristine picture of order, like a perfect Da Vinci painting, of the various sects at this time, when in reality, it was more like the splattered chaos of a Jackson Pollack painting. Hence, Constantine organized this splattered palette of colors into a single vision, which radiantly projected his new and miraculous Trinity.

The point here is that Constantine was drawn to the religion by several of its unique facets. Beyond the sublime words of Jesus were the religion's openness to outsiders, its staunch followers, and the power to interpret and manipulate doctrine, all of which were attractive incentives. In a word, the religion had magnetism.

Beyond the religion's appeal to a Roman emperor, however, Christianity had a growing allure among the pagans. For even before

Constantine's arrival, the religion seemed to inherit more and more of their pagan traits, and even important dates.

As we know, the New Testament is an anthology of recollections, not the direct words of God. This unreliable relay of communication naturally created a plethora of perspectives and opinions that caused sharp and at times brutal conflicts of interest among many feisty bishops. Along the three-centuries-long path of chaos, until Constantine intervened, many aspects about Jesus were not agreed upon, including references to his birth. This date, of which no official state record exists, was shrouded in mystery, but eventually it needed to be recorded.

History cannot give us a date for Jesus' birth but dates for other gods have been recorded. Many pagan beliefs were based upon early astrological observations, which were astute calculations about specific movements of the planets and stars. The sun was the most obvious object sustaining life in the ancient world, and as such, it was the first and greatest object of human worship. The earliest records from various cultures all shared similar experiences of worshipping the mighty Sun, as its importance reverberated among generations of all great ancient civilizations.

The sun was so captivating and so crucial to daily life that primitive men spent many years analyzing the great fireball. They astutely noticed how the sun disc mysteriously traversed the sky at different degrees upon the horizon in different seasons. As such, they cleverly charted its basic movements and instinctively interpreted its movements. Unsurprisingly, divine interpretations of these movements found their way into a majority of antique cults and religions, and even into Christianity when we examine it more closely.

The ancients observed that the mighty sun disc appeared to *die* on December 22, which today we know is quite accurately the winter solstice. The sun's movement south suddenly appears to halt until December 25, when suddenly its movement dramatically reverses for its journey back north. Hence, the ancients celebrated this movement as a new birth. In their minds, if the sun continued its trajectory southward it would disappear and cause the dark and chilling end of the world.

Therefore, December 25 was a joyous day, one that signaled divine salvation to mankind. This specific date became the nucleus of faith, as it clearly defined the saving grace of their fiery Sun god that floated in the universe. In this regard, the sublime date of December 25 appeared in numerous religions, long before Jesus arrived or his followers recorded his miraculous birth date. In fact, the birthdays of the gods Sol Invictus and Mithras, among others, were both celebrated on December 25th, and they, too, were hailed as *The Light of the World*. So it appears that Jesus' birthday was likewise implemented with divine perfection.

As the highly acclaimed religious scholar Elaine Pagels said, "...most New Testament scholars know that we have little to no historical information about Jesus' birth" and neither did these early Christian writers of scripture, who had at their disposal a long held and widely worshiped date of divine birth to incorporate into their fledgling religion. Moreover, because there had been so many failed attempts by the apostles to connect Jesus to past traditions, bloodlines, or prophecies this only increased the likelihood that this all-important pagan date was adopted.

Other astronomical occurrences or celestial entities were likewise infused into the Christian story, like the significance of the North Star during the nativity. The synoptic gospels tell a far more Judaic story than the discarded gospels, which often refer to celestial and astrological activities of a clearly pagan origin. Regardless, the church, which doesn't place any significance in the stars but only in Jesus, quite interestingly still posits the Christmastime story that places divine significance on this Northern star.

More important, however, was the cosmological importance of the number twelve. This number reverberates among almost all ancient civilizations, since as far back as 5000 BC when the constellations and movements in the heavens were painstakingly studied and worshiped. When one realizes how the Chinese and Hindu peoples also developed their own zodiacs, each featuring twelve signs (though naturally with different names), we can see the astounding and divine importance of the number twelve. Twelve signs comprise all these zodiacs, the ancient Greeks had twelve Olympian gods, the Jews had twelve tribes, and even the highly influential Roman codes of laws were conceived as the Twelve

Tables. Naturally, there are the twelve months on the calendar and our clocks are divided into twelve hours.

This brings us to the twelve disciples. Interestingly enough, John, in his gospel, simply did not mention all of Jesus' disciples' names. Additionally, the names mentioned in these four gospels do not all match, as discrepancies arise among the names of Thaddaeus, Nathanael, Lebbaeus, and Judas the Zealot. This lack of concord, especially among the accepted gospels, causes some doubt whether there actually were twelve disciples, and sheds some light on the slight possibility that the apostolic authors wished to maintain a connection to the astrologically divine number twelve, which had a strong religious and pagan precedent. Even if twelve disciples did exist, that, too, could have been to conform to this widespread pagan tradition.

The ancients attached divine implications to the zodiac and the astronomical calculations that these brilliant observers made—who we must remember worked without the aid of any modern tools or calculators—was nothing short of amazing. As mentioned, the occurrence of the winter solstice was worshiped with such divine significance that its adoption into many ancient religions and cults should not really be surprising, yet to most diehard theologians and believers it is seen as purely pagan and therefore blasphemous.

Beyond the astrological implications, even one of America's founding fathers, Thomas Paine, noted how the miraculous intervention of God impregnating Mary has been easily accepted by Christians, yet they are quick to ridicule the base and bizarre Greek and Roman Olympian gods who often did the same thing. Here again, we see Christianity strangely embracing a very pagan mindset. Paine's book, *Age of Reason*, caused a tremendous uproar in the Christian community, and their scorn caused many of Paine's founding father friends to shun the once highly admired thinker, even though some silently agreed with many of his arguments. Nevertheless, public condemnation firmly ruled the day, thus relegating Thomas Paine into the distant shadows of his peers. However, Paine's provocative point does warrant attention.

Paine's premise was that all Christians accept the story handed down to them about the earthly appearance of Jesus. Very few stop to analyze the basic notion that God could have made Jesus simply appear. Instead, God chose to impregnate a mortal woman, one who was already betrothed to a mortal man no less, forcing Joseph to step back and forfeit his beloved. Thereafter, Joseph not only faded from the big story, but quite sadly, even lost contact with his divine quasi Son.

Equally baffling, however, is that Mary was the one and only woman in all of history to be given the ultimate honor of carrying God's sacred Son within her mortal womb, yet oddly enough, she would garner relatively little mention in the gospels and a severely mitigated place by the early male founders of the church.

Although Holy Mother Mary would generate a devout following in the distant future, she certainly played a sideline role during much of the religion's founding and during the many ensuing centuries. If one contemplates the gravity of her role and her divine union with God himself, it could only be expected that after Jesus' death she, more than anyone else, would be hailed as the most divine on earth and the leader of the Jesus movement. Here was a woman who was physically injected with the Lord's essence, yet a mere mortal named Peter would be given the honor of being the founder of the church. Interestingly enough, even Peter's role has been subject to serious doubt by the pioneering actions and leadership of James, who, as we also know, was clearly documented in scripture as being the blood brother of Jesus.

However, beyond the neglect of Mother Mary's proper place in the Christian hierarchy, Thomas Paine was baffled and humiliated at how Christians were repulsed and even enraged by the sexual behavior of Zeus, who impregnated mortal women, yet somehow the same action by their own God was never questioned; instead, Paine opined, it was joyfully embraced and mindlessly celebrated.

Naturally, the miraculous birth of Jesus is one of prime importance and ultimate sanctity within the Christian religion, yet, although this is an extremely sensitive topic, this incident did cross the minds of many others before and after Thomas Paine, and as such, is mentioned here as food for thought. What is unmistakable is that the Christians, once again, embraced a miraculous occurrence that quite interestingly mirrored the reviled actions of ancient pagan mythology—a cult they supposedly despised and condemned as idol-worshipping infidels.

Attempting to construct the relatively unknown chapters of Jesus' birth and his early life, early Christians apparently gathered an assortment of oral anecdotes, and added their own interpretations (drawn from a diverse collection of Judaic and pagan sources), in a grand effort to construct a cohesive story. Yet, as mentioned, the story was by no means singular, as many viewpoints existed from immediately after Jesus' death right up to Constantine's fourth century.

That Jesus' own contemporaries were in total disagreement leaves us today with only one positive conclusion—there is no conclusive answer to Jesus' birth date or his mother's mysterious pregnancy. However, this topic raises a serious point, namely, those that believed these issues were 100 percent true now only have a 50 percent chance of being correct.

Aside from these profound issues, however, are other pagan traits that likewise found their way into Christianity. In the centuries after Jesus' death, there was a growing interest in collecting and enshrining the sacred remains of martyrs and saints, which in turn became valuable commodities. These hallowed bones and artifacts offered a visual tangibility that the illusive belief in Jesus alone did not. In turn, this attracted worshipers, many of whom prayed to various patron saints rather than to Jesus in times of special need. As Christians embraced this new trend of praying to a variety of saints for guidance or assistance, they either unwittingly or quite intentionally adopted another one of Rome's pagan traditions.

Pagan Romans used to appeal to different gods or goddesses for particular blessings or guidance, and quite interestingly, the longstanding tradition was carried on by newly converted Roman Christians. Whether this was a natural progression by the parishioners or intentionally fostered by bishops to make the new religion more comforting to Roman sensibilities is unclear, however, what is clear is that pagan Roman sensibilities did emerge within the Christian religion, which was providing more nectar to draw and maintain its growing congregation. As we know, praying to patron saints remains a strong practice today, as most Christians have their favorite saint or saints to whom they pray on various occasions.

Whatever the source, this also must have added to Constantine's agenda of easing pagans into the religion. However, more influences were yet to come, even after Constantine's death. The eventual fall of the Western Roman Empire would subject the new theocracy to invasion and disintegration, and scattered monasteries arose to offer safe haven. Moreover, the religion, and in particular monks, would continue to scrutinize and adopt various pagan philosophies that not only reshaped it but also caused some Christian sects in the distant future to reinterpret these scriptures in interesting and even harmful ways.

The friar, Thomas Aquinas, in the thirteenth century was one such Christian philosopher. Many Christians hail Aquinas as being the greatest theologian, and his book *Summa Theologica* is a study that not only instructs but also questions the scriptures. Aquinas did this very methodically by listing perturbing objections he had and then answering them using logic. As an example, here is his first objection.

Objection 1: It would seem that Christ should not have led a life of poverty in this world, because Christ should have embraced the most eligible form of life. But the most eligible form of life is that which is a mean between riches and poverty; for it is written in Proverbs 30:8, "Give me neither beggary nor riches; give me only the necessaries of life." Therefore, Christ should have led a life, not of poverty, but of moderation.

Aquinas deeply valued Saint Paul's stern opposition to the Greek philosophers, who placed logic above faith, yet Aquinas adopted the power of reason himself and applied it to theology with great effect. His religious reasoning made significant and very positive changes in Christian belief, even though his so-called logic in certain matters was questionable.

Such is the critical case of Jesus' mother Mary, who for a millennium was known to have given birth to Jesus' mortal brothers, as recorded in the earliest of scriptures. Yet, this "stain" caused much controversy, so Aquinas simply deduced, through reason, that Mary conceived as a virgin, gave birth as a virgin, and remained a virgin. This viewpoint satisfied clergymen in his day and remains intact, simply because Aquinas validated it by using his own unique brand of logic.

Some modern scholars agree with Aquinas' disregard for Greek logic or science, and even go so far as to say that Christianity adopted neither. They point out that Christians simply ignored most aspects of Greek philosophy, like the Greek concept of the universe being an essence without beginning or end—much like that in Chinese Taoism—rather than being divinely created.

Additionally, even though Plato did designate a creator, named the Demiurge, this was clearly not *The* Creator that the Christian Bible spoke of, but an impotent god of a dubious nature. They also, quite correctly, derided how the Greeks gave personalities to the celestial stars and planets, which ironically clashed with their high praises of Greek logic.

Even though the Greeks adopted the quasi science of astrology from the Mesopotamians and other ancient cultures, astrology played a significant role in many religious cults, especially during the first four hundred years of the Roman Empire. Therefore, soon after Constantine's reign, the great religious philosopher Saint Augustine promptly reasoned that astrology was a false practice, not to be embraced by Christians. This was based upon the logic that since God endowed mankind with free will, true Christians could not believe in the destinies foretold by the stars. Knowing this, it is interesting that these pagan astrological undercurrents remain in the minds of many who speak of horoscopes, or their good or bad fortunes that they hail as destiny. Moreover, if they claim that God willed these astrological destinies, then that clashes with their own free will, for according to Augustine at least, God does not preplan mankind's destiny. Hence, many people either unknowingly or intentionally hold Christian and pagan beliefs simultaneously.

It appears that subjecting religion to pure reason was quite aptly summed up by the eighteenth century philosopher, David Hume, who said, "The Christian religion not only was at first attended with miracles, but even at this day cannot be believed by a reasonable person without one."

Despite Hume's atheism and critical intention, his comment can be viewed in a reasonable light, for religion does remain a miraculous mystery, founded upon and practiced with faith alone; however, despite the miraculous storyline that demands blind faith, logic dictates that religion does enhance many people's lives, so perhaps that is miraculous.

Returning to the issue of free will, however, most Catholics today maintain Saint Augustine's interpretation that mankind has free will and can choose to accept or deny God. Meanwhile, some Reformed views state that mankind does not have free will. These Reformed authors also draw distinct references from the Bible that lend credence to the fact that man was not given the freedom of choice. Ephesians 1:11, *"...we have obtained an inheritance, being predestinated according to the purpose of Him who worketh all things after the counsel of His own will."* Beyond negating free will, this also validates how contradictions in the Bible force interpretation.

However, there are also references in the Bible to man being the Lord's sheep; sheep being animals that need to be herded by a shepherd or master due to their inability to govern their own actions, or as applied to humans, their inability to attain salvation on their own. The Reformers also rejected the Catholic perspective that God offers his love and grace to all of mankind, and hence all one needs to do is accept his divine offering. Instead, they say that the Lord has predetermined his chosen flock, and that he will call upon them. Akin to the Old Testament, where Yahweh chose the Jewish slaves fleeing Egypt, the Reformers say that in the New Testament, Jesus chose only those truly deserving from his broad Christian flock—namely these Reformed Christians—since the Catholics, Baptists, Evangelists, and all other sects corrupted Christ's message. Additionally, they claim that Jesus' Almighty Father made this selection at the predawn of creation.

Naturally, this raises many questions, too many to address here, yet their viewpoint states that mankind, due to the Fall of Adam and Eve, is born in sin and cannot and would not chose God on its own accord, for mankind is only capable of sin and error, once again, because only God can administer salvation to his chosen people.

Chapter 10 in the Gospel of John retells the story of doubting Jews who badgered Jesus about his claims of divinity. Jesus' reply was curt.

"But ye believe not, because ye are not of my sheep, as I said unto you. My sheep hear my voice, and I know them, and they follow me: And I give unto them

eternal life; and they shall never perish; neither shall any man pluck them out of my hand. My Father, which gave them me, is greater than all; and no man is able to pluck them out of my Father's hand."

This passage, allegedly spoken by Jesus, since this is John's recollection some sixty years later, likewise causes some concern. This "chosen sheep" connotation echoes Judaic exclusivity and denies God's grace and salvation to the vast majority. Just a few verses before this one, Jesus also tells the doubting Jewish High Priests:

"All that ever came before me are thieves and robbers: but the sheep did not hear them."

Here again, is another powerful statement that condemns all High Priests and religious leaders who came before Jesus as being charlatans. Only those who came through him were authentic. This at first may not sound that radical, however, it all relates to a far broader, actually global issue. Selective choosing that only embraces his predestined Christian followers—in this case, choosing only his Reformed flock out of a sprawling pool of billions—seems most unholy and unnervingly unfitting for a supreme Creator, yet what are we to make of these Biblical passages?

The Reformed sects, as well as most other Christians, also fixate on their chosen status, for John 3:5 further relates how Jesus said that only those baptized and of Christian spirit can enter heaven. *"Except a man be born of water and of the Spirit, he cannot enter into the kingdom of God."*

This line has immense implications, for it once again raises the question that has baffled many curious and rational minds, namely, why would God create billions of people since the beginning of time, in many territories outside the Judaic/Christian epicenter, only to exclude them from his loving grace?

It's understandable that not all people are entitled to be part of the divine plan—unrepentant evildoers should be excluded—however, since all the heavily populated regions across the globe, including entire continents and ethnic races, are being deliberately slighted, this does present problems for the faith. We are asked to believe that God created enormous masses of men, women, and children (which significantly dwarfed the size of his infinitesimal chosen flock) over countless millennia only to sentence them all to eternal damnation.

One can also not forget that all people from before the birth of Christ, including all the great Greek philosophers and mathematicians, Roman statesmen, artisans, engineers, and all others whose knowledge and ideas were largely adopted by Christians, were also shunned, except the early Jews, who were at that time God's only chosen people. Yet, after Christ appeared, most Christians claim that God suddenly decided to abandon them too. Those that he previously favored and made his exclusive covenant with had become "evildoers," and every Jew, along with many Christians who worshipped Jesus improperly, would be eternally condemned. And since Jews were not baptized, did this not completely negate their claim of being the Chosen People?

Since Reformers claim that mortals do not have free will and that only God can make such decisions, we must infer that it was not in the Jews' capacity to use free will and decide to follow Jesus. Following this line of reason, God alone preplanned the worldly change of events, which tore his mantle away from the Jews and passed it onto his new Catholic flock. Yet, even the Catholic flock would eventually splinter after Martin Luther arrived on the scene, so once again, God tore away his grace and salvation from Catholics and now passed it on to the specially chosen Reformed heirs. This logic, quite suitably, is reminiscent of a Greek Olympic relay race, for it actually appears mythological in concept.

Examining this particular Reformed faith further, I ask that they must then consider the following: Martin Luther was exceptionally adamant in labeling Jews as the killers of Jesus Christ. The vast majority of Christians likewise holds this view. Yet this issue causes a problem, since Jesus' own words, according to John 10:18, made it clear that no one has the power to kill Jesus, for only he has that power: *"No man taketh it from me, but I lay it down of myself. I have power to lay it down, and I have power to take it again. This commandment have I received of my Father."*

Therefore, if only Jesus had the power to actually end his transitory life on Earth, since no mortal could truly triumph over or, worse yet, execute God, then exactly what role did the Jews play in the whole crucifixion debacle? Using Reformed logic, in which God preplans destiny, and John's recollection of Jesus' omnipotence, if Jesus preplanned his own death and had all the mortal Jewish players carry out the accusations and conviction leading to his crucifixion, then Jesus deliberately entrapped these puppet-like characters—those who used to be his chosen flock—in order to have them and the entire Jewish race purposely condemned.

Such perplexingly cunning and even seemingly traitorous actions on Jesus' part should give us pause to contemplate. Naturally, Catholics, who believe in free will, would jump to the defense and say that the Jews were traitors by not believing in Jesus and plotting his crucifixion, and in so doing deserved exclusion. However, according to the Reformed view and John's scripture, the Jews were incapable of killing Jesus, or the true God, because only Jesus had that power, therefore the crucifixion was not their doing but Jesus' own handiwork. If Jesus controlled his own death, then he obviously knew beforehand and even preplanned how the Jews would refuse him as their Lord God.

If God knows all things, and even if he bestows freedom of choice upon his creations, he must know what their decisions will be beforehand. Otherwise, God does not know all things, and such a proposition would instantly negate his omniscience. This single premise alone means that free choice is impossible, since that would mean that people can think thoughts and make decisions that the Lord would not know about, and again, this is impossible for a Creator who is all-knowing.

Therefore, according to this line of thinking, the Lord had to have known of their disbelief as well as their plot to kill him (in his earthly form as Jesus) beforehand. His willingness to end his transient mortal life was merely the final act of his own preplanned tragedy. Such logic makes one ask, "Who truly is the traitorous party in this equation?"

If the word of Jesus was, *"Love your enemies, bless them that curse you, do good to them that hate you, and pray for them which despitefully use you, and persecute you,"* how then can any of his flock follow a Master who doesn't practice what he preaches?

This last argument may have come as an irreverent shock; however, it does not conclude that God is traitorous or deceitful. Rather, it leads to the next issue, namely, the scrutiny of those who wrote and interpreted his alleged words. This includes John, as well as the many copyists who translated these passages, for such unreasonable and perplexing utterances demand clarification. Naturally, these men are long gone, but perhaps the logic put forth can clear up this quagmire.

As to those who would argue about the passages I am comparing in these instances, I submit the following. It appears abundantly clear that Jesus' statements referring to loving one another would be the ones that are true to the source, as opposed to other statements that incite prejudice, hatred, condemnation, or advocate illogical favoritism for a few, while inflicting damnation upon billions.

In seeking a more logical and pious answer to the Reformed sect's burning declarations of intolerance and favoritism, I posit two antacid rebuttals. The first lies in the verse Jesus gave during an exchange with the doubting Jews. *"I am the door: by me if any man enter in, he shall be saved and go in and out, and find pasture."*

That verse can redeem Jesus' other damning words, which at first seemed totally focused upon his newly chosen Christian flock, for here an open opportunity exists for any man to enter and be saved.

(We will overlook the sexist use of the word "man," which excludes women and is used throughout the entire Bible, even though it confirms chauvinism and scriptural error, and aids in validating the forthcoming second rebuttal.)

However, as inviting as that open door offer may have been, which appears to have allowed even some doubting Jews to enter if they abandoned their Jewish faith, we are still left with the fact that Jesus' offer in this verse was made at a specific moment in time. Hence, once again, all people before the arrival of Jesus were either "thieves and robbers" or unbaptized, hence, unworthy of salvation. This still unfortunately leaves all the people of the world, prior to Jesus, excluded from grace, salvation, and naturally heaven. This partial salvation of opening the door to all, only after his arrival, is far more palatable, yet still hard to fully ingest.

The second rebuttal requires a greater degree of open-mindedness and will probably irritate many diehard conservatives. However, this point seems to be the key to unlocking the mystery and focuses on the very real notion of human error. Whether made by secular historians, Jewish rabbinical scribes, or Christianity's religious icons, errors must exist in all ancient texts somewhere and somehow, even if in small measure. As C.S. Lewis, the famous author of Christian apologetics and *The Chronicles of Narnia,* remarked, even the small contradictions found in the Bible, if not crucial in and of themselves, clearly prove that not everything written in the Bible is the truth.

Plainly put, the truth cannot be invalidated by another line of truth and remain the inerrant truth. Hence, errors *truthfully* exist in the Bible.

As such, it is very possible that John's interpretation or possible alteration of Jesus' words may be what ignited the Reformers to see Jesus' predestined and selective choosing, rather than a divine notion of brotherly love—a love that could one day embrace, if not all, at least the majority of the human race. Accepting this possible error could silence the bigotry of the Reformed voices and eliminate much intolerance, hatred, and conflict; however, this explanation would be difficult for most Christians to accept, as it means questioning the sacred canon of Christendom. However, we must not forget that this sacred canon was written by fallible mortals and hand selected by Irenaeus, not Jesus.

As such, these passages, for which even the Reformers themselves cannot be fully blamed, since they have only read John's words, have spawned intolerant condemnations that attack all non-Christians, as well as Catholics, Evangelists, Baptists, and others who supposedly interpret the Bible incorrectly, as being reprobates. In essence, according to John and the Reformers, the majority of the world has it all wrong and never even had a chance at redemption, since God made his plans at the predawn of creation.

The fervent bias against the majority of the world's population has posed and continues to pose serious threats to world peace. In concluding this particular topic, additional evidence shall be presented to shed light upon these very probable errors in scripture written by fallible human hands.

Knowing that Jesus was many times misunderstood, even by his closest disciples, leaves us to logically conclude that they quite possibly transcribed these errors into their personal recollections. Although some verses state that everything shall be clear and fully understood once endowed with Christ's divine blessing, there are other verses to refute and invalidate that statement. Even Peter (Jesus' most trusted disciple) was in the dark about certain actions by Jesus. For example, in the Gospel of

Mark, he tells how Jesus became irritated with his disciples because they remained baffled after he performed a miracle.

Jesus said, *"Have you no inkling yet? Do you still not understand? Are your minds closed? You have eyes: can you not see? You have ears: can you not hear? Have you forgotten?"*

This natural deficit, inherent in all mortals, disciples included, seriously questions the competency of the Biblical authors, and the reliability of their scriptures in conveying the true inerrant word of Jesus, or any revelation from God the Father. It is not as if the scriptures were written in the presence of Jesus, who could have monitored the work with a discerning eye and pure divine vision. Even this Reformative interpretation of the Bible leaves much open to debate, as do the variously interpreted dogmas of their many Christian rivals.

Whether through interpretation, misinterpretation, or use of verses of questionable authenticity, the bottom line is that this view has caused countless generations to condemn their brothers and even take up arms to kill their brothers for their unique interpretation of faith. This is apparently why the founding fathers understood that God must be a guiding presence for the new nation, yet why they chose not to identify any particular religious faction—clearly to avoid conflicts between Anglicans and Puritans, Catholics and Baptists, and so on.

The perpetual pang of fanatical religious factions clinging to certain scriptures has torn apart many nations: an example is the founder's own homeland, Britain, that fought bitterly to sever its Catholic ties to Rome, thus becoming a Protestant nation. Meanwhile, France and Spain fought in direct opposition to remain Catholic nations. Naturally, politics played a role in all those instances, however, it is evident that the founding fathers understood and learned from history, and it is crucial that Christians today do the same, for they must remain focused on the uplifting words of Jesus, rather than those passages that estrange or condemn fellow Christians. Yet much conflict still abounds, all due to the questionable fidelity of our sources and their numerous interpretations.

We have just analyzed portions of the Christian's New Testament. We now shall examine one of the more intriguing scriptures found in the

Hebrew's Old Testament. Many have interpreted this vivid, yet wildly futuristic story in different and provocative ways.

The *Book of Ezekiel* relates the amazing story of how Ezekiel witnessed God descending from the heavens. What makes this story so intriguing is that Ezekiel's vision was not of a humanoid figure (after all, man was made in God's image) but instead, he distinctly describes what is unquestionably a spacecraft of some sort. Furthermore, it even flew him to the Temple of Jerusalem.

Ezekiel described the craft as containing four living creatures, each looking like a man with four wings and each having a different animal's face. He then refers to them having retractable wheels, and those wheels were described as a wheel within a wheel.

"And when the living creatures went, the wheels went by them: and when the living creatures were lifted up from the earth, the wheels were lifted up."

Likewise, Ezekiel describes their feet, or landing pads, as being hooves that *"sparkled like the colour of burnished brass."* Quite startling as well is the imagery of a spaceman's glassy visor, when he says, *"And the likeness of the firmament upon the heads of the living creature was as the colour of the terrible crystal, stretched forth over their heads above."*

In describing the objects rocket-like propulsion, he states: *"As for the likeness of the living creatures, their appearance was like burning coals of fire, and like the appearance of lamps: it went up and down among the living creatures; and the fire was bright, and out of the fire went forth lightning. And the living creatures ran and returned as the appearance of a flash of lightning. Now as I beheld the living creatures, behold one wheel upon the earth by the living creatures, with his four faces."*

Here, Ezekiel plainly demonstrates his inability to describe them as actual living and breathing creatures, but rather the likeness of living creatures that burned like coals on fire. His descriptions are far more akin to a fiery machine than a fleshy being. The oscillating bright lights and their lightning speed however is quite clear and remarkable. The description of these wheels being lifted along with the creature interestingly describes what seems to be a spaceship with retractable wheels. Oddly, this creature or craft had the attributes of four part-man part-animal configurations with flapping wings, or quite possibly flaming turbines.

This miraculous sighting by Ezekiel has caused many theologians and laypersons to scoff at such aeronautical hyperbole, however, the pioneering and highly provocative theory by Erich von Däniken regarding this mysterious scripture resulted in his book and film documentary, *Chariots of the Gods?* This exposé caught the attention of millions, yet the lack of hard evidence left von Däniken's theory grounded. Nevertheless, since its 1968 release, two additional researchers have added thought-provoking material to the extraterrestrial question.

First is Walter Joerg Langbein, with his extensive theological training in the ancient Hebrew language. Langbein revealed that Ezekiel's scriptures had been altered during later translations, for the original texts do not refer to the city of Jerusalem as being the destination of Ezekiel's journey. Instead the original text tells of Ezekiel landing in a strange mountainous region where he describes spotting a huge building complex. Yet, it was clearly not Jerusalem or that city's Temple, for Ezekiel had been to Jerusalem and would have said so, if in fact it were. If not to Jerusalem, as later translators wished us to believe, then where did Ezekiel go?

We know that from its inception, the *Book of Ezekiel* had always caused a serious dilemma for early Jewish priests. Ezekiel's fantastical visions and experiences were hard for these ancients to not only fathom, but also to categorize theologically. There is no mistaking that his vision was not of a single divine entity—God—but rather four moving creatures somehow attached to a wheel-like flying object. Moreover, this contraption had transported an unspecified number of passengers.

Ezekiel's book was written in BC 571, yet it would only be added into the canon in AD 100. Later translators naturally attempted to make sense of Ezekiel's bizarre and baffling story and obviously changed his destination to Jerusalem. Yet Ezekiel's original text not only mentions a strange, unknown place, but he meticulously made hundreds of detailed measurements of the building complex, which enigmatically seems to have been a hangar to house this flying vehicle, and it categorically was not the Temple in Jerusalem.

The second researcher was Josef Blumrich. Erich von Däniken and his famous *Ancient Astronauts* theory caught the attention of Blumrich, who was the chief engineer at NASA. Blumrich played a significant role in designing the Saturn V rocket that transported man to the moon, as well as Skylab, and the space shuttle. He was also awarded the NASA Exceptional Service Medal for his work on the Saturn and Apollo projects. Therefore, he was no lightweight enthusiast, but one of our century's most brilliant engineers.

Blumrich initially scoffed at von Däniken's wild conjectures, calling them "rubbish." After a cursory investigation of Ezekiel's alluring passages, however, he soon became enamored with the ancient prophet's clear and detailed descriptions that either came from an extremely vivid imagination, or was a primitive person's admirable attempt at describing something far beyond his limited understanding. After much scrutiny, Blumrich actually designed a flying machine based upon Ezekiel's descriptions, and to his amazement, his model proved aeronautically sound. Blumrich later wrote his own book, *The Spaceships of Ezekiel*.

Whether Ezekiel was the first science fiction writer in history, who possessed a hallucinatory imagination, or a simple man of his times struggling to convey his mystical experience aboard a strange fiery contraption still remains an enigma. However, rather than flatly reject this scripture as nothing more than an odd visitation by God or the delusional ranting of a madman, it seems far more prudent to at least advocate further investigation.

The issue of science and delusions aptly brings us to our next topic. Some fanatical Catholic scholars now claim that Christianity was solely responsible for formulating true science during the Dark and Middle Ages, thus completely debunking the long held view that the church was generally its greatest opponent.

Naturally many early scientists were in fact Christians, and indeed, many were clearly motivated by their religious beliefs; however, what has emerged from this radical hypothesis was that the vast majority of scientists that they cited were carefully concealed by the church. Most important, none of these cloistered geniuses made a universal impact, or even made his revelations known to the public at large. The majority of people during these centuries were obviously Christian, yet that distinction has no connection at all to the idea that Christians were the sole impetus behind scientific endeavors, nor does it prove that science was their exclusive discovery. What this does prove, however, is that such right-winged viewpoints are based solely upon arrogance and intolerance.

As we know, the church wielded immense control, and, yes, it did provide a sound educational environment for scientists to grow. But the church had an insatiable desire to control and withhold knowledge, to which the long preservation of many texts in monasteries attests. Whether they harbored knowledge as a means of control or a safeguard against their foes remains to be seen, yet it was probably a combination of both. That they now claim so many scientists were under their tutelage—despite very few of these names having ever seen the light of day until now—only makes the case stronger that the church concealed these men's thoughts, discoveries, and findings. Building think tanks of brilliant minds, while not openly sharing the resulting knowledge, only further validates that their regime was built upon suspicion, fear, or self-interest.

Therefore their hypothesis, which condemns all previous pagan or secular thinkers as lacking the divine Christian spark or awareness that would allow them to make scientific progress, can only be deemed defective. Oddly enough, their hypothesis also extended to the scientific revelations found in the fine arts. Here they cite how the geometric principles that led to the use of perspective were supposedly spawned under the Christian domain due to Christian belief.

Ironically, they quasi acknowledge the use of perspective in ancient Roman times, however they avow that its glorious perfection and clever use by Christian artists is what made it truly magnificent and flourish. They cite Giotto as the founder of Renaissance art due to his Christian revelation of perspective, which allowed him to paint characters and tangible objects in three-dimensional form and space. Firstly, Giotto did not reinvent perspective—Brunelleschi did. Moreover, we must not underemphasize that Brunelleschi learned it by studying ancient Rome, the land of the so-called "ignorant pagans."

Furthermore, Giotto's use of perspective was not only incorrect, due to his ignorance of the geometric principle (since Brunelleschi was born 40 years after Giotto died), but Giotto's more fully rendered three-dimensional characters—compared to the previous, and purely Christian Gothic art which was rigid, flat, and drone-like—was not a new revelation in art. One only needs to travel back to ancient Pompeii to see that pagan Romans, over a millennium earlier, painted similar and even more natural characters than Giotto did, which were also in three-dimensional form. Examples of this artwork still exist today as tangible evidence not calculating conjecture.

Most importantly, these religious authors go beyond just science and art, for their main thesis was based upon the alleged fact that it was Christian reason alone that allowed progress. This was clearly a defensive argument against the long held historic account that the church suppressed progress during the Dark and Middle Ages. This they reasoned was because all despotic regimes suppress the people and their will to make progress.

Although this may hold true for most tyrannical regimes, it is instantly proven false by the glaring and undisputable fact that although Hitler's Germany was perhaps the epitome of a ruthlessly despotic regime, in the early part of the twentieth century, Germany was by far the world's leader in technological and scientific progress. This is because their leader had a clear vision of domination, which in this case happened to be purely secular, not to mention evil, and he feverishly sponsored research and development. Equally important was Hitler's grand motivational impetus of declaring all Germans the superhuman Aryan race. Hence, Hitler's sole impetus for progress was certainly not Christian belief, since several of his key scientists were even Jewish, but was pure self-motivation that propelled nationalistic motivation.

Another succinct example of how motivation, and not Christian endowment alone, is what propels progress is the invention of the transistor chip. The research and development department of the United States Army funded the project, which operated at the Massachusetts Institute of Technology (MIT) and Bell Laboratories during the latter part of World War II. This was purely a militarily motivated enterprise, with a core mission and ultimate goal of killing and subduing the enemy.

Eventually this technology led to the development of the integrated chip by Texas Instruments and Fairchild Semiconductor who pioneered the digital computer revolution. When Gordon Moore left Fairchild to found Intel during the late 1950s, the government, now entangled in its Cold War policies with Russia, still eagerly funded the technology. As such, our modern day digital world of computer technology is a result of purely secular political and military entanglements in either bloody war or calculating cold war between conflicting political ideologies, and has nothing to do with Christian benevolence or belief, even though that would have been preferable for humanity's sake.

Moreover, even secular China's many advances (such as inventing paper, gunpowder, etc.) all occurred without Christian influence. The point is that Christians, pagans, or modern secularists at certain times, have all made advances, and the impetus was pure motivation. This motivation in some instances may have been strictly controlled but certainly did not spring up as a result of suppression. Where the secular dictator, Adolf Hitler, proved effective in motivating his scientists, such as the rocket scientist Wernher von Braun, the Catholic Pope Julius II was likewise effective in motivating his artists, such as Michelangelo.

Oddly enough, this brings us briefly back to Constantine, who was instrumental in the development of these theologians' mighty Christian church that became the wealthy benefactor it has. Constantine's firm legislation provided wealth and power to the Christian church, which allowed them in turn to pursue other avenues, or more pointedly motivate others in areas not of their own expertise. All great enterprises need funding, and once the church became very wealthy, their endeavors escalated and multiplied.

This significant change immensely altered the church into sponsoring other ventures in later centuries, whereby they funded agricultural and business entities, as well as scientific endeavors. Once the church rose to supreme power, its patronage of the arts became most evident; Michelangelo's frescos and statues, Da Vinci's *Last Supper*, and

Bramante's Saint Peter's Basilica are all prime examples of artistic grandeur par excellence, and, yes, many were motivated by their faith.

However, they overlook the fact that secular leaders, such as the Medicis, started or rather revived art patronage to beautify their city and to foster the public's appreciation, respect, and loyalty. The Vatican quickly emulated the Medici's success in Florence with stunning results.

Oddly enough, these religious authors hail the achievements in art and architecture as representing the pinnacle of human advancement in their respective fields, and all because of the cultivating nature of Christianity, for they posit that nothing remotely comparable had ever been achieved under pagan regimes.

Firstly, these glorious edifices were not surges of progress that arose out of thin air or Christian belief; it is blatantly obvious that the artists revived and mirrored earlier Roman grandeur, which arose when Rome was also under great leadership.

Christian architecture was entirely based upon Roman technology, to which the barrel vaults, groin vaults, and huge domes of many cathedrals, including Saint Peter's, clearly attest. Likewise the Christian visual arts revived classical Greco-Roman statuary. For example, Michelangelo studied Roman statuary, while the rich frescos and mosaics of ancient Roman ruins offered a "revivalist" starting point for all artisans during the Renaissance.

Secondly, these authors condemn the Romans for being builders of colossal edifices, which flaunted their own egos, all the while they cast stones from equally ostentatious cathedrals. But it seems that since their edifices glorify Christ, the ostentation was and is acceptable, even though they blatantly defy Jesus' humble words and actions. Jesus eschewed temples and often preached outdoors, and his patent condemnation of wealth and excess of any kind is well known. One cannot ignore how Jesus conducted his Sermon on the Mount, while mere popes conduct their sermons in the grandest and most flamboyant palace in the world.

Unfortunately these headstrong attacks on pagan edifices were simply due to religious bias. Quite blindly, they forgot that Pope Julius was deeply inspired by the greatness of pagan Rome, which yielded the magnificent St. Peter's. However, their own intolerance prohibited them from bestowing the slightest bit of praise on these ancient achievements simply because ancient Romans honored "false" gods. This view is sadly narrow-minded, especially from a modern perspective, since all gods of other religions are deemed false, while secularists are also debased for being heretics. Therefore, by sermonizing that only Christians are capable of great deeds and progress they instill the deadly flaw of underestimating their rivals. Adolf Hitler (secularist) and Osama bin Laden (Islamic Jihadist) are two prime examples of foes that were underrated, due to such arrogance or complacency, and the costs were high.

Intolerance exists on both sides, however, and as such, modern secularists bemoan how the mighty Christian church squelched Greek philosophy and mankind's ability to reason. Although the Greeks were, and still are, prided for their profound sense of reasoning, we must also consider another, less obvious, side of the coin.

Although the church wrongfully condemned certain aspects of Greek secular knowledge, which unquestionably contained many potent seeds to stimulate inquiry and intelligence, they did embrace and integrate Ptolemy's theory into scripture, thus blindly following the path of this so-called secular genius. The adoption and strict enforcement of Ptolemy's geocentric model crippled mankind's concept of the universe for almost two millennia. Therefore the grievances of these modern secularists warrant caution, for how crucial was Greek philosophy? After all, the Catholic Church did adopt this Greek hypothesis, which proved to be *universally* damaging and later caused the church much condemnation.

We must stop to consider that even the great Ptolemy, whom these critics and most historians proudly claim was Greek, gained much of his knowledge from Hipparchus. Hipparchus was a Turkish astronomer and mathematician who, three centuries before Ptolemy, compiled the first trigonometric table, calculated solar eclipses, and charted the movements of the Sun and Moon. Therefore, secular critics who worship Greek culture, and Ptolemy in particular, should understand three important facts: first, Ptolemy gained much of his insight from a Turkish scientist, among other sources; second, Ptolemy's flawed geocentric system was a Greek concept, adopted from Aristotle and Plato; and third, Ptolemy himself was not even Greek, he was Roman. Ptolemy lived from AD 87 to

150 in the Egyptian city of Alexandria, which was a province of the Roman Empire. Yet somehow this is overlooked.

This latter issue of labeling prominent historical figures as Greek is rather prevalent and likewise warrants examination. As mentioned earlier, this is most likely due to the fact that the genius of Homer, Euclid, Thucydides, Plato, Aristotle, and other Greeks (who are rightfully called founding fathers in the realm of literature, mathematics, and philosophy) have so enamored and influenced the halls and fraternities of academia that these institutions focus on whether the subsequent figures in history merely spoke, studied, or wrote Greek, rather than their new place or their unique actions in the timeline of history. In essence, they focus more on the initial Greek impetus or Greek words used to express these new ideas than the new ideas themselves. As such, they label many prominent figures as being Greek, simply because they spoke Greek, or even studied it, regardless of the fact that they lived in the Roman Empire while Greece had clearly ceased to exist.

To call these particular Roman men Greek is like calling a descendent of George Washington, who is living in today's United States well over two hundred years after the birth of our nation, British. In a more relevant instance, simply because Americans write in English and maintain certain English traits does not make them Englishmen. Hence, men like Ptolemy who were born in the Roman Empire (which had already been in existence for a hundred years) were Romans.

Authentic Greeks, including the two most popular philosophers, Plato and Aristotle, however, also made colossal blunders similar to Ptolemy's. As noted, Ptolemy's geocentric model was adopted from both of these great thinkers, who had formulated their idea centuries earlier. Because Ptolemy's book was widely published, his name was attached to this theory as if it were his own.

Plato and Aristotle both proclaimed that all planetary orbs follow a circular, rather than elliptical, path through the heavens. Not having the knowledge to calculate these paths, Greeks simply chose the circle for planetary orbits because it logically fit their aesthetic; namely, a circle formed a perfect geometric shape and thus they deduced that the universe must be built upon similar formulas of perfection. This Greek concept of circular perfection also stymied Copernicus when he devised his hypothesis almost two thousand years later, for even though he placed the sun at the center of his heliocentric diagram, he incorrectly displayed all the planetary orbits as perfect circles.

It is interesting to note that the Greek obsession for aesthetic ideals even carried over to their architecture, as Greek theaters were designed as perfect half-circles terraced into an earthbound hillside. In contrast, and unhampered by inflexible aesthetics or earthly restraints, the Romans built the Colosseum as an elliptical freestanding structure that defied gravity. In hindsight, this oddly mirrors the anomalous but pragmatic order of the universe. That planets defy gravity and revolve in elliptical orbits may at first seem illogical and imperfect, however, jettisoning preconceived notions of Grecian perfection yielded an efficient and long-lasting Roman model, which some today even call divine, especially architects of arenas.

Carrying the flawed Greek argument forward, only this time with more *gravity*, we must recall that Aristotle likewise made a huge blunder by positing his faulty, yet (in)famous, Law of Gravity. This purely hypothetical law prevailed in Western thought for as long as that of the earth-centered universe. Eschewing physical experimentation, Aristotle posited his law that heavier objects fall faster than lighter objects. It is quite entertaining how Aristotle himself said, "It is foolish to make confident statements about these matters if one does not devote a lot of time to them. It is useful practice to question every detail."

Unfortunately, to Aristotle's shame, not a single detail was questioned, and he certainly did not devote too much time in gathering proof. If he had simply dropped two objects of different weight, he would have instantly realized that his mentally conceived law was painfully wrong. Oddly enough, Aristotle's own logical words, in this particular instance, correctly labeled him "foolish."

Naturally, Aristotle was no lightweight, and he remains one of history's great thinkers, but since he did not physically test his theories, the great thinker made many blunders that inculcated the world with blinding fluff that had profound consequences. In essence, many others didn't perform this simple test (and thus disprove Aristotle) because the theory emanated from the mouth of the eminent Greek philosopher, who was virtually glorified as an oracle. In hindsight, this is a critical point, for the overwhelming majority of people are afraid to question authorities who supposedly possess and profess the truth.

However, these failures were due to the Greek penchant for being philosophical dreamers rather than strict scientific mathematicians. Although great mathematicians existed, like Euclid, the father of geometry, or the brilliant polymath Archimedes, most engaged in cosmic speculation that dispensed with practical experimentation. More importantly, many Greeks never realized the importance of mathematics in solving many of these issues. This was somewhat due to the embryonic state of mathematics, which severely crippled their endeavors. Therefore this critique does not expect the ancient Greeks to have known more than their era afforded them, but rather focuses on two issues: the heavy reliance on idyllic, aesthetic dreaming, and the lax and unquestioning attitude by (and toward) vociferous, yet often vacuous, oracles.

The term dreamer, however, is not used negatively here, for being a dreamer is an often-slighted discipline that is extremely crucial in the process of invention. It is a key ingredient in formulating a revolutionary hypothesis, as Einstein later revealed. However, it was the mathematical work of others, built upon Einstein's dream, that eventually developed atomic reactions and nuclear energy. It is through these strict scientific methodologies that visionary dreams can become manifest and proven valid. As such, the highly praised work of many Greek philosophers were often founded upon blind conjecture and established misconceptions about the Earth and the cosmos that lasted for hundreds and even thousands of years. These concepts could only be proven accurate or false upon the advent of pure mathematical procedure.

Although the Greeks and Arabs were pioneers in math, many anomalies caused severe limitations and obvious mistakes. Having no conception of the number zero caused many setbacks for the Greeks and Romans. The reawakening of man's mind to the importance of math would have to wait for Galileo to set the precedent firmly in place, well over a thousand years later. The first true mathematical wizard to follow in his footsteps was Sir Isaac Newton. *(See page 711)*

For secular historians to hail Greek philosophy and science as being the sole light of the ancient world, which they further bemoan was suppressed by the church, falls as quickly to the ground as the arguments of their equally fanatical and dead-weighted religious rivals who claim Christianity alone fostered science and productive intelligence. Basically, polar extremes are usually biased and severely flawed.

Greece is praised for its logic-based philosophy, and rightfully so, for beyond the severe blunders, it has had a profound and positive influence on all Western cultures. But we must remember that they simultaneously conceived and believed in perhaps one of the most peculiar set of gods in all of antiquity. The Olympians were gods with base human desires and foibles who engaged in rivalry, hatred, trickery, lust, and even incest. Almost every primal tribe or great civilization has developed a belief in gods who on the whole were models of perfection, strength, or some virtuous trait that all could attempt to emulate. The Greek's illogical creation and admiration of such ignoble characters remains an oddity.

Despite their unsavory gods, we have seen how certain aspects of Greek philosophy were adopted and integrated into Christian doctrine. Saint Augustine would later say, "If those who are called philosophers, and especially the Platonists, have aught that is true and in harmony with our faith, we are not only not to shrink from it, but claim it for our own use from those who have unlawful use of it."

Plato wrote much about the soul and the unseen afterlife, which he in turn partially adopted from the Egyptian Pharos. Once again, Greek traits, when put under a microscope, yield foreign influences. Nonetheless, even Christians had no qualms about taking Greek philosophy away from the pagan infidels, who interestingly enough had unlawful use of their own concepts. Again, power breeds arrogance. This holds true for most people, regardless of their religion, creed, or race.

Some Christians of antiquity were proudly cognizant of the fact that they were accumulating followers faster than their Greek philosophical rivals. This, they proclaimed, was because Greek philosophy was too difficult for the uneducated masses to comprehend, whereas, a Christian miracle worker won over large audiences instantaneously. Surprisingly enough, many evangelical congregations today still win over large audiences with this time-tested practice. In essence, when dealing with the masses, the wow factor or mere simplicity evidently triumphs over complex reasoning.

The theologian, Origen, in the early 200s after Christ, best summed this up, by stating, "The multitude, since they lacked the time or ability to pursue the study of rational argument, would be best served if they simply believe, without thinking out their own reasons." Unfortunately, Origen's advice stuck hard, as many today blindly parrot what they are cursorily taught. Furthermore, they do so without an inkling of the sandy specifics and cracking contradictions that comprise their religious foundation. Much fiction abounds, and every parishioner should know which truths to embrace and which truths are unfounded.

However, as the early Christians were winning the uneducated masses with miracles and the purity of the good word, they also realized that to attract inquisitive intellects they needed logic to coincide with blind faith. This integration of logic evolved over time, for the more the church gained power and influence, the more the intellects of the day gravitated to the religion and became clergymen. The church accumulated ancient texts, eventually depleted secular libraries and became the sole bastion for anyone seeking knowledge. The new sanctified intellects relished studying philosophy to better understand their religion, a noble quest that continues to this day.

Therefore during these early formative centuries of Christianity, many dynamics of adoption or interpretation were working in unison, which reshaped the religion and wielded influence. As noted, most of the analysis herein focuses on lesser known foibles or oddities, yet added to this spectacular rise to power was the all-important mission of spreading the gospel. Even three centuries after the birth of Christianity internal conflict persisted, yet the religion still managed to attract our pivotal character—thus once again, and conclusively, we are brought back to Constantine.

Historians and Christian leaders have always found Constantine to be a very complex man, one overflowing with contradictions. As such, he has always been difficult to fully categorize or embrace. Constantine had unequivocally engendered many positive and earth-shattering changes, yet the unavoidable fact that his reign was soiled with blood looms over his great name. Therefore, the question remains, how should Constantine be judged?

Constantine Reprise and Final Assessment

In AD 326, Constantine was confronted with the ugly allegation that his wife Fausta and his son Crispus engaged in an illicit affair. Such a scandalous betrayal and infamy was too much for any ordinary Roman, let alone the emperor, to handle, and as such, Constantine ordered their executions. Fausta was suffocated and allegedly scalded to death in her bath.

In the eyes of many modern scholars, Fausta's incestuous incident may elicit mild condemnation, yet Constantine's brutal reprisal incites disgust and harsh criticism. The covert manner in which Fausta was executed has added to the charge of Constantine being underhandedly cruel. However, both the indiscretion and the punishment were ugly, and we must always remember Constantine's era.

Not only were the practices of the pagans more severe than today, but so, too, were the punishments by the Jews and Christians. We must not forget how the Bible meted out harsh reprisals for incest or even homosexuality, such as in Leviticus 20:13, *"If a man also lie with mankind, as he lieth with a woman, both of them have committed an abomination: they shall surely be put to death; their blood shall be upon them."*

Therefore, if even the Bible championed severe punishment or even death for what it deemed sexual deviance, then we must not judge Constantine by today's standards, for it blurs our window on history and the realities that existed. Modern critics and readers forget or simply never realize what severe and brutal punishments existed in their own pious religion. Centuries of modifying harsh ancient traditions, including those found in our own Bible, has modern Americans believing that the Bible dictated our current predilections and civilized penal code. However, as noted, this is clearly not the case.

Beyond these penal codes, the majority of Roman emperors upheld the intense belief and duty of maintaining Rome's survival at all costs.

They also lived among a vastly uneducated and even treacherous lot, where assassinations occurred more frequently than today. Conspiracies or even immoral indignities, such as those committed by Constantine's wife and son, posed a threat to the order or stability of Rome's legacy and were dealt with swiftly and harshly. This was not unique to the Romans, as most other ancient civilizations shared a similar mindset.

Constantine's wife and son did not have their day in court and were sentenced without trial, but such traitorous acts would never be allowed to stain the emperor or empire, so punishment was swift. Despite all the reasoning posited so far, this incident still remains too harsh for some today to accept, and as such, it remains a gruesome black mark on Constantine's record. But depending upon the historical analyst, it could also be seen as an unfortunate yet understandable blemish.

Aside from this seedy affair, Constantine has also been branded as an egotistical opportunist. Some, especially Catholics, take umbrage with the fact that Constantine took the role of high priest, governing over all the bishops. Some see this rise above all other men as blasphemy. However, one only needs to look at the pope to see that he, too, holds the same *pontifex maximus* position. For today, Catholics still condone that one mortal man can be held divinely above all others. Granted, Constantine did not officially rise up through the church hierarchy in the proper fashion; however, upon reviewing the long list of popes throughout history who have despoiled the honor and dignity of that exalted seat, just how harshly can we judge Constantine?

In today's politically correct environment, many cannot accept the axiom that the end justifies the means. The mere mention of Machiavelli's maxim causes condemnation and outrage. Of course, this maxim can and has been taken out of context to the extreme, condoning wanton or capricious acts of debauchery for either personal glory or an aberrant concept of good, yet that negative connotation is not what is meant here.

The fact that he believed that he was chosen by God to perform religious acts does not negate that Constantine accomplished many pious and earth-shattering deeds for mankind—deeds that were moral, ethical, and humanitarian, and despite several centuries of severe setbacks, they were deeds that ultimately enhanced civilization. This is not to say that we can turn Constantine's wrongs into rights, but rather placing him on the scales of justice, we find that those good deeds clearly outweigh his misdeeds.

While pagan religions were certainly not devoid of instilling morals, Christianity did morally groom many future leaders, along with the lives of millions of people, and would have remained in the minority if Constantine had not taken action. And while some may argue that Christianity eventually developed into an intolerant regime that enforced its faith and squelched secular knowledge, that transition occurred after Constantine's legitimate precedent. In his own words, he sought to establish "peace and concord" among all the empire's peoples and religions. Backing that up, Constantine's decrees never forced religious conversion, nor did he wage holy wars or enact inquisitions; instead his pioneering Edict of Milan offered freedom of religion to all.

Naturally, Constantine's Catholic prototype did deteriorate, until finally, only greed, power, and intolerance ruled for many centuries. Those vile mutations occurred by future hands, but they were eventually corrected in large measure. Moreover, the Crusades, Inquisition and infighting between Protestants, Catholics etc. did not consume or involve every Christian in their day. The radiant light of Jesus' message may have been partially eclipsed, but it did eventually prevail, and the influences that Christianity had, and still has today, are considerable.

What is undisputable, however, is that Constantine ran a tight and sturdy ship, and did what he felt was necessary for the religion and the empire, as well as his own ambitions. As the dusk of his life approached Constantine knew it was time to make amends. As such, the emperor finally sanctioned his own baptism upon his deathbed— a practice that was not altogether unusual at the time. However, Constantine most likely knew the baptismal cleansing of his soul could only occur after he had completed all the dubious deeds of his divine mission. Then again, it may have been a calculated gesture to incite his devout pagan followers to reflect upon their great leader's final decision, which was to officially and completely immerse himself into the Christian faith. Hence, his tainted Sol Invictus skin would now be forever cleansed by the baptismal waters of Christianity.

Nevertheless, the Emperor was buried in the Church of the Holy Apostles in Constantinople, which was specifically built as his mausoleum. Inside the cathedral were twelve empty sarcophagi, symbolic of the twelve apostles. Yet the great Constantine ordered that his body be interred in a thirteenth sarcophagus in the very center. This bold, yet considered by many to be profane, gesture typifies the god-like man who not only reshaped Christianity but also enabled it to thrive. Constantine had previously preferred to be called *Isapostolos* or 'Equal of the Apostles.' In his burial, it seems Constantine chose to even exceed their authority.

Some Christians today may still denounce these actions as irreverent, yet it is uncontestable that Constantine was as crucial to the rise and eventual dominance of Christianity as any of the apostles, and in reality, even more so. The missionary work of Saint Paul was crucial to the initial alteration and spread of Christianity, but it had only become a ten percent minority after three hundred years of proselytizing. This is when Constantine arrived and took the passive lamb by the ears. Hence, without Constantine's unprecedented gifts of unbridled power, ample funding, tax exemptions, legal endorsements, and integration into the empire's political infrastructure, Christianity would most likely never have been transformed into the dominant lion that majestically ruled over Europe and beyond.

Constantine's Christian burial in Constantinople left many pagan citizens in Rome and the Senate understandably baffled. It is not hard to visualize the assemblage of senators sitting in the great hall in Rome staring up at the huge statue of Victoria (the goddess of victory, who had outspread wings and outstretched hands holding a laurel wreath) and pondering her impotence, and their own unstable futures. Regardless, the pagan Senate deified the recently baptized emperor, who in essence ruled both the pagan and Christian domains.

It appears that the Senate had realized and even grew to appreciate that the emperor achieved the noble goal of unifying the empire, even if sharply breaking with their pagan tradition. It almost seemed a win-win situation, since the quasi peace enamored the citizens, who in turn respected the Senate. Nevertheless, the shift of power toward Constantinople would become a scar that would grow and cause much resentment in the West. We cannot minimize how crucial this new capital city was, for the East would be the lifeboat that enabled the Empire to survive another thousand years after the Western "Titanic" sank.

To this day, Constantine is regarded as a saint in Eastern Orthodox churches and his feast day is celebrated on September 3. However, Christianity's Western nucleus, stationed at the Vatican in Rome, still refuses to acknowledge Constantine's sainthood. Even though Constantine secured their power, the West ironically cultivated a bias against him, just like some of the ancient pagans had in the Roman Senate. As such, the mighty Vatican cast the colossal persona of Constantine into its shadow. This is literally evident to this day.

If you enter Saint Peter's in Rome, you might, with any luck, notice a locked gate. If you peer through the slotted wrought iron, you will see a huge statue of Constantine riding on horseback. This equestrian statue beautifully captures that significant moment when Constantine saw the apparition at the Milvian Bridge. Nevertheless, this grand statue of Constantine quite symbolically remains locked behind the ungrateful prison-like bars of the mighty Roman Catholic Church.

Constantine had also played a crucial role in the formulation of the Vatican's own Bible. Early Christian texts had been plagued with many variations and editions, and Constantine aimed to correct this unprofessional convention. Often they were copied with errors, large and small, ranging from truly important verses to merely simple mistakes in spelling or grammar. Some original Greek words were copied incorrectly—the word "evil" was mistakenly transcribed later as the Greek word meaning "sexual deviance," which was similar in spelling. Some verses were clearly added to scripture, as later copies contain verses that older ones do not. One was of a woman adulterer. She was brought before Jesus by her accusers who were looking to trap the Messiah into a conflict of core theology. They knew that God commanded in the Old Testament that adulterers should be stoned to death, however Jesus preached love, compassion, and forgiveness. When they confronted Jesus, he told whoever was free of sin to cast the first stone.

While this was happening, Jesus was said to have been scribbling words in the sand, presumably pointing out the accusers' sins, yet the words in the sand were never spoken. The accusers saw the words and in humiliation, left the scene, leaving the adulterous woman standing alone and unharmed. Jesus then absolved the woman of sin. Interestingly enough, this verse, as it appears in the Gospel of John, was actually added later by an unknown hand and is not to be found in the earliest known version. Whether this tale is fact or fiction remains anybody's guess.

Most modern theological scholars concur that the earlier editions were undoubtedly closer to the original source, and the newer copies contain added verses. Whether these additions make significant theological alterations to doctrine remains a matter for personal analysis, but the fact put forth here is that many alterations and errors in translation or transliteration exist in our present day Bible. Furthermore, we must remember that since Jesus never wrote down any of his sermons, his words and deeds were all handed down to us by the recollections of his apostles many decades after his death, and they in turn were recopied and translated into several languages, such as Aramaic, Greek, Latin, and English over centuries.

The number of copies and translations that abounds is staggering. Worse yet, the early centuries of the religion were marked by common scribes who were only moderately competent in copying texts. They were certainly not professionals by any means, nor did they understand the words or the theology as deeply as the religious scribes who materialized centuries later. These later scribes were actually theological scholars, yet eventually this crucial task fell into the hands of the scholarly monks who dedicated themselves to meticulous accuracy.

The art of faithful translation becomes all the more difficult when dealing with ancient languages that had limited palettes of words. As such, some words of the source text had meanings that could not be exactly duplicated by the destination language. It is like trying to create the color green (which can only be made by mixing yellow and blue) when the source palette only offers yellow and red. The task is extremely difficult, as it can only approximate not replicate the source.

This is especially true when transcribing from Hebrew to Greek, or from either of those languages into Latin. Even well trained scholars made mistakes, as we shall see soon enough. But the reality of the Bible's long and checkered journey clearly indicates that it is simply unrealistic and exceedingly improbable that these sacred words are fully accurate and unchanged from their inception. Constantine recognized this flawed tradition and he wisely instructed Eusebius to assemble fifty definitive Bibles. This judicious act was the very start of scholars becoming professional copyists, giving rise to the very competent scriptoria that thankfully emerged. This once again demonstrates another of Constantine's vital contributions to the religion.

Several decades later, in AD 382, Jerome was ordered by Pope Damasus to translate the existing Hebrew and Greek Bibles into a single Latin "Vulgate" Bible. The Latin *vulgate* refers to the vernacular language of the common people. The following is from Jerome's letter to the pope regarding this onerous task.

"You urge me to make a new work from the old, and that I might sit as a kind of judge over the versions of Scripture dispersed throughout the whole world, and that I might resolve which among such vary, and which of these they may be which truly agree with the Greek. Pious work, yet perilous presumption, to change the old and aging language of the world, to carry it back to infancy, for to judge others is to invite judging by all of them. Is there indeed any learned or unlearned man, who when he picks up the volume in his hand, and takes a single taste of it, and sees what he will have read to differ, might not instantly raise his voice, calling me a forger, proclaiming me now to be a sacrilegious man, that I might dare to add, to change, or to correct anything in the old books?"

Jerome validates the fact that even in the hands of competent scribes, slight changes or alterations naturally occurs, especially during translations from one language to another. Jerome was well versed in Greek and Latin, yet knew little Hebrew. He even relocated to Jerusalem to immerse himself in their language as an aid to his daunting task.

Many centuries later, in 1515, Erasmus was put to the task of forming a Bible from various Greek texts, including Jerome's Vulgate Bible, to form yet another Bible. A century later, even Erasmus' Bible would be copied and edited to produce the popular King James Edition. It is the King James Version that is used by most English-speaking countries to this day, which again makes clear how far removed our version is from the original sources. Therefore, we must be mindful of the key role Constantine played in assuring accuracy to biblical texts that had been inaccurately copied and scattered about the empire for three hundred years. Just how many inaccuracies exist can only be left to the imagination, yet we have Constantine to thank for taking logical measures to insure authenticity and fidelity, at least from that moment onward.

There has been much debate in recent years, especially after Dan Brown's earth-shattering book *The Da Vinci Code*, about Constantine and early Christianity itself. Granted, much of Dan Brown's novel was based on conjecture and pure fiction, but he did open up many people's minds to a truly obscure past. Many today have risen hard and fast against Brown, and the notion of questioning the religious past, however we must realize the importance of investigating the past to reveal the truth. As Winston Churchill said, "History is written by the victors." This doesn't always equate to the most truthful or accurate retelling, for the ancient world primarily lived under the notion that "might is right."

It is a noble endeavor to open our eyes and investigate for ourselves, rather than close our eyes and blindly accept whatever has been strategically positioned in front of us. Likewise, it is foolish to adopt the insecurities of those fearful of uncovering the past, as ugly or positively enlightening as that might be. For according to Thomas, Jesus said:

"*Let him who seeks continue seeking until he finds. When he finds, he will become troubled. When he becomes troubled, he will be astonished, and he will rule over all.*"

Therefore, it is prudent that we all continue the perpetual quest for enlightenment. Having done so in the past, many tantalizing curiosities and even blindly accepted notions that have persisted in Christian dogma and rhetoric for centuries were unveiled, and we now realize that much has been crafted or silenced. Scholars and theologians will be busy for many more centuries determining whether these falsehoods have been deceitfully fabricated, mistakenly posited, or by odd chance divinely bestowed for some unknown purpose. Perhaps imparting a childhood analogy will offer hope.

Children are led to believe in Saint Nicholas for the sound reasons that it demonstrates how good behavior is rewarded and it instills the notions of good will, love, and generosity; but cold reality strikes painfully hard when they finally realize that the benevolent old man was just a grand illusion. They initially don't understand why the deceptive fantasy was created, but later take solace in knowing that the lesson learned outweighs the falsehood. Hence, wisdom can be gained via deception.

Therefore, we might even feel that Constantine was a deceptive and false saint; however, wisdom can be gained by evaluating his munificent deeds and numerous gifts. Constantine's colossal imprint on world history defies comprehension, as does the negation of his place in religious history by the Vatican. Constantine single-handedly enabled Christianity to proliferate in ways that no assortment of clergymen could ever match. His adoption, protection, scriptural transformation, and organizational reconstruction that endowed bishops with political legislative powers, were all acts of empowerment that no one on earth but an emperor could provide. This imperial secular action is what makes the Vatican refuse to look at itself and admit their indebtedness to a pagan Roman emperor, even though he converted and made an immense contribution.

Regardless, soon bishops were rising in influence and power that spawned a reversal in aggression and discrimination that would blossom in about a hundred years after Constantine's Nicene Council. The Theodosian Code was passed in AD 438 that included an article to penalize bishops and Christians who might unlawfully or even violently attack or plunder any peaceful and law-abiding pagans or Jews. This elucidates how Constantine's laws and councils empowered bishops and the Christian community far beyond what any religion separated from state could possibly marshal. Constantine's legal and financial empowerment of Christianity and his bold decision to relocate the empire's capital to Constantinople (that later became a significant bastion of preserving Western thought amid the Dark Ages) mark two of a mere few earth-shattering milestones of Western history.

There is still another major event that has not been mentioned, for the powerful name of Constantine would emerge four centuries after his death to enact another monumental event in world history. This fascinating event caused a major mutation in the church, and it, too, has remained out of the catechism and neatly stored in silence.

In the year AD 755, Stephen, the bishop of Rome, was faced with a precarious situation, for the Italian peninsula had lost much power and wealth as many migrated to Constantine's new capital city in Constantinople. This crucial move had made the Byzantine part of the empire thrive, while Rome and the western provinces fractured and weakened. As the centuries unfolded this gave rise to many small kingdoms in the West that were not firmly united. Therefore, Stephen needed to establish a power alliance if Rome was to stay alive.

Stephen was an old man, but he and his clergy were clever; in fact, more than clever, they were devious tacticians. Their plot was to use Constantine's powerful name to subdue their enemies, and also empower Rome. More importantly, however, was the goal of elevating Stephen's own personal seat within the hierarchy of Christendom.

Stephen called upon his trusty clergyman, Christophorous, who was an astute writer with a vivid imagination. Christophorous ingeniously fabricated a historical document entitled *The Donation of Constantine*. This purely fictitious document proclaimed that during Constantine's reign, Saint Peter's heir (the bishop of Rome) cured the emperor of the plague. For this miraculous feat, Constantine decided not only to donate Rome to the bishop, but also to empower him to rule over all other bishops. In gratitude for his life, the text continued, Constantine established the new capital of Constantinople in order to continue his rule there. Moreover, Constantine proclaimed that he, too, would be subservient to the bishop of Rome, who from that moment forward would rule over both the temporal and spiritual domains. The bishop's new lofty position would be called "Pope."

This was a fabrication of astronomical proportions, yet a truly miraculous event was to follow. When bishop Stephen approached King Pepin of the Franks with this fallacious document, not only did Pepin take the bait and become his ally, but so, too, did the reigning emperor in the Byzantine capital—who legally held rule over these lands, which were ordained by centuries of Roman precedence. This extremely outlandish yet successful ploy officially inaugurated the supreme office of pope.

It must be noted that although the term pope (from Latin *papa*, meaning father) was sometimes used earlier, it did not denote the supreme significance and exclusivity of ultimate control that it would now enjoy with Stephen's masterful "Constantine" plot. It was this pivotal action that made opportunists flock from all parts of the scattered empire to Rome, for this new and most exalted Seat of St. Peter held control over all other bishops as well as their parishioners and their combined wealth.

As fate would have it, King Pepin's son was none other than Charlemagne, whose crucial role in protecting this papal seat by engaging in warfare is well documented, and it was a sign of the bloody times that would soon follow for Christianity. Charlemagne was born in what today is Belgium; he was crucial in formulating the territories that would later become France and Germany. There is some controversy as to whether or not Charlemagne wanted Pope Leo III to crown him emperor, yet he was certainly aware of the beautiful gold crown that sat nearby, while praying in St. Peter's basilica that day. Moreover, when the pope did crown him emperor Charlemagne offered no objections. Pope Leo III's gesture was more than mere kindness, it was meant to strip the Byzantine emperor in the east of power, whereby strengthening Rome and the papacy.

Eventually King Charlemagne's son Louis was crowned heir to his kingdom, and it would be Louis's sons who would splinter and divide the kingdom into what became known as the Holy Roman Empire. The growing importance of the kingdoms of France and Germany would reveal themselves in the coming centuries, thus leading into the turbulent Middle Ages.

Nevertheless, Charlemagne respected the pope's rule, as established by his father's earlier alliance, and was the key defender for the pope's lofty new position. This immensely powerful seat of spiritual and temporal rule was now the grandest prize the world had to offer. As such, power mongers all vied for the position and many bloody battles ensued between rival factions.

In the frenzy for power, this new Seat of Saint Peter also became the target for blood sport. One opportunist was just a layman. He miraculously had himself ordained as a cleric and rose up through the ranks of pope all in one day. He was instantly dethroned, however. In the meantime, another contender took the seat, but was brutally murdered, as rivals gouged his eyes out. Others held the office for short terms only to face the recurring fate of assassination, as the turbulent and bloodstained years rolled on, thus creating what became known as the Dark Ages. The origins of this miraculous position of divine power, however, are all linked to the powerful name of Constantine.

Hence, without Constantine, Western civilization would most certainly have been devoid of the Christian dominance that shaped the future world considerably. Constantine organized and united a chaotic assemblage of bishops, filled their coffers, secured new real estate for the church, inaugurated architectural practices for church construction, built the original and pivotal St. Peter's basilica, empowered the church with legal programs, bestowed judicial powers upon the bishops, indirectly formed the seat of pope, and he firmly tattooed the symbol of the religion onto the Christian faith and the military. However, future popes would transform Constantine's use of the cross from imperial conquest into religious intolerance, domination, and submission. Constantine enabled Christian bishops to rise above the Senate and eventually partnering with future emperors and kings, ultimately wrested control, conquered Europe and became the all-powerful Roman Catholic Empire.

As seen, in the case of the *Donation of Constantine*, even future kings and emperors respected the wishes of their great predecessor, Constantine, who was an able politician, an undefeated military leader, and a religious icon. We have seen the many earth-shattering changes that Constantine enacted, however, he also made many small contributions, such as his acts of charity. Constantine offered the empire's grain to feed the needy, the sick, as well as the unjustly exiled or tortured. Additionally, he helped the bishops establish churches that offered hope and tangible community services to a needy public.

Furthermore, unlike many emperors, kings, or czars, Constantine made sure the imperial treasury was an open vault, for he said to his bishops, "Ask without hesitation whatever [funds] you find to be necessary."

As such, Constantine certainly made every effort to do the right thing, despite tainted or brutal necessities, to achieve his ultimate goal. Considering these facts, Constantine is largely viewed as one of the ultimate leaders of Rome, a major force within Christianity, and an overall prime mover in Western civilization.

As Machiavelli said, "There is nothing more difficult to manage, or more doubtful of success, or more dangerous to handle than to take the lead in introducing a new order of things."

Constantine took the lead and faced overwhelming opposition from an overwhelmingly pagan empire to introduce a new Christian order, one that he managed to mediate and legislate, even against difficult odds, and he succeeded. Christianity undoubtedly prevailed, and Constantine survived, despite dangerous threats of assassination. Hence, Constantine overcame Machiavelli's extremely dangerous and highly doubtful challenge.

Therefore, despite his many failings, and those who abhor his end results, Constantine commandingly resides on that extreme summit of world influence where only a very select few reside. Perhaps it is only fitting that the name Constantine means constancy, firmness, and solidity, for Constantine exemplified all these qualities. From his faithfulness to his Christian cause, to the firmness of his leadership, to the solidity of uniting church and empire, his efforts and successes remain colossal.

In the final analysis, Constantine's name simply means "constant," and quite appropriately, his influence has unquestionably remained constant.

❄ ❄ ❄

Constantine and the long complex history of Rome and its fusion with Christianity are endlessly fascinating and multifaceted topics, which are often viewed from many different perspectives. The attempt herein has been to reveal religious facts from a historical and factual perspective, rather than a spiritual one based upon faith alone. This is because faith no longer means a faith solely in Jesus, for the wealth of knowledge available to us makes it very clear that primary sources are scant, often contradictory, and as such, they spawned a sea of dubious scriptures.

Therefore, Christians today literally worship texts written by fallible men half a century after Jesus, which were translated, judged, and edited by other fallible men two centuries later. Even they had to work with second-generation copies, as no originals exist. Faith therefore extends beyond Jesus, onto these men's deeds. This precarious leap of faith prompted Thomas Jefferson to extract only the passages that he believed Jesus spoke, rather than be misled by the contrivances of his followers. Such a task has stymied many, however Jefferson called locating Jesus' words in the Bible as difficult as spotting "diamonds in a dunghill."

For nearly two millennia, the church has groomed its congregations with a pristine version of antiquity. The story of Jesus has been crafted into a single seamless story, without conflicts of interest or ideology. As we've seen, that was not true then and is still not true today. Evangelists and neo-Christian sects are born almost daily with their own "truthful" message. Some even preach the word of Jesus in arena-sized cathedrals and collect huge sums of money to expand their church, their own pockets, and the size of their opulent palaces. From what we do know of Jesus, if he walked the earth today, he would certainly topple their glittering collection tables and instruct these practitioners to give their immense profits to the poor.

Yet even when some of these pastors are found guilty of unscrupulous activities or outright sins, the complacent masses who are accustomed to and prefer having others read and interpret the gospels for them, fall prey to their own failings and embrace their fallen angels. The names of three Jims reverberate among the fallen— Jim Jones, Jim Bakker, and Jim Swaggart. The Jim Jones case, in which he brainwashed his congregation to commit suicide, was not only sad and tragic but also pathetically shocking. As for those that were deceived by adulterous or avaricious pastors, to be forgiving is one thing but to be foolhardy is another. Meanwhile others follow reverends that spew racial hatred and unconsciously consume sin rather than contest it. In essence, ignorance, complacency, and or hopelessness are mankind's enemies in the quest to find truth, happiness, and salvation.

No doubt, religion is a highly sensitive topic, and the commentary herein will ruffle the feathers of some Christians, however the intent is not to incite anger but prompt serious reflection and reevaluation. Historical evidence has been unveiled throughout these pages that questions not only Christianity but Judaism and Islam as well. During this dissertation, even secular ideologies have been criticized that perhaps leave some readers wondering where, if at all, does God fit into this whole equation. That valid question warrants attention.

Who Truly is God?

While it is true that the existence of God cannot be absolutely proven with human logic, it is also true that humanity's cognitive limitations simply prove that God can exist. Men have often believed that they were the end-all, the philosophical savant, the mirror image, the blessed prophet, the infallible scribe, the chosen flock; some have even believed that they themselves were divine. However, from a rational standpoint, the truth is mankind has little to no irrefutable evidence to base these assumptions on. Furthermore, no one can declare with total certainty that his or her particular God is *The* God. This haggling over who is and who isn't the true God, as well as declaring sole ownership, explains why so many so-called indisputable truths have been posited—not only among different religions but within those religions as well—and conflicting truths only confirm true doubt.

At this point, it is crucial that we ask ourselves some serious questions. Has mankind explored the entirety of the universe? This question may sound odd or irrelevant, but the answer is a resounding NO. Therefore, if mankind knows nothing about the vast unknowns of space, with its many untold secrets and mysteries, then how can we have the audacity to think we can fully understand something as universally vast and mysterious as God?

Mankind's attempt to understand this grand phenomenon is like an ordinary ten-year-old child attempting to read and understand Einstein's theory of relativity. That child might acquire only the most superficial understanding, however, even if the basic core idea were somewhat understood, the child would never be able to say with total confidence and utter truth that they fully understood what was just read.

Similarly, for millions of people, many stories in the Bible have presented far more perplexing questions than logical answers, such as Adam and Eve being the sole parents of all mankind–whose sinfully incestuous children spawned the human race. Noah and his miraculously filled ark—with thousands of species of mammals, birds, and insects—that were spared God's wrathful Flood, for he allegedly *regretted* making the vast majority of his flawed creations, and then in a fit of rage, exterminated life on Earth. The sinful Tower of Babel, which was erected in the first city to arise after God's error-cleansing Flood, yet once again, God allegedly failed to make obedient creations and punished mankind by "confounding their languages". The advent of Jesus and the mysterious three-is-one, one-is-three Trinity; or even the Resurrection, which no other religious group witnessed or recorded, yet only a few Christian witnesses allegedly did, and the list goes on.

Beyond the Bible, however, even the sciences, including the Big Bang theory (which states that perfectly shaped and orderly solar systems, with revolving planets in fixed orbits, all somehow formed out of a supernova's chaotic explosion) or even the theory of evolution, offer no absolute answer to our most baffling question– that of creation. But somehow, we are here, and when we contemplate the vastness and complexity of the universe, with its trillions of stars, galaxies, quasars, comets, and planets—in their precise and complex clockwork-driven paths—containing unknown gases, rocks, metals, or even alien life forms, be it bacteria or something highly advanced, it becomes all the more clear that something had to give birth to all of this, and certainly nothing as mindless as a Big Bang, but something magnificent, which is far beyond the miniscule limits of our microscopic intelligence.

Speaking of our microscopic or bird-brained intelligence aptly shifts our gaze from the vast heavens down to our own small planet. This brings to mind the often used, yet little contemplated, phrase, "Which came first, the chicken or the egg?" This simple, profoundly deep question has baffled mankind for thousands of years, and it has best been answered with the single response, "God." But, which God? There has been a plethora of gods in antiquity and a sprawling sea of gods from a global community far larger than the small Middle Eastern nucleus where Judaism, Christianity, and Islam originated. One must also contemplate that these three major religions developed in a small territorial zone (also explaining similarities that no other religions share), and that must be contrasted with the far larger Asian territory—with its Buddhist, Taoist, and Hindu gods, as well as Confucianism—and the entire western hemisphere, with its Native American, Aztec, Mayan, and Peruvian civilizations who had their own huge assortment of gods. Upon visualizing this immense global view, along with its panoply of glittering gods, one must ask, why are there so many gods? Why all this confusion, and who was responsible? Was it God or mankind?

Returning to the small territorial nucleus of the Judeo-Christian heritage, we must also ask, why were the Jews the chosen people? Why did the Christians become the new chosen people? Why did Jesus negate salvation to Jews or anyone who does not enter his kingdom through him? Why did Muhammad and in turn, Islam, also negate salvation to both its Judaic and Christian roots? Further still, why do some Protestants and Lutherans negate salvation to Catholics?

These profound questions are merely presented to the reader to best answer for his or her own self. In essence, all humans are like adopted children on planet Earth, and we each must seek our true Creator, yet we must not blindly accept what our personal tradition or even humanly created or humanly pre-selected scriptures dictate, but rather use our own God-given logic to best surmise who God truly is. When we realize that Einstein was an agnostic and many brilliant thinkers, like the founding fathers, all had varying degrees of doubts about the total accuracy of the Old Testament, with its jealous and spiteful God, or the divinity of Jesus in the New Testament, we know that we stand in good company while searching for the truth. Henceforth, it is most fervently hoped that a deeper inquiry begins— at least for those that recognize the anomalies and contradictions —and that your particular God, once revealed, is a loving God. On that most serious note, we leave the mysteriously dense realm of God and religion and return to the prevailing winds of time.

The many centuries following Constantine are certainly not without interest, however, since our narrative focuses on the most significant events that shaped Western civilization, these bleak centuries have only been briefly touched upon during this chapter and will be again during the course of this narrative in flashbacks, during which we will draw conclusions in reference to these dark times. As such, we now move on to the tail end of the Middle Ages, when the seeds of rebirth were beginning to sprout buds that would eventually blossom into the Renaissance.

Here, perhaps more than anywhere else in history, the embryonic stage of the pre-Renaissance beautifully elucidates how studying history spurred people to break the chains of misfortune, enabling them to gallop forward and master their own destinies. The dark and plagued world preceding it, in part, offered that impetus. Immersed in a world that seemed damned and doomed, leaders sought new ways to rule, entrepreneurially-minded men sought power through commerce, architects looked back to an illustrious past, and men of letters and philosophy analyzed the chaos in order to impart a message of hope. It is under this black veil that we come upon the most influential and profound writer of the Middle Ages, Dante Alighieri.

V

PART 1:
1320 – 1600. MIDDLE AGES AND THE AGE OF REBIRTH

The Spark at Dawn
DANTE – *Morals, the Italian language and literature*
The Radiant Light
DA VINCI – *The Renaissance Man*
Debunking Modern Revisions of the Renaissance
THE MEDICI: *True Architects of the Renaissance*
GUTENBERG – *Dissemination*
BRUNELLESCHI – *Engineering*
COLUMBUS – *Exploration*
A New World | Its American Name | Its Detractors
KING FERDINAND – *Spanish Empire*
QUEEN ELIZABETH I – *English Empire*
SHAKESPEARE – *English Literature*
GALILEO – *Mathematics & Censorship*

(Quinque, Leo, Issachar, Philip, May)

The Spark at Dawn

DANTE ALIGHIERI: A relentless breeze rippled over the banks of the Ronco River and throughout Ravenna. Sitting at his wooden desk, Dante could hear the rustling of trees outside his window. He had put the final touches on his *Divina Commedia* only weeks before and was now getting ready to depart for Bologna.

Dante had recently received an invitation from the Latin professor, Giovanni del Virgilio, of Bologna's famous university. Penning some last-minute thoughts about a current poem, Dante wanted to make sure he harvested the ripe fruits of inspiration before they withered and died. He then meticulously collated the parchments and placed them in perfect parallel to his Bible.

The Middle Ages and the Age of Rebirth

Grasping his deeply treasured rosary beads, Dante looked down at them and paused. A warm grin etched his chiseled features. The beads had belonged to his beloved mother who died when he was only six. Dante reverently kissed them twice, then hung them on a brass-angel wall hook.

Wrapping his red *lucco* around his shoulders, he pulled the tie strings and wove a neat knot. Grasping his small leather satchel, Dante turned to inspect the room one last time. Noticing the bronze crucifix on the wall was slightly crooked, Dante leveled it, crossed himself, and then exited.

On his way to Bologna Dante reflected upon his first visit there, which had developed into a two-year stint several years earlier. Nevertheless, upon his arrival Dante learned that his invitation was for the express purpose of being awarded Bologna's illustrious laurel crown. Dante cordially informed Giovanni del Virgilio that he appreciated the reward but preferred waiting for that great honor to be bestowed upon him by his beloved city of Florence. Giovanni, aware that Dante was exiled from Florence, must have pleaded with the great poet to give up his fanciful dream, after all, Florence, that most beautiful flower, was under the black thumb of a corrupt pope, so why cling to her fallen petals?

Dante's tumultuous life and eventual exile from Florence by the pope will be addressed soon enough, but this illustrious award was predicated on many aspects of Dante's miraculous genius, but particularly for his epic work the *Divina Commedia*, or in English *Divine Comedy*.

Dante made bold advances on several fronts, first, by abandoning Latin to use the common Italian vernacular. Saint Francis of Assisi was actually the first to attempt this, for he wrote his song *Canticle of the Sun* in Italian some eighty years previously. Both men must have found the Italian tongue more pleasing for the beauty of its tone, but more importantly it had become the new language of the common people. Meanwhile, Latin had become more and more reserved for the clergy and intelligentsia. Therefore, all learned people wrote in Latin, however Dante wanted his work to be read by the masses, to the chagrin of most of his haughty peers. Furthermore, in time, Dante's influential work would actually define the Italian language, as it had been plagued by many different dialects previously, depending upon location or even social status. With other medieval poets following Dante's precedent, the Italian language, as we know it today, was born.

Second, Dante invented a new poetic invention called *terza rima* to construct the *Divine Comedy*. *Terza rima* was not simply a chain rhyme scheme that carried one rhyme over to the following stanza, for it also had a religious connotation. Consisting of three lines, *terza rima* was indicative of the *Holy Trinity*. Dante further supported this triplet structure when he divided the *Divine Comedy* into three main *canticas* or canticles: *Inferno, Purgatory* and *Paradise*. Each of these canticles consisted of 33 *cantos*, thus repeating and reinforcing the *Trinity* through the number 3, as well as possibly referring to Jesus' alleged age of 33 when he died. Dante's *terza rima* would prove to have its own unique poetical allure, as it was later adopted and utilized by Petrarca, Boccaccio, Chaucer, Milton, Byron, Shelley, and even twentieth century poets, including T.S. Eliot and Clark Ashton Smith among others. Oddly enough, this author/artist created the cover art for *three* of Clark Ashton Smith's reissued fantasy books.

Finally, Dante visualized the enormity and complexity of God's universe in a way that no Biblical scripture had. Dante's vivid account of Hell, in the *Inferno* canticle, was conceived as nine descending circles, each lower ring imprisoning sinners of greater magnitude until finally reaching the deepest and darkest pit of Hell. This is where the three-headed monster with wings (Satan) gnaws on the three ultimate sinners: Judas Iscariot (the traitor of Jesus Christ), along with Brutus and Cassius (the two traitors of Julius Caesar). The former king representing the ultimate Lord that spoke of his Kingdom of Heaven, who was betrayed and crucified, and the latter king representing the supposed ultimate lord on Earth who was likewise betrayed and assassinated. Interestingly enough, each king being unable to achieve the desired kingdom they preached about, as many today still await Jesus' Kingdom of Heaven, which St. Paul told his followers would appear in their lifetime but never did, while Rome would never see an empire truly envisioned by Julius Caesar. Here again, their missions would be left in the hands of their respective followers to design the religious and political superstructures that would carry on their visions of religious brotherhood and secular government, neither winning over the entire world, but certainly vast portions of it.

Despite all three canticles being ingeniously conceived and well written, Dante's *Inferno* would generate the most attention; naturally, since the evils of the world have always been more intriguing to the masses. Where the ancient Romans were drawn to watching the bloody carnage in the Colosseum, modern Americans are drawn to watching bloody kickboxing matches, where combatants ruthlessly batter and bloody up their opponents. Even those not content to witness live boxing matches eagerly watch horror films where evil villains hack apart innocent victims with chainsaws, hatchets, and other dreadful tools of death. Hence, the ravenous thirst to watch mankind attack and destroy itself resounds throughout history. Even the more civil are drawn to watching the evening news, whose programmers likewise cater to their audience's thirst for violence and dreadful bad news. With such entrepreneurs throughout time catering to the masses' primal needs it's no wonder mankind has not progressed in the most important capacity, to be humane.

Therefore this innate evil trait, to commit evil, or at least have the desire to promote it or watch it, has great significance to Dante's *Divine Comedy*. Unlike his two great predecessors, Homer and Virgil, Dante broke tradition with his grand epic by having himself appear as the lead character that travels through the *Inferno*, then *Purgatory*, and ultimately arriving in *Paradise*. Rather than great warriors or leaders making precarious odysseys to ultimately achieve greatness, Dante presents himself as the common journeyman who is guided by the brilliant, pagan poet Virgil; who happened to have been Dante's idol. In this way, any reader, from high to low esteem, could readily associate with Dante and his amazing journey.

However, despite Dante's astonishing journey being otherworldly it has as its core a practical theme, namely, that we all must confront evil and contend with sin in order to reach Heaven. We are showed all the various types of sin imaginable and can readily pause at those that we may have considered or even committed, even if only on a minor level. We are then presented with the consequences for those sins, whereby making us pause once again to consciously avoid committing that sin or seek redemption if we have erred. Meanwhile, those that simply like to watch all these various evil doers and their unique punishments, whether innocent or guilty themselves, get to see both Satan's and God's handiwork in action.

However, in reality, it is Dante's handiwork, for Dante has utilized artistic license to the ultimate degree by not only prescribing the punishment for the condemned but also judging characters that happened to be historic figures of the past or, more boldly, his own contemporaries. Therefore, the reader travels through Hell not only witnessing horrible monsters or shocking visions but is also confronted with the reality that it is *we*, mankind, that are wicked, and there a many ugly punishments we can face depending upon the degree of sin committed. Most ominously, all sinners are excluded from God's grace, as Dante powerfully reminds his readers with a placard chiseled in stone above the Gates of Hell.

> 'I am the way into the city of woe.
> I am the way to a forsaken people.
> I am the way to eternal sorrow…
> Abandon all hope ye who enter here.'

Hence the impact is extremely powerful, being direct and personal, as well as frightening and morally instructive. In this regard, Dante's *Divine Comedy* surpasses Homer and Virgil.

In addition to Dante's complex and reverent "rhythmic/numeric" structure, and his personal appearance in the *Divine Comedy*, he also presented another concept, borne in his age of chivalry. We must recall that according to the Judaic roots of the Christian religion, Eve was the reason for the downfall of mankind. When Eve enticed Adam to eat the forbidden fruit she became the symbol of *all* women, whom from that moment forward were vexed with the sin of leading men astray and causing mankind eternal woes. Yet Dante shunned religious tradition by not only placing a woman named Beatrice on a pedestal, but also made her (and thus all women) the divine symbol of purity that actually guides him (men) toward God. This occurs in the *Paradise* canticle, as Dante's pagan guide, Virgil, was prohibited from entering Heaven. Dante's praise of women influenced his peers and even later writers, like Goethe.

In essence, Dante's *Divine Comedy* was a monumental work of extraordinary breadth and depth that was wholly unique, religiously potent, and historically instructive. As such, the laurel crown that professor Giovanni del Virgilio wished to honor Dante with in Bologna was certainly well deserved. However, Dante's wish to receive that great honor from his beloved city of Florence instead would never occur. This was due to Dante's disenchantment with the moral breakdown that plagued his times, which was as noxious as the Black plague. A sharp rise in greed, intolerance, and depravity was evident everywhere, including at the highest levels of his adored Roman Catholic Church. This corruption prompted Dante's political activism whereby he rose to the city's highest office, being elected prior. Siding with the independent White Guelph faction, Dante's mission was to save Florence from papal rule.

The White and Black Guelphs divided Florence, causing much havoc. The Black faction supported Pope Boniface VIII. The pope's lust for complete spiritual and temporal control was clearly reflected in his own words, when he declared, "It is necessary for salvation that every living creature be under submission to the Roman pontiff." Thus began the pope's struggle for ultimate political and religious power as he locked horns with the Germanic rulers of the Holy Roman Empire. The White Guelphs' attempts to retain control over Florence failed, and Dante found himself convicted of corruption and bribery, and was also slapped with a fine. Worse yet, Dante was exiled for two years. When he refused to answer his charges or pay his fine the pope's Black Guelphs banished Dante for life with the proviso that he would be burned to death if he ever dared to reenter Florence.

Needless to say, Dante viewed this collective degeneration as a downward fall from grace. Being exiled from Florence may have made Dante's soul vacant, but the Lord filled that void and propelled his pen to the summit of world literature, even giving him the opportunity to condemn his sinful rivals for eternity in his *Divine Comedy*. So, I guess we can call that poetic justice.

Furthermore, five hundred and eight years after his death, the city of Florence regretted erasing the memory of Dante from his hometown, and they erected an impressive tomb for the famous poet inside the Cathedral of Santa Croce. Yet Dante's body, to this day, remains far from Florence in the city of Ravenna.

Contrary to what some people today might envision, Dante was not some frail bookish man locked up behind his desk reading and writing poetry. Like every other poet of his time, Dante worked by day and would write as time and inspiration allowed. Additionally, as a young man in the cavalry, well trained in a variety of assault weapons, Dante courageously fought in the bloody Battle of Campaldino with valor. Therefore, it is very likely that his physique was not bony and frail, but rather firm, lean, and well defined.

What's more, as a young man, Dante enjoyed hunting and the camaraderie of men that lived a rough and simple lifestyle. Thanks to his friend, Guido Cavalcanti, Dante was persuaded to stop wasting his time and virtuous talents with these crude men and pursue endeavors more in line with his vast intellect. Dante's gift for prose and poetry made expounding upon his fertile thoughts a natural fit, and *La Vita Nuova* was the result.

Oddly enough, the name Dante Alighieri in itself offers an interesting glimpse of this moralizing prophet. Dante is a shortened form of Durante, which means "enduring", while Aliger means "winged." Thus his full name offers us an enduring winged being. And certainly, Dante's *Divine Comedy* along with his genuine and perpetual quest for truth, morals, virtue, and dignity, especially during his chaotic times, was nothing short of angelic.

Beyond Dante's love for the spiritual realm, the grandeur of classical Rome had always fired his inspiration. As mentioned, Dante even placed Julius Caesar's assassins in the deepest circle of Hell alongside Judas. His ultimate idol, however, was Virgil, who, as we also know, was the most revered writer during the golden age of Augustus.

Virgil's immense popularity throughout the ages was due to two very distinct, yet overlapping reasons. Virgil's *Aeneid* was the pagan tale of Rome's long, proud history, and as such became the Romans' heirloom. A purge of classic pagan texts began after Constantine made Christianity the state-sponsored religion. The long repeated Christian story, however, is that Virgil remained a bestseller because many readers believed that the author foretold the emergence of Christ in one of his elusive passages.

However, it is quite clear that the vast majority of Roman Catholics had distant ancestors who were Roman pagans, and the *Aeneid* was the most illustrious document of their long and rich culture. We must remember; Virgil was a pagan, with no entitlement to Christ's heaven, thus he had no spiritual significance or influence. Therefore the vague prophecy of Christ in his fourth *Eclogue* was impotent and only of superficial and secondary value, as the Roman Catholics still valued their distinct heritage. Dante exemplified a devout Christian embracing his native Roman roots, for he chose not a Christian saint but a Roman pagan to guide him through his *Divine Comedy*.

In essence, pagan Roman blood still surged through the veins of many Roman Catholics, as attested by the use of Caesar's pagan Roman calendar, and how Charlemagne and countless others sought to revive the Roman Empire. Therefore, Virgil's *Aeneid* remained a bestseller because it praised the Italians' distinct Roman roots, and the author also happened to foretell of a golden new leader, which some interpreted as Christ, despite truly referring to Augustus. Moreover, with the addition of Dante's special honor, Virgil's lofty place in the pantheon of literature was secured.

Beside Virgil, Dante was also drawn to the brilliant statesman Cicero, as well as the poets Ovid and Horace, among others. In his *Divine Comedy* Dante praised many virtuous heroes as well as condemned many unsavory villains from Rome's long and eventful past.

We also cannot overlook the deep and personal motivation that came from a woman named Beatrice Portinari, for whom Dante harbored an unrequited love from childhood. Dante would later marry Gemma Donati in 1285, yet he still maintained a haunting idyllic vision of Beatrice, who had married a banker two years later. Unfortunately, Beatrice died in 1290, at the premature age of twenty-four.

When Dante wrote *La Vita Nuova,* at Guido Cavalcanti's prompting, his love poems referred to Beatrice. He attempted to conceal his burning obsession, but Florence was not a big city and gossip must have traveled fast. Dante only mentions two encounters with Beatrice—the first from afar at age eight, and the second many years later when she unexpectedly greeted him. Flushed with titillation, Dante retreated to his room and fell asleep. Thus his dreams gave birth to *La Vita Nuova*.

Dante's intense attraction was apparently based not only on Beatrice's physical beauty but also on her sweet and benevolent nature. She, therefore, fulfilled Dante's spiritual vision of the epitome of womanly grace and divine purity. Perhaps it was fortuitous that Dante never really knew Beatrice, for that pristine vision most assuredly would have paled.

Although personally heartbreaking for Dante, we must thank Beatrice, and her distant encounters, for helping to inspire the exiled Florentine to create the *Divine Comedy*, which was the grandest and most cognitively dense piece of literature ever written by a single person up to that time, and to some, in all of history. Its influence upon countless generations of writers, like T.S. Eliot, who compared it to the entire dramatic work of Shakespeare, secures Dante's lofty position atop literature's grand podium of laureates.

Dante was driven to attain greatness by his staunch beliefs, because his religion, morality, benevolence, and the destiny of Rome remained paramount. He detested the pillage by barbarians, the Muslim conquests, and the corruption by politicians and popes. Dante was painfully aware that the world had sinfully plummeted into the dismal abyss of the Dark Ages, and the remnants of that era still permeated his own medieval times. The overwhelming shroud of corruption and recklessness demanded immense change, and Dante was presented with a glimmer of hope. Dante's brief stay in Bologna years earlier was at the request of another professor at the university, Cino da Pistoia.

Cino specialized in jurisprudence, and he studied and lectured about the famous Codex of Law, which was compiled in AD 529 by the Roman emperor, Justinian. The intellectual elite of the time had committed themselves to analyzing the Romans' successful mechanisms for maintaining order. This amounted to its well-organized governing hierarchy, its well-trained military, and its strongly written code of laws.

What was painfully evident was that their beloved Catholic Church had failed miserably at attempting to govern. The long centuries of its rise and ultimate rule aided in the dismantling of the Western Roman Empire, yet the infrastructure of ancient Rome that once seemed overbearing and dispensable was now viewed with envious eyes. They might not have wished to see an emperor again, but the remaining superstructure was clearly the key to worldly survival.

The church's lack of a unified army to ward off foreign invasion had caused a splintering effect, giving rise to small city-states centuries earlier. The papacy, as well as the Holy Roman Emperor and various monarchs were now eyeing these rogue city-states for consumption; the world was in constant turmoil and had been for centuries.

This long trail of deterioration offered clear proof that the world needed more than spiritual and moral control over the masses. Likewise, it also proved that even though there were many devout and pious Christians among the corrupt, they could not prevent the outside attacks of terror that remained unabated, for the glaring reality was that not all mortals believed in their peaceful God, and mercy was likewise alien to savage raiders.

The list of bold marauders included the Vikings. This Scandinavian group of barbarians began their attacks on Europe in AD 793, when they raided the town of Lindisfarne, England. They soon realized how easy it was to prey upon, hatchet to death, and pillage one village after another. The sheer lack of military resistance made the Vikings set their sights on the mainland. Their sleek longships were ideal for sailing directly into the heartland of Europe with its webbed network of rivers. Therefore, a multitude of villages became easy targets.

These isolated settlements, which lacked a unifying central government, were at the mercy of ruthless bandits whose favorite tactic was to prey upon defenseless monks. Countless monasteries were brutally ransacked for the great wealth of silver and gold hoarded in their coffers. These terrifying waves of destruction plagued Europe for several hundred years, spanning the entire Dark Ages right up to the Middle Ages. In turn, these frightening and deadly times led to the construction of the great gothic cathedrals, particularly in France. Perched high atop the spiritual citadels were carved gargoyles and other grotesque creatures to ward off savages and other evil spirits.

The fear and inability to maintain order, safety, or unity prompted men of higher learning to seek a solution, and this inevitably led back to ancient Rome. Most did not wish to abandon their Christian faith, but faith alone had clearly failed them. Other institutions were needed to provide order and security. This is what Cino da Pistoia had been examining in Bologna. His influence on Dante explains why the poet hailed the Emperor Justinian as the world's lawgiver in his *Divine Comedy*. Dante saw Roman justice as the ultimate earthly symbol, somehow endowed by the Creator, to which all mankind should pay heed. However, the intellectuals' goal to resurrect Roman law and order was beyond their grasp. City-states would resurrect principles of the Roman Republic and build upon Roman laws, but this long process continued over the next few centuries.

As a man of his times, Dante sought political change, but held firmly to his deep Christian faith, and like many medieval men, he even condoned its spiritual zeal. In the *Divine Comedy*, Dante expressed his belief that another Crusade would be welcome to recapture the lost Holy Land from the Islamic infidels. He also realized that in spite of the corrupt popes who tarnished their reigns, their rule was transitory, and there were many others who would honor the church and humanity with God's grace. Moreover, this grace was worth defending at all costs, especially against an alien religion that not only threatened Christendom, but Western civilization in general.

Dante also gave absolution to his great-great-grandfather, Cacciaguida, whom he proclaimed was an honored martyr. His noble death occurred during the Second Crusade, almost two hundred years before, thus earning him heavenly bliss in Dante's *Paradiso*.

By Dante's time, the Christian faith had an uneasy relationship with Greek philosophy and the sciences, which for the public had become almost extinct in the West. Aristotle's works were widely banned in the previous centuries, and this was primarily the result of early Christian scholars who feared the application of logic to the many illogical mysteries of the faith. Many of Aristotle's works remained in the custody of the church for centuries, however, preserved in silence by its monastic copyists. Even during the Middle Ages, when the church was finally becoming more lenient, they issued their infamous 219 propositions, which banned many ancient works, including those of Aristotle. Dante was only twelve years old when these damning propositions, known as the Condemnations of 1277, slammed the doors once again. Dante's cantos, likewise, expressed the axiom of faith over reason, an idea which dated back to Saint Paul, who stated, "I will destroy the wisdom of the wise"; the apostle's prediction did become manifest as the centuries unfolded. As time revealed, this squelched wisdom was a hodgepodge of both profound thought and profound folly.

Although early Christians adopted Greek and pagan ideologies and rituals, they had grown more intolerant over time, particularly after their immense empowerment by Constantine. But many centuries of reckless control, coinciding with raids, plagues, and political decay had brought them to a dire state. As such, a new atmosphere of yielding to change permeated the church by the latter part of the Middle Ages.

As the saying goes, when you hit rock bottom there is no place left to go but up. So, too, the church had no choice but to share their knowledge. The church was the sole bastion of knowledge during the Dark and Middle Ages, and their concealed libraries and comprehensive archives were finally unveiled.

The famous theologian, Saint Thomas Aquinas, was clearly influenced by Aristotelian philosophy, which as we saw in the previous chapter, was reflected in many of his works. Meanwhile, Dante was caught in the midst of this immense transition. While holding fast to his strict, old world Christian beliefs, Dante was also eager to embrace new schools of thought.

Dante's complex mind absorbed many facets of the ancient world that further stimulated thought among his peers and future authors. He consumed knowledge from the classics, religious texts, philosophy, politics, and the world around him. This became a valuable commodity to modern analysts, as many texts have been lost from antiquity and even since his era. Therefore, Dante's *Divine Comedy* proved to be far more than a religious allegory, for it was infused with historical data that later became a valuable resource for understanding many people throughout history, particularly from a medieval perspective.

Giovanni Boccaccio wrote the first formal biography of the great poet called *Trattatello in laude de Dante* or "Treatise in Praise of Dante". Dante's fame cascaded down the centuries influencing numerous authors and theologians and even spawned many illustrious societies dedicated to the highest standards of scholarship, such as the "The Dante Society of America" founded by Henry Wadsworth Longfellow in 1881, who also translated the *Divine Comedy* into English, the "Oxford Dante Society" and the "Dante Society of London" among others.

Dante, along with Homer and Shakespeare, remains at the summit of world literature: a distinction that was instantly recognized. Interestingly enough, Giovanni del Virgilio, the professor from Bologna who tried to award Dante Bologna's laurel crown, took the honor of writing an epitaph for Dante's tomb, it read: "Dante the theologian, skilled in every branch of knowledge that philosophy may cherish in her illustrious bosom."

Hence, Dante had not only revealed his personal brilliance but he also appeared like a prophetic *spark at dawn*. The profound poet was a sign of his growing times; men's minds were becoming more inquisitive, stimulated, and far more active. A new light upon the horizon was beginning to beam, as a chain reaction of creativity was about to explode.

The Radiant Light

After several languid centuries, the dark medieval shroud finally evaporated, as the radiant light of the Renaissance revitalized the Italian peninsula.

Corruption would still exist, but progress and man's perception of the world would take on a completely new perspective. The church's once all-powerful grasp had no alternative but to loosen. Between a broken and splintered world and a growingly apathetic public, the Catholic Church had to swing open its musty doors. The knowledge they seized for over eight long centuries would now be put toward renewing a solid liberal arts program, one interestingly modeled after that of ancient pagan Rome.

The earlier Carolingian dynasty, during the Dark Ages and later ruled by Charlemagne, had established an education program exclusively for the clergy. It, too, was founded upon the ancient Roman model. This consisted of the seven liberal arts: logic, rhetoric, arithmetic, geometry, astronomy, music, and grammar. The Catholic Church would become a staunch benefactor of public education, even if exclusively for Christians.

The Vatican still held immense power and wealth; however, it was slowly being forced to deal with the new power lords in town—the capitalists. The fiery rise of the Italian city-states of Florence, Venice, Genoa, and Milan would be pivotal in reshaping and altering the new direction of the future world. These energetic and prosperous cities broke free of absolute papal rule as well as oppressive monarchies by establishing republican parliaments in the case of Florence, or electing a Doge or Duke in Venice.

Although the papacy continued to exert influence, these new forms of government allowed far more freedom for private entrepreneurial growth, and with it international trade, as we know it today, was born. This amazing facilitation of diverse trade reached a whole new level in Venice, while a new financial entity—*modern* banking—was officially invented in Florence. This was complemented by something else strikingly new, business trade schools. For the first time, students were trained in mathematics, not for scientific purposes but exclusively for economic calculations.

Leonardo Fibonacci from Pisa had previously published his groundbreaking book, *Liber Abaci* or *Book of Calculation* in 1202. This book used the new Arabic decimal system in lieu of the complex Roman numeral system, yet it was not merely math in and of itself. Fibonacci had devised a system of multiplication and division that he directly applied to business practices, thus devising balance sheets, calculating precise interest rates, converting weights, and other tasks that were previously tedious and extremely complex, or did not even exist.

The new training schools were inaugurated in Florence, yet they soon developed in the other four major Italian cities. In time, they slowly spread to all other major cities throughout Europe. The most elite and successful accountants and businessmen emerged from Florence, as the Peruzzi, Bardi, Medici, and Riccardi from the nearby town of Luca, all rose to prominence during the thirteenth and fourteenth centuries.

This powerful network of bankers invented risk management and insurance policies, along with revolutionizing the practice of loan management. More importantly, these were not typical modern-day bankers, but powerful mega-conglomerates that cultivated and owned many of the evolving trade and manufacturing businesses. All of this was due to their firm command of business strategy, organization, and profit accountability. Although nepotism played a small role in their upper management, the actual accountants who calculated all-important profit margins and risk analyses were impartially harvested from a rich pool of accounting talent. During the late medieval period these banking and trading pioneers set up branches across the full breadth of Europe, as every bank during these formative years were Italian entities, bar none. They used to say that if a community had no Italians, they had no bank. This amazing fact directly caused the development and rise of countless cities like Antwerp, Amsterdam, London, Paris, and many others, as Europe awakened to Italy's new capitalistic movement.

Previously, the textile industries, particularly in Flanders and England, had been making slow, steady progress, as manual tasks yielded to the use of foot-powered models and then water- and wind-powered machines. Yet these small businesses in Flanders were hampered by guilds that set production limits in an attempt to keep commerce fair and balanced. Once the Italian bankers entered these markets, however, production increased radically with their large trade networks, akin to the earlier Roman administration, thus allowing for massive growth and expansion. The port in Antwerp grew to be a primary port, as these strategic bankers relocated many of their Italian employees to the northern city. After the Spanish ravaged the city, many migrated to Amsterdam. Thus in due time, one-third of that city's inflated population were foreigners. These mega-banking tycoons coordinated an international network of trade with many foreign ports stretching from England, around the Strait of Gibraltar, down to the Middle East.

Additionally, although loans had been around since the early days of ancient Rome, the Italian bankers' new excess of wealth afforded entrepreneurial commoners the ability to rise above their family's station. The one major setback that plagued the Middle Ages when the church had vast control was that it was a sin to lend money with the purpose of collecting interest. Charging interest was considered unnatural, or *contro natura*—contrary to nature, because lenders did not physically earn the money, but sat back and slothfully collected interest upon other people's hard labor. They were labeled usurers. Dante relegated usurers to the seventh circle of hell, alongside sodomites. Both were viewed as unnatural and wicked practices.

Once the practice was brought to the fore by Renaissance bankers, however, the Vatican would not deprive itself of this "sin," and as such, it cunningly doctored its books to make loans look like exchanges or gifts. The church became the largest customer of private bankers, and their many investments further bolstered their power and influence. Ironically, the church was notorious for not paying back its loans.

Bankers and newly made aristocrats gained tremendous power by being able to purchase anything imaginable, including having their family's portraits set into religious frescoes, or even legitimacy for illegitimate offspring. Capitalism ruled the Renaissance.

At the dawn of the Renaissance, another pivotal event took place. In 1453, the Muslims sacked Constantinople, and the Eastern flank of the Roman Empire was at last consumed. This caused many intellectuals to flee back to the West, and with them returned ancient Greek philosophy, both Greek and Roman literary classics, and basic sciences. Although the Catholic Church in the west had preserved some of these neglected works, and had even begun teaching some of the texts a century earlier, this influx brought with it additional texts, including Aristotle's essential books, *On the Heavens and World*, *Physics*, and *On Generation and Corruption*. The mighty Italian bankers, as well as the church, integrated certain aspects of this long forgotten knowledge into their own ideologies, to both good and ill effect.

Many secularist historians have overestimated the importance and effectiveness of Greek philosophies and sciences, which were often based on pure conjecture. This, in several major instances, proved to be a mind-locking disaster, as many blindly adopted these theories as fact. Naturally, other texts provided much to stimulate thought, from the philosophical to the mathematical, and this contribution is undeniably significant.

Although the church released some of the Greek texts for public consumption, it didn't reap the most benefit; it was primarily the aristocracy that turned the idle rhetoric into proactive production. Establishing their own private symposia, they invited scholars to lecture and mentor promising youths, and these power lords savored the mentally stimulating discussions, which benefited them and their talented flock. Most notable of the power lords were the immensely rich banking family from Florence, the Medici.

The Medici's immense position of power and influence enabled them to shape the education of the most promising youths in their state, not to mention having a hand in almost every venture and operation within their realm. Their huge network of banking, loans, trading, construction, and an unrivalled den of artisans fueled a booming economy that was without parallel in its day and certainly surpassed any contenders from the preceding one thousand years. One of the beneficiaries of the Medici's powerful oligarchy was Andrea del Verrocchio.

Verrocchio's great talents in a variety of media brought him many commissions and fame, thus allowing him to develop the most prominent studio in Florence. His studio fulfilled many commissions for patrons like the Medici, councils and churches from various states, and it also served as the finest academy of its day. The fortunate youths who were accepted studied and worked under one roof and were taught to hone their craft to the highest standards. Being versed in sculpture, drawing, perspective, painting, metallurgy, and philosophy, the majority of Andrea's flock made an indelible mark on their city and the world. Among these gifted apprentices was the astonishingly brilliant and uncommonly versatile Leonardo da Vinci.

Leonardo's radiant mind had become the hallmark of his era, and is still relentlessly probed and discussed today. More than an artist, Leonardo *is* the quintessential *Renaissance Man*. Therefore, before proceeding on to other aspects of the Renaissance, this wizard warrants our attention.

LEONARDO DA VINCI: Even as a youth, Leonardo stood apart from his fellow brethren. Leonardo's insatiable quest for knowledge lured him into perhaps the broadest spectrum of inquiry ever ventured by a single mind. Even more astounding was that he excelled at the majority of his endeavors. Leonardo became a leading figure in anatomy, engineering, botany, optics, weaponry, flight, hydraulics, music, theater, and sculpture, and naturally, he was the ultimate master of drawing and painting.

The vast amount of notebooks left by Da Vinci, not to mention all those regrettably lost, are not only staggering in volume but also indicate a man obsessed with the creation of visionary ideas, even at the expense of failing to gain funding or having the opportunity to build them. That Leonardo was under the employ of the eras most prominent men, like Lorenzo de Medici, Cesare Borgia, Ludovico Sforza, Pope Leo X, and King Francis I, but often did not have his designs implemented or, worse yet, failed to deliver on his commissions, remains somewhat of a mystery. Although Lorenzo de Medici and his relative, Pope Leo X, had little patience and were happy to see Leonardo take on a new patron, all these great leaders had a great deal of belief in, and admiration for, this eccentric genius. That they put up with his independence and even contractual neglect only indicates that they all realized his genius and perhaps eagerly wished for an opportunity to see just one more of his fertile creations materialize. His *Virgin of the Rocks*, *Portrait of Cecilia Gallerani*, colossal *Sforza Equestrian Monument* and of course *The Last Supper* were all proof of that. If not, they would be content just to witness the endless font of ideas, odd contraptions, or even beautiful sketches that would emanate out of this man's deeply complex and radiant mind.

We know today that some of Da Vinci's sketches for machinery were most likely renderings of existing devices that intrigued the curious artist. Other great engineers existed: particularly Brunelleschi, who, many years before Leonardo's birth, invented cranes, elevators, scaffolds and other equipment that were left scattered about many years after he completed his many architectural wonders. However, those today that negatively fixate on these particular sketches by Leonardo as being mere copies have missed the far larger picture. First of all, these sketches provided Leonardo with workable solutions that acted like an engineer's study manual today. These schematics laid the groundwork for the many wholly unique and often mind-boggling inventions that Leonardo *did* devise, and these have no predecessors. Moreover, many of these inventions would only see the light of day many centuries later in the distant future.

So although some critics like to focus on Leonardo's impractical inventions, like his colossal crossbow, we can see that his notebooks were just that, personal drawing boards were the master could indulge his imagination to devise and revise, or even discard, as needed. We must also realize that Leonardo experimented with weapons that were deemed too radical and never built. One design was a horse-drawn device with a rotating gear mechanism. It spun four helicopter-like blades, each capable of being outfitted with spiked clubs or a series of metal balls that would have clearly destroyed anything in its path. We must also bear in mind that just because these mechanical devices were never built or implemented by his royal patrons does not mean they were all improbable or unrealistic. Moreover, Da Vinci designed several variations of a multi-barreled rifle or cannon and even a rotating "Gatling-type" machine gun, the latter predating Richard Gatling's Civil War machinegun by four hundred years.

As for why Leonardo's sound weapon designs didn't make it into production, first of all, bravery and gallantry on the battlefield was the order of the day, and machines to kill en masse must have been viewed with doubt and probably distaste. Even five centuries later, Adolf Hitler initially rejected the use of machine guns on the grounds that they were not honorable weapons. The ease of killing so many without a struggle was almost equated to cheating. However, the chivalrous bravado of hand-to-hand combat would indeed eventually give way to technological mass-slaughter. So has mankind really become more advanced or less chivalrous?

Secondly, those with less vision do not always embrace novel ideas. Case in point, after several successful test flights by the Wright brothers with their pioneering new flying machine, they solicited the United States War Department with plans to retrofit their new invention for military use. The military brass was not convinced of the plane's worthiness and they flatly rebuffed the inventors. Three years passed, as the Wright brothers feverishly tried to entice European countries to buy their new fangled invention. Only after prolonged and exhausting efforts did Teddy Roosevelt's administration buy into the idea. *(Photo page 714)*

Knowing the extremely curious and restless nature of Leonardo, it is not hard to see that he would never jeopardize or abandon his scientific research to become a full-time salesman, especially for the promotion of a single idea. His time and energy was far too precious and much better spent at his miraculous drawing board where even he must have been amazed at some of the ideas that materialized in his perpetually sparkling and mysterious mind.

Moreover, Leonardo is unique in that he often abandoned projects, whether being more interested in the initial creative process than with the menial or tedious chore of execution; being piqued by another alluring endeavor; or producing concepts that baffled and then humiliated his ornery patrons. Nevertheless, this self-determining behavior was a first, as no other artisan ever had the audacity to defy their patrons as often, or in the ultimate manner, as did Leonardo. Even Michelangelo, who was twenty-three years younger and had an ego the size of his colossal *David*, may have petulantly moaned about, and detested, his assignment to paint the Sistine Chapel, yet he obediently gave in to his master, Pope Julius II.

Meanwhile, Leonardo moved among his patrons clearly as their equal—or in reality their superior. This drove some of them mad, especially the incompetent and greedy Pope Leo X, whom, upon commissioning Leonardo for a painting, was infuriated that the artist began by mixing varnish. He blasted, "This man will never do anything, for he starts by thinking about the end before the work is begun."

What Leo failed to comprehend is that Leonardo was not the run-of-the-mill artist; he was a scientist, inventor, engineer etc. Leonardo had not only introduced the art of oil painting in Italy, but he was also drawn to experimenting with various paint mediums, resins and varnishes. He very likely was still seeking to find the ideal solution when Pope Leo hired him, for we know Leonardo experienced several failures previously, and as we also know, all roads leading to success are littered with failures. One was with Leonardo's famous painting, *The Last Supper*, in Milan.

Duke Ludovico Sforza commissioned *The Last Supper* for the refectory in the Santa Maria delle Grazie church in Milan. It was supposed to be a typical fresco; fresco being a rapid and laborious process of using a water-based paint in wet plaster. This severely limited the time an artist could work with the paints before the plaster dried. Obviously having an aversion to working at somebody else's prescribed pace or even a mixture's hasty pace—in tandem with being a relentless innovator—Leonardo set out to devise a new methodology.

Da Vinci formulated a new resin and gesso mixture as a base, which sealed the wall and was allowed to dry. He then used either oil or tempera paint and worked at his own leisurely pace. Spectators noticed how some days Leonardo would enter the refectory and pick up his brush to make a small change to a minor detail and then leave. Other days, he would sit and just stare at the painting for great lengths of time and then leave, only to return the next day and work like the possessed from dawn till dusk.

However, the Dominican friars were getting annoyed at Leonardo's slow progress and they appealed to the duke, who pressed Leonardo to finish the work. The final result, however, was spectacular. The new process allowed Leonardo the time and ability to create fine detail and dazzling colors that were unattainable via the fresco method. The vision was simply breathtaking. Naturally his flawless use of perspective, which not only placed Jesus at the focal point but also made the scene look as if an extension of the dining hall—along with his unsurpassed ability at drawing the human form—added to the awe. Instantly hailed by many as the ultimate masterpiece, Da Vinci's eternal fame was secure.

However, Leonardo's paint was not secure. His new technique to replace the time-tested fresco process sadly turned into a humiliating failure. Leonardo was destined to watch his glorious masterpiece slowly deteriorate, as the paint blistered and began to flake off bit by bit. By the seventeenth century, the sacred figures were mere ghosts of their former selves. Mindless restorations followed, whereby destroying Leonardo's sublime masterpiece forever.

Nevertheless, Leonardo had previously established himself as the most advanced, unconventional, and often-flawless artist of his day. Only a few years previously, in 1483, Leonardo had painted the *Virgin of the Rocks*, which exemplified his unrivalled skills. Firstly, Leonardo's composition, like the majority of his works, perfectly suited the subject and the theme that he wished to portray. The work exhibited a perfect state of balance that carried the spectator's eyes in the circular direction that *he* intended. While other artists often placed figures without rhyme or reason, Leonardo set the standard for strategically arranging many figures, as well as a single pose. Even a hand gesture or facial nuance was well calculated to achieve the desired result, i.e. the *Mona Lisa*.

Secondly, his pioneering use of *chiaroscuro*—bathing his subjects in light and shadow—was based upon his keen, scientific observational skills, which no other artist had ever exhibited as deftly. Finally, Leonardo's ability to draw and paint figures of anatomical correctness and express an inner human or even spiritual presence, when called for, were clearly talents that even Michelangelo or Raphael found difficult to rival.

Leonardo's intense technical study of the human form—being the world's first anatomical illustrator to make diagrams of internal organs, arteries, veins, muscles, and bones—clearly equipped him with the firsthand knowledge of how to draw and paint the human form in any position and with complete accuracy. And although Michelangelo became his close rival, the sculptor often painted or even chiseled figures—particularly women—as if over endowed with bulging muscles. Barring Michelangelo's early works, which were more natural, his later works all exhibited both men and women of herculean stature. In fact, Leonardo even quipped about artists of his day drawing figures as if bags filled with rocks. One look at Michelangelo's rendition of Eve in the *Garden of Eden* or his sculpture of a woman representing *Night,* on his tomb for Giuliano de Medici, clearly demonstrates his obsession with masculinity and muscles. Softness and tenderness had sadly faded from his works. *(See page 708)*

Meanwhile, although only being a charcoal sketch, the womanly grace and spiritual transcendence found in the faces and bodies of Leonardo's *Virgin and Child with St. Anne and John the Baptist (see page 708)* display talents that no other Renaissance artist fully obtained, thus explaining why Filippino Lippi, when petitioned to paint this scene, declined, stating that it should be awarded to Leonardo instead, being that he was "a greater artist."

Leonardo was viewed as the great old master, even being honored by the younger (and heavily influenced) artist Raphael, in his masterful work *The School of Athens.* In this grand fresco, which decorated the Apostolic Palace in the Vatican, Raphael used Leonardo's likeness to represent the wise old philosopher Plato, who, along with Aristotle, rightfully stood at the painting's focal point. Meanwhile, a sea of other great thinkers surrounded the two titans. While many today may have expected Michelangelo to represent Aristotle, being the younger titanic force, Raphael instead used Michelangelo to depict Heraclitus, who was known as "the weeping philosopher". Raphael placed Heraclitus in the foreground sitting on the floor in a contemplative position, bearing a somewhat disturbed mood. This was surely due to Michelangelo's utter contempt for being forced to paint the ceiling of the Sistine Chapel, which he happened to be working on at the very same time. *(See page 709)*

Several years earlier, Leonardo had been appointed to a committee in Florence that was entrusted with determining the optimal location of a new colossal statue by the young and dynamic talent Michelangelo. The statue in question was Michelangelo's *David*. *(See page 707)*

The young sculptor had managed to salvage a discarded monolith of white marble that was deemed flawed and unusable by a fellow artisan. By using it, Michelangelo not only triumphed over a physical roadblock, but also sculpted a shocking new masterpiece that won the attention of his talent-infested city. Having been accustomed to the petite and lean bronze *Davids* by Donatello and Verrocchio, all of Florence was stunned by Michelangelo's muscular gargantuan that stood almost 14 feet tall. This spectacular David, who even towered over Goliath, was ideally proportioned with pronounced and precise anatomy, except for his oversized hands, which intentionally evoked David's raw strength.

Many modern professors in the humanities have attributed these powerful hands to Michelangelo's intention of projecting the power of Florence. They were, however, almost certainly fashioned to project the indomitable power of the statue's dynamic creator. For Michelangelo had previously stunned all by boldly carving his name across Mother Mary's blouse in his stunning *Pieta*. The proud youth had heard rumors that some were attributing his work to another sculptor, an unimaginable affront. Consequently, Michelangelo signed his masterwork, and in such a blatant fashion that the entire world would never doubt who was its creator.

However, Michelangelo's *David* did also mirror the bold spirit of Florence, for both the statue and the city stood fearless, proud, and determined—to the rest of the world, they radiated invincible power.

Both Michelangelo and Leonardo would eventually leave Florence and find employment elsewhere, as the Renaissance was indeed a most turbulent era. And it was precisely these rivalries that forced dukes, princes, and even popes to seek and secure military engineers and architects, and this aptly brings us back to why these patrons eagerly sought Leonardo's multifaceted skill sets.

Ludovico Sforza of Milan and King Francis I of France proved to be Leonardo's staunchest patrons. They recognized the genius before them and allowed him freedoms no other artist/scientist/engineer/architect/musician ever enjoyed. Along with the many weapons Leonardo designed, we mustn't overlook his radical La Rocca Fortress, which he conceived for Duke Cesare Borgia. Here again, his drastic leap forward must have baffled his busy patron; however, Niccolo Machiavelli, the perceptive military thinker, had wisely approved.

The norm had been to construct towering monstrosities with flat angular walls and high turrets, which were meant to not only give the inhabitants a bird's eye view of the advancing enemy but was also intended to psychologically intimidate the invading foe. In essence, a fortress was intended to be a huge, menacing structure to thwart even the thought of breach.

Meanwhile, Leonardo devised a stealthy, low-profiled, circular building. It was actually a series of circular rings with moats in-between. A larger moat surrounded the outer ring, while four rounded turrets sat outside the walls and evenly spaced. Sitting like some futuristic streamlined complex, Da Vinci's La Rocca Fortress (or *Ringed Fortress*, as I call it) would have been able to fire upon intruders in any direction. Most importantly, any artillery or cannon balls fired upon the fortress would have clearly ricocheted off its low and smoothly rounded walls. Underground tunnels conveniently connected all the rings to the central command tower. Leonardo's *Ringed Fortress* was a design that evidently didn't impress the ostentatious patrons of his day, but was clearly an amazing concept for a distant *Star Wars* age. *(See page 710)*

Interestingly enough, when the United States War Department decided that it needed a new headquarters building in 1941 they built the Pentagon. Although not circular, the design was a low profiled building consisting of several concentric rings.

Leonardo's prophetic and inventive genius has rightfully enamored millions. Many in his day (and many today) recognized Leonardo as being a polymath of the highest order. However, due to his illegitimate birth Leonardo never received a standard education. He was fortunate enough to be accepted into Verrocchio's studio, yet he never attended school. This deficit caused some to mock and dismiss him, which irritated Leonardo. However, when we consider how many great thinkers, such as Thomas Edison or Henry Ford also had no formal education, we must realize that a college diploma is not the sole means for judging talent or even brilliance.

In fact, when we consider how Nero was educated by Rome's foremost intellectual, Seneca, only to become a madman, or how Alexander the Great was tutored by Aristotle, only to remain a warring general, we have to question just how important is education when we neglect the innate qualities of the individual being trained? We know education benefits the majority, yet it's prudent to remember that many geniuses have forged their own paths, and Leonardo rightfully sits at the apex of human brilliance, along with many other great thinkers.

When we peruse a list of seminal doers of history, such as Euclid, Aristarchus, Augustus, Constantine, Dante, Brunelleschi, Columbus, Gutenberg, as well as the many titans after Leonardo's day, we see that all of them were visionaries or dreamers, not delusional dreamers, but kinetic dreamers. We must also recall that none of these titanic figures had a college diploma. Oddly enough, it is generally regarded that after the highly influential German philosopher Immanuel Kant, many great thinkers not only sought college, but by the twentieth century, no great thinker would even be acknowledged unless they were a professional in academia. Alas, the cheap paper certificate had trumped true brilliance.

Today we have radicals like William Ayers—a confessed terrorist who bombed buildings, including the Pentagon—who is a professor at the University of Illinois at Chicago, as well as Ward Churchill, who was a professor of ethnic studies at the University of Colorado at Boulder, each promoting corrupt and radical behaviors. Therefore, how much trust should we place in those in academia that claim to be superior intellects?

Beyond the many radicals in academia today that continue to groom our youth in very proactive and harmful ways, we cannot overlook others that may not be explosively dangerous but still distort our society, even if in subtle nuances. There are many scholars and authors today positing misinformation in an attempt to revise history. Their intent is to alter our way of thinking about our past or about those who truly shaped our world. Therefore, a clear reading of history is crucial if we are to groom our children or ourselves for success.

In this regard, the works of Rodney Stark and Roger Osborne come to mind. Both criticize the Italian Renaissance in general but particularly the artistic geniuses that flourished in Italy. This new revisionary trend by Stark, Osborne and other Christian scholars seems to be gaining a gullible audience, and as such deserves a rebuttal.

Debunking Modern Revisions of the Renaissance

Roger Osborne makes many lucid points about the Renaissance, as it was not just the great art of great masters that characterizes this period. However, he belittles the importance of great men such as, Da Vinci, Michelangelo, and Brunelleschi among others, citing their artistic endeavors as being inconsequential and of no relevance to civilization. Furthermore, Osborne somehow views the Renaissance as a bittersweet ending to Italian history rather than an astonishing era of creativity—one that clearly enhanced millions of lives and civilization.

Interestingly, Osborne quotes a line conceived of and spoken by Orson Welles in the movie *The Third Man*: "In Italy for thirty years under the Borgias they had warfare, terror, murder and bloodshed, but they produced Michelangelo, Leonardo da Vinci and the Renaissance. In Switzerland, they had brotherly love; they had five hundred years of democracy and peace – and what did that produce? The cuckoo clock."

Despite the cuckoo clock being invented in Germany, Welles' statement resounds with much truth. Yet Osborne only sees a negative connotation, namely that our endeavors are better when geared towards peace and happiness for the many, rather than producing only a few super geniuses. While his opinion sounds practical at the outset, he overlooks other crucial factors.

First, it is a blaring fact that only a handful of gifted doers produce the titanic benefits for the masses. Therefore, with out them, stagnation would reign. Second, beyond the achievements of these select geniuses is the all-important aspect of influence and motivation. As a personal example, ever since I was a young boy, I have been influenced by Leonardo da Vinci. His insatiable curiosity not only led into countless fields of endeavor, but his attempts were proactive measures to contribute something of value to humanity. In this regard, I, too, have avoided society's mold of being pigeonholed. Like Leonardo, I believe that a person's interests and motivations don't always need to be limited to a single career. With Leonardo's influence, I inevitably became more multifaceted—delving into architectural design, construction, art, new media, computer programming, and even writing. Therefore, if a handful of supreme geniuses can motivate others to do the best they can, whereby giving back to society something useful, then this seems to be a far more logical, productive, and even gracious way of conducting our lives. In this regard, it certainly is better than fostering a peaceful and stagnant society that whiles away the hours admiring cuckoo clocks.

As for the Renaissance, despite the corruption at the highest levels, these Italian artists and creators were driven by a rich past, as well as by the competition that mounted among their well-trained peers, or between one city and another. This in turn spawned a chain reaction of dynamic innovation and progress. As noted, these critics failed to see that beyond the initial works of art, many influences and spin-offs projected beyond the artistic realm. Artists spearheaded research into other more advanced areas of human exploration; for example, Leonardo the painter became the first technical dissector and illustrator of anatomy and botany. He advanced map-making techniques which inspired explorers, devised schematics on optics and ballistics, along with engineering designs and inventions that inspired others and still astound us today. Moreover, this only reflects the growing advances of one man—others abound.

Too often modern scholars forget just how much of an impact art had in the Renaissance. To us it is old standard fare, yet their world had only known the stiff two-dimensional depictions of Gothic art. These new three-dimensional illusions, which mysteriously transformed flat surfaces, were intriguing; for the people of the Renaissance, they were the silver screen, television, Internet, and science all in one. Therefore, frescoes and paintings were marveled over even more than sculpture and elicited discussion, inquiry and, for some, personal investigation into other fields. In essence, they were enthralled that man had the mathematical ability to create three-dimensional wonders in paint, and wondered; what else was within man's seemingly unlimited grasp; what else could be examined to understand, manipulate, or control.

Similarly, the geometry used by Brunelleschi to invent linear perspective inspired not only other artists but also mathematicians. These newly inspired intellects sought to measure all facets of the world around them, thus becoming scientists in many new groundbreaking fields. Geology, biology, botany, astronomy, and other sciences began to emerge. This eventually fueled men of the Enlightenment, like Descartes, who not only examined and dissected nature but also made his own drawings, following Leonardo's precedent.

Dome construction reached new heights via Brunelleschi, who influenced Michelangelo and the countless others who followed. These technologies sparked other endeavors, as construction machinery (with its gears, pulleys, levers, and tension springs) was carried over and altered for other engineering and manufacturing projects. In fact, Leonardo had invented a self-propelled, spring-action motorcar, although this amazing invention never became public. Other less radical devices, such as improved cranes, complex clocks, or hydraulic winches would prove essential to producing many spin-offs that propelled inventiveness. This progressive path may have been beset with political and religious turmoil, but the efforts of a few highly motivated individuals spurred many others, thus eventually leading into the Industrial Revolution.

It is also an unavoidable fact that architectural advancements, and the arts in general, commenced in earnest after these great Renaissance men laid the foundation. Despite the trivialization of this art by critics, these were not trite little finger paintings or useless crafts for mindless enjoyment. Da Vinci's *Last Supper* is unquestionably beautiful to behold, but it also elicited intense spiritual enchantment and fascination for countless millions. Beyond those obvious benefits, however, Leonardo's startling use of geometric perspective in this fresco influenced thousands of artists and even scientists.

Of the latter, the mathematician Luca Pacioli, who was intrigued by Leonardo's abilities, recruited him to draw illustrations of complex three-dimensional designs for his treatise on geometry *(see Leonardo's polyhedron on page 707)*. This practice aided scientists and engineers in visualizing concepts that otherwise could not be accurately described or understood by words alone. Likewise, Leonardo's anatomical drawings were so accurate and instructive that they are still used in textbooks by the scientific community today. Hence, art and architecture extended far beyond its own sphere and infiltrated many others.

Beyond these influences, the Renaissance in general was a time of sweeping change, and in this regard, Leonardo was certainly not alone, for the Renaissance boasted a dazzling assemblage of geniuses that no scholar can debase or ignore. Along with Da Vinci, names like Giotto, Donatello, Verrocchio, Michelangelo, Raphael, Bernini, Botticelli, and to the north, Dürer, Van Eyck, Bosch, and Holbein dominated the visual arts. At the same time, Brunelleschi initiated the architectural boom, and Bramante and Alberti followed his lead. Christopher Columbus discovered a new hemisphere that doubled the size of the known globe, as Cortés, da Gama, Cabot, Verrazzano, Magellan, and countless others followed suit. Pope Julius II expanded Roman Catholic influence and Martin Luther and John Calvin formed new religious branches. King Henry VIII instituted the Protestant religion in England, and upon learning of the spherical geography of the world laid the seeds for the British Navy. As noted, Dante, Petrarca, Boccaccio, and Chaucer had previously inspired literature with their famous works. Copernicus and Da Vinci were pioneers in debunking the status quo and reviving true science, while the Medici, Borgias, Sforzas, and Machiavelli all made significant strides, albeit rough handedly in many instances, in economic or political affairs of state.

In contrast, we can examine the world that Stark, Osborne, and others declare outshone the Renaissance. The preceding Middle Ages, and particularly the Dark Ages before that, were deeply mired by fear, disunity, and the lack of strong economic, military, or political administration. Although not as severely devoid of progress as previously thought, these eras did face major breakdowns in organization, and a splintering effect that gave rise to feudalism, small independent villages, monarchies, and naturally the sprawling theocracy of Christendom, which included several monastic orders.

These various entities managed to maintain a modicum of order, yet only within the confines of their own realms and limited capabilities. Feudal communities and small city-states could not muster a professional standing army, while monks did not believe in armies at all. Despite the religion's peaceful core, the pope would rally devout believers to form the infamous attack force, the Crusaders. These forces were used to recapture the lost Holy Land, and were not for national security. Therefore even the pope had to seek security from Holy Roman emperors.

Incapable of warding off incessant attacks by barbarians, these feudal communities lived in fear, while the pious sought monastic sanctuary by retreating from the world. Preferring to live in spiritual solitude, monks catered to only a small populace. Their formula was one of devotion and hard work, which offered not only sanctuary from a chaotic world, but also self-sufficiency and a degree of progress.

Those outside their ring of influence remained completely severed, thus eroding foreign relations. Although many found solace and lived fruitful lives within these cloistered communities, this outwardly stagnant system likewise caused the neglect and deterioration of roads, which severely hindered communications, trade, and overall prosperity on a broad continental basis. It was this breakdown in unity and military strength that opened the monastic community's borders to repeat attacks. Hence, the Dark and Middle Ages unquestionably paled in comparison.

Moreover, it was during these dark centuries that the majority of ancient Rome's esoteric knowledge was lost. The original techniques and plans or proprietary knowledge, usually passed down by oral tradition, no longer existed. Engineering skills for developing massive building projects, intricate public works, and innovative textiles became dormant, as only provincial construction for small towns and feudal-states remained active. This compelled architects to venture back to Rome; for only by physically scrutinizing the works of those master builders could they hope to unlock their secrets.

This exploration eventually gave rise to those who forged a new architectural style, and culminated in Romanesque cathedrals, which contained Roman-styled features, infused with subtle novel nuances. The towering cathedrals in France, like those at Chartres and the famous Notre Dame in Paris, appeared in the twelfth century. These striking masterpieces of Gothic architecture arose during the tail end of many centuries of bleakness, and we mustn't forget; they, too, adopted classical Roman features, such as arches and groin-vaulted ceilings. However, to their credit, the elongated gothic windows, stained glass, and flying buttresses were distinctively new additions to the field of architecture.

Some architects, however, have criticized flying buttresses as being huge, cumbersome, ugly exoskeletons. Their sole function or structural necessity is to add lateral thrust to the towering cathedrals' walls; without them the colossal structures would collapse. This they attribute not only to poor structural planning, but also to a sacrilege of architectural aesthetics, for they distract from the beauty of a building's overall form and grace. Others even bemoan that they jut out like huge spider's legs.

There is some merit to these aesthetic and structural assessments, since they are indeed just a series of braces, and the eventual use of steel eliminated the need for external buttressing. But flying buttresses still have an intriguing mystique. They have enamored many who believe that the architects managed to create towering wonders within the confines of the engineering and structural resources of their day. Beyond the technical challenge, many, myself included, find these rows of supporting braces aesthetically pleasing, rather than viewing them as a series of obstructions.

Despite acknowledging some of that era's achievements, this returns us to the biased Catholic scholars who hailed Gothic architecture as superior to all others, while severely criticizing the competition. Topping the list were both classical Greek and Roman architecture, which their undulating tongues demolished like a wrecking ball. Although they made some very sound arguments regarding their cherished works, their outward attacks were narrow-minded and devoid of facts.

They astutely lauded the fact that many Gothic architects used divine proportions in drafting their buildings. For example, Salisbury Cathedral used the dimension of thirty-nine feet by thirty-nine feet for the transept, while its smaller naves are exactly half that dimension. Additionally, they mentioned the choir at Saint Remi, which uses three windows on three levels that symbolize the Holy Trinity, and the number thirty-three, the age of Christ when he supposedly died.

These were indeed admirable feats carried out by creative and highly devout architects. However, it is quite evident that these Christian scholars only sought to research these particular Christian cathedrals, and failed to investigate the fine details and sacred purposes of the architecture they viciously maligned. They derided pagan buildings for not stretching upward to the heavens like their towering Gothic cathedrals, which had graciously attempted to reach God.

First, these Christian zealots must temporarily deactivate their bulldozer mindset, which intolerantly shoved these pagan edifices into the shadows, so that they may clearly see them. Second, they should attempt to truly understand the beliefs and motivations of these ancient builders. Once that's understood, their designs suddenly become luminous and their achievements spectacular.

The Pantheon in Rome was designed to be a temple that honored not one god, but all their gods. As such, stretching upward to only one supreme god—in their case, Jupiter—would have denigrated all the others. Considering this, the solution that Hadrian and his planners arrived at was nothing short of miraculous. By designing a round building, they created a space that embraced all equally—a brilliant concept that King Arthur's ideal Round Table emulated. Mounted atop the circular drum stood the first and largest dome ever constructed. This engineering feat in itself is as miraculous as the Gothic edifices that came one thousand years later. Moreover, a greater number of modern buildings feature domes than they do gothic flying buttresses or stained glass windows. Therefore, in terms of influence, the dome is unmatched.

Further still, at the apex of this massive dome was a round opening, or oculus, which symbolized that most revered object of all antiquity, the Sun god. This orbital eye is the only source of light the interior receives, and this perfectly round circle sits perfectly at the center of a perfectly measured interior, and is, quite divinely, straight above their heads. In this regard, one could interpret gothic cathedrals as having light, not from God directly above, for that light is blocked by a solid gabled roof, but from sidewall windows, well below God's rightful place above. Hence, they could be interpreted as honoring earthly saints or even unknown souls, who stood on our right or left, rather than God directly above.

Added to this is the fact that the interior space of the Pantheon also contains divine dimensions, according to pagan beliefs, which is that of a perfect sphere and a perfect cube. The height of the dome is exactly equal to the circular drum's diameter; hence, this perfect configuration of absolute unity and concord had achieved its divine mission. Moreover, it did so just as well as the Gothic cathedrals, and possibly better, especially considering that the Pantheon was conceived and built over a thousand years earlier. *(See page 705)*

Another consideration they overlooked is that the cross-shaped configuration of many cathedrals was not invented by French Gothic architects; it was, in fact, created by the Romans who altered the plans of their basilicas to form cruciform churches. This slowly became the norm after Constantine's influential reign in the third century.

Furthermore, the domes that decorate many churches throughout Christendom, including Greek Orthodox churches, Saint Paul's Cathedral in London, and the Catholic Church's most holy cathedral, Saint Peter's, are also a pagan Roman invention. Therefore, they evidently don't realize or fail to mention that the vast majority of their churches, including their most sacred one, all incorporate designs emanating from the Roman Empire. Unfortunately, their intolerance for other religions and for the Roman pagans specifically, has clouded their judgment, and has done a disservice to themselves and their misled readers.

Admittedly, they constitute a small fringe, but the fact that they are published authors speaking to thousands and possibly millions demands a rebuttal. This leads to other biased attacks that warrant our attention.

As mentioned earlier, their revisionist pens were committed to revising the Dark and Middle Ages into a thriving golden age, one that was filled with innovation which boldly surpassed anything attempted by the Greek and Roman empires. According to them, these two pagan civilizations constitute an axis of evil and need to be punished by stripping them of all historic merit. Yet oddly enough, none of the so-called Christian innovations that they posited ever proved to be totally free of Roman and Greek influence.

Moreover, the minor advances in technology they mentioned only proved to be stepping-stones rather than full-blown milestones. This in no way belittles the importance of stepping-stones, for these are necessary to lead progress forward rather than backward. The abundance of documented history, tangible artifacts found in ruins of the Roman era (as put forth in this book and in thousands of others by notable scholars) clearly proves that the Middle Ages, when compared to the innovative and dynamic eras of the Roman Empire before it, and the Renaissance after it, was a long and relatively slothful period in Western civilization.

Beyond that glaring reality, however, they claim that the Roman Empire suppressed anything their aggressive hands touched, and like clumsy brutes, they mindlessly quashed invention. However, the following examples clearly indicate that the Romans enhanced invention and other cultures. A prelude to the Dark Ages was evident even earlier when Rome no longer supported, funded, or managed its province of Briton. During the Roman occupation the British Isle thrived, yet once they left, it sank into a dark malaise that persisted for many centuries. Those remaining after the evacuation had been left with the best facilities, tools, and knowledge that Romanization afforded them, yet the lack of Roman leadership, administrative skills, and economic infrastructures of trade caused Briton to slowly sink back into its previous primitive state.

Likewise, without the Romans' strong military to provide security, unchecked tribes poured over Hadrian's Wall and ransacked the once productive and civilized villas and city centers. It must also be noted that Roman villas were not small farmsteads, but huge agricultural centers that depended largely on trade with cities, not only in Briton, but throughout the empire as well. Therefore, with trade channels closed after the Romans' withdrawal, the high production rates of these centers practically came to a halt, for without the demand, the need to supply ceased. This once again elucidates how Romanization was not an aimless program that merely conquered territories, suppressed people, and simply built huge and glorious edifices. On the contrary, the Romans educated and advanced any culture that their thriving empire acquired, despite not offering the fully broadminded freedoms that we enjoy in the modern era. They were, after all, an ancient civilization.

With the collapse of the mighty, yet certainly not flawless, Roman government, later generations were politically and economically weakened, and in many instances broken. Yet during these deficient and secluded Dark and Middle Ages, many small seeds were being planted. Windmills and watermills powered tasks that many independent millers previously had done by hand; eyeglasses were invented in Italy, along with the improved compass; and greater freedoms emerged in some city-states, as the Magna Carta made its landmark debut in England in 1215.

However, all these innovations pale in comparison to those of the era's predecessor and successor. Nevertheless, these revisionists insist that Christianity was the driving force that gave rise to technological invention during the Middle Ages, and that the church even invented capitalism during the Renaissance.

As we shall see, their claim of inventing capitalism clearly falls into the lap of the Renaissance Florentine bankers, while the rural villagers in the Middle Ages, who they claim invented superior windmills, were clearly outmatched by their Roman predecessors. We shall begin with the case of watermills.

An astonishing discovery was made in the 1940s, at Barbegal in southern France, which revealed the existence of a huge Roman water-powered factory. It was, in fact, a flourmill, but no small or ordinary mill like those in Flanders or elsewhere, which were in use during the Middle Ages. Flemish windmills were not only small but remained in use without any significant improvement right up to the nineteenth century. In contrast, the Roman factory contained not one but eight colossal pairs of water wheels that milled flour in high volume for mass consumption.

The magnitude of this milling complex offers irrefutable evidence that the Romans invented and used large-scale industry that predated the petite watermills of the Middle Ages. That the Romans invented a superior watermill many centuries before also confirms how their advanced knowledge disappeared during the Middle Ages, and how Roman technology was not rivaled until the Industrial Revolution, which was over a thousand years in the future.

As for capitalism, the Renaissance bankers of Florence were the new driving force that initiated and then energized all economies throughout

Europe. These were all independent business-minded power lords that had dealings with the church, but those dealings were not for discussions of religious scripture, they were for making loans with interest and pursuing purely capitalistic ends.

As discussed elsewhere in this book, some dealings with the church ruptured into battles, as conspiracies and murderous intrigues prevailed on both sides. Popes, like Alexander and Sixtus, were mere power lords vying for their share of the market. Earlier popes, like Urban, sponsored the Crusades that killed fellow Christians along with Muslims while others reveled in nefarious Inquisitions, thus debunking the notion that Christianity only brings progress and radiant light upon all it embraces.

Perhaps the most devastating example of how Christianity thrust progress and civility into sheer darkness is the bloody fact of the Taiping Rebellion in China. During the mid-1800s, Hong Xiuquan converted to Christianity and formed the Taiping Heavenly Kingdom. This Christian kingdom was primarily a militant force of almost two million Chinese soldiers that was set up to rebel against the Qing Dynasty. Hong had emerged from the lower classes; he tried numerous times to gain civil employment but failed each time. Dejected and humiliated, he eventually embraced Christianity. Hong's obsession soon exceeded mere faith as he became convinced that he was Jesus Christ's brother and heir, thus negating the Holy Trinity.

Hong's large mass of followers embraced the Christian messiah, and together they went on to slaughter over 20 million Chinese, as they razed cities and ruthlessly killed men, women, and children. This bloodbath, over a ten-year period, was among the worst carnage known to mankind, and its leader's motivational impetus was Christianity.

Bloody milestones like the Crusades, Spanish Inquisition, or the Taiping Heavenly Kingdom are incontestable proof of the atrocious side effects that Christianity had on humanity. We should regret, yet learn from this history, not ignore or revise it to extol Christianity as the sole source of light, progress, and magnificent deeds. Christianity has many positive traits that make it the great religion it is, therefore these deceptive attempts to strip other secular or religious entities of their rightful place in history clearly defies core Christian principles of lucidity and integrity.

The Renaissance was an age of economic survival and control. Naturally many businessmen were religious, as even the Medici attended church and moreover placed their own kin within the Vatican to produce not one but three popes, namely Leo X, Clement VII, and Leo XI. However, attaining this ultimate seat of power also lends credence to their ulterior motives of maintaining power and economic control. It is rather significant that Lorenzo II de Medici's daughter, Catherine, transported Italian influence into France, when she became queen in the sixteenth century and gave birth to three future kings, namely Francis II, Charles IX and Henry III. In essence, religion for the masses was ritual, but for the ambitious elite, power was paramount.

In tandem with the rise of these secular power lords, was the advent of guilds, such as the masons' and the very powerful wool workers' guild. Guilds organized to form the powerful *popolo,* which gave a voice and a modicum of power to the working class, as they brokered with entrepreneurs and clergymen. The aristocracy and even the *popolo* became prime patrons of the arts, in order to decorate their cathedrals and paint private portraits. This explains why many religious paintings in Renaissance cathedrals include the portraits of their secular patrons acting out the roles of religious figures.

With the renewed interest in classical Rome, pagan themes also arose, such as Botticelli's paintings of Venus and other gods and goddesses. Additionally, portraiture became a new mode of fashion and prestige, as patrons sought the best artists. As we know, the *Mona Lisa* surpassed all other portraits and in popularity even rivals religious works of the era, with Leonardo's own *Last Supper* and Michelangelo's work in the Sistine Chapel being its only competition. The primary sponsors of progress were no longer to be found in the church, but rather in the new capitalistic private sector—despite how these fanatical Christian authors have unsuccessfully attempted to revise the story. This now leads us to the true architects of the Renaissance, the Medici.

THE MEDICI: *True Architects of the Renaissance*

The Medici dynasty produced an amazing lineage of shrewd businessmen, politicians, queens, kings, and patrons of the arts that more than any other person, pope, or aristocratic family, built the Renaissance. Our treatment of this powerhouse of ingenuity, however, needs to be placed within the framework of a changing world. It was shortly after the first millennium that three milestones of human advancement occurred in three different cities. The first two will be addressed briefly, and the third city, Florence, which is the foundational home of the Medici and the Renaissance, will be discussed at length.

THE FIRST MILESTONE occurred in Salerno with the advent of the first true medical center. A rich diversity of ancient medical practices was revived there, along with the development of new scientific procedures, thus Salerno became the progressive nucleus of medical science and instruction. Previously, all medical training and treatments were conducted at the infirmaries of monasteries. The primitive remedies practiced by monks were rarely beneficial, and the scholars at Salerno soon realized that human afflictions weren't the result of God's wrath, but were due to natural occurrences. The new surgical practitioners changed the use of old monastic remedies of bloodletting, folk medicine, and prayer. Roger Frugardi, who studied anatomy and devised the methods of suturing torn organs, became well known for prescribing new remedies, such as using seaweed ashes, which contained iodine. Iodine soon became the prime antibacterial solution for many centuries, right up to the twentieth century. Frugardi also penned the first Western book on surgery in AD 1170. The strict curriculum at Salerno consisted of eight years of intensive training and a one-year internship with a respected doctor. Graduates were allowed to practice their new trade for a fee, and the birth of the medical profession was official.

THE SECOND MILESTONE occurred in Bologna when the world's first university was established in 1088. This new form of public education laid the foundation of academia that still exists to this day. This was the Roman Catholic Church's grand contribution. The new guild of teachers became known as the *collegia*, and a broad liberal arts curriculum was formulated.

It was based upon the Roman model of classical antiquity, and academic degrees—baccalaureate, master's, and doctorate—were newly established and awarded. In time, Bologna's university influenced other cities, so that by 1400, two-dozen universities sprouted throughout Europe—from Paris to as far away as Cambridge, England. Of these twenty-four new campuses, ten were in Italy. Universities greatly altered social and economic paradigms and profoundly enhanced civilization. As the centuries passed, this great invention of the Catholic Church was replicated, as many secular universities arose. Naturally all great ideas and monopolies inevitably must contend with rivals.

THE THIRD MILESTONE occurred in Florence and was initiated by Giovanni di Bicci de Medici. Giovanni launches our immersion into the Medici dynasty, for he was the mastermind who founded the Medici bank. The entire Medici clan for many generations would reap the benefits of Giovanni's strong foundation, and even expand into areas that would have been unimaginable to this levelheaded patriarch, for Giovanni insisted upon maintaining a low profile.

Giovanni did not invent banking—other Florentines resurrected the age-old practice first—but his wise business maneuvers transformed the industry, making the Medici Bank a leader. Where other banks had collapsed, such as those owned by the Bardi and Peruzzi families, Giovanni devised a simple but brilliant solution. He took on junior partners to manage his banks in distant locations, which operated as quasi-independent branches, and in this way motivated his associates, built loyalty, and secured the Medici's parent holding company. This, too, operated out of a separate office in Florence, protected from the threat of total bankruptcy. Giovanni's strategy became the template of modern day banking and corporate structure, with limited liability being a key feature.

Giovanni also set the Medici standard for funding grand projects, although warning his children to "stay out of the public eye." Avoiding attention, jealousy, and scandal, Giovanni employed Brunelleschi to rebuild the San Lorenzo church, and commissioned Donatello to decorate the Sacristy. Thus began the new practice of funding talent for the good of the church, which also happened to be the Medici's main client. These traits of artistic patronage were deeply ingrained in Giovanni's offspring who continued the Medici tradition. Upon the elder Medici's death, his son Cosimo took the helm and boldly pioneered a brilliant course that procured many more wonders for Florence. He became one of the most important figures, along with his father, in spawning the Renaissance.

Cosimo, however, refused to take his father's advice about keeping a low profile and became embroiled in Florentine politics. His attempt to sway public opinion against the Albizzi family, which ruled over Florence for decades, almost cost him his life. The Albizzis were a wealthy family of landowning aristocrats who were about to face a new generation of power lords, the bankers. Cosimo had been a savvy and ambitious networker who became a very popular figure. Where landowners were wealthy in their own town or region, this new breed of aristocrat had clients and contacts across the full breadth of Europe, and included the all-important pope and Vatican States.

Cosimo was determined, ruthless when necessary, but equally benevolent to the poor, knowing that they needed funding to be productive and to regain self-esteem. He was likewise dedicated to civic improvements, including sponsoring building projects, artistic endeavors, literary studies, as well as renovating the local San Marco monastery. Besides constructing a library for the monastery, Cosimo also supplied the books. This pious gesture was actually prompted by Pope Eugenius IV, who happened to be hiding in Florence, since usurpers were vying for the holy seat back in Rome and creating havoc.

However, Cosimo's deal with the pope had two conditions. First, the Silvestrine order had to be replaced with the humbler and more easily satisfied Dominicans, and second, he needed to receive a family chamber in the monastery. Better still, for his munificent gesture, Cosimo was to receive a papal bull absolving him of all sin. Being the astute businessman that he was, verbal agreements were not good enough; Cosimo insisted that the papal indulgence be engraved in stone above his sacred chamber.

These were revolutionary times, as the church would break their isolation and enter a new, heightened phase of brokering with outsiders, for the wealth and power of the new capitalists was unavoidable.

In essence, Cosimo was a born politician, in the best and worst senses. As with anyone wielding great power, however, toes were inevitably going to be stepped on, feathers would be ruffled, and conflict would and did erupt.

The Albizzi family was not willing to give up control of the city, so when Cosimo engaged in mudslinging propaganda (while Rinaldo degli Albizzi was away on a war campaign), all hell broke loose. As soon as Rinaldo received word of the Medici maneuver, he quickly summoned his forces. Abandoning his post, Rinaldo returned to Florence and had Cosimo arrested. Rinaldo intended to behead Cosimo, but his council was wary. They knew many in Florence lived and thrived on Cosimo's generosity, and therefore outrage and mayhem would ensue.

Adding further to their concerns was that Cosimo's clients across Europe quickly dispatched messengers to Florence on Cosimo's behalf. Worse still, the pope had a voice in the matter. Fearing trade embargos and excommunication, the Florentines were adamant about sparing Cosimo's life. Essentially, the power of a banker with allies across Europe was no match for a rich local landlord. In humiliation, Rinaldo was forced to release Cosimo, but banished him to Padua for ten years.

Cosimo was too ambitious and too well connected to remain in Padua. It wasn't long before Cosimo's friends on the Florentine council managed his transfer to Venice. Not one to sit idle, Cosimo wasted no time in making lavish investments while in Venice. These budding enterprises quickly awakened many in Florence to a cold reality; namely, those improvements could have been for his home city and the proceeds in their pockets. As such, banishing their star achiever was a barefaced blunder.

Despite his absence, Cosimo managed to win even more supporters and more business. His uncanny knack for business would catapult the Medici bank to its greatest height of profitability and solvency. Riding high on a wave of success and power, Cosimo returned to Florence where he soon became the city's political and economic leader. Never one to forget a bad deal or rival, Cosimo received his payback by exiling Rinaldo.

Naturally, a few heads had to roll, but Cosimo became the munificent father figure in Florence who sponsored everything imaginable, from the Catholic Church to the new secular humanist breed. Furthermore, he provided loans for almost every type of business entity in

Florence, as well as in distant cities. These investments actually turned floundering slums or wastelands into thriving cities.

During this time, Cosimo's wealth and influence also became evident in a uniquely visual fashion. A new breed of artists was emerging that exhibited a growing awareness of the ancient practice of painting realistic scenes. Along with Cosimo's desire for immortality, this inaugurated several firsts in art history. First, rather than kings, pharaohs, or emperors being the prime patrons of the arts, now independent capitalists not only competed, but actually led the way. Second, religious scenes were painted with a new humanist realism, in direct contrast to the rigid plastic-like figures of the Middle Ages. Last, and to some people quite blasphemously, the new breed of secular patrons wanted their families to be remembered and revered; thus, religious characters in frescoes took on the features of the patrons and their family members.

It must be clarified that in this last regard, Cosimo was far more discreet. He only insisted that his patron saint, along with those of his relatives, be included in the scene, yet the religious portraits themselves did not bear any physical likeness to the Medici.

But quite subtly, the Medici emblem and color scheme would find its way into dazzling frescoes. As ancient emperors wanted to leave their imprint upon their empire, so, too, did Cosimo and his powerful group of rivals.

Most importantly, by the secular capitalists funding and infusing the new art form into the sacred realm, they truly launched the Renaissance art movement. The high visibility of these works quickly gave rise to talk, praise, discussion, inspiration, and inevitably competition. As each Florentine chapel or church outdid another, rivalry escalated, prompting churches in other villages to follow suit. Naturally, popes became fierce contenders, as it was imperative to outdo their secular subordinates. The future Pope Julius would achieve victory by commissioning Michelangelo to paint the Sistine Chapel, and Raphael and a profusion of other great talents to decorate the Vatican.

To some it seemed natural that great wealth and power were in the hands of their spiritual leader, the pope, but men like Cosimo needed to find some biblical justification or example to follow. He found it in the

Magi, and this is why that particular scene was his favorite. In fact, it was the only scene in which Cosimo allowed his portrait to be used to depict one of the three kings.

Oddly enough, even the Bible somehow managed to have a moment where the rich offered gifts to Jesus, which is ironic, since his whole ministry practically revolved around despising the wealthy. Whether it was toppling over the moneychangers' table that secured his crucifixion, or lambasting rich people, Jesus' message was clear. As He said, *"How hardly shall they that have riches enter into the kingdom of God! For it is easier for a camel to go through a needle's eye, than for a rich man to enter into the kingdom of God."*

Cosimo was not alone, as other rich men went even further in their desire for glory and eternal life in heaven. The rich banker, Giovanni Rucellai, had his tomb built to the exact specifications of the famous Church of the Holy Sepulchre. Taking megalomania to a profane new level, Rucellai had his name chiseled right on the façade of the beautiful Santa Maria Novella Church. This edifice, designed by Leon Battista Alberti, still stands today. It is clear that the humanist movement had literally etched itself upon the religious world.

Despite the extravagances by all men of power (for what is the use of being hyperambitious if nothing remains to show for it), when Cosimo died, the city bestowed upon him the title *Pater Patriae*, meaning Father of his Country. Cosimo de Medici's imprint and influence was so immense and so multifaceted that he aptly earned another title—Renaissance man.

Cosimo was pivotal in making Florence the beacon of civilization in the fifteenth century. Along with Brunelleschi's dome being completed during his reign, which was the engineering miracle of the early Renaissance, and the array of artists under his employ, Cosimo also managed to hold the Council of Ferrara in Florence. This council temporarily united the Eastern Orthodox and Western ecclesiasts who had been divided since the fourth century. The Eastern Roman Empire, or Byzantium, lasted longer than its western counterpart, but faced a perilously fast decline as Ottoman Turks encroached dangerously closer. In an effort to gain support from the West, the Greek Orthodox were finally open to discussion.

In 1439, Cosimo had the meeting held in Florence, due to the plague that was afflicting Ferrara at the time. With Pope Eugenius IV presiding, the Italian ecclesiasts won not only the Greek delegates' obedience to be ruled by the pope, but also their sworn testimony to finally embrace the notion of the Holy Trinity. This was colossal, for the Greek Orthodox never believed in this concept that Constantine cemented into Catholic scripture. It had been another major reason for them to split centuries ago, yet now a forced epiphany seemed to have struck these worried Greeks.

When the clergymen returned home, their colleagues burst into rage. They were initially receptive to kowtowing to the pope's wishes (obviously to gain financial and military support), but they were not prepared to cave in on such a crucial article of faith—that their Lord was not one, but three entities. This was something they would never sell out on. Hence, they terminated the negotiations. The Byzantines would somehow face the Turks alone.

Unfortunately, they signed their own death warrant, as fourteen years later harsh reality triumphed over faith. To their horror, the great city of Constantinople fell. The Muslim forces were stronger and they made the first-ever naval attack on the port city. The Byzantine Empire crumbled in 1453. Christianity in the East was irrevocably overrun, as the Islamic invaders stormed churches and cathedrals and stripped them of their Christian glory. The streets ran red, as men, women, and children were butchered in the wake of Islamic forces.

Similar to the time of Hitler's rise to power, many people recognized the warning signs and fled Byzantium before a major tempest struck. A century before Cosimo's time, Byzantines arrived in Italy. The Byzantine scholars moved to Florence, most of whom were well versed in the writings of Plato, Aristotle, Homer, Pindar, and many others, including an assortment of Roman classics that had likewise been lost to Western Europe. Although the Eastern Byzantines preserved and transported these precious texts, it was the Western Florentines and other Italians who utilized the information that truly influenced Western thought.

One example was Barlaam of Calabria, who was born in Italy in 1290, and then moved to Constantinople. Barlaam later returned and taught Greek and Roman classics to the famous Italian scholar and poet

Petrarca (also known as Petrarch). Originally born in Arezzo (some forty miles south of Florence), Petrarca infused this newly acquired Greek and Roman classical knowledge with his own sensibilities, thus becoming a strident voice for the new breed. In fact, Petrarca first used the Latin term *humanitas* or humanism, the term still used to describe this entire movement in history. Petrarca is likewise credited with labeling the appallingly dim centuries before his time, which apparently disregarded knowledge, as the "Dark Ages."

With his three primary role models being Virgil, Cicero, and Seneca, Petrarca's own philosophy was an amalgamation of these famous ancient Romans', as well as the new Greek philosophical texts he ingested. Petrarca's influence extended to other scholars, writers, artists, and politicians, and he has rightfully been called the "Father of Humanism."

Furthermore, although later Byzantine diplomats, like Manuel Chrysoloras, effectively taught Greek for several years in Florence, it was primarily their Italian protégés who would instill ancient Greek and Latin literature into the Florentine mindset. Leonardo Bruni, also from Arezzo, was pivotal in that while others converted ancient Greek texts word for word, whereby the Latin equivalent seldom conveyed the proper meaning of its direct Greek counterpart, Bruni actually rewrote the sentences in a fluid and more comprehendible style. Bruni's innovative process not only captured the original concept more clearly but it was also more eloquent and engaging. Bruni actually coined the term "translation".

Bruni's many translations, and perhaps more importantly, his influence on prominent Western leaders, including those in the Vatican, were vital to unshackling the rigid gothic and monastic mindset that had crippled the West for many centuries. Bruni gave lectures at the Vatican and also exposed them to his own books, such as *In Praise of the City of Florence* and *The History of the Florentine People*, which advocated Petrarca's humanist ideology. This more open-minded period allowed many forgotten or discarded ideas of the ancient Romans and Greeks to reemerge and thus bind with the once resistant Catholic mentality.

The Western protégés of Eastern Byzantine scholars demonstrated an amazing ability to quickly ingest knowledge and become the new and enduring experts who inspired future generations. Where the Eastern

Byzantines savored and preserved ancient relics, which was crucial in itself, from the impending doom of an Islamic invasion, the Western-minded Italians, in contrast, turned those dusty old pages into vibrant and scintillating ideas—ideas that spurred a whole new era.

Some still posit the belief that Byzantine and Greek thought were solely responsible for sparking the Renaissance and this warrants some attention. First, as discussed thus far, not only Greek texts were used, and second, not only texts spurred the Renaissance. Furthermore, the Italian Renaissance, for the most part, possessed Italian and Roman factors for several prominent reasons.

First, the Eastern Byzantines held this information for centuries yet the East never exploded into a Renaissance as the Italian peninsula did in the West. This indicates that other profound influences were unquestionably involved. It also indicates that either the Greek Byzantines did not know how to use or build upon that knowledge, or that they were just sentinels preserving the texts. Probably both are true, since many of the scholars that came to Italy did in fact teach this information. Therefore, the Byzantines were certainly adept at reiteration but not at stimulative recreation. Furthermore, the majority of prime movers in the West were born in Italy, and their profound interest in their own tradition validates why the Western Renaissance blossomed while the Eastern Byzantine Empire not only withered but also disastrously fell.

Second, even visual comparisons of the two cultures make this quite clear. The Greek Byzantines and even the invading Muslims had clearly avoided humanism and wholly embraced iconoclasm. In essence, they eliminated all human imagery from their religious symbols, churches, and mosques. This visual vacancy in Eastern art is in sharp contrast with the art that has come to personify the Western Renaissance. It is extremely difficult for anyone to claim that Byzantium gave the West its visual splendor or that it was the sole impetus for breaking the West out of the long Dark and Middle Ages. As the old adage goes, "seeing is believing," and the visual evidence proves otherwise.

Beyond this Greek Renaissance hypothesis, we also have Muslims today asserting superiority to the West. Their claim is that at the end of the Renaissance and well into the Baroque period, Muslims surpassed

Western engineering feats. They point to the architectural complexity of the Suleiman Mosque, built in 1550; but this Mosque was simply a plagiarism of the Roman-designed Hagia Sophia basilica, with only minor variations. The Emperor Justinian ordered the Hagia Sophia to be built in AD 532, preceding the Muslim design by over a thousand years.

Furthermore, no completely new or original designs developed in the East, while centuries earlier in the West, the cathedral in Florence, with its octagonal dome, was a first in world history. Likewise, the gothic cathedrals, built two centuries earlier in France and Germany, also boasted unique designs, with nothing comparable to be found in the East. Beyond architecture and art, however, advancements in education, medicine, manufacturing, business, and of course, banking flourished in the West, while the East, even with its stockpile of Greek texts or Arab influences, pales in comparison.

Arabic numerals, as credited to Muhammad ibn Musa al-Khwarizmi, were the most obvious and important advancement in the East, which have greatly benefited the West. However, the more precise calendar, devised by Omar Khayyám for the Sultan Malik-Shah in 1079, was nothing earth-shattering in the grand scheme of historical progress. Even the often-quoted gift of paper, which came through Byzantium, and ended the use of inferior papyrus, was not invented by Byzantines or Muslims, since paper originated in China.

The humanist thought and inventiveness that pervaded Renaissance Italy not only came from ancient Greek texts from Byzantium, but more so from other sources. Moreover, some of these sources were visually evident all around them in the grand and magnificent edifices that remained from classical Rome, as well as the rich texts of Cicero, Cato, Seneca, Tacitus, Livy, and other Roman notables, which furthermore was inherent in their blood. This gravitational pull was evident in the poetry of this time and in the fine art, politics, business, and every other facet of their reawakened sensibilities. As noted, the intervention of the Medici and their capitalistic innovations remains paramount in this Renaissance picture. In essence, all these sources in unison had a huge catalytic impact on fueling this bold generation to resurrect the past and resolutely build upon it to make an unprecedented leap forward.

The Middle Ages and the Age of Rebirth

The dynamic Medici family eagerly harvested both ancient Greek and Roman literature, as their friend Roberto Rossi personally tutored Cosimo de Medici. Cosimo also enjoyed the lectures of Pletho—who although being a fanatic that advocated the reinstatement of the Greek Olympian gods—was also influential in introducing Cosimo to Plato. Plato's antidemocratic stance happened to coincide with Cosimo's broad authoritarian agendas, which made it easy for the adventurous entrepreneur/ruler to infuse secular ideas into his well-funded workshops and private academies.

The renewed interest in classical Rome prompted the excavation of Cicero's house along with literature, plays, and the all-important histories left by Livy, which simultaneously entered Florentine workshops. These new bastions of learning eventually spawned the humanist breed in Florence that would help establish at least part of the Renaissance mindset. This was an inquisitive, and at times mystical, outlook, which revitalized the arts, philosophy, and even religion.

We must also not forget that the most influential author of the Renaissance by far was Machiavelli; and aside from *The Prince*, his *Discourses on the First Ten Books of Titus Livy* was a direct study of the Roman historian's works. Furthermore, Machiavelli's comedy *Clizia* was a reworking of a play by the famous Roman playwright, Plautus, while Machiavelli's *The Art of War*, was a thorough study of classical and contemporary Roman military tactics. In fact in large part Machiavelli's sources were drawn from ancient Rome along with his own experiences in Florence. That is also why he was selected by Giulio de' Medici (who later became Pope Clement VII) to write the *History of Florence*. What is abundantly clear, however, is that Machiavelli's most ardent desire was to groom a new leader or prince who could rekindle the glory of ancient Rome.

Meanwhile, beyond the realm of philosophy and books, the influence of the majestic ruins of ancient Rome, which tantalizingly mocked the younger neophyte generation, single-handedly propelled early Renaissance engineers to rekindle the lost technologies of their forefathers. The grandness of classical Rome also impelled entrepreneurs to seek capitalistic trade infrastructures that once powered the mighty

Roman Empire, while prodding artists and sculptors to explore classical Roman frescos, mosaics, and statues. Naturally, the study of the Roman Republic and Imperial Rome taught rulers how to structure a regime, like the republic of Florence, and maintain firm control, like the Medici or various dukes among a sea of city-states.

This included the papacy, which always maintained Roman influences of authoritarian rule. This elucidates why the pope adamantly denounced the new wave of Greek Orthodox immigrants who strongly favored rule by council. Greek Orthodox Christians preferred a socialistic configuration, like the ancient Greek form of democracy, and this long-held preference even turned to coercion.

In 1431, the Greek conciliarists, who advocated administration by council, effectively drove Pope Eugenius IV into exile, and so he moved to Florence. The pope remained there for ten years, along with his court. A major schism had erupted earlier in 1309, when Avignon in southern France became the new seat for several popes. Some of those popes ruled concurrent with Roman popes, but were later annulled and reviled as antipopes. However, the diehard Catholic Church eventually regained its stronghold, and indelibly fixed itself back in Rome; the Roman pope would retain ultimate control. As noted, this ultimate executive seat of power was adopted from the Roman Empire. Christianity's older paternal relative, Judaism, and its younger sibling, Islam, both rejected the Roman hierarchy of power and governance, as did the Greek Orthodox.

The resolve of Catholics to maintain their Roman form of rule is further validated by other events. When the new wave of Greeks first arrived, they sought to sway public opinion into advocating rule by council rather than having the executive office of pope. However, their attempt to convert the Italians failed, as they themselves converted to Roman Catholicism. Men like Barlaam, and a century later in the fifteenth century, John Bessarion, who actually became a Catholic cardinal, eventually surrendered to the Roman Catholic hierarchy of administration. The vast majority of these Byzantine scholars, which also included George of Trebizond, or even Lorenzo de Medici's tutor, John Argyropoulos, all converted to Roman Catholicism.

Making the Byzantines' conversion to Catholicism much more palatable was the fact that later in 1446, the Italian Tommaso Parentucelli became Pope Nicholas V. As it turned out, Tommaso had been a close friend of Cosimo de Medici and his humanist entourage, which included Cardinal Bessarion. Pope Nicholas V was more of a scholarly bookworm himself, and is best remembered for establishing the Vatican Library. Cardinal Bessarion played a key role in building the library, which housed existing and newly commissioned translations of ancient Greek and Latin texts.

One such translator was the Italian, Lorenzo Valla. Valla not only translated works by Thucydides and Herodotus, but he also determined that the famous document, *The Donation of Constantine* (which 700 years earlier invented the papal seat, and gave the pope dominion over both the religious and temporal realms) was in fact a fraud. This revelation must have come as an embarrassment to Pope Nicholas V; however, with the papacy and Vatican now firmly rooted, this unsavory piece of history would remain nicely locked in the Vatican's vaults for several more centuries. What mattered most was that the humanist agenda now had support by the pope himself.

In summation, ancient Greek and Roman texts did reinvigorate Western theological, academic, and philosophical realms of learning, however, these influences would more fully reveal themselves during the distant Enlightenment era of the eighteenth century. Far more crucial were the pragmatic political, military, technological, and capitalistic aspects gained from ancient Rome, as these caused the most dramatic and life-altering events during the Renaissance. The Florentines not only revived Roman architecture, engineering, and visual arts to build prestige as well as civic and spiritual pride, but of equal or perhaps even greater importance was their new banking system and expansive trade network. As stated, this bolstered their economies and living standards, and it pervasively swept throughout Europe. Naturally, the emphasis on capitalism and entrepreneurialism altered not only their own era but quite significantly all others that followed.

While the great artists, such as Leonardo, Michelangelo, and Brunelleschi, stole our attention with magnificent paintings, dramatic statues, majestic cathedrals, and opulent villas, the Medici, Riccardi, Pazzi, and other power brokers (who ignited these dynamic capitalistic empires) were the silent architects who created the economic foundation for all capitalistic enterprises in the future. Naturally, this includes all democratic and republican nations, such as England and America.

In their day, this ingenious capitalistic machine took precedence over the visual arts or the philosophical and literary exchanges in which social groups, even academics, would politely engage. But today, as many peer back to assess the Renaissance, the artistic and intellectual landmarks blindingly dazzle us, yet the daily balance sheets and business transactions that ushered in this prosperous new age still remain hidden in the banker's dark vaults. In essence, it was this dynamic duality of capitalist patron and creative talent that truly built the Renaissance.

As for the Catholic Church, it not only engaged in business and politics with dukes, kings, and various city-states, but the influence of Greek thought likewise had some effect on dogma as well. For many centuries, the church rarely encouraged science, and more often prohibited it, for men were taught not to question the world or their place in it; the church's exclusive doorway to God was all men needed for enlightenment. Most of us are well acquainted with the church being criticized for suppressing science, however, the church, especially during the Middle Ages, did adopt and unwittingly enforce Greek scientific paradigms. However, certain aspects of the Grecian order of the universe were already compatible with some verses of scripture. Nevertheless, Aristotelian thought was incorporated into new liturgy to the extent that the Jesuits strictly enforced it well into the seventeenth century.

However, these Greek scientific truths, which were in reality unchallenged hypotheses, would prove to be devastatingly flawed, and caused a great deal of havoc and harm. Inquisitive minds that refuted those Greek paradigms were imprisoned, like Galileo, or even sentenced to death, like Giordano Bruno. Bruno was a sign of the times. More than a decade earlier, Bruno delved into Copernican theory and Neo-Platonist philosophy, both of which opposed Catholic dogma. After being brutally burned at the stake, Bruno was hailed as the first martyr for science. The Roman Inquisition by the Vatican regrettably lasted until the mid-1800s.

Therefore, the influx of Greek thought, through the corridors of Byzantium, brought with it both positive and negative attributes that both stymied and propelled the Renaissance to varying degrees.

The Renaissance was also marked by other major events outside of Italy. As mentioned, far off to the east, the Byzantine Empire, with its grand capital city of Constantinople, fell to the Turks. The eastern half of the Roman Empire had finally fallen to the Muslims, while even further east, Ivan III, better known as Ivan the Great, made successful conquests that established Moscow as the preeminent capital of Mother Russia.

Interestingly enough, Cardinal Bessarion had written a letter to Ivan, suggesting that he wed the last reigning Byzantine emperor's niece. Being enamored with Roman/Byzantine heritage, Ivan took the cardinal's advice and married Sophia Paleologa. Ivan symbolically styled his new imperial order with Constantinople's double-headed eagle, which naturally was an adaptation of the Roman eagle. Ivan inspired Russian literature that heralded their new city as the Third Rome. Several decades later, Ivan IV, better known as Ivan the Terrible, took the title Tsar, which is Russian for Caesar, once again, indicating the all-powerful fascination and influence of Rome, which motivated countless leaders and whole nations.

During the reign of Ivan the Great, in 1455, a truly major milestone occurred. This took place to the west in the German city of Mainz, where a newly improved invention would eliminate the long and tedious process of copying manuscripts by hand.

JOHANN GUTENBERG: In 1450, Gutenberg was looking to expand his fledgling printing business and borrowed 800 guilders from Johann Fust. During the next few years, Gutenberg printed short poems and his first book on his new movable-type printing press.

Gutenberg then borrowed another 800 guilders from Fust to begin printing the Bible. In 1455, he printed 180 Bibles, yet he found himself embroiled in a legal battle with Fust, who claimed that Gutenberg embezzled funds. Gutenberg lost the case and Fust and associates took over the printing business, which subsequently developed into a successful enterprise. Meanwhile, Gutenberg fell into debt and almost total obscurity. It would be many long years before Gutenberg would finally be credited with initiating this new process of printing.

Although Gutenberg did not invent the printing press, or movable type, which were invented in Korea four hundred years previously, Gutenberg's reinvention allowed the written word to reach the masses at an accelerated rate. For within two decades, more than one hundred printing presses across Europe were churning out books by the thousands. Previously, books were laboriously written by hand, or printed on presses that required long and tedious preparations that yielded a fixed unalterable plate.

For centuries, the church controlled all publications, and with that, all thought contained within those pages. With the advent of Gutenberg's printing press, independence and unrestrained thought were given wings. As such, the dissemination of human knowledge more readily took flight.

Also taking flight was man's desire to achieve architectural wonders. Quite regrettably, the esoteric knowledge of engineering and technology that had given rise to the Pantheon and Colosseum had sadly vanished. As the church rose in affluence and busily propagated dogma, the loss of this knowledge caused serious repercussions, and their own quagmire. At the predawn of the Renaissance, architects in Florence ambitiously began constructing a huge cathedral, yet lacking knowledge of dome construction their grand efforts came to a screeching halt. Standing perplexed at their technological dead-end, they eagerly awaited a miracle.

FILIPPO BRUNELLESCHI: Born in Florence in 1377, Filippo Brunelleschi was well known by all Florentines, for he had invented the mathematical laws of linear perspective that the ancient Romans apparently exercised. Brunelleschi's geometric invention gave a whole new generation of artists and architects the primary tool to develop earth-shattering wonders in paint, like those created by Verrocchio, Leonardo, Michelangelo, and countless others, not to mention 3D architectural plans.

Brunelleschi was also remembered in Florence for losing the bronze door competition to his rival Lorenzo Ghiberti. Ghiberti's magnificently sculpted doors adorned the Baptistery and immediately enthralled the entire city. In turn, Ghiberti was garnished with the utmost adoration and world fame. In humiliation, Filippo left Florence, only to return many years later when a golden opportunity presented itself—the new dome competition.

Finally, here was Brunelleschi's chance to regain his stolen title, and the respect he knew he deserved. The design was for the city's huge Santa Maria del Fiore cathedral. Originally designed in 1296, the huge project lingered for over a century, facing revisions and cutbacks. By 1419, the building had finally reached completion, except for the massive void at the top, which somehow was to be capped off with a dome.

Brunelleschi was dismayed to learn that his old rival, Ghiberti, also entered the competition, but more problematic, however, was that the project posed an additional conundrum. The dome's drum foundation was not round like the Pantheon, but octagonal. This was a first, which naturally entered the participants into new and uncharted realms of engineering. Brunelleschi had previously traveled to Rome and meticulously studied the Pantheon. Despite the obvious differences, Brunelleschi had deciphered many of the hidden tricks and traits of the Pantheon's unique anatomy. Confident that this covert acquisition gave him the edge over his archrival, Ghiberti, and every other contender, Brunelleschi feverishly set to work on his own master plan.

When the day finally arrived, the hopefuls submitted their grand plans. As the judging committee sifted through the entries, their jaws must have dropped when they gazed at Brunelleschi's radical plans. For not only was his design astoundingly unique *(see page 707)*, but Filippo had the audacity, or sheer stupidity, to do away with the use of wooden centering. Centering had long been the established and mandatory approach for erecting arches. It entailed creating huge wooden arches whereby masons would lay and set their bricks on top, thus following the curved wooden form. Some Florentines ridiculed Filippo for abandoning this only-known procedure, while the contestants anticipated new solutions.

The octagonal obstacle, along with its unprecedented height, demanded a new approach. At first skeptical, the committee slowly recognized the validity of Filippo's engineering skills when his flawless miniature model awed the public audience. Brunelleschi had even penciled out plans for constructing his own proprietary cranes, jacks, and scaffolding to complete the daunting task, all without the use of centering. No detail was left out, for nothing had escaped Filippo's discerning eye.

With the backing of the highly influential Medici banking family, the committee initially commissioned Brunelleschi to construct a smaller dome in the city to test his theories in practice. It was soon evident that Filippo was the engineering savant that Florence had long prayed for, and to his everlasting delight, Brunelleschi won the contract.

Filippo engaged the project with fervor, and cautiously supervised every facet of the operation. The master even constructed his new-fangled hoists and machinery, in addition to safety mechanisms that saved many lives. Years later, young Leonardo would be intrigued by these devices, and they deeply influenced his own array of mechanical creations. Ingenuity begets influence, influence begets inspiration, and inspiration begets ingenuity—a perfect circle.

But Brunelleschi was in for some aggravation. A few judges on the advisory panel were still skeptical of his abilities, and they insultingly appointed his rival, Ghiberti, to become the project's supervisor. Resolved to never fall in Ghiberti's shadow again, Brunelleschi soon made it abundantly clear that he, not Ghiberti, was the grand master. As engineering obstacles arose, Ghiberti stood mute. The complex project was far out his creative or technical reach, thus proving that Brunelleschi alone possessed not only all the concepts but also all the solutions. Filippo's solutions single-handedly escalated engineering, architecture, and the art of dome construction to new heights.

Brunelleschi's mesmerizing dome even inaugurated the first double-dome construction in history, which even facilitated a staircase sandwiched in-between. Located inside one of the vertical ribs, it was conveniently used to ascend to the apex of the cupola. In total, these radical and daring features not only perplexed the committee but also made Brunelleschi's design seem ridiculously unfeasible.

Therefore, on the heavily anticipated day of the dome's completion, the architect was presented with a double reward, for his biting critics fell into an eerie silence, while the rest of the city showered him with praise and glory. Brunelleschi's masterwork broke many astounding records, and rightfully boosted Filippo into the stratosphere of world fame. Not only was Filippo's design an instant success, but his double-domed blueprint would even be adopted by Michelangelo and Dela Porta many years later when they designed Saint Peter's dome.

Thus, with Brunelleschi's new masterpiece, Florence became the technological focal point and crown jewel of the budding Renaissance.

This aptly brings us to the following chain of events, which also validates how the influence of artistic genius spurs others to greatness.

In 1475, Brunelleschi's friend, Paolo Toscanelli, was enamored by Filippo's new architectural wonder. Paolo was a brilliant physician and astronomer, who had even taught Filippo geometry.

Toscanelli was anxious to conduct celestial experiments atop the soaring lantern (which was designed and mounted by Verrocchio) that crowned the new dome. With the committee's consent, Paolo rigged up a plate with a small aperture at the base of the lantern; this allowed sunlight to pass down the drum directly to the distant floor below.

In essence, Paolo created a highly accurate sundial, and this allowed him to make precise mathematical corrections to the prevailing calculations that charted the sun's movements. This led Toscanelli to calculate the vernal equinox and summer solstice with complete accuracy, and also to devise a new and superior form of navigation.

The existing methods of navigation, whereby navigators used maps with astrolabes to calculate their position by tracking the Pole Star, had reached a dead end. It worked in the Mediterranean Sea, but as mariners traveled south, they realized the Pole Star's position lowered on the horizon, thus becoming insufficient for global navigation.

Toscanelli realized that the sun was the best source for global navigation, and with his superior maps, he was the first person in his age to put forth the idea of sailing west to reach India.

Six years before in 1453, the Turks conquered Byzantium. That conquest severed land travel for Europeans attempting to reach the Far East, which was a vital trade route. As such, another route became a necessity. Hence, Toscanelli was extremely eager to make his theory known as a viable solution.

Toscanelli promptly appealed to his friend, Fernão Martines, who worked at the court of King Afonso in Portugal, for Paolo was well aware of their great strides in vessel construction and exploration. However, Paolo's new plan fell upon deaf ears. Seven long years passed before a zealous relative of Martines finally contacted Toscanelli. It was the gutsy navigator from Genoa, Christopher Columbus.

CHRISTOPHER COLUMBUS: Intrigued by Paolo Toscanelli's new maps and bold route plan, Columbus eagerly tested the waters further south off the coast of Africa, near the Canary Islands. Finding that the currents appeared more favorable, he quickly adopted Toscanelli's plan.

As an additional reinforcement, Columbus was also aware of the provocative theory by Augustus' tutor Posidonius, fourteen hundred years previously, who also believed that the Indies could be reached by sailing westward. Hence, with Toscanelli's recent studies adding mathematical validity to this intriguing proposition, Columbus fervently sought to secure a sponsor for his daring expedition.

Unfortunately, like Toscanelli, Columbus also hit a dead end with the Portuguese, thus prompting his appeal to King Ferdinand and Queen Isabella of Spain. It would take almost a decade before the Italian navigator won their patronage, for the monarchs had been heavily preoccupied with other affairs.

As it happened, King Ferdinand was in the process of sterilizing Spain of all infidels of the Christian faith, and his pogrom began with the expulsion of Muslims. However, the cost of the long purge seriously drained the imperial coffers. A new source of revenue was mandatory and Columbus' proposition sounded rather enticing, as the promise of rich spices, textiles, and gold from Asia seemed the ideal remedy to the Spanish crown's immense debt.

Marco Polo's famous journey and enlightening book, *Il Millione*, had previously opened up the Orient to Europeans in 1298. However, in 1453, Sultan Mehmet II sacked Constantinople, whereby severing the land route. Now, thirty-nine years later, Ferdinand and the pope shared the fear of Muslim expansion. Therefore, the notion of spreading and strengthening Christianity also added a vital incentive. As such, the Spanish monarch's had no choice but to authorize the bold exploratory mission, and as we know, Columbus courageously sailed into history.

The year 1492 indelibly marked that historic voyage, which became a colossal milestone in human history. It cannot be understated that Columbus' tenacity and unrelenting resolve opened the new door to an entire hemisphere, doubling trade and spreading Christian influence across the globe. Furthermore, even though most educated men knew that the world was round, navigation of the vast expanse of the Atlantic had never been attempted in the bold fashion that Columbus mapped out. Up to that time, all European navigators were trained to hug the coastline, and only rarely ventured out to the precarious point of losing sight of land. When they did, their journeys were for a maximum of seven to eight days. Meanwhile, Columbus took his men out into a vast and uncharted ocean for two terrifying months.

That feat alone displayed Columbus' courage and determination; however, it also revealed the immense belief in his abilities, for his men put their lives in his hands, while abandoning safety and civilization, to challenge the unknown. This is crucial to understanding Columbus, who in recent years has been maligned for, among other things, being a cruel administrator. This indictment shall be challenged in due course. Most are familiar with Columbus' famous discovery in 1492, but not with his other exploits or how unanticipated events hurled Columbus into a deadly tempest of ravaging seas and personal ruinous slander.

Columbus journeyed to the New World four times, yet before his last voyage, the Italian navigator had lost favor with his Spanish patrons. This was due to his failure to generate enough profits for the Spanish monarchs and his poor management of the newly formed colonies that he established in the West Indies. Columbus rightfully argued that they expected him to govern over a wild tropical island, inhabited by naked natives, as if it were a cultivated Spanish city. Hispaniola (present day Haiti and the Dominican Republic) was a large island in the Caribbean that Columbus discovered, and where he was later asked to establish his primary colony. Unfortunately, many factors had quickly aligned that turned Columbus' governorship and his life into a disaster. To better understand his misfortune, we need to backtrack to his first voyage.

Upon discovering Hispaniola, Columbus encountered the Arawak natives, whose chief was Guacanagari. Four supreme kings ruled the island and the natives told Columbus of the cannibalistic Carib tribe that stole and raped their women while ferociously eating men and children. Soon after, fifty-five Caribs attacked seven of Columbus' men, but the Spaniards' weapons scared them off, thus proving to the Arawaks their superior might. Meanwhile, Columbus ordered the shipwrecked *Santa Maria* to be used to build a fort (naming the site La Navidad), and had a small garrison of thirty-nine officers remain with the friendly Arawaks. Meanwhile Columbus returned to Spain to break the astounding news.

The king and queen were enamored by stories of exotic tropical islands inhabited by naked natives, but mostly by the prospects of gold and other riches. Columbus was outfitted with seventeen ships and was sent on his second return voyage; this time, however, with the added responsibility of establishing a fully functional colony, and being the governor of Hispaniola. Despondent over his new political assignment, Columbus was yet to face the real catastrophe that was to await him when he returned to the picturesque island. To his utter horror, all his officers had been brutally massacred and their fort burnt to the ground.

Guacanagari had been injured and claimed that two rival kings, Caonabo and Behechio, had attacked his village and killed the Spaniards. The motives included their taking of women, possibly to reclaim those abducted by Caonabo, and disease, yet the Spaniards' belongings were found in the friendly natives' huts. Equally suspicious, Guacanagari's injury, once revealed, showed no visible wounds. The mysterious massacre was a bloody omen of worse things to befall Columbus.

Therefore, right from the fatal start, Columbus faced a dangerous uphill battle. Making a new settlement further east, Columbus and his crew of fifteen hundred established the town of Isabela. Only this time the natives would be handled more cautiously—some were converted to Christians and others enslaved. While the slaves and colonists panned for gold, Columbus and his brother amassed two hundred men and hunted down Caonabo. Upon his capture, the hostile king confessed to killing twenty Spaniards at La Navidad, and worse yet, admitted to being friendly to the new wave of Spaniards in order to replicate the first massacre. Rather than kill Caonabo, Columbus imprisoned him for deportation to Spain. The victory ensured peace on Hispaniola for a year.

Nevertheless, with the governor spending most of his time exploring the Caribbean, slanderous rumors arose. Evidently, the Spanish settlers from the second voyage were all greedy vagabonds that only sought the riches of gold. Like the Dominican priest, Bartolomé de Las Casas, said, these unscrupulous souls expected to find gold in abundance and sitting readily available for the taking. The prospect that to find gold required digging, sifting or mining caused these lazy Spaniards to mistreat the natives by working them harder while also drifting from location to location in their frenzied quest. King Ferdinand and Columbus had expected these people to be true settlers, thus building homes and churches and nurturing families. Instead, their licentious and selfish ways only incensed the natives and caused Columbus undue anguish, as they blamed Columbus for their financial misfortunes.

This growing rebellion prompted Columbus to return to Spain, along with Caonabo in chains, to update the sovereigns. Before departing, Columbus appointed Francisco Roldan as mayor to rule in his absence. However, Bishop Fonseca detained Columbus for two humiliating years in Spain, while back on Hispaniola, order quickly degenerated into chaos. Dissension ran wild and reprisals grew wicked. Both natives and Spaniards who committed crimes were recklessly sentenced, jailed, tortured, or hung. When Columbus finally returned on his third voyage, he faced an unruly mass of rebels reveling in anarchy.

This chapter of Columbus' career has caused the most outrage and vilification. Previous to his governorship, Columbus generated deep loyalty and admiration. However, the ugly situation on Hispaniola is the root cause for modern analysts to besmirch Columbus. However, the evidence largely points to others as being the villains, such as the traitorous mayor Roldan, who wreaked havoc in Columbus' absence, the whimpering citizens that blamed Columbus for their financial woes, and other factors that need to be woven into the Columbus story.

As we know, men of the past cannot be judged by modern American standards. Despite the centuries that separate us from Columbus, we can actually find third world nations today with similar sensibilities as Columbus' fifteenth century Spain, and we can also find primitive tribes located in remote corners of the world that mirror the sensibilities of the natives that Columbus faced. Therefore, because our cultivated society is the result of countless centuries of refinement and progress we cannot expect third world nations today to miraculously behave like Americans, nor can we expect archaic tribesmen today to be more than what they are.

That said, some records indicate that Columbus engaged in cruel practices while reprimanding rebels on Hispaniola. This resulted in cutting off men's ears or slicing their lips. Naturally, this makes any modern American cringe, and it instantly elicits condemnation. Although we rightfully would never tolerate this today, we need to ask what the standard practices of Spanish law were. For that matter, what were the practices of many other nations throughout the fifteenth century? We have all heard of the hostile treatment of even petty criminals having their hands chopped off for theft, nonbelievers burned at the stake, or even the brutal practice of pouring molten metal down a traitor's throat, so were the brutalities on Hispaniola so extraordinary? It certainly appears not, especially when we take this a step further.

Was it Columbus, or his administrative officers who committed these acts? Records indicate that Alonso de Hojeda cut off a deceitful chief's ear, not Columbus. And how innocent were the rebels? We also know that Columbus spent very little time on Hispaniola. His digest and charts detail his many discoveries of various islands in the West Indies, and we know he loathed the position of governor. Naturally, his being the governor makes him responsible for his men's actions, which included his brother Bartolomé, and in that regard, we can administer varying degrees of dissatisfaction or blame. Since he was a man of his times, we can also ask what exactly did his superiors in Spain do. Were they ethically above this sort of treatment? We know Columbus was reprimanded, shackled in chains, and then shipped back to Spain for questioning. But we need to probe the royal actions further.

King Ferdinand was furious that his new colony was in disarray, as law and order was mandatory for maintaining productivity. We must have no illusions—productivity was first and foremost for the crown and filling Ferdinand's empty coffers. Ferdinand was obliged to take swift action to pacify the humiliated settlers and natives, especially those that were innocent: after all, these abuses were occurring a vast ocean away from their king and under the administration of a partially absentee governor. The devastating massacre of the first colonists and news of the cannibalistic Caribs were also constant reminders of this raw and untamed world, and with communications alone taking a month or more to arrive, Ferdinand could have received word that his entire expedition and colony was annihilated months after the fact. His investment needed to be protected so a stern reprimand was indeed in order.

This brings us to the all-important issue of comparing the Italian governor to his Spanish king in the matter of meting out punishment. Columbus was stern but judicious. The earless chief, that Hojeda hacked, pleaded for forgiveness and Columbus pardoned him. Rebels who threatened the very survival of Hispaniola were indeed punished; yet, most often, Columbus tried to prevent his men from committing sinful acts. In fact, on his previous return voyage to Spain, Columbus had to prevent his men from throwing the natives overboard. They were driven off course and food supplies were scarce, hence the Spaniards wished to eliminate some of the competition for rations by killing the natives. Fortunately, Columbus' lecture about Christian compassion prevailed.

Furthermore, the naïve comments made many years later by Las Casas that fueled modern historians to alter the Columbus story must be addressed. The Spanish priest certainly made valid criticisms regarding the cruel mistreatment of natives, that are deplorable and regrettable, however, the mayhem that grew was certainly not Columbus' intentions, and this malevolence grew while he was busy exploring or building the new town of Isabela. Working the natives to pan for gold was prompted by Columbus' dire need to accrue gold, not for himself, but for Ferdinand. For to return to Spain empty handed would have certainly eliminated funding and terminated the New World project.

Moreover, Las Casas had become unwittingly biased. He tells of *two million* natives being so overworked that their numbers dropped to *two thousand*. These massive amounts of deaths we now know were largely due to the invisible diseases that the Europeans innocently brought with them, not cruelty. This epidemic, mistaken as genocide, caused Las Casas to piously say "the Indians were not so much guilty of one single mortal sin." Moreover, he changed his opinion and ironically blamed Columbus for ignorantly calling the natives hostile. However, Las Casas somehow forgot how the thirty-nine Spaniards at La Navidad were slaughtered, or how Columbus personally encountered many native tribes that attacked his crew without provocation and clearly with hostile intentions. Therefore, Columbus had far more on his plate than most realized.

In stark contrast, the Spanish monarchs were steering Spain into its most ugly period by initiating ferocious pogroms. They had begun expelling Jews, Muslims and Protestants, some being tortured or killed, as they embarked on their brutal initiative—the Spanish Inquisition.

With the aid of their second in command, Bishop Fonseca, the royal couple began to purge Spain of all its Jewish inhabitants, as well as forcing all nonbelievers to convert to Catholicism or join the thousands of others who were set ablaze as human torches or had their skin removed with hot pincers. The enormous barbarism that ensued under Ferdinand's reign was monstrously wicked. There is controversy over the total death toll, with numbers ranging from 10,000 to 150,000, but regardless of the actual number, King Ferdinand was a mass murderer. But this is never mentioned by modern historians that hastily criticize and dishonor Columbus for being a cruel governor. Columbus certainly was deficient in his political duties and could have performed a better job, yet in comparison to King Ferdinand, Columbus was far more just. Furthermore, Columbus was unfortunately the subservient pawn of a duplicitous king.

Most revealing, is that King Ferdinand dropped the charges against Columbus, yet took this opportunity to strip him of his monopoly. The savvy navigator had initially made a deal securing sole enterprise of all voyages to the New World. This had always irritated the rapacious king, yet with the current turmoil, this gave the crown some legal elbowroom. Columbus would be allowed to return, but he no longer held a seafaring monopoly. Furthermore, a full fleet of ships would even proceed to the New World before Columbus, with some men being covert operatives.

Adding further to Columbus' misery was King Ferdinand's top advisor, Bishop Fonseca, who proved to be even more intolerant and devious in his plotting to destroy Columbus. Harboring a strong prejudice against Columbus and Italians, Fonseca had previously purloined the financial bid for Columbus' second voyage to gain firm control, almost bankrupting the Italian banker Gianotto Berardi. The bishop had also sent Alonso de Hojeda to the New World to undermine Columbus.

Meanwhile, in May of 1499, Francisco de Bobadilla was appointed governor of Hispaniola while Columbus was detained in Spain. However, after Bobadilla's inept and cruel, yearlong reign, he was replaced by another devious Spaniard, Nicolás de Ovando. The atrocities grew.

Columbus' honor was tarnished by his dismissal, his lands in the New World were stolen, but at least the Crown had dropped the charges and he could explore the Caribbean once again. This had always been his ultimate quest, and this now brings us to his fourth and final voyage.

Upon leaving the Spanish port—on May 9, 1502—Columbus immediately headed westward to find that elusive passageway. To his credit, Columbus actually made landfall on current day Martinique and then found the exact spot where the future Panama Canal would link both oceans. It was a relatively narrow section of land, but to Columbus, it looked like Asia or perhaps just another large island.

The natives he encountered told of another huge body of water just across the landmass, but it was a nine-day hike. Columbus was not thrilled with the idea of his seafaring crew hiking through the dense, bug-infested forest, and he had good reasons not to. The intense heat, thick jungles, and mosquito-swarming swamps were notorious for inflicting illness (although they had no idea what malaria was), and the earlier unexplained deaths of many of his men clearly must have aided his decision. Furthermore, Columbus was seeking a water route to India not another land route. Therefore, logic dictated that this huge body of water could be easily reached by sailing around the obstruction; so the admiral weighed anchor and set sail once again.

Traveling along the coast, the crews and their ships were bedeviled by the scorching tropical sun. To their dismay, the ships began taking on water. Shipworms had latched onto the fleet's hulls and were gnawing their way through the soggy timber. The watery parasites eventually sank the small fleet near the shore, as Columbus desperately ran his ship aground on the beautiful but uncharted island of modern-day Jamaica.

With his half-eaten ship beached, Columbus was further burdened by a severe decline in health. Wracked by gout, arthritis, and other debilitating ailments, Columbus was confined to minimal activity, and worse yet, with an irritable and restless crew. Sailors only knew how to busy themselves with daily chores upon the rolling seas, so idle time on land became a major quandary, especially for an ailing admiral.

It wasn't long, however, before the castaways encountered natives. Although they were a primitive race, they fortunately appeared friendly. Columbus quickly established a rapport with the natives, bartering various beads and trinkets for food. This vital exchange went on almost daily. Here again, the digests clearly reflect how Columbus approached each new encounter; namely, by open signs of friendship and making every effort not to incite or threaten them; however, if they attacked, a firm response would follow. Nevertheless, as uninvited guests, Columbus ordered his men to return to the beached ship routinely at nightfall and log in for good measure.

Again, many primary sources indicate how Columbus interacted with the natives, and they clearly dispel ruthless hostility. On Columbus' third voyage, he encountered natives that curiously rowed out to his ships. He ordered his crew to wave and invite them closer. After some failed attempts, Columbus said, "I had a tambourine brought up to the poop and played, and made some of the young men dance, imagining that the Indians would draw closer to see the festivities. On observing the music and dancing, however, they dropped their oars, picked up their bows, and strung them. Each one seized his shield and they began to shoot arrows at us. I immediately stopped the music and ordered crossbows to be fired." Here we clearly see how the natives initiated hostilities. However, there is the slight possibility that the natives mistook the friendly gesture of dancing to music as a war dance. That both peoples were not familiar with each other's traditions also added a deadly dynamic. Therefore, unfortunate calamities arose from both purely hostile actions as well as misunderstandings, and modern revisionists should not be too quick to assume that the white man was always the one in error.

The Middle Ages and the Age of Rebirth

Nevertheless, weeks passed on the strange island, and Columbus' crew grew increasingly unnerved, and rightfully so, for it was clear that they were dreadfully marooned. The sailors' ships had served as their propelling legs and now they were frightfully crippled. Columbus knew their situation was desperate, as the odds of a Spanish caravel passing their uncharted isle were astronomical. But although Columbus was physically ill, his mind was never idle, for he had indeed devised a plan.

Columbus discreetly summoned his courageous crewmember, Diego Mendez, and secretly relayed the plan. Secrecy was necessary to avoid ruffling the egos of his crew, as he knew that none would volunteer. The plan was for Diego to set sail on a small native canoe in search of Hispaniola by using Columbus' astute coordinates. There were no illusions, the perilous rescue mission, even if successful, was beleaguered by the fact that Columbus' adversarial replacement, Governor Ovando, now ruled in Hispaniola. Furthermore, Ovando had already made his position well known—Columbus was banned from returning to the island. But every sailor knew that the nautical rules of distress must prevail; after all, they were all fellow seamen loyal to the Spanish Crown.

As expected, when Columbus openly presented this plan to the crew, they quickly exchanged glances and then peered back at their commander with blank stares. The crew knew the plan was a death sentence; however, as planned, Diego Mendez boldly stepped forward and volunteered, while Bartoloméo Fieschi followed. Outfitted with only three days of food rations, Diego, Fieschi, and six natives climbed aboard two log-hollowed canoes, and set sail into the choppy Caribbean Sea.

Meanwhile the island's natives started to grow more impatient with their white-skinned guests, who now appeared more like well-settled gatecrashers. To Columbus' dismay, many stressful months passed without word. There was no way of knowing if Diego drowned, made landfall on Hispaniola, or even got stranded on another island.

During Diego's disquieting absence, Columbus' crew grew even more restless and divided. Half had conspired secretly and broke out in open mutiny. Taking arms and wreaking havoc, the mutineers faced an equal band of loyalists, but failed to prevail. Angrily, they fled, heading deep into the heart of the island. During their rampage, they prodded the natives to kill Columbus, and also demanded food and raped their women. Worse still, the mutineers began killing the natives who didn't comply with their demands, thus provoking a direct reprisal. This forced the brutal mutineers to retreat and regroup.

Columbus and his loyal crew, who remained defenseless on the open beach, were further endangered. Worse yet, Columbus was running out of items to barter for food, and the natives were growing more impatient and hostile. With Columbus' resources and his clever peace negotiations failing fast, the shipwrecked crew had to respond fast or face certain annihilation.

Columbus was painfully aware that he was not only outnumbered but ill equipped militarily. All that remained between life and death was his intellect. As the greatest navigator in his time, Columbus was fortunately well read in the sciences. This naturally included astronomy, for Columbus had even advanced the art of navigating by the stars. Knowing that a lunar eclipse was scheduled to occur in the next three days, Columbus hatched a brilliant scheme.

Setting his plan in motion, Columbus summoned a meeting with the natives. As the suspicious tribesmen gathered around, he assertively proclaimed that his God was superior to their lunar idol. He then ceremoniously hailed himself as his God's personal messenger. As the natives nervously listened, Columbus demanded their full obedience, or they would insult his mighty God and reap his deadly wrath. As a demonstration of his omnipotence, Columbus confidently declared that his God would blacken their cherished lunar orb in three days hence.

The fateful evening finally arrived, and the natives' eyes were anxiously fixed upon the night sky. Suddenly, they were horrified by a diabolical spectacle—for right before their eyes their all-powerful lunar disc was indeed blotted out of the sky! Filled with fear, mixed with humble praise, the natives repented. Columbus peacefully stood his ground and assured them that his laudable God would restore the moon if they continued to bring food. Delighted with the reprieve, the natives eagerly complied. Due to Columbus' astronomical knowledge and astronomical wit, he was able to turn the tables without bloodshed, and in so doing, managed to save the lives of his entire crew.

Meanwhile, braving the restless seas on his weather-beaten canoe, Diego finally spotted land. To his amazement, he found Hispaniola exactly where Columbus had plotted. Once again, Columbus' keen knowledge saved the day. As the tiny canoe made landfall, Diego ran to the governor and summoned for help. To his astonishment, Ovando flatly refused immediate assistance, and instead, showered him with lame excuses.

Interestingly enough, the shady governor was racking up a bloody record of barbarism on the island, yet ironically this did not make waves. Being appointed by Bishop Fonseca, Governor Ovando did not have many worries, nor did he have any desire to rescue Columbus. In fact, both he and the bishop would be delighted to see the troublesome Italian fade into oblivion. As for Columbus' Spanish/Italian hybrid crew, they, too, were expendable. Most shockingly, Columbus and his crew were to remain shipwrecked for over a year.

Diego tried everything possible to gain favor and secure a vessel, but to no avail. Diego's appalling story quickly spread, however, and did not sit well with the residents of Hispaniola, some of whom still admired Columbus. Even those who were mistreated under his administration knew this was outright murder. Under growing pressure by the Hispaniolans, and fear of the Queen receiving word of his gross negligence, Governor Ovando was forced to make a move. His grand gesture was to send a single caravel. But the scheming governor only ordered the ship to locate the island, deliver food, and naturally quench his devious curiosity—was Columbus even still alive?

The caravel set sail and followed Diego's reverse coordinates. Slicing through the uncharted waters, the obedient captain duly spotted the island. Locating Columbus and his crew, the captain requested permission to board the beached vessel. The admiral invited the captain into his rotting cabin, while the castaways buoyantly cheered outside. As the captain ducked and entered the moldy hull, he immediately informed Columbus that Diego Mendez was alive, and then handed him a letter from his loyal crewmember.

Columbus began reading Diego's note, while the captain nervously imparted the Governor's bad news. Columbus abruptly stopped reading and lifted his eyes with a sinister squint. As the captain uneasily finished relaying his orders, the admiral sprung to his feet in disbelief. Columbus was momentarily speechless: there would be no rescue!? The captain meekly added that he was only instructed to drop off some wine and pork. Columbus exploded! The captain recoiled and frantically tried to reassure the infuriated admiral that Diego Mendez would very likely be making a rescue voyage in the near future. Yet his words couldn't quench the fire.

As the captain anxiously exited the cabin, his eyes inadvertently met those of the stranded castaways. Quickly, he turned about, and made a beeline to his ship. Columbus' crew stood momentarily dumbfounded.

As the ship raised anchor and began to set sail, the crew likewise exploded. Running and surrounding the beached ship, they vehemently cursed Columbus for his rivalry with Governor Ovando, as that—in their minds—caused their predicament. Even some of the loyal crewmembers threatened mutiny. Columbus stood firm; pacifying them with the news that Diego was still alive and would come soon. Hence, any revolt would be severely punished under Spanish law. The crew backed down.

Back in Hispaniola, Diego's laborious task reached fruition. He had finally managed to purchase a ship on Columbus' sterling reputation and good credit, which had always remained intact among seamen. Quickly setting sail, Diego made his way back to the dreaded island.

As Diego's ship came into view, the stranded castaways couldn't believe their eyes. When their fellow shipmate landed ashore, they turned toward their admiral with huge grins, saddled with remorseful eyes. They had blamed their commander for being stranded for over a year and facing almost certain death, yet Columbus had ensured their survival. They could finally leave the godforsaken island, with all its pain, death, and sin, far behind.

Despite Columbus' obsession, which often drove his crew to the limits of human endurance, the admiral managed to survive the trials and tribulations of a seemingly orderless and merciless world by using his sharp intellect and sheer determination.

Bitterness, however, filled Columbus' heart. He was unable to fulfill his life-long quest, was stripped of his discoveries by a greedy king and devious bishop, and left for dead along with his entire crew by a soulless colleague who refused a mandatory rescue mission and personally stole his dominion. Unfortunately, this ultimate insult added to his already withering health, and the tired admiral only sought the solitude of home. Upon his return to Spain, Columbus refused to even lay eyes upon the contemptible king or his foul bishop. Avoiding the limelight that once beamed over him, Columbus sank into obscurity.

This final and gloomy chapter of a spectacular man and colossal achievement is a sad and tragic ending for a man who had been a life-long servant of God and loyal subject to his king and queen. Beyond the shipwrecks, hurricanes, mutinies, reprimands, demotion, insults, thefts, and near-fatal abandonment, Columbus also had to look forward to his great name being practically forgotten during his last years on Earth, and quite deplorably, completely forgotten for over two centuries thereafter.

Worse still, after his death, Columbus' name would be passed over and another explorer's would be used to name the New World's two huge continents. His sacrifices and suffering, like those of many famous Christians, was for a monumental cause, and for that the Western world owes Columbus its eternal debt and gratitude.

A New World | Its American Name | Its Detractors

The world was changing drastically during and especially after Columbus' eventful life; cartographers could not keep pace with the windfall of new discoveries and the world map's ever-changing form. Portugal was Spain's ultimate rival, and with its superior naval fleet, they eventually managed to discover the eastern route to India. This was due to Vasco da Gama, and his new course of sailing south around Africa's Cape of Good Hope in 1497. Additionally, the Portuguese had previously signed a treaty with Spain, claiming dominion over large portions of the unexplored seas.

Nevertheless, King Ferdinand, with the aid of his cunning companion, Bishop Fonseca, wanted nothing more than to curb Portugal's expansion. Most importantly, they wanted to prevent the Portuguese from learning about or pilfering Spain's treasure trove of new discoveries, which Spain in turn had wrested from Columbus. Therefore the bishop contacted the reigning pope, who also happened to be of Spanish descent, with a request and an offer. The request was to aid the kingdom of Spain, but the alluring offer was for the Vatican to expand their Christian kingdom into a New World. The pope, who eagerly took the bait, was none other than the infamous Borgia barracuda, Pope Alexander VI.

Pope Alexander promptly drafted a series of very devious papal bulls. Amid the sanctimonious rhetoric, Alexander devised an imaginary demarcation line, which ran north to south in the Atlantic Ocean and just west of Portugal's Cape Verdi Islands. To the loss of any others, all points west of that line, which constituted the Atlantic Ocean and all unknown territories beyond the visible horizon, would belong to Spain and, in a religious sense, the Vatican.

With the firm alliance of Spain and the Vatican blatantly sealed, Portugal and other nations seemed unwilling to intervene, especially since they viewed these newly discovered islands as wastelands inhabited by primitive natives. This gave Spain a significant lead in discovering more lands in the New World, while completely stripping Columbus of his lands, dreams, tribute, and wealth. Unfortunately, another disappointment awaited Columbus.

As early as 1499, a fellow Italian explorer followed Columbus' route, and with far less talent garnered even greater acclaim, or at least his name would. Amerigo Vespucci was born in Florence and actually lived in the house next door to the famous artist Sandro Botticelli.

After working in a lackluster string of menial and even unsavory professions, Amerigo found employment in the Medici's service, yet soon relocated to Seville, Spain. While there, he eventually became associated with Gianotto Berardi, an Italian banker who, upon envisioning Christopher Columbus as the golden goose, devoted all his time and financial resources to the courageous navigator. After losing the bid to finance the entire second voyage (only receiving a small portion of the journey to outfit, since Bishop Fonseca opted to power-manage the fleet), Berardi fell ill and subsequently died.

Being his primary beneficiary, Vespucci was left to manage Berardi's affairs. With Columbus falling out of favor with the Spanish monarchs and amassing hefty debts, the magnificent golden goose had instead become a malignant white elephant. Vespucci needed to cut his losses and move on to another profession. Being Columbus' major outfitter, Amerigo naturally heard many of the famous navigator's amazing stories firsthand. Furthermore, although Columbus had initially failed to procure financial rewards during his early explorations, he had informed the king, and Amerigo, about the abundant pearl fisheries he located off the shores of what today is Venezuela. This was a compelling lure—one that seemed to promise Ferdinand a stellar fortune and Vespucci worldwide fame.

Without training or experience for any position aboard a caravel, Vespucci secured passage to the New World with one of Columbus' former mates turned-captain. At that point in time, several new independent expeditions were sponsored before the king even allowed Columbus to set sail again, as this was during King Ferdinand's policy of stripping Columbus of what he called a monopoly. As Columbus' star faded even his revelations of potential windfalls were stolen when Vespucci's ship sailed directly toward the pearl fisheries.

The new captains of these fleets all understood the importance of securing something financially tangible, since future sponsorship, as well as personal wealth, rested upon results. In a phrase, the New World was open game.

One of Vespucci's former jobs was as a jeweler; hence his selection as a crewmember seems to have been initially granted for this reason. Vespucci wasted no time, however, in gaining recognition, not to mention the titles of pilot and astronomer. Much of this was due to Vespucci's aggressive drive for success and even stardom. This habitually involved the use of pretense and self-promotion, and successfully led to his securing a second voyage in 1501.

Vespucci's second journey took him along the shores of South America, and allegedly south of the equator, where he made many observations about the natives and the exotic flora and fauna. He also seized the opportunity to conjure up fallacious astronomical claims, which included having a secret mastery of the astrolabe. Amerigo also drew his own maps in addition to his romantic and illusory notes. Many of his observations, however, have recently been noted as being almost direct quotes of those made previously by his hero, Christopher Columbus. Nevertheless, Vespucci had come to realize that the huge land mass was not Asia, as Columbus assumed, but actually a new continent.

Upon his return, Amerigo wasted no time in professing to be an astrolabe expert and the most qualified cartographer of the New World. Selling himself as a scientist rather than a simple seafarer, Amerigo won the confidence of the royal court. During this time, Amerigo stayed at Columbus' house, picking the brain of the dejected but still brilliant master.

Their relationship was nothing short of odd, for while Amerigo deeply admired the admiral, and even won his confidence as a fervent supporter, it seems his own burning desire for glory and recognition led to a series of events that undermined his friend and master even more. Whether this was intentional or out of his control has been debated, but it appears his own hype and spin enthralled publishers who were likewise eager for fame and fortune, and thus started a chain reaction that quickly became uncontrollable and most unfortunate.

Nevertheless, armed with Columbus' astute input and his own experiences at sea, Amerigo's confidence and verve won him favor and high office. He not only managed to win a financial reimbursement for Columbus, but his new official role of Pilot Major entrusted him with establishing an academy in his own house. Here, Amerigo would train all of Spain's sea captains in the use of the astrolabe and be solely responsible for commissioning or declining their service to the crown. Furthermore, Amerigo was assigned the task of compiling charts from all New World voyages to construct new and updated maps of the rapidly emerging western hemisphere.

Amerigo's observations of the New World were immediately published in a small book called *Mundus Novus*. It became a bestseller and quickly hurled Amerigo's name into the spotlight. Rapidly overshadowing even Columbus, Amerigo's name resounded in almost half of all the travel books being published at that time.

Adding weight to this momentum was a letter allegedly from Amerigo to Piero Soderini, who was a member of the Medici regime in Florence. The thrust of the letter laid claims to an impressive array of observations and discoveries. This mysterious document later became known as the *Soderini Letter*, which evidently was compiled by an anonymous author. The letter contained many fragments of observations by Vespucci that mirrored Columbus directly, as well as the bogus claims of landing first and making four voyages, none of which Amerigo could lay claim to. More importantly, however, Amerigo's maps were sent to his German friend, Hylacomylus in France, who happened to be a premiere publisher of maps. (Hylacomylus was a fanciful Greek pseudonym, as his original German surname was Waldseemüller.)

Even though Columbus had lost all favor and fell into almost total obscurity, Hylacomylus cautiously withheld publication until the ailing navigator was safely dead. Whether this was intentional or happenstance is not known, however, when Columbus died in 1507, Hylacomylus published Vespucci's maps. Hylacomylus' successful publication not only displayed the intriguing design of the New World but he allegedly took it upon himself to label both huge continents "America."

Either this was a genuine gesture to honor his friend Amerigo for the rights to print a spectacular map or more likely was part of a prearranged agreement between mapmaker and publisher where the mapmaker declined royalties in favor of eternal fame. Whatever the deal, the instant success and volatile ignition of sales quickly sparked other mapmakers to follow suit. Spreading like wildfire, even the Spanish monarchs could not suppress the hot news, as the New World would be forever branded with the fraudulent name of Amerigo rather than Columbus.

For over two hundred years this error prevailed, and the world hailed Amerigo Vespucci as the discoverer of the Americas. Meanwhile, Columbus was marginalized to the point of being almost forgotten. It was only during the late eighteenth century that the true story of the Vespucci sham was revealed. Today some historians have reassessed Amerigo's complicity in this naming convention, and insist that it was largely instigated by Hylacomylus and then amplified by others in an unbridled chain reaction.

Serendipitous events have occurred throughout history, but Vespucci's successes did not seem to be the result of pure luck: his modus operandi consisted of weaseling his way into official positions of power without a proper resume, being in charge of mapmaking for King Ferdinand, and using his personal contact with Columbus to hone his own boastful claims. Between his ultimate authority in the map industry and his long established record of self-importance and being a glory hound, it seems evident that Amerigo had his hands in the inkwell for penning his name on not one but both colossal continents.

Nevertheless, the revelation of Amerigo's deceit had sparked the beginning of Columbus' long overdue rise out of the ashes of neglect, and, like a phoenix, he soared to the summit of his field and received universal acclaim. Yet while the founding fathers of the United States and their generation were the first to catch wind of Columbus' disgraceful plight, the maps of the Western hemisphere had already been branded with Amerigo's name and irrevocably burnt into history. Vespucci and/or Hylacomylus had pulled off a monumental caper of global proportions.

For many Americans, it probably comes as a disappointment that two flawed characters, driven by the fortunes of fame and greed, hatched their continent's name. Yet beyond their dubious actions, the United States of America likewise had a long and checkered history in its rise to power. From its earliest settlers through the fight for independence and beyond, American history is filled with imperfections and bloody events. As such, it should come as no surprise that during America's founding, the Liberty Bell cracked and symbolically remains flawed. That symbol should offer a constant reminder of how the trail to grand and noble ideas is always flawed, for even though many believe America was constructed under divine guidance, it was essentially left to the fallible and even unsavory hands of mortal men and women to build.

Therefore, fantasies of a utopian founding should remain in the books of ancient history, such as Homer's attempt to recreate a glorious and purified past for Greece, or Virgil's attempt for Rome. In contrast, the recorded history of America's founding should remain true and sobering, in the sense that we must understand the unpleasant actions that were taken while also understanding human nature well enough to know that those actions were often necessary to arrive at where we are today. Amerigo's burning need to better himself drove him to take risks based on his personal motives, but it also added momentum to a new exploratory development—one that needed a proactive spokesman or propane salesman to keep the flame burning. In a sense, Amerigo had innate

American traits, for the world never saw a greater PR man, advertising wizard, or *Continental* car salesman than Amerigo Vespucci.

Too often history has shown that even great discoveries or ideas can lapse into obscurity, and although the New World was exotic and exciting, sponsorship was the only way to continue the quest. Therefore, salesmanship in portraying the New World as being more than just beautiful islands, inhabited with primitive natives and pretty flora, was mandatory to encourage investors as well as adventurous souls willing to risk life and limb. Amerigo, more than anyone else, sparked the intense media hype being generated at the time, and that was crucial to the cause, despite his being undeserving of the high acclaim and honor his name would garner.

Columbus' pioneering courage, and Spain's egregious attempt to strip him of his rightful discoveries, rank, and possessions, was somewhat mirrored by our brave fledgling nation and its fight against imperial Britain, which likewise tried to oppress and strip the colonists of their rights. Although Columbus made mistakes, his intentions were noble and largely selfless, and his spirit was emboldened with an indelible drive that is nothing short of remarkable. In this crucial sense, it is quite fortunate that the future United States of America would inherit his bold and courageous spirit. Even though Columbus never had the opportunity or resources to regain his rightful land or title, the revelation of truth two centuries later did restore his honor.

Among all the ancient explorers who sailed the rolling seas, Columbus majestically rides the crest, which not only dwarfs his rivals but also eulogizes his courageous name and spirit. Unfortunately, unmerited claims have always been part of human nature and America's history was certainly not immune. Over the years, there has been a rising tide to discredit Columbus. The first signs appeared at the 500th anniversary of Columbus' discovery. The politically correct apologists mounted a huge smear campaign that maligned the courageous navigator by raising suspicious accusations of his heavy-handed governorship of Hispaniola and his mistreatment of the natives.

Beside the fact that this unwanted position was thrust upon Columbus by King Ferdinand, who had ulterior motives, it's odd how

Ferdinand and Governor Ovando literally got away with mass-murder, yet only Columbus was shackled and maligned, despite his documented plea of innocence and the evidence of foul play to discredit him. What we do know is that Ferdinand and Bishop Fonseca plotted to undermine Columbus, and they succeeded in stripping him of his possessions, with the added bonus of defaming him in the process.

Moreover, these critics have gone a malicious step further by denying Columbus his rightful entitlement of discovery. Their attack is based upon the fact that the Vikings had previously crossed the Atlantic and hence they discovered America first. Most are well acquainted with Leif Ericsson's discovery of Vinland, which is modern day Newfoundland, however, several key issues must be considered.

First, Columbus and Europeans had no knowledge of any previous discovery or Northern routes. Although the Vikings used the icy waterways along Iceland and Greenland to reach the island of Newfoundland, which the Vikings eventually abandoned, the most important fact is that they never publicized this discovery. Hence, it remained completely unknown to all others.

Second, the Vikings even deceptively named the landmass that was green and lush, Iceland, and the icy lands, Greenland. This was simply a selfish and ultimately vain attempt to deter followers. Although some modern scholars speculate that the so-called Little Ice Age caused Greenland to become icy and that the land was actually green when the Vikings, Eric the Red, and his Norsemen first landed, the fact remains that their refusal to share knowledge or intermix with the natives doomed their existence when the frigid icy weather did come.

The native people of these frigid landmasses had developed superior ivory spearheads with reverse jagged edges that efficiently killed fish. This enabled the natives to survive, while the Vikings' land-based animals (which they brought with them) died in the cold climate. The Vikings believed that they were superior to the natives, however, so they never bothered to adopt their hunting skills. This mistake, coupled with their isolationist mentality, caused their own demise. Therefore, in the final analysis, the Vikings' secret ventures remained just that, for their discovery died due to their own selfish mistakes, and for the rest of humanity they remained completely unknown and utterly useless.

In contrast, the explosive and international acclaim of Columbus' initial discovery, which was immensely amplified by Vespucci, began the volatile chain reaction that opened up an entire hemisphere to a new era of exploration. Furthermore, this single action profoundly altered world history forever. For as Thomas Edison would say centuries later, "The value of an idea lies in the using of it." This was true of Gutenberg, who did not invent the printing press yet bequeathed it to the world, and it would be true of Columbus, who though not technically the one to land first, officially introduced the western hemisphere to the rest of the world.

As mentioned, word of Columbus' discovery spread so fast that shortly after, exploration and trade routes were bustling with caravels sailing along Columbus' mid-Atlantic course. Like a portal to another dimension, Columbus bequeathed to the Old World the golden key to a glorious New World, a gift to humanity that defies calculation.

KING FERDINAND: The great Spanish empire that emerged during the Renaissance came about due to the strategic marriage and territorial union of Isabella from Castile and Ferdinand from Aragon (Aragon being a significantly smaller region). Both rulers cared little for bookkeeping, and as such, it wasn't long before their budding empire was faced with dire fiscal problems.

Added to these dismal internal affairs were serious external dilemmas, such as the threat of Portugal's growing navy, and the recent conquest of Constantinople, which severed all trade routes east. As such, the funding of Columbus' bold expedition was aimed at replenishing their ill-managed vault and getting them out of the red.

Upon Columbus' miraculous discovery, Ferdinand lost no time in not only plotting to conquer the entire western hemisphere, with the aid of the equally corrupt Spanish pope, but also in eradicating Spain's internal woes as well. While Queen Isabella was said to have been superior in intellect to her husband, Ferdinand had a raw lust for power, which he gained by common street-savvy and deceit. Despite the ugliness of his motives, Ferdinand was extremely capable and ruthlessly effective. After stripping Columbus of his lands, rank, and honor, Ferdinand and his wife built a world-class navy, and became master helmsmen of the Spanish Inquisition, with the aid of their wily first mate, Bishop Fonseca.

Ferdinand and Fonseca appealed to their fellow Spaniard at the Vatican, Bishop Rodrigo Borgia, who later became Pope Alexander VI, to put pressure on Pope Sixtus IV to issue a papal bull that would endorse their inquisition. It was nothing more than religious cleansing to scour Spain's "tainted" populace with a Christian wire brush. Pope Sixtus may have silently appreciated the Muslim cleansing agenda, but he truly needed Ferdinand's military aid, so he allegedly conceded with reluctance.

Ferdinand then appointed the infamous Tomás de Torquemada, who directed the *auto-da-fé* "act of faith" campaign, which vigorously hunted and condemned Jews, Muslims, and atheists. Those under the Inquisition's Gestapo-like eye were forced to convert, while those who refused were tortured, executed, or forced to flee Spain.

These broad persecutions were the invention of an unholy trinity, with the Royal Crown and Bishop Fonseca being the ultimate architects and Torquemada being the fanatical head foreman and executioner. Meanwhile, the pope was a disheartened accomplice who sold his soul and the dignity of the Catholic Church in exchange for military defense.

Previously, Ferdinand had cleverly managed to broker a deal with the Vatican, whereby the pope granted Ferdinand power to appoint his own bishops in Spain. From his position of power, Ferdinand also prohibited the pope from passing a bull without first getting his royal consent. The French monarchy had managed to do the same, which was the reason Spain and France never revolted against the Roman Catholic Church. Meanwhile, Germany and England never managed to broker such deals with the Vatican, and as a result this further motivated Germany's feisty monk, Martin Luther, to establish his own Lutheran sect, as well as England's King Henry VIII to depose the Catholic Church in favor of his own English Protestant sect.

King Ferdinand was a tyrannical tactician who knew how to use valuable connections to achieve ultimate control. Recently, some theologians have pointed to perhaps Ferdinand's one good gesture when he passed laws in favor of treating the American natives with benevolence.

This gesture warrants scrutiny, however. First, this good deed was prompted by Father Montesinos who witnessed the oppression firsthand, and as such brought it to Ferdinand's attention. When Ferdinand's actions are compared to Father Montesinos' it becomes clear that only the good Father deserved being called benevolent.

Second, and most importantly, King Ferdinand was locked in an alliance with the pope; therefore, he had to make a visibly pious gesture or risk losing the Vatican's support. Despite his military superiority over the Vatican, Ferdinand faced other nation-states that posed a threat, so the Vatican, with its wealth and multinational congregation, was a crucial ally.

Most revealing of all is that Ferdinand did little to nothing to enforce these laws, which further validates his lack of concern in this regard, for his sights were set upon the selfish mission of world conquest. In this capacity, Ferdinand did rather well.

The Spanish empire grew as the heirs of Ferdinand and Isabella carried it forward, yet it was doomed to failure from its very inception. The sprawling empire, which has impressed many, was actually like a glittering matador adulated by the masses. Standing proudly with his huge distracting red cape, the crowd was unaware that the powerful engine actually running the show was the foreign beast. Once the flamboyant matador squandered his funds, he could no longer afford another powerful beast. That is when the grand spectacle ended and it became clear that the essence of the show was, in fact, bull. Bull, in that it was a hollow empire sporting a dazzling façade, and bull, in that the real engine that made the empire run was the foreign bull market.

To clarify this fanciful analogy, this amazing empire rested solely upon foreign imports, for Spain did not have adequate terrain or resources, besides sheep for wool. Therefore, Spain relied upon foreign eatables, clothing, textiles, loans from Italian bankers, Italian-made cannons and weaponry—it even imported warships along with their international crews. In effect, all the major necessities for maintaining an empire came from outside sources.

Spain even exported whatever raw materials it had, only to re-import them as finished goods. The Spaniards were, in large measure, consumers only. Therefore, the gold and silver that Spain reaped from its

New World settlements were turned into coinage that once again left Spanish soil to buy imported goods. Thus only a fanciful aura of glittering magnificence was created, which was precariously based upon negative cash flow. *(This lazy approach of outsourcing and relying on other nations for manufacturing goods brought about the eventual demise of the Spanish empire and serves as a warning to the American empire today.)*

Hence, Ferdinand and Isabella founded the Spanish empire, which although exerting immense influence worldwide, ran itself into debt. Their kingdom was bequeathed to their grandson, Charles V, who in turn sought huge loans, totaling some 29 million ducats. Charles was an able leader and through royal family inheritance, war, and intrigue managed to expand the Spanish empire. Charles—like his grandfather, Ferdinand—inaugurated another brutal inquisition when the Reformation threatened to overtake the Netherlands. The matador king slaughtered over 100,000 fellow Christians for simply being tagged as Protestant, which to Charles meant heretic. When his son Philip II inherited the throne, along with the royal family's chronic debt, the younger matador was only able to keep the grand red cape flowing for one year. That is when the bull market died, and the Spanish empire collapsed.

Ferdinand's great name has long been remembered in history due to his powerful partnership with his wife, Isabella, both of whom are credited with uniting Spain, and more importantly, establishing the first global empire, spanning two hemispheres. However, the latter was only made possible by Columbus' courageous discovery. Moreover, it can no longer be ignored that Ferdinand was one of the principle architects of the Inquisition, the power hungry king who, while frantic to refill his empty coffers due to poor management, allowed many of his minions to wreak havoc in the New World, and was the deceitful schemer who robbed Columbus of his just rewards and even temporarily besmirched his great name. As such, the dirty truths of Ferdinand's crimes are like oil in water, and have risen to the top.

Approximately seventeen years after King Ferdinand's death, another imperial titan would be born, however, this one was born in England and instead of wearing trousers, wore radiant gowns.

QUEEN ELIZABETH I: Elizabeth was the illegitimate child of King Henry VIII and his eventual second wife, Anne Boleyn. Born in 1533, Elizabeth proved to be a sharp-minded girl who relished learning. Unlike her hedonistic father, who had six wives and numerous mistresses, Elizabeth never married. Despite her unflattering looks, Elizabeth was known to be flirtatious, like her parents, and had received several marriage proposals. After all, she was the most powerful woman in the world and the first woman in European history to reach such stellar heights. Elizabeth's half-sister, Mary, may have been the first female ruler of England, but her short, five-year reign had been a disaster, earning her the epithet "Bloody Mary," and she didn't have the brains, power, determination, or successes that Elizabeth exhibited.

Like Augustus Caesar, Elizabeth ruled for forty-four years and learned from her father's mistakes. As Augustus wisely took advice from the Senate, yet ruled largely upon his own good judgment, Elizabeth likewise solicited the advice of Parliament, and she, too, ruled with Augustan vision and vitality. But unlike Augustus, Elizabeth had emotional insecurities, such as constantly demanding that she was prettier and smarter than her cousin, Queen Mary of Scotland.

Her father had earlier severed ties with the Catholic Church, due to the pope's refusal to annul his first marriage to Catherine. This was because she only produced a daughter. Determined to get his way, Henry not only became Protestant, but so, too, would all of England by royal decree. Out of six wives, Henry would only produce one legitimate son.

When Catherine's daughter, Mary, took the throne, mayhem ensued when she reversed her father's religious ruling. Entering into marriage with King Philip II of Spain *(see pg. 711)*, Mary joined him as a crusader for the Catholic faith. Philip was none other than the great grandson of King Ferdinand, and he continued his family's religious tradition of intolerant conquest. Queen Mary charged many of England's Protestants with heresy, and her executions even included some of her father's close ministers. Upon Mary's premature death, her half-sister Elizabeth ascended to the throne.

Elizabeth faced a nation religiously torn between Roman Catholics and Protestants, a treasury nearly broken, as well as political pressure by

Spain that by this time had amassed the world's largest naval fleet. Elizabeth tactfully defended the Protestants and defiantly refused a marriage proposal from her brother-in-law Philip. This refusal, plus the Spanish king's irritation over Francis Drake and Sir Walter Raleigh's influence on behalf of England in the New World, persuaded Philip to unleash his Spanish Armada.

The much smaller British fleet, as fate would have it, took advantage of the bad weather and made some effective maneuvers, thus managing to win the battle. This serendipitous victory propelled England into becoming a world power. As such, Elizabeth's successful reign secured for England religious independence and a primary role in the future exploits of the New World.

Catholicism takes a lot of heat for its ruthless endeavors, yet in the New World, the Protestant settlers in North America proved to be just as brutal, if not worse than their older counterpart. During the reign of Queen Elizabeth's successor, King James, Captain John Smith *(see pg. 711)* was commissioned to sail to the New World. Smith's mission was proudly lauded by King James as a noble endeavor to bring their Protestant religion to the hapless natives who were ignorant of the true knowledge and worship of God. Oddly enough, the charter for this religious expedition predominantly spoke of searching for gold, silver, and other valuables, while only a mere third of this document mentioned anything of a religious nature.

Captain Smith landed in Jamestown, aptly named after the English king, in 1607, and established a small settlement with a makeshift chapel. After the sudden death of their only minister, the chapel was abandoned and not used again by the carefree adventurers for two years. During that time, skirmishes occurred with Native Americans. Captain Smith was captured, yet he managed to escape death primarily thanks to the chief's sympathetic daughter, Pocahontas. When Smith returned to the settlement, he was aghast to find that two-thirds of his men had been slaughtered. As soon as word reached King James, he furiously sent Sir Thomas Gates sailing to revive Smith's failed mission.

Sir Gates' assignment was to administer a religious scolding for the lax and disloyal attitudes that pervaded Smith's camp. Once ashore, Gates enacted the king's strict, "Laws Divine, Moral, and Martial," that were designed for the English settlers. These laws demanded stringent religious observance, twice daily, with severe punishments ranging from whipping to confinement, and even death for adultery or sex-related perversions. The severity of this religious expedition-turned-concentration camp was by no means characteristic of their original missionary goals. The Protestant religion that Queen Elizabeth strenuously advocated and King James cultivated had shown its dark and ugly underbelly, as had its Roman Catholic precursor. Yet the question of whether England's religious state was beneficial or detrimental would have to wait another century and a half before men gathered to evaluate a new form of government that separated church from state.

During Elizabeth's long reign, another prominent personality emerged. He, who would later be hailed by many as the greatest playwright of all time, was named William Shakespeare.

WILLIAM SHAKESPEARE: Born in 1564, in a small hamlet called Stratford-upon-Avon, this dramatic poet/actor bequeathed to the world a solid output of literature that, despite criticisms by some of his contemporaries, like Ben Jonson who later altered his opinion, would captivate the ever-growing English-speaking domain that eventually spread across the entire globe.

Taking ancient Roman stories as his sources for *Julius Caesar*, *Romeo and Juliet*, *The Merchant of Venice* and *Othello*, Shakespeare managed to recreate these stories with realistic character portraits and articulately conveyed their overt actions as well as their subconscious or psychological motivations. Weaving storylines filled with intense drama and tragedy, Shakespeare captivated not only all of England, but eventually a worldwide audience.

Interestingly enough, Shakespeare's story *The Tempest* incorporates waves of verse that were inspired by Sir Thomas Gates' stormy voyage to the New World. Gates had encountered a hurricane near Bermuda that destroyed his vessel. Fortunately, his crew fashioned two rafts out of the wreckage and managed to sail into Jamestown a month later. Whether Captain John Smith viewed Gates arrival as fortunate is another matter.

Much speculation abounds regarding the authenticity of Shakespeare's writings. There have been many claims bestowing true authorship upon Christopher Marlowe, Edward De Vere, Sir Francis Bacon, William Stanley, or even Queen Elizabeth herself. Even the famous American author Mark Twain took a special interest in this matter, citing many flaws in the reasoning by devout Shakespearians who made their case based solely upon assumptions rather than hard factual evidence. As such, Twain admitted that he had no way of knowing for sure who actually wrote these works, but that his suspicions pointed to the highly erudite Sir Francis Bacon.

Twain arrived at this hypothesis because the biographical history of William Shakespeare indicates many factors that don't add up. For example, Shakespeare was born in the quaint village of Stratford-upon-Avon. This backwater village, whose populace was largely illiterate, had no library and spoke the unsophisticated Warwickshire dialect. Yet quite miraculously, Shakespeare somehow became the English language's highly proficient and highly polished wordsmith. The claims that he learned or ingested this worldly knowledge are purely circumstantial. Added to this are strange occurrences of complete "silence" or voids, both during his life and after his death, which aroused the suspicions of many historians. Therefore, it is worth citing an excerpt by Mark Twain on this highly controversial matter. *Note: words in all caps are by Twain.*

"For seven years after Shakespeare's death nobody seems to have been interested in him. Then the quarto was published, and Ben Jonson awoke out of his long indifference and sang a song of praise and put it in the front of the book. Then silence fell AGAIN. For sixty years. Then inquiries into Shakespeare's Stratford life began to be made, of Stratfordians. Of Stratfordians who had known Shakespeare or had seen him? No. Then of Stratfordians who had seen people who had known or seen people who had seen Shakespeare? No. Apparently the inquiries were only made of Stratfordians who were not Stratfordians of Shakespeare's day, but later comers; and what they had learned had come to them from persons who had not seen Shakespeare; and what they had learned was not claimed as FACT, but only as legend—dim and fading and indefinite legend; legend of the calf-slaughtering rank, and not worth remembering either as history or fiction."

Furthermore, Mark Twain makes a clever and very comical analogy of how Shakespearians crafted vague assumptions about their hero's education and environment, and then turned them into fact. He does this by creating a scenario where two cats are placed in an inescapable cell with a mouse. One cat is a lap-bred house kitten and the other is a sharp and worldly tomcat. When the cell-door is opened, the mouse is missing. The analysis of whether the kitten or tomcat is the culprit follows:

"The Shakespearite will Reason like this…He will say the kitten MAY HAVE BEEN attending school when nobody was noticing; therefore WE ARE WARRANTED IN ASSUMING that it did so; also, it COULD HAVE BEEN training in a court-clerk's office when no one was noticing; since that could have happened, WE ARE JUSTIFIED IN ASSUMING that it did happen; it COULD HAVE STUDIED CATOLOGY IN A GARRET when no one was noticing—therefore it DID; it COULD HAVE attended cat-assizes on the shed-roof nights, for recreation, when no one was noticing, and harvested a knowledge of cat court-forms and cat lawyer-talk in that way: it COULD have done it, therefore without a doubt it did; it could have gone soldiering with a war-tribe when no one was noticing, and learned soldier-wiles and soldier-ways, and what to do with a mouse when opportunity offers; the plain inference, therefore is, that that is what it DID. Since all these manifold things COULD have occurred, we have EVERY RIGHT TO BELIEVE they did occur. These patiently and painstakingly accumulated vast acquirements and competences needed but one thing more—opportunity—to convert themselves into triumphant action. The opportunity came, we have the result; BEYOND SHADOW OF QUESTION the mouse is in the kitten."

In addition to Mark Twain's well-crafted Mississippi humor in addressing a serious historical enigma, many prominent people, such as Walt Whitman, Henry James, and Sigmund Freud have also questioned the authenticity of Shakespeare's writings. All crafty kittens aside, most scholars today somehow believe that Shakespeare was in fact the author of at least the majority of works. Even though his personal life remains in a shroud of mystery, the name Shakespeare has almost become synonymous with the term, English Literature. His works have been cited by other authors, staged, and even been made into movies, perhaps more than any other playwright in history. Whatever the source, the writings themselves stand as pinnacles of literature and documents of human nature.

Also born in 1564, like Shakespeare, was another highly influential individual, yet this man lived almost eight hundred miles to the southeast, and his eyes gazed upward, away from the theater's humanist stage, in order to examine and challenge the order of God's universe.

GALILEO GALILEI: Galileo was born in Pisa, Italy. As a young man, Galileo contemplated entering the priesthood but at his father's request entered the university at Pisa to study medicine. He was quickly drawn to math and science and eventually became the university's Chairman of Mathematics. Three years later he moved, teaching math and sciences at the University of Padua. This formal training prompted Galileo to debunk Aristotle's conjectural observation method in favor of a systematic and statistical experiment-based approach. In essence, Galileo pioneered the "experimental scientific method," which is why many scientists, including Albert Einstein, honored him as the Father of Science.

Scientists say that the astronomer must be of a unique character, for astronomy demands patience, assiduous concentration, strict adherence to data collection, and a dedicated, one-pointed perseverance. This explains why the great Leonardo da Vinci only dabbled in astronomy, for his restless nature would never allow him to make the protracted efforts required to accomplish what Galileo resolved to do.

Galileo's intense interest in the celestial heavens prompted him to invent the telescope. Although recent evidence suggests that others possibly designed similar instruments first, those devices or their inventors never bequeathed anything significant in their day, and as such, never garnered world attention. Therefore, they were inconsequential. Galileo cleverly fashioned his working telescope from primitive lenses developed earlier. He quickly improved the lenses and arranged them in a tube, greatly increasing the new device's magnification. Becoming the first being to ever examine the heavens with a telescope and astutely record those sightings, Galileo opened a new window to the universe, about which he made significant astronomical discoveries and detailed drawings.

In 1604, Galileo discovered four moons orbiting Jupiter, sunspots, and mountains on the moon that he documented with detailed drawings, and he analyzed and drew the phases of planet Venus, which he noted were similar to the phases of Earth's moon. Observing Venus and Jupiter's moons' phases later aided Galileo in positing his heliocentric system.

Galileo's other inventions include the microscope, thermometer, and military compass, the latter being used to accurately aim cannon fire. His experiments on falling bodies, conducted at the Leaning Tower of Pisa, and his studies with inclined planes proved that all objects fall at the same velocity, depending upon outside forces, like friction. More importantly, beyond being just a hypothesis, Galileo formulated the mathematical equation to prove the rate of velocity—32 feet per second per second. This indisputably disproved Aristotle's long-accepted theory that heavier objects fall faster than lighter objects. With a stroke of mathematical genius, Galileo had jettisoned the Greek philosopher's two-millennia-long, mind-locking anchor over the side of the gravity-laden balloon, and science finally began to rise calculatingly upward.

In addition to cracking the code of the laws of gravity, Galileo also confronted another conundrum posed by Greek antiquity. Earlier, when Galileo was a professor at the University of Pisa, he was required to teach the Ptolemaic/Aristotelian theory, which stated that the Earth was at the center of the universe. This, to the ancients, explained why the sun and all the planets appeared to revolve across the sky. Later, as a professor at the University of Padua, Galileo learned of Copernicus' heliocentric theory. Interestingly enough, because Copernicus' theory was viewed by the Catholic Church as mere conjecture, it wasn't seriously considered harmful to church doctrine.

Galileo realized that the lunar effects on tides and the phases of Venus lent compelling support for the heliocentric theory. Furthermore, his discovery of Jupiter's moons sparked a new revelation. Astronomers had long believed that if the Earth moved, the moon would be left behind. Galileo now understood, however, that moons revolve around another heavenly body in their own orbits, thus debunking the old worldview.

This prompted Galileo to seek permission from the pope to publish his findings, yet without blatantly endorsing them. Galileo managed to convince the Vatican by citing how its rival, the Protestant Church, was not blindly bound to the theories of Ptolemy or Aristotle, which had been cemented into Catholic liturgy three centuries earlier by Saint Thomas Aquinas. Moreover, although Aquinas integrated a great deal of secular philosophy into the Catholic religion, he warned his fellow ecclesiasts that if new evidence proved anything in the Scriptures to be false, then logic dictated that it must be adopted. This further eased the Vatican's concerns.

However, in 1630, Galileo attempted to publish his book *Dialogue Concerning the Two Chief Systems of the World—Ptolemaic and Copernican*. Several clerics at the Vatican scrutinized Galileo's work, and thwarted its publication. They weren't convinced that Galileo's evidence was conclusive, and many scientists today agree. This was unfortunate for the church, for although it had grounds to challenge Galileo, its harsh sentencing backfired. Nevertheless, Galileo stubbornly believed otherwise, and despite acquiescing, he ignited an historic altercation and precedent.

Galileo's book was, however, permitted publication in the more secular-minded city of Florence in 1632. Galileo's clever treatise took on the guise of a discourse between two protagonists in the form of fiction rather than scientific treatise. One character was Simplicio, an Aristotelian philosopher defending the Earth-centered universe advocated by the Catholic Church, and the other was Salviati, an advocate of the Copernican heliocentric solar system. Their names alone offered a subtle hint at Galileo's intentions, Simplicio being simple-minded and Salviati being the salvation of free thought.

Galileo's unique book, however, did not resonate with devout Christians, or Jews for that matter, for a passage from the Old Testament was raised that clearly refuted Galileo's poorly camouflaged claim. Moreover, this passage was not from some questionable secondary scripture, but from the indisputable Bible itself. The verse comes from the Book of Joshua, and reads:

"Then spake Joshua to the LORD in the day when the LORD delivered up the Amorites before the children of Israel, and he said in the sight of Israel, Sun, stand thou still upon Gibeon: and thou, moon, in the valley of Ajalon. And the

Sun stood still, and the moon stayed, until the people had avenged themselves upon their enemies. Is not this written in the book of Jasher? So the sun stood still in the midst of heaven, and hasted not to go down about a whole day."

If the Lord made the sun stand still amidst the heavens, and did not let it go down for a whole day then it was irrefutably clear that the sun was the object that moved, not the stationary Earth. As such, on June 22, 1633, in the Convent of Minerva, the church's relentless inquisition convicted Galileo of heresy. The sentence spelled out in clear and harsh terms that Galileo... "believed the doctrine which is false and contrary to the Sacred and Divine Scriptures, that the Sun is the center of the world and does not move from east to west and that the Earth moves and is not the center of the world...Consequently, you (Galileo) have incurred all the censures and penalties enjoined and promulgated by the sacred Canons and all particular and general laws against such delinquents."

Ironically, Galileo's condemnation took place in a convent named after Minerva, who was ancient Rome's goddess of wisdom, learning, and inventiveness. Alas, the Christian usurpers of pagan Rome had unwittingly denounced what Minerva and Galileo blatantly possessed.

The strict papal edict banned publication of Galileo's book, and he was sentenced to life imprisonment within the dungeons of the Holy Office. But due to the influence of his former academic student and friend, Cardinal Barberini, who was seated on the hearing committee, the sentence was reduced to house arrest. Cardinal Barberini also happened to be the nephew of the reigning Pope Urban VIII. The Barberini clan, like other families before them, had done well by engaging in nepotism.

The Barberini pope had wasted no time in appointing many relatives to high office shortly after his election ten years earlier. During Galileo's trial, Pope Urban VIII commissioned Rome's newest and most famous artist, Gian Lorenzo Bernini, to construct the gargantuan *baldacchino* over the altar in Saint Peter's. To fulfill the demands of the project, Pope Urban ordered enormous amounts of bronze to be stripped from Rome's pagan masterpiece, the Pantheon. In anger, the Romans jeered, "What the barbarians did not do, the Barberini did!" Alas, despite the Barberini's skill in illuminating the Vatican, the light of knowledge was quenched.

Galileo remained in his villa, just outside of Florence, for the remainder of his life. For ten years, Galileo continued to experiment in his home prison, and even invented the pendulum clock in 1640. Two years later, Galileo died, but fortunately his universe-shattering manuscript managed to be smuggled into Holland and was widely published.

Galileo's place in the timeline of science is pivotal. Where the ancients made many basic and noteworthy attempts, they likewise burdened countless generations with an overabundance of rhetorical ballast. Fortunately, Galileo emerged after two thousand years to finally cast much of this dead weight overboard. In retrospect, Galileo was astonishingly innovative in the way he formulated his scientific method of analysis. Despite his questionable zeal to prove the heliocentric model, Galileo's many successes at proving theories based upon scientific experimentation and mathematics paved the way for modern physics. Years later, Isaac Newton used Galileo's mathematical "Law of Inertia" as a foundation for his "First Law of Motion." Interestingly enough, Newton was born in 1642, the same year that Galileo died—the torch of enlightenment had been passed onto the next influential runner.

Even Galileo's contemporary, philosopher René Descartes, who was an avid Jesuit Christian, was enamored by Galileo's ideas, some of which he had simultaneously pondered, yet only in vague outline. For the most part, Descartes was deeply disheartened and frightened by his church's harsh censorship, for he thought that if they condemned even the mere mention of a hypothesis, this meant that inquiry and free thought were dead. In personal letters, Descartes confided that he would abstain from such public expressions, and hoped that the pope, who to his knowledge was not involved in these trials by the cardinals of the Inquisition, would one day see the light. This fear warrants attention.

Descartes was raised during the tumultuous time of the Counter-Reformation, and as a child was a boarding student at the Jesuit school, La Flèche. The French king, Henry IV, established the Catholic school in 1604. Before becoming king, Henry had been the unofficial head of the Huguenots, which was a distinct group of French Calvinist Protestants. His arranged marriage to Margaret of Valois, the Catholic daughter of King Charles IX of France, was made to quell the religious rivalry that had torn France apart. But six days after their wedding, a bloody massacre ensued during which Catholic assassins began killing Huguenots en masse. Protestant leaders and parishioners were ruthlessly slain. From Paris to Toulouse to Bordeaux, French cities turned red. One of the prime orchestrators of this bloodbath was the mother of King Charles IX, Catherine de Medici *(See page 707).*

Amid this chaos, Henry managed to remain in the fray diplomatically by converting to Catholicism, yet King Charles IX's mother, Catherine, kept a deadly eye on him. Henry briefly reverted to Protestantism, but when he later rose to be king, he once again converted to Catholicism. Though he was Christian chameleon, Henry never wavered in his support for education. After allowing the Jesuits, who he had banished eight years previously, to return to Paris, he remarkably established the Jesuit school, La Flèche.

The Jesuits used a new model of education that encouraged and rewarded their students rather than the traditional approach, which was to jam as much knowledge into their little heads as possible. The Jesuits correctly saw this as filling a thin-necked bottle too fast; too much material overflowed and much knowledge was wasted. Their slow and well-nurtured forums of open exchange were ideal for Descartes, who found this atmosphere of open-mindedness a natural way to cultivate learning. Therefore, the Church was also progressive.

Ironically, to the dismay of many, a Jesuit, who probably had suspicions about the king's true sympathies, killed King Henry IV. Descartes was present that day, and even attended the royal funeral. The religious warfare that surrounded Descartes certainly must have troubled the young student, yet the long history of religious conflict was probably easier for him to understand than the condemnation of Galileo thirteen years later. Fighting over different ideologies was one thing, but despotically silencing free thought was another, especially for a brilliant philosopher who was sympathetic to his fellow scientist's endeavors.

In the years ahead, when Descartes published his book *Discourse on Method* he would also find himself submitting a copy to Cardinal Barberini at the Vatican. As he himself said, he did this to "test the waters." He wasn't so much looking for their assessment of his theory, but for its compatibility to doctrine. Even though the majority of Descartes' work dispelled Aristotelian theory, his book luckily made no mention of the Earth, or its theoretical movements like Galileo's had, therefore, his work went on to become a staple in almost every university. Descartes' famous quote, "I think, therefore I am" survived the Catholic Church's censorship and can still be heard in philosophy classrooms today.

Although fear suppressed many critical thinkers during the Counter-Reformation, the highly exposed trial of Galileo Galilei sent shockwaves throughout Europe. Many scientists that followed found the allure of his work more compelling than the severe repercussions they possibly faced. The fact that Galileo proved that mathematics was the essential and missing ingredient in the adventurous task of scientific inquiry naturally drew mathematicians like moths to a flame.

For countless centuries, the entirety of Western mankind viewed the physical world through Aristotle's eyes. Aristotle had fashioned his geocentric model of the universe after Plato's more mystical model, yet it still contained metaphysical explanations, such as Plato's belief that the moon's close orbit to the earth contaminated it, explaining why the moon has dark spots. All other planets shine clearly and are perfect bodies, all floating in perfect circles around the earth. Centuries later, Ptolemy compiled a book, called the *Almagest*, containing many ancient theories, including Aristotle's geocentric model, which became the official account on the subject—the Ptolemaic system. Yet this model firmly has its roots in Aristotle, Plato, Pythagoras, and even some earlier Greek philosophers who hypothetically concocted this abstract system.

These views were adopted from the realm of Greek pagans, embedded into Christian scripture as if handed down from God above, and then strictly enforced as incontrovertible laws, despite Aquinas' warning. Galileo's use of mathematics to prove new observations, as well as disprove old and uncontested hypotheses, intrigued a whole new generation of inquiring minds. The shock and humiliation that most intellectuals must have experienced at the crucial turning point presented by Galileo's theory ironically mirrors Plato's famous *Allegory of the Cave*. Basically, Plato's mind-game exercise presents a scenario where groups of prisoners have been fooled by a visual illusion from birth, whereby they perceive shadows as reality and truth. When one prisoner is released, however, he soon finds out that they all were deceived and actually living a lie, for reality and truth are found elsewhere, not in the shadows.

It's profoundly sad and a bit ironic that this allegory became manifest in Plato and Aristotle's own shadowy geocentric model, for it blindly kept mankind in the shadows for almost two millennia. Yet fortunately a small handful of men were able to release themselves from this delusional Greek tragedy and were able to see and reveal the truth elsewhere. The onerous task of confronting the world on this crucial concept fell to one man—Galileo. Standing alone against the mighty church with the entire world looking on, Galileo rose like a phoenix out of the ashes of religious persecution and philosophical folly to become the guiding star that all others followed.

Many brilliant individuals precede others who seem to rise to the heavens and receive all the glory, but there are reasons for Galileo's praise. To evaluate his importance we need to compare his deeds to those of other luminaries. Although Leonardo da Vinci clearly preceded Galileo, and is perhaps the first true scientist of the post-medieval era, two crucial aspects stymied the scientific genius of Leonardo. First was the fact that he never published his many codexes, since he was a perpetual thinking-machine who habitually reworked his thoughts. He probably could never think of them as finalized and ready for publication. Coupled with this was the technological handicap of the printing process during his age. The printing press had only recently been invented and it could not economically reproduce his intricate drawings and schematics, for it would require the laborious and expensive method of etching copper plates. The mere thought of this full-time project must have certainly hampered Leonardo's desire to publish his robust codexes, which contained thousands of pages and illustrations. Because Leonardo's works were never published, the world remained much darker for several centuries longer than it had to in numerous disciplines.

Second, and more importantly, Leonardo da Vinci was only fundamentally proficient in mathematics and this severely curtailed his endeavors into certain realms of experimentation. He recognized math's importance but never attained expertise. Galileo's superior understanding of math actually became the official procedure for proving theories. This formed the scientific method that all subsequent scientists, engineers, physicists, and the like would need to use, since math was the critical key for unlocking the most difficult and abstract mysteries of nature.

Likewise, although Copernicus put forth the basic premise of a heliocentric system (which in fact was first hypothesized by Aristarchus in the third century BC), Copernicus had nothing to support his theory, and more importantly, like Aristarchus over a millennium earlier, neither theorist took the world's attention by storm, as did the mathematical scientist named Galileo. Galileo's highly publicized book that heralded this theory, its unfortunate harsh denouncement by the Church, and his eventual imprisonment was irrevocably etched into the minds of a growingly inquisitive and freethinking world. As a result, Galileo would inherit the illustrious title, The Father of Science.

When we review history, and the many great minds like Galileo's, that made a huge impact on civilization, we are often disappointed by the overpowering resistance they faced, not only by the political or theocratic authorities but also by the masses, who generally oppose change. As such, it's worth our while to briefly reflect upon mankind, for the popular notion that "time advances, yet mankind remains the same" can be attributed to a prevalent condition of human nature.

While only a select few make the monumental changes that alter the course of human progress, most of them either submit to the ignorance of the masses–and sacrifice their dreams as well as progress–or they endure personal hardship and hold their ground. This entails, in most cases, foregoing financial rewards, or any other benefits that society deems most important, in order to forge forward with what seems to the majority as a frivolous waste of time. In this regard, Leonardo's secret scientific endeavors that were rejected by several dukes, or Columbus' bold endeavor that was rejected by royalty come to mind.

Dedication to such sublime principles, which remains invisible to the masses, is extremely crucial and deserves the utmost praise, but success often only occurs after they have suffered from neglect, adversity, or even worse, and many times recognition only occurs generations later. The expression "starving artist" can easily be transferred to scientists, inventors, explorers, musicians, and many other practitioners who dedicated their lives to a higher cause. Unfortunately, too often, those sacrifices do not bear fruit in their lifetimes. Leonardo, Columbus, Mozart, and many others faced financial troubles and periods of neglect, while countless others have never emerged from obscurity.

This is why years or centuries, pass before the brilliant ideas of a select few can rise up to penetrate the dense masses. However, with the growth of educational facilities from the pre-Renaissance onward, and the dedication to a higher standard of excellence, each succeeding generation managed to produce greater numbers of geniuses, as knowledge and cognitive horizons expanded. As we have seen, the Middle Ages evolved into the Renaissance, which gave birth to a broad spectrum of dynamic individuals who supercharged the mighty winds of progress. Amidst this grand collection of talent there were others who are also worthy of our attention, yet for quite different reasons. Despite the amazing advancements in science and engineering, the intrinsic traits of mankind sadly remain unchanged. In this regard, we continue our study of the Renaissance, yet with a different focus on the innate behaviors that have persistently afflicted mankind—namely nepotism and corruption, for one or both are employed by every power seeker, be they sacred or secular.

PART 2:
1480. POPES, THE BORGIAS, AND THE MEDICI
Nepotism and Corruption

THE BORGIAS: *The Pernicious Pope and Devious Duke*
Leonardo Da Vinci as Borgia's Military Engineer
NICCOLO MACHIAVELLI: *Pragmatic Political Guru*
MARTIN LUTHER: *Protestant against Catholic Corruption*
THE MEDICI: *In the Crosshairs of the Catholic Church*
SAVONAROLA: *Transient Theocratic Ruler and Precursor to Martin Luther*

THE BORGIAS: *The Pernicious Pope and Devious Duke*

A swirling wind blew across the Tuscan hills, twisting the towering cypress trees like a manic Van Gogh painting. In the midst of this gale stood Duke Cesare Borgia wearing his typical black velvet suit with a flamboyant black beret and white plume. Walking cautiously toward him was his newly appointed military engineer, Leonardo da Vinci.

The turbulent weather mirrored the turbulent times, as the city-states of Renaissance Italy were marked by a constant turnover rate by ambitious and even deadly hands. One owner of such deadly hands happened to be Cesare Borgia. Cesare, with his many military successes, was like a razor-sharp magnet; he had charisma and bravado that drew talent, yet he was also cutting and deadly. However his most attractive quality was that money was no object. Being the illegitimate son of the immensely powerful and underhandedly slick Pope Alexander VI, it was clear that Cesare had few financial worries and could easily compensate his personnel.

Meanwhile, the uncommonly brilliant Leonardo was highly recommended to Cesare by many who witnessed his magnificent works of art and mastery of perspective, which likewise garnered the highest praise. All who had seen Leonardo's revolutionary *Last Supper* in Milan were astounded by the master's unrivalled skills. However, Cesare was not the type of patron to care one iota about the sublime qualities of art.

The ruthless and power hungry duke had been informed of Leonardo's impressive architectural skills and secret obsession with military engineering, coupled with an impressive gift for invention.

Leonardo had recently fallen upon hard financial times. His former patron, Duke Ludovico Sforza *(see page 710)*, had lost his dukedom of Milan to the invading French under King Louis XII. The French king also happened to be in league with Pope Alexander VI and Cesare. Therefore, Leonardo at first refused Cesare's invitation, being skeptical and knowing well his deadly intrigues. However, after failing to secure solid commissions the temporarily starving artist/polymath conceded.

Also recently lured into the fold was the insightful bureaucrat, Niccolo Machiavelli. The Florentine official of foreign affairs and defense had initially been dispatched to Borgia's camp to negotiate a truce, for Cesare's notorious troops were in the Romagna conquering city-states north of Florence. The Florentine heads of state, or the Signoria, worried about Cesare and his lack of good faith and evidently sent Machiavelli as not only a diplomat but as a spy. Needless to say, Machiavelli was soon captivated by Cesare's vibrant—yet lethal—charisma.

Oddly enough, this would be the only time that the two greatest minds of the Renaissance, Machiavelli and Da Vinci, would unite. This startling encounter has only become public knowledge in recent years, and with good reason. Not only was their mission top secret but their services for the coldblooded ruler were not something anyone would care to publicize.

Nevertheless, Cesare Borgia now proudly stood on a hill in Tuscany, as Leonardo approached his new patron. The seemingly infallible warrior had just completed a successful assault on the La Rocca Fortress, whereby adding the township of Imola to his growing kingdom. Looking up at La Rocca, Cesare informed Leonardo that he wished to make the old fortress his primary stronghold in the region. As such, he needed Leonardo to assess the damages and prepare plans for its refortification. Leonardo took off to engage his new task, and renovations promptly commenced.

However, during Leonardo's evaluation process his mind, as usual, had wandered far beyond the menial task of retrofitting outdated features and devices by medieval architects. It was at this opportune moment that the farsighted inventor conceived of what came down to us, via his notebooks, as the radical *Ringed Fortress (see page 710).*

That Da Vinci's stunning fortress was never built, yet was highly admired by Machiavelli, only indicates Cesare's lack of vision, or lack of desire to squander funds on a futuristic defensive complex. Then again, Cesare was facing mounting opposition and he feared losing his ground.

However, upon taking a closer look at Leonardo's notebooks, we now suspect that other things were on Leonardo's mind, beyond retrofitting or designing a futuristic fortress. Cesare had given Leonardo a high degree of clout upon entering the fold, which is rather odd considering that the duke of Milan, Ludovico Sforza, previously employed Leonardo, while the Borgia's were allies of the French that dethroned him. Moreover, Leonardo was a Florentine by birth, and Cesare was deviously seeking to force Florence into submission via a power play. Nevertheless, Cesare allotted his new military architect/engineer free and unhindered passage among his ever-expanding principality. The royal pass that Cesare issued to Leonardo is worth reading:

To all our lieutenants, castellans, captains, condottieri, officers, soldiers, and subjects who read this document: We order and command this: that to our most excellent and dearly beloved architect and general engineer Leonardo da Vinci, bearer of this pass, charged with inspecting the places and fortresses of our states, so that we may maintain them according to their needs and on his advice, all will allow free passage, without subjecting him to any public tax either on himself or his companions, and to welcome him with amity, and allow him to measure and examine anything he likes. To this effect, provide him with the men he requests and give him any aid, assistance, and favor he asks for. We desire that for any work to be executed within our states, each engineer be required to confer with him and to conform to his judgment. Let no man act otherwise unless he wishes to incur our wrath.

Once again, Leonardo's prestigious title of being Cesare's general engineer, who outranked all others, and the free access to travel and inspect anything he desired, with the proviso that anyone who interfered would incur Cesare's wrath, speaks volumes about Leonardo's impressive new status. Overlooking the obvious grounds of loyalty was the question of Leonardo's qualifications. Cesare certainly knew Leonardo performed many different services for Sforza in Milan, and it's quite possible that he performed military projects of which we have no records. We know that Leonardo's surviving notebooks indicate architectural designs and various gadgets, both practical and military, however there were other architects and engineers with formal backgrounds and highly publicized reputations that were known to Cesare, yet he overlooked them all to appoint Leonardo as his chief military architect and engineer.

Here again, many modern historians have a difficult time understanding this mindset, however we must keep in mind that even Pope Julius II—when seeking to raze the existing St. Peter's basilica built by Constantine a thousand years earlier—was surrounded by many prominent architects that felt the commission would easily be theirs, yet to the chagrin of all, Julius appointed Donato Bramante. Bramante was a relatively unknown architect; yet Julius sought someone who shared his bold vision, someone who wasn't afraid to think different, think big.

Interestingly enough, Bramante had been a good friend of Leonardo's in Milan, serving as Duke Ludovico Sforza's court architect. Bramante and Leonardo must have exchanged many ideas, as Bramante is believed to have designed the apse in the Santa Maria delle Grazie, the church where Leonardo painted his *Last Supper*. However, after leaving Milan, Bramante traveled to Rome where he built his small but impressive *Tempietto*. The martyrium, or tomb for a martyr, sat in the courtyard of the hilltop church San Pietro in Montorio. The *Tempietto* displayed the style of classical Roman that deeply impressed Julius, and so this relatively minor architect trumped and bewildered all his preeminent peers, thus becoming the envied yet famous architect of the most colossal and captivating church in all of Christendom, the new St. Peter's basilica.

Therefore, Cesare's decision was probably based upon the same criteria, for Leonardo was known by all to be a remarkably innovative thinker, despite having an extremely restless mind that was hard to harness. Additionally, it was known by those of high rank that Leonardo was officially hailed as *The Duke's Inventor* while serving Sforza in Milan.

However, the even greater mystery was how Leonardo took advantage of his new authority, whereby investigating and recording a wealth of information that never seemed to be authorized by Cesare. Nor did this information ever reach the duke's hands. That is, while inspecting castles, fortresses and villages, Leonardo was keenly surveying the town of Imola in excruciating detail. In fact, Leonardo broke pioneering grounds, once again, by devising aerial maps of such astounding precision that it makes it easy to fantasize the notion that Leonardo managed to build his bizarre flying machine and surveyed Imola from the skies above.

However, landing in the world of reality, we know that Leonardo's mathematical measurements and keen artistic eye melded together to create detailed and accurate maps; maps that not only outlined the city and surrounding mountains but, more importantly, the canals and river systems that ran through this region. And here is where the mystery unravels, or rather flows into our consciousness.

Leonardo had many years previously entertained the thought of controlling the mighty Arno River. If he could bend the river to his will he would then be able to better irrigate the region, whereby bolstering Florentine farming and economic influence. However, with the military concerns of the Signoria now presented to him by his new acquaintance, Niccolo Machiavelli, the two Florentine masters set into motion a covert plot to undermine Cesare and ignite their own power play to skyrocket Florentine power. Whether the two were working together as secret agents from the very start or Machiavelli persuaded Leonardo to engage subversive activities upon meeting him at Cesare's camp remains unclear. However, we do know that the Florentine Signoria loved their bold idea, one that would consume their time and financial resources for quite some time. After all, Florence was precariously close to the clutches of Cesare, and they were prepared to do whatever possible to defend her. Moreover, the ambitious Florentines had far grander ideas in mind, and Leonardo now made those ideas plausible. The audacious plan was to divert the Arno River to deny their rivals at Pisa of the very water they needed to survive. Rather than engage the Pisans in a bloody battle, this technological ploy would peacefully force Pisa to reenter the fold of being under Florentine rule. However, this would only be phase one of a far larger plot, for Leonardo envisioned an even greater possibility.

Being friends with Amerigo Vespucci—even having drawn a sketch of the famous explorer—Leonardo had firsthand information about the

New World discovery, a mindboggling discovery that had many Italians flocking to Spain, Portugal, France, and England to secure charters. Leonardo, Machiavelli, and the Signoria all agreed that Italy—or actually Florence; being the most influential city in Italy at that time—should not allow foreigners to strip them of their rightful place. Therefore, Leonardo and Machiavelli's plan was to not only divert the mighty Arno River, but also make a system of canals that would lead to a new miraculous inland seaport, one that would make Florence the leading hub and ultimate power in the race to monopolize the New World. This was indeed *grand*.

The engineering expertise required to pull off this grand scheme was so advanced that it literally required the knowledge of future engineers. However, Leonardo's calculations of manpower and the tonnage of earth removal required were sound and meticulous. Furthermore, realizing the setbacks of using manual labor to achieve this massive project, Leonardo designed a colossal canal-digging machine, which appears to have been capable of executing—and certainly expediting—the immense project. However, after expending a great deal of time and creative energy on the covert project, Leonardo faced a rapidly changing environment.

Leonardo completed many projects for Cesare, but then, quite suddenly, left his service. Whether Leonardo felt uneasy working for an unpredictable and unstable patron like Cesare Borgia or, perhaps, fulfilled his secret mapmaking mission for the Florentines and left remains unclear. But he did return to Florence, where he soon secured various commissions and his next patron. It would be at this time that Leonardo would paint the most famous portrait in all of Western history, the *Mona Lisa*. The Arno River project, however, was dropped.

Meanwhile, the Signoria hired a new engineer to take over the Arno project, with Colombino as project supervisor. It was Colombino who actually attempted the miraculous feat, but he decided to reject Leonardo's calculations and strategies for controlling the raging river. Colombino not only cutback on digging the number of ditches prescribed by Leonardo, but he also foolishly discarded his canal digging machine, his calculations of manpower, and the most crucial factor—the required depth that the ditches and canals had to be in order to successfully redirect the massive flow of water.

Daniel Bernoulli received world acclaim for his Bernoulli's principle of fluid dynamics in 1738. He learned that water pressure and rate flow significantly increased when channeled down from a large body into a smaller one, something Leonardo observed and clearly understood over two centuries earlier. As was often the case, Leonardo exhibited an uncanny and prophetic trait of anticipating the future, and many times by multiple centuries. At any *rate*, not heeding this dynamic principle would prove to be the bane of Colombino's attempt to conquer the Arno or the science of hydrodynamics. The deluge of water raged through his shallow channels overflowing onto the plains. The plains were too high to maintain the flow, so the waves either dissipated or rolled back, as the mighty Arno continued business as usual. Henceforth, the only thing that Colombino managed to alter was Leonardo's sound plans—the Arno remained unchanged and victorious.

This was just another *what if* moment for Leonardo da Vinci. Like so many other farsighted visions of the great master, the immense feat to control the Arno River never materialized, nor did Florence's chance to be a world player in the New World. As with any great inventor, Leonardo also experienced many setbacks and even utter failures. After the Arno project, Leonardo was commissioned to paint a huge fresco in the Palazzo Vecchio, entitled the *Battle of Anghiari*. All who saw Leonardo's sketch were in awe. The impassioned vision featured men riding on horseback all twisted and contorted in the deadly heat of battle. However, once again, Leonardo decided to test out a new procedure in lieu of the standard fresco method. In an attempt to dry the oil based paints that he applied, Leonardo lit small furnaces to expedite the process. However, to the horror of all, the oily colors ran, and the painting that was ardently hailed as not only a masterpiece, but also a school for all artists to study, painfully dripped into ruin and faded from history.

The key was, however, that Leonardo was a perpetual innovator, and despite his many humiliating setbacks, he *always* forged forward and *always* sought new ways to advance any project his fertile mind engaged. And that fortitude and determination to enhance knowledge, despite the agonizing pains of failure, is a powerful lesson that we all can learn from, as well as admire.

As for those whose failures we can also learn from and even applaud, were Cesare Borgia, whose reign of terror was quashed, and his brutal father, Pope Alexander VI, who was poisoned. The exploits of this notorious father and son team often read like a seedy thriller and, as such, it pays to backtrack to the world they inherited and the world they forcefully shaped.

Almost two hundred years previously, in 1309, Pope Clement V had boldly moved the papacy to Avignon (modern day France), which at the time was a fiefdom of the King of Sicily. This relocation, known as the Babylonian Captivity, was allegedly due to the havoc that was ravaging Rome. This expedient maneuver ended up lasting sixty-eight long years. Over that time, the papacy lost control over much of its territory, as a lack of unity further plagued the Italian peninsula. Life in Italy was doomed to perpetual waves of invasions and short-lived reigns by homegrown Italians as well as French and Spanish foreigners. The Italians viewed this as intolerable, yet, as time would tell, they wouldn't be able to unify their peninsula for several more centuries.

Nevertheless, in 1455, with the papacy back in Rome, a number of Italian clergymen were not pleased when a Spaniard entered the holy walls of the Vatican itself to become Pope Calixtus III. Worse yet, Calixtus was determined not to remain alone, as he flooded the Vatican with his bawdy Borgia brigade; among them was his young nephew, Rodrigo.

Rodrigo Borgia quickly rose to cardinal and just as quickly established a telling reputation for himself. Pope Pius II, who succeeded Rodrigo's uncle Calixtus, learned of the lewd sexcapades that Rodrigo engaged in while at Siena. Admonishing him for shameful activities unbefitting a cardinal, Pope Pius' letter reeked with utter humiliation, charging: "All of Siena is talking about this orgy... Our displeasure is beyond words... A cardinal should be beyond reproach."

However, the papacy would soon find itself falling deeper into depravity as Giovanni Cibo became pope; being the first to openly admit having illegitimate children. Worse yet, Cibo flaunted this insult by choosing the pontifical name of Pope Innocent III. Rodrigo must have felt relieved that Innocent paved the way for his own licentious behavior.

However, along with Rodrigo's lust for women was his lust for money, and the crafty cardinal amassed great wealth by any underhanded means possible. He eventually became the second wealthiest man in the College of Cardinals, whereby he boastfully proclaimed that he had enough gold to fill the Sistine Chapel: the chapel having been built by and named after Pope Sixtus IV in 1480.

Interestingly enough, the nephew of Pope Sixtus IV was Cardinal Giuliano della Rovere. Giuliano felt sure of his ascension to pope, however he painfully realized that the crafty Spaniard, Rodrigo, also had his eye on the lofty throne of Saint Peter. With the death of Pope Innocent III, both Giuliano and Rodrigo scuttled to secure votes. Della Rovere believed he had the upper hand; after all, he had his bloodline to Sixtus, his Italian heritage, and held the eminent position of being Pope Innocent's primary manager of affairs. And for good measure, della Rovere even charged Rodrigo with simony. However, the Borgia briber managed to buy a majority of votes; his massive wealth literally paid off. Rodrigo had successfully power politicked his way to the top.

In searching for a pontifical name Rodrigo Borgia decided upon Alexander VI, probably after the great Macedonian warrior rather than his five pious predecessors. To allay the fears of some in the Vatican and the larger Christian community, Alexander prudently announced that simony would be eliminated. These words, however, were spoken by a hypocritical politician rather than an honest pope, and simony was only one sin of many that would plague Alexander's iniquitous and turbulent reign.

Pope Alexander shamelessly followed Pope Innocent's lustful lead, as he made no attempt to conceal his many children. Worse yet, Alexander proudly flaunted his many love affairs, including the ultimate scandal where he had the portrait of his mistress made to look like the Virgin Mary, and then had the gall to mount it over the door to his bedchamber.

Despite his many mistresses, Alexander took a vested interest in his children and made sure each received higher appointments. Cesare and Lucrezia rose to become the most popular, as a shroud of intrigue even enveloped Lucrezia. Before Alexander became pope, he married off his daughter twice before she was twenty-two. Moreover, he made sure each husband was disposed of once they were deemed useless.

Lucrezia's first husband was Giovanni, from the powerful Sforza family in Milan. Rodrigo eagerly awaited the young couple to bear fruit, yet Giovanni proved to have seedless prunes. As such, Giovanni was humiliatingly forced to declare his impotence to secure the divorce.

Rodrigo then arranged Lucrezia's marriage to Duke Alfonso of Bisceglie. Despite their loving marriage, once Rodrigo became Pope Alexander, he, too, was deemed expendable. Alexander pressed Alfonso to sign the divorce papers, but, still being in love with Lucrezia, he refused, and then fled. Alexander appointed his wild boar son, Cesare, to be the enforcer, however, as fate would have it, Alfonso foolishly returned upon Pope Alexander's command. Entering back into Rome, Alfonso was confronted by a team of assassins and was wounded. Escaping in fury, he then tracked down his boorish brother-in-law and attempted to shoot Cesare while he was walking in the Vatican gardens. He missed. With his courageous attempt foiled, Alfonso retreated to his wife's chambers. Cesare took off in hot pursuit and burst into the room. He looked at Lucrezia and demanded that she leave. Unable to condone her brother's lethal intentions, yet also unable to defy him, Lucrezia fled the room in tears. No sooner had the door closed, did Cesare lunge at his wounded victim's throat and strangle him to death.

However, Lucrezia was no angel, and she gained the lurid reputation for poisoning numerous victims at her father and brother's beckon call. Modern historians, however, claim that enemies of the Borgias concocted many of these vile allegations, yet, although that is certainly true, it is highly doubtful that Lucrezia was saintly.

Meanwhile, Lucrezia's ruthless brother Cesare cannot escape the brutal reputation that he carved in blood for himself. Although we know he had charisma and charm, like his father, his escapades and personality traits, both good and bad, were well documented.

Pope Alexander had big plans for Cesare. With the growing wave of nepotism in the Vatican reaching high tide, Alexander made sure that Cesare received the vestments of a cardinal at age eighteen. Yet, to his utter dismay, his brutish son quickly shucked the cloth. A glorious temporal life like Julius Caesar was more in line with his wild constitution, and Cesare's blacksmith even branded his sword with the apropos maxim: "Either Caesar or Nothing!"

A year earlier, in 1497, Cesare's older brother Giovanni had been his father's precious gem, carefully polished to be the shinning diamond of the flawed Borgia family. However, the diamond was horribly defaced and then tossed away in the blackness of night. Giovanni was brutally murdered, being stabbed repeatedly and dumped into the Tiber River. Giovanni had been made Duke of Gandia with Alexander's utmost strategic care; however, Giovanni's unexpected and gruesome death caused Alexander to sink into a numbing depression. The pope languished in despair for almost two weeks, hardly eating. Giovanni's death awoken in Alexander a new desire to cleanse his soul and the papacy, as he painfully made the following decree:

"…God has given us this punishment for our sins, for the Duke has done nothing to deserve such a death. Therefore, we are resolved to amend our life and reform the church. We renounce all nepotism. We will begin the reform with ourselves and so proceed through all levels of the church till the whole work is accomplished."

However, Alexander's noble aspirations were fleeting and, in time, he resorted to his old evil ways.

Those nasty traits were well known right from the very day Rodrigo took the tiara in 1492. In fact, a plot to skewer the Spanish bull had begun immediately, resulting in a bold attack that would commence a year and a half later. Pope Alexander was very close to literally losing his head.

In the summer of 1494, King Charles VIII of France stormed into Italy on a daring crusade that took him right to the Vatican's doorstep. In fear, Pope Alexander fled the Holy palace via an underground tunnel, whereby emerging inside Hadrian's massive mausoleum across the Tiber. The huge circular edifice had been converted into a fortress and Christianized with the name Castel Sant' Angelo. However, the scheming that prompted King Charles VIII to make his audacious attack needs to be illuminated.

Quite understandably, Alexander's election as pope was strongly contested, especially by the feisty clergyman, Giuliano della Rovere. As noted, della Rovere believed that the seat of Saint Peter's was his, but he humiliatingly lost the bid. Upon Alexander's ascension, della Rovere fled

Italy and secured a meeting and firm ally with King Charles VIII. This wasn't all that difficult, primarily for two reasons.

First, King Charles was not particularly bright. As such, he was easily manipulated. Second, taking advantage of that deficit, Duke Ludovico Sforza of Milan had done a superb job of goading Charles into making a raid into Italy. Ludovico had illegally placed his nephew—the rightful heir to the Milanese throne—in confinement. Unfortunately his nephew's wife was the granddaughter of the King of Naples, and she was stirring up her relatives to attack Ludovico to restore her husband to the throne.

Therefore, Ludovico wasted no time in persuading the pliable French king to attack Naples, since the Neapolitan king had actually stolen the crown from a Frenchman of the Angevin dynasty. King Charles happened to be an Angevin himself and naturally relished the idea. However, Ludovico had other schemes up his sleeve, as he also manipulated Holy Roman Emperor Maximilian I to get involved, too. This would eventually ignite the Italian Wars, which would plague and further divide Italy for the next seventy years.

However, things went terribly wrong for Ludovico, and he later found himself fighting the French for survival. He was even forced to use the precious bronze that he was storing—which was to cast Leonardo da Vinci's colossal equestrian statue of his father—to make cannons. Hence, Ludovico robbed Leonardo and history of a colossal masterpiece (the beautiful clay model being destroyed by the French) and he thrust Italy into countless wars by inviting foreigners to manipulate Italian politics. Greed had proven deadly for Ludovico who, five years later, would lose his Milanese dukedom to Charles' successor, King Louis XII, in 1499.

Nevertheless, Ludovico's scheming plan in 1494—to prod and aid King Charles to invade Naples—happened to be augmented by another prodding schemer. This returns us to Cardinal della Rovere, who actively prompted Charles to invade the Italian peninsula, not only to seize the lost kingdom of his kinsmen in Naples, but for a truly noble and Christian cause; dethroning the evil Spanish pope that defiled the sanctity of all Christendom. Naturally, della Rovere allayed Charles' fears of attacking the Pontiff by recommending himself as the ideal replacement, a cardinal of stature and dignity that would not upset the vast Christian flock.

Della Rovere, however, added even more divine grandeur to the pot. He goaded King Charles to follow up that mission by routing out the Ottoman Turks, whereby recapturing the lost Holy Land of Jerusalem. With a glorious Holy War that would make all of Christendom applaud his efforts, combined with personal glory for France, King Charles set his plans into motion and stormed the Italian peninsula. To the shock of many, Cardinal della Rovere would ride with Charles and 25,000 French soldiers on their historic mission. It wasn't the last time he would strap on armor.

Upon hearing of King Charles' frightening advance, Pope Alexander scuttled to secure aid. He happened to have one extremely valuable commodity right in his possession; namely, the younger brother of the Turkish Sultan, named Djem.

Djem had been banished by his brother Bajazet for staging a coup. Shortly thereafter, Pope Innocent VIII craftily held Djem hostage and received 40,000 ducats a year from Sultan Bajazet just to keep Djem from returning home. Pope Alexander inherited Djem upon his taking the Seat of St. Peter. However, Alexander took a liking to Djem, who became an extended part of the tawdry Borgia family. However, now, with his own neck on the line, Pope Alexander had no compunction about using his young friend as a bargaining chip to pressure the Sultan to aid his cause. He told Bajazet that King Charles's intentions were to remove him and make Djem pope, whereby his brother would surely mount a full Christian attack upon his Ottoman Empire. Therefore, Alexander urged Bajazet to not only send his annual payment early but to also force his Venetian friends to send troops to Rome immediately.

However, Bajazet devised a much easier solution. He sent a message requesting that if they kill Djem he would gladly fork over 300,000 ducats upon receipt of his dead brother's body. As fate would have it, King Charles' troops intercepted Bajazet's messenger. The Sultan's letter, which confirmed Pope Alexander's underhanded and lethal negotiations with Christianity's ultimate infidel, stunned the French king and added more fuel to Cardinal della Rovere's already burning fire of papal desire.

As the French troops surrounded Rome they managed to capture Pope Alexander's favorite mistress, Giulia Farnese. Alexander was panic-stricken. Fortunately for his tattered nerves, King Charles was not savvy and he foolishly offered away his ace in the hole for a mere 3000 ducats ransom. Despite the deluge of mayhem that surrounded Alexander and the papacy, the pope managed to gather the funds and quickly rode out to retrieve his beloved mistress. Upon hearing of King Charles' mindless maneuver, Duke Ludovico Sforza was livid, knowing that Alexander would have bent like wax if they used his sultry flame to torment and mold him. However, worse was yet to follow.

This brings us to the point where Pope Alexander quickly gathered his essentials and escaped underground to the well-fortified Castel Sant' Angelo. As King Charles and his troops surrounded the fortress, Alexander's nerves rattled inside the castle tomb. However the Christian king was beginning to have doubts. Despite his advisors pleas to unseat the unsavory pope—who was guilty of simony, racketeering and nepotism, in addition to his numerous sexual sins and allegations of murder—King Charles, to their dismay, backed down. Evidently he feared the response of the Christian majority that would damn him as the usurper of an incumbent pope. Cardinal della Rovere was livid, they had Alexander trapped like a rapacious rat, even most aptly in a pagan tomb, and the fearful French king forfeited his prize. Pope Alexander buoyantly emerged from Hadrian's mausoleum to remain the Christian Pontiff.

Looking to fulfill the rest of his mission, King Charles then headed south towards Naples, taking along Alexander's son Cesare as collateral. Cesare, however, was too wily for the feeble Frenchman and he managed to escape. Nevertheless, Charles easily stormed into Naples, as they offered no resistance. News traveled fast of the French king's conquest, and the quarreling Italians temporarily united to eradicate the foreign invader. Charles barely managed to escape the peninsula with his life.

Meanwhile, Pope Alexander had an odd epiphany; *maybe his life was spared because he had done nothing wrong*. As such, Alexander's evil escapades would grow ten-fold, as a wave of retaliation, corruption, secret alliances and conquest ensued. In the years ahead, after the death of Alexander's eldest son, Cesare would become the pope's ultimate rake for devouring Italy. However, even Alexander had no idea of what he unleashed. With violence and vengeance in his gut, Cesare formed an alliance with King Charles' successor King Louis XII, and he quickly mushroomed into an uncontrollable dynamo that, at times, even had his hefty father walking on eggshells.

Cesare swept through the Romagna region, devouring city after city. Meanwhile, his doting father made sure that he could finance his son's insatiable appetite. Alexander even resorted to extorting the belongings and property of noblemen, as well as his own clergymen, to pay for his pernicious policies; in fact, he even passed a papal bull granting such confiscations. The Borgia policy was straightforward; rich people would be bogusly accused of an offense, imprisoned and, if troublesome, disposed of by outright execution or silently poisoned. They would then confiscate the innocent victims' property, possessions, and wealth, which further funded the pope and his son's warring campaigns.

Seething at the Borgias seemingly uncontrollable and wicked reign, perhaps more than any other man, was Cardinal della Rovere. His covert mission with King Charles to dethrone Pope Alexander had failed miserably, only emboldening the corrupt Pontiff and his deadly kin. However, della Rovere would finally achieve his payoff a few years later.

In August of 1503, Alexander fell gravely ill, some suspecting that he was poisoned along with Cesare who fell ill at the same time. However, Cesare recovered in a few days, and no evidence ever arose to confirm foul play. Meanwhile, Alexander lay in agony for a week. The excruciating pain turned ugly as Alexander was mauled by the violent clutches of death.

Cesare stormed the Vatican only to see his father's purple face writhing in pain and hideously spotted with bluish-black boils. Not too surprisingly, hardly anyone cared, as the pope drew his last breath. As he exhaled, all of Christendom must have sighed in unison; it was the last and least damaging breath that the Borgia pope ever uttered.

The hatred for the extorting, nepotistic, lustful, homicidal pope was thick and it even choked the air in the papal chambers. As one clergyman noted, "No candles were lit, and no priests or other person of dignity attended the corpse."

Cesare wasted no time in gathering whatever valuables he could and then made a hasty exit. However, he would not relinquish what he and his father worked so hard to accrue. Many ambassadors had to be called upon to prevent Cesare from disrupting the conclave, which even had to be secretly moved from the Vatican to the Santa Maria sopra Minerva basilica, near the Pantheon. Then on September 22, 1503, the College of Cardinals made their *safe* decision. Francesco Piccolomini—an old and sickly man that would give the papacy a brief respite, and who ethically refused to be bribed at Alexander's conclave—would become Pope Pius III. Being only a deacon, Pius had to be ordained a priest and consecrated a bishop in record time. However, Pius didn't even give the conclave the time they expected, for he only held the seat for three weeks, and died.

Cardinal della Rovere quickly went to work securing favor and even stooped to bribing his archenemy, Cesare Borgia, with entitlements. Stepping out of the shadows, della Rovere finally grabbed the Holy Seat, thus becoming Pope Julius II; choosing the name Julius not for the previous Julian pope but rather for his idol– Julius Caesar. Unsurprisingly, Julius became known as the warring pope, even riding in the lead with full body armor to overtake the cities of Perugia and Bologna. However, his grand Caesarian vision would also transform the Vatican into the most impressive and talent-infested enterprise in religious history.

Nevertheless, Pope Julius still had to contend with Cesare Borgia, who was still on the loose and creating havoc. Julius had him hunted down, but Cesare managed to flee south to Naples. Fortunately, Julius had been in contact with King Ferdinand of Spain, who now controlled Naples. Ferdinand's governor caught the fugitive and transported Cesare to Spain, where he was incarcerated in the massive Castle de la Mota. However, the wily firebrand escaped, and the fugitive duke found refuge with his brother-in-law, King John III of Navarre. Cesare joined the ranks, and continued his fighting spree in Spain. However, he died a year later, in 1507, in the battle for Viana. Cesare was only thirty-one.

Despite his ruthless nature and devious tactics, Cesare managed to win over a vast string of city-sates throughout Italy, which Pope Julius conveniently took possession of, thus Cesare unified Italy in ways he never intended. Oddly enough, in the years ahead, Pope Julius would manage to cause a split that he likewise never intended. This began with his decision to raze the original St. Peter's basilica, built by Constantine, to erect a new gargantuan masterpiece. However, the grand scale of this project, which Julius entrusted to Bramante, became a financial black hole.

As such, all of Julius' efforts and financial worries fell to his successor, Pope Leo X, who likewise struggled to keep the monstrous project moving forward. However, all it caused was protest and revolt, particularly in Germany, thus leading to the irrevocable split of Julius' beloved Roman Catholic Church.

However, Pope Julius also took a vested interest in decorating the Sistine Chapel; built by and named after his uncle, Pope Sixtus IV. As noted, Alexander (while still a cardinal) boasted that he could fill the Sistine Chapel with his many bags of gold. Yet even during Alexander's reign as pope, the chapel still featured a bare plaster ceiling. Although he amassed great wealth, the uncultured Alexander had no intentions of squandering money on art or producing devotional works to glorify God; that was left to his ambitious successor—Pope Julius II. It was Julius that commissioned Michelangelo to paint the Sistine Chapel's ceiling, and later the wall behind the main altar with *The Last Judgment*. Hence, Julius transformed the cold and empty chamber—which the Borgia pope neglected—into a glowing masterpiece of Renaissance art.

Pope Julius' Caesarian ambitions, quite understandably, did not reverberate with many, as his warring campaigns and passion for grandeur unnerved much of his poverty-loving, Christian flock. However, despite the Vatican's immense size and ostentatious aura, which defies the message of Jesus, we must realize that it was Julius' grand and majestic vision that today attracts millions of people every year; not only to see the Holy shrine of St. Peter, but to see the magnificence of its colossal architecture, which never ceases to amaze, and the thousands of pieces of the world's finest artworks by some of the world's greatest artists. Despite his obvious faults, Pope Julius—with his grand vision—was dedicated to his beloved Roman Catholic Church, and he left behind an awe inspiring *Basilica of Wonder* that fascinates peoples of all races, creeds and religions.

In stark contrast, Pope Alexander's sole goal was selfish power at any cost, a cost that cost the papacy and even his Borgia family dearly. His dark reign despoiled his office and put a new distaste in the mouths of the faithful. The foundations established by the Borgia pope caused many in the clergy to continue the Vatican's lopsided policy of making secret alliances and abrasive decrees. This corruption existed throughout the reigns of Julius and Leo thus compounding the financial burdens placed on the public by the latter two, which, in total, led to the Reformation. Hence, the Borgia regime had a strong yet negative impact on much broader events than just moral indiscretions or nepotism within the papacy. This was just a sign of the corrupt and bloody times that would follow, and the father and son team of Pope Alexander VI and Duke Cesare Borgia were like two savage Spanish bulls that killed the matador (human morals) and then bullied their way to ultimate power. However, the power hungry trail that they carved and the blood that flowed in their wake was not lost on a keen observer who analyzed their every move.

NICCOLO MACHIAVELLI: *Pragmatic Political Guru*

Machiavelli's careful observations of Cesare Borgia's antics proved to be an odd but necessary godsend, as they would materialize years later in his powerful little book on political and military theory, *The Prince*.

This groundbreaking work was based upon Niccolo's assessments of men in power. This he acquired during his fourteen years acting as Head of the Second Chancery for the Florentine republic. For beyond reading and analyzing history, Machiavelli also gained first-hand experience of how contemporary leaders operated, and this naturally included Cesare Borgia with his cunning antics and ruthless campaigns.

One such observation was how Cesare allowed one of his deputies to cruelly rule over a new village, only to have him publicly executed, thus making himself appear as though a benevolent savior. However, Machiavelli astutely valued how Borgia never relied on mercenaries, who often showed loyalty only to the highest bidder. As such, they could never be expected to fight with the zeal of natives defending their homeland.

These experiences filled Machiavelli's curious mind with some of the raw data that was needed to formulate his political theories. Additionally, Machiavelli made it a point to make a distinct departure from all other theorists, such as Plato with his *Republic*, who merely sat in solitude and speculated on what might and could be. Instead, Machiavelli dispensed with idealism and created an extremely shocking work that viewed politics through uncolored eyes. Moreover, Machiavelli offered clear instructions on how to rule, based upon practical experience and a careful analysis of history.

Achieving the lofty title Head of the Second Chancery, Machiavelli was a very successful and powerful political figure in the Florentine republic. But when the Medici reclaimed power in 1512, Machiavelli was viewed as a threat. He was captured, tortured, and then soundly stripped of power. As an added kick in the teeth, he was banished from the city, living on the outskirts in near poverty. This immense fall from grace, and from the center of action, was devastating. As such, Machiavelli pondered how could an invincible lion lose his pride, only to be left roaming the gutters like a starving alley cat? Furthermore, he pondered a burning question that always plagued his entire political life, namely, why was Italy a mere disjointed shadow of its former unified Roman self?

Machiavelli's exile is what allowed him the time to search himself and the history books about great leaders to find these answers. *The Prince* had evolved into a treatise with a provocative new perspective regarding leadership that broke tradition in every regard; however, it also offered Niccolo two valuable possibilities. First, were his working solutions that, if followed, could enable a prince to unite Italy. Second, this powerful manual could actually become Machiavelli's own ticket to freedom. His intention was to offer it as a gift to Giuliano de Medici, yet he unexpectedly died. Therefore, he dedicated it to his new overlord, Lorenzo de Medici, duke of Urbino (not to be confused with Lorenzo the Magnificent).

However, the younger Lorenzo viewed Machiavelli as a diehard republican and an untrustworthy adversary. Therefore, anything the author wrote would be held suspect and not worth the prince's time. Machiavelli would languish in exile for eight long years, where he would also write his *Discourse* on Livy's *History of Rome*, his *Life of Castruccio Castracani*, and his comedic masterpiece, *The Mandrake Root*.

However, a small glimmer of fortune shone when Lorenzo died in 1519. Machiavelli's works had impressed several men of high esteem who now approached Giulio de Medici on his behalf. Giulio was more open-minded and received Machiavelli shortly thereafter. Recognizing Niccolo's talent and fervent patriotism, he appointed him to be the historiographer of Florence, and placed him on the payroll. Machiavelli would embark upon his *History of Florence*, where three years later he had the honor of dedicating it to Giulio under his new title Pope Clement VII.

The Prince was officially published after Niccolo's death, in 1527, and became legendary. Its blunt and effective tactics would later become a How-To-Bible for many successful leaders as well as tyrants.

Machiavelli's keen observations had an immense impact on Western history, and unlike other political theorists whose ideas were never implemented or were found to be useless, Machiavellian principles have continued to this day, for good or ill. We must also bear in mind that some of Machiavelli's principles have been distorted by evil men to fit their own agendas, as *"the end justifies the means"* can be taken as merely unconventional methods or murderous means. Then again, with even the Bible or Koran being grossly misinterpreted, why should a genuinely controversial book like *The Prince* be any different. However, Machiavelli's name recurs throughout the ages, just as his name appears throughout this book's many pages, and being history's most pragmatic political guru, Machiavelli remains a powerful icon.

Machiavelli lived amid turbulent times and, as we saw earlier, among corrupt popes as well as princes. The accruing abuses in the Vatican eventually stirred a young German monk to rebel against the arrogance, greed, simony, and nepotism that the Borgias and the Medici pope, Leo X, personified in Rome; his name was Martin Luther.

MARTIN LUTHER:
Protestant against Catholic Corruption

Martin Luther initiated what would become the largest split in Christianity when he defied the Roman Catholic pope and nailed his ninety-five theses to the door of the Wittenberg Church. This public display was an open challenge to debate the "power and efficacy of indulgences" by the Catholic Church, which offered forgiveness of sins for monetary contributions.

Pope Leo X had also been collecting money for the reconstruction of St. Peter's Basilica, and one of Luther's arguments, or thesis, directly targeted the rich Medici pope. Thesis 86: "Why does not the pope, whose wealth is today greater than the riches of the richest, build just this one church of St. Peter with his own money, rather than with the money of poor believers?"

Pope Leo X had privately called Luther a loud-mouthed drunkard who would forget about his tirade when he sobered up. However, the sobering effect took hold not of Luther but of Pope Leo when Luther gained instant popularity with his bold dispute.

Interestingly enough, this landmark event occurred on October 31, 1517. As such, it has become known to Protestants as Reformation Day, yet this date has since become far more popular for celebrating Halloween. Consequently, some Catholics may take spiteful solace in the fact that Reformation Day occurred on, and is eternally bound with, evil spirits day.

Halloween, itself, is said to have originated by the early pagan Celts, but was annually practiced by the Romans. This became a visual eyesore to the Christians once they controlled power. The pagan ritual consisted of a fire festival where huge bonfires were lit to ward off the evil spirits. This was because they believed that on that night the dead revisited the earth. However, the new Christian overlords would eventually try to appropriate this ritual to strip the pagans of their day of celebration. Therefore, in AD 835, Pope Gregory IV transformed October 31 to All Saints' Eve, or the Hallowed Eve, thus declaring November 1 as All Saints' Day, the latter being a happy celebration of Christian Saints and Martyrs. In the end, the Christians' attempt to wrest this celebration from the pagans failed, as very few celebrate All Saints' Day, while hundreds of millions celebrate the evil pagan ritual, now labeled Halloween.

Nevertheless, Luther's Reformation was nothing short of seismic. The Christian movement had struggled for three centuries to finally attain unity under Constantine, and then for over a millennium the Roman Catholic Church grew and eventually solidified into one huge monolith. Although independent city-states sprawled across Europe, the church still maintained the devotional faith of many who populated those various regimes. Therefore, Martin Luther's bold maneuver was not only like a shaft of steel that chipped off a shard of rock from this great monolith but, in time, his deep fissures would spread and crack, thus breaking the monolith into Lutheran, Methodist, Protestant, Baptist, Evangelist,

Presbyterian, Episcopal, Mormon and a myriad of other new sects. Christianity would be splintered into more shards than in its infancy over a millennium and a half earlier.

However, by 1520, Pope Leo X was irritated by the quick growth of followers Luther attained, especially those in the German states holding political power. This growing threat prompted the pope to issue a papal bull called the *Exsurge Domine*, or "Arise, O Lord". The intent was to silence the troublesome monk by threatening him with excommunication if he didn't retract forty-one of his ninety-five theses. Luther's response was patent; he burned the papal bull in a bonfire for all the people of Wittenberg to observe and applaud.

A year later, in 1521, Luther was summoned to appear before the Holy Roman Emperor, Charles V, at the Diet of Worms. This was not a disgusting punishment that required Luther to eat slimy invertebrates but rather an assembly (diet) that took place in the town of Worms. Here, once again, Luther was asked to recant or face excommunication. Luther refused; however, before sentencing took place, Prince Frederick III had Luther safely abducted and escorted to the Wartburg Castle in Eisenach. Luther was marked as a fugitive and heretic, but his fiery words spread.

Luther's blazing rebellion would soon ignite the French-born, John Calvin, who, in trying to develop his own sect in Geneva, Switzerland, was exiled. Returning to France, Calvin preached for three years in the city of Strasbourg. Meanwhile, some of Calvin's associates had managed to gain positions of power back in Geneva and invited Calvin back. Once in power, Calvin ruled Geneva firmly, attempting to gain full control over both religious and state affairs.

Calvin's rise was in part due to his influential *Institutes of the Christian Religion* along with his many powerful commentaries. However, although he gained much admiration, Calvin also sparked sharp criticism.

Jacques Gruet wrote openly about Calvin and his French cohorts who he felt were strong-arming the Swiss city. Gruet was arrested, tortured and beheaded. The theologian, Michael Servetus, would also be tried for heresy, and sentenced to death on the stake. Calvin approved of these torturous executions, yet his staunch followers flocked only to the light of his words, words of deep religious conviction and enlightenment, while overlooking his other words that convicted, condemned and, in some cases, killed his critics.

Calvin advocated the Reformed concept of the *Five Solas*, which was Latin for "by grace alone", "by faith alone", "by scripture alone", "by Christ alone", and "by the Glory of God alone". Calvin's new Presbyterian order would also center its thought on the concept that the Bible alone was the final authority, and that salvation can only be attained by the grace of God, as good deeds alone are insufficient. Like many provocative figures in history, John Calvin won the confidence, love, and praise of many, as well as the contempt of others. Nevertheless, Calvin's new order was vast in scope, as well as deep in faith. Despite the ugliness that taints Calvin's personal actions, he gave birth to the Huguenots, Puritans, Dutch Reformed, Anabaptists, and Presbyterian sects, thus inspiring millions who have lived by the word of God and honored the religion.

However, this broad movement all began with Martin Luther, and the eventual growth of Luther's Protestant sect swept its way up into England, the Nordic countries, and even the New World, as the Catholic popes would never again control all of their Christian flock. The corruption by a staggered selection of popes had caused this monumental break, proving that even the papacy was not immune to human foibles, be it simony, greed, or more pointedly nepotism. In fact, Alexander's predecessor, Pope Sixtus IV, who had ordered the construction of the Sistine Chapel, even surpassed the Borgias by appointing six of his nephews as cardinals. Nepotism, however, was only one minor flaw of Pope Sixtus, for evil intent was another. Thus begins the story of a pope who deviously orchestrated a brutal conspiracy to assassinate his rivals.

THE MEDICIS: *In the Crosshairs of the Catholic Church*

This dark tale has deep roots and, as such, requires a little background. After the ravaging Black Death swept through Europe in 1350, killing an estimated 25 million people, or a staggering third of the continent's population, the Catholic Church rapidly began losing parishioners. Many felt that faith no longer offered them protection from the plague or the corruption in the Vatican itself. The shock of witnessing devout clergymen dying just like commoners meant that no one was granted divine protection or spared from the disfiguring death of the bubonic plague. As such, many decided to live more adventurous and even reckless lives.

During this transition, oligarchies, some run by rich bankers, eventually rose to power. The Riccardi, Peruzzi, and Bardi were all powerful pioneers, yet the Medici of Florence grew to be the most powerful bankers in Europe, and established a dynamic regime. By the 1400s, the Medici family was one of the primary forces that fueled the Renaissance by bolstering the economy and being patrons to the arts, science, music, philosophy, education, and architecture.

Lorenzo de' Medici became heir to his family's long and rich heritage, and although he proved to be a great politician and patron of the arts, Lorenzo had to contend with running the powerful Medici bank. Financial matters were not his forte, yet in his vast dealings he and his younger brother Giuliano also funded the Vatican with loans. However, Pope Sixtus eventually began to grow wary of the increasing power, wealth and influence that the Medicis wielded. As such, when Lorenzo endeavored to purchase the town of Imola, the pope immediately decided to buy it himself. Worse still, Pope Sixtus brazenly asked the Medici bank for the loan.

Lorenzo adamantly refused, whereby Sixtus quickly terminated all Medici relations, and then turned to a rival banker to secure the loan. Lorenzo retaliated by forging alliances with Milan and Venice, thus weakening the papacy's control. An infuriated Sixtus fiendishly countered by sponsoring a coup d'état, with the intent of assassinating both Lorenzo and his brother, Giuliano. The carefully chosen coconspirator was the Pazzi family, who were fierce rival bankers who eagerly sought to destroy and replace the Medici's rule. Interestingly enough, the name Pazzi means madmen, and on Easter Sunday, the pope's madmen set their strategy into motion.

During mass, in Florence's magnificent Santa Maria del Fiore cathedral, the band of conspirators patiently waited for the Cardinal to offer communion. As the host was raised, the congregation devotedly bowed their heads, this being the deadly signal to attack. One assassin,

Bernado Baroncelli, skulked up behind Giuliano and thrust his dagger deep into his skull. Giuliano fell flaccidly to the cold, marble floor. In a brutal frenzy, Baroncelli repeatedly stabbed the quivering body eighteen times. During this blaze of debauchery, Baroncelli even slashed his own leg.

Simultaneously, two conniving priests on the opposite side of the cathedral lunged at Lorenzo. As one priest grabbed Lorenzo, the other attempted to skewer him. However, as the amateur assassin's blade grazed Lorenzo's neck, he nimbly recoiled. Swiftly seizing a sword, Lorenzo lacerated his assailants and then hurdled over the altar's railing. Quickly, several companions escorted Lorenzo inside the sacristy. Safe inside, one comrade quickly sucked the blood from Lorenzo's wound, just in case the priest's dagger was laced with poison. Oddly enough, the name Medici means doctors, and Lorenzo's wounds would fully heal. Filled with anxiety, Lorenzo quickly inquired about his younger brother, but alas, they could no longer conceal the bad news, Giuliano was dead.

The pope and the Pazzi family, however, foolishly underestimated Lorenzo de Medici, for not only did he survive, but he also rounded up all the conspirators—except for his brother's fugitive murderer—and all suffered horrible deaths. The leader of the Pazzi clan, Jacopo, was hurled out of a towering window, as the Medici loyalists in the crowd further mutilated the smashed body, and then tossed it in the Arno River. Vengeance would be savage, just as the murderous act had been, which we cannot forget was committed in church, and on Easter Sunday no less. Hence, Lorenzo had made it painfully clear—the Medicis would *not* be intimidated.

What's more, Lorenzo never abandoned his burning quest to find his brother's murderer. When he later learned that Baroncelli had fled to Constantinople he successfully persuaded the sultan to have him extradited. Once returned to Florence, Lorenzo had Baroncelli publicly hanged. Recording this historic event, with an illustrious sketch, was the legendary spectator, Leonardo da Vinci.

Despite the bloody episodes, Lorenzo de Medici ruled Florence during its golden age, and fostered the humanist mindset along with the talents of Michelangelo, Botticelli, Da Vinci and Verrocchio, among many others. Many have criticized Lorenzo for being a ruthless oligarch who manipulated the republic to secure ultimate influence. This naturally is true, however, those opposed to the Medici family were mostly influential families themselves who simply lost their bid for the same unofficial seat of ultimate power. Therefore, their complaints can only be embraced with minimal enthusiasm, for despite the political shenanigans, the Medici family was crucial to empowering trade, various businesses, and igniting the whole cultural movement, which for many, defines the Renaissance.

As for the political structure, the Florentine republic had been cleverly designed to avoid the rise of tyrants by limiting public office to two-month terms. That hardly allowed anyone enough time to wield influence, yet the loophole, or new mode of wielding power, was through stealth. Wealth bought loyalty and rigged elections, so nepotistic officials could sit in office while the true executive pulled all the strings completely apart from government, hence becoming the city's father figure.

This back door policy is what destined the Florentine Republic to be manipulated, and explains why many wealthy families vied desperately for this coveted position. That also explains why things could get quite bloody. However, even after Lorenzo's death, the wealthy capitalists all lost the bid to control Florence to a seemingly unlikely man, a man of no financial means, no political or military connections, but oddly enough, he was a man of the cloth.

SAVONAROLA: *Transient Theocratic Ruler and Precursor to Martin Luther*

Upon the death of Lorenzo de Medici, all of Florence mourned his passing, even the radical Dominican friar, Girolamo Savonarola, who allegedly blessed Lorenzo on his deathbed.

Savonarola had been making a name for himself by denouncing the humanist movement, which focused inwardly upon man's unbound abilities rather than upwardly at God's graceful gift. Naturally, Savonarola's prime targets were Lorenzo and the Medici family, which he believed exemplified the decadence that now thrust Florence into worldly sin. As such, Savonarola's blessing of Lorenzo might have been genuine Christian forgiveness, or possibly thanking God for the opportunity to seize control, whereby he could finally put an end to what he saw as errant endeavors and moral degradation.

Lorenzo's son, Piero, had assumed control, but he was immediately confronted by French forces near Pisa. King Charles VIII had set his sights on Florence; and Piero, unlike his father, easily buckled. With the Medici removed, and with the pope's support, Savonarola emerged as the city's new leader. His day had come.

Savonarola quickly launched his political ministry by inculcating his listeners with guilt. The friar made it clear—the reason why France had taken control over much of Italy was due to *their* sins. Although Savonarola's theological guilt-trip won over the faithfully blind, Machiavelli pragmatically summed up the reality of Italy's woes. Namely, popes and small city-states could not, or did not, amass armies; hence, they were forced to hire mercenaries. As mentioned, Machiavelli loathed these hired guns, which he said were unwilling to die for a fee, disloyal, unruly, and gravely detrimental, thus, why foreign invaders overran Italy in his day.

Nevertheless, the friar then engaged the task of cleansing the city of sin. Caught up in Savonarola's searing sermons, many Florentines followed his instructions to burn all items that depicted or represented moral corruption. Thus began the infamous Bonfire of the Vanities at the start of 1497. As the fires roared, pagan books, women's cosmetics, fine dresses, fancy hats, musical instruments, statues, paintings, and immoral poetry by contemporary artists were destroyed. Among these artifacts were masterworks by Botticelli and Michelangelo, which allegedly the artists themselves tossed into the flames; all would be lost forever.

However, Savonarola's arrogance grew as rapidly as the destructive flames he ignited, which had maliciously burned the remnants of his rivals. Once his tongue began lashing the pope, however, Savonarola sealed his own fiery fate, for the pope happened to be Alexander VI, the infamous Borgia ogre.

On May 13, 1497, Pope Alexander VI excommunicated Savonarola, and ordered his arrest and execution. After a bloody seizure, Savonarola and two of his closest clergymen were charged with heresy and tortured on the rack. A year later, Savonarola and his two cohorts were ushered to the Piazza della Signoria, the same place they reveled in their bonfires, and all three were hung on huge crosses. With many in the crowd eager for revenge, the flames were lit and Savonarola burned; his rebellious body reduced to black ashes. Although the Florentines were glowing in retribution, the dark shadow of the Borgia pope still blanketed the Piazza.

However, unlike the books and works of art that Savonarola burnt, which were unfortunately lost forever, the stern friar's message prevailed. Savonarola prefigured what lay ahead, for a rebellious monk from Germany would follow his fiery footsteps by defying the pope, and successfully ushering in a new, but separate, Christian regime. This monk was Martin Luther. However, Luther would confront a different kind of pope, for this pope emerged from a rival camp, his name was Pope Leo X, and Leo was a Medici. Hence, the vicious alternating cycle of royal and religious blood, which had feverishly spun for centuries, would now intertwine.

As demonstrated, nepotism, and even deadly intrigue, know no bounds, as even the sacred realm is tainted by human weakness. Likewise, the decisions and actions of the Borgia pope and his two successors caused seismic shifts in political alliances. This also led to religious persecutions and rebellions, as well as the proliferation of Christianity, which spread into the newly-discovered Western hemisphere; however, not as a single Christian entity, but rather as a splintered and, at times, antagonistic diversity of sects.

Beyond the religious turmoil of the Catholic Church losing its hold on the Lutherans, Anglicans, Quakers, or Puritans, among others, Europe was going through major philosophical, social, and political changes. These changes caused a chaotic and unsettling atmosphere, one that many were willing to flee in order to start a new life elsewhere. Bravely taking to the seas, many found this promise for sanctuary across the Atlantic...in the New World.

VI
1492 - 1812. AMERICA: THE NEW WORLD, THE NEW ROME

Intro | The Founders: SAMUEL ADAMS, THOMAS PAINE, GEORGE WASHINGTON, JOHN ADAMS, THOMAS JEFFERSON, JAMES MADISON, ALEXANDER HAMILTON AND BEN FRANKLIN

(Sex, Virgo, Joseph, James, June)

The maritime winds of the north Atlantic blew from east to west, forming a cascade of whitecaps that mirrored the deluge of exploration that would soon follow. Columbus had already discovered the New World, and subsequent explorers, mainly from Spain, Portugal, France, the Dutch Netherlands, and England, all vied for territory. The bounty seemed enticingly endless. However, one nation would eventually monopolize the prime real estate of the North American continent, edging out the Dutch, Spanish, and French, while remnants of those races became part of the new unified settlement. That nation was England.

These imperial acquisitions, however, were largely made possible by courageous navigators who charted and harnessed the untamed seas. Although kings or merchants would fund most of these expeditions, it was often the incessant prodding and salesmanship of these brave adventurers that turned their monarch's head away from their narrow-minded self-interests to look at a broader more glorious future, one that remained elusive yet awfully compelling. Naturally, the lure of gold, precious herbs or foodstuffs would be part of the salesmanship process, but this did require a huge investment. This also required the development of vessels worthy of these great undertakings, and although the Portuguese led this race with their caravels, other nations soon followed suit in the daring race for unknown glories and ultimate conquest.

The British Royal Navy did not officially develop until the 1700s; however, as mentioned, two centuries earlier, King Henry VIII initiated the development of shipbuilding facilities in England, which did yield several prominent ships. Henry's daughter, Elizabeth, did much to enhance the British fleet, which managed to score a victory over the famed Spanish Armada. This unexpected victory bolstered not only England's reputation but also their desire to build more ships.

Nevertheless, it was not Elizabeth, but one of her courtiers, Sir Walter Raleigh, who conceived of and funded his own expedition to make the first settlement in the New World; this he generously did on behalf of the English Crown. The new territory he hoped to acquire would be named Virginia, which was in reference to England's virgin queen. However, Raleigh's small colony on Roanoke Island did not take root and England abandoned their efforts, at least until John Smith was commissioned to settle territory near this *Lost Colony* by Queen Elizabeth's successor, King James I.

Sixty years prior to these British expeditions, however, the French had claimed this Virginia territory, as well as much of the east coast of North America. The first European to discover this vast territory, from South Carolina up to Nova Scotia, was Giovanni da Verrazzano, an Italian explorer sailing for King Francis I of France in 1524. Verrazzano's many discoveries would be abandoned by the French king, who favored the northern territories near Newfoundland, which were explored even earlier by John Cabot. Cabot, whose real name was Giovanni Caboto, was also an Italian navigator who sailed for merchants in the English city of Bristol as early as 1497, only five years after Columbus' famous discovery. This concentration by the French on the northern "Canadian" regions, which the British had claimed first, left the heart of North America open for the taking, hence, the British had little qualms about seizing this bountiful opportunity.

Henceforth, after John Smith established the first permanent English settlement in America in 1607, which was named Jamestown in honor of King James I, other explorers had made their own discoveries. In 1609, Henry Hudson, a Londoner sailing for the Dutch East India Company, explored modern day New York Harbor and the Hudson River (named in his honor, despite Verrazzano finding it first), while the Pilgrims, several years later in 1620, would set sail from Plymouth, England to establish the settlement of Plymouth Colony in present day Massachusetts.

During the course of the next century, adventurers from England would populate this new rich territory until a confederation of thirteen colonies was finally established. It would consume much of the east coast of North America, extending from present day Georgia up to Maine. Much farther to the west was a large expanse of seemingly uninhabitable territory claimed by the Spanish, yet speckled with tribes of natives who were erroneously called Indians. Henceforth, these semi-cultivated British colonies were the root of what would one day become a new nation, one that would soon be diametrically opposed to oppression and monarchy.

This was due to the British Empire's methodology of conquest. Unlike the Romans, who cultivated and outfitted their new provinces with booming cities that mirrored Rome, England's worldwide colonies never fully mirrored London. English rights or even London-styled cities, with Parliament or Tudor buildings, were not to be found in North Africa, the Middle East or China, but only somewhat in America. Colonies only served their superior masters. As such, the escalating demands and unfair trade acts established by the King of England caused a backlash, which resulted in the American colonists aggressively seeking a solution.

This quest for an independent nation would not be the brainchild of one motivated individual who would rise to supreme ruler—like history often demonstrated—but rather by an amazingly rich assemblage of talent that worked in unison to craft something exceedingly unique. Due to this broad spectrum of glittering talent no one man or even duo can be singled out as a focal point, so we shall address the eight most prominent titans.

Although George Washington stands as the strong, iconic leader of this rebellious movement, which spawned a new regime, we must always be conscious of the dazzling support team that, in reality, were never his subordinates, but rather his equals and near equals, for many became presidents themselves. However, although none of these great men ever attained the lofty title of Commander in Chief of the Continental Army, they were extremely crucial to the cause, and in no lesser terms should some of them be addressed. Ben Franklin was certainly such a person who contributed far more than what most presidents could ever hope to achieve in office, however, our story begins with other men who, although their names ring familiar, their stories often do not.

SAMUEL ADAMS is a name most are familiar with, beyond the popular beer, yet few realize just how crucial Samuel's actions were in steering the thirteen colonies away from British oppression. Adams was a man of deep conviction; coming from a very religious family, well educated at Boston Latin School (the oldest school in North America), then later at Harvard College. Samuel was also well connected, his cousin being the feisty lawyer, John Adams. But, most importantly, Samuel was not one to simply talk about grand ideas; instead, Samuel preferred to take aggressive physical action.

Samuel's dynamic personality cannot be understated, for many Colonists harbored deep humiliation during the Sugar Act in 1764, which unfairly favored British merchants over Spanish and French suppliers of sugar, as well as the Stamp Act of 1765, which required that all articles utilizing paper must use a special paper containing a stamp. The proceeds from this higher priced paper were allegedly to be used for British troops to protect the Colonies. Not content to sit idle, Samuel Adams became a prominent spokesman and organizer of protests and riots, which eight years later, in 1773, eventually led to his most famous revolt, the Boston Tea Party. That sparked a revolt in Delaware, nine days later, which even destroyed twice as much tea. Meanwhile New York harbors followed suit by prohibiting sales of tea, this all due to Samuel Adams' initial and well-publicized revolt.

By this time, the Colonists were saturated with one oppressive Act after another, so the Boston Tea Party became a clarion call well beyond Adams' noisy band of conspirators known as the Sons of Liberty. Along with his Boston Latin School classmate, John Hancock, Samuel Adams was forced to flee Boston, for British General Thomas Gage had issued a proclamation granting a pardon to any conspirators who remained loyal to the crown, with the exceptions of Adams and Hancock. As a prominent member of the Sons of Liberty, Samuel expressed his desire to unify and revolt against Britain, which deeply motivated his fellow members, such as Patrick Henry, John Hancock, Paul Revere, and of course his cousin John Adams.

John Adams would later state: "Without the character of Samuel Adams, the true history of the American Revolution can never be written.

For fifty years his pen, his tongue, his activity, was constantly exerted for his country without fee or reward." Samuel Adams was also hailed as the *Father of the Revolution* by many of his peers, including Thomas Jefferson.

However, Samuel Adams was not alone, for at this early stage, many others aided the noble cause, but perhaps the most unsung hero of this rebellious gang was the Forgotten Founder, Thomas Paine.

THOMAS PAINE was a radical intellectual that moved others to action with bold words, rather than personally leading the charge. Paine's brilliant but unpredictable philosophies caused both profound inspiration and profound indignation. However, this does not mean that Paine was one to sit idle behind a desk and only write, for Paine eagerly joined the Continental Army.

Paine's book, *Common Sense,* published in January of 1776, became an instant best seller, but more importantly, its call to fight tyranny for independence deeply moved George Washington and John Adams to action. Once the Revolution got under way, Paine joined the ranks of soldiers and began writing a series of reflections with the title *The Crisis*. The first essay caught Washington's interest in December of that year. Washington was preparing for his famous crossing of the Delaware River *(see pg. 712),* which was laden with ice by a bitter cold winter. Seeking appropriate words to boost morale, Washington ordered Paine's essay to be read to his troops. Paine's inspiring words captured the moment.

"These are times that try men's souls; the summer soldier and the sunshine patriot will, in this crisis, shrink from the service of his country; but he that stands it now, deserves the love and thanks of man and woman. Tyranny, like hell, is not easily conquered; yet we have this consolation with us, that the harder the conflict, the more glorious the triumph."

However, by 1781, Paine was focusing on the importance of not only keeping France as an ally, but also helping France with its own tumultuous civil disputes. Paine traveled to France and soon published his influential book *Rights of Man,* in 1791, which supported the French Revolution. With the chaos fermenting in Paris, Paine was eventually arrested in 1793, due to his protesting the execution of King Louis XVI, and the additional fact that Paine was British born. Paine argued that he was an American citizen, and as such was an ally of France, yet his pleas fell upon deaf ears.

Worse still, Paine's appeals to the American ambassador to France, Gouverneur Morris, likewise fell upon deaf ears. Morris was close friends with George Washington, and even hatched the famous words that launch the *Constitution* "We the People..." However, Morris and Washington both turned their backs on Paine, who was scheduled for execution. Worse yet, Paine was to be beheaded by that gruesome contraption, the guillotine. As fate would have it, Paine lingered in prison for almost a year.

Washington, who had become America's first president in 1789 while Paine was in France, was evidently not the flawless white marble icon that most modern Americans believe, but rather a flesh and blood man that made flesh and blood decisions. Whatever his motives, Washington made the cold decision to abandon his once highly respected fellow American, who now sat fearing for his life in a dank prison in Paris.

What we do know is that Paine was extremely bitter that Washington actually took the newly invented seat of president. Paine had strongly believed that the new nation should never allow any one man to rule over the Republic. This action alone caused Paine to personally lambaste Washington in a letter that preserves his venom and humiliation, which even went on to attack Washington's leadership abilities as general. An excerpt of Paine's long letter is worth our attention...

"The part I acted in the American Revolution is well known; I shall not here repeat it. I know also that had it not been for the aid received from France, in men, money and ships, that your cold and unmilitary conduct (as I shall show in the course of this letter) would in all probability have lost America; at least she would not have been the independent nation she now is. You slept away your time in the field, till the finances of the country were completely exhausted, and you have but little share in the glory of the final event. It is time, Sir, to speak the undisguised language of historical truth. Elevated to the chair of the Presidency, you assumed the merit of everything to yourself, and the natural ingratitude of your constitution began to appear."

One is immediately flabbergasted to hear George Washington, our country's great hero and Father, being criticized; and worse yet by such a crucial fellow founder. However, this brings to light one of many instances, which will be expounded upon in due course, that clearly dispel the fabled notion that America's founding was a harmonious and monolithic undertaking. The combatant seeds of bipartisanship had begun to grow not gradually but rather instantaneously. America would be split between conservatives and liberals from day one.

Furthermore, Paine's letter continued to expound upon Washington's willingness to emulate the British crown, by having one head of state, and he derided the favoritism that Washington and his French ambassador, Gouverneur Morris, lavished upon Britain to the exclusion of France.

Britain and France were at war, and the Jay Treaty, crafted by John Jay under Washington's administration, allowed American trade ships to sail unchecked into British waters, yet the British fleet was allowed to stop and confiscate American ships and their cargo traveling to France.

Naturally, the French were not enthralled by Washington's treaty or his appointment of Gouverneur Morris as ambassador. Additionally, French intelligence knew that Morris was conducting covert operations with British spies from his apartment in Paris. As such, the French government pressured Washington to relieve Morris. This action became Paine's salvation, as Washington appointed the young and patriotic James Monroe. In stark contrast to Morris' cold and heartless snubs, James Monroe's profound admiration and strong benevolent desire to secure Paine's release came as a luminous light from above.

Upon his release, Paine remained in France, and even met with Napoleon, who, appearing as France's great redeemer, highly praised Paine's book *Rights of Man*. However, once Napoleon seized absolute power, akin to Washington, at least in Paine's mind, Paine caustically labeled Napoleon the *"biggest charlatan that ever existed."* Evidently, the great German composer Ludwig von Beethoven shared Paine's views, for he had dedicated his third symphony to Napoleon, but after he seized power, Beethoven scratched his name off the score and renamed it *Eroica Symphony*, whereby honoring the heroic dead that fought in the Revolution.

Taking a step backward, as Paine sat humiliated, abandoned and physically deteriorating in prison, thoughts about the bizarre and baffling order of the universe flooded his restless mind. This prompted Paine to write the first part of his deeply personal tome *The Age of Reason*. With the encouragement of James Monroe, Paine finished and published the book in 1795. This powerful and provocative document, which criticized the Christian Church and other religions in general, would have an immense impact on the new group of liberal and secular intellects that were emerging in Europe. However, it would have a devastating effect on his personal life back home, as the overwhelmingly Christian and devout public would soon reject and relegate Paine to the dismal abyss of blasphemous condemnation.

Disappointed with the direction that America was heading, Paine remained in France. However, in 1802, Paine finally returned to America, yet only due to the gracious invitation by America's new and third president, Thomas Jefferson. To the president's dismay, Paine received a cold reception, as his new rebellious affront to religion excluded him from most circles. Although the Enlightenment movement was well under way and thriving in Europe, America was firmly founded upon and entrenched with Christian religious factions, which, although butted heads with one another over dogma, still collectively embraced the Bible and its teachings. Ben Franklin had even forewarned Paine that he should burn his book if he valued his reputation, for as the old sage put it, it would be like pissing against the wind.

Franklin's perceptive prophecy came true, as Paine became the black sheep of the founding flock in his own day, as well as tarnished and neglected in the great story of America's founding. This is not only unfortunate but also ironic, for the new nation, which although established under the eye of Providence, did proclaim freedom of religion as one of its major principles. Yet, Paine's Deist belief in a creator (yet not Jesus or any other god revealed in religious scriptures) was a belief openly condemned, and he became perhaps America's first victim of religious intolerance. Although the American government did not persecute Paine directly, the founder's estrangement certainly added to the perception of profane guilt and ultimately Paine's demise. That this prominent national prejudice would destroy one of its own founding fathers, and the man who even labeled our country the United States of America comes as a veritable disappointment. This becomes even more justified and irksome when we view Paine's beliefs alongside those of his fellow founders.

Paine's open and blunt critique of Christianity naturally exceeds anything penned by the other founders; however, other members did share some of his beliefs, except they cleverly cushioned their remarks, such as Thomas Jefferson.

Thomas Jefferson sits at the apex, along with Washington, for many Americans who rate or praise the founders. Jefferson is often credited with having the most radiant philosophical mind, as President John Kennedy once remarked to a full assembly of Nobel Prize winners: "I think this is the most extraordinary collection of talent and of human knowledge that has ever been gathered together at the White House—with the possible exception of when Thomas Jefferson dined alone."

However, despite Jefferson's brilliance, political achievements, or public adoration, few are aware of his true religious beliefs. A point of fact is that Jefferson scoured the Bible to extract only passages spoken by Jesus, for he did not believe the questionable or even fanatical words of the four Evangelical writers of the Gospels. Further still, Jefferson did not believe in Jesus' divinity, or the whole concept of the Holy Trinity, which to his rational mind seemed convoluted. Jefferson's work became modestly known as the *Jefferson Bible*, yet its true title was *The Life and Morals of Jesus of Nazareth*.

After much serious scrutiny and contemplation, Jefferson concluded that Jesus was a mortal prophet, and that the church was the fabricated byproduct of mankind. Henceforth, Jefferson dispelled the full breadth of Christian dogma, which the scriptures professed as truth, except for the writings of Jesus, which he said were *"the most sublime and benevolent code of morals which has ever been offered to man."*

Jefferson's religious beliefs, although not as radical as Thomas Paine's, were certainly not devoutly Christian in the purest sense, as some even called Jefferson an atheist, hence, this explains Jefferson's kinship and invitation to Paine to return home. Despite Jefferson not being a pure Christian or an atheist, the fact remains that Jefferson escaped persecution and condemnation while Paine suffered the pain of professing his personal philosophical perspective. Rattling off all those pesky "P's" perfectly personifies how Paine's persecution was pathetic.

Additionally, although Jefferson's personal spiritual beliefs did eloquently flow in the *Declaration of Independence*, again without any reference to Jesus being God or the Creator, we must also realize that Jefferson was the prime advocate for building a wall of separation between church and state. As a voracious reader, Jefferson was quite aware of how the church perpetually failed as a political entity, as fanaticism taints all religions and their efforts to govern in the temporal realm. However, he clearly understood the necessity of religion to ground a populace with morals and benevolence.

We shall return to Thomas Jefferson in due turn, but having covered how the critical groundwork was established by Samuel Adams and Thomas Paine to incite rebellion, this now brings us to the man who led the Continental Army against the British and won independence for his nation; George Washington.

GEORGE WASHINGTON was born in Virginia in 1732. At sixteen years old, George became a surveyor and acquired considerable knowledge about the broad terrain ranging from his home state of Virginia over to the Ohio Valley, Pennsylvania, and the surrounding areas. Unbeknownst to him, this knowledge would prove quite useful in the years that followed. The French had set their sights on the Ohio River, which, if controlled, along with the Mississippi River, would link their two polar settlements; namely Louisiana to the south and Quebec to the north. More importantly, it would create a longitudinal border that would cut off the British colonists from westward expansion. Naturally, the British colonists understood the importance of controlling this vital waterway, so inevitably tensions flared.

Interestingly enough, in 1752, Washington had no college education or any military experience, yet he did recently inherit the large and wealthy estate of Mount Vernon from his half-brother Lawrence that recently died. Evidently, this aristocratic influence, along with his tall and commanding stature, impressed Governor Dinwiddie, which enabled him to enter the Virginia militia as a Major. Although this favoritism nicely dispensed with the demanding process of achieving this rank, it likewise dispensed with the crucial experience acquired during that natural process. Hence, George's lack of experience would become evident in the very near future.

Two years later, in 1754, Washington (now promoted to Lieutenant Colonel) was placed second in command of a regiment of three hundred men to protect the vital and volatile Ohio country, along with its crucial rivers. An Ohio based troop attempted to build a fort as they awaited Colonial and British reinforcements, however, French forces, numbering over a thousand strong, seized the unfinished fort and renamed it Fort Duquesne. This strategic location sat upon a bird's eye mountaintop, at the junction of the Allegheny and Monongahela rivers (in present day Pittsburgh).

Washington received intelligence of these actions from his long-time Indian friend and ally Tanacharison. Tanacharison's message was wracked with fear; as he witnessed the sprawling French forces consume the high peak, which strategically overlooked both rivers, thus making a superb sentinel's post. Grossly outnumbered by the French, Washington called upon Tanacharison to secure whatever local warriors he could muster to buttress his small regiment. Tanacharison's response to Washington was laden with foreboding, namely, that if sufficient forces weren't generated the two would never lay eyes upon one another again.

The impact of this imminent and ominous threat upon the young and inexperienced Washington cannot be underestimated. Moreover, since the proceeding events would contain the crucial spark that ignited the French and Indian War, historians have analyzed Washington's actions and state of mind to uncover the all-important fact of who fired the first bullet. With that in mind, this nerve-racking news by his Indian warrior friend along with his severely outnumbered regiment must have played a decisive role in Washington's actions; actions by a novice lieutenant colonel that would later elicit praise by some for being gallant, and harsh condemnation by others for being a savage murderer.

In any event, Washington merged with Tanacharison and his small band of Indians, and they began their slow and cautious advance. As they proceed toward Fort Duquesne, recon soon revealed a small French unit of thirty-two soldiers that were camped in a deep wooded glen. This is when Washington formed a detachment of forty soldiers, accompanied by Tanacharison and his warriors, and encircled the French camp. The proceeding event is the one most shrouded in speculation, but Washington's report to Governor Dinwiddie portrayed a rather standard tactical maneuver, namely that he moved in and engaging a battle, whereby killing ten soldiers, including the French Commander, Monsieur De Jumonville.

However, other eyewitnesses, and even Washington's personal diary, portray other events that were suppressed in Washington's official version. These other events seem to indicate a cold-blooded massacre. This version posits that after Washington and his Indian brigade stormed the campsite—shooting and killing one third of the French posse—they moved in and found Commander Jumonville injured and sitting prostrate. While Jumonville rattled off in French that he was on a diplomatic peace mission, Washington struggled to comprehend his words. Meanwhile, Tanacharison, who spoke fluent French, abruptly stepped in and cried, "Thou are not yet dead," and sunk his hatchet into his head.

Gruesome details followed, for after Tanacharison split open Jumonville's head he scooped out his brain matter and began washing his hands with the bloody substance. His Indian cohorts then began scalping the remaining injured in a bizarre Indian blood-fest that must have sent chills down Washington's spine. Yet, this brutal massacre evidently happened so spontaneously that Washington might very well have stood there shocked and mute. This version seems quite plausible, especially knowing that this was Washington's first active encounter in warfare, not to mention his first time witnessing the horrific practice of scalping in real-time.

Washington's personal diary mentions more details, such as the scalping, yet his decision to encircle, engage, and possibly even condone the massacre might have been due to his lack of experience and momentary shock. Although innately brave, patriotic, and optimistic, Washington was a first-class rookie who had entered the army as a major, received promotions due to the deaths of his superiors, not service or merit, and was shaken earlier by Tanacharison, who made clear their grave situation. Knowing that he was greatly outnumbered and inexperienced thrust Washington into a life and death situation, which his previous scouting and military drills never presented or conditioned him to properly respond to accordingly. Where a more seasoned veteran might have approached the situation with more composure and diplomatic forethought, Washington seemed to act more on impulse, beginner's fear, and the heightened notion of ultimate survival.

News of Washington's encounter traveled fast, and even his private comment that there *was something charming about the sound of bullets whistling by* made it into the Virginia newspapers. While some American colonists hailed Washington as America's first war hero, back in England, King George II flatly dismissed Washington as a youthful braggart.

Whether Jumonville was really on a diplomatic peace mission or harbored evil intent, as Washington later claimed, we can only surmise, but the bloody hatcheting by the Indians did send a clear message, one that Washington even possibly hoped to convey. The French at Fort Duquesne were now painfully aware that a savage force was in the neighboring wilderness and would do whatever was necessary to prevail. And this necessity becomes even more pronounced when we realize what happened next, namely that Washington ordered his men to construct a temporary fort, aptly named Fort Necessity.

In carving out this little oasis, Washington had his men cut back the brush some sixty yards around the Fort's perimeter. Evidently, as the future would soon reveal, this, too, would prove to be another mistake by the rookie commander. In the interim, Washington received word that reinforcements and rations were on the way. Added to this was another serendipitous promotion, as his commander, Joshua Fry, had fallen off his horse and died. Now a colonel, Washington relayed news back to the governor that he and his new Fort Necessity stood ready and confident.

Washington's appraisal was either charged with unrealistic bravado, due to their previous victory/slaughter, or wishful thinking. The fact remains that they were grossly outnumbered and the French were gaining Indian support in the region. This is where Washington can be viewed as extremely courageous or extremely naïve. Then again, at this juncture, Washington was probably both.

In any event, the French and Indians took advantage of the brush just outside Fort Necessity's perimeter, and then rained bullets and arrows upon the confined encampment. For nine hours, the French forces pummeled the rickety fort, while rumors of more Indian reinforcements further panicked Washington's men. Interestingly enough, another Jumonville was leading the French campaign; the grieving brother of the dead diplomat that Washington and his Indian warriors savagely mutilated.

Washington's later account, once again, varies greatly from French reports, as both sides claimed killing hundreds of soldiers. Here again, Washington's truthfulness is seriously doubtful, for the result of this battle was spelled out in the Articles of Capitulation that Washington himself signed. The surrender even referred to the assassination of Monsieur De Jumonville, which Washington later claimed he had no recollection of, due to the document being written in French. First, we must assume that even if Washington did not know how to read French that one of his subordinates surely would have. Furthermore, a trained and certainly competent commander would not sign anything they did not fully understand.

Second, the fact that this humiliating defeat severely damaged Washington's reputation, as many blamed this fiasco on Washington's inexperience and impetuous nature, we must conclude that the French version is more accurate. That being the case, a third of Washington's men was killed compared to only minor casualties by the French. As for the dynamics of this battle, it seems bad weather, along with a more seasoned and very honorable French commander, ended what might have been a personal vendetta resulting in Washington's annihilation.

This calamity caused so much bad press that Washington was faced with a demotion and shame, thus causing him to resign. As such, Washington returned to Mount Vernon deeply disappointed, but not beaten, for the military life was in his blood, and somehow he knew it was his calling. As such, when the British crown appointed General Edward Braddock, with his successful record of European campaigns, to sail to the troubled colonies, Washington saw his chance for redemption. By reenlisting under Braddock's wing, Washington could not only ride on the coattails of this successful commander but also gain his friendship and all the benefits that go along with being part of the inner circle.

However, General Braddock was a born and bred European, and his old world tactical inclinations would prove disastrous. Upon his arrival, Braddock was approached by various Indian chiefs who all sought territorial protection for their aid. Being commissioned to conquer Fort Duquesne, Braddock was outfitted with a huge force of over two thousand men and heavy artillery, so the Indians pleas for an alliance were meaningless. Braddock was the epitome of British bravado and majestic might, and the humble gestures by a seemingly primitive race were coldly rebuffed. Braddock's arrogance and prejudice however incited the Indians to flock to the French, thus causing severe ramifications in the coming days and months.

With Washington under his wing, Braddock set out to conquer Fort Duquesne and in essence expel the French from the Ohio territory. However, Braddock soon found out that the rugged American wilderness posed too many obstacles for a huge entourage, one laden with cannons, artillery, ammunitions, foodstuffs and the like. After being delayed by erecting numerous bridges, scaling huge mountains and hacking their way through dense forests, Braddock was forced to adopt Washington's advice, which was to form a mobile lightning brigade that could attack the fort. Consequently, Braddock assembled thirteen hundred soldiers and rode off ahead, while Washington stayed temporarily behind due to illness. Oddly enough, Washington's early experiences in battle sometimes mirrored those of Augustus, not to mention both men becoming the first to rule over their hard fought, and in many ways similar, empires. Nevertheless, before Braddock even reached Fort Duquesne, he encountered a large reconnaissance team of nine hundred French and Indian scouts. That's when all hell broke loose.

No one knows who truly fired the first shot, but General Braddock soon found himself in a surreal situation that turned nightmare. The British were trained to fight using European military formations dating back to the ancient Greek phalanx. These were large rectangular masses, where the front line would fire and then kneel to reload, as alternating rows stepped forward and engaged in similar firing sequences. These engagements likewise occurred with a sense of military honor by both armies to obey these rules on an open battlefield.

The French, however, adopted the native tactics of the Indians, who used trees for cover and made random guerilla attacks. This chaotic stealth-tactic proved very successful, and it thrust General Braddock into modern warfare. Maintaining his suddenly outdated tactic of order and decorum, Braddock rode gallantly, yet mindlessly, into an open field of ambushers, as bullets and projectiles flooded the sky. Braddock's pierced body fell flaccidly to the grass, looking like a reused target from a shooting range. Virginian soldiers scurried to take cover, but were caught between enemy and British fire. Washington's diary recollected the painful and panic-stricken massacre, as over nine hundred British and colonial soldiers were killed in comparison to two-dozen French and Indians.

Once more, Washington was associated with a humiliating defeat, however, this time he was cushioned by the blame that was leveled against his dead commander, General Braddock. Nevertheless, once again, Washington gained a promotion due to the death of his commander. The upshot, however, was that Washington was finally acquiring the military experience and knowledge that he never obtained previously with all his unqualified promotions.

The French and Indian War was now afoot and Washington would continue his practical education of military warfare in the field. Contrary to other great military leaders throughout history, Washington did not lead a long succession of overwhelming victories throughout his career, and even during the French and Indian War Washington was forced to retreat in several battles. However, his acquired strategic and tactical experience proved that Washington was a man that continually learned from his mistakes and, most importantly, never quit. By the end of the war, Washington had gained the rank of Commander himself and he finally won the confidence and respect of many politicians.

Over the following years, however, the British Empire escalated its imperial demands over the colonies. These Acts of taxation and indoctrinating dependency upon British imports aroused the ire of many colonists, including Washington, who felt firsthand the humiliation of trying to keep his huge enterprise at Mount Vernon afloat. This personal frustration led Washington to actively engage the cause that others had already deliberated upon in silence. As Washington admitted, he was not the most knowledgeable in political matters but once apprised of the details, he was a man of action.

In fact, George Mason was perhaps the colony's prime maven of British law, and his influence and ghostwriting became apparent in Washington's letters, which were now more refined and erudite. Then again, without a formal education, Washington was perceptive enough to always rely upon others to polish his voice, such as Hamilton and Laurens in the years to follow. Furthermore, in a revealing personal letter, Washington stated how he relied upon their ability "to think for me, as well as execute orders."

Nevertheless, Washington's impetus and motivation to take action emanated from his own personal repugnance toward the British Lords, which ironically made Washington complain that he felt like one of his own slaves. However, the widespread notion at the time was that the Negroes were an inferior race, so their treatment was to be expected, however, for the colonists, such insults were degrading and caustic.

With the Boston Tea Party escalating matters, by inciting King George III to reprimand Boston by instating martial law, tensions flared and thoughts of vengeance mounted. As Washington became more involved with the Patriots' cause, he simultaneously began to resuit his military uniform. Quite symbolically, Washington was the only one to sport a uniform during their meetings. Furthermore, he had already begun to buy and read several books on military history. Washington knew bloodshed was imminent, and he would make sure that he was the most prepared and the most obvious to his fellow countrymen to lead.

By 1775, the reality of a full-blown revolution struck the colonists, and the Second Continental Congress unanimously voted Washington as their commander-in-chief. This vote of confidence was based upon several reasons, namely, that Washington had a commendable military record, he was a Virginian and would best serve those in power in Virginia, as it was the largest colony, and one final criterion, which seems juvenile but was often mentioned by his peers, and that is Washington's tall and commanding stature. Where others were more erudite, vociferous or emotional, Washington, in contrast, exuded a silent and indomitable strength that was almost paternal in its psychological intensity.

Washington's many battles during the Revolutionary War did not always result in victory, as his many losses and retreats during the New York/New Jersey campaign was a major debacle that enabled the British to occupy New York Harbor and the surrounding territories for seven years, right up to the war's end. Paine's critical letter comes to mind when viewing these major blunders. Furthermore, Washington's defeat against British General William Howe, whereby losing the city of Philadelphia, was another damaging blow that even prompted some in Congress to petition for Washington's removal.

Despite these major setbacks, however, Washington remained resolute and in full command of his senses and his men. What was clear to others in Congress and the colonial citizens was that Washington was relentlessly optimistic, and his strength and paternal charisma somehow turned even disasters into resolve. Without his reassuring presence, the Continental Army would certainly have been demoralized, and nothing could be more disastrous.

The Revolutionary War was by no means an easy victory, as the decisions and actions of many generals and diplomats were crucial in keeping the momentum, as well as distracting the British from taking advantage of America's numerous weaknesses. Washington was well aware of just how close America came to loosing the fight for independence, as he called the victory "little short of a standing miracle."

Nevertheless, Washington undoubtedly stood as America's greatest beacon of hope, and his unyielding fortitude, along with those of equal fervor, secured a tremendous victory for the underling colony, now turned independent nation, which likewise captivated the world and won its admiration.

With the Revolution ending in 1783, Washington was in a powerful position. With the love and respect of his troops, his founding peers, and all the freed citizens of the new leaderless nation, Washington could have easily powered his way into a British-styled kingship; however, with the utmost humility, he opted to emulate the Roman general Cincinnatus. In a similar fashion, Washington likewise returned to his simple agrarian lifestyle, relinquishing all claims of personal gain and ultimate control.

However, over the next four years, Washington would not enjoy the peaceful calm of retirement. The war may have been won but his loyal peers made sure he understood just how unsettled and vulnerable the new nation was, for it was like a feisty crew aboard a captainless ship, sailing without a compass. This is that fascinating period when all these great minds gathered to build the greatest constitution known to mankind, human flaws included. Madison drafted the *Constitution* in 1787, and two years later, George Washington would take office as the first president of the United States.

Being the first to hold this undefined position, Washington had to contend with significant as well as petty issues, such as the menial task of devising a title. While John Adams suggested "His High Mightiness" and other pompously royal names, Washington opted for the simpler "President of the United States." Matters of greater importance included the question of salary. The founders were eager to pay Washington a handsome sum, yet Washington refused, offering to serve the people freely. However, this munificent gesture would have unwittingly established a precedent whereby only aristocrats could hold office, therefore, those opposed to emulating Britain or other monarchies insisted upon a moderate salary.

Additionally, since no term limits were established, Washington indicated a four-year policy, yet after his second term, Washington humbly stepped down. This unofficial precedent was maintained throughout U.S. history until the advent of the Second World War, when Franklin D. Roosevelt was elected to four terms. However, after that anomaly the 22nd Amendment was passed to officially indoctrinate the two-term ruling.

However, after Washington's request to step down, the young nation faced the dilemma of electing a new president. Although John Adams garnered the second most electoral votes for the first bid for president, as well as serving as Washington's vice president, he certainly was not the larger-than-life military hero turned president that George Washington epitomized. In fact, while Washington held office, he overlooked Adams completely when seeking advice and instead relied upon his right-hand-man, Alexander Hamilton.

As the near future would reveal, even when Adams won the Presidency, Washington continued to secretly plot with Hamilton and others behind the new president's back. One agenda was to build a new national army, and Washington was even actively engaged in the selection process where he rated veterans from the old Continental Army. However, it finally dawned upon Washington that if rumors of their covert actions reached the new president it would cause, as he put it, "unpleasant consequences." As such, in his correspondence with James McHenry (one of Adams' cabinet members), Washington asked that their secret letters be destroyed, but McHenry opted to save them instead, leaving firsthand evidence of the back-channel operations of Washington, Hamilton and others. In these instances, however, Washington was resigned to taking a back seat, as the highly ambitious Hamilton clearly orchestrated the opposition.

Hamilton's fears rested upon the fact that Napoleon *(see page 713)* was in the process of conquering Europe by storm, leading him to believe that the Americas would eventually be added to the French dictator's list. In hindsight, we can easily see that Napoleon would exhaust his own efforts, but in his day, Hamilton's preemptive proposals were not as radical as some then and even some today claim. However, private correspondence did indicate that Hamilton was considering marching his new army across Virginia, hence silencing the Republican protestors, and then conquering the French and Spanish held territories from Louisiana and Texas down to Mexico and beyond to expand the American empire. Hence, going beyond national defense and into the realm of offensive conquests would have not only caused great concern, but would have been illegal, requiring congressional approval.

Interestingly enough, discounting the legality or moral implications of Hamilton's hypothetical maneuver, some historians today believe Hamilton's mission would have been suicide for the young nation. However, it is worthy of examination, because it quite probably could have gone without a hitch.

In addition to the small Mexican forces, Spain and France posed the major obstacles. However, Napoleon had all of Europe tied up with imminent threats of danger, leaving Mexico and the Central Americas partially cutoff and vulnerable. Furthermore, as the near future would reveal (under Jefferson's administration), Napoleon was very eager to sell the French occupied territories in the Americas for almost nothing to further his military objectives in Europe. If a suitable time existed for aggressive expansion this window of opportunity was it, and Hamilton's astute and perceptive mind, even if also being imperialistic, must have foreseen this moment.

Additionally, in regards to the moral issues leveled by today's politically correct, Hamilton still lived in a young nation where size and strength offered the best chances of survival. Although Hamilton didn't do so, other Americans would eventually recognize the threats and roadblocks and engage expansion, despite its condemnation by some now and then. Nevertheless, Hamilton's objectives stood at strict odds with many in his day, including the new president, John Adams, who took action to thwart Hamilton's military ambitions.

As mentioned, the founders may have pulled together to sever the oppressive strings of Britain, which strangled their freedoms, but their latent differences soon became blaringly manifest, especially when Alexander Hamilton founded the Federalist Party. In fact, the election for the second president of the United States would be the first to reveal the bipartisanship of the nascent government, which would become a permanent fixture in American politics.

With Washington retired, the new nation immediately began racing in new and divergent directions, especially as military necessities vanished and the demand for administrative and legal positions materialized. Despite Washington acknowledging his lack of political aptitude, his presence and leadership in not only winning stiff military encounters (many times outnumbered) and the Revolutionary War itself, coupled with being part of the founding process, was beyond critical.

Actively engaged in every crucial step leading up to war, Washington's role in this chain of events was the miracle that the new world needed. Washington proved that although not a military genius, like Caesar or Trajan, he did manage to remain resolute in his mission and self-confident. That was bolstered by his own unique brand of spirituality along with his deep love for his country and belief in liberty. This potent combination was the driving force that turned insurmountable odds into ultimate victory. But, alas, the sun had finally set and Washington's long and eventful day had expired. The young nation would now be in the hands of a new president.

JOHN ADAMS had a long and active connection with the Patriots and the Colony's tumultuous rise to revolution. In fact, Jefferson even called him "Colossus of Independence". With the initial impetus from his proactive cousin Samuel, John Adams sought separation from Britain early on and never wavered in his zeal. Oddly enough, however, despite Adams' wishes to be free of the royal yoke, he still maintained some of the British crown's pompous predilections.

While Adams sought autonomy for the Colonists, he had hoped to marry off his son, John Quincy, to the daughter of King George III, with the hopes of establishing a royal bloodline that would allow his family to rule the confederate states. Even later on, when Adams was vice president, he suggested that Washington establish the precedent of a royal bloodline. Although willing to allow Washington and his heirs to take the primary seat of power, he naturally hoped that Washington would respond in kind, and grant the Adams family (not the creepy one with Gomez and Morticia) the royal and perpetual seat of vice president in gratitude. Washington, however, was exactly the wrong man to make such a repugnant offer to and he flatly refused.

Regardless, John Adams maintained his royal aspirations and made sure his son, John Quincy, was immersed into the political arena. His persistence, to some extent, paid off, as the short-lived Adams dynasty continued into the first quarter of the nineteenth century, when John Quincy became the sixth president of the United States.

Often outspoken, stubborn, jealous, deeply religious, and deemed unpredictable by his peers, John Adams was a feisty individual, even if short and rotund, especially in comparison to his iconic predecessor. Previously an avid supporter of George Washington, even falsely claiming that he was responsible for electing Washington as the Continental Army's commander-in-chief, John Adams grew to despise how Washington received what he called "superstitious veneration." In a personal letter to Benjamin Rush, he sarcastically vented, "The essence of the whole will be that Dr. Franklin's electrical rod smote the earth and out sprang General Washington."

Adams further whined how Washington and Franklin seemed to be given all the credit for the new nation's policies, legislations, and negotiations, as well as winning the war. This was only marginally true, for although Washington did garner an almost mythological aura, the roles of Jefferson, Madison, Hamilton, and even Adams himself, were often on the tongues of proud Americans. However, even Adams' deep Christian faith failed him in this regard, as he was never able to control his jealously and ego.

John Adams' election as America's second president, however, was in small part aided by Alexander Hamilton and his new Federalist Party. This does not insinuate that the two were friends, for Hamilton only saw Adams as the lesser of two evils. In fact, the two men would soon become open rivals. Adam's opponent was Thomas Jefferson, whose idealism, advocacy for state's rights, and grass roots predilections stood at polar ends to Hamilton's fiscal visions for big business, industrialization, and a strong Federal government. However, even though Hamilton was a man of action and intrigue, and might have played some minor role in swaying votes, what has been uncovered is a private correspondence by Thomas Jefferson to James Madison, whereby asking Madison for his opinion about a letter he intended to mail to Adams.

Jefferson's letter aimed at alerting Adams that it was "possible that you may be cheated of your succession by a trick worthy of the subtlety of your arch-friend of New York."

Fortunately, Jefferson was wise enough to ask his brilliant friend for advice, as Madison advised him not to send the letter. Madison believed the letter would have aroused suspicion regarding Jefferson's motives, and he firmly believed that Adams already knew of the plot. Furthermore, Jefferson's Republican mindset was at odds with Adams, hence any future opposition to the new president's policies would give Adams tangible evidence of Jefferson's initial support and hypocritical opposition.

Despite the great amount of finger pointing at Hamilton being a man of intrigue, which he was on certain occasions, we must similarly strip away our pristine notions of Jefferson being flawless and above such actions.

Nevertheless, John Adams slipped into office, with or without Hamilton's aid, yet he would not win a second term. Hamilton would have run for office himself, but the *Constitution* denied the office to anyone of foreign birth, and unfortunately, Hamilton was from the island of Nevis, in the British West Indies.

A year after Hamilton founded his Federalist Party Jefferson retaliated by forming his own party, with the aid of James Madison and his newly conceived campaign manager John Beckley. This operated under a variety of names, from the Democratic-Republican Party to the Jeffersonians and other variants; however, many followers at the time referred to themselves as Republicans. Jefferson's party stood firmly opposed to the Federalists, and advocated better relations with France, a rejection of the biased Jay Treaty, mentioned earlier, as well as against most of what Hamilton's Federalist plan proposed. This included Hamilton's petition for a national bank, and his belief that all states should share the burden of national debt, which was incurred by some states more than others during the Revolutionary War.

During Jefferson's run for president in 1800, the new phenomenon of partisan politics, established previously during the Adam's election, would once again rear its ugly head, and unbeknownst to all Americans at the time would forever prevail. Jefferson tied with Aaron Burr in electoral votes, and this left the House of Representatives responsible for deciding the election. The House consisted of a majority of Federalists, and, here again, Hamilton's powerful hand played a role in gaining influence, which consequently did decide the fate of the presidency. In a similar vein, Hamilton found himself, once again, endorsing the lesser of two evils, as Jefferson took office. Consequently, this brings us back to Thomas Jefferson, the third President of the United States.

THOMAS JEFFERSON, as mentioned earlier, stood as a vital component of the founding brotherhood. Unanimously chosen by his peers to author the *Declaration of Independence*, Jefferson later claimed that it was not a personal document but rather a collaborative effort that spoke of an entire nation's spirit. Although Jefferson did write the vast majority of the document's hallowed words, it did reflect an accurate picture of all the founders' idyllic vision. Some finer points needed to be revised, as the issues of religion and slavery caused deep concerns, but the result was nothing short of amazing.

Thomas Jefferson's *Declaration of Independence* draws upon previous sources, such as the *Virginia Declaration of Rights* authored largely by George Mason and adopted into law only weeks earlier; from his Italian neighbor, Philip Mazzei, who spoke of the natural rights of man; and from John Locke, Cicero, Thomas Paine, and other philosophers who believed in the right to defend those rights against oppressive governments. Being well read, Jefferson was a font of brilliant ideas, yet beyond mere retention, Jefferson's genius enabled him to further shape and develop these ideas to create a brand new political mindset. With his natural gift for writing, Jefferson enshrined those ideas into a solid and powerful document that would ground a nation and impress much of the world.

Beyond the conceptual realm of politics, however, is the tangible realm of visual identity, which any great visionary or government will also attempt to mold. Hence, in addition to constructing this masterful text, Jefferson was also crucial in constructing a new American architecture. Jefferson drew most of his inspiration from Italy, yet by utilizing local building materials (such as red brick) the hybrid he created resulted in edifices of stately quality yet with a rustic charm.

As mentioned earlier, the Pantheon of ancient Rome clearly figured into Jefferson's building plans at Monticello, but he was likewise drawn to the works of the High Renaissance architect, Andrea Palladio. The neo-Palladian movement had already influenced eighteenth century Britain, which preferred Palladio's clean classical lines to the heavily ornate Baroque style that was still prominent throughout Europe. Jefferson likewise adopted these clean and reserved lines and in the process aided in pioneering an American style.

Although Jefferson joined Britain in its adoption of architectural principles, he adamantly rejected the British system of government with its aristocratic principles. Here again, the early founders butted heads, as Jefferson was a prime proponent for American Republicanism, based upon an agrarian model, while Alexander Hamilton favored a strong Federalist government, based upon big business that would fuel a capitalistic economy. Here we can see how Jefferson's lofty philosophical ideals may penetrate the hearts and minds of many Americans, and even provide a strong foundation, but Hamilton's pragmatic system of banks and big business is the towering superstructure that unequivocally dominates the aspirations and financial objectives of Americans, which, in larger measure, made America the indomitable world leader it is today.

Jefferson's affinity for a republic and Hamilton's for an empire had a profound a long lasting impact on defining America. Here again, the spirit of ancient Rome is revived in its distant heir across the Atlantic and across the centuries; except, where the great Roman Republic lasted for almost 500 years before giving way to the mighty empire, the embryonic American Republic, in the course of a decade or two, evolved into a hybrid of Republic and Empire. America would maintain its liberal system of government, without ceding to dictatorship; yet aggressively engage in industrialization, broad networks of trade, intensifying its military power, and spreading its culture worldwide.

Although America visibly followed Hamilton's bold and aggressive model, as mentioned, Jefferson's philosophical and moral underpinning likewise prevails to this day, and this duality is what makes America a unique entity. America's unyielding determination for progress and world influence, despite its at-times reckless capitalistic ventures, is fortunately balanced by its moral obligations, restraints, and noble aspirations. In essence, America adopted the best aspects of both the Roman Republic and Roman Empire, and Jefferson and Hamilton best represent those traits respectively.

Jefferson was by no means an idle philosopher, and as president, he proved to be an effective administrator. Jefferson's method of administrating differed from others in that being a solitary man he opted to delegate via written communiqués rather than face-to-face meetings.

Nevertheless, as odd as this was to some in his cabinet, Jefferson did manage to accomplish his objectives and get things done.

Jefferson also surprised his colleagues by his humble manners and lifestyle. Upon his inauguration, he refused all aspects of pomp and even returned to his boarding house that evening to wait on line with others to eat dinner. Moreover, he would even wait two weeks before moving into the large and regal White House. As president, Jefferson also dispensed with all the gala dinner parties and opulent festivities that his predecessor enjoyed. Jefferson wanted to make clear that he was not only acting on behalf of the people but was indeed one of them. In stark contrast to John Adams—a devout Christian who oddly enough cherished royal elitism—was Thomas Jefferson, whom although not a follower of the organized faith did attempt to live the humble life of a true follower of Jesus. Naturally, Jefferson fell short in other respects, such as his distaste for slavery yet never freeing his own. Contradictions afflict most people.

Jefferson was also a pacifist by nature, once again, being influenced by the sublime and peaceful words of Jesus, for he was firmly opposed to building a national army or using force. Yet, as history proves time and time again, a pacifist's ideology must change when living in the real world, or the aggressors will prevail. During Jefferson's administration, tensions flared in regards to commercial trade with Britain and France, who were both engaged in war and each seeking exclusivity with America. In response, Jefferson decided to cut relations with all foreign nations and ordered an embargo as a peaceful remedy. The Embargo Act of 1807 caused tremendous animosity, commercial chaos, black markets, and even ridicule, as political cartoons cleverly used the word embargo in reverse to scornfully claim "O grab me!"

To his dismay, Jefferson's peaceful remedy failed miserably, as it also caused many to flee his Democratic-Republican Party to join the Federalists. However, quite unintentionally, the Embargo literally forced his agrarian homeland to invest in industrial enterprises and bolster its military. Although the Embargo only lasted a year, the taste of commercial independence, which demanded industrialization, had already been swallowed, and the craving for more would never end. By pure folly, or luck, Jefferson's actions ensured the nation's sweeping transformation into not only an industrial nation but also a military one, just as his wise pragmatic rival, Alexander Hamilton, suggested. And as time passed, Jefferson's pacifism eroded further.

Jefferson envisioned a larger America, beyond the thirteen colonies, and the Louisiana Purchase was instrumental in building a stronger nation. This huge chunk of territory, which more than doubled the size of the fledgling nation, was a provocative maneuver by Jefferson. Many declared it unconstitutional, since federal powers of this magnitude would conflict greatly with states' rights, which ironically, Jefferson always fought for. But most importantly, it was not authorized in the *Constitution*. This initiative clearly displayed Jefferson's ability to adapt and make decisions against his personal beliefs for the security and enhancement of the nation.

Fearing the close proximity of French occupation, Jefferson wisely felt that a peaceful acquisition of New Orleans would defuse any future conflicts. Jefferson's intent was to only purchase this crucial hot zone with its busy port, not the entire Louisiana region, which at the time constituted roughly fifteen modern day states. More pressing was the fact that Napoleon was beginning to demonstrate his designs of conquest; hence, Jefferson closely monitored intelligence to keep one step ahead. As such, he assigned James Monroe and Robert Livingston to broker the deal.

Meanwhile, Napoleon was eager to amass a costly naval fleet to invade Britain, and he advised his minister to sell the entire region or nothing at all. Monroe had only been authorized by Jefferson to purchase the port city for $10 million. So when he was presented with the ultimatum, he was at first taken aback by the vast territory being offered. However, upon hearing the French diplomat demand $15 million for the entire region, Monroe took it upon himself to make the purchase.

Jefferson was gleefully shocked, and the nation hailed Monroe as a brilliant statesman. The purchase likewise secured Monroe's rise and eventual nomination as president, which would occur after Jefferson and his successor, James Madison, completed their terms.

The Louisiana Purchase now added a huge expanse of uncharted territory (530 million acres) that needed exploration and, once again, Jefferson had to secretly gather federal funds to accomplish the task.

Securing the necessary capital, Jefferson then hired the expedition team of Lewis and Clark. The results of their efforts revealed a variegated terrain of land that was a mixture of raw and fertile ground, thus being a rich gift of monumental importance for the growing nation.

In essence, Jefferson's overall contribution to the development of the United States was monumental, and many decades later in 1927, the sculptor, Gutzon Borglum, would rightfully include Jefferson in his monumental carving of Mount Rushmore. Several years later, in 1934, President Franklin D. Roosevelt likewise felt compelled to honor Jefferson. Up to that time, Washington DC had only honored Washington and Lincoln with memorials (both being built in the previous century). Now FDR felt that it was time for Jefferson to finally take his rightful place in the nation's capital. The Jefferson Memorial proved to be a model of sheer perfection. Four years later, in 1938, Roosevelt also had the Indian Head nickel, with buffalo on the reverse, changed to bear a portrait of Jefferson on the obverse and Monticello on the reverse.

The founding of the new nation is inconceivable without Jefferson's brilliance, both as a philosopher and as a national leader, yet he found superb company among his amazing peers, who all shone with brilliance in their own way. This brings us to Jefferson's successor, the man many recognize as perhaps the most intellectual of the founders, James Madison.

JAMES MADISON was the mastermind who crafted the largest part of the *United States Constitution*. Where the *Declaration* was one of philosophical ideologies, imbued with lofty spiritual overtones, the *Constitution* was a hard secular document dealing with the mechanics of government. Madison was likewise pivotal in drafting the later Amendments, thus gaining the names of "Father of the Constitution" and "Father of the Bill of Rights".

This petite man, standing at only five feet, four inches tall and weighing in at one hundred pounds, was the smallest president America ever elected into office, yet certainly one of the most influential. However, Madison's influence was largely relegated to his magnificent documents, where his full genius reigned, for his administrative role as president was mired with poor and even terrible decisions, most notably with his declaring war on Britain, thus starting the War of 1812.

The British were already entangled in a war with Napoleon, yet due to their massive naval fleet, they were still able to send a large fleet to the Americas (three times the size of the United States' fleet), which began seizing American ships to cut off trade with France. Meanwhile, the United States still did not have a standing army and relied solely upon local militias. Similarly, its naval fleet was a mixture of small vessels with a few larger frigates, such as the *USS Constitution*, which did make a valiant effort during the war. Nevertheless, the British managed to sail into Chesapeake Bay and continued their raids inland, thus reaching their final destination, Washington DC.

The terror raid was in retaliation for the Americans' attack and burning of the British held city of York (present day Toronto, Canada). As such, a small troop of British soldiers stormed the Capital and began burning all the government buildings. James Madison and others were not present, but First Lady Dolly Madison held her ground, while most people evacuated the city. Although she managed to salvage the *Declaration of Independence*, a priceless portrait of George Washington, and other valuables, she, too, was inevitably forced to flee. The British soldiers entered the White House, ate the dinner that had been prepared for a function that evening, and then set the building on fire.

The attack on Washington DC was a devastating blow, as the Capitol building, Treasury building, White House, naval yard, and the Library of Congress were all burnt. In the aftermath, Jefferson—owning the largest personal library in the nation—sold his collection to the government to replenish the great loss of books. However, this attack would remain the last major attack on U.S. soil from a foreign force until the tragedy of 9-11 in 2001. Some historians have labeled Madison's blunder as the sixth worst presidential mistake ever made.

However, here, too, James Madison, like his close ally, Thomas Jefferson, who favored states' rights, small federal government, and no standing army, was likewise put in the position of contending with real life issues. Hence, the pristine beauty of ideas on paper does not always hold fast in reality. Therefore, Madison had little choice but to change his stance and embrace some of the policies voiced by his rival, Alexander Hamilton.

While serving in Washington's administration, Hamilton pushed for a standing army, and he established the Bank of the United States. The national bank, however, was only granted a twenty-year charter, and was due to expire in 1811, which happened to be during Madison's second administration. Madison eagerly looked forward to terminating Hamilton's fiscal initiative, but the hardships of funding the War of 1812 made Madison realize that a national bank was crucial. In 1816, Madison passed legislation to reestablish the National Bank, and he likewise saw the need for a standing army.

In conclusion, Madison's administrative role as president failed to match his brilliance at crafting ideas on parchment. Hence, the sparks of genius that are found in the transcending world and the tangible world are not always found in a single individual. Nevertheless, James Madison's contributions to the founding of the United States were of seismic proportions. Although petite, the atom was atomic.

ALEXANDER HAMILTON has appeared rather consistently throughout these assessments of our nation's founders, and rightfully so. Hamilton's influence upon our burgeoning nation was immense, and the mere fact that he was prohibited from attaining the high office of president in no way diminishes his role. *(See page 712)*

Although many are familiar with Hamilton's portrait on the ten-dollar bill, few Americans today know who this man really was, or why he was chosen for such an honor. The points made thus far have given a good indication of some of his assets, yet we shall now look at this special founding father a little closer.

Alexander was born in the Caribbean, on the isle of Nevis. Nevis means snow, and was the name that Christopher Columbus gave this island, since the billowy clouds that hovered over the mountain peaks appeared to be white as snow. Although the island itself exuded great charm and beauty, Alexander's childhood did not. He would later prefer not to mention these years, yet they did have a positive as well as negative effect on the remainder of his life and, as such, are necessary to explore in order to fully understand the man and his actions.

Alexander and his older brother, James Jr., were born out of wedlock to Rachel Lavien. Rachel had married the fortune-seeking Dane, Johann Levien, on the isle of St. Croix, but due to an unhappy marriage, the spirited Rachel sought her amours elsewhere and became an adulteress. Under Danish law, Johann was entitled to imprison his wife for these transgressions, and eagerly did so. However, after serving several months in a dank prison cell, Rachel did not emerge tamed or even emotionally submissive. As such, Rachel promptly left Levien and the island to live with the Scottish vagabond, James Hamilton, whereby settling on Nevis. It was upon this tiny, rustic island that Alexander and his brother would enter the world.

However, Johann Levien had previously fathered a son with Rachel, named Peter, and made sure his adulterous and abandoning wife would be legally severed from all claims of his estate. This included making sure that his son Peter's inheritance was protected from the two bastards, Alexander and James Jr. Lumping more shame onto these unpleasant affairs, economic factors forced the new Hamilton family back to St. Croix, thus forcing Alexander and his brother to live in open disgrace with their notorious mother.

Due to his illegitimacy, Alexander was prevented from attending school. As such, he was relegated to attending a private Hebrew school, yet even this was short-lived. Adding further emotional turmoil to his life, Alexander's transient father, James, abandoned the family and apparently moved to a neighboring island. It appears that James Hamilton was a part-time clerk, or most probably a loafer, as no tax records exist to support steady employment.

Many years later, Alexander offered the excuse that his father was simply not a successful businessman, and being unable to support his family, he left the island when the boys were old enough to seek employment; evidently, eligibility for employment in James Hamilton's mind meant only ten-years-old or older. Nevertheless, the greatest blow was yet to come when Alexander's mother died, leaving the thirteen-year-old boy an orphan.

Early life was unsympathetic and hard for Hamilton on both Nevis and even St. Croix. As mentioned, the island of Nevis may have been a tropical paradise, but the island's economy provided a bleak environment. Entrenched with slave-ridden sugar plantations, as was customary on most Caribbean Islands, the Nevis population consisted of an eight-to-one ratio, where enslaved blacks dominated the landscape. Treatment was harsh, and reprisals for disobedience were brutal. These visions of unjust persecution and bigotry would remain with Alexander forever, as even among the otherwise enlightened men who populated his future, Hamilton would remain one of the few who viewed slavery, and the notion that blacks were intellectually inferior, with realistic and sympathetic eyes.

Along with the slave traders, and other underhanded enterprises, were the bands of pirates that periodically entangled in skirmishes. This is where the young Alexander first learned about the art of dueling, as swashbuckling men defended their honor in open and lethal confrontations. This deadly habit was adopted by the impressionable lad, as Alexander engaged in duels for the rest of his life. Sadly enough, this ancient ritual of honor would ultimately dictate Alexander's demise.

However, St. Croix was more than just a band of roughians, slaves, and corruption, for it was coupled with the equally influential aspect of international traders who frequented the island and drove a booming economy. Now older, Alexander found employment as a clerk for Beekman and Cruger, which was a primary trader that imported the vast array of goods that St. Croix needed to survive. The staggering volume and variety that Alexander had to examine, from building materials, to foodstuffs, to shipping equipment, to livestock and incidentals, opened the youngster's eyes to a much broader world beyond the island's busy wharf and sandy shores. These lessons in fiscal exchanges and international enterprising would have a deep and lasting impression on the young teenager.

Alexander also displayed a voracious appetite for reading, and he soon found a vehicle to give voice to his own thoughts via poetry. Some of these works were submitted to the local gazette for publishing, and many display his wavering search to understand life, as new perspectives arose from ingesting new books, gaining life experiences, or simply renewing evaluations. For example, from praising pious and wholesome women, Alexander's next poem lauded the adventure of engaging jaded sluts. This, too, would come to haunt him in the future when he had a scandalous affair with Maria Reynolds. Alexander claimed that Maria intentionally seduced him in order that she and her husband could blackmail him, all the while remaining genuinely in love with his wholesome (yet now mortified) wife Eliza. Yet, this tainted tale will be addressed in due turn.

Nevertheless, Alexander's ability to write at an early age began to mature rapidly. His gift to project powerful and moving thoughts would become manifest many years later with the Federalist Papers, which he conceived, among many other crucial documents of early Americana, including ghostwriting much of Washington's Farewell Address.

Alexander's great mind and sturdy character caught the eye of a local Presbyterian minister named Hugh Knox. Knox quickly realized the boy's potential, and became somewhat of a mentor. With this, a new religious air infiltrated Alexander, and it would soon become publicly apparent after a severe hurricane ravaged the island. In the aftermath, Knox held services and issued a sermon that evidently moved the seventeen-year-old. Alexander was already struck hard by the devastating effects, which pummeled the island into rubble, but now he was motivated to compose a highly moving, yet religiously histrionic, rendition of this account that he would mail to his father. (Oddly enough, Alexander maintained a sporadic and only written correspondence with his father, despite his abandonment).

As fate would have it, Knox caught hold of this letter and managed to get it published. Alexander's insightful perspective, which was saturated with religious overtones of fire-and-brimstone and divine retribution, caught the dejected and bewildered imaginations of the hurricane's victims, who now pondered the meaning of this massive catastrophe. The public's response was so genuine that despite the devastation and financial ruin, some contributed funds to further the education of this talented young wordsmith.

Adding greatly to this effort was Alexander's cousin, Ann Lytton Venton, who quite possibly became the principle benefactor. Ann was involved in her own family discord as her father's death left her an inheritance, which she refused to share with her deadbeat husband, John. In response, John Venton's malice extended into his placing an ad in the Gazette that threatened all ship captains not to transport his wife and daughter off the island. In defiance, Ann took her daughter and fled to New York, and in her wake, made Alexander the executor of her father's estate.

It is implicit that once Alexander received the final disbursement of the inheritance, that Ann kindly donated a healthy share to her cousin so that he, too, could leave the island. Meanwhile, Minister Knox had done his part to make Alexander aware of the importance of a good education, and he aided in establishing contacts that would ensure Alexander's voyage to the American colonies. After a disastrous three-week voyage that ended with his ship catching on fire and drifting lame into Boston Harbor, Alexander disembarked and entered the new world alone.

Alexander was only eighteen years old, but thus began his transformation into the titan that would brush shoulders with the greatest men that the restless American colony had to offer. Here is where the illegitimate and orphaned boy, Alexander, becomes the history changing man, Hamilton.

Making his way down to New York, Hamilton enrolled in King's College (present day Columbia University). Hamilton quickly became known for his fiery debates and his many sound political articles that aroused attention and admiration. However, with the heated atmosphere of 1775, and a growing obsession for his new homeland, Hamilton joined a militia group in New York. Studying military history of his own volition, Hamilton quickly demonstrated a command of the psychology and strategies involved in warfare. It was during the New York/New Jersey campaign of 1776 that Hamilton's bravery caught the attention of George Washington, who astutely took the young dynamo under his wing, making him one of his secretaries.

Hamilton formed a close relationship with Washington, and rode by his side during many campaigns. Washington's high regard for Hamilton's perceptiveness, bright mind, and efficiency, firmly cemented Hamilton into all of Washington's future endeavors, thus becoming a fellow foundation builder and cabinet member for the future first president.

A few historians have commented on Hamilton's letters of affection that he wrote to Washington, and especially to his fellow army secretaries, John Laurens and Marquis de Lafayette. They are not sure of whether to classify them as homosocial or homosexual in content, although some lean toward the latter. However, if one contemplates the times, the atmosphere, and Hamilton himself, a pristine picture arises.

Firstly, the times were marked by a more flowery expression in words, as the literary style of men of the eighteenth and nineteenth centuries differs greatly from modern technique. Any student today reading passages from the great poets of the past would be apt to call some of them gay or, at a minimum, effeminately over-emotional. Moreover, Hamilton's melodramatic flare for writing was established early on, and whatever topic he engaged was always saturated with passion.

Secondly, the atmosphere in which Hamilton was immersed was one of a soldier during wartime. Survival depended upon a close camaraderie, for entrusting one's life to a fellow man does form a bond of love and devotion that exceeds the norm. In fact, John Laurens' own love and admiration for Washington made him challenge the recently court-martialed General Charles Lee to a duel. This was on the grounds that Lee insulted not his but rather Washington's honor. This provocative act defied all the rules of dueling's long history, but validates the intense loyalty, honor, and even love among soldiers.

Lastly, Hamilton himself was an orphan from an early age, and that void could have easily been filled by Washington's acting as a father figure, and his two secretaries, acting as brothers. Hamilton's deep appreciation for his peers embracing him as family could easily explain this filling of the emotional void and his love.

These three reasons in unison, and the fact that Hamilton happily fathered eight children with Elizabeth Schulyer, seem to be sufficient evidence that these accusations appear to be snow, just as much as the white clouds that hovered over his distant birthplace of Nevis. The evidence may appear like cold hard facts, but the exposé is vaporous.

Nevertheless, Hamilton served in the Revolutionary War with distinction, and as a lieutenant colonel, he even led a special infantry battalion in the battle of Yorktown—the famous confrontation that helped conclude the war. Interestingly enough, Hamilton's future adversary, James Monroe, who was similar in age, had also served under Washington. Monroe was even depicted in the famous painting, *Washington Crossing the Delaware*, being the man directly behind Washington, holding the American flag *(see page 712)*. However, unlike Hamilton, Monroe never attained the rank to command a platoon, and this is something that Aaron Burr made note of decades later when Monroe ran for president. Despite Burr's assessment, Monroe did succeed James Madison, and served two terms as America's fifth president. Meanwhile, the commander, Aaron Burr, only attained the rank of vice president. Henceforth, a person's ability to command troops is not the only criteria for winning the Oval Office.

Nevertheless, after the Revolutionary War, Hamilton served on the Congress of the Confederation, and a year later opened up his own law firm in New York City. With the British troops finally evacuated from New York, Hamilton was eager to set his fiscal ideas into motion that would boost the economy. Consequently, he founded the Bank of New York in 1784 (the oldest bank in America still in operation). Interestingly enough, the bank's first president would be Aaron Burr. Little did Hamilton know then that he and this man would be historically linked; first, as his mediator during his most embarrassing scandal, and second, as the grim reaper that would terminate his life.

Three years later, Hamilton became an assemblyman in the New York State Legislature. Hamilton's reputation was rising fast, and in 1786 Hamilton made the prudent decision to attend the Annapolis Convention in Maryland (which at the time was the temporary capital of the United States). Interestingly enough, many other delegates chose not to attend, thinking it unimportant. Although this meeting itself was uneventful, it did afford Hamilton the opportunity to once again meet James Madison, and the two intellects, despite their differences, bonded.

With the suffering condition of the present confederation on both men's minds, it appears this meeting was where Hamilton formed the basic concept of his famous *Federalist Papers*, which he would begin publishing two years later along with Madison and John Jay. These insightful papers offered commentaries and critiques on the budding American system, and won much attention and influence. More importantly, it was here in Annapolis that Hamilton and Madison first realized the need to not simply amend the Articles of Confederation, but to terminate them in order to construct a completely new government. This decision was just as momentous as the Revolution itself, for the Articles of Confederation was a weak and separatist document that, if left unaltered, would have thrust the leaderless colonies into the hands of foreign manipulation, causing internal rivalry and discord, and ultimately shackling them all into submission.

Hamilton and Madison both clearly recognized that the current system could never operate efficiently in its present form. The war had caused huge amounts of debt, and the independent states were disproportionately taxing their citizens; some so heavily, that it thrust many into dire hardship and near poverty. Worse yet, this led to Shays' Rebellion in western Massachusetts, where farmers, led by Daniel Shays, rose up in arms. Owing to state sovereignty, a federal army could not be amassed nor could they legally intervene, so a state militia had to be assembled to put down the rebellion. The eyes of the Confederation's leaders were drawn to this grave situation, including Washington's, who now seriously contemplated rescinding his retirement. Washington had wished to maintain his honorable Cincinnatus role-playing deed, by retiring from the limelight, yet with conditions now shockingly similar to being under the oppressive British system, change was mandatory.

Additionally, Hamilton believed that the unity of a loose confederation of states without a singular army, could never survive in an internationally-constructed world economy. Firstly, states would compete against their fellow states for foreign trade agreements, and secondly, if a crisis arose, the rivaling states would be reticent to fight for another state's grievance, especially if that state opposed one of their steady and lucrative foreign business partners.

This quagmire prompted Madison and Hamilton to press their fellow delegates for the necessity of a Constitutional Convention. With their motion confirmed, the famous convention was slated for May 25, 1787, and would be held in Philadelphia. However, the radical initiative of eliminating the prevailing Articles for a new government, which would build a new centralized federal government and partially strip the states of their separate and sovereign power, would not be revealed to the attendees until the convention actually began session.

The notion many Americans have about the Constitutional Convention is that after the turmoil and hard won battle to win independence, all these great men gathered in harmony and cordially fashioned a novel constitution. However, like the apostles attempting to construct the church after the turmoil of Jesus' death, the founders did not share a common vision of how to construct their new government. In fact, once the newspapers exposed a glimpse of the new plan, it immediately stirred dissension and rivaling factions. Right from the outset, the state of Rhode Island refused to even attend, and never signed the final draft of the *Constitution*.

Men in power, namely state governors and their underlings, had intense anxiety over the possible ramifications. New York's governor, George Clinton, who ruled over his state like a royal monarch, was naturally opposed to any talk of stripping him of power. As such, he made sure that New York was represented by two other delegates who would overrule Hamilton's radical voice.

Meanwhile, Thomas Jefferson had been in France, but he managed to send James Madison a barrage of books to fill his huge cranial database with historical precedents for evaluation and emulation. Henceforth, once at the Convention, Madison posited the Jeffersonian/Madisonian concept, known as the Virginia Plan. This clever plan formed the essential layout of our present system, as it designated a single executive leader (elected to office and serving a seven-year term) who would be checked and balanced by both a legislative and judicial branch. The senate and house, however, would be filled with representatives proportional to their state's population. This proposition gave Virginia more voice, being the most populous state at the time and, as a result, intense opposition ensued.

The Revolution had been fought on the grounds of humanitarian and God-given rights, without a plan or even basic concept for the aftermath. Hence, the unity of fighting for a common cause, suddenly hit a red brick wall in Philadelphia. The discrepancies were so varied and profound in nature that the Convention would linger for four long months. During this time, many delegates opted not to attend every meeting, which became burdensome to their official duties back home. This included Hamilton's two rivaling sidekicks who, displeased with the directives expressed, refused to return, although making clear their opposition to Hamilton as well as a centralized federal government. This came from the top man down, as Governor Clinton wanted no part of the proposed regime change.

After Madison proposed his Virginia Plan, William Paterson of New Jersey countered by proposing his New Jersey Plan. Meanwhile, Hamilton had remained silent, due to the stifling position Governor Clinton imposed upon him, tinged with a bit of humility being among such an illustrious congregation. However, Hamilton was always aware of the bigger picture, and knew just how crucial this moment in history was, for this very congregation would be establishing the functional doctrine that would either make or break the young, leaderless nation. This prompted Hamilton to rise and express his own concept of government, for as he said, "My situation is disagreeable, but it would be criminal not to come forward on a question of such magnitude."

The congregation was not only numbed by his six-hour-long speech, but also by Hamilton's inclination toward an old-style monarchy. Although some, like John Quincy Adams, would feel in concord with many of his propositions, the majority felt that Hamilton was a threat, attempting to restore a monarchy that they had just fought to eliminate.

Hamilton believed that an elected monarch should rule for life, however, as a preventative against tyranny, any signs of bad behavior would summon a process of removal. Despite this disappointingly backward suggestion, Hamilton did espouse the lucid notion that America could not operate in tranquil isolation, as many states sought, and that foreign affairs were crucial for trade and national solvency. Moreover, establishing a strong federal government with a standing army would demand international respect.

Additionally, Hamilton foresaw and forewarned that the vast Atlantic Ocean did not offer absolute immunity against foreign intrigue or invasion. Interestingly enough, this issue would become painfully evident during Madison's presidency when the British burned Washington DC. Moreover, this notion of protecting America from foreign invasion would be firmly indoctrinated into law by Hamilton's rival, and America's future president, James Monroe. The Monroe Doctrine declared the entire Western hemisphere off limits to European interference. As it turned out, the future Cuban Missile Crisis would find the Soviet Union at direct odds with America in the twentieth century, as well as the 9-11 attacks by radical Muslims that ushered in the twenty-first century, for these events finally shocked Americans with the reality of a homeland invasion and the need for national security.

Therefore, despite Hamilton's old-world, conservative view of monarchy, he was a visionary in many other respects, with national strength and security always being a priority. Hamilton saw beyond his nation's present separatist and agrarian mentality, and he advocated and steadfastly implemented designs for building a strong centralized federal government with a standing army and a robust industrial economy. Moreover, this vision, despite being accredited to some of his fellow founders—who were forced to adopt Hamilton's pragmatic stance when reality shattered their idealism—remains intrinsically and blatantly, Hamilton's vision.

As such, much of America's hard-line strength is primarily Hamilton's legacy. Moreover, although this air of arrogance, which is truly survivalist, ruffles the feathers of some foreigners and some pacifistic Americans, it is pragmatically clear that this hard-line quality is not only what made America the strong nation it eventually became, but is the only quality that will ensure America's present lead. As history has shown repeatedly, the meek do not inherit the earth, for the code of survival is benevolence with strength. As Teddy Roosevelt aptly said, "Speak softly and carry a big stick."

In hindsight, it is worthy to note that despite Hamilton's difference of opinion at the Constitutional Convention, firstly, his radical plan suddenly made Madison's Virginia Plan appear more appetizing and, as such, it helped win supporters who were previously noncommittal. Secondly, once Madison's Virginia Plan was adopted, Hamilton did embrace it wholeheartedly, and became the only New York delegate to sign the *Constitution*. Therefore, regardless of how determined, or even stubborn, Hamilton might have been, he did know when to relinquish personal opinions for the good of the nation.

The same cannot be said of New York's governor, George Clinton, who gravitated to seats of power for ego and selfish indulgences. After flatly rejecting the Convention, Clinton was suddenly confronted with a new federal order and a downgrade in rank. As the future would reveal, Clinton's lust for power drove him to abandon his once-sovereign state after it lost its supreme power. Clinton embraced the new federal government, which only Hamilton endorsed on behalf of New York, and became the future vice president for both Jefferson and Madison. Meanwhile, Hamilton always remained committed to the higher cause, and he aggressively debated the issues, despite opposition, to forge a new government, one that would be structurally sound and durable.

However, Hamilton's role in establishing this unique system along with his peers was just the beginning. Once the new government began operation, Hamilton immediately found himself appointed Secretary of the Treasury by George Washington. During Washington's first term, Hamilton's strong views in his *Federalist Papers* began to draw a loyal following. In time, this devout audience prompted him to found the Federalist Party. Hamilton's party not only promoted his provocative views about banking, industrialization, commerce, and the military, but it also impelled Thomas Jefferson to form his own party in response, thus creating the two party system in American politics.

Along with these two parties came much intrigue, as propaganda, ruthless smear campaigns, and seedy scandals, brought to life a world very much like our own. In this regard, it is a welcome breath of fresh air that we did not fall from a pristine and cordial state of grace to the petty and unscrupulous smut of the modern era. However, that little to no progress has been made in this department does come as a pessimistic memorandum about our human plight, which remains a perpetual scar upon humanity.

This brings us to the scandalous event in 1797, when Hamilton was forced to confront the most humiliating embarrassment in his life. The key players were James Monroe (who twenty-years later would become president), James Callender (the typical gutter journalist), Alexander Hamilton (the quasi-guilty victim), and we will include Aaron Burr (the fair-minded mediator, and long-time Hamilton adversary).

It was in the summer of 1797, when Hamilton was shocked to read a newspaper advertisement promoting a newly-published book with the misleading title *The History of the United States for 1796*. This book was a compilation of pamphlets that claimed to reveal unethical and seedy truths about the corrupt Secretary of the Treasury, Alexander Hamilton. As Hamilton began reading, curiosity soon turned to rage, as slanderous charges defiled his official activities in public office, and revealed his extramarital affair. Hamilton immediately accused Monroe of leaking this information to the press, which exposed his adultery with Maria Reynolds, along with the accusation that he and her husband, James, were engaged in fraudulent business speculations by skimming federal funds.

Several years earlier, in 1792, Monroe had been a key operative in investigating the Hamilton and Reynolds transactions, believing the payments to be an abuse of Hamilton's federal office. The Republicans quietly approached Hamilton, who then explained the tawdry affair, and assured them that the payments were for blackmail, and made from his personal account. The Republican committee was satisfied with Hamilton's confession, and decided not to pursue it further. As such, James Monroe was entrusted with filing the papers in confidence.

Subsequently, Monroe was then sent to Paris by President George Washington to replace Gouverneur Morris as Minister to France. This is when Monroe came to the aid of Thomas Paine, who was not only imprisoned, but also abandoned and rightfully outraged. Unfortunately for Monroe, he shared Paine's desire for an alliance with France, which broke completely with Washington's pro-British agenda. This became blaringly evident in the Jay Treaty, which clearly affronted the French. As such, Hamilton, along with others in Washington's administration, called for Monroe's removal. Washington wholeheartedly agreed, and without offering an official reason for this action, which was later revealed in

Washington's private and scathing letter, whereby he called Monroe a "mere tool in the hands of the French government", Washington ordered James Monroe to return home. Upon Monroe's return, the dejected and angry statesman met and dined with Aaron Burr and other Republicans in New York City.

The timing of these slanderous papers being published about Hamilton curiously coincided with Monroe's return to New York, and this led Hamilton to believe that Monroe turned over the papers for revenge. Furthermore, as stated, Hamilton knew that Monroe was the man entrusted with these secret papers, so any breach whatsoever, would logically have emanated from his hands.

As it was, James Callender—the shady newspaper reporter whom Thomas Jefferson first applauded for this exposé, then later derided as an unethical worm—published the pamphlets. Interestingly enough, Jefferson had used Callender's seedy services during his election campaign against John Adams, yet something ultimately went awry, as Callender was the man who first reported Jefferson's own indiscretion with Sally Hemmings. That provocative controversy, however, quickly faded, only to resurface two-hundred-years later in recent times.

Nevertheless, the secret documents that accused Hamilton of committing fraud by money laundering Federal monies with James Reynolds, did turn out to be personal blackmail payments to silence his adultery. Public integrity and honor were most precious to Alexander Hamilton so, rightfully, he exploded. However, to the surprise of all, Hamilton dragged this volatile battle into the public arena by publishing a ninety-five-page rebuttal. Hamilton came clean, vindicating his public honor and shamefully confessing adultery.

Evidently, Alexander's lack of family honor during childhood made him hypersensitive about his own. However, honor, to Hamilton, would now apply to his public service for the greater good, rather than his personal affairs. Hamilton's twofold attitude and willingness to confess his tryst with Maria Reynolds very likely emanated from his own mother's lack of moral fiber in this same regard. Then again, Hamilton was a voracious reader and had much to draw on to construct his own moral code. Titans throughout history, right up to our modern age, have often been allotted special treatment. For as the thinking goes, for all the great things they bequeath to mankind, it somehow seems compulsory to pardon their vices, and even favor them with sexual gratuities.

This moral double standard was certainly understood by a few of Hamilton's associates, but certainly not all. Where John Adams viewed extramarital affairs as severely damaging to character and infectious to one's abilities, others engaged their libidos with complete ambivalence and effectively conducted their business affairs in complete detachment. With the wealth of great men who indulged their licentious appetites while simultaneously performing highly admirable deeds, it remains a perplexing matter to completely condemn one's entire character because of sexual misconduct, despite the severe moral sin. Many have certainly caused national disruption by recklessly spiraling out of hand, as Bill Clinton's impeachment and the costly and distracting Starr investigation attest, yet others did manage to maintain ballast and sail a steady course.

Nevertheless, Thomas Jefferson, who allegedly had skeletons in his closet, called for caution and political decorum during Hamilton's public escapade. Jefferson was well aware that Hamilton could and would attack him directly and mercilessly if the trail led back to him personally. However, Hamilton had quickly surmised the rupture and honed in on the culprit, that being James Monroe.

As mentioned, Hamilton had publicly detonated a fiery rebuttal, and since Monroe was conveniently in New York, he demanded an immediate face-to-face meeting. This included the stipulation that both men bring along one witness to ensure the fidelity of their exchange. Upon their heated encounter, Monroe claimed to have no knowledge of how or who released the papers to the press. Hamilton, in turn, called Monroe's plea "totally false." As Hamilton saw it, even if another person handed them over to Callender for publication, it was still Monroe's breach that started the chain of events. Monroe, being of the same headstrong, honor-defending stock, refused to admit wrongdoing and, in defiance, called Hamilton a "scoundrel," followed by the lethal challenge, "I am ready; get your pistols!"

Fortunately, their two levelheaded witnesses stepped in and separated the two men. Although death was averted and the initial meeting terminated, the two gourami-warriors parted, seething. At Monroe's request, Aaron Burr was later called upon to intervene, whereby Burr deftly insisted that Monroe was innocent. Never one to trust Burr, Hamilton all the more remained fixed against Monroe. The feud lingered for several months in written duels, which never materialized on the open field of honor.

One might conclude that Aaron Burr was biased in his defense for Monroe, since Burr and Hamilton were life-long rivals, however, the personal letters of Burr display a sagacious mediator, who actually defended Hamilton's honor (excluding the charge of adultery), and advised Monroe of his duty to clear Hamilton of the false charges of fraud. Instead, Monroe remained unyielding, and even though a duel was avoided, the two men never reconciled their differences.

Oddly enough, current sources indicate that John Beckley, who was a clerk, made a copy of the document before Monroe deposited them with his secret and reliable source, which must have been Jefferson. Hence, the breach seems to have been made by Beckley, especially since Monroe had even challenged Hamilton to a duel to secure his honor.

Meanwhile, tensions grew between Burr and Hamilton, especially when Hamilton learned that Burr was Maria Reynolds' lawyer, whereby suspecting Burr of plotting the affair. Hamilton and Burr never clicked. This was primarily because Hamilton was a black and white visionary, with a one-track mind. Hamilton's innate genius for constructing policies to financially and militarily strengthen the new nation would not be derailed by someone who was wavering, fruitless and elusive. Burr's fickle nature was clearly displayed when he accepted Governor George Clinton's support to win a seat in the Senate and then later ran against Clinton, attempting to steal the governor's seat. Hamilton stepped in and won support for John Jay to eventually derail Burr in his bid for governor. Hamilton's animosity grew. As far as Hamilton was concerned, Aaron Burr was a selfish and untrustworthy turncoat.

Aaron Burr was atypical, in that he took no firm side in partisan party politics which, as we now know, Hamilton actually created. This independent position made both parties reluctant to fully embrace Burr. In hindsight, Aaron Burr remains an enigma, for despite being erratic and conniving, his personal letters indicate a man of great intellect with a judicious nature. Nevertheless, he was perceived as a threat, or at least a high risk. Burr's other peculiar, yet innovative, behavior didn't help matters either. Forsaking the prevailing and stylishly "dignified" trend of campaigning, whereby citizens were expected to simply read articles, then vote, Aaron Burr traveled the country, meeting people face-to-face, and shaking the hands of mere commoners. This degrading and suspicious "fad", which would soon become the norm, did not resonate with early American politicians. The burgeoning government, with its free elections, had caused rapid change, evidently too rapid for many stately politicians in the eighteenth century.

Furthermore, Aaron Burr and Alexander Hamilton were very different men. Where Burr was a sly and crafty lone wolf who preferred the company of tender felines, Hamilton was a fiery, red-haired stallion who boldly ran with the herd and preferred to lead the stud brigade.

Additionally, Burr had served under Washington along with Hamilton during the Revolution, yet despite his commendable service (which didn't match Hamilton's), he did ask to be relieved of duty. Burr was disgusted by the partisan camaraderie of military life; and naturally, with Hamilton being fully committed, and an integral part of Washington's loyal brotherhood, Burr simply didn't mesh. Here again, Burr's independent nature prevented him from bonding to what he perceived as a macho clique. And, although Aaron Burr would be the man to kill Hamilton in a duel, Burr's own bravado only got him entangled in two confrontations, one ending with Hamilton's death and an earlier one with Hamilton's cousin, John Church, which ended in a draw after both men missed and Church apologized.

Meanwhile, Hamilton formerly held the age-old tradition in high esteem, engaging in eleven duels during his eventful life. However, after his son Philip's death during a duel in 1801, Hamilton was overcome with melancholy, as the middle-aged firebrand was transfixed by death.

That same year, Burr's career was on the rise, as he tied with Thomas Jefferson in the Electoral College in their bid for the presidency. Hamilton was enraged; besides Burr's managerial incompetence, he was mounting up huge personal debts, which Hamilton feared would make him even more susceptible to corruption out of sheer desperation.

With the House of Representatives being left to decide the winner, Hamilton saw his chance to avert disaster. Despite the House being a majority of Federalists, Hamilton needed to convince them that Thomas Jefferson, who was their chief rival and leader of the Republican Party, was now to be chosen over Aaron Burr. Many couldn't comprehend Hamilton's strategy, but Hamilton's gift of persuasion finally prevailed, whereby ensuring Jefferson's election. Hence, Burr's burning desire for fame and fortune was effectively terminated by Alexander Hamilton.

Due to the unrefined electoral policy of that time, Burr was now uncomfortably forced to serve as vice president under Thomas Jefferson. Jefferson didn't trust Burr either, and Burr found himself abandoned by both parties and sinking further in debt. During May of 1804, Burr and Hamilton exchanged heated letters, whereby inciting Burr to challenge Hamilton to a duel, a duel that would live in infamy.

The gloomy event took place on July 11, 1804, on the Palisades cliffs in Weehawken, New Jersey. Interestingly enough, the calculating Hamilton, who hated to lose and had fixed ideas as to how history should remember him, had written a document just before the deadly confrontation. He made clear his refusal to fire at or kill Burr in this unfortunate yet unavoidable challenge. The two witnesses, each being a friend of one of the combatants, both confirmed that Hamilton's shot veered four feet away from Burr and lodged in a tree. Whether it was an involuntary reaction after being mortally shot or an intentionally wasted shot is not known, but it appears that Hamilton never intended to kill Burr. Burr would soon be charged with murder, and he fled to Philadelphia. The charge was eventually dropped, but Burr's career effectively died, just as his fallen foe had long wished. Hamilton had managed in life, and in death, to finally destroy the man he most feared would ruin the great nation that he and others struggled to build.

As noted, Hamilton exerted great influence in several presidential and gubernatorial elections. As in the Burr and Jefferson election, when Hamilton was unable to secure victory for a Federalist candidate, he rallied for the "lesser of two evils". This strategy allowed him to continue his political objectives, even if at a compromised pace. The downside was that Hamilton often toiled away behind the scenes and never basked in the limelight like his five illustrious co-founders; all of whom, save one, managed to become president.

Although some have viewed Hamilton as ultra radical, ultra manipulative or ultra hotheaded, he was also ultra sharp, ultra visionary and ultra effective. In essence, where many others contributed to the great story of our nation's birth, such as Aaron Burr, John Jay, John Hancock, Ethan Allen, Patrick Henry, Samuel Adams, Thomas Pinckney, Thomas Paine, George Mason, Gouverneur Morris, George Clinton, or even James Monroe, only Hamilton became an Ultra Founder.

Quite remarkably, the illegitimate Scottish orphan from Nevis had come to the budding nation, and powered his way up into the highest echelon of a country teaming with brilliant men and cutthroat rivals to become one of the mighty six pack, residing with Washington, Jefferson, Franklin, Madison, and Adams.

Henceforth, from a current perspective, it is abundantly clear that Hamilton's influence, although abrasive, was enormous, for after the revolutionary battles won by Washington, the philosophical *Declaration* composed by Jefferson, and the functional *Constitution* constructed by Madison, it was largely Hamilton who shaped the new burgeoning Republic into the centralized and industrious federal empire that would become the new Rome.

Interestingly enough, Hamilton's affinity for Rome over Greece was typical of the pragmatic politician and enterprising facilitator that he was. While some of his compatriots were more adept at philosophizing, Hamilton was propelled by a practical desire to make his divinely-guided empire a bold world leader, rather than a passive backwater academy. For Hamilton, bargaining with France and England from a position of power and economic strength was preferred to submissively kowtowing to overlords. That America mirrors Rome, rather than Athens, is a foregone conclusion and a Hamiltonian conclusion.

As subsequent years passed, and succeeding presidents engaged in expansionism, the frail thirteen colonies multiplied into a healthy fifty. At the very fundamental core, however, Alexander Hamilton was the man who established the political and economic paradigms that were necessary for future presidents and entrepreneurs to build the great and powerful American civilization that we know today.

Like Hamilton—who rose from near poverty and family turmoil to the highest level of American society—another, and much older, fellow founder followed a similar path. And, once again, just like Hamilton, this man is the only other person to appear on our paper currency who was not a president. Although not ten times as great as Hamilton, this man resides on our one-hundred-dollar bill, and his name is Ben Franklin.

BEN FRANKLIN was one of those rare individuals who could generate love, respect, and idolatry from the middle class, contempt from some of the high-browed upper class, cautious veneration from the clergy, or admiration and even ridicule from his brilliant peers. Yet, of all the founders, Franklin remains the most approachable, the most unusual, and certainly the most inventive. When we view his precarious rise from a lowly provincial family to the pinnacle of fame and super stardom (well before his younger rebellious peers), we can only be proud to call him one of our founders or, as H.W. Brands calls him, "The First American."

However, Franklin's road to success differed from Hamilton's in that a magnanimous cousin and clergyman funded Alexander to migrate to America, and he was educated at one of the country's best colleges. Benjamin Franklin, on the other hand, was forced to contend with a far different situation.

Benjamin was born in 1706, being the fifteenth child, and last son, in a line of seventeen children. His father, Josiah, was a candle and soap maker. And being one of the lower classes, he only understood that hands-on-labor yielded security and survival. Nevertheless, despite Josiah's simple heritage, financial difficulties and large family, he did manage to send young Benjamin to the prominent Boston Latin School. This he could only manage for one year, leaving the inquisitive-minded Ben to receive one additional year of formal training at a standard school. Despite how unfortunate this may seem in hindsight, formal schooling was not the standard practice in colonial America, as most children learned their parents' trades and continued the family businesses. However, because Ben displayed an aptitude for learning, his father wished to provide at least some sort of a start. With school a dead issue, thoughts of the priesthood were considered, but eventually Ben had to submit to custom, thus becoming an apprentice to his father.

Benjamin certainly wasn't indisposed to working with his hands, but the monotony of making candles and soap must have driven him mad. As it happened, Ben's older brother, James, opened the first independent newspaper, the *New England Courant*. Ben eagerly jumped into the business of printing, which entailed messy inks, hauling heavy loads of paper, setting type, and running the presses. At the time, printing was also considered a menial job—especially by upper class gentlemen who were schooled to work with their minds—yet Ben quickly gravitated to the end results of this messy mechanical endeavor, and that happened to be the power of the printed word.

Even though Benjamin was thought too young and insufficiently educated to write for the paper, the crafty teenager decided to fool his older brother and the Boston community by writing under the pseudonym of Mrs. Silence Dogood. Franklin's provocative letters stirred much controversy and interest, yet once James discovered the hoax, he wasted no time in reprimanding his young, spirited brother. Since Ben's term of apprenticeship was legally binding and dictated by the employer, James extended that timeframe to last several more years. Furthermore, because James couldn't expose the scandal, knowing it would ruin his business, his only recourse was to humiliate his disobedient brother with extra hard labor. However, Benjamin would not submit to his brother's callous demands, and he decided to flee Boston, thus breaking his legal contract and becoming a petty outlaw.

Ben traveled several hundred miles south to Philadelphia, where he landed a printing job. Philadelphia, we must remember, may have been a new and upcoming city, but it only consisted of roughly six thousand people. As such, it didn't take long for Ben's wit and personality to catch the attention of almost everyone in town, including Deborah Read (to whom he would become engaged), and the governor, Sir William Keith. Sensing the young boy's energy and motivation, Keith suggested that with his financial support, Ben should travel to London to acquire his own printing presses, whereby he could start his own newspaper. Benjamin jumped at the fiscal opportunity and the bold adventure. Leaving his fiancée behind, Ben excitedly sailed to England. However, after many distractions, the young adventurer soon found that he lost Keith's patronage as well as his interest in going home.

Young Ben spent two years of hedonistic freedom in London where he matured into a worldly man. With the funding of an American merchant who offered him a job, the seasoned Franklin returned to Philadelphia, and thus began his long, illustrious career. Franklin quickly proved to be a remarkable polymath, for whatever Franklin contemplated, he eagerly sought to improve or, at the very least, contribute to the field. This included devising the first lending library, designing the more efficient Franklin stove, basic contributions to the new field of electricity, the lightning rod, bifocal glasses, the glass harmonica, and more. With Franklin's creation of the *Poor Richard's Almanac*, which offered commentaries, advice, and even sayings that would become national adages, it didn't take long for the colonists to know the name Ben Franklin, as well as Europeans, who eagerly sought the oracle's thoughts and advice on a broad range of topics.

This international stardom made Franklin the most popular man in the colonies. Oddly enough, by the time of the Revolution in 1776, Franklin was in his seventies, making him two to three decades older than his young-blooded friends. This huge gap in age is seldom considered, and it adds greater mystery to this old man who by this time was well established, had firm connections to local and British politicians, was independently wealthy, honored by great universities and foreign governments, and in no obvious need to rebel. What many have learned about Franklin, however, is that his long rise to world fame was accompanied by a sound philosophy that ensured his success. This philosophy becomes very apparent in his actions, and was likewise revealed in his personal letters.

Ben Franklin's father was a religious man who instilled a formal account of Christianity in the young boy; however, Franklin astutely recognized the divisions that religion caused, even between fellow

Christians, let alone those of different faiths. As such, Franklin made it his business (business likewise being paramount to the industrious boy from meager beginnings) to ensure that one should follow the sound advice of doing good to one's fellow man rather than fixating on questionable dogma, which habitually divided men. This is why Franklin belonged to no particular church, stood as a legal advocate for several denominations to protect their rights to practice their religion without prejudice, and why he even joined the Freemasons.

As mentioned earlier, Franklin advised Thomas Paine to burn his book, *Age of Reason*, which condemned the irrationalities of organized religions, for Franklin understood the depths of faith and tradition that the vast majority held. And as he predicted, it spelled suicide for Paine. As a wanton young man in London, Franklin had written a provocative article himself regarding religion. It was called *Dissertation on Liberty and Necessity, Pleasure and Pain,* and in it, Franklin claimed that since only God knew the truth, it was useless for mankind to bicker over such matters. Yet years later, he burned every copy he could get his hands on.

That incident appears to have been one of Franklin's final lessons regarding his public views on religion as well as the public response it provoked; his first lesson had come earlier when he wrote those articles in his brother's newspaper under various pseudonyms. The teenager's religious attacks had caused sharp rebuttals and unforeseen consequences, which Franklin later reflected upon, saying, "my indiscreet disputations about religion began to make me pointed at with horror by good people, as an infidel or atheist."

As such, Franklin became a charismatic chameleon, one who would openly embrace all religions, assist all religions, and appear to be a believer in all religions. However, he would not become a parishioner of any of them, at least not in the fullest sense. This amiability toward all religions carried over to politics as well. Franklin learned that avoiding conflict garnered broader acceptance and broader rewards. This philosophy served him well in not only achieving a good reputation, but was also crucial to his later diplomatic efforts in France during the Revolutionary War.

Franklin remained a calming mediator and unbiased public figure until the last years of his life, when he took offense at some of the new congressmen of the new regime. The issue happened to be slavery. Franklin had been like most other eighteenth century white males, in that slavery was a tradition, as deeply ingrained in society as much as religion; as odd and ironic as that seems. Beyond tradition, blacks were perceived to be intellectually inferior. However, a few decades earlier, during the 1750s, Franklin noticed the ill effect that slavery had upon the young, white generation. Being an industrious hands-on type of guy, Franklin was furious to see how young whites became lazy when placed in settings where blacks did the majority of hard labor. Franklin observed that the few blacks who were educated did manage to comprehend and memorize just as readily as whites, yet Franklin was not prepared to make a public assault on the issue.

Twenty-five years later, in 1775, his fellow Philadelphia Quakers founded the first abolitionist group in North America. Still not ready to confront the volatile issue, Franklin kept his feelings to himself. Twelve more years would pass before Franklin made his public move, by becoming the president of the society in 1787. This radical and forward-thinking group had even realized that the assimilation process would warrant a completely new educational and vocational program for moving blacks out of the labor fields and into the mainstream. Their doctrines naturally attacked the atrocious behavior of the white supremacists who treated their fellow black men as animals. Three years later, in 1790, Franklin finally launched his attack on Congress with a formal request to abolish slavery in the United States. The request fell upon deaf ears, but the word was out and the sentiments were spreading. The nation would have to wait another seventy years for the final conflict and resolution, but of all the founders, only Ben Franklin took physical action to eradicate slavery.

Beyond Franklin's many attributes as a moral defender, industrious businessman, scientist, inventor, or statesman, his role as foreign diplomat was certainly his most crucial contribution to the formation of his fledgling nation. Without the financial and military support of France, which Franklin single-handedly won, the American Revolution would have very likely lost steam and fallen into the dustbin of failed revolts.

The amazing feat that Franklin pulled off was no easy task by any means. While pursuing the fragile business of securing confidence and transmitting the same, Franklin was forced to contend with jealous rivals, such as John Adams, who almost sabotaged Franklin's delicate diplomacy.

As a preface to Franklin's mission in France, it is crucial to note that it was Franklin's lifelong foundation, which he thoughtfully and industriously constructed, which opened doors for him throughout his long and eventful life. The opening of this section focused on Franklin's self-made rise from peasantry to prosperous pop icon with the intention of revealing how one's actions transcend the present and project into one's future. The groundwork that Franklin established with his industrious life and amicable ways enabled him to achieve what no other American could in the imperially aristocratic world of snobbery that constituted eighteenth century France.

Franklin had achieved world recognition with his scientific contributions and inventions, not to mention his humble workingman's form of philosophy, which intrigued and delighted all of Europe and particularly the French public. This fact added immensely to Franklin's acceptance and influence while in Paris during the 1780s. In stark contrast to Franklin's worldly prestige and his worldly experience, was the bumbling loudmouth John Adams who, by sheer folly, the United States sent to replace Franklin.

John Adams despised every aspect of Franklin, whom he perceived as a charlatan without the knowledge or moral fiber to represent America. Upon his arrival in Paris, Adams immediately found himself in an alien world, which he openly and quite foolishly badmouthed, especially considering the critical mission he was sent to accomplish. His account of when Franklin met and even embraced the famous French philosopher, Voltaire, reeks with jealousy as well as repugnance.

Adams' jealousy arose from his belief that he was the better man for the diplomatic job, while his repugnance most likely arose from his staunch Christian core, which instantaneously rejected and despised secular philosophers. With Voltaire being the leader of the pack, Adams sarcastically labeled the two old sages Solon and Sophocles.

Beyond petty jealousy and ideological repugnance, Adams was a born and bred American colonist, one who was accustomed to the small-town puritan ways of rustic Boston. The highbrowed aristocratic world of Paris, France, with its rigid and ostentatious monarchy, yet extremely liberal lifestyle, was as if Adams descended into one of Dante's infernal rings of hell. Meanwhile, Franklin understood the ways and customs of the French better than any other American, and being the charming chameleon that he was, Ben knew how to play the game of diplomacy. Meanwhile, Adams saw issues in black and white, and if America represented the white luminous glow of freedom and Protestant perfection, then France was the black hole of elitism, doused with a fatal mixture of Catholicism and secular decadence.

Adams' black view of France also carried over to his view of Franklin, whom he thought acted more French than American, at least in certain ways. Proud of his culture, Franklin was the only American diplomat to wear the common clothing of his humble heritage, and even a large fur hat, while every other American conformed to French etiquette, wearing posh linens, powdered hair and other fineries. However, Franklin's apparent fondness for French women drove Adams nearly mad. Adams had observed the wife of an elderly aristocrat named Madame Brillon, sitting on Franklin's lap and giggling, while her husband seemed completely unaffected. Worse yet, Adams later found out that a woman who had always stood close by (and whom he thought was the Madame's friend) happened to be the mistress of Monsieur Brillon.

Hence, Adams' own private confession sums up his distaste for the French and his own diplomatic shortcomings: "I was astonished that these people could live together in such apparent friendship and indeed without cutting each others throats. But I did not know the world."

Indeed. John Adams did *not* know the world, nor could he understand or appreciate the delicate matters of state that Franklin so aptly performed with ease and grace. Again, this points to the blaring reality of how Machiavellian methods, regardless of how repugnant to one's personal moral beliefs, are unavoidable if one wishes to successfully deal with people or nations that have alien ways and lifestyles. Franklin was the only American to form a bond with the French statesman turned foreign minister, Charles Gravier, Comte de Vergennes.

Franklin quickly targeted Vergennes as the key man to form a relationship with, since Vergennes sought revenge against the British for the Seven Years' War, which had devastating effects in both the North American and European theaters of engagement. Yet Vergennes was easily incensed by the other American delegates, especially John Adams, who lacked all tact and understanding of French pride. Adams refused to believe that America needed France as much as it did, and would not forget America's own position in the Seven Years' War, better known to Americans as the French and Indian War. Adams even tried desperately to have Congress relieve Franklin, yet thanks to Franklin's winning ways, Vergennes firmly requested that all diplomats be retracted, except Benjamin Franklin.

If John Adams had succeeded in undermining Franklin's crucial position—and mission to gain financial and military aid from France—the American Revolution might never have ended as America's victory, regardless of Washington's resolve and strategic acumen. As stated earlier, even Washington knew that the victory they had won was by a very narrow margin, or as he said, "a miracle."

Henceforth, the old self-made man from Boston, who made Philadelphia a symbol of Americana, and bequeathed to the young nation a broad variety of pioneering innovations and infrastructures, solely managed to secure the foreign support required to complete the grand and precarious task of winning America's independence. For this, Benjamin Franklin's larger than life persona and his honorary title as "First American" are indeed justified.

While the newly-established nation struggled in semi-isolation, its European ancestors were struggling to keep pace with a rapidly changing world, one that often trampled tradition. The Enlightenment era of the eighteenth century was quickly compounded by the Industrial Revolution, political turmoil, social migrations and mutations, and the quest to understand mankind and nature. In essence, by the nineteenth century, Europe was in a volatile state of hyperactivity and unrest, as ideologies and beliefs were turned topsy turvey.

Scientific endeavors forged earlier by Galileo and continued by Kepler, Newton and others, now led into areas that profoundly challenged the order of the universe. Along with this universe-altering new revelation came the desire to analyze the human mind as well as the conjuring up of new philosophies of how mankind should best govern itself. These evolutions and revolutions in ideologies disseminated so quickly that they were often adopted in haste. It would take many decades for people to finally realize that not everything that appeared indisputable in concept would hold true in reality.

VII
1800 - 1900. DARWIN, MARX, AND FREUD: EVOLUTION, REVOLUTION, AND PSYCHOLOGICAL SCIENCES

Intro | Communism: MARX, LENIN AND STALIN | *Psychological Sciences:* SIGMUND FREUD | *Evolution vs. Creation:* CHARLES DARWIN

(Septem, Libra, Judah, Thomas, July)

Blistering winds filled the sails of the H.M.S. Beagle. Salt water sprayed from the bow as the British ship sliced through the Pacific. Upon its slippery decks stood the young and recently self-titled naturalist, Charles Darwin. Darwin had graduated Cambridge University as a clergyman, with the intention of entering the Church of England, but instead accepted the invitation to join the Beagle's five-year voyage of exploration.

Scouting the South Pacific and South American coastlines in 1832 was no easy task, especially for a neophyte observer unaccustomed to the hardships of life at sea. However, Darwin was deeply motivated by the concept of evolution, which was previously put forth by writers such as Thomas Malthus, with his *Essay on the Principle of Population* (1798), and Charles Lyell, with *The Principles of Geology* (1830).

Lyell made the geological observation that the Earth appeared to have evolved, rather than come into being by spontaneous divine creation, while Malthus focused on living creatures, and how fierce competition for food resulted in survival of the strong. These provocative claims were made without scientific proof, thus this crucial deficit incited Darwin's critical determination to find that proof. For five years, Darwin observed and collected data from various islands and shorelines, both biological and geological, which he meticulously recorded in numerous journals.

Upon landing back on English soil, Darwin spent several years in London. The Industrial Revolution had transformed the city into a dismal smog-laden sewer as its smoke-stacked factories multiplied malignantly. Darwin's disdain for the destruction of the city quickly engendered his eagerness to leave it. Eventually Darwin, along with his new wife Emma, who was his cousin from the famous Wedgwood family, settled in the tiny village of Downe, just sixteen miles from London.

Interestingly enough, though many years passed after his long sea expedition, Darwin did not attempt to collate and publish his findings. In fact, twenty-one long years would pass before he was alarmingly compelled to publish *On the Origin of Species by Means of Natural Selection* in 1859.

Earlier, in 1858, Darwin found himself nervously pacing back and forth, his mind reeling. In his hands was a letter from the naturalist Alfred Russel Wallace, accompanied by Wallace's most recent essay. Darwin read Wallace's essay with trembling hands, as beads of perspiration slowly moistened his body. To his utter surprise, Wallace had been in Malaysia collecting and analyzing data. His extensive fieldwork had taken him across the globe to Brazil and then to Indonesia. But the shocker was that Wallace had independently arrived at the same conclusions as Darwin, and now furnished him with his essay on natural selection. Worse yet, he entrusted Darwin with publishing his earth-shattering discovery.

Darwin's procrastination had now caused a most uncomfortable situation. Should he honor Wallace's request and lose all twenty plus years that he invested in research? Or should he tell the young naturalist that he somehow beat him to the draw many years ago, but never published it? Then again, would Wallace even believe such a claim?

Darwin decided to pass the buck, and begged for advice. He contacted Sir Charles Lyell, England's foremost geologist, and Joseph Hooker, a prominent botanist. Together they wielded great influence over the scientific community. Lyell had warned Darwin against holding back his theories, and now he was confronted with an ethical dilemma. Since Darwin shunned complicity, rightfully fearing scandal, Lyell and Hooker took it upon themselves to handle the situation. They published a brief outline of Darwin's views that was cleverly positioned above Wallace's completed essay, thus making the two co-discoverers of the theory of evolution, although prominently favoring Darwin in the process.

When Alfred Russel Wallace finally received word of the publication, he remarkably conceded with great poise and dignity. He believed an earth-shattering theory, such as evolution, could only impact the world if it came from a prominent figure, and Darwin's status clearly exceeded his own. Wallace's magnanimous gesture thus ensured his own eclipse, for evolution did have a tremendous impact on the world, and Wallace's name vanished in the immense and dense shadow cast by Charles Darwin. As one axiom of the new theory proved—the strong, albeit shrewd, would survive.

Darwin and Wallace both realized the religious implications of their discoveries; like Galileo before them, they had turned core beliefs topsy-turvy. The mid- to late-nineteenth century was at a crossroads. The sparks of scientific, philosophical, and political awareness—created earlier by Newton and his scientific laws that proved what Galileo pioneered, namely, that mathematics held the key for decoding many of the world's secrets; Hume and Voltaire, whose philosophy and atheism mirrored that of the ancient Roman statesman Cicero, which helped ignite the Enlightenment; and the American founding fathers who drafted a new republican government—all ignited many nineteenth century minds to rethink their fundamental belief systems to chart new courses.

Three figures of this volatile era stand out the most: Darwin and his theory of evolution challenged religious beliefs and spawned new scientific ones; Freud and his pioneering psychoanalysis deeply influenced views regarding the human psyche; and Marx and his political creation, communism, enchanted countless nations. They questioned three major areas of human existence—mankind's true origin and spirituality, the workings of the human mind, and how mankind should best govern itself on Earth. Their powerful influences would infiltrate the world's population and have profound effects, both good and ill.

Yet of these three nineteenth century shakers, only Darwin remains the least scathed. Although it cannot be understated that Freud is primarily responsible for igniting the fields of psychology, psychiatry, abnormal psychiatry, and a slew of tangential sciences dedicated to unlocking the mysteries of the human psyche, Freud's personal methodologies and interpretations of analysis has, in most circles, been ruled inaccurate, necessitating new directions. Karl Marx's communism, which at first appeared promising, soon revealed its catastrophic flaws and hurled numerous nations into complete economic ruin or oblivion. The amazing fact is that these three individuals profoundly altered and reshaped the human mindset on a global scale, proving that the pen can be mightier than the sword.

Communism: MARX, LENIN AND STALIN

The writings of Karl Marx have created a tsunami of repercussions that have affected many nations over the course of several decades. Whereas in the ancient world only a handful of individuals formulated and plotted their rise to power, in the modern world the disseminating power of books, newspapers, and pamphlets created a new dynamic in which rebellions and authority could be achieved by influencing the masses. The most noted forerunner to have an immense impact on politics was Machiavelli. However, his book, *The Prince,* was not only geared toward those in power, but access to it was often limited to the privileged few. Several centuries later, book printing and distribution had grown exponentially; the volatile words of Marx spread like wildfire, even landing in the hands of uneducated Russians, like Josef Stalin, who was living in near poverty.

Wildfire brings to mind another man worthy of our attention, hence a small sidebar. With the current state of affairs, it appears that one day the Egyptian poet, Sayyid Outb, will follow Karl Marx's fiery lead as being a highly influential writer who spawned a new regime. However, Outb's notorious role will be as the founder of Islamic Jihad terrorism. Outb had opted to be educated in America, yet utterly loathing what he saw as American materialism and soulless prosperity, he returned to Egypt. Outb was imprisoned and tortured for allegedly trying to kill Egyptian President Gamal Nasser. This induced Outb's merely provocative words to become radically militant. His last book, entitled *Milestones,* was written in prison, and it outlined his vision of creating *hakimi,* or a "Godly society." Sayyid Outb was executed in 1966, thus he became the first and most revered Jihadist martyr.

Like Karl Marx, Outb's words were a call to action that ignited radicals, such as Kamal el-Said Habib and his Egyptian guerillas decades later. They, in turn, influenced Osama bin Laden, thus becoming the explosive *al-Jihad/al-Qaeda* movement we know today. Along this radical path of influence, however, the Ayatollah Khomeini (who ranked America as enemy number one, labeling it the Great Satan) became a figurehead back in the late 1970s. Khomeini, however, was content to kill Americans on his own soil, whereas bin Laden took *jihad* to American soil. Nonetheless, while we already know the disastrous outcome of Marx's Socialist society, in Outb's case, the outcome remains to be seen and written.

A hundred years before Sayyid Outb, however, Karl Marx was the first political writer to move millions with his provocative words. Marx had originally posited his new political system, called communism, in his book *The Communist Manifesto*, which was published in 1848. This book was actually co-authored with Friedrich Engels, yet Marx became the front man and spokesman for the cause. Marx would later follow that up with his equally famous book *Das Kapital*, in 1867.

Marx drew his inspiration from a broad spectrum of sources, such as philosophers like Hegel, economists like Adam Smith, and even politically-minded individuals like Ben Franklin, yet he clearly formulated his own concepts that departed from these sources in distinct ways. Marx abhorred the capitalist movement, which allowed tycoons to enslave workers in factories; hence, communism, later called socialism, would hypothetically empower the workers. Furthermore, *The Communist Manifesto* advocated that the working class should revolt and overthrow the ruling class. These volatile words of action would have profound repercussions. When Vladimir Lenin led the Bolshevik Revolution in 1919 to overthrow the Tsarist regime in Russia, he fulfilled the Marxist manifesto, and simply labeled it Soviet Communism.

Lenin's new communist nation seemingly started off with good intentions, for Lenin espoused democratic ideas, decried the anti-Semitism that was tearing apart the nation, and proposed the electrification of Russia to bring power and prosperity to the distant reaches of the expansive nation. However, Lenin's premature death, in January 1924, caused disarray and a major shift in Soviet events. Lenin's long underground struggle to lead the Bolsheviks into open revolt against the three-century-long Tsarist regime certainly appeared hopeful, yet once they succeeded, Lenin failed to establish a concrete code or political constitution for his fellow revolutionaries to follow. This was the tragedy of Lenin's long and hard struggle for a better Russia.

Lenin's sudden death caused the remaining Soviet councilmen to be left standing helplessly in their leader's wake. Each may have had embryonic potential but certainly no clear direction or political savvy, thus enabling Josef Stalin, who was the least mentally and morally qualified, to rise to power. The theologically educated Georgian, who never held a job, and was an often-imprisoned rebel, adopted the name Stalin, which means "man of steel". He had befriended Lenin early on, initially through letters, in their united quest to overthrow the entrenched Tsarists. After the Revolution, Stalin was awarded the seat of General Secretary.

However, Lenin soon realized his error in judgment, and cautioned some of his associates about Stalin's dictatorial designs. Lenin even left a warning in his will about Stalin's malicious tactics and his position that could lead to unlimited power. But the broader communist party was not privy to Lenin's unnerving prophecy. The dead leader's suspicions became manifest when Stalin strategically seized full control and turned Lenin's communism, which was actually Marxist communism based upon communal socialism, into the maligned dictatorial concept that became known as communism.

Two members from the reigning communist council, Zinoviev and Kamenev, were particularly instrumental in swaying other members into letting Stalin remain in the post of General Secretary, thus allowing Stalin to wield greater power. Lenin realized that holding this key position could allow Stalin unbridled power, which is why Lenin astutely recommended in his will that Stalin be replaced. Lenin also believed that Stalin was too crude and coarse to rule, and in his last letter—which he demanded not to be published but only read to the council after his death—Lenin made this painfully clear, along with other formal requests. To the council's astonishment, Lenin also mentioned that none of the remaining members was fully capable of leadership, not even Alexander Trotsky, who was a brilliant orator and theoretician. Lenin believed that Trotsky was not pragmatic enough and that the council should find a new leader without taking on an outsider. It didn't matter—Trotsky was later murdered by Stalin's assassins while in Mexico. He was brutally hacked to death with an ice pick.

Additionally, the democratic minded Lenin spoke of the necessity of incorporating the needs and rights of the people into the new government. Yet, with the steel-fisted Stalin already welded into the key seat of power, consideration for the working class was the furthest thing from his selfish, power-hungry, and provincial mind. True to form, after Stalin secured his dictatorship, his two earlier advocates, Zinoviev and Kamenev, were executed, due to differences of opinion. The two foot-soldiers realized too late that the man they cheated for and lied for, to make appear like shining steel, had become a deranged death sword, one not only poised to slice their throats, but more importantly, had already cut down countless rivals to achieve the ultimate goal, that of duping and subduing Mother Russia.

For over thirty long years, Stalin shaped every aspect of Soviet life, from his strict and orderly bureaucratic regime right down to the coerced, and in many instances, gullible people who believed in their deified leader. Because Stalin was a loner and a terrible public speaker, he resorted to propaganda to mold and cultivate a false belief of national pride, based upon the premise that he was one of Lenin's close comrades who continued the noble cause. Stalin became adept at concealment and smoke screens that kept many of the Soviet people blissfully proud, at least initially. It soon became apparent, however, that Mother Russia would become devoid of liberty, devoid of religion, denied of hearing or speaking the truth, and denied the ability to pursue genuine progress, creativity, or true prosperity.

The growing and suppressive dictates of the unsophisticated ruler had glaringly become all too real, as Stalinism pathetically shackled the intelligentsia and cultured elite. Their creativity was now to be monitored, severely reprimanded, or even extracted from the world of the living.

In 1934, the gifted composer Dmitri Shostakovich would soon catch the watchful eye and untrained ear of Stalin. The composer's avant-garde opera, *Lady Macbeth,* had just premiered, and it received accolades from both the public and some officials; however, it wholly displeased Stalin. He strongly condemned the work in an article entitled *Muddle Instead of Music*. The composer would not realize the full gravity of Stalin's wrath until two years later, when in 1936, Stalin began what became known as the Great Terror. During this sweeping purge, many of Shostakovich's relatives and artistic friends were imprisoned or murdered. Shostakovich, along with Sergei Prokofiev, Igor Stravinsky, and all other artists, had to bend to the dictator's artless will. The avant-garde suddenly became traditional, and only those like Sergei Rachmaninoff, who fled Russia during the Bolshevik Revolution, managed to escape Stalin's wrath.

However, despite the empty-headed tyrant's attempt to silence creativity, Shostakovich brilliantly mocked Stalin in his *Eighth Symphony*. Instructed to create only upbeat music, Shostakovich composed one of the most unrelentingly gloomy, obstinately harsh, and aptly symbolic pieces of music ever composed. Created during the horrors of World War II, Shostakovich could be excused for the solemn tone and brutal outbursts, for it echoed the destructive death march of war and the pain and anguish of the millions who suffered.

However, the third movement symbolized more than the brutality of war, for its stubborn *ostinato* scoring was mindlessly plodding and tainted with bizarre and hollow orchestration that aptly mirrored and mocked the deranged dictator. Quite fittingly, Dmitri's machine-like death march climaxed with a cataclysmic explosion and an ominous gong, which resonated the horror and cold inhumanity of war, as well as that of Stalin's icy regime. Not surprisingly, Serge Prokofiev's Seventh Piano Sonata is also a masterwork with a *precipitato*, or rapid and thoughtless third movement, which likewise captures the repetitive drone-like sensibility of the coldhearted Stalin.

Beyond the artistic or public abuses, Stalin's personal life was also marked with coldness of heart and tragedy. His second wife, Nadezhda, was twenty-two years younger, and desperately tried to involve him with his three children (two from their marriage and one son from his previous marriage), however Stalin was obsessed with one thing only and that was power. Nadezhda was habitually assaulted by verbal abuses and outright neglect that psychologically mangled her spirit and tender heart. One evening, during a house party, Nadezhda finally had enough of her husband's cold and demeaning jibes. In humiliation and utter desperation, she went to her room and shot herself. Stalin was said to be devastated, but managed to get over the incident, which in typical fashion, he viewed as an affront to his good graces. Stalin also cruelly tested the loyalty of his closest comrades by having several of their wives or relatives imprisoned or shot. They all managed to carry on their daily activities with the cold and sadistic ruler, yet only God knows what emotions truly traversed their hearts and minds.

It appears that the Russian people did have one small consolation. It is splendidly apropos that when Stalin fell to the floor from a stroke, his bodyguards (who found him hours later) could not even phone for help because that defied protocol. Stalin's paranoid procedure only permitted the Chief of Security to make such calls. Therefore, Stalin lay helplessly paralyzed and dying for twelve long hours, all due to his own steel-headed handiwork.

Upon Stalin's death, his Chief of Security, Lavrenty Beria, suddenly found himself in a powerful position. His bloodstained hands were also linked to the deaths of well over ten million Soviets under Stalin's regime, and made him a prime target. Hence, Beria was duly executed by Stalin's successors.

Despite his own evil defects, Beria was only the high-ranking foot soldier of his ruthless master. Stalin was the paranoid architect who built his new Soviet Union, killed his real or imagined opponents with broad executions, imprisoned political adversaries in *gulags*, and by intentional neglect, caused famine and death to whole communities. Most Americans remember that six million Jews were killed by Hitler, yet few realize just how monstrous Stalin was, for he ruthlessly killed four-times as many people. His heinous crimes have long been obscured by the grand spotlight on Hitler, and have been conveniently kept secret behind closed doors by the tight-lipped Soviet nation that Stalin personally built.

Stalin's oppressively die-cast Soviet Union was passed down to a series of leaders, each of whom adamantly fought to defend and expand their militarist regime. These leaders in total, who intentionally discarded their initial socialist credo, habitually neglected their own people and economy; hence, as the decades progressed, so, too, did poverty. When President Reagan further subjected the Soviet regime to economic and military hardships, it could no longer bear the weight of its massive façade, and the vast Soviet Empire collapsed. Today, Russia and its satellite nations are still struggling with their fledgling democracies, marred by Stalinist sympathies.

As Soviet historians embark upon a massive reassessment of their misguided past, many former members of the Politburo and military are finally beginning to speak of the secrecy, misinformation, and cold-blooded atrocities of Stalin's steely reign, which is chiefly responsible for Russia's current decrepit and rusting regime. In 1990, former Colonel General Dimitri Volkogonov called for the Soviet government to openly condemn Stalin for his blatant contempt of the Soviet people, which deprived them of freedoms that are natural and inalienable. This was ascertained directly from that famous republican document the *Declaration of Independence*, written by their former rival, the United States.

Meanwhile, China, which Stalin strong-armed into becoming a communist nation in 1949, has grown economically in recent years due to American corporate interests. This has clearly allowed China to replace the reconstructed Japan of the 1960s; however, whereas Japan was a democratic nation set up under American Marshall Law, China remains a totalitarian regime with many anti-American traits, not to mention its awful track record on human rights. With a rapidly growing economy and a new military alliance with Russia, China is positioning itself to be a world superpower to rival and surpass the United States.

In conclusion, the births of both Russia and China, which subsequently imposed communism on a spectrum of third world nations, all began with the influential words of Karl Marx that were penned in *The Communist Manifesto*.

Psychological Sciences: SIGMUND FREUD

Sigmund Freud's words likewise affected change on a global scale. Here, too, many forerunners, such as Plutarch during the reign of Hadrian and Trajan, attempted to analyze the human character. Plutarch pitted Romans of great stature against Greeks of great stature in his book *Parallel*

Lives. His purpose was to compare and contrast these figures but also gain insights about their virtues and foibles—in essence, what made them tick. However, this admirable effort was not based upon the scientific method that would only develop over a millennium later, and in this regard, Freud's work was pioneering, even if severely flawed.

Although Freud knew that a scientific methodology was necessary to gain academic respect and global acceptance, he was unscientifically shrewd and careless about gathering and recording his new theories on psychoanalysis. This was especially true when he analyzed his own childhood, which was the launching pad for his long psychoanalytical expedition. In thus doing, Freud was often intentionally blind to his results, or more to the point, he was intentionally deceptive in documenting them. This is now believed to be due to his strong and obsessive desire to create a new science and emerge as a heroic figure. He did this in a vainglorious effort to be like the idols he read and fantasized about: Darwin, Copernicus, Alexander the Great, Napoleon, or even Oedipus, who he honored with his famous Oedipal complex.

Beyond his largely self-fabricated persona, and rightful title "Father of Psychoanalysis," Freud's views on sexuality, the unconscious, neurosis, and the interpretation of dreams have largely been proven false after decades of careful study. This has also been painfully proven by many analysts who made erroneous Freudian diagnoses and implemented erroneous Freudian therapies that yielded results which ranged from imperceptible to disastrous. As many therapists today assert, Freud's overall failure emanated from his radically zealous desire to formulate a science of psychoanalysis that he constructed and dictated, rather than allowing the data to speak for itself.

An examination of Freud's numerous cases shows that he would receive negative results from patients who complained about their worsening state of digression, yet he adamantly refused to modify or change his formula for treatment. Instead, Freud would angrily lambaste his clients, and then intrepidly document his glorious results, which deceitfully advocated his initial prognosis and therapies. Sadly, these sessions often fixated on sexual desires or fears, such as penis envy, Oedipal complex or castration anxiety, rather than platonic emotional needs. Moreover, the science of genetics was not yet born, which added significant understanding about an individual's mental and physical states. Despite this lack of information, however, Freud was reckless.

He was also noted for creating universal doctrines based upon his own personal experiences. For example, Freud was prone to anxiety attacks on trains, so he fashioned an elaborate explanation that somehow linked neurotic compulsions to sex. He also formulated a similar deduction after witnessing young boys in a shoe store. Because they were fidgety and uncomfortable when a salesman slipped on their new shoes, Freud ludicrously deduced that they feared losing their foot (which frightfully disappeared into the shoe) because they feared castration. As such, Freud not only invented universal truths based upon personal experiences, but his hyperactive imagination distorted these observations to the point of lunacy. Sigmund Freud invented his own megascience on his own misdirected terms, which were inundated with absurd sexual oddities, thus he became perhaps history's greatest practitioner of pseudoscience. How the scientific world could have bought into Freud's world of madness is equally fascinating.

Some of Freud's fantastical interpretations may have been due to his heavy use and reliance upon cocaine. Early in his career, Freud formed a very close relationship with Ernst Fleischl von Marxow. Some speculate that Freud even adventured into sexual relations with his friend, for whom he expressed his love in personal letters. A photograph of Ernst was the only one to hang in Freud's office for many years after his beloved friend died at an early age. Ernst was a sickly young man who had become addicted to morphine; the intensity of the drug concerned Freud, who then prescribed cocaine. Cocaine was the new wonder drug that spread across Europe and America, even becoming wildly famous in the American soft drink Coca-Cola. However, once the medical authorities denounced the drug, Freud had no option but keep his usage secret, which he did for ten years. The effects of cocaine, as well as other drugs he might have been taking, might very well explain some of his bizarre theories. However, the lion's share of his actions appears to be pure unadulterated Freud, and certainly his zeal for fame was unclouded and fixed.

After the publication of Freud's *The Interpretation of Dreams* in 1900, European and American practitioners began to engage in Freudian psychoanalysis. In fact, America would soon become the new Mecca of psychiatric science. In 1909, the president of Clark University, in Worcester, Massachusetts, was the first to offer an honorary degree in the burgeoning field of psychology. As such, Freud was invited to receive this distinguished award. Freud was ecstatic, as academic recognition would be a crucial first step in the justification and acceptance of psychology. Hence, Freud anxiously made his first and only trip to America to receive the degree and to present five lectures. The audiences sat enthralled, as Freud's German-spoken lectures were interpreted into English.

William James, the prominent American psychologist (and brother of author Henry James), was present. Afterward, he took a walk with Freud. James was not won over like the college audience. He could not equate Freud's dream theories with any of his own cases, as he said, "…obviously 'symbolism' is a most dangerous method." James also clearly recognized in Freud's obstinate lectures that he was a man with fixed ideas. This, too, would prove dangerous, as Freud's unintentionally, as well as deceptively fixed theories would all crumble decades later, regrettably after millions were improperly diagnosed and treated. Nevertheless, early American psychologists embraced Freud's rhetoric as sacred doctrine and his Freudian absurdities infiltrated the masses.

Interestingly enough, even beyond the analysts' offices, laymen evaluated themselves, their friends, and relatives based upon Freudian principles. This influence extended into child rearing and the "supposed" ill effects experienced during child development, like how all people need to fight the natural desire for incest, or how all females desire a phallus. Radical measures were taken to adjust for these misdiagnosed children, however that only added more doses of idiosyncrasy to the psychological soup. It would take far too many years before Freud's psychoanalysis was gradually denounced by purists of the scientific method. Soon, they all mocked Freud's work on psychology as being pseudoscience, which oddly enough was created by a psychotic.

Freud's misinterpretations of some of his own experiments have now become almost comical. Laced with all its subconscious sexual desires or perversions, these views, amazingly enough, gripped much of the world for the greater part of the twentieth century. Early movies, like *Spellbound*, seriously addressed Freudian theories, while the later comedies of Woody Allen made a mockery of its absurdities.

In the visual arts, Freud deeply influenced Salvador Dali. Intrigued by the powers of the subconscious, Dali became the grand master of Surrealism and the fascinating world of dreams. In turn, Dali's Surrealism, along with that of Giorgio de Chirico, Max Ernst, René Magritte, and later M.C. Escher would permeate the world of modern advertising and countless science fiction and fantasy films to become one of the most effective and lucrative vehicles of visual communication. That only humans experience dreams makes Surrealism a potent new art form.

Therefore, despite Freud's personal flaws and the falsehoods he espoused, his books on the subject initiated a revolution in how mankind views the inner workings of the human mind. Men before Freud, however, had naturally evaluated others to understand their motives. Machiavelli is a prime example; his scrutiny of what made leaders tick and become successful was one of many earlier attempts to understand a man's actions, not so much his mind; moreover, it dispensed with science or therapies. Freud was the first to attempt making a science of inquiry into the broad spectrum of this mysterious realm, and although he himself failed miserably, he must be credited with at least spawning the many other avenues of inquiry that have yielded positive results. Still, many people, especially those wrongly diagnosed, had nothing but contempt for Freud, while practitioners of his method likewise became painfully embarrassed and humiliated. In the final analysis, it has become quite clear that many doctors and clients were duped by the demented personal fabrications that emanated from the reckless mind of Sigmund Freud.

Evolution vs. Creation: CHARLES DARWIN

Unlike Freud's revelations about the personal psyche, Darwin's revelations shook the foundations of divine creation with his famous treatise, thrusting Christianity, Judaism, and all world religions into a strong defensive stance. This immense impact was so profound that we must return to Darwin and his earth-shattering theory of evolution.

As noted, Darwin wasn't the first to put forward the concept of evolution, but no one else supplied concrete evidence to substantiate the claim. Hence, this was Darwin's major contribution (with the aid of Wallace), even though this theory was incomplete, not fully supported by natural selection, and contained the famous "missing link," among other enigmas and unsupported claims. However, that the world stood up and took heed is solely due to Charles Darwin, with Wallace's impetus.

Darwin's provocative theory took root rather quickly, as advocates, like Thomas Henry Huxley and others, spread the word at universities and conferences. Equally important were the philanthropists who began building natural history museums in American and England, which promoted the theory of evolution to the public. Similarly, the westward expansion that was still occurring in nineteenth century America had opened up a goldmine of discoveries to support evolution, as fossils of dinosaur bones were unearthed and excitedly shipped back to paleontologists for reconstruction. The breathtaking displays of colossal dinosaur skeletons instantly captivated the public, and Darwin's new theory was on its way, overshadowing the research necessary to validate some of his theory's genetic gaps. This issue took a backseat to the fanfare at museums, or the deftness with which Darwin's theory filled classrooms and textbooks in public schools.

Nevertheless, many parts of Darwin's underlying foundation held firm and likewise have firmly held the attention of scientists ever since. The advent of newly discovered fossils was compelling, and offered tangible proof of evolution. This included the five-toed eohippus, which developed into the single-hoofed horse we know today, or the saber-tooth tigers and woolly mammoths that were clearly ancestors of modern-day tigers and elephants respectively. This phenomenon of nature was never mentioned in any biblical text, for Genesis simply states that all land animals, birds, and sea creatures were created on a single day.

Furthermore, the carbon dating system, which is highly accurate, placed the development of certain species in chronological order, and was used to dispel the Creationists' Biblical notion that the world is only 6,000 to 10,000 years old. Additionally, Genesis claims that man was created on the sixth day, hence no older than 10,000 years old. The fact that fossils of modern man (Homo sapiens), are found to be 200,000 years old clearly dispels the Biblical dating hypothesis. Taking this further, even while the rise of Homo sapiens exceeds the Biblical account of Earth's creation, it comes nowhere near the earliest found human-like creature, Homo habilis, which lived 2.5 million years ago.

Extending far beyond the appearance of human-like creatures on Earth exists a huge catalog of prehistoric dinosaurs, reptiles, and other creatures that are extinct and are never mentioned in any Biblical text. Genesis very briefly states that on the fifth day whales and all creeping things were created and that man followed on the sixth day. Ironically, this places mankind only one day after the creation of the whale and all other creatures on Earth, yet the whale has been dated to be 50 million years old, and the earliest form of man only 2.5 million years old.

Furthermore, the Earth is approximated to be 4.5 billion years old, not 10,000 years old. That no human-like creatures appear in the earliest strata of Earth's physically layered constitution (nor does the carbon-dated timeline of history place mankind within the first six days of Earth's creation, which extends far beyond thousands and into billions of years), thrusts the notion of Adam and Eve into the realm of fanciful mythology or gross human error in regards to recording biblical facts.

Additionally, as new sciences evolve, like embryology or microbiology, with their evolutionary development, or "evo-devo," more discoveries add weight, such as the discovery that DNA has a very slight but confirmed mutation rate per nucleotide per cell division. Naturally, there are still crucial areas of evolution that remain obscured by misinterpretation or missing pieces to the development process, however, the core concept, such as the several evolutionary variations of prehistoric men that are nowhere to be found or explained in the Bible, all offer impressive evidence of an alternate beginning for mankind.

Despite missing evidence, one cannot escape the fact that the Homo habilis, Neanderthal, and other ape-like humanoids, which irrefutably existed, find not a single mention in any Biblical text. This is simply because they happened to be discovered several millennia after the writings of the Old Testament—given that early sacred authors knew nothing of their existence. This once again provides compelling evidence that mankind has been fundamentally involved in the crafting of Biblical stories, the extent of which remains as mysterious as the missing link.

Even though the theory of evolution cannot prove exactly how the world was created, these prehistoric variations of humanoids that existed long before modern Homo sapiens have unequivocally raised serious questions about Adam and Eve, or just what sort of man was created in God's image on day six. Here again, a crucial verse from the Bible itself leaves us pondering exactly who did God intend to be made in His image—the Homo sapien or the ape-like Homo habilis? With such tangible and lucid evidence, as these skeletons clearly attest, evolution had become a huge thorn in the side of religious texts ever since.

However, despite the breakneck speed at which evolution entered public schools, Darwin's theory just as quickly elicited a stern response from devout Christians. In 1925, a Tennessee farmer named John Butler realized that many children were coming home from school and telling their parents that the Bible was all nonsense. This prompted Butler to draft a law that would prohibit the teaching of evolution in all public schools in Tennessee. The bill was instantly ratified within a week by an overwhelming vote of 71 to 5, thus establishing the Butler Law.

At this time, the ACLU (American Civil Liberties Union) was just being inaugurated, and the defense of evolution was its very first cause. As such, only four months after the Butler Law was in effect, the ACLU scouted for a teacher—finding John Scopes—who would stand trial to defend Tennessee teachers who were still teaching evolution in class. The premise was that the textbook supplied to teachers contained a chapter on evolution, thus forcing teachers to break the new Butler Law.

Rallying to the ACLU's side was the famous defense attorney, Clarence Darrow. Darrow's high profile and publicity had little effect as the trial moved from the textbook's content into a heated debate on religion. Interrogating William Jennings Bryan (who acted as a Bible expert), Darrow drilled him on such questions as how old was the Earth, how did Cain find a wife, and other perplexing matters. Bryan said he did not have to attempt to explain it—faith in the Book was enough. Bryan did however contest the dating theory on the crafty grounds that a "day" during the time of God's Creation did not necessarily mean the twenty-four hour day that we use today.

With the trial swelling into a heated frenzy over theology, the judge shut down the case, asking Darrow what the relevance was of such questions. Darrow replied, "We have the purpose of preventing bigots and ignoramuses from controlling the education of the United States."

With the judge expunging all testimony from the trial, the jury ruled against Scopes, fining him $100, which the ACLU offered to pay. Thus, not only did the ACLU, Scopes, and Clarence Darrow lose, but the evolution theory experienced its first big setback in public education. The Butler Law was eventually overturned in 1965, and the theory of evolution has been taught in classrooms ever since.

However, Creationists and Evolutionists have always been vying for supremacy, and religion and science are once again butting heads, as a new wave of right wing Christians want evolution eliminated from public schools' curricula.

We know Christianity was pivotal in creating the university to enhance human knowledge, yet as seen in the Dark Ages or the Counter Reformation, it has also gone through long spells of backward intolerance. We also know that the Church adopted many secular theories in the past, such as Aristotle's and Ptolemy's earth-centered universe, only to later reprimand Galileo, and then later receive harsh criticism and ridicule for doing so. But in the case of evolution, the Church was not defending itself against theories based on conjecture or adopted philosophies that proved false, since evolution scientifically challenges the Holy Scriptures with solid facts and tangible fossils, that even if not wholly conclusive do offer an alternate explanation for mankind's origins and certainly unexplained life forms. This is why Darwin's theory remains so dangerous to religion.

As a sign of reconciliation, some Christian scientists have recently attempted to explain God's hand in evolutionary science, yet this becomes transparently unconvincing, since the two are diametrically opposed. A world 6,000 years old can never be one that is now estimated to be 4.5 billion years old. Any slight thought of mankind evolving from some previous ape-like ancestor, as the remains of Neanderthals and other primates compellingly insinuate, can never explain Adam and Eve. That is of course, if we take each and every detail in the ancient scriptures, which were committed to papyrus by fallible humans, as being the unerring word of God.

In hindsight, however, the stage had already been set when Darwin's theory challenged Creationism. The questioning attitude of the Renaissance had previously supplanted the Middle Ages; then came Galileo's earth-shattering discovery in the seventeenth century; followed by the Enlightenment philosophers of the eighteenth century, such as Hume, who applauded Galileo's scientific revelation debunking the religiously-ordered universe; and then came Voltaire, who boldly attacked religious dogma.

Voltaire used reason and logic to dissect the Bible and its teachings, and spoke of it as a sort of brainwashing from infancy, rooted in mankind's primal fears. He purported that since God is an entity inconceivable to man, that basic lack of comprehension leaves man as an infant, or basically ignorant. In one verse, Voltaire states: "Men believe in God only upon the word of those who have no more idea of him than they themselves. Our nurses (guardians or catechists) are our first theologians; they talk to children of God as they talk to them of were-wolves; they teach them from the most tender age to join the hands mechanically. Have the nurses' clearer notions of God than the children, whom they compel to pray to him?"

Such thoughts have opened a can of worms that has been squiggling ever since. In this debate, philosophical questions still arise about the divinity of a God, who is praised for being flawless and perfect, yet created flawed and imperfect subjects. Coupled with this intrinsic creational flaw, some evolutionists saw God as being unkind and even cruel. One such example comes from the Book of Genesis 6:7, *"And the LORD said, I will destroy man whom I have created from the face of the Earth; both man, and beast, and the creeping thing, and the fowls of the air; for it repenteth me that I have made them."*

Here evolutionists ask, how can God be flawless or even kind? He clearly spoke of having repented or regretted making his flawed creations, including, shockingly, mankind. Therefore, even if it was men's highly controversial *free will* that caused their flaw, rather than God's *admitted flaw* in Creation, God also condemned all the innocent beasts, creeping things, and fowls that committed no wrongdoing. Hence, God decided to drown *all* his creations, save for Noah and his select crew.

We know the theological answer is not to question that which is inconceivable to mankind, but that throws us right back to Voltaire and his repugnance of shackling mankind in ignorance, which, in another sense, can also be viewed as a cruel punishment by the Divine Creator. But do we have the right to even think such thoughts? The verdict is still out and remains unsolved.

Despite all the controversy, Darwin's aim was pure science, not a pogrom against religion. His quest was to unravel the truths regarding the mysterious beginnings of mankind, the animal kingdom, and plant life, by tracing their specific developments using critical analysis and precise data collection. The results of his noble quest presented the world with radical ideas that sparked many other intelligent minds to follow his lead, as well as igniting an array of air-headed imbeciles, who infected the thoughts of others with almost equal fervor.

As with the reaction to many illustrious ideas, there will always be a select few who misconstrue and misinterpret, such as Arthur de Gobineau with his *Essay on the Inequality of the Human Races*. This document of racist hatred proclaimed whites, and in particular Germanic Aryans, to be superior to all other humans. Naturally, this was one of many sources that later fueled Adolf Hitler. This variation became known as Social Darwinism, which unjustly blemished pure Darwinism.

The concern over the ill effects of social evolution also surfaced in the famous nineteenth century novel, *The Time Machine* by H.G. Wells. Interestingly, Wells was a student of Huxley, who, as mentioned earlier, advocated Darwin's theory. Wells' novel told of a time traveler who, upon reaching a destination in the distant future, came across two species of humanlike beings. The Eloi lived above ground, and had limited intelligence, while the Morlocks lived underground, and provided food for the Eloi wandering above. However, the traveler soon discovered that the Morlocks fed the Elois like cattle, only to slaughter them later for consumption. This leads to his unnerving discovery that both species evolved from his very own human roots. Hence, H.G. Well's posited a frightening question: could the evolution of man bring advanced malignancy? With such primitive roots, maybe so.

Another interesting set of genetic roots exists between Darwin himself and his cousin Francis Galton, literally and figuratively. After Galton read his cousin's theory on evolution, he recognized some discordant survival traits between humans and animals, and wrote several books, coining the term eugenics. Eugenics is a social philosophy that advocates various forms of intervention to ensure the strongest line of heredity. This philosophy of ensuring that only the strongest humans survive, analogous to the animal kingdom, meant selective breeding must be facilitated between individuals or families who were not only physically healthy but also more intelligent. The mentally and physically weak would then die away according to natural law. Being a well educated man, akin to his famous cousin Charles, Galton naturally sat perfectly at the summit of his ideological philosophy, one that would decades later inflame the imaginations of Ernst Rüdin, a Swiss psychiatrist/geneticist, and other German scientists who would be instrumental in shaping and implementing Hitler's genocidal mass exterminations.

However, there is another side to this fanatical variation of Social Darwinism. Many progressive thinkers—Theodore Roosevelt, Woodrow Wilson *(see pg. 714)*, Alexander Graham Bell, George Bernard Shaw, and Margaret Sanger—also embraced eugenics. Their idea of control, however, was often far less radical. Margaret Sanger, who actually had an affair with the aforementioned author H.G. Wells, was the founder of Planned Parenthood in the United States. Her battle against civil and religious leaders to advocate "birth control" (a term she coined) was not easy. During her quest for the right of women to decide, and for the use of contraceptives, Sanger was once even arrested and jailed for 30 days. Worse yet, Sanger used Hitler's geneticist madman, Ernst Rüdin, as an advisor, and she strongly advocated the sterilization of hereditarily inferior humans. Both euthanasia and abortion, which are themselves the social offspring of Darwinism, remain hot topics today.

H.G. Wells' thoughts and fears of evolutionary degeneration, along with the grandiose notions of racial superiority held by countless people, were all philosophical mutations that evolved out of Darwin's scientific exposé. In a similar fashion, the growth and continued interest in euthanasia, abortion, genetic counseling, stem cell research, cloning, and other controversial procedures falling under the umbrella of genetic sciences, are all outcrops of Darwinism.

Therefore, the revolutions in human thought by Darwin, Freud, and Marx profoundly altered the world in very positive and negative ways. That these ideas became entrenched on a global level and at such a rapid pace, should offer a warning—one's own logic and moral code must not be easily swayed when adopting unproven ideologies, even if the majority embraces them.

However, pure Darwinism, as noted, has influenced and spawned countless areas of positive exploration. His meticulous scrutiny of the developmental process of various species opened cognitive doorways to a broader and brighter horizon of possibilities. For if we consider how the succeeding sciences of genetics, microbiology, molecular biology, and biochemistry materialized, which also offer tremendous medical and medicinal benefits, we see that Darwin's roots aptly evolved into a fruitful tree. Furthermore, the benefits of DNA testing and the future prospects of the controversial yet groundbreaking study of stem cells have their roots in Darwin's thinking.

Additionally, thanks to Darwin, many have learned to better analogize, and as such, develop devices or products that are fashioned after the refined specialties of certain species, such as an airfoil designed after a bird's wing, camouflage designed after leopards or chameleons, submarines designed after whales or dolphins, pliers designed after a crab or lobster claw, and so on.

Darwin's scrutiny and the subsequent investigative sciences have proven that all things in nature serve as keys—keys that are mandatory to unlocking mankind's quest to better understand the world around us, to advance, and ultimately to survive. Furthermore, they should awaken us to conservation and preservation, and, of course, to the sanctity of all life on Earth. For to destroy or exterminate anything in nature only serves to destroy these keys and their ability to unlock vital doorways to knowledge, thus inevitably crippling our own grand journey of advancing toward total enlightenment and revealing God's handiwork.

From the theory of evolution we return to the winds of time and inevitably to the evolution of progress by mankind. This leads us to our next titanic topic, for today, we clearly realize the benefits and necessity of wireless communications, yet few know who was responsible for inventing this astonishing innovation.

VIII
1900 - 1937. MARCONI – Radio and Wireless, Global & Space Communications
(Duodeviginti, Scorpius, Levi, James, August)

A frigid Canadian blizzard hammered the sides of a cast-iron locomotive, as it chugged and swayed its way southward along the frozen tracks. Snowflakes melted rapidly as they slammed into the steam engine's coal-fired boiler tank. Peering out one of its rear windows was Guglielmo Marconi, who nervously watched, as his towering communications aerial disappeared under a blanket of driving snow.

Over the past several years, Marconi's notoriety for pioneering wireless transmissions sharply escalated the demand for his presence. Having just finalized his progress-check on his new broadcast antenna in Nova Scotia, Marconi was now heading south to Massachusetts.

Arriving in Cape Cod, in January of 1903, the beleaguered steam engine finally thumped to a screeching halt. As Marconi made his way to the exit door, he hunched over slightly to peer out the train's long series of windows. Through a thin veil of steam, he could see a line of officials standing among a crowd of spectators. Suddenly, the doors slid open, and Marconi exited the train. Meanwhile, dignitaries flocked to greet the Italian inventor and shake his hand.

Walking toward Marconi, with a valiant gait, was a stocky man with a mustache and round spectacles; it was none other than America's twenty-sixth president, Theodore Roosevelt.

Roosevelt was there to test out Marconi's wireless device, and, as always, the firebrand was glowing with anticipation.

An antenna had already been setup at Cape Cod to accommodate the historic event. Four years previously, Marconi's wireless apparatus was used at the cape to cover the American Cup. The sailors marveled over the new fangled technology, calling it "not of this world."

Teddy Roosevelt was a true-blooded American that thrived on innovation and adventure. He also loved to push the barriers of engineering and science as much as he would love to push an attacking bear to the ground. Roosevelt viewed his efforts of building the canal locks in Panama as being the world's grandest engineering feat of his time, and it was. However, the notion of transmitting messages through the nothingness of ether must have seemed as fantastical as a magic trick performed by the new sensation of their time, Harry Houdini.

Actually, Marconi's magical *wireless* act had begun when he was only twenty-one. He traveled to England, in 1897, where he premiered a series of radio transmissions, thus securing a commission. The Germans were soon captivated and took a vested interest in wireless communications. However, the Germans and Marconi were unable to reach an agreement; as such, Karl Braun founded the Telefunken Company. Despite their best efforts, the Germans lagged far behind.

A few weeks before Marconi's arrival at Cape Cod he had sent several radio messages from Canada to England. Marconi even received a congratulatory telegram from the illustrious inventor Alexander Graham Bell. However, the feat Roosevelt would perform that day would be a significant piece of public relations to further amplify Marconi's miraculous radio waves.

As the two iconic men walked towards the broadcast station, Roosevelt gazed at Marconi with his big trademarked grin. It would be an exhilarating day of presenting another of the world's firsts. However, underneath his tepid smile, Marconi had concerns about sending his message over the Atlantic. He had realized that, due to the Earth's curvature, light and sound waves shoot straight out into space after 200 miles. So the trick was to find a solution, which Marconi believed he found, but a few glitches still existed.

Upon reaching the control center, Marconi instructed the president to send the British king, Edward VII, a simple greeting. With a few clicks, Roosevelt's Morse-coded message was sent off. Roosevelt stood silent, looking at the equally silent gadget. The president must have found it a bit unnatural not speaking to someone face-to-face. However, to both men's delight, the message had indeed traveled across the Atlantic Ocean and reached its destination. It was the first transatlantic radio transmission in history, traveling from the United States to Great Britain.

Marconi had a good reason to be nervous, for as he later admitted to a journalist: "The mere memory of it makes me shudder. It may seem a simple story to the world, but to me it was a question of the life and death of my future." Marconi's future, however, was secure, as was his amazing wireless invention.

Despite the setbacks Marconi had faced at that time—with static and the need for higher-powered stations—he informed the president of its many possible uses, the most important of which was its use at sea. Many nations expressed an interest but still hadn't mandated its use in naval vessels, including the United States.

Unfortunately, Roosevelt was persuaded to stand by the U.S. Navy Department's position, which was to wait until all the glitches had been worked out. However, as far as Marconi was concerned, sailing the vast oceans, while severing contact with land, was surely a recipe for disaster.

The world of travel in the early 1900s, before the advent of flight, was firmly dominated by the sea. Therefore, all ships leaving port were instantly rendered mute, leaving their fate to the unpredictability of carrier pigeons, a messaging system that was literally for the birds. Hardwired telegraph cable was an up and coming technology, but it left any movable land vehicle or sea vessel severed and perilously isolated. Eventually, Marconi's wish was realized when it became mandatory for all vessels to carry wireless. However, even open communications at sea had to be manned by fallible humans.

A few short years later, on April 15, 1912, the *SS Titanic* set sail on its maiden voyage. In the dead of night, amid the frigid North Atlantic seas, the colossal vessel struck an iceberg. The horrific disaster shook the world, as over 1,500 people died, drowning in the icy, dark and desolate waters. Yet, it was solely due to the *Titanic's* wireless distress signals that 700 people survived. In a British report the next day, Marconi was rightfully praised for making that miracle possible.

Strangely enough, Marconi was scheduled to travel aboard the *Titanic*, but at the last minute rebooked an earlier passage safely aboard the *SS Lusitania*. That ship, too, would later face its own disaster; hence, Marconi escaped death twice.

Marconi's wireless miracle had previously attracted the attention of many other nations. In February of 1904, Russia and Japan broke out into war. Each side purchased Marconi's apparatus. The Japanese equipped their entire naval fleet, while the Russians only outfitted their ground forces, foolishly sparing expenses with their navy. A mere three months later, the Japanese triumphantly defeated the Tsarist's in battle, which in turn gave rise to Russia's Bolshevik Revolution.

By 1909, the impact of Marconi's invention became universally clear, and he was awarded the Nobel Prize for Physics. However, by 1922, Marconi was already predicting further uses of his wireless technologies. He spoke of microwaves, which later developed into a broad array of modern uses, and described how waves, when transmitted and bounced off objects, could be calculated on their return. This became known as radar, and subsequently that spun-off sonar. These two technologies had their first and most profound application in WW II.

Notwithstanding the brilliant leadership of FDR and Churchill, the most important factors in WW II were wireless communications, radar, cryptography, LCVP landing crafts, and aircraft technologies. The engineering feats of R.J. Mitchell's Spitfire, and his pre-war determination to advance his airplane during competition rivalries with German aviators, were likewise critical to England's early survival. Additionally, Marconi's wireless communications, and later radar, became England's most crucial defense mechanisms against Germany's blitzkrieg.

Many scientists contributed to the early developmental process of radio. Akin to other inventions that borrow ideas from others to gradually build and obtain a solution, Marconi's radio was no different. Scientist/inventors, such as Nikola Tesla, Karl Braun, Heinrich Hertz and most importantly, David Hughes, who actually made the first basic wireless transmission years earlier, all made preliminary and crucial developments. Yet Marconi is the one who persisted in the venture, utilized new research, connected the dots, added his own genius, and made it functional on a broad global scale. David Hughes, who probably had the most claims to this new technology, was even interviewed regarding Marconi's world fame, thus he stated, "His efforts at demonstration merit the success he has achieved."

This explains why large British investors maintained a steady interest in Marconi, because he had the ability to provide steady results. Meanwhile, other scientists, like Hughes, could not generate interest and gave up; or men like Tesla, who had a greater brilliance for invention, lost funding due to poor business management or simply being distracted by too many other alluring endeavors. Hence, this is how and why Marconi succeeded while other brilliant minds failed.

Additionally, this clarifies why Marconi's radio transmitting devices became prominent in England, rather than America. Fortunately, England seized Marconi's inventive and industrious skills early on, for without the eventual development of wireless transmissions or radar, England would have suffered far greater losses during Hitler's blitzkriegs and naval assaults. Some analysts even say England would have been annihilated.

Therefore, Marconi was crucial to England's effective use of radio and radar during WW II, and the war effort. Furthermore, this explains why the Americans during the war attempted to discredit Marconi—who at the time lived in Fascist Italy—by rallying behind the newly Americanized citizen and scientist, Nikola Tesla. This conflict erupted into the Marconi vs. Tesla case in 1943, which naturally resulted in the Americans overruling Marconi in favor of Tesla. Interestingly enough, the American government had awarded Marconi the patent for radio decades earlier, overlooking Tesla. Henceforth, the American government blatantly sided with the party whom they would not be required to pay royalties to in their own quest to control radio.

However, while Marconi admitted that his early progress owed much to ideas borrowed from Karl Braun, Tesla, Hertz, and others, his success was a result of personal research, trial and error, inventiveness and his laser-focused determination. This materialized into his successful transmissions across the sea between mainland Ireland or even Wales, to surrounding islands, thus leading to his development of stronger frequency waves, which then led to his famous transatlantic transmission. Marconi was obsessed with finding the solution to make wireless waves travel even farther. The Earth's curvature had many believing that longer wavelengths might be the solution, yet Marconi found the opposite to be true. His quest led to the answer and ability to send wireless waves around the world.

After the Second World War, the Cold War between Russia and the United States had immediately spawned the Space Race. All space communications, including ground-control's wireless remote systems, which guided the space vehicles, were all made possible by Marconi's wireless technology. Moreover, satellite communications, cell phones, GPS, Bluetooths, wireless Internet, microwaves, and all remote control systems all evolved from the one driving force that perfected and then brought wireless to market, Guglielmo Marconi. *(Photo on page 713)*

Along with Marconi's great invention of wireless technology, the world was in a mode of rapid change. From the mid–to–late nineteenth century, engineering and industrial progress were rampant.

In 1896, Henry Ford built his motorized Quadricycle, which led to his forming the Ford Motor Company in 1901. He would forever change our concept of personal transportation, while his brilliant production-line technique would revolutionize the world in the mass production of every product imaginable ever since. In the first decade of the nineteenth century, English engineer William Hedley made early models of steam engines that were later improved upon by fellow Englishman George Stephenson, who built the first useful flanged-wheeled locomotive. Public transportation would likewise be forever changed.

In the 1870s the French attempted to build a canal in Panama, yet failed, as thousands of workers died. President Theodore Roosevelt power managed his way into controlling Panama and bought the French equipment. With his engineer, John Frank Stevens, Roosevelt made sure the immense task would see fruition. Hailed as one of the largest and most difficult engineering projects undertaken, the Panama Canal connected the two largest oceans; eliminating over 8,000 miles of travel for a trip from New York to San Francisco, as compared to traveling around South America's Cape Horn.

In 1889, Gustave Eiffel had completed his landmark iron tower as part of the World's Fair, which not only became a symbol of Paris, and even France, but most importantly of man's ingenuity. The Eiffel Tower was fashioned together with over eighteen thousand metal pieces, and over two million rivets. The tower, which many artists, writers, and architects of the day, including Alexander Dumas, decried was an eyesore and a useless monstrosity, soared over one thousand feet high and held the record for the tallest structure for forty-one years, until New York City's Chrysler Building dethroned it in 1930, immediately followed by the Empire State Building in 1931. The Eiffel Tower was even fitted with an antenna in the early twentieth century for wireless transmissions.

Meanwhile, scientists in Germany were making astounding breakthroughs in a variety of other fields. However, a very unsuspecting individual granted these scientists this ability. The Germans had previously lost World War I and, consequently, in 1919, the Versailles Treaty harshly penalized them for their ruthless aggression. The strict sentence caused economic decline, demoralization and, more importantly, bred contempt. However, this most unassuming individual would sense the pulse of his German people and amass a regime the likes of which the world had never seen and, as time would tell, would ever care to see again.

This is the story of Adolf Hitler, a man who would rise from nothing to the pinnacle of power, only to enact the most diabolical atrocities known to mankind. Where the Dark Ages plummeted mankind into despair while making only minimal to marginal advances, Hitler, in contrast, would push advances in technology to unprecedented heights. The progress being made in Germany during the early twentieth century was astounding by all accounts, however, one man would take a leading role in turning that progress toward destroying nations, hope, and humanity. This darkest chapter in history belongs to Adolf Hitler.

IX
1889 - 1945. HITLER – Poverty, Propaganda, Power and Hatred
The Influences of Art & Music
(Novem, Sagittarius, Naphtali, Judas, September)

Dark ominous clouds loomed over the cobbled streets of Vienna, as an unusually cold and damp April wind howled. Down a grimy brick alleyway in the ghetto district stood the Stumpergasse. Peering out of a cracked and dilapidated window of Flat 29 was the recently-turned orphan, Adolf Hitler. The year was 1908.

It was Adolf's nineteenth birthday and he was sharing an apartment with his friend August Kubizek, nicknamed Gustl. His beloved mother Klara had died a year earlier, yet more was on Adolf's mind. As he gazed out of his window all he could see was the back wall of a grimy brick building. The air reeked of kerosene and his life now seemed to fit the dank domicile that now entrapped him like a prisoner.

Hitler had visions of becoming a great artist, while his friend Gustl had aspirations of being a musician. However, despite Adolf's love for art, the Academy of Fine Arts Vienna rejected him not once but twice, finding him unfit for painting. The verdict was blunt: "Drawing exam unsatisfactory." Adolf was devastated. His bright and glorious future had come to a dead-end. His mother had even supported his decision, yet now all doors to the highest echelon of the art world were closed.

Being a dropout and having no other skills, Adolf had few choices, but would somehow carve out a meager existence. After all, his friend Gustl was right there beside him in the struggle for life.

Evidently, Adolf harbored a greater interest in architecture, which, as we now know, would truly blossom over the next decade. In 1925 he designed a colossal *Arch of Triumph* in honor of the veterans of the Great War. Its projected height was to be 386 feet, almost six times higher than the *Brandenburg Gate*. It was obvious that Adolf harbored a grandiose vision of imperial splendor and immense national pride.

However, while Kubizek was in school, Adolf was left jobless and living off his inheritance. Money was so tight that Adolf made sure he got home at nights before lockdown, as latecomers were charged a small fee. Never telling Kubizek of his second rejection, Hitler abruptly parted ways and eventually began selling watercolor paintings. Oddly enough, Adolf entrusted the sales of his artwork to his Jewish friends, Reinhold Hanisch and Josef Neumann. Despite Kubizek mentioning in his memoires many years later that at this early stage Adolf was anti-Semitic, some historians disagree; citing that there were no venomous outbursts like those in later years. However, that Adolf and Josef Neumann engaged in idle conversations where Neumann proudly claimed that if Jews were to leave Austria the nation would lose all of its money, while Adolf countered, saying, that the money was Austrian not Jewish, hence, they'd have to leave with nothing, certainly indicates a strong predisposition, one that we know would blossom into Hitler's outright expulsion of Jews and far worse. Hence, we must conclude that the seeds were certainly present during his teens, but just didn't sprout stems, *yet*.

However, beyond managing to squeak out a living as a watercolor artist was another passion of Hitler's that actually had a greater impact on his life. Hitler utterly adored music, and most of all, German music. Even here we can see the nationalistic preference, pride, and prejudice that dominated his thinking. And the man that dominated Adolf's very heart and soul was the masterful orchestrator of massive operas...Richard Wagner. *(See page 713)*

Adolf was only a little boy of twelve when he experienced his first opera by Wagner. Actually, the maestro called them music dramas, and rightfully so. Wagner's lush orchestration not only dominated the libretti, which he also wrote, but also the listener. Wagner had learned, and in many cases stolen, this highly advanced and emotionally charged form of music from his friend and father-in-law, Franz Liszt. Wagner even managed to take Liszt's young daughter Cosima as his second wife, being twenty-four years her senior. Wagner was married but impregnated Cosima while she was still married to Hans von Bulow, a talented musician and friend to both Wagner and Liszt. Liszt refused to speak to Wagner for many years because of this tawdry affair. Although Liszt was a womanizer, the handsome Hungarian bachelor seemed to draw the line when it came to hawking a friend's married daughter.

Franz Liszt was a world-renowned pianist who garnered more media attention for his electrifying performances than did royalty on matters of state. Beyond his unrivalled talents at the keyboard, Liszt invented the master class, the piano recital, selflessly offered free lessons, was a prophetic innovator that wrote massive oratorios, unconventional symphonies (the *Faust* and *Dante* being pinnacles of the era), and he invented the symphonic poem. Liszt's new forms of music were so dynamically advanced and emotionally penetrating that they literally tore apart tradition. Like Martin Luther splitting apart Christianity to form his Protestant sect, which later spawned an array of new sects, Franz Liszt split apart traditional classical music with his radical *Music of the Future* faction (the Romantics), which then splintered into new genres, such as Late Romantic, Impressionist and Atonal. More impressive still, Liszt personally pioneered each of these new schools; an accomplishment unrivalled by any composer in all of music history, including the giants, Bach, Mozart, Beethoven, Chopin, Brahms, or Wagner.

Nevertheless, Wagner learned quickly, studying Liszt's musical scores in detail and even silencing his colleagues when they noticed his tactless plagiarisms. The evolution, however, was brilliant, as Wagnerian innovations beautifully complimented and compounded the Lisztian core. Wagner's lush blankets of sound, that enveloped his audience, would make a colossal impact on history, not only music history but political history. For the young Adolf Hitler was consumed, as if by a drug, by Wagner's intoxicating power.

As a teenager, one of Adolf's favorite operas was Wagner's *Rienzi*. Kubizek later documented Hitler's first viewing of the opera, in 1906. He recalled how Hitler was wholly captivated, and admired how it rallied the people's loyalty to support their leader and tribune. Moreover, even Richard Wagner openly praised his operatic hero for being a powerful liberator who, although initially an outcast, rose like a shining star to enlighten and lift his people. This was indeed a powerful message, one that even Wagner could identify with, having been a struggling musician that often fled the authorities due to his seditious political activism.

Nevertheless, Hitler readily identified with the opera's brave leader and eagerly adopted Cola di Rienzi's persona. Many choruses in the opera would prophetically resound with the chant "Heil!" Hence, it was most fitting that when Adolf later rose to be Führer, he adopted the *Rienzi Overture* as the anthem to his Third Reich, not to mention how his followers barked the unnerving chant "Heil, Hitler!"

As the years progressed, Hitler cultivated intense admiration for Wagner's *Götterdämmerung*, which in English translates to *Twilight of the Gods*. It was Wagner's fourth and final opera of his grand Ring cycle, in which the ancient Norse gods are annihilated in an emotionally-charged immolation scene.

These two operas, in particular, paint a dramatic portrait of the young and impressionable Hitler. As a lonely orphan and dropout, stricken by poverty, Hitler was desperate for role models. In hindsight, it becomes clear why Hitler psychologically immersed himself into opera, especially the emotionally charged music dramas of Wagner, which boasted courageous warriors and valiant gods.

Deploring alcohol, loose women, vulgarity, and many other vices, Hitler fervently sought to escape the dismal and degenerate world about him, seeking solace and answers. Hitler's belief in God, however, was brief. He initially claimed to be Christian but later vented—in private— that science would eventually prove all religions false. Hitler was a habitual liar and his beliefs did oscillate; yet he grew to loath religion. However, the most remarkable aspect of his earlier belief in God was how he viewed Jesus.

As Hitler told a friend, "My Christian feeling tells me that my Lord and savior is a warrior. It calls my attention to the man who, lonely and surrounded by only a few supporters, recognized what they [the Jews] were, and called for a battle against them, and who, by God, was not the greatest *sufferer*, but the greatest *warrior*." *(See pg. 706: Jesus as the warrior god Apollo)*

Hitler's view of Christ being a valiant warrior rather than a sufferer is a fascinating and very telling interpretation. His view, when overlapped with Rienzi's courageous persona, is one of a heroic-underdog turned supreme-warrior who bravely confronts adversity, and is *not* the passive lamb so deeply ingrained in Christian philosophy. For Hitler, the meek shall *never* inherit the Earth.

Hitler gravitated to heroic figures, and in Jesus' case, altered his entire persona to fit his own needs, for however long that was necessary. Hitler clearly sought empowerment and these role models endowed him with a profound sense of higher purpose. However, Hitler's obsession with these brave warriors and gods (Roman, Christian or Norse) would eventually convince him that he himself was godlike. Many close acquaintances noted, when Hitler focused on something that he deemed crucial, he became obstinate and abnormally obsessive. But there was more to it than simple obsession, most importantly, Hitler *transformed himself*.

The young Adolf could closely identify with Wagner's powerful leader, Rienzi, and set out to do likewise. In this regard, Hitler did become a powerful leader who rose from obscurity to lead his own people. Hence, Hitler became Rienzi. Equally eerie, and pathetically prophetic, was that after wielding great power and causing destruction, Hitler then emulated Wagner's *Twilight of the Gods*. After Hitler's war machine incinerated much of the earth and millions of people, the self-proclaimed god committed suicide in the infernal ruins of Germany. Hitler had brought Wagner's dramatic immolation scene tragically to life. Hence, life can imitate art.

Hitler's obsession with Wagner motivated him to form ties with the Wagner family. Eventually he met and befriended Winifred Wagner, and established a deep and loving relationship. Winifred had married Siegfried Wagner, Richard Wagner's son, and had four children. When Hitler was in a Munich prison in 1923 for a failed coup d'état, known as the Beer Hall Putsch, Winifred sent him the paper on which to write his famous *Mein Kampf*. The book was published in 1925, and dedicated to his older friend and mentor, Dietrich Eckart. The book clearly demonstrated the political influence that Eckart had on Hitler and his new radically, *uninhibited* mindset. Nevertheless, Adolf and Winifred became ever closer as the years progressed. After Siegfried died, Winifred gained full control of all operations at Bayreuth in 1930. There were rumors after the war that Winifred and the Führer had contemplated marriage, but the Hitler-Wagner blood bond never materialized.

Back in Vienna, at the Stumpergasse, Kubizek and Hitler were only destined to remain roommates for a few months. Spending many hours attending Wagner operas, which they could ill afford, and discussing the master's works, the two aspiring artists parted ways in the latter part of 1908. As noted, Hitler silently left his friend, feeling dejected and bitter.

Thirty-one years later, while Kubizek was still struggling to make a living, his old friend, Adolf, had astonishingly risen to Führer. Kubizek wrote a congratulatory letter to Hitler previously in 1933 for his election to Reich chancellor, but the two never managed to physically connect. Finally, in 1939, Adolf sent a warm invitation to Kubizek to rendezvous in Bayreuth. Kubizek eagerly accepted.

Bayreuth was the city where Wagner built his custom Festspielhaus. After many years of struggling and asking Liszt and other friends to lend him money—which he never paid back, explaining to others that his artistic genius deserved it—Wagner finally managed to secure a devout patron. King Ludwig II was the mentally unstable, homosexual ruler of Bavaria. Ludwig is most noted for having built the beautiful Neuschwanstein Castle, which Walt Disney imitated in his fairy tales and physically emulated at Disneyland. Ludwig loved Wagner's music, and most probably Wagner, and granted the composer his ultimate wish; the ability to construct his own opera house that would not only feature Wagner's new stage design, which cleverly concealed the orchestra pit under the stage, but would also be used exclusively for Wagner's operas. In essence, Wagner had his shrine. Wagner's Festspielhaus would be the Mecca for his adoring fans, and this included Hitler and Kubizek.

The Führer and Kubizek enjoyed a rousing performance; Kubizek elated to be in the shrine of his musical god and sitting next to Germany's ultimate new god. Their reunion was a happy one; Adolf reminisced about the old days in Vienna, and even showed his generous side by not only introducing Kubizek to the Wagner family but even offered to pay for his three children's education. Kubizek was numb with gratitude.

However, in contrast to Hitler's small personal acts of kindness were many other malignant initiatives that were telling signs of the melanomas that would metastasize into a unified, massive stage 4 cancer.

In 1937, villagers in the small Spanish town of Guernica were enjoying market day. As they greeted friends, and bought or bartered goods, they faintly heard an alarming rumble. As the roar got louder and louder the sky suddenly blackened. Gazing up, they saw a fleet of warplanes. To their horror, twenty-five bombers released their loads, as twenty fighter planes swooped down and opened fire. As civilians ran for cover they were mowed down with bullets or blasted with explosives. For three hours the attackers flew in various formations and turned the peaceful town into a bloody graveyard of mauled cadavers and weeping survivors. As the planes veered off, sixteen hundred civilians lay dead in their wake. The village had been turned to rubble.

Hitler's Condor Legion had performed the world's first aerial attack on a civilian target. Led by Wolfram von Richthofen—cousin to the famous WWI ace Manfred von Richthofen, aka The Red Baron *(see pg. 714)*—the mission was a test flight by Luftwaffe commander, Hermann Göring *(see pg. 713)*. Göring had been anxious to test out the effectiveness of his new squadron and the Spanish dictator Francisco Franco happened to provide the live testing-ground, complaining that Guernica harbored resistance fighters. At first Franco and the Germans denied responsibility, but eventually they offered excuses that only military sites were targeted. However, the local railway station, arms factory and bridge were not even touched. It was a premeditated slaughter of unarmed civilians and a precursor to the disasters that would soon befall several continents, as millions would die and many cities would be reduced to rubble.

The massacre at Guernica was so brutal that the Spanish artist, Pablo Picasso, was moved to paint a cubist rendition of both the human horror and technological debauchery at Guernica in order to document this disturbing act of inhumanity. This bloody event aptly offers us a moment where we can reflect upon human actions and technological progress.

Mankind thrives on believing that they are eminently superior to their ancient predecessors. This is ingrained in us by the unavoidable fact that technological progress is an upward progression. Yet we rarely ever stop to analyze the ramifications of progress. We can certainly see the benefits of progress, but does it change humans themselves?

Ancient warriors first learned how to battle with clubs, and then shaped bronze into swords. Soon, it dawned on them, that the power and speed of horses would be more effective in killing, thus they formed the cavalry. Then the brilliant development of engineering allowed warriors to kill more effectively, as crossbows, catapults, muskets and cannons wiped out their foes from a greater distance. Then mankind learned of invisible diseases and they quickly utilized this deadly but unseen weapon to kill their brethren. Colonial American troops issued blankets to the Indians laced with smallpox, being perhaps the first exercise in germ warfare. Eventually, man invented poison gas, and thousands were blinded or choked to death in WW I. Then Hitler used that gas to slaughter six million captives like insects. With the advent of the atomic bomb thousands were vaporized in the blink of an eye, and the quest continues.

Meanwhile, modern mankind still foolishly believes that they are superior to and more civilized than their ancient relatives. We often blind ourselves with the brilliance of new technologies, marveling at how smart and civilized we are, after all, we cured polio and even landed men on the moon. Yet can we compare Hitler's mass slaughters, by the most destructive and inhuman means possible, to the battles of Julius Caesar? Even eliminating the technology, would those ancient chivalrous warriors have even used gas or germs to kill their enemy? One thing is abundantly clear; man does make progress with his mind, but not with his heart. In this regard there is no religion today that can claim that mankind has *innately* improved since the inception of their respective religions. There has never been a holocaust throughout all of history as brutal, wicked and inhuman as that inflicted by Adolf Hitler, a product of our *modern* world.

Hitler's transformation from a puritanical, quasi-tolerant starving artist into an overtly obsessive pro German, anti-Semitic, ruthless dictator, who slaughtered innocent people en masse, is one the most baffling yet intriguing mysteries in human history.

To better understand this transformation it's important to journey back to Hitler's early childhood development, for it speaks volumes of his later actions. Contrary to popular Freudian belief, Adolf had a natural, loving relationship with his mother, Klara. However, he did have issues with his oppressive father, who was prone to intoxication and its darker backlashes. Maintaining only a small group of close friends, the introverted Adolf was a keen observer but, interestingly enough, lacked the will to intervene. It was said that only among friends would Adolf become animated, and then engage in lengthy monologues. These sessions would groom Hitler's public-speaking skills so that by the time he made his rousing speeches in beer halls, he quickly attracted a strong following.

Hitler's charisma was infectious and eventually grew to the point of idolatry, as even men of greater stature bowed to his unrivalled ability to ignite an audience. Hermann Göring, who was a national war hero, said his heart dropped into his trousers whenever he met the Führer. Likewise, Joseph Goebbels recorded his outright love for Hitler in his diary, while the highly unstable Heinrich Himmler stated, "Believe me, if Hitler were to say I should shoot my mother, I would do it and be proud of his confidence." Moreover, as time would tell, soulless and mindless jerks like Adolf Eichmann would obediently and eagerly cart millions of people like cattle to be exterminated all for his beloved Führer. This was far from mere politics; rather it was a deep and dark cult that was built upon the ideologies of superiority, hatred, and revenge. However, this pathogenic weed would fully blossom many years later. As for the young Adolf, he had begun to bud in the bogs of poverty-stricken Germany, a condition that was largely due to the harsh reprimands of World War I.

Hitler had become parentless by the age of nineteen, and moved to Vienna. It was these years that later proved most influential. The Viennese press was infected with partisan rags that spewed flagrant and noxious slander. As an orphan who had mediocre grades, dropped out of school, and was socially apathetic, Hitler was relegated to a world of self-education. Unfortunately for the young and impressionable Adolf, most of what he read was Vienna's toxic rags. Freedom of speech had an ugly bite.

Likewise, many German minds became saturated with thoughts of racial superiority and vile hatred, and not only for the Jews, but equally for the Slavs, as well. The noxious rhetoric of these articles used terms like rats, infestations, crooked-nosed Jews, and other racial slanders that further advocated firm action to rid their nation of this growing pestilence. They vehemently disapproved of how the Jews infiltrated the arts and publishing industry to disseminate their modernist views. Meanwhile, the majority of impoverished Germans seethed in silence. This deeply agitated Hitler, who saw a dire need to counter this degenerative malaise, which immobilized his people. However, without a strong leader to fend for their rights, the Germans, for the time being, remained hopeless.

The Austro-Hungarian Empire was a hotbed of multi-national factions living precariously together. The Hapsburg monarch, Emperor Franz Josef, found it difficult trying to keep this powder keg from exploding. The vast differences in education and religion, and the high incidence of illiteracy among these impoverished groups helped fuel the propaganda of a superior German race. They harbored deep resentment against the Poles and the various Slavs who infiltrated their country. In most cases, the Czech population managed to assimilate, however, many Jews lived in segregated communities, such as Leopoldstadt. Moreover, while many of the previously settled Jews assimilated, at least in business activities but not in marriage, the new wave of Jewish immigrants remained orthodox, or became Zionists.

An additional factor was the effect that Rabbi Israel ben Eliezer had on Poland during the 1700s. Eliezer had started a new branch of Judaism, called the Hasidics, and by the time of Hitler's day, this sect grew and eventually spread into the Ukraine, Lithuania, Hungary, and beyond. Their fervent isolationism and alien lifestyle was in stark contrast to any community they settled in, and over time, the Hasidics, as well as the Zionists and orthodox Jews all became blaring targets.

Years later, Hitler made a point of this in his book *Mein Kampf*, by stating, "The cleanliness of this people, moral and otherwise, I must say, is a point in itself. By their very exterior you could tell that these were no lovers of water, and, to your distress, you often knew it with your eyes closed. Later I often grew sick to my stomach from the smell of these caftan-wearers. Added to this, there was their unclean dress and their generally unheroic appearance."

But the rise of the Jewish population was characterized by yet another element, a shift in status. The Jews were education-oriented and made swift progress in the new industrial world, while the incumbent aristocrats became passive spectators. With a strong focus on individual trades, especially lawyers, doctors or business owners, the Jews rose in affluence. Their ornate lodgings and liberally progressive cultural events, that glorified anything modern, quickly supplanted the static and traditional Austro-Hungarians. The thriving and modern metropolis was now booming with Jews who had adopted German traits, language, and culture, and flaunted it as their own.

Their beloved Jewish maestro, Gustav Mahler, who converted to Christianity to secure the directorship, was one of the blatant eyesores that the humiliated Germans wanted to see purged. Mahler had dominated Vienna, and rightfully so, as even Hitler admired his unrivalled abilities to make Wagner's music soar. However, nepotism prevailed, and the concert halls, both in the orchestra pit and in the audience, slowly filled with Jews. Hitler angrily vented at how Bruno Walter and other conductors and musicians were of mediocre talent, yet they not only rose to the top of the Playbill but were also lauded in the Jewish press as *the greatest*, thus grooming the German public to believe in and embrace second-rate performers. Moreover, they even attempted to supplant the adored works of Beethoven and Wagner with Mahler and Mendelssohn. They didn't mind the masterworks of foreigners, such as Puccini's *Tosca* or Verdi's *Aida*, but when Mahler attempted to premiere his oversized Romantic symphonies, featuring cowbells and other odd instruments, their patience faded, as would the performances of Mahler's personal works in due time, despite being masterworks by today's standards. Nevertheless, as the Germans gained more influence, Gustav Mahler was pressured to resign.

As Hitler matured, he became increasingly curious as to how the Viennese government operated. Upon viewing parliamentary proceedings, Hitler was appalled by the chaos, as multiethnic factions clamored to be heard. To Hitler, these riotous discourses appeared like a Tower of Babel. However, disorderly outbursts by a variety of people with alien languages were only part of the problem. In an effort to pacify the vocal minorities, the government granted them more concessions. This reverse discrimination infuriated the majority, which was now left powerless. This irritation permeated the large Germanic constituency even further, and gave rise to the false impression that democracy itself was flawed. To the young Hitler, that was more than enough proof that another system of government was necessary, one that would not cower to the minority.

Despite all the anti-Semitic press that Hitler ingested in Vienna, many of his closest friends were Jews. As a starving artist whose main advocates for selling his watercolors were Jewish entrepreneurs, Hitler had nothing but good experiences. As noted earlier, there were really no *outward* actions to indicate that Hitler was anti-Semitic during his Vienna years. However, the idol-worshiping Adolf had read Richard Wagner's racist book "Judaism in Music", and knew of Martin Luther's religious treatise "On the Jews and their Lies", hence he certainly was ingesting a good deal of venomous food for toxic thought.

However, it was during his stay in the military between 1914 and 1920, when Adolf began to express his real distaste for the Jewish liberals who would eventually take over Germany. For, as he noxiously said, he preferred to see these Jews at the war's front, being exposed to poison mustard gas. However, this was recorded several years later in *Mein Kampf*, when his hatred was well underway. Nevertheless, those sentiments do reflect how and when the toxic seed began to grow, and quite unnervingly with the prophetic allusion of poison gas.

Mustard gas was the new, terrifying weapon during World War I, and in that vein, it is understandable why Adolf would later use gas for his Final Solution. The fact that the teenaged Bavarian Reserve Gefrieter (Private) had been at the front and witnessed this chemical toxin, and was even temporarily blinded and hospitalized for mustard gas himself, makes Adolf's later decision a little more clear. Although Hitler never utilized poison gas during his own Nazi war campaigns, for Hitler oddly had an old world view of bravery and honor on the battlefield, the irritating pain and memory of the deadly gas might have seemed an appropriate solution for a race that he viewed as parasites.

Anyhow, the teenaged Adolf had left Vienna humiliated, and settled in Munich, where he became politically obsessed. After being discharged from the army, Hitler had lost his only sense of belonging, for he had won several Iron Crosses for bravery. And despite not achieving a high rank in the military, he now faced unemployment in a country that was poverty-stricken. After the First World War, Hitler, along with the vast majority of Germans—including his future Reichsmarschall, Hermann Göring, who even commanded the Red Baron's Flying Circus after the hero's death—all took major blows to their national pride and self esteem. They were dishonored by their leader's unexpected surrender, and profoundly angered by the armistice drawn up by the international treaty at Versailles, which even excluded the Germans from the table.

Field Marshal Hindenburg had been Germany's most popular military champion, but was merely a figurehead, for General Erich Ludendorff was the genuine brains and operations maven. Ludendorff had secured substantial victories that brought the prospect of a complete victory within arm's reach; however, the extremely high number of casualties (which they kept secret) drained the small country of soldiers. Regardless, Ludendorff falsely kept up his countrymen's morale so that while they all expected news of a victory, the bombshell of surrender came as a devastating blow. Adding insult to injury, their illustrious hero, Erich Ludendorff, likewise abandoned his countrymen, as he sheepishly fled to Sweden, wearing a disguise. The Kaiser likewise fled, he to Holland. The memories recorded by Hitler in *Mein Kampf* expressed the utmost rage over this debacle, yet also the utmost determination to never allow Germany to witness such a humiliating defeat again. However, the young Hitler's country was now broken and further humiliated by a painfully unfair treaty.

The prevailing German government, which had been run by the Hohenzollerns, along with all the other royal houses that ruled over Bavaria and other German states, were all, in a random moment, terminated by Philipp Scheidemann. Scheidemann was a socialist who knew other factions were plotting to announce a new regime for their country, so he rushed to the Reichstag Library and mounted its balcony. Addressing a huge audience, Scheidemann proclaimed that the monarchy was dead, and that the new German Republic was born. In an odd and impulsive instant, a few words vaporized a thousand years of German and Austrian rule.

The new German Republic brought with it many Jewish Social Democrats who, in short time, consumed many political, legal, economic, and cultural positions. Thus, the Germans not only lost the war, but now their country as well. Adding further to the Germans' humiliation was another dynamic occurring simultaneously. When the Bolsheviks toppled the czar during the Russian revolution of 1917, it caused many Jewish refugees to migrate to eastern Europe. This fear of Jewish domination plagued the minds of most Germans. Henceforth, the anti-Semitic press, which for decades groomed popular opinion, now felt justified in amplifying their harsh and brutal accusations. This paranoia helped galvanize German nationalism, as they now felt the imminent threat of a Jewish invasion or revolution.

Although Hitler felt abandoned, since he had lost the only family he had in the army, and was distressingly unemployed, the able and cunning youth now saw his chance to enter politics and make his mark. Hitler realized that the majority of Germans were now actively engaged in an anti-Semitic craze, and this gave him pause to reevaluate, not only his thinking, but his entire life. Previously, Hitler had only good experiences with Jews as a young artist, but the times had changed. The Jews had infiltrated and now dominated almost every aspect of German life. In writing his autobiography, *Mein Kampf,* Hitler tactfully constructed a new unbridled persona, and thus emerged as a staunch anti-Semite.

Among the pages of the heavily biased *Mein Kampf,* Hitler did espouse some lucid political and social arguments, yet the influence of others on Hitler's words, including his cellmate, Rudolf Hess, would later reveal themselves. Still, some of Hitler's so-called authentic claims would later prove to be the ravings of a charlatan. For once Hitler became the Führer, he claimed to have struggled as a hard laborer working in construction. Yet, he never revealed actual details or names, only vague scenarios. Years later, no record or eyewitnesses ever emerged to validate his fallacious employment.

However, the prevalent notion that Hitler swayed the German people into becoming violently anti-Semitic is a misnomer. The Germans were already ripe with hatred, for they were deeply rooted with humiliation and fertilized by anti-Semitic writings which, like manure, sullied their newspapers and rancid books.

Equally noteworthy, is how this hatred dates back to the sixteenth century. Martin Luther launched his Reformation for valid reasons, yet his own shortcomings were forcefully preached, documented, and even ingested by his German flock. Luther's hateful words rang loud and clear and could not be easily forgotten, "Know, my dear Christians, and do not doubt that next to the devil you have no enemy more cruel, more venomous and virulent, than a true Jew."

Like the Germans of the early twentieth century, Luther had also witnessed changes that incited contempt in both him and his ilk. The notoriously wealthy Jews who were tax collectors for the Roman Catholic popes deeply incensed Luther, yet Christianity itself also provided him with fertilizer. Had not the Christian sect become fierce rivals with their former Judaic brethren right from Jesus' conflict and death forward? Then again, even the pagans constantly butted heads with the Jews, causing some to become irate. The famous Roman historian Tacitus venomously railed, "The Jews are the abomination of the human race. Everything that to us is sacrosanct is contemptible to them, while they are permitted to do anything that is an outrage to us. They are the lowest of all peoples."

Therefore, Martin Luther was not alone in his hatred, but he certainly was an outspoken and prominent voice throughout Germany, even if other Christians did not harbor or vent this hatred. Therefore, Luther's blunt remarks were perhaps the clear starting point, or virulent seed, of anti-Semitism in Germany. This is not to say that Luther's vile seed suddenly mushroomed into the full-blown cancer that would arise under Hitler, but four centuries of hatred, condoned and ingrained by their spiritual leader, did influence many Germans. This would also include those who abandoned the religion, yet held onto the hatred.

Even a moment in ancient Jewish history lent itself to being a lesson that Hitler and the Nazis would vow not to repeat. Long before Moses, when Jacob and his son Joseph lived during the reign of a peaceful pharaoh, who was very much like the liberal Austrian leader, Franz Josef, he allowed the Jews to settle and build in the land of Goshen. This territory soon gained power and influence that infringed upon and stole Egyptian culture, so much so that when a new pharaoh came into power, he enslaved the Jews. Could Hitler have seen himself as this new pharaoh who would corral and enslave the Jews that stole German culture?

However, the dark lesson continues. Moses would later emancipate those Jewish slaves, and likewise destroy the Egyptian army. If Hitler and his demonic crew were aware of this Biblical tale, then certainly they would have learned that merely enslaving the Jews was ineffective, hence only extermination would provide a Final Solution.

Naturally this is only one scenario drawn from history that may have been read and analyzed by any one of Hitler's henchmen; however, many documented seeds of mental corruption and anti-Semitism abound, including the effects of Napoleon Bonaparte's failed military campaign.

Napoleon seized upon the realization that assisting the Jews became beneficial to winning his battles. As thousands of Jews rallied behind the emancipation afforded them by Napoleon's victories, the strategic leader used their support, along with espionage, to topple the entrenched leaders of the opposition. After Napoleon's demise, this association tagged the Jews as scapegoats, making them look like revolutionaries and terrorist threats to the establishment. However, in reality, the Jews did not initiate the violence; Napoleon was the expansionist aggressor, hence, being caught in the middle, the Jews opted to aid Napoleon's efforts. Once more, engaging war for the purpose of conquest was not the modus operandi of the Jews; theirs was one of educational, social, capitalistic and political elevation that eventually offered them sizable degrees of control within their host country. Hence, being one of infiltration, not annihilation. So, many Germans wrongfully tagged the Jews as being Marxist militants.

Although Karl Marx's mother was a Jew, and his father only converted to Christianity just months before his son's birth, Karl wanted nothing to do with Judaism or Christianity. To Marx, both religions seemed like shackles to mankind. His cry was for the large and downtrodden working class, which extended across national and religious lines. Yet his being tagged a Jew carried much weight upon the Germans' minds who feared these Jewish radicals were serious militant threats. Henceforth, it became quite easy for the German newspapers in the 1900s to reek with intense hatred against these rebellious Jews.

Hitler easily adopted the hatred in these newspapers, and like all his other bad sources of influence, Hitler learned to excel at whatever he needed to believe in to reach his political goals. This hatred played well into Hitler's early political career, which began with the aid of Ernst Röhm, the battle-scarred veteran who took Hitler under his wing. Röhm facilitated the introductions and financing of Hitler's German Workers'

Party. By making public speeches, mainly in beer halls and small auditoriums, Hitler's gift for oration quickly became evident; as such, his small party grew rapidly, even changing its name to the National Socialist Party and, ultimately, the abbreviated Nazi Party. Hermann Göring, upon first sizing up the party, astutely commented, "Even its anti-Semitism served a purpose – it won over those who needed something more elemental than a political error as a focus for their emotions."

Göring quickly joined the party, and even admitted later that he did so, not so much for the party's political ideology, which he had little interest in, but because Hitler showed guts. It took guts to denounce the Versailles Treaty, the liberal pacifists who stole their country and, most importantly, Göring admired his pledge to use militant action to regain honor for Germany. Göring, the WWI ace and recently discharged captain, quickly noticed that the majority of Hitler's followers were all non-entities, without any pedigree, intelligence, or social influence. They were the dispossessed, the downtrodden, and even the drunkards. Only Ernst Röhm had an impressive background, and only Röhm posed a threat to Göring's own aspirations of becoming the president of the new Reich. It is interesting to note that Hitler at this moment (having never achieved above the rank of corporal) envisioned the famous war hero as possibly being Germany's new leader. Still lacking complete confidence, Hitler viewed himself as the leading spokesman for the new and monumental Third Reich, but the fledgling party still awaited its glorious and demanding leader. Hence, to Hitler and many in his sordid party, Göring looked like a gift from the gods.

However, a year after Göring's induction as commander of the *Sturmabteilung*, or Storm Section, Hitler was becoming more confident and convinced of his own abilities to become the movement's leader. This was predicated on the visible fact that his rallying spirit is what significantly increased the size of his Nazi Party. Additionally, the growing adulation he received was already showing signs of cult worship. However, also quite significant was the addition of Ernst 'Putzi' Hanfstaengl. Putzi's wealth and connections to high society strengthened Hitler's image, for this finally made the Nazi Party more than just a band of working-class ruffians.

Hanfstaengl's parents were world-class art dealers who sent their son to Harvard to cultivate a cosmopolitan air to add to his business degree. However, Putzi's true love was music. Although he officially became Hitler's foreign press secretary, a role he showed considerable ability in, Putzi became better known as Hitler's personal piano player. Ripping through Wagnerian opera transcriptions like Hitler's old friend Kubizek once had, Putzi's percussive beat often aroused Hitler, so much so that others in the inner circle would try to distract their leader from engaging in these intimate recitals, for they didn't want Putzi gaining an edge. However, as this lionizing Nazi mob became an occult, Hitler became proudly aware that he was to be the Cola di Rienzi who would lead Germany to ultimate glory.

Hitler's Nazi Party attracted new members, such as Himmler *(see page 714)*, Goebbels, and others, who also played a vital role in influencing Hitler, and escalating the intensity of their ruthless and racist regime. Hitler's small handful of devious disciples all vied against one another to gain his favor and, more importantly, the tantalizing title of successor. Hitler, likewise, played into their cutthroat desires for power by pitting them against each other, probably as a sadistic exercise to keep his omnipotent control honed, but most certainly to thwart secret unions that could result in a coup. As such, to gain favor with Hitler often resulted in extreme deeds, which included sheer brutality. This toxic breeding ground sadly escalated their diabolical schemes to unimaginable heights.

In addition to these acts of rivalry, Hitler's henchmen each brought their own personal visions and baggage to the new regime. Although most hated the Jews, Goebbels enacted the first physical attack on the Jews by ordering his men to smash windows on Jewish businesses and beat up anyone who looked Jewish. Meanwhile, Himmler was obsessed with the contrived Aryan race and its odd history, which claimed that 2000 years BC, the imperial Indian caste system included the Kshatriya warriors who overthrew the old regime for the Aryans. This model of an elite rebel force prompted Himmler to turn Hitler's bodyguards into the ruthless SS, with the similar intent of overthrowing their socialist government. Himmler handpicked his troopers, rejecting anyone looking remotely foreign, and shaped them into a special praetorian force that would wield great power in the years ahead. This entity was the sole brainchild of Himmler, and was never something envisioned by Hitler. However, as Germany's supreme ruler, held accountable for the Nazi's sins, the ultimate scar of diabolical sin and disgrace can never be erased from Hitler's name for, like Satan among his fallen angels, Hitler fanned the flames of the Third Reich.

Nevertheless, Hitler's satanical Nazi occult did have many other hands in the virulent vat, each adding their own toxin to the evil stew. Before and during Hitler's Third Reich, authors and philosophers in Germany sought all sources, proven or not, to confirm their fabricated beliefs. Keywords appeared frequently, as the term *degenerate* became increasingly synonymous with the Jews. Adopting Darwin's use of the term, regarding certain animals that in lieu of establishing their own food began living off the efforts of others, they now saw the Jews as parasites or sub-creatures, living off German culture.

Darwin's theories were recklessly misappropriated, eventually forming Social Darwinism. This led to the notion of being able to breed a superior superhuman race, which was mildly advocated by Friedrich Nietzsche but, far more caustically, by Houston Stewart Chamberlain. Chamberlain was born in England, lived in France, then met and married Richard Wagner's daughter, Eva, whereby settling in Bayreuth.

Naturally, Hitler met with and discussed these theories with Chamberlain when visiting the Wagners. Chamberlain's theories on race were widely published by his colleagues in Vienna. He advocated selective breeding, and abandoning the inferior to procure a master race. Additionally, he asserted that Jews could never assimilate or be converted to a superior race.

Social Darwinism spurred numerous half-witted philosophers to conjure up twisted theories of racial development and superiority, such as the illogical tale of the Aryan race, supported by the "World Ice Theory". This tale professed that the Aryans emerged from an ancient, yet mystical, civilization in the icy northern regions of the globe. This also helped to explain the traditional influence of Norse gods and myths found in German culture. But in time, these Aryans allegedly ventured south to germinate and cultivate Egypt, Greece, and all other highly advanced ancient civilizations, thus explaining the reason for their greatness. Yet quite inexplicably, these Aryans somehow mysteriously vanished within those cultures. However, the miraculous end result was that nature and God chose this semi-divine breed to be the master race.

Hence, the Aryan nation's ancestral saga, in some ways akin to the Romans' *Aeneid,* was born. There were now historical and divine justifications for the Germans' rise to power. However, unlike the early Romans who embraced foreign races, Aryan Germans thought themselves superior to all others, and even the elimination of all inferior races was acceptable to preserve their supreme bloodline. Furthermore, purity would be maintained by the eugenic breeding plan of Ernst Rüdin. The plan entered Nazi law in 1933, whereby they eventually sterilized 70,000 "defective" people, and killed over 200,000 people with disabilities to ensure only genetically perfect offspring. Astonishingly, these absurd theories and inhuman practices spurred the demoralized Germans into believing that they were invincible and that their shining destiny was upon them. Alas, desperation devoured logic and morals, while motivation, of any kind, was better than demoralization.

Additionally, Guido von List, whom Hitler and most Germans admired, had prophesized that a new and infallible leader would emerge in Germany. This partially explains Hitler's intense and, at times, violent reaction to rebuttals, as his need to appear infallible was crucial to fulfilling this prophecy. In addition to Guido von List, many others influenced the German people and Hitler, such as: Georg von Schönerer, who was a political leader of the Pan-Germans who wielded great influence; Wolf, who was a pioneer in preaching of a dominant German folkdom that the Führer naturally admired; Karl Lueger, being Vienna's famous tribune who knew how to rally a crowd, and also resurrected the ancient Christians' anti-Semitism by calling the Jews Christ killers, and claiming they were turning Vienna into another Palestine; Hans Hörbiger, who put forth his Aryan "World Ice Theory" as an ancient master race; Weininger, the traitorous Jew who turned radically pro-German, then committed suicide; Lanz von Liebenfels, who changed his name to conceal his partially Jewish ancestry, then founded the Christian *Order of the New Templars* and pushed for pure-breeding colonies; Hans Goldzier, who emphasized that stronger races were superior while weaker ones were parasites, and the incredibly insane list went on.

Quite strikingly, Hitler, himself, best summed up the German's propaganda of being a superior ancient culture, when he questioned Himmler's ironic archeological find: "Why do we call the whole world's attention to the fact that we have no past? It isn't enough that the Romans were erecting great buildings when our forefathers were still living in mud huts; now Himmler is starting to dig up these villages of mud huts... All we prove by that is that we were still throwing stone hatchets and crouching around open fires when Greece and Rome had already reached the highest stage of culture. We really should do our best to keep quiet about this past. Instead, Himmler is making a great fuss about it all. The present-day Romans must be having a laugh at these revelations."

However, as we have seen, Hitler had also deceived himself in many ways. In Hitler's unpublished *Second Book*, which is the sequel to *Mein Kampf*, he clearly reveals his paranoiac fear of an international collusion against Germany. Granted, the Treaty of Versailles planted seeds of humiliation, but Hitler's outlook became narrowed to the point of self-interest for Germany and Germany alone.

Hitler believed all other nations were not only unworthy, but also inferior. Additionally, he clearly mentions how alliances are solely for national self-interest. This explains why he broke his word with Neville Chamberlain and Stalin, among others. However, Hitler's narrow-sighted view of German nationalism was even further funneled down to the ludicrous notion of Aryan racism. Aryanism was likewise based upon the fear of being dominated or, worse yet, becoming extinct, and fear devours logic and benevolence. As Roosevelt aptly said, "The only thing we have to fear is fear itself."

It was this fear and lack of international goodwill that caused Hitler to miscalculate America's relationship with England. Hitler perceived America's formidable navy to be a threat to England; he presumed Britain would rise against America in fear. Hitler clearly failed to realize the inherent bond that the two nations shared for democracy and freedom which, in essence, are founded upon benevolent principles. This proved to be just one of Hitler's many blunders. Interestingly enough, all tyrants seem doomed to run the same course. Furthermore, dictatorships only have a select few in high offices who pull all the evil strings. Therefore, when the Clock of Fate tolls…in horror they all find themselves at the end of those bloody strings, like Mussolini and his bloody hoods, or Saddam Hussein. Hitler, like Hussein, would likewise be hunted to the point of being trapped like a rat in a bunker, yet Hitler defiantly took his own life.

Still, to most people, it defies logic how a nation that was rapidly advancing in so many fields, and easily surpassed their rivals in so many instances, should falter, and at such a horrific magnitude, no less. This illustrates the power of mental conditioning and propaganda, especially upon a downtrodden people whose hopes and morals are exhausted. These factors can clearly rally a nation into committing unthinkable deeds, especially to obtain what they believed was salvation.

So it was that Germany appealed to the people's primal instincts, rather than logic or a moral code. The list of offenders is large, as we have seen, for it includes many writers of the Viennese press, countless half-witted German authors and philosophers and, naturally, Hitler and his many cohorts of the Third Reich, who politically embraced and enforced this fanatical hatred to make it manifest. They all played a vital role in systematically germinating and reviving the Teutonic barbarian, unfortunately to the world's chagrin.

As we have seen, Hitler did not act alone, for many in his inner circle were mentally corrupt and morally bankrupt, but so, too, was the brutal Soviet, Josef Stalin. The untold atrocities that Stalin committed against his own people dwarf Hitler's in number, yet the high profile of Hitler and his Nazi regime's premeditated and diabolical procedures to exterminate people, as if inanimate waste, defies all human sensibilities. Hence, Hitler remains burnt into our minds as the ultimate in evil. Nevertheless, evil of such a magnitude shall never be permitted to proceed indefinitely, so long as strong-minded and righteous individuals have the courage to stand up, and aggressively confront such demons. This leads us to the valiant men who faced down this evil, and with miraculous resolve, they prevailed.

X
1933 – 1945. ROOSEVELT & CHURCHILL
SAVIORS OF WESTERN CIVILIZATION
(Decem, Capricornus, Reuben, Matthew, October)

Blazing through the wind in his shiny blue Ford convertible, Franklin's polio-ridden body showed no sign of burden as he deftly manipulated the custom hand levers. Above all things, Franklin loved driving and swimming, as it was only during these times that his crippling paralysis, which robbed him of the use of his legs, seemed to vanish. Only then could Franklin regain the full vigor of his youth. Dashing to Hackensack airport, not far from his home in Hyde Park, New York, the president rapidly approached the crudely constructed airfield. It was Friday, June 19, 1942.

With the landed airplane now in sight, Franklin cut the wheel and fishtailed onto the airstrip's dirt runway. Squeezing the accelerator lever with his hand, the Ford's whirling Firestones churned up huge billows of dust, forming a long amber wake. With his hair flapping in the breeze, Franklin rumbled up to the small plane and came to a sliding stop. As the dust cloud passed by his head and over the front hood, Franklin could see the plane's tiny passenger hatch fling open.

Franklin's fingertips anxiously tapped the steering wheel as he awaited his guest. The plane's air-cooled engine cut back to an idle and the small prop gradually whooshed to a stop. It was then that Franklin could vaguely see a stout figure slowly emerging from the fuselage's threshold.

Impulsively, Franklin's arm energetically shot upward and sturdily waved, as he greeted his friend, Winston Churchill. The stocky prime minister looked over and cracked a nervous grin, as he irritably pushed his way past the pilot. The tiny plane was not Churchill's cup of tea. After eagerly exiting the plane, Winston walked towards Franklin and bellowed, "That was the roughest bump landing I have experienced!"

As Churchill swung open the car door his eyes jolted, having caught a glimpse of the customized control levers. Immediately, they darted back up at Franklin, who probably said, "Don't worry; you're in good hands!"

It's not hard to imagine Winston replying, "Y-y-yes, ol' chap, I can see. Good hands, indeed! But how in blazes can this bloody thing move without foot pedals?"

In fact, Winston later confided that he had said a silent prayer: "I hoped the mechanical devices and brakes would show no signs of defects."

Nevertheless, Winston nervously hopped in and shut the door. Franklin squeezed the accelerator lever, and the two leaders took off. As Roosevelt raced along the perilous cliffs of the Hudson, Winston was further unnerved. However, the prime minister's concern for veering off a cliff was soon replaced by a greater concern once the president relayed his fretful, new military proposition.

Here again, it's not hard to envision Franklin positing his serious war strategy while his long, trademark cigarette holder flapped with each syllable. Roosevelt told the prime minister that he had intentions of staging a massive assault against Hitler in September. Churchill listened carefully, and then offered his rebuttal, a rebuttal built upon the British Empire's long battle against Germany. It was a rough mixture of painful experience and English pride. The latter for having been the key defender of freedom until America finally joined the fray.

Although their discussions in this car ride were not fully disclosed, a letter by Churchill to his young American ally revealed the intense topics. Moreover, it revealed their intense differences in strategies and innate perspectives. Churchill's letter was laden with grim, paternal gravity:

"No responsible British military authority has so far been able to make a plan for September 1942 which had any chance of success unless the Germans become utterly demoralized, of which there is no likelihood."

Although Churchill was the rock of England—the optimistic public powerhouse who told his people failure was *not* an option—his personal statement reflects a stark and even dark reality that had been kept secret, not only at that time but more so after the victory of war.

This is not to infer that Churchill's statement revealed that he was defeatist by nature—he most certain was not. However, at this point in the war, he and his entire military command had faced a grim reality. The German war machine, with its superior generals and superior armaments, was irrefutably *superior*. And Churchill's letter clearly states this grim fact.

In stark contrast, during their car ride, Franklin had firmly expressed that it was imperative to move boldly and decisively with an aggressive assault to penetrate Germany. It was just a matter of firming up a plan by logically weighing all the options, and any possible reprisals, so the Allies could knock the wind out of Germany's massive sails.

The following is a brief scenario that I envision of these two great leaders discussing this topic.

With his cigarette holder clenched in his teeth, Franklin says, "Winston, defensive maneuvers will *not* bring about victory. We Americans believe in establishing aggressive goals, and achieving them at all costs."

Winston blinks as the peppery smoke of his cigar rises into his eyes. Taking another puff, he replies, "Franklin, ol' boy, we Britons are most comfortable with improvisation. The battlefield is like a raging sea; you never know when a gale will snap a mast, or a wave will roll a ship. I guess you can say we Brits like to roll with the punches."

"Well, Winston, we Americans like to *throw* the punches!"

Both men were diehard optimists, however, Churchill and his staff had faced the utter humiliation of perpetual defeats that put them on a defensive war footing, and that was completely alien to Roosevelt.

This brings us back to their famous little car ride, as Franklin blazed over the tree-lined roads in rural Hyde Park, New York. Their chat was so intense that Churchill would later say: "We made more progress than we might have done in formal conference."

Driving up the pebbled driveway of the Roosevelt estate, which picturesquely overlooked the Hudson River, Franklin and Winston were greeted by Harry Hopkins.

Hopkins was Franklin's personal envoy who was sent to London several years prior to secretly assess Churchill. It was Hopkins who relayed to Roosevelt that, despite popular rumor (especially put forth by Joseph Kennedy), Churchill was not a rhetorical drunkard, but in fact, the firm and lucid spirit of England itself. Over the ensuing years, Hopkins and the two world leaders became comfortable friends.

Hopkins, as usual, was waiting with a wheelchair. Franklin swung open the door, and slithered his body into the chair. Grasping the chair's large front wheels, Franklin pushed himself forward with an affable smile, and entered the house. Winston was overcome with admiration; Franklin's indomitable inner strength and outward buoyancy was as poignant as it was inspiring. With a mindful nod, Winston looked at Harry and followed.

Excitedly, Franklin wheeled himself over to a glass showcase and turned, showing Winston his prized stamp collection. Amicably, Winston listened, while Franklin expounded upon his philatelic passion since childhood. Afterwards, they all enjoyed a cordial dinner in the Green Room.

Franklin then retreated to his study, as his two guests followed close behind. As they entered the small and dimly lit room, Franklin quickly swiveled about in his wheelchair. The dimly lit room appropriately suited the dim subject that would soon commence.

Franklin told Winston that earlier in October of 1939, an advisor of his, Alexander Sachs, handed him a letter from the famed Nobel Prize winner, Albert Einstein. Einstein's letter began with a miraculous revelation:

"Some recent work by E. Fermi and L. Szilard, which has been communicated to me in manuscript, leads me to expect that the element uranium may be turned into a new and important source of energy in the immediate future."

Then came the explosive bang: *"This new phenomenon would also lead to the construction of bombs, and it is conceivable - though much less certain - that extremely powerful bombs of a new type may thus be constructed. A single bomb of this type, carried by boat and exploded in a port, might very well destroy the whole port together with some of the surrounding territory."*

We can see Winston pulling his smoldering cigar away from his moistened lips as he extrapolated on the burning destruction of this new uranium bomb. Not to mention the burning need to beat Hitler in this deadly race to unleash the destructive powers of Hell. It was, indeed, a dark moment that was aptly discussed in a dark room, for the two great leaders were plotting to open Pandora's box.

Churchill informed Roosevelt that they had already begun a plutonium bomb project, code-named "Tube Alloys". Two Jewish scientists, Otto Robert Frisch and Rudolf Peierls, had earlier fled Germany in 1933 upon hearing of Hitler's rise to power. In 1940, Frisch and Peierls jointly posited the basic theory of how to construct an atomic bomb, despite their gross miscalculations that called for tons of uranium.

This discussion proved to be the catalyst for Roosevelt; he had already established a small research team after receiving Einstein's letter in 1939, and Churchill's revelation solidified its importance. It was now evident that this theoretical nightmare would certainly become a reality. It was just a matter of time, and which team crossed the finish line first; a grand prize that would exceed just winning the atomic race, for it would very likely dictate the war's victor and the world's ultimate superpower.

It was at this moment that the generously funded Manhattan Project was born. Being a military operation, General Leslie Groves would be appointed as the project's director with Robert Oppenheimer as scientific director. With the Italian born scientist Enrico Fermi being hailed by Einstein and others as America's leading expert, Roosevelt was compelled to loosen up U.S. restrictions on Italian immigrants just to secure his employ. In short time, the Manhattan Project would mushroom in size, just like its nuclear end product, costing over $2 billion in funding and employing over 130,000 workers.

Meanwhile, back at Franklin's house, the two leaders agreed to share information. This would expedite progress and hopefully beat the deadly clock that was ticking ever faster toward a new hour when only one nation would possess the awesome power and advantage of atomic weaponry.

After this momentous discussion, Franklin and Winston enjoyed a few moments of much needed respite. However, by dawn on Sunday, it was time for them and Hopkins to catch a train to Washington D.C.

The balmy June air peacefully blanketed the mountains, yet as they traveled southward, clouds began to form on the horizon. Upon their arrival, the sky turned gray. Making their way toward the White House, gusts of wind swirled, while drizzle speckled the pavement.

The three men quickly entered the building, when FDR excused himself. Meanwhile, Winston opted to kill some time reading newspapers and catching up on some telegrams.

As the president entered the Oval Office, several aides readily stood by, each anxious to update the president. One hurriedly walked over and handed the president a telegram.

Unfolding the document, Franklin's eyes oscillated left to right and steadily downward. Suddenly his arm fell limp. He slowly gazed upward and asked them to summon Churchill.

As the prime minister entered, Franklin looked up, his face grim. He informed Winston that the piece of paper in his hand was a telegraph regarding his British troops in Tobruk. As Winston spotted Franklin's solemn expression, a porcelain-like pallor washed over his ruddy face.

Franklin sat speechless, as his empathetic eyebrows wilted. Winston suddenly felt alienated and alone. There he stood, in a foreign office with foreign dignitaries, with all eyes locked on him in a cold stare. A wave of discomfort rattled his entire body. Taking a deep breath, the British prime minister advanced toward the American president.

Churchill grasped the telegram tightly with his meaty hand. He could sense the weight of anticipation by all the watchful eyes surrounding him. With a feeling of dread, Winston lowered his head to examine the ominous slip.

An eerie silence befell the room. Only the sound of the pounding rain, with occasional murmurs of thunder, reverberated within the oval chamber. As Winston read further and further his heart became weaker and weaker. Then his eyes came to the lethal lines. His soul dropped.

Standing in silence, Winston was enraged and appalled. Over 30,000 men surrendered in Tobruk to much smaller German forces, forfeiting 2,000 vehicles, 2,000 gallons of fuel and 5,000 tons of rations. Only a short while previously, 85,000 men surrendered at Singapore to the Japanese. For Churchill, surrender was *not* an option. He couldn't comprehend what his men were thinking. His mind must have reeled *how could they disgrace the Crown like this? Don't they realize civilization and freedom teeter in the balance?* What frightened Churchill most, however, was that this surrender foretold a most dark and ominous future.

Erwin Rommel—the legendary German Field Marshal, known as the Desert Fox—had been undefeated in his North African campaigns. This pivotal victory would now ensure Rommel's obvious next step, which would be the mother lode of all conquests. The desert rouge would soon have easy access to seizing Cairo, the Suez Canal, and the Middle East. Germany would occupy the entire breadth of Northern Africa and all of the oil-rich nations of Asia. Compounding this grave thought, Japan was moving in from the east, and if the two armies met, the Axis powers would easily devour the rest of Europe. Hence, Churchill quickly deduced a most horrifying chain of events...*all would be lost!*

As Winston stood paralyzed with shock, Franklin broke the dense silence. Overwhelmed with empathy, yet tinged with vengeance, he declared, "What can we do to help?"

As if awoken from a hellish nightmare, Winston gazed at Franklin awkwardly. He was completely overwhelmed by his friend's heartfelt offer, which Churchill later confessed was perhaps his most humiliating moment. Moreover, Franklin's words were saturated with resolve and compassion. Here Winston stood dejected, aghast, ashamed, and awaiting a barrage of criticism, yet Franklin rallied to his side like a heavenly angel.

Looking about, Winston could see and feel the same spirit and benevolence in the eyes of Franklin's aides. With renewed vigor, Winston barked energetically: "Give us as many Sherman tanks as you can spare, and ship them to the Middle East as quickly as possible!"

Immediately, Franklin picked up the phone. Jamming his finger into the rotary dial, he made direct contact with General George Marshall, and duly put in the request. Marshall responded promptly; the new Shermans were allotted to one of America's own divisions, yet sensing the gravity of the president's request, Marshall assured him that not only would the Shermans be sent immediately, but so, too, would the Army's newly developed 105-mm automatic weapons. *This call* was truly momentous.

Roosevelt's supply of Sherman tanks and artillery in the Middle East played a decisive role in the British victory at El Alamein. This battle was a turning point in the war, being the first *major* victory for British forces.

Furthermore, it effectively quashed Rommel's designs for moving east into the oil-rich nations. By supplying the British with tanks, weapons, and ammunition, Roosevelt also made the world understand that his earlier reference to American manufacturers being the Arsenal of Freedom now proved to the entire world just how crucial America's industrial might was to the war effort. England's bright imperial star would now begin its slow descent as a dynamic new supergiant was forcefully rising.

Even Churchill's chief officer, Lord Ismay, later reflected on how different the outcome could have been if Churchill received that telegram anywhere else. Would Churchill have even called Roosevelt? Considering his deep humiliation, utter embarrassment, and pride, possibly not. Moreover, if this request were handled by the bureaucratic chain of command, the American military would have most likely rebuffed the British request and sent the Shermans to American troops as intended.

Hence, the Tobruk debacle could have been the beginning of the end, but thanks to Roosevelt's firm action and America's unrivalled arsenal, the victory at El Alamein changed the course of the war from one of almost certain failure to one of hope.

These momentous and serendipitous chains of events were only made possible by the solid partnership of Franklin and Winston. Their deep and ever-growing friendship was the result of long and difficult struggles together that only hardened their resolve. After the devastating shock of Pearl Harbor, Roosevelt could readily empathize with Churchill when he faced his own humiliating defeats. It cannot be understated; this dynamic relationship was the most important in the twentieth century and was paramount to the Western world's very survival.

As noted, before America officially joined the war, the British were primarily engaging in responsive tactics, striving to hold the Germans at bay. As Great Britain faced several major setbacks, Roosevelt vigorously rallied support for his friend personally, by lifting his spirits, and physically, by supplying the British with armaments. Due to Roosevelt's struggles with Congress and an isolationist public, America entered the war late; as such, it was not fully mobilized. Fortunately, Roosevelt was perceptively shrewd and anticipated this day, as he already had factories retrofitted and engaged in military production. Hence, while Americans were fixated on their personal concerns, Roosevelt had been actively maneuvering America onto a solid war footing.

Meanwhile, Churchill had made no illusions about Britain's primary role and the world's indebtedness to their being the sole defenders of civilization. However, in the days and months ahead, the astounding rise of American ingenuity and facility proved awe-inspiring, not only to Churchill but more so to Josef Stalin. At their famous meeting in Teheran, Stalin stated point blank that the success of the war, at that point, was due to the Americans, since their unrivalled production of military machines surpassed that of Britain and Russia combined. As such, the dynamics of world power were inevitably shifting, to Churchill's chagrin.

As a staunch imperialist, Churchill advocated his king and queen's policy of worldwide colonization. This caused a major rift between Roosevelt and Churchill, as the president was already assessing the order of the postwar world. This led to Roosevelt's evasive actions at Teheran that baffled and even hurt his sentimental British friend. They may have been close friends, but America's future weighed heavier on Franklin's scale of priorities.

At Teheran, Franklin tried desperately to pierce Stalin's cold, emotionless shell. The Russian leader, dressed in military garb, was a man of few words, but when he spoke, he was clearly a dictator accustomed to absolute control. Born Iosif Dzhugashvili, the young Bolshevik rebel fashioned a new name in 1912, Stalin, meaning quite appropriately, "man of steel." The steel-headed tyrant was even called "the most outstanding mediocrity" by his fellow Bolshevik, Alexander Trotsky, during the early days of the revolution. After Lenin's premature death, however, Stalin seized control, thus outmaneuvering Trotsky, who was far more intelligent, but evidently, nowhere near as cunning. With his intemperate will and steely hands, Stalin smashed his rivals and hammered out the rigid laws that would shackle the Soviet people.

Against their better judgments, Churchill and Roosevelt had to align with Stalin in order to make use of his large standing army. For Roosevelt, the manpower alone was worth every temporary moral concession to this soulless tyrant, for the imminent threat of Adolf Hitler demanded unconventional thinking and unholy alliances.

Therefore, during the Teheran conference, Franklin Roosevelt enlisted all his charismatic and cunning resources to scrutinize and reveal the slightest inkling of a human connection. The inscrutable Stalin remained cold and impenetrable, however. During their three-way discussions, hampered by a translator, Roosevelt made a mild gibe at Churchill's expense. It was then that Roosevelt observed the Soviet barbarian's weakness. Stalin grinned! Demeaning others apparently aroused the sadistic dictator. Franklin had now found that elusive diplomatic key.

The following day, before their next meeting, Franklin told Churchill not to be sore about what he was going to do. Churchill, meanwhile, had no idea what the president had up his sleeve. Roosevelt then played into Stalin's confidence by whispering mild ridicules, such as, "the prime minister seems a bit cranky today." This unlocked Stalin's frozen façade, and quite miraculously, the Russian bear slowly emerged from his Siberian slumber.

Later on, while discussing postwar operations, Stalin made a bold suggestion. In his thick Georgian accent, he stated that all of Hitler's top officials should be exterminated—all fifty thousand of them! Churchill exploded, and adamantly denounced Stalin's ruthless proposal. He further stated that even if war-frenzied Britons initially approved, they would immediately protest after the first round of murders.

Stalin remained firm, demanding, "Fifty thousand must be shot!"

Roosevelt calmly interjected, "My good fellows, hold on a minute!" Churchill sighed with relief, content that his civilized friend had finally intervened.

Roosevelt continued, "I see that perhaps a compromise is in order. May I suggest that only forty-nine thousand be shot?"

Stalin's thick mustache unfurled, as he burst out with laughter. Yet the joke did not reverberate with Churchill. Unable to harness his disgust, Churchill sprung to his feet and stormed out of the room. In his momentary burst of humiliation, Winston mistakenly entered a dark empty room. Trying to regain his senses, he quickly turned about, only to find himself face-to-face with two broad silhouettes. Standing abreast, they solidly blocked the doorway. As Winston's pupils dilated, the vision of

Stalin and his translator appeared. With a thick Russian accent, the translator assured Churchill that it was all said in jest. Not believing that it was a joke, Churchill unhappily accompanied the two Soviets back to the conference table.

Neither Churchill nor Roosevelt really knew if the dictator was in fact jesting or serious. In view of all the mass murders covertly committed by Stalin on his own people, however, it would appear the Soviet dictator was dead serious.

Stalin would later ignore the terms of the triple alliance, as his troops proceeded toward Poland and Hungary. At the Polish capital of Warsaw, the Soviet troops stopped just outside the city's perimeter. Stalin then called upon the Polish resistance to rise and attack the German occupation. Much blood was shed, as both factions ravaged the city. Stalin heartlessly waited for his contemptible subjects to slaughter each other, knowing very well that Poland would soon be his.

At that moment, Roosevelt had already won his unprecedented fourth-term election, but his health was declining rapidly. In a panic, Churchill contacted Franklin about Stalin's advances. Franklin immediately telegrammed Stalin and issued a stern warning. He had been trying to bide his time with Stalin, for his ultimate goal was to gain the tyrant's assistance against the Japanese. Nevertheless, Roosevelt's deep commitment to a future world of peace forced him to neglect his cordiality, and sources say FDR reprimanded the Soviet dictator.

Despite the strained relations, a glimmer of light shone, for it was clear that the end of the long and bloody war was near. Now all three leaders faced the uneasy task of securing territory to ensure their own vision of a postwar world. Stalin vied for communistic occupation, Churchill imperial colonization, and Roosevelt democratic globalization.

Roosevelt believed the new superpowers had a duty to humanity to police the world. At Yalta, FDR outlined the foundation for the United Nations. He proposed four major police states: the United States, England, the Soviet Union, and China. Churchill and Stalin rebuffed the inclusion of China, but FDR contended that it would assist in the balance of power. This would have benefited American interests, for FDR intended China to act as a safeguard against Soviet expansion, and the spread of more British colonies beyond Hong Kong or India. A close alliance with China might have also prevented the communist takeover that did occur after the war.

Unfortunately, time and the war had taken its toll on the president. FDR was deathly ill. He had even suffered a stroke before his third term. However, despite his handicap and fatal condition, Roosevelt managed to maintain a quasi air of strength, as well as his unique charisma. Some have criticized FDR for being too weak physically and mentally to engage in this important conference, and persistently blame him for losing Poland. The Yalta transcripts indicate that FDR convinced Stalin to allow Poland to have free elections, yet his premature death allowed the deceitful Soviet dictator to break his agreement and engage in his own plans.

Earlier in the war, Roosevelt was confronted with many other vital considerations and predicaments that demanded solutions. Stalin had previously chastised his two allies for not making the significant strikes that they had alluded to earlier. This caused the deaths of hundreds of thousands of Soviet soldiers while the Germans aggressively invaded Russia. FDR had only authorized the low-risk attack in Northern Africa. Intended as a morale builder for the American troops, as well as the American public, the strike offered no reprieve for Stalin's soldiers who were being slaughtered. Therefore, Roosevelt knew that a major assault to seriously rattle the Germans was unavoidable and necessary to salvage his waning alliance with Stalin. Roosevelt's unfailing perceptions were correct, since after Stalin recaptured his lost city of Stalingrad—at a loss of one million Russian lives—the wary Soviet leader attempted to make a secret peace treaty with Hitler. Hitler, however, flatly refused.

Roosevelt's massive assault on June 6, 1944, under the skillful direction of General Eisenhower, was the famous D-Day invasion of Normandy. Interestingly enough, Churchill had adamantly rejected the strike, due to a long string of demoralizing British defeats, but eventually he conceded. Fortunately for the Allied forces, Roosevelt and Eisenhower prevailed, as this massive assault was the major turning point in the war. Of equal importance, the American-led initiative redeemed Roosevelt in Stalin's skeptical eyes, and made it clear that America was a formidable ally. Further still, it established that America could also be a deadly foe.

Roosevelt understood the absolute necessity of maintaining a relationship with Stalin; hence, by clearly demonstrating America's strength in a monumental battle, he knew the negotiations at the conference table would run smoother, particularly in the war's aftermath. Although Roosevelt wouldn't live to engage in these future meetings, the agreements that he made at Tehran and Yalta, under a veil of grim and dangerous circumstances, were better than anyone else could have possibly managed, including Churchill. That the headstrong Briton stood firm and ethically unyielding set him at polar odds with the sly and homicidal Soviet. Simply put, Stalin was dirty oil to Churchill's pure water and the two could never mix. That said, it was solely Franklin D. Roosevelt who charmed his way into the cold Soviet's confidence, as much as anyone possibly could, and was chiefly responsible for securing deals that protected America's stature and leading role in modern-day international affairs.

After the war, America's military dominance was indisputable, and was the result of Roosevelt's firm leadership founded upon insight, strategy, guile, and determination. As time unfolded, it became clear that Roosevelt's free and democratic worldview held fast. The British Empire ceded India, Hong Kong, and its other colonies to their native inhabitants, and released their firm political grip over Egypt and Middle Eastern territories. Churchill's imperial empire had dissolved. Decades later, President Reagan would pressure Gorbachev into tearing down the oppressive Berlin Wall, which was symbolic of Stalin's deadly communistic grasp that shackled and suppressed millions. The eventual collapse of the Soviet Union clearly ushered in a new dawn—one that comes close to Roosevelt's glorious world order, even if somewhat curtailed by modern events.

Roosevelt's appearance on the world stage during America's most devastating depression and most militarily demanding confrontation was uncanny in its timing and irreplaceable. His early rise to power, however, was not easy, even for a man of privilege. Constantly being compared to his famous cousin, Theodore, Franklin's early actions never seemed to rival the elder Roosevelt or impress the critics. His first claim to victory came when, as a New York senator, he boldly confronted the powerful and corrupt band of Irish tyrants that ruled Tammany Hall in New York City. Despite not securing substantial change, the public took heed.

Succeeding the popular Al Smith as New York governor, Franklin vigorously opposed President Hoover, whose passive stance on the rapidly tanking economy was to let it revive itself. Franklin championed New York State farmers, perceptively realizing that without food the state would literally starve. His winning good nature and oratorical poise likewise endeared him to the public, even if prompting his rivals to call him a superficial dandy. However, underneath his lightweight exterior was a perceptive and shrewd tactician with an unassailable determination.

It is also significant that this energetic and dashing young man, who served previously as President Wilson's Assistant Secretary of the Navy, was suddenly stricken with polio and confined to a wheelchair for the rest of his life, yet he still pressed forward—further testament to his unyielding determination to overcome adversity. Roosevelt's disability profoundly transformed the once aloof and haughty politician to empathize with the needy, focus his priorities, and strengthen his resolve, for it would surely be tested to the maximum when World War II unleashed its fury upon the free world. After the cataclysmic collapse of the American economy in 1929, compounded by President Hoover's stagnant administration, Roosevelt appeared like American's sole hope and savior. The Depression was toxic, as it thrust the nation into dire poverty and spiritual despair. Undaunted, Roosevelt stayed the course and won the presidency.

As a man of action, Roosevelt made bold mandates with his New Deal in an attempt to rescue the deflated economy. Roosevelt's agenda included revising the Federal Reserve Bank, unemployment relief, aiding agricultural and industrial recovery, establishing Social Security, FDIC, the CCC, and many other sweeping programs. Although these reforms were hit or miss, they clearly illustrated a man aggressively seeking solutions, rather than one paralyzed, literally or figuratively. His wife Eleanor added to that list, thus becoming a role model for all future First Ladies.

With Hitler's antagonistic offenses escalating, and the prospect of war looming, Roosevelt sought proactive measures; but instead, he was confronted with numerous enemies who were hell-bent on sabotaging his efforts. The country desperately needed to manufacture tanks, jeeps, weapons, warships, and aircraft, yet John L. Lewis led the national coalminers on strike, disgracefully boycotting the War Labor Board.

Another rival was the famous aviator Charles Lindberg, who began producing a long series of antiwar broadcasts and news articles after Hitler's invasion of Poland, no less. Lindberg's ideology grew in scope to include Nazi-like endorsements about racial superiority, while also revealing his personal disgust of Roosevelt. Calling the president a dictator, which amazingly influenced some of his naïve listeners, Lindberg claimed that America's deepest threat came from Roosevelt, not Hitler. Lindberg's prestige made his voice reverberate nationwide, thus spawning the lame notion that America's only danger came from within, not from without—something many wartime presidents, including Lincoln, Reagan, and George W. Bush have faced. Additionally, even after the aviator's many visits to Nazi Germany, Lindberg insisted that Hitler had no designs of world conquest. That Lindberg grossly failed to recognize Hitler's objectives and condoned racial intolerance only blackens the aviator's once pristine legacy, while further attesting to Roosevelt's profound and moral sense of judgment.

Meanwhile, shortly before the outbreak of war, Joseph Kennedy, whom Roosevelt had appointed ambassador to England, had the temerity to defy the president by promoting his own pacifistic agenda. However, his pessimistic stance did not sit well with the American public, despite its desire to remain isolationist. For years, Joseph Kennedy had displayed a flagrant craving to become the nation's first Irish Catholic president, however, his lack of moral conviction did not resonate with the American people. As such, Kennedy committed political suicide, and had to resort to marketing his son John years later to achieve that presidential milestone.

Therefore, aside from the Axis powers, Roosevelt also had to combat many influential Americans who were causing dissension and forming crippling roadblocks. Roosevelt was also painfully aware of the covert German emissaries sent to America to shatter unity and play upon America's isolationist and antiwar sentiments. They strengthened his critics' cause and aided the Nazi's agenda. As such, FDR made a speech addressing this deadly issue along with indirectly criticizing Lindberg,

Kennedy, and others for their mindless yet destructive philosophical and moral allegiances. An excerpt from FDR's speech is worth our attention.

"They exploit for their own ends our own natural abhorrence of war. These trouble-breeders have but one purpose. It is to divide our people, to divide them into hostile groups and to destroy our unity and shatter our will to defend ourselves. There are also American citizens, many of them in high places, who, unwittingly in most cases, are aiding and abetting the work of these agents. I do not charge these American citizens with being foreign agents. But I do charge them with doing exactly the kind of work that the dictators want done in the United States. These people not only believe that we can save our own skins by shutting our eyes to the fate of other nations. Some of them go much further than that. They say that we can and should become the friends and even the partners of the Axis powers. Some of them even suggest that we should imitate the methods of the dictatorships. But Americans never can and never will do that."

— Excerpt from FDR's Fireside Chat. December 29, 1940 (9:30 PM)

Considering how pro-democratic and pro-American Roosevelt was, it's surprising how some Americans still believe he had dictatorial designs. Like Lincoln, FDR did make unconstitutional maneuvers—such as his attempt to control the Supreme Court—yet both men sought only to save the nation. To use the cliché, *"Desperate times call for desperate measures."* Aware of the people's ultimate power, Roosevelt had even expressed his concerns of possibly losing his last election. Additionally, Roosevelt repeatedly pressured Churchill to free the oppressed British colonies to engender a truly free and democratic world community. Sadly, few people then (and today) truly understood this unique president and his unique four-term administration. As noted, many wartime presidents were forced to take unconventional steps that had some critics screaming "unconstitutional," however, FDR's personal traits and political actions irrefutably attest to a man deeply devoted to championing freedom and democracy, certainly not an immoral or selfish despot seeking a throne.

Meanwhile, while Americans passively balked, Roosevelt astutely assessed that Hitler was a global threat, and shrewdly established his Lend-Lease program. This allowed arms to be leased to the Allies in exchange for military bases. Although unconventional and disturbing to some, it was voted on and passed by Congress. For a nation unwilling to engage in war or help Britain, this crafty workaround was vital to keeping the Allied forces adequately supplied. Moreover, with MacArthur's and Ike's advice, Roosevelt initiated the subtle yet effective plan of silently retrofitting factories for military production. These were clear and decisive steps for mobilizing a slumbering nation that otherwise would have remained in its isolationist malaise. It is irrefutable that without Roosevelt's firm and preemptive leadership, America and all other free nations would have fallen victim to Hitler's tyrannical war machine.

The military data is clear; toward the end of 1941 and most of 1942, Hitler was categorically defeating the British at every turn. It must be remembered that Britain's first major victory was in November of 1942 at El Alamein, under Montgomery's command. This battle, which finally turned the tide, was heavily supplied with American Sherman tanks and automatic weapons by Roosevelt. Although it is true that Churchill's early defense, even if steadily faltering, did offer the United States more time to mobilize both strategically and industrially, two critical issues remain. First, Churchill's Allied war effort was only able to sustain its shaky, defensive posture because of the military supplies and aid that it covertly received from Roosevelt, and second, once America did enter the war, its swift and unrivalled production rate secured the dominant role for America in every theater of war against the Axis powers.

One of Hitler's major blunders was that he severely underestimated the will and tenacity of the American people, who appeared to be bankrupt and suitably doomed. The Depression had seemingly given Hitler ample proof that a capitalistic republic was a broken and unsalvageable system. The cocky dictator even trumpeted his deep hatred and repugnance for Americans, claiming that the nation had fallen due to placating the Jews and Negroes. To Hitler, America was a pathetic nonentity.

Hitler's personal traits and beliefs likewise crippled his own nation, which could have produced far greater weaponry and technological wonders. Although Germany was scientifically more advanced than the Allies, one critical key issue limited their abilities—Adolf Hitler. When presented with a new technology that exceeded his limited grasp, Hitler would scrap the project. In fact, Hitler rarely ever spoke to scientists face-to-face, and preferred having intermediaries relay their dialogue. This buffer zone allowed Hitler to dismiss concepts without a direct rebuttal, which in an open forum would have certainly revealed his limited knowledge, and belittled the egotistical grand master.

Interestingly, Hitler's nostalgic admiration for chivalry made him limit machine gun development, since he believed that the use of the automatic weapon would eliminate hand-to-hand combat and produce only cowards. Hitler also limited jet propulsion development, claiming that the excessive speed would prevent pilots from engaging in dogfights, as they would pass their opponent too quickly. The new effects of G forces at such high speeds caused pilots to get light-headed and black out, as such, this added strength to Hitler's nearsighted argument, and in turn, he curtailed or even canceled more projects.

Perhaps most detrimental, however, was Hitler's prejudice. His policy of purging Jewish, Hungarian, and other non-German scientists drastically crippled his own efforts. From 1900 until the 1930s, Germany maintained perhaps the most brilliant array of scientific minds. This included Edward Teller, Leo Szilard, and of course Albert Einstein, among others. Their cutting-edge lead in physics, along with the number of breakthroughs in aircraft and weapon design by many skilled engineers were staggering, yet once Hitler rose to power, many of these scientists either fled the country or were ignorantly relieved of duty.

One scientist that Hitler expelled was Fritz Haber *(See pg. 714)*. The Kaiser had even awarded Haber the title of Captain for developing chemical warfare during WWI. Haber's wife detested his work on poison gas and his loyalty to the German army. Tragically, she committed suicide at a dinner party by shooting herself with his army pistol. Fritz, however, remained a loyal German and continued his work of outfitting the army. After the First World War, Haber's lab developed cyanide and Zyklon B. The Nazis later used cyanide for their heroic suicide pills, and quite horrifyingly, Zyklon B in their extermination camps. The Jewish chemist little knew that his government would use the poison gas he invented to kill millions of his own people. Nevertheless, because Haber was a Jew, Hitler demanded his exile. This occurred in 1933, the very year Hitler became Reich Chancellor. The famous German physicist Max Planck, who was crucial in the formulation of quantum theory, even tried to persuade the new leader to rescind the exile, yet Hitler's prejudice prevailed.

Oddly enough, Fritz Haber had even converted to Christianity, yet his Jewish bloodline was enough for Hitler and his Nazi bloodhounds to chase Haber out of Germany. From 1911 up through the early 1930s, Haber did much of his work at the Kaiser Wilhelm Institute for Physical Chemistry and Elektrochemistry. He would even befriend the young wizard Albert Einstein at the Institute. However, once Haber showed his blind loyalty to the Kaiser during WWI, and his eagerness to develop chemical weaponry, Einstein severed the relationship. In 1914, Einstein even confronted the entire German scientific community by signing a manifesto advocating a pacifist agenda, yet the majority were fervent nationalists. Haber's chemical weaponry development was augmented by the development of gas masks with filters for the German troops. His work even won him the Nobel Prize for Chemistry in 1918. But again, all this mattered little to Adolf Hitler, Fritz Haber was still seen as a Jew in his hateful Aryan eyes, and so Haber was banished.

Hitler's blatant anti-Semitism is almost the dictionary definition for the word, but what may come as a surprise is that some people have recently tried to label both Roosevelt and Churchill as anti-Semitic. These accusations are tactless and shouldn't even elicit a rebuttal, yet the sad fact that some people have bought into these disturbing accusations warrants some attention.

As the Germans engaged in their cold-blooded exterminations in concentration camps—a process they code-named the "Final Solution"—reports of these diabolical machinations were leaked to American newspapers, yet most were tagged as rumors or vengeful fabrications. During WWI, false reports of atrocities were used as propaganda to weaken the morale of the Allies. As such, during WWII, the American media used extreme caution and never placed disturbing or fallacious-sounding articles on the front page. Moreover, they often used the term "alleged" and other similar phrases when describing these incidents, since no hard evidence existed. It was only near the close of the war, when the facts became known, that they finally hit the press. But, alas, by this time it was too late, the shocking death toll had already been amassed, for the

Nazis devilishly increased their processing rate to incinerate as many Jews as possible before being forced to shut down and flee.

Other reasons exist for the initial lack of belief by the media, or the lack of hard evidence by reporters. First, the Germans had never concealed their hatred of the Jews. They had always publicly harangued or even assaulted them; therefore, many believed the same would hold true in this instance as well. Second, and more importantly, the vast majority, including Jews living in occupied German territories, simply found the whole concept unthinkable and far too heinous to ever be a reality.

Even America's top generals, Eisenhower and Patton among others, could only partially believe the reports. It was only at the close of the German war, after visiting the death camps, that the full horror truly sunk in. In hindsight, we all know what transpired, we have seen the horrific footage and the utterly disturbing photos, but back then the thought of humans being capable of doing something so outrageously morbid and demonic had to be held suspect. They, like all others, fell prey to human nature's defense mechanism, which purges such unfathomable descriptions from the mind. Hence, only by witnessing the horror firsthand did it become manifest as real. Moreover, these generals were all exposed to the many iniquities and debaucheries on the battlefield; therefore, if they could not believe these initial reports, then certainly Roosevelt or Churchill cannot be blamed either. Moreover, to implement such a plan on the grand scale that was being purported by Jewish sources only made the reports seem unnaturally bizarre, or even prejudicially contrived for the sake of racial vengeance. By all accounts, it was a truly tragic yet unbelievably surreal situation, one that most thought unreal.

As for the lack of hard evidence, the Nazis had implemented their Final Solution in a systematically covert manner. What's more, they covered up their nefarious actions by spinning a huge propaganda campaign. By heavily publicizing their relocation program as a harmless and routine method to move Jews to labor camps, they successfully hoodwinked the Allies, and even the majority of prisoners at the outset. The German commandants cleverly designated certain stables in their death camps to house Jewish captives who would not be terminated, such as those at Work Camp Birkenau. The Germans then gamely coaxed these inmates to write postcards and letters to their loved ones, which deceptively validated that they were alive and well. In effect, the Germans appeared to have standard labor camps, yet unbeknownst to outsiders, their sinister furnaces burned day and night.

Additionally, modern research indicates that America's head of the State Department, Breckenridge Long, allegedly suppressed the news of Germany's mass-murders, falsified cables, and even deceptively coached Roosevelt with misinformation. Some have labeled Long an anti-Semite, and this may or may not be true. Long was cited by all of his coworkers as being statistically cold and calculating, so perhaps Long placed more importance on the core war mission than a rescue attempt that would drain crucial resources, time and manpower.

However, far overshadowing Long's subterfuge, Roosevelt and Churchill had Hitler, Mussolini, Hirohito, and even Stalin to contend with in order to rescue civilization from global annihilation. The Allied war effort looked painfully bleak. By 1942, Hitler's war machine was at its peak, as they made significant victories and even boldly advanced on Stalingrad. Meanwhile, Roosevelt feared losing the November election due to these setbacks, as well as the fact that the Republicans gained nine seats in Congress and a staggering forty-four seats in the House. The brutal attack on Pearl Harbor, less than a year earlier, and the huge American and British losses in the Philippines in the early part of 1942, weighed most heavily on Americans' minds, and it was unfortunately at this crucial time that rumors of Hitler's death camps leaked out.

Compounding this whirlwind of madness were the incoming news reports of the heartless Japanese, who oddly enough, even made the Germans look good. Eyewitness accounts reported how the Japanese sadistically tortured and beheaded Allied captives for pleasure. The Japanese had even translated Hitler's *Mein Kampf*, although deleting his derogatory remarks about the Japanese, and savored his hateful words. Like Hitler and his Aryan cronies, the Japanese also believed that they were the master race. This air of superiority made killing all other races as easy as killing insects, and the atrocities proved it. The Japanese killed more American POWs than the Nazis, for while the Nazi Germans killed four percent of their prisoners, the Japanese killed over thirty percent.

Furthermore, the Japanese gruesomely tortured their victims, using soldiers for bayonet practice, nailing them to trees, or even burying them alive. In the minds of many Americans, these brutal debaucheries overshadowed the European conflict.

Additionally, the Jews in Poland were not the only ones being diabolically slaughtered, for the Japanese experimented with germ warfare, killing almost a half-million Chinese along with an unknown number of Allied fighters. Japanese scientists, led by Shiro Ishii, even went so far as to vaccinate Chinese babies with their germ-infested syringes. Between the atrocities breaking out across the globe and the direct threat of the Japanese, who slyly slaughtered Americans at Pearl Harbor and were torturing American soldiers, the priorities of national security became a profoundly difficult pecking order to address. This nationwide phobia is what directly pressured FDR into interring Japanese-Americans. In fear, Americans had lashed out against their alien-cultured neighbors, who suspiciously maintained their own language, looked different, and rarely intermarried. The world seemed to be crumbling apart and the fear at home was a further distraction from what evil might allegedly be taking place against the Jews in distant Germany or Poland.

Furthermore, it must be noted that Roosevelt appointed Henry Morgenthau Jr., who was Jewish, to serve as his Secretary of the Treasury. Morgenthau was even put in charge of postwar planning for Germany, as his Morgenthau Plan proposed dismantling German's capacity for heavy industry to prevent the manufacture of weapons. Roosevelt also maintained consistent contact with Rabbi Stephen Wise and other Jewish leaders, and had done everything in his power, under the dire circumstances, to address the Jewish issue. The State Department had shot down some of these proposals due to their unfeasibility or fear of the huge influx of refugees if a rescue plan succeeded. In this last instance, the logistics, manpower, money, and resources required would have severely hampered the war effort, which still showed no signs of clear victory.

Other prominent Jews, like future Israeli prime minister, Golda Meir, were adamantly against the guerilla Revisionists and Irgunists, who wanted to militarily establish a nation of Israel in Palestine. These rebel groups included another future Israeli prime minister, Menachem Begin.

Begin was in charge of the Betar, which trained Jewish youths in military tactics. However, opposition to their militant strategies for a Jewish state and their unrealistic rescue plans were all resoundingly denounced. One rescue plan consisted of air bombing the death camps themselves, since they believed the confusion would allow some Jews to escape. Nevertheless, all their ideas were quashed as impractical, dangerous, and, in the case of killing innocent Jews in the process, extremely reckless.

Most importantly, however, when Hitler's genocide was confirmed in 1943, the Allied forces were so overwhelmed in the fight for survival that rescue missions could not even be entertained. However, the bombing of railways leading to Auschwitz was authorized at this time. Unfortunately, the Germans not only repaired these damages with lightning speed, but several weeks later, after many bombing raids, they located the Allied airbase and destroyed over 75 Allied planes and over a half-million gallons of fuel. Therefore, the air raids to save the Jews at Auschwitz turned into a disaster and had to cease. But a legitimate and valiant attempt was made, especially in light of the huge losses, and the massive onslaught of German and Japanese attacks around the globe that took precedence. That Roosevelt's mind and his nation's physical resources were tapped to the maximum is an understatement, and one that is easily overlooked in hindsight.

The immense barrage of information that Roosevelt had to process and absorb is mind-boggling, as wires and letters of international outcry flooded his desk daily, along with covert intelligence communiqués and war room meetings. These covered activities spanning Europe, Asia, North Africa, and the vast Pacific. Most important was how many huge operations, projects, and objectives required his full attention and quicksilver decisions at all hours of the day and night. Yet it is always easy for peacetime critics to denigrate those in the heat of battle and utter chaos.

Roosevelt was also criticized for dealing with unsavory characters, like French Admiral Darlan; yet, here again, these critics fail to recognize Franklin's skill at being a consummate tactician. While some leaders, like Churchill, were straight shooters who distanced themselves from their foes by openly displaying their firm opposition, Roosevelt joined the inner circle of wolves and kept his enemies close. This enabled him to gain the confidence and objectives of dubious leaders under the beguiling veil of friendship. (In this instance, Eisenhower initiated the union with Darlan.)

Admiral Jean-Francois Darlan led the Vichy military that ruled over French North Africa, and he was known to be unscrupulous, and in league with the Nazis. The American press lambasted Roosevelt for dealing with Darlan, yet Roosevelt lashed back, stating that Darlan had given him Algiers—Eisenhower being the point man. Roosevelt realized that making temporary negotiations, regardless of what or whom he had to deal with, was a fair price to pay in order to attain the ultimate goal of victory. Operating like a Machiavellian undercover CIA agent, Roosevelt had his own method that others saw as unsavory and undignified; however, FDR was simply a brilliant *Prince* that understood the deadly game of survival.

Roosevelt had a myriad of potential warlords strewn around the periphery of Hitler's war-torn Europe, and any one of them could have caused further disaster. Aside from Darlan, Francisco Franco of Spain was unpredictable and could have sided with Hitler. More threatening still was Haj Amin al-Husseni, the Muslim ruler of Palestine and the ancient city of Jerusalem. Roosevelt realized the potential danger of over 20 million Arab Muslims joining Hitler's anti-Semitic regime. Not only would Hitler be massively empowered, but the British stronghold over Arabian oil would be lost. These volatile kegs of dynamite needed to be cajoled by a charismatic Roosevelt, not admonished by an imperialistic Churchill. Roosevelt had to engage and juggle an immense amount of delicate yet critical diplomacy, and he did so with outward calm, grace, and strength. It by far dwarfs all the lilliputian naivety of his detractors, who simply could not comprehend FDR's precarious position and stellar abilities.

Beyond his beguiling gift of diplomacy, Roosevelt was a hands-on leader who engaged in many phases of the American and Allied forces operations. General George C. Marshall held the highest regard for Roosevelt's lucidity, determination, and strategic wisdom. Also attesting to Roosevelt's insight was his very risky, somewhat doubtful, and highly expensive Manhattan Project, which, as time would tell, would prove crucial to ending the war with Japan, although not with Germany. Despite delays, it did expedite the war's eventual end, and as a far greater reward, it summoned in the Atomic Age.

In essence, Roosevelt prepared America for the arduous and vital mission it was about to face. Before America committed to the war, the horizon was extremely bleak, far darker than most Americans realized then or can even fathom today. As noted, although Britain and the Allies were defending the free world, not a single major victory occurred before the battle at El Alamein. Losses were rapidly mounting, as Field Marshal Rommel in Northern Africa pulverized the British with his panzers, and even the Japanese sank Britain's two largest vessels. The death knell was tolling louder and louder as Hitler and Hirohito rancorously raped sand and sea, leaving a trail of brutally tortured corpses in their wake. The ghastly specter of Western civilization's grim and seemingly ultimate demise profoundly plagued the free world's failing spirit.

Hence, it is without question that America's firm and dynamic entrance turned the mighty winds of war against the death cloud of the Axis. It was American foresight, ingenuity, industry, and utter determination that won the day and that commitment cleared the sand, seas, and skies of nefarious evil.

And while it's imperative to give credit to the Soviets, who were engaged in a long and bloody battle on the Eastern front, which amassed the largest death tolls, we must keep in mind that their efforts were substantially aided by Allied forces fighting Hitler on the Western front, which tied up huge resources of the Nazi's war machine. If no Western front existed, it is highly doubtful that Stalin would have prevailed. In fact, one could say it's a foregone conclusion. As such, despite the Soviets' higher losses and bloodier battles, the United States involvement in WWII, which also supplied the Soviets and British with armaments, was unquestionably *the* critical component for winning the war.

Naturally in a war of such magnitude, many individuals contributed immeasurably to the ultimate victory, and the sacrifice of millions deserves our utmost respect and gratitude. Yet without Roosevelt's swift and effective leadership, the Allied engines would have certainly stalled. And while some understandably wish to place Churchill on par with FDR, there is one major unavoidable fact, which is that Roosevelt's tactics enabled America to not only defeat its formidable enemies but also surpass England as a world superpower. At the same time, Churchill's

England lost its preeminent prewar stature and quickly began losing its grasp on all its colonies worldwide. Churchill managed to weather the storm but the once mighty British Empire faded into a relic of history. In direct contrast, Roosevelt did not weather the storm, dying weeks before victory, but the dynamic America that he created emerged as the ultimate leader of the free world. That is not only astounding but also indisputable.

Furthermore, Americans must realize that they have been well groomed by the British, who both during the war and after took great strides in touting their superiority. Not only did General Montgomery try to strip his American peers of just glory to laud his own, but even after the war his British comrades exaggerated British efforts and victories.

Aptly enough, Churchill is well noted for saying, "History is written by the victors." And after the war the British took the most active lead in the publication of books and films. One only needs to think of the immensely popular and highly lauded film series "The World at War" to see that the British victors eagerly jumped at documenting history.

The series was undeniably spectacular, as it compiled impressive and often riveting archival footage, thus producing an exemplary visual history of the war. However, once the audio chimes in, the British narrator clearly documents a war that was won by the British with—as British rock star Ringo would say—*a little help from my friends*.

This is evident by the fact that in relaying the story of the violent Battle of the Bulge, for example, they hail General Montgomery as being the heroic genius of this famous battle. Worse yet, they fail to even mention American General George Patton, who was pivotal. An omission of this magnitude from a comprehensive war documentary, which boasted over *30 hours* of footage, can only lead to two words, sad propaganda.

This is not to say that the entire series is of no use or totally flawed, on the contrary, it remains an invaluable and extremely moving documentary. However, it is crucial for Americans to be aware of the bias in the narrative, which *does* diminish its historical accuracy. Not to mention the great disservice and insult that it heaps upon the six-hundred-thousand American soldiers that fought and died in this particular battle under their brave American generals, which in Patton's case, did not even merit the courtesy of being mentioned.

However, even great soldiers and great generals all fall under the ultimate command of their executive leader, and, here again, Roosevelt's perception, cunning maneuverability, and firm, forward-prodding actions rightfully place him at the apex of this grand American pyramid.

These amazing feats are all the more remarkable when we consider that his legs were shackled in iron and his paralyzed body confined to a wheelchair. We know today that this has no effect on one's intellect, to which Stephen Hawking surely attests, but the 1940s were different times. People with physical disabilities were often frowned upon as being inferior or impotent. Further still, no world leader had ever been a cripple, and this psychological weight added ten-fold to Franklin's physical leg irons. Roosevelt was forced to deal with terrifying adversaries, including his evil ally Josef Stalin, who certainly judged strength in leadership by physical standards. Most macho dictators would scoff at or threaten physically handicapped people, yet Roosevelt's resolve, strength, and courage stymied Stalin. This truly makes Roosevelt a giant among men.

It is this extensive litany of admirable qualities and astounding results that make many hail Franklin D. Roosevelt as the most crucial president in American history. However, the sad fact is that apparently more Americans lack the ability to fully comprehend, appreciate, or even respect his grand and noble efforts. This is painfully evident in national polls. Although polls have little factual merit, they often rank Abraham Lincoln either first or second, while FDR lags behind. We know that the typical complaint about FDR was that he was duplicitous; yet again, many missed the significance of his cunning craft, impeccable timing, or blessing of being in office at the world's most perilous crossroads. Most importantly, they missed the lesson that all Americans should have learned in the aftermath of the war. The fact remains that Roosevelt utilized his special gifts not for selfish interests or even corruption, but rather to empower America to defeat the Axis powers, emerging free of conquest or annihilation, and more strikingly to become the ultimate superpower and defender of liberty.

As mentioned, WWII involved many nations and many leaders, some of whom were sordid characters, even outright psychopaths. Roosevelt's ability to not only deal with these leaders, but also win their confidence required skill, tact, perception, and of course, deceit. A straight-shooting president would have never been able to manipulate these leaders or the war effort as brilliantly as FDR. It was one of those rare moments when the ideal leader was somehow destined to command, and that FDR was the only American president to ever be elected four times only seems to validate this divine occurrence.

Many are also deceived by the notion that America was a superpower well before the war, for even Franklin's great cousin Teddy did much to bolster American prowess. Moreover, World War I forced President Woodrow Wilson to raise America's military stance somewhat. However, Germany and Britain unquestionably dominated the scene, while Russia, Japan, and Italy held competitive positions among the second tier. Shockingly enough, the United States Army only had 100,000 men in 1915 and in 1938, and it was ranked below Bulgaria in size. Hence, FDR not only ensured America's victory, but he also skyrocketed America into its stellar lead position with an unprecedented show of strength.

Despite these immense achievements, many national polls often favor Lincoln, or Honest Abe. In most situations, honesty is the best policy, but precarious and complex situations, such as the myriad of national forces and leaders that FDR was forced to face, are exceptions, at least if survival is deemed paramount. Oddly enough, Abraham Lincoln performed many provocative acts that should have had many Americans up in arms, yet they remained amazingly mute. Lincoln terminated habeas corpus in order to detain Confederates and suspects that he and his administration simply deemed suspicious. Lincoln also performed many other Machiavellian unconstitutional acts, yet those who emphatically despise Machiavellian principles curiously embrace them in Lincoln's case or simply ignore them. Quite interestingly, however, the same does not hold true for FDR or any other president, except perhaps Washington.

Lincoln also brazenly wrested control of several states, such as Kentucky and Maryland, by literally rounding up state legislators and arresting newspaper editors. Not too honest. Lincoln also confiscated the newspaper's printing facilities, simply because they printed disparaging remarks about him—namely that his actions were dictatorial and unconstitutional. It would be very interesting to see how people today, especially newspaper editors, would react if a president arrested them for exercising their constitutional right of freedom of speech. Oddly enough, Lincoln not only silenced freedom of speech, without being admonished, but on the contrary, he received the utmost praise from duplicitous or simply unknowing admirers. The issue is not to criticize Lincoln's actions, since his goal evidently justified his unconstitutional means, but rather to elucidate the colored attitude that pervades many Americans, particularly when judging these two presidents.

This double standard becomes clearer when we see that Lincoln was forced into situations just like FDR, yet only Lincoln gets the free pass. When asked about the Civil War, Lincoln said, "I claim not to have controlled events, but confess plainly that events have controlled me." Despite our immediate and cordial response to Lincoln's self-effacing gesture, this is a truism. One never knows what one will be forced to do when unknown or unpredictable events arise. Just as Lincoln never anticipated revoking constitutional rights to save the nation, so, too, did Roosevelt engage in unpremeditated controversial measures. The spontaneous chain of events that escalated for both men demanded quick, firm, and atypical responses, which may offend purists who expect fidelity to the system, but those actions actually preserved the *Constitution* in the end. Both men faced tremendous obstacles not only from their enemies, but also from within their own ranks, yet the scales of justice always tip in Lincoln's favor.

In trying to understand America's misguided mentality in these polls, we need to look at other reasons as well. First, is the oddity of how most *modern day* Democrats have discarded Roosevelt (a fellow Democrat) in favor of Lincoln (a Republican). This is not because they adopted Republican sympathies, but rather because the Democratic Party has mutated and abandoned many of its once unyielding principles, as well as its convictions to a worthy cause, regardless of hurting a minority's feelings, popular opinion, or the sacrifices required. This new leaning toward the extreme left has injured the once mighty Democratic Party of FDR and Truman, thus becoming the weakened platform of the politically correct. And Lincoln simply fits much better into that correct agenda.

Second, most Americans (both Democrats and Republicans) have an isolationist or small worldview that blinds them to the immense gravity of the much broader world around them. Just as many Americans feel no compulsion to learn foreign languages, most prefer to focus on national issues. We must, however, open our eyes to the broader picture if we are to assess these two great men with any sense of logic.

As we know, Lincoln presided over the bloodiest home battle our country ever faced to unite a divided country, and of course to abolish slavery, which is undoubtedly the key element in this decision. Yet compare the outcome of the North losing the Civil War, with America and all the free nations of the world losing to Hitler and Hirohito. If Lincoln lost, Americans still would have maintained some variation of America, beset with racist Southerners perhaps, but still offering the broad spectrum of freedoms that were established by the founding fathers, not some tyrannical regime. People somehow forget that before Lincoln came into office, America was a young resilient nation that boasted of presidents like Washington, Jefferson, Madison, Monroe, Jackson, Polk, and others, and all their noble efforts would not have been lost even after a defeat to the South in the Civil War. The result would have been a flawed variant of America, or possibly two nations, but there still would have been a republic offering hope for future change.

However, if Roosevelt did not stand up against an entire nation's initial weakness and then boldly confront the largest assembled alliance of mass destruction the world had ever known—the Axis powers of evil—Americans would all be wearing swastikas and living under a brutal dictatorship, all rights and freedoms terminated. A conquest by the Japanese would have been equally horrific. Under a dark Nazi regime, all would have certainly been lost, without the slightest hope of ever having freedom or emancipating blacks. For Hitler's next program, after killing the Jews and Slavs, most assuredly would have been to exterminate the blacks and quite possibly many other non-Aryan groups after that.

Therefore, the gargantuan divide between the supreme leadership required to confront the Confederate Army and that needed against the diabolical Axis powers, which sprawled across the globe and featured a whole new assortment of advanced naval, air, and space weaponry, is astronomical. The horrific consequence that Americans, and countless free nations around the world, would have suffered by losing WWII is never seriously contemplated, nor is the immense gravity of the topic ever truly understood.

One thing, however, remains unavoidably clear:

As the world sank into its darkest and most evil bog, while deranged despots desecrated life, turning captives into carrion, aspiration into desperation, facility into futility, and hope into hell, the salvation of civilization was largely due to one man…

Franklin D. Roosevelt.

The turn of the twentieth century was a volatile era with so many advances occurring simultaneously that we need to go back slightly to address important advances that preceded and accompanied the two great wars. The nineteenth century was one of the horse and cart, tasks powered by hand or steam, and dark nights lit by candlelight. All this would effectively change over a mere handful of decades. A small and miraculous group of men, who played a part in putting the word 'modern' into modern world, would give light to the new world.

XI
1880 – 1955. EDISON & EINSTEIN
THE ELECTRO-ATOMIC AGE
VOLTA, BELL, TESLA & WESTINGHOUSE | FERMI & VON BRAUN

(Undecim, Aquarius, Simeon, Simon, November)

THE ELECTRIC AGE

Relentless winds swept over the rolling seas of the North Atlantic as its biting chill froze the decks of *L'Amérique*. En route to New York, the famous actress, Sarah Bernhardt, stepped out of the steamship's coal-heated cabin to encounter the raw elements. As gas lamps flickered inside the ship's hull, cylindrical beams of light radiated out through a series of portholes, each being eerily truncated by the darkness of night. The distant silhouette of the New World was backlit by a faint yet warm and shimmering glow. It was late November of 1880.

As the steamship *L'Amérique* entered New York's harbor, it quietly sailed past the vacant spot that in six years would host America's colossal icon, the Statue of Liberty. As the ocean liner reached port, Sarah grasped her luggage and disembarked.

Not far from the cold harbor, on the Jersey mainland, was Menlo Park. It was the famed site of the inventive wizard, Thomas Alva Edison. Sitting behind his oil-stained desk, the prematurely gray-haired alchemist scribbled diagrams with illegible notations, resembling a Da Vinci codex.

Oddly enough, on this day, Sarah Bernhardt, the brightest star of the day, paid a visit to Thomas Edison, the brightest electrical leader of the day. Her journey across the Atlantic on a steamship outfitted with smelly gas lamps was the standard equipment of their time, equipment that Edison was determined to change.

Edison may not have been the brightest inventor of his day but he was certainly the brightest electrical leader of his day. Edison had that true American "I can do it" attitude that even made him surpass his more brilliant rivals. This kinetic ingredient was not only crucial to Edison's success but was crucial to the vast majority of his peers' successes in other fields, as brilliant ideas that sit idle on a drawing board or in a lab remain static unless kinetically jolted into action.

For example, the incandescent bulb was actually invented a year earlier by the British inventor, Joseph Swan. Yet, Edison put his mind to making it a practical utility and did everything in his power to bring it to market. As Edison said, "Anything that won't sell, I don't want to invent. Its sale is proof of utility, and utility is success."

Taking advantage of Sarah Bernhardt's visit, Edison recorded her dramatic voice with his new phonograph that became a huge success. She made the first vocal recording of dialogues from the play *Phèdre,* among several other recitations.

Edison even perfected Bell's telephone, by adding two carbon buttons formed out of lampblack carbon that made it truly useable. Basically, Edison was in perpetual motion, constantly seeking solutions. As the Wizard of Menlo Park said, "Genius is one percent inspiration and ninety-nine percent perspiration."

There would be many blunders and failures, but like a raw bolt of lightning, Edison's path may not have been perfectly straight, but quite often he struck pay dirt.

However it must be emphasized that Edison did not work in a vacuum, he had many helping hands and many brilliant thinkers that made contributions to his electrical crusade. It wasn't long before Edison not only illuminated New York City, but the entire nation, as well as parts of Europe. His dispute with Joseph Swan over their incandescent bulb was resolved in England by a merger that formed the Ediswan Company. Edison effectively promoted his new invention as not only being more cost effective than the malodorous gas lamps, but even slighted the outdated and dangerous device by stating, "Gas was a light for the dark ages."

The railroad tycoon, J. Pierpont Morgan *(see page 715),* perceptively recognized the lucrative future of electricity and became Edison's primary financier. J.P. Morgan invested in many peripheral industries, and by routinely holding a majority of shares, he omnipotently power-managed each of them. This finally enabled Edison to implement his modern marvel, and at an accelerated rate. One of his first feats was to retrofit Morgan's New York office with electric lighting. Other affluent families, such as the Vanderbilts, utilized Edison to electrify their estates, while business offices and factories soon followed. Eventually, in 1881 the city of New York commissioned Edison to install lampposts and wiring throughout the city. In time, subsequent mergers allowed Edison's lighting system to spread across the nation, illuminating streets and homes, while his European satellite followed suit. Edison was effectively snuffing out the archaic age of gas lamps.

However, Edison's eventual success was not void of obstacles. One of Edison's early roadblocks was how to solve the immense power source that his direct current network required. Batteries were the only known source of electricity during his pioneering days and they couldn't sustain the vast network Edison envisioned.

ALESSANDRO VOLTA had made the astounding invention of the battery over a century earlier, in 1799. By first devising the electrophorus, in 1775, Volta managed to produce static electricity. However, static discharges yielded nothing useful. Volta then discovered that when certain metals and chemicals encountered one another, they produced electricity. For the first time, man could not only create, but also harness the raw power of nature, which previously had merely fascinated them. This opened a huge doorway to electrical research and experimentation. His revolutionary invention attracted the attention of the famous emperor, Napoleon Bonaparte, who even presented Volta with a cash award and minted gold coins in his honor. The term *volt* was applied to the electro current in 1881, which is still used today, thus commemorating his electrifying achievement.

Yet, it was only after witnessing the dynamo generator, built by William Wallace, that the key to successfully lighting large networks dawned upon Edison. It was Edison's improvements to this generator that finally enabled him to power his broad direct current network with some modicum of stability.

At the outbreak of WWI, Edison was invited to Washington DC, and protected by the Secret Service, where he developed over forty inventions for the navy. Some of these inventions were as follows: fitting naval searchlights with rapid-action Venetian-blinds to send visual Morse Code; devising a chemical, soda-based fire extinguisher that stripped fire of its oxygen; developing a gyro-like platform for mounted guns to correct aim in rolling seas; modifying periscopes to enhance clarity; devising underwater parachute-like bags that, when deployed, could more quickly turn or slow down a ship.

Edison then devoted much time to developing a new and more cost-efficient rubber that aided Henry Ford's rising automotive needs. The post-WWI years had marked a tremendous shift in innovation. One that even Edison was growing uncomfortable with. The new age made clear how trains confined to tracks were yielding to automobiles on an open road, or how Bell's telephone, confined by wire, was yielding to Marconi's radio, which was wireless and boundless.

Edison strongly opposed radio, in particular, as it rivaled his interests in the telephonic, telegraphic, and phonographic industries. He even declared it a "fad" that wouldn't last. However, it would later become President Franklin Roosevelt's favorite medium, as his fireside chats were broadcast into American homes via the invisible wireless signals. A new rapidly progressive world had emerged, one that even Edison was finding hard to keep pace with.

Nevertheless, Edison's impressive list of inventions includes: the electrical vote recorder; universal stock ticker; electrical fuses, sockets and regulation meters required for the massive electrical network; the fluorescent lamp; the nickel-iron-alkaline storage battery; the miner's helmet with safety light; as well as over forty naval innovations and many others. Last, and certainly not least, is Edison's patent of the motion picture camera. This was actually developed by Thomas Armat and Charles Jenkins, from whom Edison bought the rights, and this device would likewise have an incalculable effect on modern culture.

As a young boy born in Ohio, Thomas' family soon moved to Michigan where his schooling would soon prove brief. After only three months, Edison's humiliated teacher pronounced him incapable of focusing or learning. Thomas was homeschooled by his mother, who prompted his appetite for reading. As such, Edison soon became a voracious reader.

However, by age twelve, Edison already had profound hearing loss, which most likely accounts for his learning debacle at school. Edison's hearing progressively deteriorated. Finding it an asset to close out the outside world and better focus on his experiments, Edison later denied pleas from deaf people who begged him to develop a hearing aid.

In 1837, the young Edison became infatuated with Samuel F. B. Morse's telegraph. By the end of the Civil War, telegraph cables stretched across America from San Francisco to Washington DC. Edison eagerly became a telegrapher and relocated several times, each time gaining promotions in the new industry. Eventually, the innovative youngster was given corporate backing to develop a new and faster stock ticker.

By 1876, ALEXANDER GRAHAM BELL had invented the telephone, and for the next two years, Edison worked on perfecting his speaking telegraph. He even perfected Bell's telephone by adding two carbon buttons formed out of kerosene lampblack. This finally made the device consumer-ready. However, during this experimentation, the partially deaf inventor needed to place a metal plate between his teeth that was connected to a sounding apparatus in order to hear.

Despite his stubbornness in some instances, Edison always strived to find a solution to overcome adversity. In fact, during these hearing tests, Edison realized that if he could record these signals, he could then possibly reproduce and playback the sound. This endeavor would inevitably give birth to Edison's phonograph. Yet Edison's primary focus was on lighting, and by initially electrifying New York City, his enterprise soon expanded nationwide and caught the world's attention. As mentioned, J.P. Morgan's calculating financial grip enabled Edison to form a monopoly over the electrical consumption industry. By the early 1880s, Edison had his lab in Menlo Park, New Jersey, and power plants in New York City as well as Europe. But, Morgan's immense power would change all that in the future.

In 1884, Edison was introduced to NIKOLA TESLA *(see page 715)*, a Croatian-born Serbian immigrant, seeking work. Tesla was a young wizard in his own right who worked as a troubleshooter for Edison's power plants in France and Germany. In fact, Tesla first witnessed Edison's Dynamo DC electric generator in his college class at the

Polytechnic Institute in Austria. Fortunately for Tesla, Edison had just received a distress call regarding broken dynamos aboard a ship he recently outfitted. Tesla was employed on the spot to remedy the electrical malfunction, which he did at lightning speed.

Tesla was instantly hired and diligently aided Edison in the struggle to invent generators powerful enough to transmit current over a broad network. Tesla was a workaholic and put in fifteen to seventeen hours a day, prompting Edison to remark, "I have had many hardworking assistants, but you take the cake!" However, a recurring dispute kept erupting as Tesla kept suggesting his favored AC (alternating current), which he knew was superior. Edison was deeply invested with labor and patents on the existing DC (direct current) system, and kept his focus on DC. In essence, the equally headstrong Tesla was becoming a nuisance, even if Edison realized his genius.

Tesla was a rare individual, yet even Tesla's amazing discoveries were in small part indebted to previous patents by other inventors. His alternating current motor was a modification of the works that several scientists had previously developed, yet most prominent was Elihu Thomson, who had already designed and operated motors on the AC system. Thomson was a prolific inventor, and secured more patents than even Tesla. Thomson had also established his own electric company when he partnered with a friend to form the Thomson-Houston Company.

However, hovering above all these geniuses was a hawkish titan, who was now eyeing up the unsuspecting Thomson, and this, once again, was J.P. Morgan. Morgan's typical cutthroat practice was to establish rival companies, only to undercut prices, which forced his rivals to renegotiate contracts and company shares, allowing Morgan to consume a fifty-one percent majority holding. Morgan had appointed Charles Coffin in charge of leading this devious capitalistic assault. Eventually, Thomson was forced to merge with Edison Electric to form a new powerhouse company, whereby Morgan effectively erased both inventors' names from the nameplate, thus becoming General Electric.

Morgan once again controlled his lilliputian subjects, and quite appropriately, his appointee had the perfect name, for as far as name recognition went, Charles Coffin had nailed both Thomson and Edison's coffins shut.

However, before this merger, the young and brilliant Tesla would secure many new patents for the Edison Company, until irreconcilable differences peaked and he decided to quit. This was due to personal as well as serious financial conflicts with Edison. Although both men were geniuses, they came from polar molds. Tesla was academically educated, quiet, and extremely fastidious, while Edison was self-educated, often brusque in manner, and unkempt. Tesla would even mock the older genius for being appallingly disorganized. However, beyond inventive genius, Edison also possessed an intuitive business acumen, which Tesla lacked. This would plague Tesla for the rest of his long and inventively fruitful life. Nevertheless, Tesla then found employment with Edison's rival, Mr. Westinghouse. *(See page 715)*

GEORGE WESTINGHOUSE was a dynamic force in his own right, and his interest in the AC motors and transformers of earlier inventors persuaded him to challenge Edison's DC system. Westinghouse had previously developed the first commercial AC system, consisting of thirty plants in Buffalo, New York, in November of 1886. Therefore, when Westinghouse heard of Tesla's amazing breakthroughs, with his recent patents that included polyphase AC motors, transformers, and all the accessories necessary to run a new and infinitely far superior AC system, Westinghouse jumped at the opportunity to secure Tesla.

Yet even Westinghouse was caught in the snare of dealing with J.P. Morgan and his electrical wizard, Edison. Westinghouse was a man of strong principles, and a staunch advocate for progress, not just financial progress, but scientific progress. This meant that even if an existing and expensive system was already in place, it would be prudent, and in everyone's best interest, to change it if a superior system presented itself. This was not always true with Edison, and especially the moneyman Morgan, who was mainly concerned with bottom-line profits.

Interestingly, Mark Twain summed up this era of robber barons rather nicely when he said their credo was, *"Get money. Get it quickly. Get it in abundance. Get it dishonestly, if you can, honestly, if you must."* However, Westinghouse was a different breed, for Westinghouse knew that AC was superior. And now with the advent of Tesla's patents, thus making AC unequivocally far superior, Westinghouse, like David, stood up to the Goliaths that monopolized the industry. This duel became known as the "War of the Currents".

Yet while Westinghouse unveiled his slingshot of truth and progress, Edison unsheathed his sword of underhanded greed and suppression. Edison's subordinates engaged in many smear tactics that today would be crimes. They had dogs, cats, and even an elephant electrocuted in public using the high voltage of AC as a demonstration of the system's many dangers, while labeling the dead victims as being "Westinghoused". They even took this to an unprecedented level when Sing Sing Prison decided to make a first in history by electrocuting the criminal William Kemmler. The executioner's stage was set and the switch thrown, yet the Edison technicians miscalculated the voltage required, since they had previously killed only small animals. Kemmler would suffer a torturous death, as the electrical jolt had to be repeated to terminate his quivering nerves. Westinghouse was mortified. However, this spurred respected scientists to rally to Westinghouse's side, whereby they published proven statistics that soundly countered the unfounded hype.

Edison, however, was wielding a double-edged sword, for on one side, although he originally refused AC (perhaps out of stubborn jealousy), as an inventor he had to have known that AC was a superior technology, which he unfortunately did not invent or legally possess. Meanwhile, Edison also had the fiscal-minded J.P. Morgan to contend with, who inevitably called all the shots. As the man who pulled all the strings and controlled Edison's purse and fate, Morgan would not jeopardize his profits by overhauling an entire system just to accommodate the public. Edison may have been the brilliant puppet, but Morgan was the puppet master.

However, while battling these titans, Westinghouse's market share dropped, and he now found himself in a crisis. Upon the recommendation of top-notch financial advisors, Westinghouse was advised to repair the gaping hole that was internally sinking his ship. This hole was the over-generous royalty that he agreed to pay Tesla for his AC polyphase system. If this leaking fissure persisted, the Westinghouse flagship would surely sink. Being an inventor himself, Westinghouse believed in royalties for scientific ingenuity. As such, he detested the admiral's call to duty, which forced him to order his first mate to either sacrifice his share of the treasure, or watch the entire ship sink. Therefore, with heavy heart, Westinghouse approached Tesla and relayed the ultimatum, "Your decision determines the fate of the Westinghouse Company."

Tesla paused and then questioned Westinghouse about his loyalty and dedication to the AC System cause. Westinghouse professed his dream and determination in succinct terms, "It was my efforts to make it available to the world that brought about the present difficulty. But, I intend to continue, no matter what happens, with my original plans to put the country on an alternating-current basis."

Tesla was a diehard scientist; the benefits of his endeavors for society came before his own personal gain. Moreover, he knew that if he was cast out to sea there were no other flagships to climb aboard. His patents for his new AC polyphase system would sink with him, while the resolute Westinghouse would rise and establish another fleet to continue the assault, even with a whole new crew if necessary. Tesla realized the sincerity and goodwill of the man before him, and conceded to the inevitable. Many years later, Tesla would recollect that Westinghouse was the only man in the struggle who was a true friend, a genuine man of honor, and a true benefactor of progress. Likewise, Tesla knew that Westinghouse supported him and his dazzling invention with his own hide, but desperately needed a sacrificial compromise to stay afloat. Tesla would receive a flat fee of $216,600 for his AC patents, and Westinghouse remained in business.

Under the revised contract, Tesla was required to move to Westinghouse's Pittsburgh plant to conduct the implementation and development. However, Tesla soon became embroiled in intense arguments with the plant's engineers who wished to maintain standard practices. Tesla, meanwhile, endured as best he could. Upon completing his consulting, Tesla decided he had had enough, and established his own laboratory in New York City with money he had saved. This is when Tesla invented the Tesla coil, which transformed high voltage down to safe levels for use in appliances. He also began research on radio transmission.

While Tesla was consumed in his own world of research and invention, Westinghouse phoned him from Pittsburgh. Westinghouse was ecstatic; he had won the contract for powering the upcoming World's Fair in Chicago. This event was scheduled to celebrate the 400th anniversary of Columbus' discovery, and was projected to attract millions worldwide. They would finally have their chance to show the world the awesome power of AC. Moreover, they would also set an historic benchmark by being the first to use AC current to power a World's Fair. However, not only would the eyes of the world be focused on the event (which would feature exciting new inventions by Edison, grand classical architecture and, of course, their new AC system), but the country was in a slump with unemployment, bankruptcies, and foreclosures, as Grover Cleveland took office for a second term. Therefore, the country also needed a grand spectacle to boost morale and incite new markets of interest and development. It was January of 1893, and they only had four months to complete the huge task. Henceforth, Tesla had to drop everything he was laboring on in New York to make the fair a success.

The Chicago World's Fair (Columbian Exposition) opened on May 1 and exceeded expectations in all spheres. By September, over 25 million people attended, as new fangled wonders of all kinds were on display, including the 250-foot rotating wheel with seats, which was designed by Mr. George Ferris. This also allowed Westinghouse to display his own contributions to the AC system, which included transformers that could convert AC to DC, making it universally adaptable to preexisting appliances or even trolleys. Westinghouse and Tesla scored a huge success, and by October of 1893, Westinghouse already received a call for their next big project. He would be awarded the contract of building the first two generators to harness the power of Niagara Falls.

As a young boy, Tesla was fascinated by watermills and turbines, and even saw a photo of the mighty Niagara Falls in one of his father's books. The sheer size of the falls, and the waste of water not being utilized enamored Tesla. Now he had the expertise and opportunity to tackle his childhood dream. With the superior AC System perfected by Tesla, and the perseverance and sound business acumen of Westinghouse, Niagara Falls became a milestone in electrical engineering. The initial facility produced a staggering 150,000 horsepower of electricity, and with General Electric being awarded the task of installing the power lines as a fair contractual compromise, the city of Buffalo was set ablaze with current. The Westinghouse/Tesla success at this facility made clear that AC was, in fact, the better solution, and in the years that followed, it ultimately replaced Edison's DC system.

Edison had previously strung wires across cities using his DC network, yet as the years passed, the harsh reality of this system's inherent flaws mounted and became painfully evident. Fires were prevalent and DC generators often required repairs. The DC system could only transmit electricity short distances, and only allowed for a single voltage. Hence, although being sufficient for light bulbs, since bulbs all drew an equal amount of current, appliances such as the new refrigerators and fans being invented, required more voltage, thus confirming that DC was obsolete. In contrast, the AC method, developed initially by others, yet perfected by Tesla, effectively allowed for this variance. Tesla became the unsung hero.

Tesla maintained a small circle of friends, but was predominantly a loner, as many creative minds are, and was erroneously described by some as insane or a mad scientist. This image was further enhanced by his invention of the Magnifying Transmitter in the late 1890s, which produced huge, flaring arcs of electricity 20 to 30 feet long. This wildly charged apparatus became synonymous with the mad scientist, as similar mock devices were used in Hollywood for the early Frankenstein films. However, the real basis for these people's assessments was his odd behaviors. Tesla was known to circle a building three times before entering, demanded that eighteen clean linen napkins be neatly folded at every meal, and he required a similar amount of towels for every bath. Tesla's servant also recorded other repetitious oddities that promulgated the rumors. However, modern analysis of Tesla's condition indicates he had OCD, obsessive-compulsive-disorder. This nagging affliction, however, did not have an effect on his lucidity or inventiveness, which remained extremely active.

Tesla was also a close friend of Mark Twain for many years, and a photograph actually captures Twain in Tesla's lab, standing near one of Tesla's illuminated spheres. These spheres where illuminated by an ambient oscillator nearby, making them completely wireless, and could be held or even moved freely around the room. Tesla also demonstrated to Twain and an English journalist, Chauncey McGovern, his red ball of flames. Tesla snapped his fingers, and this odd phenomenon (without a glass tube or container, or an apparent power source) appeared in his hand. He then placed this glowing red ball of flames on his clothes, in his hair, and even on his bewildered spectators' laps, all without the slightest burn or injury. Tesla proved to be an astounding scientist with many bold ideas that, unfortunately, weren't brought to fruition by investors and, even more unfortunately, were never fully documented by Tesla, hence these intriguing experiments died with their luminous master.

Tesla's earlier battle with Edison over the AC/DC systems caused both men to become more embittered as the years progressed. When the nomination for the Nobel Prize in 1915 was rumored to include both Edison and Tesla sharing the honor, each inventor rose in heated opposition, swearing never to share the award. It's ironic that neither would receive this prestigious award, yet the inventiveness of both men helped immeasurably in shaping a nation, a nation positioning itself to be a world leader.

The turn of the century saw many new inventions, and the Industrial Revolution, with its earlier roots in England, now became more pronounced on American soil. In fact, this trend was well charted; in the 1870s, America produced about 23 percent of the world's manufacturing output and by 1929, it was producing over 42 percent. Meanwhile, England produced 32 percent in the 1870s, which dropped down to 9.5 percent by 1929.

Henry Ford's automated production line technique ushered in advances that would prove crucial to both World Wars, and the potential benefits were incalculable to modern manufacturing needs in general *(see page 714)*. Like Edison, Henry Ford had no formal education yet his contribution to American society and the war effort was colossal. Edison's phonograph, movie camera, and the original concept and installation of an electrical network that powered appliances, machinery and lights, indelibly changed the world. His DC System may have been defective, but it was Edison who first conceived and implemented this system well before Tesla perfected it with AC. Tesla and Westinghouse, on the other hand, made this system extremely adaptable, electrically safe, cost effective and resoundingly universal.

The beginning of the twentieth century had closed its doors on the listless nineteenth century of gas and wicks, thus opening its doors to the lightning fast world of electricity and light. This shocking transformation was largely due to Edison's pioneering role, while the additional inventive genius of Tesla and the business acumen of Morgan and Westinghouse completed the circuit.

THE ATOMIC AGE

In 1931, the streets were well lit and new appliances hit the market, but Thomas Edison, the pioneer of electricity, died. However, the world did not blink, for it was irrevocably lit, and on an accelerated course to an unpredictably blinding future. In fact, only fourteen years later, many new brilliant minds arrived on the scene. However, these savants were tackling abstract areas of physics that entered a radically new dimension of human thought; namely, they were attempting to understand the secrets of the most basic, yet essential, particles in nature in order to unleash the most explosive and radiant power in the universe. It was the summer of 1945.

The midnight sky crackled as thundershowers drenched the parched desert sand of New Mexico. Upon the horizon, huge mountains stood, as if towering sentinels guarding their masters' secrets below. The rains tapered off as the agitated sky sighed, quelling into an eerie silence. In the distance, a solitary metal tower stood amid the flat sandy floor of the Alamogordo desert.

Six miles away, a small gathering of men lie on the ground, face down with their feet toward the tower, and nine miles away, another cluster of men did the same. The darkness of early morning maintained its peaceful calm. As the clock ticked the stroke of 5:30, the dark sky suddenly exploded, as a flash of silent light illuminated the desert. It was as if the sun were instantaneously born before their eyes, as the miniscule tower incinerated under the enormous fireball. Jumping to their feet, while safely wearing thick, dark-tinted glasses, Enrico Fermi and the scientific team gazed in awe.

Instantaneously, a massive shockwave of extreme heat, accompanied by a deafening roar, rattled the earth. As the sand rippled under their feet, Enrico simultaneously dropped a few pieces of paper. It was a brisk attempt to assess the explosion's discharge. Within seconds, Enrico calculated what elaborate instruments only arrived at days later. To the amazement of his peers, Enrico's preliminary results were unnervingly close. The explosion was actually brighter than the sun, as its megaton force surpassed all expectations.

This top-secret, wartime endeavor—initiated by Franklin Roosevelt and codenamed the Manhattan Project—was directed by Robert Oppenheimer. From 1942 until 1945 the elite team, which eventually employed 130,00 people, worked clandestinely to reach this historic day. The project's test, or operation Trinity, was a success. Within that split second—on July 15, 1945, in a remote desert in New Mexico—the world officially entered the Atomic Age.

Despite Oppenheimer's managerial role, however, the maven who most scientists revered was Enrico Fermi. Fermi had fled Italy in 1938, shortly after receiving the Nobel Prize, due to Mussolini's Fascist rise as dictator. Settling in at Columbia University in New York City, Enrico spent several years assimilating into American culture. However, after the Japanese attack on Pearl Harbor, the newly conceived theory of thermo-nuclear power became crucial to the war effort, and Fermi was invited to Chicago. Enrico initially faced security roadblocks, since the Italian-born physicist was by law an enemy alien. However, on Columbus Day in 1942, President Roosevelt lifted the alien status of Italians, which somewhat eased Fermi's situation.

Two months later, on December 2, under a volleyball field at the University of Chicago, Enrico successfully produced the first controlled chain reaction. The Atomic Pile, which Fermi later called it, was a landmark event in the development of nuclear energy. It also spotlighted Enrico's firm grasp of various sciences and applied theory, for he had meticulously planned and calculated every detail. Fermi's Atomic Pile became the critical foundation for the Manhattan Project's research and development, which enabled the successful creation of the atomic bomb. At Los Alamos, Fermi became a project leader and (as verified by his peers) was called upon, as almost an oracle, to answer the many baffling questions that stymied their research.

As Fermi's fellow physicist and later biographer, Emilio Segrè said, "This was one of those occasions when Fermi's dominion over all physics, one of his most startling characteristics, came into its own. The problems involved in the Trinity test ranged from hydrodynamics to nuclear physics, from optics to thermodynamics, from geophysics to nuclear chemistry. Often they were closely interrelated, and to solve one it was necessary to understand all the others. Even though the purpose was grim and terrifying, it was one of the greatest physics experiments of all time. Fermi completely immersed himself in the task. At the time of the test he was one of the very few persons (or perhaps the only one) who understood all the technical ramifications of the activities at Alamogordo."

Enrico Fermi's role in the development of the atomic bomb was so significant that when the Manhattan Project secretly premiered the first self-sustained nuclear chain reaction in history, the celebrated phone call to one of the absent project leaders stated, *"The Italian navigator has landed in the new world... The natives were very friendly."*

Today, physicists are still devising new theories upon fermionic fields, which consist of particles called fermions, all of which are named after Enrico Fermi. The Compact Muon Solenoid (CMS), for example, is an experiment in particle physics that is attempting to prove supersymmetry, which is to hypothetically find and measure symmetric particles in nature. This is a mind-bending noumenon that current quantum physics cannot locate or mathematically measure; yet, Fermi's great name lives on in all these grand endeavors.

However, to reach this highpoint in physics, we must backtrack to the origins of man's quest to understand basic laws of nature. The theory of gravity had been initially posited by Aristotle, which as we know was mere conjecture and seriously flawed, and was only finally understood by Galileo two thousand years later. However, even Galileo's laws required refinement.

On Christmas Day, in 1642, Isaac Newton was born. By coincidence, it was the same year that Galileo died. Essentially, the baton was passed from Galileo (who had first discovered the correct and basic laws of gravity and motion) to Newton (who formulated the physics and mathematics required to establish his own famous laws of gravity). These laws would dominate Western thought for 250 years, and were deeply ingrained into the scientific community, as well as the public's awareness...until the dawn of a new century.

The 20th century commenced with a bang in 1905, when the twenty-six-year-old ALBERT EINSTEIN put forth his theory of relativity. Over a ten-year period, Einstein would refine his theories and publish his theory on gravitation in 1916. This would eventually replace Newton's laws of gravity and motion.

Scientists in the late 19th century were baffled that the orbit of Mercury was shifting and making the planet appear to wobble in space. Newton's laws of gravity failed to address any such occurrence, and it was Einstein's theory that posited the notion that matter in space was not rigid, and could become elastic. This hypothesis was even ridiculed by the genius Nikola Tesla. However, Einstein maintained that space actually bending near the sun accounted for Mercury's wobbling path. As mentioned, bold theories or inventions do not materialize in a vacuum, as small stepping-stones lead to others finding new and supposedly correct answers. In this regard, it is now believed that the atomic theory posited by Rudjer Boscovich, a Croatian-Italian scientist in the 18th century, was perhaps the first stepping-stone in the process leading to Einstein's own theory.

At an early age, Boscovich moved to Rome and was educated at the Collegio Romano, where he later became its professor of Mathematics. He was inspired by Newton's mechanics and he, in turn, influenced Michael Faraday to develop his theory for electromagnetic interaction. That sparked Einstein, who then grappled with it further. Henceforth, we must be cognizant of the fact that science is an ongoing process, and one day even Einstein's laws and theories will be challenged when attempting to explain other mysteries of the universe.

Another quandary faced by late 19th century scientists was whether light was a particle or a wave. Newton himself wasn't sure, so he assumed it was both. Newton had designated several key anomalies to God's unquestionable creation. This disturbed Einstein and the growing factions of scientists who were no longer hampered by religious constraints or philosophical conjecture. This did not mean some of these scientists didn't believe in God, but simply that they did not believe in mankind's religious dogma or the Bible's questionable sources that suppressed thought. However, many, believing that light traveled in a straight line, leaned toward the particle explanation. The two camps were diametrically opposed.

However, earlier, in the late 1700s, the British scientist, Thomas Young, devised an experiment that indicated light had a wavelike pattern. In 1868, James Clerk Maxwell introduced his shocking revelation that light was both an electrical force and a magnetic force. It would be upon Maxwell's model that the young Einstein pondered, using his stellar mind-games, to formulate his own theory that proved to be light-years ahead of a world chugging along on steam.

In 1919, the Royal Society in London, which Newton himself had once chaired as president, confirmed Einstein's theory, thus officially negating the findings of their old Sir Isaac. As such, Einstein instantly skyrocketed to world fame. In 1921, Einstein won the Nobel Prize for his photoelectric effect, yet not his theory of relativity. Since only a handful of scientists in the entire world grasped this profound concept, it relegated that intriguing mind-bender to the back burner.

However, other things were smoldering in the world. In 1928, the Nazi Party was elected to the Reichstag. Hitler quickly rose in the ranks and influenced the anti-liberal factions, whereby legally seizing the position of Reich chancellor in January of 1933. Witnessing the rising tide of anti-Semitism, the once pacifist Einstein soon realized that only force could remove Hitler and the Nazis. Unfortunately, many of his colleagues thought the reign of terror would pass. On October 7, 1933, Einstein sailed to America and landed in New York harbor ten days later. He then settled in Princeton, New Jersey, and became a professor at its progressive university.

Once an American citizen, Einstein had more to contend with than just teaching physics. In the summer of 1939, Einstein was enjoying his customary vacation on Peconic, Long Island. This was the only place where Einstein completely forgot about his forced exile, six years earlier, due to Hitler's pogrom. As soon as Hitler became Reich chancellor in 1933, he passed the Restoration of Civil Service Law that terminated all Jewish college professors. Fortunately, Einstein had been invited to America the year before as a guest professor at Princeton University and had decided to stay. Despite being safely out of Hitler's anti-Semitic clutches, Einstein still had bouts of melancholy.

Driving out to Long Island in a frantic hurry were Eugene Wigner (a nuclear physicist that fled Germany three years prior to Einstein, and had been recruited by Princeton University) and Leo Szilard (a physicist who had been a student of Einstein's at the Institute of Technology in Germany).

Wigner and Szilard were of Hungarian birth, yet both men had been German citizens, until Hitler's Nazi swastika crossed out any signs of hope for anyone of Jewish faith. This included Einstein, even though he abandoned his Jewish faith to become an agnostic. As he told a rabbi, "*I believe in Spinoza's God, who reveals Himself in the lawful harmony of the world, not in a God who concerns Himself with the fate and the doings of mankind.*"

Nevertheless, Wigner and Szilard had dashed out to Long Island to inform Einstein that Enrico Fermi and Szilard had been conducting experiments in nuclear fission, and they now believed that uranium could be turned into an immensely powerful form of energy, energy that could be released as a bomb.

Einstein was intrigued. He knew his famous theory allowed for such a massive release of energy, but he believed it to be beyond his era's mental capacity: an explosive hot potato better left to future scientists to juggle. Szilard informed Einstein that he had stumbled upon the basic concept of fission back in 1933, but with the brilliant work of Enrico Fermi, this possibility would become a reality, and hopefully soon.

Being a staunch pacifist—who even ended his friendship with Fritz Haber when he developed chemical weapons for the Kaiser—Einstein was at first hesitant. However, once he realized that his old comrades back in Nazi Germany were well aware of nuclear fission, it was clear that the race to build this weapon first was an ugly necessity. More importantly, contemplating the consequence if Hitler beat them was simply terrifying.

Realizing that Belgium had uranium mines in the Congo, Einstein was eager to contact the queen of Belgium; not only to purchase the ore for their project, but also to protect these resources from Hitler. If Poland fell in a month, one could only imagine how fast Belgium would fall.

Einstein dictated a letter to Szilard and Wigner, which they delivered to the Belgian ambassador. As it would turn out, Szilard felt hard pressed to expose this colossal danger, and he eagerly set his sights on the president. Through an associate in New York, he managed to contact Alexander Sachs, who was an aide to President Franklin D. Roosevelt. Sachs agreed to hand deliver the letter; however, to be effective it would need to be authored by the eminent Nobel Prize winner Albert Einstein. This meant Szilard needed to drive out to Long Island, once again.

Unfortunately, Wigner had by then left town, so Szilard persuaded another Hungarian-born friend, physicist Edward Teller, to make the trek. Teller would later rise to prominence as being the mastermind who developed the hydrogen bomb, which was tested in 1952. Nevertheless, Teller drove Szilard out to Einstein's retreat on Long Island, and the three physicists sat and drafted two letters, both signed by Einstein. The longer version eventually made its way into President Roosevelt's hands approximately two and a half months later. This was partially due to Hitler's invasion of Poland a month after the letters were written. Yet, even in hindsight, and knowing of the war's successful outcome, a delay of information this vital seems shameful.

As noted before, the war effort consumed American resources, and Roosevelt could only invest so much money on a hypothetical gamble. However, once he realized the genuine feasibility, raw power and ultimate danger, he fully funded the Manhattan Project. As fate would have it, FDR's death and Germany's surrender would occur before this highly secretive bomb reached completion, yet its use was not undermined.

During the bomb's development, thoughts of its devastating power had begun to morally plague the project's director, Robert Oppenheimer, as well as other scientists. However, the team eventually completed their task and fashioned not one, but two bombs. The Japanese, however, were proving to be extremely obstinate, and increased their desperate kamikaze raids, thus making it abundantly clear that surrender was not an option. The controversial ultimatum to drop the first atomic bomb rested with the new president, Harry Truman; who even chided Oppenheimer for his weakness at such a critical moment. As the American High Command calculated the death tolls of either dropping the bomb or using conventional armed forces, all estimates favored deploying the bomb. Upon weighing this conclusion, Truman ordered the mission a go.

However, even after the blazing disintegration of Hiroshima, which initially killed over 60,000 people, the Japanese still refused to concede. Hence, three days later, a second blast at Nagasaki (initially killing 10,000) was required to firmly shock Japan into surrender. The aftermath of these two blasts had caused an unpredictable side effect, as countless thousands were exposed to radiation poisoning. Yet many still assess that the death toll on paper still defends Truman's decision to end a long and bloody war, especially against Japan, who silently and maliciously started the war by attacking Pearl Harbor. The atrocities between the two countries had come to a cataclysmic end, and a new door to future friendship and prosperity opened. General MacArthur would be pivotal in this regard.

Although Einstein didn't work on the atomic bomb, his earlier theories presented the possibility to other inquiring minds that utilized his key principles. Through trial and error, these brilliant scientists made the seemingly impossible manifest. Oddly enough, Einstein's mystifying powers of invention emanated from his profound imagination. For the professor said, *"Information is not knowledge,"* and more surprisingly, *"Imagination is more important than knowledge."*

As a young boy, Einstein faced difficulties in school due to its standardized rote method of learning. It was only after he transferred into a revolutionary new school founded by Johann Pestalozzi, in Arrau, Switzerland, that his imagination was truly able to flourish. Pestalozzi was an educator whose family came from Chiavenna, Italy. His radical approach to learning inaugurated grade levels, grouping by ability, field trips and other practices that focused on learning concrete elements of nature first, which could then be applied and connected to abstract ideas. His provocative curriculum deeply influenced Friedrich Froebel, the inventor of the kindergarten, and other pedagogues. Einstein highly praised the Pestalozzi method, which obviously nurtured his imagination and helped to bestow upon the world his mind-boggling theories.

Interestingly enough, most people today literally "grade" a person's so-called genius by their intelligence quotient or IQ. However, research indicates that people of true "creative genius"—not merely encyclopedic knowledge retention—almost never attain IQ's over 150. Here again, modern standardized tests focus on the wrong criteria for truly gauging creative genius. As I like to say, *"Genius is measured not by static volume but by kinetic vision."* Basically, acquiring a wealth of static knowledge proves useless if it can't kinetically engender creativity.

As a boy, Einstein scored highly in physics and math, while only scoring average in his other classes. And according to Einstein's father, young Albert even received "not-so-good grades."

Additionally, it took Einstein a solid decade of studying and performing his imaginative mind exercises before his true genius flourished. Interestingly, Einstein was an accomplished violinist, and his music idol was Wolfgang Amadeus Mozart. Mozart, too, wrote only standard music for approximately ten years before bequeathing his masterpieces to the world. Einstein found Mozart's music not only sublime and therapeutic but also as a stimulus for his own creativity. This is acquired by not merely listening to the beauty of the sound but by analyzing the mastery of the composer's careful arrangement of notes; the rhythmic pulse, transitions, and intricate interplay that shapes the color and mood of the piece. After all, music is built upon a mathematical progression of various notes, clefs, time signatures, dynamics symbols etc. Therefore, underneath the aural beauty of music is a complex mathematical scheme that is carefully crafted by the creator, which most music lovers—including this author—clearly recognize and appreciate.

Therefore, the acquisition of knowledge that is pertinent to fertilizing creativity seems to be unrecognizable by the so-called academic oracles that devise our educational systems and testing procedures. Nevertheless, Einstein and others have found their own off-the-beaten-path methods to get to where their instincts drove them, and for this, we must be thankful.

Even though the advent of nuclear energy is wrongly associated with his great name, he still assisted in altering the preconceived notions regarding atoms. Einstein had been encouraged by Robert Brown's experiments that indicated atoms exist, since he observed their random movements under a microscope. The scientific community was growing rapidly, and governments began to invest heavily in atomic research, the result being the devastating atomic bomb, which later gave way to the dynamic use of nuclear power plants. The world had drastically leapt from a physical one, utilizing horsepower, to one of physics, utilizing atomic energy, and Einstein was vital in facilitating that stellar leap.

Einstein has been more than just equated with ultimate genius; he has become its new icon. Yet even this awe-inspiring genius was left baffled after forty years of toiling over the intricate details of his quantum theory; a theory he never resolved. The indelible stamp of a mortal lurks underneath this towering figure that, in ancient times, would have undoubtedly been hailed as a god or divine oracle.

Einstein's universe-shattering theories, which only a handful of scientists were able to comprehend, rightfully astonished the world. The reality, however, was that Einstein's name and the field of science had entered the limelight in world affairs. Science and technology would now push America into a vast lead over all other nations, both economically and militarily. As a result, the demand for scientists escalated in addition to their rise in stature. The names of Oppenheimer, Fermi, Teller, Planck, Bohr, von Braun and countless others, would reside in the twentieth century's Pantheon of Scientific Genius, with Einstein heading the dais.

However, where Einstein was a master thinker who was content to have his theories remain in the philosophical realm, there was another genius who strove hard to propel his own soaring concepts into the physical realm. It was during the latter years of the Nazi conflict that this mega-genius skyrocketed to world prominence. Naturally, the Allied commanders all had their eyes trained on this stellar scientist.

WERNHER VON BRAUN was Adolf Hitler's ace in the hole that, fortunately for the free world, reached the war's poker table too late in the game to alter its outcome. For if this great inventor of the V1 and V2 rockets had been able to deploy these aerial weapons sooner, it would have seriously jeopardized Allied victories. Von Braun's rumbling V1 jet-propelled missiles, which rained upon England from the sky, were like winged demons from hell that terrified its victims. Meanwhile, the supersonic speed of the V2 rocket meant that its impact and explosion occurred first, while the whizzing sound of its powerful rocket engine arrived moments after impact, thus offering no warning to the shell-shocked Londoners.

While Allied planes used piston engines to spin their props, von Braun jettisoned into the future with his liquid explosive jet turbines in his V1s, and his solid rocket propellant in his vertically launched V2s. Although others tested rockets earlier, it was von Braun and his terrifying missiles that effectively ushered in the rocket age. At the near conclusion of the war, von Braun was hastily requisitioned and transported to America, along with his secret papers that he stashed months earlier; he knew Hitler's Third Reich was imploding. He would become an American.

Years later, with the advent of the space race, NASA was formed in 1958 with von Braun playing a vital role. Von Braun's ingenuity and drive, along with a vast and brilliant team, enabled America to surpass the Soviets, who initially held the lead. When Sputnik was successfully launched in October of 1957, von Braun made sure President Eisenhower and others knew that he could do the same. He even made the challenge more enticing by stating that he could do so in sixty days. Von Braun was allotted ninety days to complete the task; he completed it in eighty.

Von Braun's stellar flight to success is fascinating. From being Hitler's leading aeronautical weapons developer for the Nazi regime's diabolical effort to annihilate America, to eventually defecting to America under Truman, then being an integral part of NASA under Eisenhower, and ultimately influencing a young John F. Kennedy to put a man on the moon, von Braun's life reads like science fiction. It was von Braun's childhood dream to fly a rocket to the moon, and during his stint under Hitler, he was even arrested and thrown in jail when word of his lunar fantasy hit the German high command. The SS tolerated only a clear focus on the war effort; however, that power plays within the SS often led to rash arrests didn't help their cause. Once Hitler caught wind of their heavy-handed actions, he immediately had his boy wonder released.

Despite popular belief, Kennedy did not truly initiate the bold undertaking to land a man on the moon. Nor does he fully deserve the immense credit lavished upon him for this huge milestone in human history, for he was merely the spokesman for von Braun's ambitious lunar venture. Von Braun personally sparked Kennedy's enthusiasm with his childhood dream of flying to the moon, along with his expertise in rocket design to accomplish the bold feat. Quite amazingly, Wernher von Braun would witness his spectacular sci-fi dream some twenty-four years after defecting from Hitler's nefarious Nazi Germany. Von Braun's transition from the diabolical dark-winged scientist to the inspirational techno-angel, flying to the heavens, has enthralled many, yet his many successes still fail to reverberate with everyone.

A number of concentration camp survivors, many handpicked by von Braun to work at his rocket factories under Nazi control, detest him for allowing the cruelty and slavery to continue while he developed highly destructive weapons for a madman. Close acquaintances of von Braun, however, tell of a man fixated on his own goals, regardless of the politics at hand. The fact that he readily embraced America to fulfill his personal dream certainly seems to bear this out.

Hence, von Braun is clearly another example of how a person obsessed with a luminous dream or goal can blindly forget about his fellow man or morals. Despite his lapse in moral judgment, or possibly his fear of refusing Hitler, human history would have been void of the many successes of NASA in space exploration, including all the spin-offs in computer technology and other fields, if it weren't for the amazing—amoral or apathetic—scientist named Wernher von Braun *(See page 715)*.

The twentieth century had built upon the previous Industrial Revolution to produce a bold collection of inventors and scientists that ushered in the Electro-Atomic age. Where previously brute strength ruled, it was now clear that cerebral knowledge was power. After the ravages of World War II, America would take advantage of this talent by luring scientists to universities and research centers, thus creating what became known as the brain drain effect. America was not alone in this race, as the Soviets quickly abandoned their ally status to engage this frenzied consumption of talent. However, the Soviets primary aim was to use these brilliant minds to bolster their brute strength with new military wares. Realizing that peace in the aftermath of WWII was a fleeting dream; America would enter a whole new world with a whole new array of deadly threats. Thus began the race for military and aeronautical superiority and the long and almost catastrophic Cold War.

XII

1950 – 2009. KENNEDY & McCARTHY – TO THE PRESENT
The Charade of Camelot
The Crusade Against Communism
From Communism to Islam

JOHN F. KENNEDY: *Charismatic yet Reckless Leader*
McCARTHY & REAGAN: *Crusaders Against Communism*
AFRICAN AMERICANS: *Slavery and Civil Rights*
MODERN PRESIDENTS: *Strength vs. Weakness*
RICHARD NIXON: *Scandal and the Scapegoat*
JIMMY CARTER: *Given the Reins after a Republican Debacle*
RONALD REAGAN: *Reviver of a Demoralized Nation*
OSAMA BIN LADEN: *Islamic Jihad and American Weakness*
BILL CLINTON: *Dismantler of State Security + Moral Vacuum = Disasters*
GEORGE W. BUSH: *Prejudged by Speech and Academic Grades* |
UNDERSTANDING ISLAM | *Religious Cowboy vs. Religious Fanatics*

THE IMPETUS FOR GREAT LEADERSHIP &
CLOSING COMMENTARY FOR AMERICANS

(Duodecim, Pisces, Zebulun, Thaddaeus, December)

JOHN F. KENNEDY: *Charismatic yet Reckless Leader*

A cold breeze tenderly massaged the unripe cherry buds along Pennsylvania Avenue. Sitting apprehensively in the Oval Office was John Fitzgerald Kennedy. He had just received another injection in his lower back, containing amphetamines, to ease his perpetual infliction from both Addison's and venereal disease. Sitting with his eyes closed, he felt the potent drug surge through his veins, numbing his pain.

The good-looking and highly charismatic young president had grown accustomed to his poor health from childhood, as well as to the string of call girls that he often managed to squeeze into his busy schedule. His Secret Service men either dutifully or humiliatingly carried out these discrete services, whether the president was in Washington D.C. or out touring on business. However, his younger brother Bobby grew concerned about these routine injections, which were being administered by Doctor Max Jacobson; better known among insiders as Dr. Feelgood. Bobby had the drugs tested by the FDA, and even confronted his older brother about the possible dangers, but John remarked, "I don't care if it's horse piss, it works!" So the treatments and the exhilarating affairs continued.

John Kennedy's amours also extended to movie starlets, like Angie Dickinson and Lee Remick, which FBI Director J. Edgar Hoover had fully documented. Hoover was a meticulous and devoted officer who, during his total tenure, served under eight presidents, amounting to more than fifty years. After Charles Joseph Bonaparte (the Italian-American relative to Napoleon Bonaparte) founded the FBI, Edgar was immensely influential in the structuring and effectiveness of the bureau, yet Hoover had his own baggage, as well. He harbored racial prejudices, engaged in various forms of corruption, and he had to keep his intimate relationship with his associate, Clyde Tolson, a secret.

Hoover enjoyed collecting tawdry data on high profile figures to keep an eye on their actions as well as their effects upon the nation, not to mention being a valuable bargaining chip for job security. Hoover had information on John Kennedy dating back to his obscured marriage to Durie Malcolm, his early childhood, and even extending back to his father Joseph's long and dirty past. Edgar's extensive FBI records included the surveillance of many politicians, corporate executives, celebrities and even included recordings acquired by illegal wiretapping. One such person happened to be John Kennedy's Civil Rights friend, Reverend Martin Luther King Jr.

Hoover believed King to be a communist, and although never acquiring evidence to support that claim he did manage to capture the Reverend's shockingly adulterous voice on tape, as King said, "Fucking is a form of anxiety reduction."

As such, Hoover grew to loathe the man that he saw as a hypocrite, calling King "a tomcat with obsessive, degenerate sexual urges." Naturally, Martin Luther King was a reverend, which made his sins all the more egregious. However, in light of the speculation that surrounds

Edgar's gay relationship, it's hard to tell if he would have fared much better with the moralizing public of the fifties and sixties. Also, would he have received the same forgiveness that King received? However, Hoover's sexual actions still remain an allegation.

More importantly, Hoover and other sources collected information on Kennedy's suicidal affiliation with Mafia bosses Sammy Giancana and Johnny Rosselli. Giancana had used the beautiful Judy Campbell Exner as a conduit to the president. Delivering dirty money, and then allegedly gratifying them both with dirty deeds, Exner was viewed by many as a double-dealing floozy. Exner was even tagged as one of the runners who transported Joseph Kennedy's payoffs that got his son elected.

John Kennedy didn't have the greatest affection for Hoover either, sarcastically calling him "J. Edna" or telling friends like Kenny O'Donnell "I bet he needs to squat to pee!"

However, the records clearly indicate that John Kennedy was not only irresponsible, but he also felt untouchable. Kennedy even allowed his old buddy, Dave Powers, to arrange orgies while his wife Jackie was away. Skinny-dipping pool parties with an ever-changing parade of women had even grated on some of Kennedy's Secret Service men. Agent Joseph Paolella was torn; he was proud to be the first Italian-American to become a Secret Service agent, but was humiliated by his first presidential assignment. Sworn to protect the president from danger with his own life, he was soon left guarding the privacy of an impulsive party-animal with an unquenchable libido. Equally unnerving was that these women gained direct access to the president without clearance of any kind, and could have been spies or assassins. With the Cold War escalating on every front—from Berlin to Korea to Cuba to the next and ultimate hotspot, Vietnam—Kennedy's actions could only be viewed as reckless.

Many years later, doctors realized that some of the pain-killing drugs that Kennedy was taking further enhanced his already over-active sex drive. However, the president evidently had a stronger sex-drug running through his veins, and that was the blood of a true Kennedy, inherited from his father Joe.

Joe Kennedy established the fervently promiscuous trait that affected his offspring. Five years earlier, in 1957, Rose Kennedy invited Lyndon B.

Johnson, then Senate majority leader, to their house for dinner. As Lyndon and his wife Lady Bird sat at the table, with Joe oddly missing, they suddenly heard the front door swing open. Prancing in was old man Joe with a young teenage girl. Without so much as even saying hello to his dinner guests, Joe rudely escorted the girl upstairs. The rumble and giggles from upstairs unsettled the Texan couple as they dined with their companionless hostess. Oddly enough, Rose maintained a sense of calm and normalcy that further baffled her Texan guests.

Joe Kennedy had risen to tremendous power and wealth by being an aggressive entrepreneur who embraced action and thrived on risk. His early dealings with the Mafia's top boss, Frank Costello, during the Prohibition years showed his reckless zeal for money at any cost. He was even known to have screwed the Mafia out of its commission by claiming that a shipment was hijacked, only to turn around and sell the un-stolen liquor to another party. Thus, Kennedy more than doubled his profit. Joe also had his hands in Hollywood for several years, which also cultivated his lustful appetite for starlets, which he obviously passed onto his sons.

Consequently, John F. Kennedy, who was Harvard educated, handsome, charismatic, and wealthy, found it extremely easy to satisfy his lust for women and his innate compulsion to live on the edge. John's younger brother, Bobby, also indulged in sexual indiscretions, but rarely, and was certainly no match for his hyper-crotched brother, who had reportedly slept with well over a hundred women. The two brothers differed, in that, Bobby was emotional and intense, while John was cool and detached. So much so, that John didn't even remember the names of the countless women he sexually devoured. In light of all his affairs, and knowing he had venereal disease, one can only wonder how many illegitimate or even ailing children he fathered. However, in the final analysis, women were fleeting physical objects of lust for John, while men were his cognitive comrades and preferred company.

Even John's affair with the sex goddess Marilyn Monroe was one literally destined to die. Their romantic beginning had quickly turned cool, and the emotionally unstable starlet was thrust even deeper into a depression. Resorting to drugs, Marilyn nose-dived into a pathetic, downward spiral. This prompted her actor friend, Peter Lawford (who was also the president's brother-in-law), to come up with a plan to lift her spirits. He arranged a gala event where the beautiful actress would sing "Happy Birthday" to the president. It was a mindless and heartless idea, for to subject an emotionally torn woman to her unattainable lover in a public arena was nothing short of cruel.

Perhaps Peter Lawford foolishly anticipated that the president would somehow ease Marilyn's despair, but it was not to be. Aloof, John mechanically slapped on his gracious, politician's smile for the cameras, as Marilyn commenced with a seductively erotic performance. It was so overblown and so revealing, in hindsight, that it tastelessly exemplified the president's secretive, yet hyperactive, libido.

Later that night, according to sources, the president laughed mockingly when he spotted his brother Bobby trying to console the love-torn starlet. Meanwhile, Bobby had suddenly found himself becoming the new beacon of light in Marilyn's dark and crumbling world. Unable to resist the beautiful diva's charms, Bobby joined her long list of seducers.

A short time later, an FBI bug, planted in Peter Lawford's Santa Monica house, recorded their sexual liaison. Soon, Marilyn was divulging to others that Bobby planned to get a divorce and that their own marriage was imminent. However, the Kennedy family was obsessed with politics and power; therefore, divorce, scandal, or even placing love above their ultimate destiny, was *not* an option.

Then tragedy struck! Marilyn was found dead of a drug and alcohol overdose. Some speculated that the Kennedys put a hit on Marilyn to silence her loose tongue, which could have easily destroyed the Kennedy Kingdom. However, in all probability, the emotionally distraught diva just yearned to escape the cruelty of a world that habitually used and abused her. Either way, both Kennedys certainly played a role in her desperate state of affairs and ultimate demise.

The Kennedy boys, and their father, had a strong attraction to the glamour of Hollywood. John, however, seemed more fascinated by and drawn to Frank Sinatra and his famous Rat Pack. This talented partying group consisted of Dean Martin, Sammy Davis Jr., Joey Bishop and Peter Lawford, with Frank Sinatra as the leader. It was said that the Mafia, who most likely secured early engagements for the singer/actor, managed

Sinatra, but Sinatra became an iconic American figure on his own drive and talents. He seldom used the muscle that backed him, and has been highly praised by not only those who knew him, but by the many who were graced by his generosity, be it indirectly, charitably, or financially. Yet, the Rat Pack enjoyed playing up the bad boy image, and lived in the fast lane, a lane that John Kennedy desperately wanted to be in.

As such, Kennedy befriended the pack and used their influence, fan base and financial backing to assist his being elected president. Yet in typical Kennedy fashion, once he was elected, he severed relations with the pack, particularly snubbing Sinatra. The Kennedys were notorious for using people and then cutting them off or, worse yet, hunting them down to legally destroy them, like Bobby did to his Mafia buddies. The Kennedy brothers were brazenly burning many bridges, and as time would tell, it would ultimately guarantee their own demise.

Despite the smut and scandal, Bob Kennedy's aggressiveness and particularly John Kennedy's brilliant and moving speeches, engendered a new and bold age that quashed the stale air of tradition. Assisting in this endeavor was John's wife, Jackie, who entertained artists, musicians and writers, thus refining the White House into a cultural palace; one fashioned after European tastes and tradition. Moreover, with an eye toward certain modern trends, Jackie enlivened dusty, old politics with a youthful buoyant energy that was infectious.

Adversely, her husband John had little interest in these matters, for the pragmatic politician, who was perpetually wracked by life-threatening pain since childhood, lived for the moment. Sensing his life was destined to be brief, John lived full-throttle, with little care for posterity. Even when confronted about his lewd affairs by his party-going friend, Senator George Smathers, John stated, "While I'm alive, they'll never bring it out. After I'm dead, who cares?"

John Kennedy was just a neophyte upon entering the Oval Office, and he quickly fell under the influence of the CIA, which was in the midst of a highly secret mission in Cuba. Under former President Dwight D. Eisenhower, the CIA, led by Deputy Director of Plans Richard Bissell Jr., was already working with the Mafia to assassinate Fidel Castro. Adopting the war-room's tactics and affiliations that were already established, the rookie president adhered to their stratagem.

The U.S. military was training and preparing Cuban exiles for a massive naval invasion, which was to be preceded by two aerial raids by American fighter planes. These two aerial strikes were deemed paramount to the mission's success. During this Cuban invasion, now known as the infamous Bay of Pigs, the first air strike was unsuccessful. Hence, the military awaited orders from President Kennedy for the second, and most crucial, strike.

However, the first strike created an immediate outcry in the United Nations, especially by the Cuban and Soviet ambassadors. Kennedy was troubled; he had already arranged a summit meeting with Soviet premier Nikita Khrushchev, and felt this air raid would jeopardize their meeting. Coupled with this political dilemma was the logistical problem of not knowing what to do with all the Cuban exiles if the mission was scrubbed. Overcome with anxiety, Kennedy called off the vital second air strike.

Meanwhile, the Mafia's assassination plot never materialized, allowing Castro to rally his troops, which mutilated the Cuban exiles who had landed by sea. These events led many U.S. officials to later charge Kennedy with intentional mass-murder, since the administration knowingly abandoned the Cuban invasion forces.

Meanwhile, the Mafia had their own agenda, for Bobby Kennedy was outrageously engaging in highly publicized measures to destroy leading Mafiosi, while at the same time covertly dealing with them. As Johnny Rosselli said, "Here I am helping the government, helping the country, and that little son of a bitch is breaking my balls."

Bobby was seen as a two-faced dirty-dealer and was accumulating enemies faster than flies on dung. Even his own staff called him "a sinister little bastard!" Therefore, it is quite plausible that the Mafia intentionally failed to assassinate Castro in order to screw Bobby, the little ball-busting bastard.

Johnny Rosselli and Sam Giancana weren't the only ones hell-bent on wishing Bobby dead, for the notorious teamster leader, Jimmy Hoffa, likewise had him in his sights. Bobby continually badgered Hoffa with repetitious indictments, and he complained to his turncoat contacts in the mob. Hoffa was eventually convicted in 1964 for jury tampering. However, while serving his prison sentence, Hoffa fell out of favor with the mob. Upon his early release, Hoffa was observed getting into a car with a group of men. Then quite mysteriously, he vanished from the face of the earth. Various mobsters from New Jersey and Detroit were suspects, but none were ever convicted.

Meanwhile, Bobby Kennedy was extremely focused, and when he engaged in a project, he became obsessive. This obsession, and his intense dislike for the Mafia, was something he couldn't prioritize while planning Operation Mongoose, the codename for the Castro assassination plot. Digging into the tax records of Johnny Rosselli and other mobsters (trying to emulate the tactic used to bring down Al Capone), Bobby lacked the common sense to fry his comrades/hit-men *after* their joint mission was completed. Despite Bobby's transgressions, he was said to have a genuine and moral desire to rectify the ills of society, yet his obsessive and overzealous nature sabotaged his efforts.

However, where Bobby attacked his opponents head-on, like a raging bull, his brother John was discreet and tactful, like a toreador. Despite John's early greenhorn blunders, after the disastrous Bay of Pigs operation, he learned never to rely solely upon the CIA or FBI. He later established back channels and even inaugurated the famous *hotline* to have a direct link to Khrushchev. Cold War tensions were wildly escalating, and he astutely knew prompt communication was mandatory.

Although John made moves to precipitate the Cuban missile crisis, in the War room he displayed a sensible mindset that eventually steered him and the world clear of nuclear disaster. The Soviets were secretly supplying Cuba with nuclear missiles when American intelligence spotted their clandestine maneuvers. Later, John Kennedy met with Soviet foreign minister Andrei Gromyko who, when asked about the missiles, denied that they were offensive nuclear weapons, stating they were merely defensive. Kennedy, for some unknown reason, chose not to press Gromyko further.

Kennedy was certainly trying to repair his injured ego after the Bay of Pigs debacle and he needed a new strategy. He would force Khrushchev into a showdown that, if failed, could be peacefully negotiated under the table. Either way, Kennedy was intent on somehow emerging as a victor. The Kennedy family's pride was embarrassingly tarnished, and he needed a ploy to polish it clean.

As the Joint Chiefs deliberated in the war-room, Bobby observed his brother's facial expressions as various options were presented. The room was divided, with two thirds being recklessly aggressive, and the remainder reservedly cautious. During the meeting, Bobby passed a note to his brother, stating, "I now know how Tojo felt when he was planning Pearl Harbor." This overtly rude and secretive exchange naturally ruffled feathers, for they were all supposed to be open with their thoughts, and in agreement, if, and when, a final executive decision was made.

Afterward, several members caught wind of Bobby's Tojo analogy, which further compounded the earlier insult. Here they were attempting to overthrow an oppressive dictator, and Bobby was equating *them* to Tojo, Japan's unscrupulous mass-murdering prime minister.

After the meeting, John told his brother he would no longer attend their committee. He personally felt his absence would eliminate a quick and hasty decision, which could have irrevocable results, namely that of a global holocaust.

Tensions further flared when a U-2 spy plane photographed a Cuban site and confirmed that the weapons were, in fact, nuclear and capable of reaching any major U.S. city. Dean Acheson, former Secretary of State, led an aggressive stance for attacking the Cuban missile sites before they became fully operational. However, when a military advisor began estimating the U.S. casualty rate if hit by a Soviet retaliatory strike (which numbered in the millions) John Kennedy stood up and walked out. He couldn't bear to witness how these top-notch military advisors were coldly calculating the demise of millions of Americans, and most probably civilization itself, with such cool and bizarre ease.

Maintaining his wits, Kennedy ordered a blockade to prevent Soviet ships from transporting the military contraband. The Soviets then scuttled two warships and a nuclear-armed submarine, forcing the president to scramble helicopters toward the approaching vessels. Fully aware of the sub's nuclear payload, the tensions in the war room mounted further.

Fortunately, the Soviet ships retreated, but the next phase of the crisis now unfolded. The Cuban missile launchers were being constructed at a rapid pace, and Kennedy somehow had to force or cajole the Soviets to quickly dismantle and remove the missiles.

Khrushchev then sent a letter stating that only if Kennedy made assurances that the U.S. would not attack Cuba, would he consider removing Soviet missiles. Khrushchev further asserted that Kennedy started this tense situation by his persistent attempts to overthrow Castro, whom the Soviets now felt inclined to assist. The Soviets clearly saw the implications of thermonuclear war and urged caution.

The next day, before Kennedy could respond, Khrushchev sent another letter adding a new condition. He demanded that U.S. missiles in Turkey be removed. The Soviets now sought to walk away from this showdown with a clear victory. Kennedy wished to avoid a confrontation over this issue, as he viewed the missiles in Turkey as being outdated and useless to NATO. As such, he believed they weren't worthy of provoking World War III. However, many U.S. leaders saw it differently. Turkey was a key military outpost. What's more, they didn't wish to bargain with a terrorist like Khrushchev, for to give in would be a clear sign of weakness, and could further escalate Cold War tensions throughout the world. Therefore, submission to the Soviets would be seen as defeat.

Time was of the essence, yet without divulging his intentions to the Joint Chiefs, the president asked his brother Bobby to have a last-minute meeting with the Soviet ambassador, Anatoly Dobrynin. The brothers had already decided that a trade for the Turkish missiles was key to ending the nuclear crisis, yet it had to remain secret at all costs.

At the Soviet embassy, Bobby firmly elucidated that his brother wanted the Soviets to remove the missiles, or the Americans would do it themselves. Additionally, he told Dobrynin that there were plenty of hotheaded military hawks in DC eager for war, so the president needed an immediate answer. As Bobby anticipated, Dobrynin then inquired about the missiles in Turkey. Conceding to the Soviets, Bobby assured him they would be removed, but in due time. This delay was part of the Kennedys' strategy, for to remove them promptly would clearly indicate a concession, thus destroying the illusion of victory, which was paramount.

Content with his Turkish victory, Khrushchev quickly broadcast his response to disengage and withdraw all their missiles from Cuba. The tense crisis finally ended after thirteen nerve-wracking days. However, Khrushchev was soon flabbergasted when he saw how the crisis was cleverly spun into a total victory for Kennedy, since no word of the Turkish compromise was publicized. In the art of deceitful stagecraft, Kennedy was a pro, and in that regard, Khrushchev appeared beaten.

With John Kennedy fully redeemed for his Bay of Pigs debacle, the nation rose in affection and admiration for their young hero. The aura of Camelot, inspired by Jackie Kennedy, of the righteous King Arthur reshaping and cultivating a barbarous world with his mighty round table, began to take root. Oddly enough, the Arthurian legend had little in common with John's tastes, for he preferred Shakespeare or the Greek tragedies. Yet the love-torn couple (albeit in reverse, with King John committing adultery) did have a suitable connotation, most notably the tragic ending, whereby Camelot imploded.

The fateful day of November 22, 1963, in Dallas, Texas, shook the nation to its core. The handsome young king, full of hope and promise, was brutally shot dead, falling limp into his wife's arms, as the world watched in horror on their colorless black and white TVs.

Jackie was caught on film, as she crawled on the trunk of the car to retrieve a piece of brain matter that was blown away by a shot to his head. Returning, she cried, "I have his brains in my hand," yet realized he was already dead. Brain matter and blood splattered her dress yet, for the remainder of the day, she never washed it off or changed clothes, for she wanted the world to see and feel the intensity of the dreadful murder.

A villain was needed immediately, and duly found. Lee Harvey Oswald would be captured wielding a rifle that would convict him outright before a trial. Yet a trial Oswald would never see, for Jack Ruby shot him dead amid a maelstrom of emotions. Upon hearing the news, Bobby Kennedy immediately wondered who was behind this mentally unstable assassin who had a full FBI record. Was it Castro or the Mafia?

Johnny Rosselli was quickly interrogated and put forth the story that American agents were sent to eliminate Castro, but were captured and returned to America by Castro to fulfill a retaliatory hit. Some journalists caught wind of the story and promptly published his conspiracy theory that quickly overshadowed Oswald as being the lone sniper.

Unbeknownst to many was that Jack Ruby was one of Johnny Rosselli's boys, and had met with him and other mob bosses several times before the assassination. Ruby's promptness to silence Oswald seemingly had a clear purpose, other than a patriotic American's emotional frenzy. Additionally, little publicity was initially given to the fact that Charles Harrelson was one of three men detained and questioned by Dallas Police for mysteriously stalking about the grassy knoll. Harrelson was a hit man for New Orleans' Mafia boss, Carlos Marcello.

Rosselli, along with racketeer leaders Santos Trafficante and Carlos Marcello, comprised part of an elaborate and powerful network, called La Cosa Nostra. Its web stretched across the United States and into Cuba, and rivaled the government itself. Their age-old organization that wielded absolute authority over their own, as well as anyone who came into their sphere, made them the most powerful civilian force in the country, and formidable rivals to the police force.

Santos Trafficante had a profitable casino in Cuba before Castro seized power, and had a vested interest in regaining his goldmine. Carlos Marcello of New Orleans was a ruthless Sicilian with a long, murderous history. Bobby had attempted to skewer Marcello on his McClellan Committee to convict the gangster, along with many other thugs who were all eloquently handled by the diplomat of darkness, Johnny Rosselli.

For years, the Mafia was under fire by Bobby Kennedy's ruthless crusade that also targeted Jimmy Hoffa. Hoffa had approached Marcello, who likewise had his own gripe against Bobby, complaining that the bastard should be hit. When later discussing this issue with a cohort, Marcello, the old-world Sicilian, said, "If you want to kill a dog, you don't cut off its tail, you cut off its head."

All the compelling evidence acquired indicates that the Kennedys felt arrogantly superior to their partners in crime. Therefore, many speculate that the Mafia, true to tradition, apparently shot off the dog's head. Of course, no single conspiracy theory has firmly taken root, but the Mafia's motives and abilities do seem compelling for making them the masterminds of this baffling murder. Yet, other theories also seem feasible.

The supreme marksmanship of the sniper(s) who assassinated John Kennedy is also worthy of note. As Jackie sat next to her husband, a bullet tore through the back of his neck and hit the front passenger, Texas governor, John Connally. Seconds later, a second shot hit Kennedy in the head, blowing a portion of his skull out. This second fatal shot has caused much debate, as many believe that only a single bullet killed Kennedy. From the Texas School Book Depository's sixth floor, Oswald fired downward and struck both the president and Connally from behind. However, there were many witnesses and indications of three shots, and most certainly at least two shots, one sounding 4.9 seconds after the other.

The Zapruder film shows Connally also being struck by the first shot and then turning around. The second shot shows Kennedy's head either being snapped back by the recoil of a shot from behind or forced back from a shot from the front-right of the vehicle, and this insinuates the grassy knoll. Of the 104 eyewitnesses that day, 56 claimed to hear shots from the depository's window and 35 claimed to hear shots from the grassy knoll. Therefore, there is some credibility to these accounts, and some credibility to there being more than one shooter. Miraculously, throughout this assault, with certainly more than one bullet flying, the First Lady was unharmed. Oswald, the accused lone assassin, was arrested and quickly snuffed out two days later, in typical mob fashion, which further adds to the thickening plot of there being accomplices, rather than a sole deranged renegade seeking vengeance or immortality. Despite the controversy and endless theories, the once flowery world of Camelot had come to a horrific and bloody end.

The assessments of Kennedy's administration run from hot to extremely cold, with the latter gaining the lion's share of votes in recent years. During his reign, much was concealed from the public, just as he planned. However, as the decades passed, much was revealed about what transpired behind closed doors, and about Kennedy's personal traits and beliefs. Although being the first Catholic president, Kennedy's affinity for religion appeared charismatically cosmetic. His gift for making eloquent speeches enabled him to praise God, with the honorable intent of instilling civil unity and harmony, yet his personal lifestyle blatantly and routinely broke the strictest of Commandments.

Although Kennedy did speak of God, he inevitably gave some people signs of his personal philosophy from the very day he took office. During his inauguration, Kennedy made some telling statements that, they believe, reveal that even when he was speaking of God, he did not expect anything from him, but rather placed all the responsibility on mankind for our survival and salvation. Kennedy said, "Let us go forth to lead the land we love, asking his blessing and his help, but knowing that here on earth God's work must truly be our own." This was not the *pure* Catholic faith of "ask and ye shall receive," but rather, "ask, but expect nothing, for what you reap is what you sow."

Kennedy's reliance upon asking the Lord for help appeared to be perfunctory, and any notion of his deep belief in his faith must be further confronted with what transpired in his mind during his taking the oath of office. As Kennedy placed his hand on the Bible to be sworn in, he later confided to Tip O'Neill that what ran through his head at that moment was "how the hell" did the Boston businessman, George Kara, get a seat right behind his family. Rather than contemplating the divine gift of his taking office, he instead was focused upon political posturing, something that was paramount throughout his entire life, as well as that of his idol, advocate, teacher, and father, Joe. And, of course, there was his adultery.

Despite his many foibles, John Kennedy did play a minor role in the Civil Rights movement, even if Johnson passed the bill in 1964. Despite using religion as a political tool, Kennedy did have a genuine moral belief in the cause of equality for all human beings. Against tremendous odds, whether by racist political opposition from the south or by a factional populous ingrained with a malignant tradition, Kennedy knew that racial prejudice destroyed the American dream and made the republic look like a two-faced hypocrite in the eyes of the world. Moreover, and most importantly, it appears that he simply knew it was wrong.

Furthermore, Kennedy's gift for rousing speeches must be given credit, for the power of words, especially from a dynamic figure such as the one he carefully cultivated, could manifest huge results. His rallying speeches and his challenge to Americans to be the first to land a man on the moon did energize the space race, even if it was von Braun's dream and genius that truly made it happen. The space race was a crucial test of political wills, as well as scientific bravado, and the entire world anticipated the winner.

During the previous administration, Eisenhower was forced to challenge Khrushchev's advances when the Russians launched their first satellite back in 1957 with Sputnik. That feat prompted Eisenhower to retaliate with the Explorer satellite, which was launched a year later. The Russians again made a great stride forward by launching Lunik, a satellite that would pass the moon and explore outer space. Khrushchev's spokesman stated that this was a clear indication that the balance of power was shifting in Russia's favor. In 1959, the Russians took the first photographs of the moon's dark side with Lunik III. Other satellite advancements continued by both sides, but Eisenhower's term ended and Kennedy took the oath of office in January 1961. At this moment in history, however, the Russians had a clear advantage in space.

Three months later, in April, the Russians reported the shocking news that they successfully launched the first man into space. Yuri Gagarin had flown their Vostok rocket around Earth's orbit and safely landed. A month later, the first American astronaut, Alan Shepard, briefly flew for fifteen minutes to an altitude of 115 miles, and then returned safely. The Americans' inability to orbit the Earth, and being second, struck a deep chord with John Kennedy, who not only opposed communism and all it stood for, but also never liked to lose.

The Russians would continue to surpass the Americans, even after Kennedy's death, by sending the first woman into space in 1963. That was furthered by having the first cosmonaut walk in space in 1965. As such, Russia's startling advances in space left America little choice but to move forward, hence, Kennedy had to embrace the cause. However, winning over the public to buy into an extremely expensive enterprise that appeared to have no real value other than national bravado, was a hard sell. Kennedy's youthful enthusiasm and his "anything is possible" attitude were pivotal in inspiring and motivating the masses in a way that Eisenhower or Johnson probably never could have. Where their speeches would have sounded like stale political rhetoric, Kennedy's supercharged charisma was the rocket fuel that publicly propelled NASA and a nation upward.

Furthermore, Kennedy's rousing speech peacefully aimed mankind's technological genius up toward the stars, rather than down toward the hellish pit of thermonuclear war. The multitude of spin-offs generated by NASA profoundly accelerated and secured America's lead, not only in space, but on Earth as well. Computer technology was a direct result, as were medical and industrial advances. From the atomic ashes of Hiroshima, and the deadly missiles of von Braun, rose new technologies that would ironically benefit civilization and propel it to unprecedented heights.

Both Kennedy brothers contained strains of skill, vitality, and idealism mixed with their DNA, which engendered recklessness, deceit, and corruption. Camelot may have crumbled, but some of the noble aspirations of the Kennedy king and his sibling knight did live on in the American spirit; a dreamy spirit of what might have been.

McCarthy & Reagan: *Crusaders Against Communism*

Joseph McCarthy was a hard-line Republican who, in 1950, made the bold claim that he had a list of 205 communists who had invaded the State Department. After the press noticed this shocking news, McCarthy, under a barrage of inquiry, changed his story to 57, citing he never said 205. This immediately gave rise to allegations that McCarthy was reckless, misinformed, and a publicity hound.

The nation was communist-conscious; especially after Richard Nixon had two years previously won a major victory by revealing and convicting the communist spy, Alger Hiss. As such, McCarthy's bold assertions amassed rapid and fervid attention, whereby he was given the power to investigate and prosecute communist sympathizers.

McCarthy's obsession with his newfound cause—and his growing ego that was bolstered by the national attention—made him devour data in a frenzy. This caused him to blur details, and ultimately distort and misdirect his actions. The backlash was that his slipshod handling of this sensitive material created a massive tidal wave of hysteria. As his accusations grew more erratic, he even targeted many in Hollywood, simply because they were liberal Democrats. Others were indeed members of the Communist Party, but they seemed to use it more as a social club rather than the political vehicle it truly was for serious-minded activists. Nevertheless, under McCarthy's powerful lens, many innocent lives and careers were brutally scorched by his haphazard aim. Blacklists were established that eventually destroyed the careers of 90 percent of those on the list, while others struggled to recover like Orson Welles, Ruth Gordon, Dalton Trumbo, and Zero Mostel.

Interestingly enough, young Ronald Reagan was the president of the Screen Actors Guild. Reagan was a staunch defender of the American republic and harbored a profound repugnance toward communism, yet he wasn't pleased with McCarthy's reckless methods. He later condemned McCarthy by stating he "was using a shotgun when he should have been using a rifle." Reagan clearly saw that the fear being generated by this frenzy played right into the communists' hands. He was incensed that the communists were taking advantage of America's constitutional freedoms in order to secure the demise of the *Constitution* itself and, in effect, the death of the republic. While the rights of actors and actresses were being trampled on, Reagan jumped to the defense of a young actress named Nancy Davis. She was evidently mistaken for a woman with the same name who was involved with the Communist Party. Rallying to her defense, the two met for dinner and eventually fell in love. She would soon become his lifelong devoted wife, Nancy Reagan.

However, Ronald Reagan's obsession with combating communism materialized into his extremely focused, sniper-like objective, which blatantly climaxed a little over two decades later when he became president. It was due to Reagan's unwavering and long-term agenda that the very public death knell of communism was sounded when he demanded Gorbachev to tear down the Berlin Wall.

Few today realize that Reagan rallied for the dissolution of the Soviet Union and the destruction of the Berlin Wall as far back as the late 1960s. This mindset developed even earlier, during the 1950s, when he became discontented with President Eisenhower's allegedly weak administration, which, he felt, preferred not to engage or question the Soviet's expansionist maneuvers. Reagan had hoped the former five-star general would have had more backbone, but once the Soviets flaunted their new hydrogen bombs—and made clear their intentions to use them if need be—Ike and company applied the brakes and played a cautious, reactionary role. One positive maneuver was that Ike shifted money from defense into the new NASA space race, since, as noted earlier, America lagged embarrassingly far behind the Soviets.

However, in 1956, the Hungarians were under siege and desperately cried out for help; meanwhile, America stood silent as Soviet tanks swallowed up their country. Reagan was livid, and his speeches about the Cold War became more passionate. "There can be only one end of the war we are in…wars end in victory or defeat." To Reagan, America's policy of trying to broker peace accords with an aggressive regime seemed futile. Reagan also chided how the Soviets engaged their new war tactics with growing success. "Communists gauge their aggression by slicing each new gain just thin enough so that we'll say, 'that isn't worth fighting for.' They have harnessed the fear of war instead of war itself."

Beyond their slicing tactics, however, the communists did make solid attempts to infiltrate and manipulate Hollywood. The cinema was an extremely valuable target, for it would enable the creation of movies that could be used as propaganda. After all, even Vladimir Lenin had stated that the cinema was the most important of all art forms. As such, Herb Sorrell, who was fronting several Communist Party operations and was the leader of the World Federation of Trade Unions, took aggressive action to seize operations by forming a picket line. Being a former boxer, Herb aptly threatened to break heads and more, if anyone crossed the line. Additionally, he sought an alliance with the American Federation of Labor with the hopes of gaining full control over Hollywood itself. Sorrell even tried to persuade the Screen Actors Guild to join the picket line, but they refused—and for one primary reason, Ronald Reagan was on the board.

When Reagan crossed the picket line to begin filming *Night Unto Night*, he received a phone call after his very first scene. The mysterious caller stated that his face would be disfigured with acid if he continued his breach. Reagan refused to back down. His determination was fully tested as he endured constant threats to himself and his family. Yet, instead of acquiescing, Reagan decided to pack a pistol. Further still, Reagan contacted the FBI and became an informant, codenamed T-10, and relayed bits of information that did eventually uncover communist operatives.

Reagan's strong-willed retaliations put him under the constant surveillance of the Soviets, who clearly realized that Reagan was a man of action who confronted fear with courage. Moreover, once Reagan became president, the roles reversed, as the communists' utmost fears were realized. In fact, only two weeks after entering office, Reagan approved a 32 billion dollar increase in the defense budget. Furthermore, his futuristic SDI program, better known as the Star Wars defense plan, which Reagan openly played with a solemn poker face, was readily believed to be a possibility by the Soviets and, as such, caused much panic in the Kremlin.

Top Soviet scientists were immediately gathered to assess Reagan's fantastical defense plan. After several months of deliberations, they informed the Kremlin that although it would take tremendous scientific research and capital investment, it could produce enough military results to give the United States an unassailable advantage. Of equal importance, they logically conceded that a Soviet attempt of entering into a technological research and development race would buckle their economy. Nevertheless, because of Reagan, they were impelled to increase their defense budget by 45 percent. This became a huge burden on the regime that needed those funds to aid its limping economy; one inundated with millions of disgruntled and poverty-stricken civilians.

Reagan's broad spectrum of offensives included aiding Poland, Nicaragua, Grenada, and other rebel forces to destabilize their ruling communist occupiers, and repetitious radio broadcasts that penetrated deep behind the Iron Curtain. These broadcasts, and those by Pope John Paul II, did inspire and call to arms thousands of oppressed citizens to wreak havoc upon their communist leaders. With the Russian economy in dire straights, Gorbachev was forced to cash in his chips, and lost the Cold War poker match; a deadly game that had persisted for over forty years. The threat of communism and the Cold War were finally over.

Reagan's earlier comments that the Soviet Union was only strong militarily and that its ideology and economy was lifeless had finally materialized for all the naysayers to see. His famous speech declaring that the Soviet Union was an *"evil empire"* and that it would fall to the *"ash heap of history"* was monumentally prophetic, as well as beautifully crafted, both in words and as the physical result of his life-long deeds. And even though some highbrowed critics had earlier ridiculed Reagan's powerful words, as being simplistic or antagonistically sectarian, it was their own lack of vision that prevented them from comprehending Reagan's brand of power politics, which now valiantly ruled the day.

Reagan's affable and buoyant spirit had given many the impression of a shallow, carefree soul. However, his highly-focused covert operations, military foray into futuristic technological initiatives, economic sanctions, and public speeches, of which many were cleverly crafted to psychologically condition friends and foe alike, clearly indicated a man with a very serious agenda. Reagan cleverly concealed his agenda with a genial smile, yet he ultimately achieved its very pointed and powerful goal. In the final analysis, Reagan and America proudly stood tall, as Gorbachev and his once mighty Soviet Union painfully crumbled. Reagan's life-long mission was accomplished, yet reflecting back to the precarious 1950s, either regime could have been the victor if Reagan hadn't stepped forward. This also returns us to how Reagan, despite being an equally devout anti-communist, didn't relish McCarthy's tactics.

Reagan's beliefs differed significantly from McCarthy's in that he believed communism was a false hope that attracted the weak-minded, very much like a false religion. Furthermore, once rigorously exposed, it would reveal to all how misguided and useless the system truly was. Meanwhile, McCarthy viewed communism as something powerfully menacing, and something to be feared. His own fears were perhaps what escalated his approach to near panic.

However, despite the corona of hype, McCarthy did have burning evidence and a legitimate cause at its molten core. In his opening indictment, McCarthy prophetically said: *"The reason why we find ourselves in a position of impotency is not because the enemy has sent men to invade our shores, but rather because of the traitorous actions of those who have had all the benefits that the wealthiest nation on earth has had to offer--the finest homes, the finest college educations, and the finest jobs in Government we can give."*

Like so many crusaders who embark on a valid mission and then go awry, McCarthy mismanaged his tremendous power. Conspiracies have always been a part of civilization, but the communists, under the KGB, brought this to new heights, and the defamation of McCarthy only helped.

While the American Communist Parties had their open member list—that even included passive sympathizers like Albert Einstein or Lucille Ball—the real operatives remained on the fringe and invisible. Many years later, investigations and post Cold War information supplied by the Soviets, revealed hard-evidence that 350 communists did, in fact, infiltrate the U.S. State Department along with thousands of lower-profile assistants secretly pushing forth their agendas.

Therefore, Americans today must realize that ever since the demise of McCarthyism, foreigners have entered America to clandestinely utilize its colleges, military, and aeronautical training facilities for evil intent, such as Osama bin Laden or the terrorist bombers of 9-11, thus proving the validity of such threats as well as McCarthy's poignant prophecy.

Regrettably, McCarthy's recklessness had maligned a very serious and worthy cause. The Democrats—being the primary targets accused of harboring communist ties—led the counter-offensive against McCarthy in order to maintain a political balance of power. Meanwhile, the liberal press fanned the Democrats' retaliatory flames by labeling the prosecutions unconstitutional "witch hunts". Hence, the over-hyped charade, which became known as McCarthyism, had at its core a very real and sinister reality that to this day has not fully emerged or truly been understood.

However, the story of a communist threat to America precedes that of McCarthy and the early 1950s. It was the Bolshevik revolution of 1918 that first made clear the viable threat of the Communist Party. The Bolsheviks had made tangible their Communist manifesto, which proclaimed that their intentions were not merely to capture, but to conquer and destroy.

A year later, in 1919, a New York postal worker detected over twenty mail-bombs all set to explode, quite symbolically, on May Day. All were defused in time except two. One exploded in a senator's house, and the other at Attorney General Mitchell Palmer's house. The bomber miscalculated and blew himself up, along with the front of Palmer's house.

A few months later, in 1920, a senate resolution empowered Attorney General Mitchell Palmer to lead an aggressive campaign to eradicate all radicals attempting to overthrow the government. The communists were the clear focus. Interestingly enough, these convictions resulted in rapid deportations, and were issued without hearings or trials by none other than Palmer's lead assistant, J. Edgar Hoover. Hoover would also assist McCarthy in his roundups some thirty years later.

However, in 1927, with the high-profile executions of Sacco and Vanzetti—who were alleged communists—liberal sympathies grew, despite their links to the bombings. With the stock market crash of 1929 painting a bleak picture for capitalism, more liberals embraced communism. This naturally included Hollywood's famous Screen Writers Guild and a sea of actors. Hence, through the 1930s, communist sympathies grew in America.

In 1938, Texas congressman Martin Dies and his assistant J.B. Matthews pushed for a resolution that eventually became the Un-American Activities Committee. Its purpose was to eradicate sympathizers of Europe's rising Communist, Fascist, and Nazi regimes. Dies and Matthews, along with Palmer and Hoover before them, not only set the precedent for McCarthy, but also supplied him with crucial advisors. Both Hoover and Matthews would arm McCarthy with their experience and wealth of damning data.

During the 1940s, Vice President Henry Wallace, serving under Franklin D. Roosevelt, had grown to admire communism and its leader, Josef Stalin, for ostensibly demonstrating that their system worked. At the latter part of World War II, when Truman became president, Wallace, along with Dean Acheson and others, advised the administration to share nuclear research with the Soviets. Meanwhile, J. Edgar Hoover adamantly rejected the idea. President Truman, who previously trusted Stalin, eventually took a hard-line stance against the dictator and duly forced Wallace to resign.

In 1947, with revenge in his gut, Wallace attempted to run for president to oust his old rival, Harry Truman. It was later revealed that Wallace's campaign was inundated with KGB spies, and was largely funded by the Soviets. Naturally, Wallace denied being a communist, yet he might have been a quasi-oblivious puppet. His speech writer, Charles Kramer, later a confirmed Soviet, even had Wallace denouncing J. Edgar Hoover as an "American Himmler." But Wallace's campaign, which was the closest the Soviets ever came to securing the White House, only secured 2 percent of the votes.

Meanwhile, some critics have claimed that communist spies were in FDR's administration, citing that the concessions made at Yalta allowed the Soviets to occupy portions of the Far East and Poland. Although Alger Hiss and chief of staff, Duncan Lee, were later revealed as communist spies, it is believed, Harry Hopkins and FDR manipulated these traitors to mislead Stalin. Additionally, what these detractors fail to recognize is that America was still bitterly embroiled with Japan, as the atomic bomb had not yet been developed. Roosevelt clearly knew of Stalin's intentions, especially after the Soviet premier halted his troops outside of Poland to allow Hitler's armies to destroy the resistance for him.

Therefore, Roosevelt was forced to bide his time with Stalin, at least until Japan was eliminated from the equation. Additionally, his insistence of including China in the postwar tetrarchy was his way of keeping the Soviet Union at bay. Unfortunately, FDR never lived to negotiate the final transactions. What Roosevelt would have done, had he lived, is open to speculation, yet his clever and wily tactics long before and during the war, all attest to his being someone quite successful in the art of negotiation, and not easily duped.

Additionally, recently released transcripts of the Yalta conference clearly show FDR in typical form, despite rumors criticizing his failing health as causing bad decisions. They, likewise, confirm that Roosevelt did not give anything away, for it was Truman who ceded China and North Korea to the communists. As for Poland, Stalin was adamant that Poland was crucial to Soviet security, and non-negotiable, yet he promised FDR that he'd allow Poland free elections. However, true to form, Stalin later reneged on his word. Hence, Roosevelt cannot be blamed for what transpired after his death.

However, deeply embedded into the U.S. government were Soviet agents that did manage to relay information back to the KGB. It took American code breakers several years to decode some of the messages, but in 1947, one breakthrough finally identified a secret agent named Liberal. He successfully passed secret information regarding the atomic bomb back to Russia with the aid of his wife, Ethel, whose name he failed to encode. This oversight led to their capture, as Julius and Ethel Rosenberg were sensationally exposed. The notorious couple was finally convicted, and they were condemned to death in 1951 for espionage. Their "...shocking and loathsome..." deeds, as the judge put it, were unfortunately discovered too late, for the spies had been relaying vital information to the KGB since 1944. Roy Cohn, who successfully prosecuted the Rosenbergs, was later recruited by J. Edgar Hoover to join McCarthy's staff in 1952.

In 1949, three other major events struck a deep chord in America. In May, the Soviets invaded China's largest city, Shanghai, and overthrew Chiang Kai-shek's Nationalist army. President Truman refused to aid Chiang's army, and the Soviets quickly pressured the Chinese to support Mao Tse-tung's Communist Party. In September, President Truman conveyed the shocking news that the Soviet Union had developed the atomic bomb. Appallingly, America's technology and military advantage was literally stolen. Then in October, Mao Tse-tung declared that the communist People's Republic of China was indeed official.

Communism, under Stalin's military influence, had succeeded in engulfing almost of all of Asia, thereby quadrupling the communist population to a staggering 800 million. Americans detested their own government's passivity, since their inactivity permitted this perilous chain of events. Hence, the stage was set for McCarthy when he made his famous speech in 1950, and rightly so.

President Truman promptly denounced McCarthy's speech, and denied all access to security files. The Democrats also established the Tydings Committee to govern and scrutinize McCarthy's charges. With a lack of hard evidence, and the cross-examining road blocks, McCarthy was forced to embellish and bluff his way through some cases, hoping that his team would eventually uncover facts to support his gut feelings. McCarthy's hands were tied, but he continued to fight.

In April of 1951, the shocking news that President Truman dismissed General MacArthur appalled the Republicans and many Americans. MacArthur—who had successfully democratized postwar Japan, and had initially made progress in Korea—had disobeyed Truman's command. MacArthur didn't like civilian bureaucrats dictating his battlefield commands, yet his latest blunder was losing all his gains in Korea due to China's unexpected attack. As such, MacArthur feared that a Soviet-backed China would engulf not only Korea but eventually Europe as well.

This added more fuel to McCarthy's fiery campaign, as he violently condemned Truman for this traitorous act. However, besides MacArthur's blunder and insolence, Truman was looking at the broader dynamics, for the Soviets now had nuclear capabilities, and the situation had to be handled more discreetly. However, the Republicans also blamed Truman for blocking their efforts to uncover communist spies in D.C., which had allowed the Soviets to gain access to U.S. nuclear secrets in the first place.

What many Republicans knew, yet for lack of an intrepid leader were unable to reveal, was passionately embraced by their "grassroots" crusader, Joseph McCarthy. Perhaps naïve to a backlash, McCarthy committed himself fully to the noble cause; but for a myriad of reasons, it mutated into a colossal disaster. Crucial setbacks included his inability to access information that had been sealed off by Truman, his impetuous and reckless nature, his ego fueled by power and sudden fame, the Democrats roadblocks, and the liberal media's eventual death knell, which reveled in extolling the repulsiveness of McCarthyism. Henceforth, all these factors contributed to sentencing McCarthy to eternal shame.

Despite the many valid flaws of McCarthy's tactics and his smear campaign, which violated civil liberties, it had at its core a vital message that got lost under the mist of McCarthyism. For under that cloaked fog, Soviet spies did, in fact, operate in Washington and throughout the country. Most importantly, these operatives stole and supplied the Soviets with aeronautical, nuclear, and military secrets. Hence, not only does McCarthy deserve reexamination, but so, too, does our current intelligence system, which must be screened for Russian, Chinese, and other spies.

The broad topic of communism and the Soviet Union as it relates to America, inevitably ends with Reagan and, as such, he deserves our attention once again. It was during the early 1970s, when Reagan suddenly found himself standing at odds with his fellow Republican, President Richard Nixon. This was because Nixon had changed his stance from being a staunch anti-communist to being the faint-hearted draftsman of détente. Reagan firmly believed that the Soviet Union could never keep up in an arms race without American aid. In essence, the Soviets came to rely primarily on stealing American science and technology, for it was much easier for them to recruit and pay for spies, rather than brilliant scientists, engineers, and the research and development labs and resources they required. Furthermore, they also had to contend with a nation crippled by poverty. This is why Reagan astutely realized that the Soviet people could actually become allies if exposed to the truth. After all, their government was directly responsible for shackling them in silence, fear, and poverty ever since its very inception by Josef Stalin.

The Soviet regime had remained a mystery to many senior American officials; however, when Senator Daniel Patrick Moynihan chaired the newly-formed Senate Select Committee on Intelligence in 1975—which was established to scrutinize governmental secrecies—he gained access to top-secret FBI and CIA files. Moynihan was awestruck by the intelligence that remained departmentalized; worse still, it was restricted from top-ranking politicians. Since President Wilson enacted the Espionage Act of 1917, intelligence agencies had accumulated and concealed millions of top-secret files, and Moynihan was infuriated by how often the lack of sharing this information caused mistakes in federal objectives and policies.

The intelligence, which Moynihan uncovered, showed a Soviet Union in dire straights. Moynihan even reproved Henry Kissinger for making the Soviets appear more formidable than they really were. However, not only was Kissinger not privy to this intel, hence his error in assessing their true capabilities, but this also proved what became inevitable, namely, the Soviets had no recourse but to invade and conquer other nations. This became a desperate measure to create new streams of economic activity or, more plainly, to drain these acquisitions of their vital resources, which the Soviets desperately needed in order to resuscitate their struggling economy. However, while Moynihan's philosophy was to simply wait and let the Soviet Union fall apart on its own ideological frailty, Reagan took action, for he cleverly recognized the Soviets' hardened determination to survive, and their widespread aggression both militarily and politically, had made clear their resolve and intentions.

When Ronald Reagan took office, he not only increased the defense budget—since Nixon and Kissinger gave the Soviets a clear military advantage with their Strategic Arms Limitation Treaty (SALT), which Carter followed up with SALT II—but he also engaged in covert missions of psychological operations, or PSYOPS. Reagan instructed the air force to conduct aggressive missions near their military units and randomly fly into their air space for the sole purpose of intimidation. The U.S. Navy performed similar operations. Under the tenure of most Cold War presidents, the Soviets had practiced tactical PSYOPS on the United States, however, Reagan's brash reversal in maneuvers caused considerable panic in the Kremlin. It is noteworthy that with the collapse of the Soviet Union, many former agents in the KGB have openly revealed just how much Reagan was feared. It was clear; Reagan turned the tides. For the first time in the Cold War, the Soviets were backpedaling.

The KGB maintained a long dossier on Reagan, dating back to his early years in the 1950s during McCarthyism. It included many of his public speeches over several decades, some of which decried how America lost its will, especially after Vietnam, and needed to stand up and take an aggressive stance against communism. These documents all showed how Reagan was a man who habitually held to his convictions and, more importantly, actively followed them through. As a result, the Soviet Union had no alternative but to change their aggressive policies accordingly.

Some Americans misread Reagan as not being a strong leader, as his gregarious attitude and sharp Hollywood wit concealed his objectives and firm constitution. However, among his political entourage, he was noted for rejecting much of his cabinet's advice and charting his own course, even against popular opinion. Reagan had many Americans and several European countries at odds with his foreign policies, particularly when he sought to stop the Soviets from building their two Siberian gas pipelines to feed Europe. Reagan perceptively recognized that the Soviets could have monopolized European gas dependency if this project were completed. As such, Reagan stood firm and unyielding as France, Germany, and even England's Margaret Thatcher opposed him. In the face of opposition, and aware of their intentions to supply the Soviets with special turbines, Reagan made the bold maneuver of commercially cutting off American technology to Europe. This act restricted Europe's transactions with the Soviets, because their companies licensed American technology. Moreover, defective U.S. equipment was sold via third parties to sabotage the project. As planned, a huge explosion did signal America's covert plot. This not only delayed the Soviets by four years, but Reagan further depleted their resources and revenue with other initiatives, which cumulatively led to the Soviet Union's instability and ultimate collapse.

During his long and productive life, Reagan witnessed the rise of Stalin and his tyrannical successors, and personally contributed to the demise of the Soviets' communist regime. He witnessed the paranoia and fear that gripped his beloved nation, and took a firm role in the grand drama. Along his trails, he came across all the major players battling against communism, including J. Edgar Hoover and naturally McCarthy.

McCarthy's procedures and practices were certainly flawed and in dire need of revamping, yet intelligence issues concerning national security are a vital asset, and must never be ignored or impeded. This, Reagan understood, as Vice President George H.W. Bush religiously supplied him with intel at the start of each day. Sadly, America's current terrorist situation bears testimony to when a nation neglects intelligence.

Many factors since the demise of McCarthyism, such as the complete breakdown of the CIA under the Clinton administration, contributed to the sharp rise of subversive terrorist actions on our own soil. McCarthy's dismantled committee was also a green light for anti-American aliens to reap America's wealthy resources, all while under our very noses. Many foreign dignitaries have been educated in America's finest colleges, only to return the favor with vindictive fury. More importantly, the lesson of Mohammad Atta and his death squad—who all trained in Florida to fly airplanes into buildings like deadly missiles—is something never to be forgotten. Nevertheless, many have already forgotten, as the ACLU and the politically correct (PC), strip their nation of its vital defenses.

The PC mantra of multiculturalism—which professes to be more civil and polite to all ethnic groups—in reality, is mindlessly stifling our right to defend ourselves. This is evident by their successful action to eliminate racial profiling surveillance when lethal and unique situations arise; namely, how it was all dark-skinned Middle Easterners, not white pearly-faced Caucasians who committed 9-11. Equally damaging, the PC have silenced freedom of speech. By silencing viable ideas, and even raw facts, from even being expressed (fearing that it may hurt someone's feelings) they likewise eliminate the crucial forum to even analyze, debate or, most importantly, remedy these situations. Hence, by silencing the issues the PC crowd is breeding ignorance. This ignorance, I believe, has led us to the pitiful state we are in today.

The PC's open-door policy of cordiality has allowed our airports, seaports, and our country's very borders to be widely open to friend and deadly foe alike. As Newt Gingrich aptly, and quite chillingly, stated, we are *"sleepwalking into a nightmare!"*

Hence, it is imperative that Americans embrace the reality of protecting their rich heritage, especially from the barbarians who still exist and shall always exist. Time advances, but unfortunately not all of humankind. During the rise of the great Roman Republic, they felt invincible, much like Americans today who fail to see the fervent determination and threat by Jihadist Muslims. However, when the Gauls shockingly sacked the capital city of Rome, they were devastated by defeat and numbed with disbelief. Fortunately, their deep resolve enabled them to not only recapture their city, but also build the world's greatest empire. However, the greater part of history indicates that such a miraculous recovery is extremely rare. That painful incident taught the Romans that victory does not ensure peace, or grant people the right to become lax or overconfident, but rather it brings with it new and far greater challenges that demand solidarity, vigilance, and action.

In essence, the Romans' self-esteem, determination, and unity was so great that it enabled them to defy the odds, rally to regain their beloved city, rekindle the republic, and go on to build a colossal civilization. To a lesser extent, America, too, had lost its self-esteem after Vietnam, yet President Reagan, at least temporarily, had restored that pride, unity, and determination. This was evident in many of Reagan's initiatives. This even extended abroad, when Reagan actively supported Poland's solidarity to confront Soviet Communism, which had firmly subjugated the nation since its Stalinist takeover. Like George W. Bush fighting terrorism, Ronald Reagan stood firmly alone, as all of America's European allies—including England—refused to back Reagan's sanctions, which wisely cut economic and technological aid to both the Soviet Union and their puppet regime in Poland. Yet, it was Reagan's pride in America, his deep belief in freedom for all the innocent peoples of the world, his spiritual foundation, and his inflexible determination, which eventually caused the communist regime to collapse.

Joseph McCarthy and Ronald Reagan were the two most prominent crusaders who combated communism (with J. Edgar Hoover being equally yet secretly committed), however, a long and deep-rooted scar plagued America internally. Although the American republic remains an imperfect system, as it has leveled injustices against women, and even the Japanese, Germans, and Italians during World War II, another internal pang has caused numerous outbreaks for over two hundred years. Major and minor battles ensued over this volatile topic, hence, prompting the need to address this issue in plain black and white.

AFRICAN AMERICANS: *Slavery and Civil Rights*

President Lincoln may have abolished slavery in 1865, but alas, a hundred years later racism persisted. The civil rights movement legally began with President Johnson in the 1960s, with the crucial aid of the peaceful black community leader, Martin Luther King Jr. However, the enslavement of blacks was a shameful stain on the United States from its very inception. To modern sensibilities, it is a hypocritical eyesore that the *Declaration of Independence* eschewed this issue. The key author of that famous document was none other than Thomas Jefferson. Therefore, we must pause to reflect upon Jefferson, who in recent years has been labeled a hypocrite by some, because he authored an illustrious document that declared freedom and equality, yet not for the blacks or women. Further still, Jefferson was a lifelong slave owner himself.

To try to understand Jefferson's dilemma and actions, we must place the man within his times and proceed from there. As we know, slavery was very much a part of the colonial American world. White slave traders were not alone; we must remember, Africans started this dirty business by selling their own kind. By today's standards, this was an unimaginable practice, yet in colonial America, this was the status quo. That is not to say that many in the day didn't silently despise or morally reject this practice, but with powerful plantation owners unwilling to release their slaves or stranglehold of profits, these voices of reason remained publicly mute. To understand slavery amid those eighteenth century sensibilities it becomes necessary to delve even further back into history.

The sad truth extends far beyond the Americas and onto mankind as a whole, for slavery has existed since the beginning of time. Even the loftiest book in human creation, the Bible, did little to advise on this topic. Few realize that Abraham and the patriarchs all had slaves yet, worse still, nowhere in the scriptures did God ever advise them to abolish slavery. In fact, even Moses allowed his Hebrew flock to keep Hebrew slaves, however, they could only keep them for six years and then should set them free. Moses went even further in regards to a master's ownership of a slave's potential family. Exodus 21:4 *"If his master have given him a wife, and she have born him sons or daughters; the wife and her children shall be her master's, and he shall go out by himself."* Here we had one of the Bible's all-time mega prophets, who actually led his own enslaved people to freedom, openly advocating slavery.

Beyond the Old Testament, the New Testament states that even the apostle Paul directed slaves to obey their masters. Therefore, what are we today to make of those directives posited by mega religious leaders? Obviously, this proves that even the most reverent of mankind made mistakes. Hence, we all need to view the slavery issue more open-mindedly and even forgivingly, rather than blanketing all these actors of the past as evil villains, and, worse yet, demanding reparations.

Likewise, this does not accuse the entire Bible of wrongdoing, on the contrary, the Bible offers far more positive and instructive passages, such as love thy neighbor as thyself, and countless others that give direction about loving one another as equals. Furthermore, during the Renaissance, Pope Paul III issued a papal bull threatening excommunication to those who enslaved natives in the New World. It would have been nice if the founding fathers had given that more consideration, along with giving women equal rights, when drafting the *Declaration of Independence*. Yet, as mentioned, even the great books that form the Old and New Testaments, which have been viewed as the inherent truth by countless millions, contain puzzling passages about condoning slavery.

We must also remember that America's influential overlord, Great Britain, only abolished slavery in 1833, and there were still many other nations dealing in this ugly practice, including the Spaniards who operated with the Vatican, while unscrupulously and habitually ignoring the pontiff's decrees. Therefore, most of South America and Central America engaged in slavery well into the mid-1800s. Most importantly, however, the southern colonists who formed a large part of colonial America's citizenry and Continental Army were deeply set in their iniquitous ways. Jefferson and the other founding fathers had a new coalition that they needed to unite, and concessions had to be made if their fight against the British were to succeed.

It is clear that Jefferson personally disliked the idea of slavery, yet between its deep-rooted tradition and the vital need to partner with the south to oppose the British, his true dream of liberty could not be fulfilled in his lifetime. It is known that Jefferson's first draft of the *Declaration* proposed liberation for the blacks, but he was asked to revise it by his fellow founders, knowing those words spelled suicide for their cause. Concessions are often ugly but necessary occurrences in the state of human affairs, and this was certainly one of them.

As for Jefferson's hypocrisy regarding his maintaining slaves, this falls into a gray area, but might fall upon one of those lesser-known flaws of the great man. Although Jefferson is one of the most brilliant and famous men in American history, he was also one of the worst businessmen. Jefferson was born into wealth and managed to live in the lap of luxury; however, financial disasters almost perpetually plagued him throughout his entire life. In fact, when Jefferson died he was deeply in debt, therefore, maintaining lodgings, meals and steady work for his slaves was probably the most humane thing he could manage at the time, for to let them go would not only cause his own financial ruin, but they, too, would suffer the consequences. Finding suitable and self-sustaining employment in those days was extremely difficult for blacks. To set them free would certainly have subjected them to a perilous existence and possibly death. That many slaves would have welcomed that risk, however, remains a constant reminder of a dark time. This appeared to be one of those no-win situations in a time that was not ripe for change, and one that would unfortunately afflict far too many people of both high and low esteem.

Fifty years after Jefferson penned the *Declaration of Independence*, President John Quincy Adams had likewise privately pondered the dilemma of slavery, which was only later revealed in his personal letters. Adams knew slavery was a terrible injustice, yet faced with a vehemently strong opposition and a limited amount of supporters, John Quincy felt that his hands were tied. Hence, he, too, was unable to break the chains of slavery.

In a modern sense, which will be far more comprehensible, it is like America or the United Nations dealing with third-world nations that commit crimes against humanity; concessions often need to be made until a majority is joined in sentiment. We still permit not only injustices, but also atrocities today. One only needs to be reminded of Rwanda or Croatia to see how even today, we can sit passively by as horrendous injustices and even genocides take place. So who are we to criticize or condemn what concessions people like Thomas Jefferson had to make several hundred years ago?

Adding further to the topic of injustices and atrocities leveled against a people or race, we must also remember that blacks have not been the only people subjected to suffering and misfortune. Naturally, black suffrage and discrimination deeply stained early America, and lasted well beyond Lincoln's supposed emancipation. Additionally, the blacks' pain and suffering unquestionably summons deep sympathy and a proactive need for change. However, the plight of other races is likewise a topic that deserves equal attention, attention to not only their plight but also their own actions and remedies, for how a persecuted race responds to their condition becomes just as important as the original offense.

In that regard, if we look at how the Jews were openly insulted and stripped of all possessions and then insidiously starved, tortured, and incinerated in Hitler's death camps, we instantly see that some races suffered far more wicked and frightful conditions than blacks. Moreover, this atrocity occurred within recent memory, hence, many others today know firsthand how it feels to be victimized and enraged by past deeds. And those deeds, in this case, were not only enslavement, they were accompanied by cold and barbaric murder; a diabolical genocide carried out by deranged commandants who engaged in gassing, starvation, and incineration, and by genetic assassins, like Dr. Josef Mengele, who engaged in ghastly tortures hailed as scientific experiments.

Naturally, due to the gross intensity of this bizarre crime, a harsh and uncompromising retaliation was expected. However, little to no fighting ensued between Jewish and German factions. Despite the controversial solution of creating the state of Israel (which given the extreme abnormality of this particular persecution, Britain and America hastily warranted its sanction), the remainder of negotiations remained considerably civil, orderly, and just. Although some Jews may have presented unreasonable demands, while the Zionists wanted no reparations or dealings with the Germans, the final legal outcome was peaceful. Essentially, West Germany paid 3 billion marks in reparations, as Israel's new coalition leader, David Ben-Gurion, sensibly used the money to build the new Jewish state.

No militant reprisals or gang mob riots ensued in Germany, like those of the Black Panthers, and legal actions of crimes against humanity understandably commenced with the Nuremberg trials and miscellaneous personal trials to prosecute sadistic murderers. The Jews military actions would arise, not against their German persecutors, but against their new religious neighbors in the Middle East, thus being a distinct and separate issue outside our topic of Jewish persecution by the Germans and the expectations of reparations.

As for the Jews who remained in Germany, their concerns were to ensure that new, yet fair, laws protected them from another act of genocide. This was initially summed up in the Morgenthau Plan that also put restrictions on manufacturing; it became manifest in the Marshall Plan. Additionally, they made sure that educational facilities would be available to them once again, Jewish owned businesses would not be boycotted or shut down, and beyond legal rectifications, the Jews strictly maintained their core traditions of education, a strong family bond, and hard work.

However, the Jews did not pursue laws that would penalize all Germans by giving them jobs that they were not trained for, or try to be placed in positions by a biased quota system, and they did not expect long-term welfare programs. They also did not demand that a special Jewish History Month be embedded into Germany's national calendar to publicly lecture about their exclusive history. Instead, they were satisfied that truly equal employment opportunities prevailed, and that public education was properly retrofitted with their history, along with establishing museums to further enlighten others to their plight. In essence, they received only funding and legislation, and would work hard to regain their lost ground.

In contrast, despite the highly respectable actions of Martin Luther King Jr., who quelled the riots by black militant factions and inaugurated his new peaceful movement, the laws that blacks, and particularly white liberals, would eventually push through Congress were welfare acts, affirmative action, and quotas. Initially directing President Johnson's war on poverty, Sargent Shriver's noble efforts yielded VISTA, Head Start, and other valuable programs. However, they were swept aside by affirmative action, quotas, and welfare, which did not sponsor education, learning a trade, or institute plans designed to build a foundation. In essence, these programs were legalized handouts and unjust favoritism, rather than truly enabling the black community to grow in a natural and healthy fashion.

Shriver keenly recognized the errors of these bad policies—knowing that they would not truly uplift the black community. He knew education, housing, family infrastructures, self-sufficiency and, most of all, hard work from the blacks themselves were required to escape poverty. Regardless, by President Johnson implementing all these controversial programs, black employment levels radically increased. All businesses were legally required to go beyond being the so-called Equal Opportunity Employer and were pressured to hire blacks, thus robbing opportunities from those with better resumes. Despite some motivated black applicants, most were unskilled or idly sought lawsuits, prompting Newt Gingrich to say four decades later, "When you create that kind of backward-looking, grievance-looking system, you teach people exactly the wrong habits."

It was essential to integrate blacks into the business community, however, the backlash effects of these poorly-conceived programs were significant, for any person, regardless of color, will resent being denied a position by someone with an inferior resume; this is simple human nature as well as common sense. Unfortunately, because President Clinton signed a bill to continue affirmative action (which his aides admit was to win black votes) he has only added his signature to the problem.

Lastly, beyond the controversial push for Martin Luther King Day by black Rep. John Conyers, which President Reagan opposed yet reluctantly ratified, the blacks implemented what would become the biggest display of racial favoritism in U.S. history when, in 1976, Black History Month was officially embedded into the nation's calendar.

Henceforth, not only were the policies drawn to protect the German Jews more practical and just but, as noted, their suffering far exceeded slavery, yet the legal remedies that have prevailed proved more civil and equitable than their black counterparts. Additionally, even though much of the world looked upon the persecuted Jews with empathy, we must recognize that many countries simultaneously displayed their open bias, for most nations refused to accept the large migration of Jews who sought a safe haven. This is what made the state of Israel more palatable to most post WWII nations. German Jews faced prejudice on a multi-national level, and not just from their home or host nation like black Americans. In essence, the prejudice and the atrocities leveled against German Jews far exceeds anything that black Americans were forced to endure, yet the final remedies by Jews were more civil and fair minded.

Then again, the Jews were not the only victims of Hitler, for we can also look at the unfortunate Germans who were innocent pawns of Hitler's war machine. After the war, they faced tremendous worldwide scorn and discrimination to the point of repugnance, as well as extreme personal hardships. Their whole nation was completely destroyed and on the brink of eternal ruin, yet with the aid of the Marshall Plan, which was not welfare paid out for inactivity, or affirmative action to place unqualified Jews above legitimate others, the Germans performed a miracle. Against the cautious concerns and even contempt held by much of the world, the Germans committed themselves to being productive and rose above the obstacles to become a major success and a major voice in European affairs. Like the innocent Jews who suffered under the Nazi regime, the Germans also turned disaster and a dismal state of affairs into success, which earned them dignity and respect.

Naturally, all races face different obstacles, however, it's upsetting that the black situation still lingers today. Obviously, their suffering, despite being less severe than the Jews, lasted longer, and they had to deal with racist white politicians who ignored their presidents' mandates and bucked change, however, other factors beyond white suppression and cruelty have plagued their just cause.

As we know, many civil rights laws were designed by whites eager to remedy the shame or quench the riots that reached a climax during the sixties, but the rise of the NAACP and other black groups had strong legal and lobbying voices that made sure they were heard. Furthermore, they readily endorsed programs that employed reverse discrimination, so long as their ultimate goal was met. They certainly had reasons to be humiliated, but as we shall soon see, that resentment was too often leveled against the entire white community rather than the offenders.

Moreover, black Americans had other dynamics working against them that actually retarded their rate of ascension. Beyond apartheid in the southern states, Jim Crow laws, and the racist white politicians in Washington—that Martin Luther King rightfully said wanted slavery and injustices to cease, but did not want to live next door to them—were three crucial factors that seriously crippled their progress. Oddly enough, those setbacks were self-inflicted, namely crime, marriage, and new leadership.

In 1995, it was reported that roughly 32 percent of black males had varying degrees of criminal records. Studies prove that high crime areas cause businesses to suffer higher insurance premiums or break-ins that hinder viability or force relocation, thus further handicapping black communities. Beyond this indirect, yet self-inflicted, deterioration of businesses in urban areas, is the fact that employers seldom hire people with criminal backgrounds, hence, further compounding the trend of stagnation or even turning promising neighborhoods into crime-infested slums. Additionally, many of these crimes are related to drugs and gang wars. The riches that a black teen can acquire make for a strong vice, one that habitually turns into a deadly vise. Naturally, this lucrative lure also adds to the higher rates of school dropouts and a breakdown in knowledge acquisition and morals.

The second factor is marriage, which has taken a drastic drop since the 1940s and 1950s. Statistics indicate a 40 percent drop in black marriages from 1960 to 1994, with only 30 percent of the black community remaining bonded in marriage. These studies indicate that even social status had no bearing, as low to high-income families ended in divorce or abandonment, not to mention all the births out of wedlock. Many have speculated as to why the black community suffers such high rates of single parents, and after years of analysis, the main culprit appears to be welfare. Welfare programs allow single moms to earn more income per child, per year if they remain single. However, even this incentive leaves much unsaid, as money issues alone cannot be the sole reason why so many black women opt to go it alone. Giving up an intimate personal bond with a spouse and his assistance in rearing children would appear to be a poor tradeoff just for additional funds, hence, the full answer to this baffling question remains open to further speculation.

The last factor is new leadership, for despite Martin Luther King's infidelities, King was an icon whose sublimely inspiring and powerfully healing mantra of peace and concord broke racial divides. In contrast, the new breed of spokesman has primarily been Reverend Jesse Jackson and Reverend Al Sharpton. The black community certainly needs leaders, and both men have done a great deal to aid their people, but when that advocacy comes at the expense of all white people, and all other races, this turns King's luminous dream into a lamentable nightmare.

The media has clearly documented how these leaders' overzealous passions for a good cause are too often laced with bad tactics, and these tactics have proved destructive. As the news reels verify, Jackson and Sharpton have both slandered whites as racists, which blaringly backfired in the Tawana Brawley or Duke lacrosse team cases, yet they never get censored or reprimanded. Sharpton's blind ambition to aid Tawana Brawley of rape and other charges by six white men immediately exploded into a major racial issue. However, the evidence concluded that Tawana was not abducted, assaulted, sodomized or raped. Therefore, it is painfully evident that defamation of character, legal turmoil, and the abuse of those six white men never mattered to Reverend Sharpton.

Meanwhile, joining Jackson's Rainbow Coalition was the New Black Panthers Party (NBPP), which likewise jumped on the Duke lacrosse team incident before any facts were known. Flocking to the scene, Jackson impulsively gave full financial and legal support to another black woman claiming rape, only this time it was allegedly by a gang of white college students. As is well documented, Jackson likewise took every opportunity to trumpet racial abuse in the media.

In unison with Jackson, the New Black Panthers rushed to the scene, all while innocently claiming that their intentions were not to play the race card. However, they instantly harassed the white news cameramen, by stating that their forefathers had played the race card for the last 450 years. Therefore, was race truly not on their minds? Moreover, were each and every cameraman's relatives slave owners? Or even prejudiced against blacks? However, the lid was sealed when they shouted "Black Power!" — eerily resurrecting Stokely Carmichael's racial supremacist slur from the 1960s; Carmichael had urged his black activists to "take over" the whites.

In contrast, whites who make remarks about blacks are decisively censored or penalized, as one only needs to look at Michael Richards or the firing of Don Imus.

Unfortunately, the term "freedom of speech" has taken on a new one-sided meaning nowadays, as the PC (politically correct) piously uphold injustice. It is clear that the liberal media enables blacks to lash and trash the white man, yet will muzzle and persecute any white person who says anything remotely unsavory in return. The PC crowd may feel righteous in defending the underdog, but have instead emboldened the bad behavior by only punishing whites. This one-sided censorship exceeds the present and even has PC revisionists scouring our country's history to reprimand whites of the past. This can be seen by looking at the stature of Elizabeth Stanton.

Stanton was once the leader of the Women's Rights movement, and a crucial figure in getting the right for women to vote. She was a figurehead for all women who had their own injustice to battle, yet Stanton has now been downgraded and obscured by the rising stature of Susan B. Anthony. As we know, Susan B. Anthony was even minted on the dollar coin. If you wonder why, it is because Stanton needed to be censored for her racial comments; hence, the new history books spotlight Susan B. Anthony and Lucretia Mott, while Stanton has been cast into the shadows.

This in no way condones Stanton's racial remarks but, on the contrary, it clearly points out how publicly verified racists like Jesse Jackson and Al Sharpton remain in the spotlight without condemnation, simply because they are black. Hence, if Stanton and Imus can be firmly reprimanded, so, too, should Jackson and Sharpton. However, true justice is not served in modern America when it comes to blacks and whites, as even the exoneration of OJ Simpson stands as a blazing testament of how many blacks want the black man to be set free, regardless of his committing two brutal murders. Meanwhile, the deaths of two white people simply did not matter. Here is where that awful double standard is most horribly evident.

Additionally, Sharpton and Jackson, as well as many of their colleagues, continually demand reparations for slavery, whereby holding all whites accountable. This sensitive topic needs to be understood in a realistic and logical context. Millions of white families in modern day America are first or second generation Americans. As such, their ancestors never even lived in America, let alone subjected anyone to slavery. Therefore, for these black leaders, and their misguided followers, to hold every single white person in America personally and financially responsible for something that the vast majority had absolutely nothing to do with is a colossal injustice. This aimless and racist approach simply persecutes over two hundred million innocent white people, and severely destroys race relations in the process.

Therefore, if many whites today appear overwrought by this topic it is because they have innocently become the ultimate villains in the eyes of not only these black leaders and black advocacy groups, but also many in the black community who have been racially-groomed to view all whites as evildoers. This often triggers Vesuvial eruptions in their dealings with whites, thus giving rise to the overused race card, which has been played with increased recklessness over the past four decades.

Although much of our focus has centered on reverse discrimination by blacks, since it seldom, if ever, receives a public voice, this does not insinuate that all blacks hold this viewpoint, as many do not. But unfortunately, only this negative perspective is broadcast in the media, whereby imparting that mindset as being the only one held by all blacks. This is deeply regrettable. Nor does our focus herein eschew or deny the racism of many whites. Naturally, there are whites today who are still outright racists, either self-induced or onset by the blacks' reverse discrimination, however, the above-mentioned black leaders and black supremacy groups, along with their polluted followers, including the leftist white liberals who advocate their racist "overkill" cause, have had the most damaging effect on race relations in recent years.

Beyond the issue of reverse discrimination, is this overkill factor, for blacks have made immense strides due to unjust legislation that attempted to remedy this situation, but has instead exceeded its goal. The Civil Rights movement started with Kennedy's agenda in 1961, but only went into action in 1965 with President Johnson's Executive Order 11246. What cannot be overlooked, however, is that after four long decades of Civil Rights laws (particularly Johnson's affirmative action and quotas), blacks have risen in almost every field of endeavor to astounding heights. These heights obviously include the true achievers who made it on their own accord, which includes people like Colin Powell and Condoleezza Rice, who both attained positions of immense power. *(It is crucial to note that many other ethnic groups have not come close to achieving these high positions in government, yet today's black leaders still seek overkill and demand more.)*

In contrast to the true achievers, however, are those who were unqualified and were unjustly pushed up the ladder; Jason Blare is only one example out of countless thousands. Equally damaging, entrance exams and standards of excellence for fire and police departments, for example, have been lowered to accommodate this flawed policy. The sad result is that both race relations and the efficiency levels of these organizations have been severely compromised. Fortunately, however, newer generations of properly trained blacks have made up for much of the dead weight imposed by their predecessors, and this new talent is impressive. They stand as clear and shining examples of how education and training should have been the first priority of addressing racial discrimination—like Shriver advocated—rather than harmful employment remedies that forced both blacks and whites into uncomfortable situations.

The quota system likewise continues to be a policy that some black leaders want reinstated, however, this, too, should be viewed with a judicious eye. If they wish to go by the numbers, then they should go by the factual numbers, not arbitrary or whimsical numbers. The fact remains that blacks constitute roughly 12 percent of the United States population. Therefore, theoretically, if a quota system were to be implemented then it would need to assert that available job openings in various fields should contain 12 percent blacks. How, then, can black leaders justify professional sports like basketball that have nearly a 95 percent black ratio, or music genres like rap, hip-hop, etc., that have a nearly 99 percent ratio?

Likewise, do cable and TV programs in general feature only 12 percent blacks or more? Does the vast spectrum of civil service jobs contain only 12 percent blacks or more? The answers to all these questions are clear; blacks have gained far more positions than the size of their population dictates, as they even dominate some fields in astronomical proportions that skyrocket off any fair-minded or even biased quota chart. Under a truly fair quota system, every race would be included, however, quotas have always been fallible and only end up being biased agendas that create friction, resentment, and ultimately division. Hence, quotas should be avoided at all costs.

Meanwhile, black leaders still aggressively push for more positions even in these already over-saturated fields of sports. In Jessie Jackson's Invited Testimony to the House of Representatives on February 28, 2007, he stated: "Forty-five percent of the players in these colleges are African-American. Only five percent of Division 1A head coaches were. And *worse*, exactly zero conference commissioners."

Worse? As noted, blacks consume the playing fields in numbers that exceed their quota, but now Jackson wants to dominate the managerial and commissioner offices as well. Again, with blacks constituting only 12 percent of America's population, it must be understood that they will not obtain employment in every level or position, just like all other races. Jackson also stated in this testimony that "the times they-are-a-changing," and indeed they are, yet in a very negative and bigoted fashion.

Added to the Civil Rights agenda, as mentioned earlier, was the inauguration of Black History Month. This policy, which shuns every other race (in a melting pot nation) to exclusively honor the black race, has many people of many races grumbling. In essence, they know Black history needed to be properly integrated into the educational system, but instead it was callously cemented into the nation's calendar.

It is abundantly clear that blacks had very serious and legitimate grievances that needed to be redressed, however, other races have suffered even worse conditions. Beyond the Jews in Hitler's Nazi Germany, and even more succinct, is the plight of the Native Americans. As many have argued, can slavery be compared to the devastating toll that Manifest Destiny had upon the Native Americans? Their slaughter and near annihilation far exceeds the enslavement of the blacks, yet Native Americans did not ask for or receive a special month of favoritism. The crux of the matter is that an annual, month-long "reprimand"—that blankets an entire nation, of which the majority are innocent of the initial crime—is no remedy, as education belongs in the classroom and not federally ingrained into a country's civic tradition, because favoritism turns education into punishment, and produces the wrong result.

Beyond the psychological reprimand that whites and other non-black races endure—and far more destructive—is how Black History Month colors the judgments of many young blacks. Many programs, and even textbooks and museums, now give the impression that most white men were, and still are, wicked and suppressive monsters, and are the black people's enemy. Unfortunately, exposés and visuals, such as shackles, neck irons, or slaves with thrashing scars, are unwelcome necessities to show the evil inflicted by *some* whites, but more importantly, this information must be counterbalanced by exposés on white people who stood up and fought this injustice. This is very crucial in order to ingrain the reality that not all white men are evil, just as the high crime rate of blacks today does not mean that all blacks are evil.

A balanced program is mandatory, because a malignant viewpoint has emerged from the present model that negatively colors the minds of many blacks, and simultaneously condemns and punishes an entire white populace, which has been eternally saddled to the deplorable misdeeds of a small faction of whites—who, unfortunately, stained the entire race. Furthermore, the white race consists of numerous European and Asian nationalities, again, most of which did not take part in this crime; hence, the blanket of condemnation that many blacks cast, and liberal whites endorse, is extremely vast, extremely multi-ethnic, and extremely unjust.

This blatant reprimand is further evidenced by the White House's Web site. The site features a link for African Americans under "History", but highlights no other ethnic groups. This is a Web site conceived and published by the United States government, and it blatantly shuns all other races, while offering information only about blacks. As such, is favoritism the lesson the United States government wishes to endorse? Is this part of the proper educational requirements to really educate or eradicate racism? Of course not. What every educator should know is that people learn by education, not castigation. Additionally, to procure a positive minded and proactive individual, they need positive reinforcement, not negative reinforcement.

To understand this more fully, we need to backtrack to a pivotal moment in United States history, the Civil War. The Confederate South had endorsed slavery since the nation's inception, and the Union soldiers of the North heroically rose to abolish this archaic tradition. Those Union soldiers already had their freedom, yet they fought, and many died for the freedom of all black people. Henceforth, if they didn't have stalwart consciences or strong moral fiber they could have left things as they were, but, no, they stood up, fought, and over 360,000 Union soldiers died for a noble cause, only to be ignobly forgotten by the majority of the black community. It is often amazing how the lives and freedom of black slaves matter, yet the lives and the hundreds of thousands of deaths of all these heroic white freedom fighters do not.

This is where Black History Month as well as the newly-revised educational programs and museums all fall short. There is a one-sided tunnel vision that many blacks and white liberal educators have about this whole story, and that's because they think the title of this story is simply "Slavery", when the true title should be "Slavery and the Courageous People Who Fought to End Slavery." Although we certainly need to learn about the villains who shackled blacks into slavery, it is far more edifying and racially healing when students learn about all the white, and even black, heroes who fought and died for the black people's freedom. When we only expose students to the immoral abuse, it generates negative feelings, humiliation, and even hatred, whereas giving these students heroes and role models will actually shape their lives in a positive fashion.

Only teaching black students about the errors of white people makes many think *okay, we can never tolerate this,* or more pointedly *those bastards had some nerve,* but it does not show them the other side, which would instill the proactive moral compass that these white heroes can offer, making them think *Wow! These guys stood up against their own race and courageously fought and died for injustices not leveled against themselves, but against us, and humanity. That's the kind of person I want to be!*

Moreover, this is something that would be exceedingly beneficial to blacks and whites, rather than the continual blame game mentality. Almost every depiction by these new programs, whether on TV or in books or museums, entails condemnations against whites, or stories of black heroes, yet all these programs fail to shed light on or honor these brave white souls. This is a truly unfortunate state of affairs, and a damaging lesson to impart to our youth.

Beyond the lack of focusing on the countless whites that fought against their own kind to free the blacks, are the effects on modern minds that have become groomed by reverse discrimination. To claim that a white person is superior to a black person in the field of education, for example, would ignite a volcanic outcry of racism. However, blacks and even many whites have come to believe that blacks are superior in sports. Because many decades of affirmative action made sports like basketball, almost entirely black, the mindset has become that only blacks can play outstanding basketball. In this same fashion, Jews have primarily been typecast as being intellectuals and, rarely, if ever, are viewed as athletes. However, let us view this issue more closely.

Let us take Mark Spitz. Spitz was once the greatest swimmer who ever lived, and he was Jewish. The fact remains that Jews, in general, simply do not foster athletics, they pursue academics, and that is why they excel in those areas. Conversely, it is not that others cannot compete academically with the Jews, or athletically with the blacks, as Asians in higher learning and Latinos in sports respectively attest, hence, it just boils down to cultivation and fair access. Jewish tradition focuses on education and nurtures it, while the blacks seized the new opportunities legally granted to them. This incited many black youths to dedicate their lives to practicing daily, thus enhancing their abilities beyond other races that only practiced part time or even gave up, finding the effort futile.

Moreover, sports have always been good for minorities in general, for it allowed the Italians and Irish to rise up the ladder in their heydays. However, it is unavoidable that teams of yesteryear never became entirely Italian, Irish, or any other race; only today do we see teams that are almost entirely black, hence validating the end results of an unfair legal agenda that also lowered education requirements for black athletes.

Colleges have once again opened their doors to whites, even for basketball, which has been almost entirely black for decades. This is why we not only see more white players today, but why some have become the top players. In college basketball, Adam Morrison and J.J. Redick were the top two scorers, and countless other white players, like Steve Nash and Tyler Hansbrough, have regained their rightful places on the courts. This simply proves that truly equal opportunity, as well as equal guidance and cultivation will yield great results no matter what color, creed, or race a person is.

However, despite the much-needed attention herein to the unfair laws that have over-saturated many fields with blacks, the rise of the countless millions of blacks that have escalated their stations in America with hard work and dedication has been remarkable and astronomical. This brings us to the other glittering side of the African American coin.

Many talented blacks have topped the charts, securing success, fame, and affluence, and despite the ill-effects of some rappers who promote hate, and even worse in their lyrics, the names of people like Colin Powell, Condoleezza Rice, Alan Keyes, Allen West, Roy Innis, Oprah Winfrey, Eddie Murphy, Michael Jordan, Quincy Jones, and countless others form a highly respectable array of role models that the black community and, more importantly, every community can draw on for inspiration. Even during the most difficult times in the past, black people like Frederick Douglas, George Washington Carver, Jessie Owens, Louis Armstrong, Ella Fitzgerald, Marian Anderson, Jackie Robinson, Sidney Poitier, Sammy Davis Jr., Duke Ellington, Ray Charles, Jimi Hendrix and many others won a solid place for themselves, their community, and a firm place in the nation's heart.

Beyond these high-profile role models are the millions of middle-class and upper-middle-class blacks who have likewise made that respectable climb up the ladder to become respected citizens and role models in their own right. Again, the black community has risen to unprecedented levels in only a few decades, and their future only looks brighter. Likewise, Obama's presidential election by a white majority speaks volumes of how whites view blacks. With numerous black executives, mayors, governors, etc. the black community has a large share of high achievers who hopefully one day will subdue the negative factions in their communities, and help make racism a dead memory of the past. As Martin Luther King Jr. proved, working with, not against, people is what generates positive results.

As noted throughout the course of this sprawling historical tome, mistakes and injustices have been leveled against many races, hence, a need to look positively forward and upward, rather than bitterly backward and downward is crucial to progress and success. Treating people with fairness and justice is the only manner to procure peace, and the unfortunate abuse that some whites initiated with slavery in America cannot be remedied with abuses in return. A new and fair mindset needs to prevail, one that will enact fair new laws, repeal bad policies of reverse discrimination, instill better educational programs that are based upon positive actions and setting positive goals, and silencing destructive racial groups and racist black leaders that cloud, corrupt, and cripple the cause. These changes are mandatory if we are ever to overcome this deep-seated discord that still reverberates under the rich fabric of this great nation.

In conclusion—and, perhaps most suitably—are final points, not by this white author, but by prominent black men. Larry Elder, a noted lawyer and host, stated in his 1994 book "The 10 Things You Can't Say in America" that racism was *not* the barrier to the success of Black men and women. Elder denounced the victimhood narratives that blamed whites and evaded personal accountability. Meanwhile, Martin Luther King Jr., Morgan Freeman, Allen West and others rightfully stated the ultimate truth: That all people should be judged by their character, not their color.

MODERN PRESIDENTS: *Strength vs. Weakness*

Moving beyond the presidencies of Kennedy and Johnson, which led into the Civil Rights movement, we shall now continue to examine key presidents in succession, leading us to the present. However, here we shall rate each president as being either a strong or a weak leader. This is not always easy or apparent, for many took wavering stances as they engaged in military actions or peaceful negotiations. However, in many instances this duality of mindset, which was either prudent statesmanship or political posturing, was hampered by personal traits that are often singular, and this, especially in hindsight, did make more of their actions fall into one of these categories, which, for the sake of simplicity, we shall call strong or weak.

The reasons for these assessments are that the overall actions of these leaders affected not only the security of our nation in their own time, but also the future course that our nation took because of those actions. Therefore, it becomes crucial to evaluate these innate traits, which inevitably dictate a leader's political constitution, with the far more important goal of revealing the consequences of these actions to the nation. Our primary focus, however, will be on how they handled international affairs, for those actions have the most direct effect on America's place on the world stage. This examination begins with the highly controversial figure, Richard Nixon.

RICHARD NIXON: *Scandal and the Scapegoat*

Most will never forget, or forgive, Nixon's dubious actions that stripped the Oval Office of its dignity with Watergate. Likewise, Nixon's resignation, to avoid impeachment, deeply demoralized the nation. This deep scar profoundly tainted the office of president, for not only would that lofty position never regain the full respect it enjoyed in the past, but all succeeding presidential candidates would be forced to endure grueling, petty, and often tasteless scrutiny. Nevertheless, just like many leaders who fell from grace, including religious ones like Jimmy Swaggart, Nixon has maintained a devout following. Most Americans either love or hate

Nixon, yet that is nothing new, for Nixon faced adversaries ever since his strong anti-communist stance after WW II.

As Nixon later confided to Monica Crowley in his twilight years, no strong leader is without strong opposition. In recent years, there have been several authors who are much more sympathetic and understanding of Nixon, especially since he did not order the Watergate break-in, and for his role in opening the doors to China. However, his actions on the international front, particularly in regards to America's security, are another matter. Nixon projected an image of strength and confidence, yet did his actions truly mirror the man or the image? To assess these actions it becomes necessary to review Nixon, the man, and his rise to power.

Richard Nixon gave every outward indication of being a strong leader. Graduating first in his class in high school, he was awarded a full scholarship to Harvard. Yet due to his parents' financial difficulties, he opted for his local Whittier College in California. At Whittier, Nixon graduated second in his class, and with a full scholarship, he moved on to Duke University School of Law, where he graduated third in his class. By all standards, Nixon was a consistent and brilliant student.

In the hard-hitting realm of sports, however, Nixon practiced with the football team, but remained benched. From a psychological viewpoint, this might explain why Nixon envied and longed for power as well as the praise that follows. Furthermore, this exclusion was indicative of how Nixon always remained a distant outsider, one that preferred individual control rather than a real team effort.

During World War II, Nixon served in the reserves as a Lieutenant Commander in the navy. Avoiding direct combat, Nixon was stationed in the South Pacific where he handled operations for supplies and cargo. Here he managed to save money that launched his career into the political arena.

Nixon soon made a name for himself with the highly publicized trial of Alger Hiss in 1948. Hiss was a government official in the State Department who was accused of being a Soviet spy. Nixon's intense and searing investigation led to Hiss' conviction, which was in perfect tune with the new anti-communist frenzy that was beginning to sweep through Washington and the nation. Nixon took full advantage of the communist fever two years later when he was elected to the Senate, effectively ousting Congresswoman Helen Douglas.

The long-standing history has been that Nixon ran a dirty campaign, whereby slandering the congresswomen with accusations of being a communist, or "Pink Lady", and that Douglas retaliated with the prophetic slur "Tricky Dick". However, recent files of the campaign, released after Nixon's death, indicate otherwise.

Evidently, it appears that Helen Douglas was in a war of words with her other rival, Sheridan Downey, who was also a fellow Democrat. Douglas was an extreme left-wing liberal, and she was losing touch with her own party. Due to illness, Downey then dropped out of the race, and he endorsed Ralph Boddy, who happened to be the editor and publisher of the *Los Angeles Daily News*. Hence, it was Boddy's *Daily News* that labeled Douglas the "Pink Lady", not Nixon. Even though Nixon did make defensive remarks, he allowed the bickering Democrats to slander each other, while he stepped over the wreckage and into office. This tactic, of allowing rivals to destroy themselves, would be well remembered and used by Nixon in future years. Interestingly, the nasty slur "Tricky Dick", as spewed by Helen Douglas, would resurface two decades later, thus becoming Nixon's most enduring cognomen.

However, in 1950, Nixon appeared as a man who was intelligent, capable, moral, and confident, which enabled him to quickly rise to prominence. Two years later, Nixon found himself on Eisenhower's ticket running for vice president. However, a charge of fraud was leveled against Nixon, prompting party members to insist that Eisenhower drop Nixon from the ticket. Nixon demonstrated his crafty talent by making a public speech, and won over the public with his famous "Checkers speech". This was in regards to Nixon's dog, named Checkers, who was given to him as a campaign contribution. Defiantly, yet with a sense of humor and wit, Nixon publicly stated that he would not return it, because his daughters loved it. Ingratiating himself with the public, Nixon remained in the Eisenhower campaign and they won the election.

Serving as vice president, Nixon took every opportunity to use Eisenhower's administration as a platform for self-promotion. With his ambitious sights set on the presidency, Nixon's rapport with Eisenhower became strained. However, Nixon's highly-publicized television debate with Soviet leader Nikita Khrushchev, at the American National Exhibition in Moscow, clearly displayed his sense of timing and tenacity. With all the pieces now in place, Nixon knew his nomination to run for president was secured. However, what was not secured was winning.

Nixon's far younger, far more handsome, far more articulate, and far more charismatic rival was John F. Kennedy. The real death knell, however, came from the young statesman's father, Joseph, who would use his immense wealth and connections with the Mafia to buy his son's election. A defeated Nixon now learned, and fully understood, the dirty business of politics. Yet, quite graciously, he did not contest the election. Instead, Nixon left politics completely to become a senior partner in a New York law firm. However, this humiliating and fraudulent defeat was a hard and sobering lesson about the dirty and underhanded rules of political survival.

At this point, it is important to briefly reflect upon the times and situations Nixon confronted. Although Nixon was raised with a strict set of Quaker morals, and certainly believed in loyalty, his harsh experiences in the field of politics would not inspire him to become a pious crusader that played by the "idealized" book. Instead, Nixon would play by the "real" book, the book used by the Kennedys, which just so happened to be *The Prince* by Machiavelli. Nixon craved the presidency, and the lesson he learned was that it's a dog-eat-dog world.

Nixon limped away from this defeat, but, two years later, he ran for governor in California. To his complete dismay, Nixon would lose this race as well. This loss, however, proved too much for Nixon, who scorned the press, saying they would no longer have Nixon to push around. Nixon even broke down and wept. By all appearances, it looked like Nixon would fade from public life forever, yet the remarkable feature of Richard Nixon is that he never quit, and this is his most impressive and admirable quality.

Six years later, Nixon would reenter politics, and to his surprise, he finally won his bid for the presidency, defeating Hubert Humphrey. It would be a memorable election, as Nixon won by less than 1 percent of the popular vote. Nixon may have squeaked into office, but the tenacious

Quaker had worked hard and scratched his way up to the top against considerable odds. Taking office on January 1969, Nixon wasted no time in surrounding himself with a respectable assemblage of talent. Yet, of that pool, only a small and elite taskforce would remain in the know. Nixon erected a barrier that excluded many from the covert core, meanwhile, wielding an air of silence and deception that would theoretically pacify or confound the external bureaucracy. In reality, it humiliated and deeply angered many, who called this barrier the "Berlin Wall", due to the two German staffers Nixon would appoint, namely Assistant to the President John Ehrlichman, and White House Chief of Staff Bob Haldeman.

Nixon was, by nature, a solitary man and preferred dealing with a small handful of trusted advisors rather than a sprawling mass of dubious officials, especially ones from a huge bureaucratic government that was habitually mired in red tape. Added to this systematic roadblock were the Democratic liberals who loathed Nixon, as their duplicity did impede many plans he had for progress. This is why Ehrlichman and Haldeman held extremely powerful seats under the Nixon administration. Beyond these two men, Nixon collected an impressive group of talent, as it featured men like George H.W. Bush, Lawrence Eagleburger, Casper Weinberger, Alexander Haig, Donald Rumsfeld, Colin Powell, Frank Carlucci and George Shultz, among others.

However, Nixon's most important and famous colleague was Henry Kissinger. Kissinger served as Nixon's National Security Advisor and then during Nixon's second term concurrently as Secretary of State. Kissinger was an intellectual who graduated from Harvard College *summa cum laude,* and received his PhD from Harvard University. Kissinger had become a professor at Harvard and was beginning to make strong connections with New York's governor, Nelson Rockefeller, and his elite crowd. It was during this time that Nixon recruited Kissinger for his new political role. Kissinger recalled their first meeting, saying Nixon was very awkward and timid, yet they both instantly recognized certain parallels. They both had a penchant for deceit, and Nixon immediately proposed that he would shunt the State Department, and make the White House staff his command center. Since this presented Kissinger with significant power and endless opportunities, he readily agreed to Nixon's covert scheme. Hence, the die was cast.

It's interesting how many have maliciously defamed Nixon for not stepping forward to speak out against the Watergate break-in, which we must recall, he did not order; instead, Nixon made the decision to keep it quiet. Conversely, Kissinger, likewise, did not step forward to denounce Nixon's policy of bypassing the State Department, and instead chose to keep his mouth shut. Yet, where Nixon kept his mouth shut to help protect the lives and careers of friends implicated in the break-in, along with his own hide, Kissinger kept quiet solely for self-interest.

As for Nixon's unjust methods of bypassing other departments to wield control, this he later expressed remorse for, since in hindsight he realized that he had overlooked the talents of men like Secretary of State William Rogers. This does not excuse his mistake, but Nixon's admission of guilt and remorse, as well as his objectives, which were not for self-interest, but for what he believed would secure the best interests of the nation, mark a strong separation point in both men. Despite some of Kissinger's genuinely good ambitions, his huge ego and thirst for fame always took a front row seat, and by Nixon closing the doors to other department heads, this gave Kissinger what he craved, boundless control.

As mentioned, Nixon only envisioned making progress with well-known and trusted individuals, so this closed-door policy unfortunately severed relations with competent officials who were never given the opportunity to prove themselves. Naturally, the upside was that this likewise excluded the incompetents and many adversaries as well.

After Kissinger's acceptance, Nixon exhibited his mendacious stagecraft by telling the press that he would appoint a strong Secretary of State to handle tactics and operations, while Kissinger would only handle long-range planning. Kissinger eagerly followed his leader in deception, yet his lust for the limelight made him become far more endearing to his beguiled audience. Meanwhile, Nixon always suffered from a poor public image. This deficit wasn't his speech or intellect, but rather his nervous physical appearance. This was established during his early TV debates against John Kennedy, where his sweaty face and awkward mannerisms projected an uncomfortable image that bred suspicion. However, Nixon and Kissinger also shared a common academic bond. But despite Kissinger's broader intellect, it would soon prove both beneficial and seriously detrimental.

It is also prudent to appraise the opinions of those who were close to both men, and while Kissinger was said to be pompous and prone to belittling people behind their backs, which included Nixon, whom he once said had "a meatball mind", Nixon, on the other hand, was said to be introverted, elusive, and even coarse. For example, Nixon had described the State Department as "incompetent fags", and he used vulgarity in the countless tapes later sequestered during Watergate. Yet, although Nixon was prone to using foul language in private conversation, which his staff used as well, we must remember that even the stately Henry Kissinger could spew obscenities, such as when he wailed about his failure with the North Vietnamese. "They're just a bunch of shits. Tawdry, filthy shits. They make the Russians look good, compared to the way the Russians make the Chinese look good when it comes to negotiating in a responsible, decent way!"

Oddly enough, despite their dynamic partnership, Nixon and Kissinger never formed a truly close bond. Then again, it is said that many in high office, likewise, could not bond with Nixon, who was uncomfortable around most people. Evidently, Nixon loathed making small talk and only became animated when he found the topic to be of interest. Some have criticized Nixon for this trait which, in reality, is not uncommon. Reagan also preferred others to initiate conversation and many times preferred listening. Additionally, even Thomas Jefferson was a solitary man who eschewed face-to-face meetings. Nevertheless, as noted, many shunned Kissinger, whom they saw as egotistical, snobbish, self-serving, condescending, and hypocritical.

Nixon's solitary nature was compounded by his growing distrust of key staff members. This eventually caused him to construct an even tighter cocoon around himself, which further severed access. However, Nixon actually aspired to achieving a persona that was elusive and unreadable. Years after Nixon resigned, Bob Dole expressed his concern that he would forever remain misunderstood because he was too complicated a man.

Nixon beamed at the comment, replying, "Aha! Now you're getting somewhere!"

Perhaps Nixon thought that remaining an enigma would cushion him from criticism, rejection, or blame, while simultaneously allowing him to maintain his own idealized vision of himself, a vision that he, too, had difficulty perceiving while still in office. In personal notes to himself, Nixon asked how he would be remembered. He offered one-word answers for other presidents, such as gutsy, charm, or vitality, yet his name was followed by a cold and blank question mark (Nixon = ?). In another note, Nixon jotted down *Maintain mystery*.

Nixon was said, by some, to be indecisive and prone to brooding over the many possible solutions to an issue, yet at other times the exact opposite prevailed. This was part of his enigmatic character that prevented many from succinctly characterizing Nixon. At times, Nixon appeared idealistic and generous, or at other times, vindictive and petty. Then again, he would appear reflective and philosophical, or impulsive and erratic. Hence, Nixon was maintaining mystery not so much by design, but most probably by disposition.

Nixon was a complex individual; he was intelligent, yet he liked to prove that he was one of the regular boys, and this might explain why he used vulgarities or told jokes, as bad as some were. It was an attempt by a semi-secluded, deep-thinking man to make himself more readily acceptable to an outside world. Many political figures and historians have condemned Nixon for taking on the public role of president when he knew that he was a solitary man. However, men of ideas can delegate to others how to accomplish something grand; hence, Nixon may have been solitary and uncomfortable dealing with many people on an intimate level, but he had grand and noble intentions of changing the world, and that could best be accomplished in the Oval Office.

Nixon knew he had flaws, and he knew he often failed, yet he always pushed himself to succeed. Nixon made a very revealing comment to Chou En-lai when he visited China, stating that all he wished to accomplish was to achieve one more win than his losses. This was clearly not the most brilliant or tactical thing to say to a foreign world leader, especially one who was isolated and had been an enemy to America for twenty years. However, it reveals the fact that Nixon was very aware of his perpetual flaws and failures, yet strived exceedingly hard for that last and ultimate triumph.

As for the state of world affairs which Nixon now faced in the Oval Office, the Cold War was still presenting a very real and persistent threat, as Soviet aggression seemed unstoppable. With Soviet support, Syrian tanks stormed into Jordan in September of 1970. Kissinger was in a state of panic; he feared the Soviets were aligning themselves for another Cuban Missile showdown, only this time with an infrastructure set to succeed. Haldeman jotted down notes that day, capturing Kissinger's frenzy, and in stark contrast, Nixon's firm and calm resolve. The staff, and even Kissinger, was impressed by the president's commanding presence.

This incident, although not truly major in the grand scheme of world affairs, holds real significance. First, it indicates Kissinger's deep fear of imminent threats of war, and why securing peace treaties at any cost was paramount. Second, it demonstrates Nixon's tenacity when under extreme pressure, as well as his firm anti-communist stance. It was during this crisis that Nixon made it clear that his purpose was to concentrate on broad directives when he declared, "I am not going to get bogged down in the details."

This is the crux of why Kissinger's role would grow radically in scope and unabated, whereby even stepping on the toes of others who were the rightful administrators of certain tasks. As Kissinger's unfettered power grew so, too, did his impudence, as he even kept the president in the dark about many small but significant details. This is a situation where Nixon, the director, opened the stage door for his aspiring actor, Henry Kissinger, who hedged out all his colleagues so that he could become the sole writer and performer to bask in the limelight. Naturally, he would receive all the cheers, good press, and even a very *Noble* prize nomination.

As the real world turned, and real threats of Soviet aggression mounted, Soviet relations with Red China became strained to the point of rupture, thus causing the Sino-Soviet Split. Nixon wisely seized the moment. China had always appealed to Nixon as a worthy objective, because opening relations with the most populated nation in the world, which just so happened to border America's archenemy, the Soviet Union, seemed to make good tactical sense. With the Vietnam War still raging on, and Americans protesting and rioting at every turn, Nixon hoped the new ties with China would humble the North Vietnamese into a truce. However, Nixon would not make this initiative a public parade with bells and whistles, at least not yet. Instead, Nixon's elite team covertly bypassed the State Department completely. With Henry Kissinger as his secret point man, Nixon's plans went into action.

Kissinger flew ahead to meet with both Premier Chou En-lai and Chairman Mao Tse-tung. With the opening exchanges being both positive and reassuring, Kissinger excitedly wired Nixon. With all systems go, the media was alerted and Nixon made his historic flight into Peking. News cameras captured Nixon exiting *Air Force One,* and shaking hands with Chou En-lai. The mysterious country which had been cut off from American contact since President Truman, was finally opening its doors to Nixon, the first American president to ever step foot in China.

Before Nixon's arrival, Kissinger informed the president that Chou confided that the Chinese distrusted Khrushchev, who came off as a bully and a man without direction; hence, evidently, having a clear objective and understanding China's objectives were paramount. Additionally, although Mao was far better known of the two Chinese leaders, Chou was the true administrator and thrust of the regime, while Mao was the philosopher. In this vein, Mao was very much like Nixon, being the reserved figurehead with ideas, while Chou and Kissinger were the men implementing the physical transactions.

Chairman Mao was especially anxious to meet the president, yet he was extremely ill and wished to keep his health a secret. His paralysis from strokes prevented him from speaking clearly or for long periods, but Nixon and Kissinger managed to break the ice. Kissinger even complimented Mao by telling him that he assigned Mao's works to his students at Harvard. Nixon followed by saying Mao's works moved a nation and changed the world, yet the aging and sick Mao humbly replied that they only affected local regions throughout China, and not the world. Mao evidently looked at it in a physical territorial sense, while not realizing that those ingrained philosophies did affect the world in how it viewed and dealt with China.

The essential conversations, however, were conducted with Chou, as he expressed his concerns for regaining control of Taiwan and his apprehensions about Japan and Russia. Nixon assured Chou that Taiwan would be slowly restored to China, but that Japan was a volatile and renewed nation that had previously caused great harm to China, the United States, and even the Soviets. As such, this strengthened Nixon's position, for removing an American presence would be detrimental to all. Additionally, America shared China's concerns about the Soviets, which further strengthened their alliance.

Of crucial interest is that during these discussions Nixon recommended that both nations should begin exchanging intelligence, whereby Kissinger interjected, saying that it had already been implemented. Hence, the ardent diplomat was clearly handling the details, which were not minor, and without first consulting the president.

Before departing, Nixon spoke with Mao and told him that since Mao didn't know him, he shouldn't trust him, but that his actions will prove that he does what he says, and often does more than he says. Likewise, he made the comparison that although they both came from very poor families, they both managed to rise and lead two great nations. History, Nixon said, had brought them together, and what they did to benefit not only their own countries, but also the entire world is what mattered most, despite their different philosophies. By all indications, Nixon's trip was not only historic in breaking two decades of silence, but for truly opening the doors of two very different and powerful nations that have since continued the effort of finding common ground.

Meanwhile, the heated burden of Vietnam still plagued America and the president. In an effort to lessen the mortality rate of American soldiers, Nixon decided to intensify air strikes. As such, it was determined that bombing Cambodia, which was a supplier to North Vietnam, would be a way to weaken their momentum and resolve. The secret bombing mission, however, failed to remain secret, thus igniting an explosion of riots throughout America, particularly in college campuses. This gave rise to the Kent State debacle, where four students were shot and killed by Ohio National Guards.

A year later in May 1971, Nixon and Kissinger finally came to terms with the Soviet Union with his Strategic Arms Limitation Treaty (SALT) after a deadlock of over a year. This initiated Nixon's famous policy of détente. As mentioned earlier, upon hearing this, Ronald Reagan strongly criticized Nixon for his lack of will to confront this aggressive enemy that threatened democracy and worldwide peace. As Reagan saw it, merely relaxing tensions was not victory, for war only procures winners and losers. Regardless, Kissinger and the new Soviet leader, Leonid Brezhnev, made plans to negotiate the SALT treaty.

Brezhnev had been equally motivated to make an agreement to not only control their soaring defense budget, but to also seek solutions for a stagnant economy. Added to this was the fact that the Soviets didn't appreciate the media's pomp over Nixon's landmark meeting in China, for it appeared as though America and China were the two superpowers. Brezhnev, it seems, was jealous, but far more importantly, he was becoming wary of their unexpected alliance.

The SALT agreements, at that time, appeared to most Americans as being logical and equitable limitations on the production of nuclear warheads, with the intent of securing a balance of power, however, they also handed over many harmful concessions. This caused many conservative right-wingers to vehemently jeer, as William F. Buckley's caustic headline in the *National Review* squalled "Veni, Vidi, Victus" — or, we came, we saw, we were conquered.

Therefore, before we can truly pass judgment on Nixon's SALT, two very important issues need to be examined. This entails all the players in this agreement, and the true outcome of this agreement. First, Gerard Smith, who was appointed chief negotiator for Secretary of State William Rogers, was supposed to lead the SALT negotiations. However, Henry Kissinger deliberately sabotaged Smith's involvement. Being a glory hound, Kissinger sought carte blanche in all foreign relations, and with his nomination for the Nobel Peace Prize added to the pot of glitter, he became even more stringent. By slyly eliminating Gerard Smith from the negotiating process, Kissinger did indeed draft all of the fine details that Nixon only briefly outlined. More importantly, where the Soviets had the advantage of consulting the Politburo, this lone-wolf approach now left

Smith and the entire National Security Council out of the loop. In essence, Kissinger took it upon himself to act for the entire United States. Yet Smith was the number cruncher whose expertise was in military inventory and weaponry. In contrast, Kissinger was always more concerned with securing a settlement, regardless of the fine details and ramifications. For Kissinger, America's true security objectives—which were hampered by his innate fear of confrontation—usually took a back seat to the praise he would receive in the press for being a great deal maker.

Therefore, contrary to popular belief, Kissinger didn't truly attempt to secure a balance of power with the Strategic Arms Limitation Treaty; he actually sold out America in his zeal to secure any kind of peace. The treaty allowed the Soviets to build 1,600 launchers, while the United States could only build 1,000. Next, the Soviets had 1,500 ICBM missiles, but they were permitted to build 250 more every year, while America had 1,054 ICBM missiles and agreed to stop production. The development of many new tactical weapons by each side was also deeply discordant in number—always to the Soviets' advantage. Worse still, Kissinger sold them grain, industrial technologies and, of all things, computers, which were America's latest spin-off technology from NASA.

Furthermore, actual statistics collected after the Cold War revealed very embarrassing results. It confirmed that Kissinger and crew might have predicted that the Soviets would dishonor the agreement, but it clearly demonstrated just how much they miscalculated their devious adversary. While they estimated that the Soviets would amass 30,000 warheads, they actually manufactured 45,000. Likewise, where they estimated that the Soviets would probably produce 500 tons of enriched uranium, in reality they manufactured 1,200 tons.

This brings us to the all-important second issue, which is why did they, primarily Kissinger, make these sell-out concessions? Americans may have felt a sigh of relief as Nixon and Kissinger confidently reassured them that America had the upper hand, but with the advent of the Freedom of Information Act, we now know the private correspondence that transpired in Washington, which revealed a whole different mindset. Here we need to look at Nixon and Kissinger independently to see what drove them.

Nixon had always been a strong and outspoken anti-communist during the 1950s and 1960s, and his public exchanges with Soviet leaders clearly demonstrated his unflinching abhorrence of communism, even gaining a few uneasy laughs in return. Nixon's stance may have slightly softened during these personal encounters, but under the façade, he still maintained a hard edge. In fact, directly before Kissinger set up the Soviet summit, Nixon was furious about the rising hostilities in Vietnam. He wired Kissinger, who was in Moscow making plans, and expressed his intentions to cancel the summit meeting, and instead move forward with massive strikes in Hanoi and Haiphong. Naturally, Kissinger tried to pacify the president, but Nixon was aggravated for several good reasons.

Nixon was determined to go for broke, and pummel the North Vietnamese into submission, but he had to contend with Congress, who held the purse strings. Additionally, even though he managed to increase air strikes, which even received approval ratings in the polls, Nixon's directives were thwarted by the Pentagon. Nixon complained that there were too may "McNamara" cronies still remaining in the Pentagon who sabotaged his orders. Even on the battlefield itself, Nixon scoffed at how commanders, after a decade of conditioning, were playing "how not to win" rather than "how to win."

Nixon was likewise discontented with the CIA. The left-wing liberals within the agency had interfered with his objectives so often that he requested that a study be made to see how CIA agents could be removed by executive action. In scouting out replacements, Nixon suggested that they look at graduates from standard colleges, as he loathed the Ivy League liberals. This same crop of left-wing liberals also inundated the press and media, which sabotaged Nixon's objectives at every turn. In a private letter to Pat Buchanan regarding the upcoming election, Nixon stated his views clearly. "The right wingers would rather lose than give up any one iota as far as principle is concerned. The left wing's primary motivation is power. They are always willing to compromise their principles in order to get power…"

On that note, the Ivy League graduate, Henry Kissinger, likewise, was willing to compromise America's best interests in the SALT agreement for the sake of personal power, prestige, and one other very powerful motive. This now shifts our attention to Kissinger himself.

Kissinger made these agreements not solely with the intent of personal glory, the Nobel Peace Prize, limiting nuclear weapons, or softening up the Soviets to ease tensions in Vietnam, but out of *fear*, fear that the Soviets were unstoppable and superior. This fear, which as we saw earlier could build into outright panic, clearly crafted Kissinger's policies. Therefore, rather than confront the Russian bear with a show of strength, Kissinger meekly offered agreements that pacified the beast. In essence, Kissinger made America the humble slave partner that gave their master resources, technology, and the right to produce more weapons. In fact, Kissinger was so eager to secure a deal that he authorized the shipment of grain even before Nixon arrived in Moscow or even heard of the deal. Kissinger was constructing his own policies with little to no censorship. This becomes even clearer knowing that Kissinger admired Prince Metternich and his axiom that *personality dictates policy*.

Thanks to the Freedom of Information Act, Kissinger's pessimism was revealed in several key statements. The highly intellectual statesman also happened to have a deep appreciation for ancient history, particularly that of Greece. In 1974, Kissinger confided to a military commander that America was unfortunately like Athens, while the Soviet Union was like Sparta. His analogy meant that it was inevitable that the brilliant-minded Americans would one day be conquered by the militant Soviets. This explains why the Athenian-minded Kissinger sold America's cutting-edge intelligence, grain, and very soul, because fear incited capitulation. Hence, as discussed in Chapter I, with academia's Grecian conditioning, the irresolvable Greek tragedy was unavoidable.

Kissinger's intellect had long served him very well in many instances, as he was celebrated for his ability to uncover Gestapo agents in post WWII Germany, and his terms in office and many consulting roles afterward have been a huge asset to American politics and business in many other capacities. However, Kissinger's success and fame for securing so many treaties and negotiations came at a price. His many successes were not solely based upon his firm intellect, but more so on his pliable philosophy. In the SALT agreement, as in many other instances,

Kissinger's intellect evidently failed him due to this innate weakness in character. To recall history is one thing; to learn from it is another. Oddly enough, Kissinger himself said, "It is not often that nations learn from the past, even rarer that they draw the correct conclusions from it."

Understanding this truth, Kissinger should have sought avenues to change America's course through strength, as Nixon was more inclined to do, and not simply repeat the ill fate of the Athenians. Nevertheless, as if stricken by a bad omen, Kissinger submitted to the ill fate of history, as if America was tragically destined to fail. Sadly enough, America did fail, at least temporarily, as Kissinger's passive precedent caused America to begin spiraling downward from a position of strength into the lowest pit of impotence under the succeeding Carter administration.

As history would bear out, Ronald Reagan's strategy of pushing the militant Soviets to the breaking point, which had no economic foundation, proved to be the most effective method of ensuring their collapse. Naturally, the good timing of Nixon and Mao opening dialogue aided in making the Soviets only marginally more cautious, however, the future events of Nixon's crumbling administration and Carter's inept administration would prove that the American-Chinese relationship was not very significant in subduing the Russian beast.

Interestingly, while Ronald Reagan was president, he was visited by Kissinger who, in typical fashion, made disparaging remarks behind his back, namely that Reagan wasn't very bright. This shouldn't come as a surprise, since, as we must recall, Kissinger called Nixon a meatball. Nevertheless, in recalling ancient history, as Dr. Kissinger also likes to do, this incident is reminiscent of two famous Romans. Kissinger comes off as the intelligent Roman statesman, Cicero, who condescendingly and quite seriously underestimated Octavian, while Reagan is reminiscent of Octavian, in that he may have been a simple country boy, but he had the conviction, foresight, and drive to achieve an amazing goal, regardless of the cost or danger.

Therefore, many Americans may have felt secure with Kissinger, the *summa cum laude* intellectual, managing international affairs, yet it clearly proves how smart people can make serious miscalculations and grave mistakes. Cicero and Kissinger remain men of stature and admiration, yet

Octavian, hailed as Augustus, and Reagan, hailed as one of the greatest of American presidents, have both dramatically altered Western civilization in significant ways, and valiantly tower over their scholarly peers.

Accordingly, Nixon had many good intentions, but extended far too much power to Kissinger. Nixon may have been the initial idea man who outlined objectives in broad strokes, but Kissinger was undeniably the key draftsman and salesman. Beyond this, Kissinger, as noted earlier, made policies upon his own accord without even consulting Nixon. During Nixon's second term, Kissinger was confronted with the criticism that he was practically a one-man show in foreign affairs. Kissinger partially conceded to the charge by saying that all future negotiations would be open to the whole bureaucracy for input, since this new phase would entail institutionalizing the framework he had laid in place. This flagrant abuse is as much Nixon's fault for allowing Kissinger so much autonomy and power. Extending power is one thing, but extending unbridled power is another, and this is where Nixon plainly lost control in certain key respects. However, with the arms superiority that Kissinger bequeathed to the Soviets, along with the economic aid, and the huge $80 billion in loans to build more weapons, the Soviets shifted into overdrive with a massive plan of world conquest.

Unbeknownst to many, the Soviets stored a large assortment of mysterious goods in a large cellar in East Germany. These items exceeded mere weapons and artillery, instead they manufactured new street signs, such as Karl Marx Place, and minted a brand new currency, and military Medals of Honor, all in advance of their premeditated conquest of Europe. The Soviets' intentions, which some liberals said were not threatening, were irrefutably tangible.

The dire consequences of détente escalated far beyond hidden objectives in cellars, or the military and economic concessions mentioned, as Soviet aggression became emboldened and invasive. Adding to the pangs of détente, America would embark on one of its most demoralizing milestones in history as Nixon became mired in Watergate. It was during this painful process that Nixon further loosened his grip, thus allowing Kissinger complete and total reign. Kissinger's prestige and world renown skyrocketed to unprecedented heights, yet his fixation and success for securing a deal would meet a sobering roadblock.

Vietnam was a painful rupture that slowly tore the American fabric for almost two decades. However, real U.S. involvement began with President Kennedy's approval of a coup that would assassinate South Vietnamese president, Ngo Dinh Diem, on November 2, 1963. General Nguyen Van Thieu, who was backed by the Kennedy administration, would eventually ascend to the presidency in 1967. It was in 1972, while Kissinger was still pursuing his secret negotiations with Thieu and North Vietnam's Le Duc Tho that Thieu defiantly refused to sign Kissinger's treaty. Once again, Kissinger's fixation to close a deal made him concede to the offer that the North Vietnamese could leave troops in South Vietnam even after the peace accord. Thieu fired back with the following analogy.

It would be like catching a thief in your house. Then you call a policeman, who enters and quickly reholsters his gun. He then turns to you, and says, *"This guy doesn't seem that bad. Why don't you just try to live with him? Who knows, maybe he'll even eventually leave."* Thieu then looked at Kissinger and added, *"Then again, he might rape your wife!"*

Hence, Kissinger was willing to leave the South Vietnamese in bed with their enemy. When Nixon heard this, he cabled Kissinger telling him that he should not be arranging a shotgun wedding. Kissinger went back to the negotiating table with the North Vietnamese, again to no avail. This failed negotiation is what infuriated Kissinger to spew forth his derogatory slur, *"They're just a bunch of shits! Tawdry, filthy shits..."*

This again points to Kissinger's personality, which had a different concept of the word *treaty*. Fortunately, hindsight offers us the ability to review the actual details of his more important negotiations, and many display anemic concessions of one type or another. Kissinger had likewise spoken candidly about his concern for maintaining American credibility regarding Vietnam. However, Kissinger's concept of credibility did not mean maintaining strength and honor, or holding firm to a noble cause. Instead, Kissinger stated that in terms of ending the Vietnam War, America only needed to achieve a "decent interval" of time between withdrawal and South Vietnam's collapse to the communists. In plain

English, Kissinger admitted that his insipid concept of credibility meant that America only needed to create a deceitful aura of credibility, as genuine credibility was immaterial. Hence, Kissinger was more of a charismatic charlatan securing vaporous victories than a masterful mediator securing valiant victories.

Quite interestingly, Kissinger engaged these negotiations, which concerned Vietnam's future, without South Vietnam's leader, Thieu, even being involved. Beyond this deceitful ploy, Kissinger sent only very brief cables back to Nixon, which were intentionally cryptic and void of details. Furthermore, Kissinger reprimanded the Foreign Service officer, John Negroponte, for drawing up resolutions that were too demanding. As such, Kissinger had it rewritten, whereby giving further concessions that would later prove disastrous and embarrassing for the United States. Oddly enough, where Nixon impressed upon Kissinger to represent America as if a "hawk not a dove", Kissinger would make America look like a beaten turkey.

In 1973, Kissinger and Le Duc Tho finally came to a resolution, and they signed the Paris Peace Accords. This peace treaty was to end the war with a full American withdrawal, yet it allowed North Vietnamese troops to remain in conquered territories, while offering no firm objective as to what South Vietnam's future entailed. Nixon promised Thieu that America would use the air force to secure a peaceful transition during America's ground troop withdrawal.

As Watergate and motions for Nixon's impeachment rose to fever pitch, Nixon was forced to waste more hours of each day with Watergate drivel than with serious world affairs. Vietnam was one major casualty, as Nixon could not fulfill his promise to Thieu to offer any additional air cover or support. Meanwhile, the Soviets and Chinese renewed their support to North Vietnam, which aggressively positioned itself to consume South Vietnam. As America exited Vietnam, full-scale massacres ravaged the region in one of the ugliest and heart-wrenching moments, which was certainly a disgraceful low-point in American foreign policy, a policy designed and signed by Henry Kissinger.

Furthermore, the Soviets gainfully seized this opportunity and actively began sponsoring coups, such as their campaign in Angola with the aid of Castro's Cuban troops. Many Americans falsely assumed that after the failed Cuban Missile Crisis, Castro had faded into his degenerative world of squalor; however, the wily Cuban leader remained infectiously active. Castro was instrumental in establishing communism in the western hemisphere, first with Nicaragua, then Grenada, and eventually every other South American nation that followed suit. Even the modern dictator of Venezuela, Hugo Chávez, was inspired and nurtured by Castro. Therefore, Americans who think that Castro was some penny-ante radical who just sat around on his poverty-stricken island, in his army fatigues and smoking his stinky cigars, should think twice.

Consequently, the repercussions of Watergate exceeded the demoralization that Americans experienced toward their leader, as it had international ramifications as well. Nixon's time in office was finished and he knew it. Nixon had reached the highest summit, and to his utter despair, the steep cavernous fall awaited. He had served office for six years and experienced a number of triumphs, but all that awaited now was one of the greatest tragedies to afflict the presidential office.

Richard Nixon was a complex and intelligent man with many commendable attributes. His penchant for foreign affairs established relations with China, which had been sealed off for over twenty years. He oversaw the greatest aeronautical feats of mankind, being the first president to speak to a man on the moon by phone, as well as endorsing and overseeing every Apollo moon mission. He oversaw the creation of the Environmental Protection Agency (EPA) and initiated dialogue with the Soviets, which also engendered the joint Apollo-Soyuz space project. And Nixon ended the long war in Vietnam, despite Kissinger's ham-fisted treaty, which betrayed the South Vietnamese and ruined America's prestige. Yet, the shadow of disgrace shall forever plague his name.

Nixon knew firsthand that other politicians, particularly the Kennedys, dealt in even worse covert and crooked operations, yet somehow he would be the one to be the fall guy. Is this fair? No. Is this forgivable? Perhaps. However, is life always fair? No. Will Nixon ever be fully absolved of this mistake? Most probably not.

As Nixon confided to Monica Crowley in his later years, "I've been around politics for a long time, and it's a dirty and cynical business, always has been and always will be. Scandal has been around forever. But to express shock over one situation and not another is just not right. That's where the double standard comes in."

Nixon knew that Kennedy utilized payoffs and the Mafia to secure his election, and later plotted with the Mafia to assassinate Castro. Moreover, during the election, Kennedy unscrupulously ordered IRS investigations to harass and intimidate Nixon. Additionally, Nixon knew that President Johnson ordered wiretapping to bug his office, yet Nixon, alone, would be the fall guy for all the others. This is categorically a double standard. However, Nixon's elite White House staff—that ran all operations in secrecy and excluded all other departments—was clearly in excess and their actions unconstitutional. Then again, was that more detrimental to national security or the integrity of the Oval Office than all the corrupt transgressions committed by Kennedy? Most today think not.

Hence, the immense burden of disgrace that Nixon was forced to endure for the rest of his life is tragic, especially when compared to how Kennedy escaped such defamation of character and torment, albeit paying the price by being assassinated. Naturally, Kennedy's death was tragic, but could he have endured the trials and tribulations that Nixon did if he had lived and all the dirt of his administration had been revealed? By all indications, the answer is a resounding no. If his father Joe's political life dissolved simply due to his anti-war stance, John would have been buried under the trash heap of disgrace for his many crimes and tawdry affairs.

A sad aspect of Nixon's demise was that he handed over the tapes fully believing that the American people would exonerate him. Nixon truly believed that once Americans heard that he did not order the Watergate break-in forgiveness would prevail. But, alas, it did not. Unfortunately, people only seem to remember the opening discussions, where Nixon and crew tried to cover up the incident or how hush money was proposed to pay off Howard Hunt. However, not a single cent was paid, and not a single person in the Watergate scandal profited a dime. It was an oddball plan hatched by an oddball team (sprinkled with a few good men who should have known better), but Nixon had no knowledge of this senseless caper. To bug the Democratic Convention Center would have yielded nothing substantial for the Republicans, and this oddball choice mirrors the oddball conviction that made Nixon the scapegoat, as if he was the most scandalous of all presidents.

Watergate was a foolish error that warranted prosecution, but Nixon's major flaw was that he bestowed far too much power and freedom on Kissinger. The initial commands and objectives were sound, as they emanated from Nixon, but the quick-dealing, passively conceding, ego-eating nature of Kissinger caused profound repercussions. For under the glitter of Kissinger's successful peace dealings were many fissures in the foundation, which caused America to lose its foothold, as the Soviet Union grew more emboldened and volatile. Likewise, the question of modern day China, and its objectives, still poses serious questions.

China has grown immensely due to embracing capitalism, namely by allowing American entrepreneurs to invest billions in their economy. If we recall how Japan rose to be a formidable rival in the 1980s, with the aid of Americans—like consultant William Deming, and his method of Statistical Process Control that improved quality and productivity—we can see that a small nation, in twenty years time, can become an economic dynamo. Therefore, China, with a population four times larger than America's, will surely be a colossal challenge. However, we also must be mindful about the jobs that America is losing to cheap Chinese labor, as well as the billion-plus people who are becoming richer, as they are now demanding the same limited resources that the rest of the world utilizes. This presents a new economic dynamic that needs to be studied and regulated, or many national economies might crash, not to mention the increased pollution and erosion of resources.

Beyond competition, America has become extremely lax in its trade agreements with China, thus accepting inferior merchandise. Automobile tires made with inferior materials have exploded, killing many Americans on the road, harmful lead-based paint has been found in children's toys, toxic pet foods recalled, while Chinese-made pharmaceuticals have also killed many Americans due to a total lack of federal regulations.

Furthermore, many of America's best colleges and universities now cater to Asians, especially Chinese in the sciences, while blatantly rejecting Americans. Many of these students are educated in the States, and then return home. Utilizing this talent, China has been proactive in establishing universities that cater to producing graduates in these high tier positions, as keeping common laborers gainfully employed is not their only goal. A brain drain agenda is clearly in operation, as Chinese universities are now attracting students worldwide. Engineers, military technicians, scientists, computer programmers, and many other highly trained individuals are filling a huge workforce that dwarfs America and its allies combined.

In this regard, America must be aware of secret agendas. China is not a democratic nation, and with their growing interest for oil in the Middle East and South America, many international conflicts are already mounting. In addition, with the FBI's computers being hacked daily by Chinese agents, America needs to be more vigilant. Therefore, this modern chapter of China's great reawakening and global interaction, which Nixon unleashed, truly remains to be seen and understood.

In attempting to analyze Nixon and his place in history, many aspects need to be considered. Beyond the harsh realities of politics that Nixon faced during his rise, was the fact that the new medium of television was a growing enterprise with enormous and unforeseen power. This crucial factor has rarely, if ever, been a point of focus in the downfall of the Oval Office, of which Nixon became the sole scapegoat. We know that Nixon committed a crime, yet so, too, have many presidents before him. Even many highly respected presidents harbored indiscretions that were only revealed decades or even centuries later. Again, Lincoln committed many unconstitutional and illegal actions, some surpassing Nixon's, yet Lincoln remains the top ranked president of all time by most popular polls, and even those conducted by scholars.

As for the issue of moral indiscretions, there is the alleged charge that Thomas Jefferson fathered children with his slave, Sally Hemmings. If the television media existed in the eighteenth century, Jefferson would have been instantly lambasted nationwide. Jefferson's name would have been smeared to the point that there would be little to no veneration, no Jefferson Memorial, no portrait of Jefferson on Mount Rushmore or on the nickel or even that odd two-dollar bill.

(Despite a high likelihood of guilt, this charge against Jefferson has not been proven, as DNA testing indicated that it could have been any number of Jefferson males living at or near the plantation, of which there were many.)

Nevertheless, the fact that the media has grown into an aggressive and invasive Secret-Service-like agency has had a profound effect on politics and our world in general. Their use of covert agents, called journalists, who finagle their way into uncovering secret information or the wrong information, especially during wartime, has long proven their unregulated excess and even abuse of power. The instantaneous broadcast of audio/visual news to an entire country, as it happens, is a factor that never affected any president before Truman. It was only after WW II that televisions first became a peculiar fad for the rich under Eisenhower, and then grew into a permanent fixture for an entire nation under Kennedy.

Although President Eisenhower sent financial aid to the volatile Vietnam region, Kennedy initiated the Vietnam War by sending in the Green Berets and small troops. However, the war truly took on its toxic nature during the Johnson administration. Johnson not only took the full brunt of the new war, but his docile approach enabled the war to continue without any plan for victory or withdrawal. This lack of executive vision and leadership provided the fuel for the media to broadcast their depressing reports into every American home. This mental conditioning, via intensive multimedia, which featured maimed soldiers, POWs, MIAs, draft dodgers, and daily listings of the dead, was the driving impetus that created perhaps the most manipulated and reactionary generation in history, the hippie generation. As they rallied for peace and love, while also engaging in anti-war demonstrations, the respect for the office of president was simultaneously corroding into a new and contemptuous seat of distrust and even disgust.

Presidents before Johnson had been treated with a sizable degree of respect, even if they were reckless and corrupt like Kennedy. This is evident by those who still absolve Kennedy of his transgressions and crimes, as they remain devout followers who worship the golden days of a picture-perfect presidency, which the media took a major role in crafting. Their memories are locked into a black and white time zone that captured an effervescent young man with his Hollywood good looks and moving speeches. Yet, anyone who truthfully looks beyond the beautiful façade at Kennedy's dark and numerous criminal actions, political transgressions, and immoral sins, could never maintain the idyll of Camelot. Sadly, this delusion still exists for many even today, but the point here is that Kennedy was indeed portrayed as a pure and noble king while in office.

During the Johnson years, however, a slow but invasive disenchantment ebbed into the media and the mindset of their captive audience. By the time of Nixon's arrival, the nation and the media knew no bounds as far as scrutiny or respect—regardless of rank or privilege. And although we know that smear campaigns existed even as soon as America's second presidency, the public's awareness and respect remained very different before TV as compared to afterward, especially after the painful and, to many, deceitful Vietnam War.

That those in the Nixon administration were caught, and instantly televised, does not absolve Nixon and company of their crimes, or blame the media for reporting criminal activity, but it must make us pause to ponder just how pure were all the other presidents and their administrations before Nixon, and just how severe were *their* particular transgressions. Furthermore, would their actions constitute impeachment? One must ask the ethical question, what is worse, a president like John F. Kennedy who had the leader of Vietnam assassinated, conspired with the Mafia to assassinate Castro, illegally bought his presidency, and had numerous affairs that jeopardized national security, or a president like Richard Nixon whose subordinates were caught wiretapping?

In the final analysis, Kennedy's criminal record exceeds Nixon's by far, yet, as noted, this does not absolve Nixon of wrongdoing. The point is that all presidents have engaged in dubious acts to varying degrees, however, the fact that Nixon stands essentially alone as the man who made the Oval Office fall from grace is not only unfair but also untrue.

As mentioned early on, the only fair method for evaluating a leader is to weigh their good deeds against their misdeeds, and then assess if those deeds affected greater positive influences or negative influences upon their era and future generations. In this regard, the Watergate scandal was indeed criminal, but in comparison to other violations, it truly is minimal. What does matter, however, is what Nixon and Kissinger bequeathed to America. Nixon's folly for extending so much power to Kissinger must be included in this assessment, along with including Kissinger in the overall results, since he played such a significant role.

Henceforth, even beyond Nixon's blaring Watergate scandal and resignation (which had long-term ill effects), he, and particularly Kissinger, did make secret agreements and implemented policies that had significant consequences for the nation, which persisted or escalated in the years that followed. As mentioned, China's relations with America and the world, as it grows in power and influence, remains to be seen, yet their current negative effect on the American economy, and their toxic military stance indicate that it very likely might be more of a danger than enrichment.

Meanwhile, despite the SALT talks, the Soviet Union unquestionably grew to new militant heights, with both higher stockpiles of weaponry and an increase in global aggression. Coupled with the Vietnam War's abysmal abandonment, Nixon truly weakened America. And while China offers its cryptic contribution, and Nixon's advocates believe he might regain his stature, there is little mystery to his prediction of Nixon = ?, as all the deficits mentioned herein tips the scale toward *weak*.

Nevertheless, with Nixon's resignation, and Vice President Spiro Agnew's earlier resignation, the Republican Minority Leader, Gerald Ford, was quickly moved up through the ranks to become vice president and then president. This was an unprecedented rise to Commander in Chief, making Gerald Ford the only president not to be elected as president or vice president. Then, in a highly controversial maneuver, Ford granted a full pardon to Nixon for all possible crimes committed against the United States. Ford's act of loyalty would prove his own undoing when he lost his bid for reelection and Jimmy Carter took office. Then again, it would have taken a miracle for the Republicans to remain in power at this volatile time; hence, Ford's decision was prudent as well as loyal. Ford's short two-year term yielded little of major influence, and this appropriately leads us to our next presidential examination.

JIMMY CARTER: *Given the Reins after a Republican Debacle*

Jimmy Carter is viewed by the vast majority as a weak president, as even a 2005 Wall Street Journal poll placed Carter in thirty-fourth position out of all forty-three presidents. Moreover, when we evaluate President Carter's overall actions, this becomes patent. Cold War tensions were still rising after the Nixon/Kissinger SALT agreements and Carter feebly followed suit with signing SALT II. The Cold War was never a priority for Carter, who, upon taking office, cut the defense budget by $6 billion. This, we must remember, was at a time when Soviet aggression was rapidly escalating. Instead, Carter built an administration dedicated to a very idealistic and certainly noble cause, namely his Human Rights policy. However, Carter's extremely passive nature even crippled his own righteous agenda.

Quite revealingly, Carter's Human Rights policy only made provisions for congenial objectives. In this regard, Carter targeted many third-world nations as being violent offenders of human rights. Therefore, rather than taking action to mentor and cultivate these weak regimes, which were floundering in political and economical turmoil, Carter decided to eliminate all U.S. aid. This ironic gesture was due to the Soviet Union's interest in these targets, and Carter's innate fear of entanglement. Unfortunately, this gave free passage to the Soviets to intimidate and consume these helpless countries. Where the Johnson, Nixon, and Ford administrations were flashing yellow lights, merely waving mild caution, the Carter administration flashed a green light. In one of America's most reticent moments, one nation after another fell to the Soviets, who devoured these nations unchecked.

As we know, every action causes an equal and opposite reaction, yet inaction is likewise an impetus that causes a reaction. Carter's stance against the Soviets can be equated to a gardener who passively fails to attack the aggressive weeds in his garden. The inevitable consequence is that the weeds grow wild and unabated. Carter went beyond sending indirect signals of inaction, as he made it quite clear in his communications to Brezhnev that America had no intentions of getting involved in the domestic affairs of other nations, and more specifically not antagonizing the Soviets. In very clear and direct terms, Carter was saying that the gardener is not only off-duty, but also leaving the premises, so do what you please. As a result, the malignant sphere of communism proliferated from South America to Central America to the Eastern European block, Asia, Africa, and beyond.

Carter's lack of stature quickly reverberated around the globe, and made him a target to even third-world leaders like Fidel Castro. While

Carter was conducting cordial negotiations with Castro, the wily Cuban leader was simultaneously dealing arms to anti-American revolutionaries behind his back. The takeover of Nicaragua and Grenada occurred right under Carter's nose, while Castro took pleasure in the fact that Carter was forced to remain silent. Carter knew that his passive Human Rights policy caused these debacles, and would only be fuel for the Republicans to roast his administration. Yet Carter wasn't through with caving in to third world nations.

Carter is also attributed with signing over the Panama Canal to Panamanian dictator, Omar Torrijos. The famous canal lock dated back to 1901, when President Teddy Roosevelt ordered its construction. Roosevelt went to great lengths to secure this vital parcel of land, which separated the Pacific and Atlantic Oceans. As noted earlier, this was the exact spot where Columbus reached in his quest to sail straight across to India, and it was here that the manmade canal linked east with west. The canal locks became crucial investments, and Roosevelt took a vested interest in gaining and maintaining its control for the nation's economic growth and safety. The canal's use by commercial trade vessels, oil and ore tankers, as well as war ships was, and still is vital, yet in a show of good will, Carter gave it all away. Carter might have hoped to soften relations with the tyrannical dictator, but the only thing that truly remained soft was Carter.

Carter also followed Nixon's lead with China by inviting its new despotic leader, Deng Xiaoping, to visit America. Carter opened up American intelligence and economic initiatives that firmly gave China the economic and military boost Deng sought. When Deng informed Carter that he intended to attack the Vietnamese "to teach them a lesson," Carter passively "urged restraint" rather than commandingly denouncing the unprovoked act of war. Emboldened, Deng attacked Vietnam days later. Furthermore, during Deng's visit he firmed up business relations with several American firms that set China on its course to become the new and perhaps dominant threat to America, both economically and militarily.

It can also not be forgotten that it was Carter's weak stance, once again, that enabled Ayatollah Khomeini to easily overthrow the Shah of Iran. As they occupied the country, they captured fifty-two Americans who they defiantly held as hostages. To America's shame, the Iranians kept them in captivity for a year. In another very revealing moment, on the very day Ronald Reagan became president, the hostages were quickly released. It had become painfully evident that Carter's passive idealism had become America's pitiful straightjacket.

In contrast to Carter's numerous blunders and weaknesses, we now turn to his extremely able successor, Ronald Reagan.

RONALD REAGAN: *Reviver of a Demoralized Nation*

We have covered many aspects of Ronald Reagan previously in the McCarthy & Reagan section, but here we shall focus on his actions that directly reversed Carter's debacles, and simultaneously revived a nation that languished in the doldrums of infirmity.

As a preface to Reagan's political policies, a note about Reagan's and Carter's religious beliefs helps to clarify their polar personalities. Interestingly enough, both men were religious, yet even worshipping the same God had yielded almost disparate results. Although some claim that Carter's faith was more firmly rooted, being clearly defined and more genuine, one must not dispel Reagan's unorthodox amalgamation of Christian and even astrological beliefs. Because a person refuses to be labeled Presbyterian, Lutheran, Catholic, Baptist, or the like, does not mean they do not have an understanding or genuine belief in God.

That said, the main difference between the two was that Carter was akin to a Calvinist, where the emphasis is on mankind's dark and ailing soul, and repentance is mandatory for redemption. Taking that further, Carter burdened the nation's spirit with a jeremiad of sacrifices, skepticism, and a call for limitations that dimmed the soul and darkened the horizon. In contrast, Reagan's exuberant view of mankind, particularly Americans, was one of divine providence with limitless possibilities upon a glowing horizon. It was this optimistic spirit of unbound energy and illumination that captured the attention and admiration of many clergymen and evangelicals, not to mention the hearts and souls of millions of Americans. Despite his undefined faith, Reagan's positive concept of religion, and the belief that he was chosen to perform God's work, set the mental and moral foundation for what he achieved, thus America's skies and horizon rarely ever shined so brilliantly.

As we know, Reagan was an anti-communist from his earliest days, and again this had at its root the basic Biblical dichotomy of good and evil. However, several decades later, Soviet expansion was at its peak. As such, Reagan was now forced to contend with the Soviets who had previously invaded Afghanistan under the Carter administration. This was a rare moment when Carter attempted to take action, by covertly sending aid to train Mujahideen forces, yet it was too little and too late. The Soviets had already stormed the presidential palace and massacred the ruling family. Quite cunningly, the communists made it appear as though it was an internal revolution by broadcasting fallacious cries for Soviet aid. Soviet tanks stormed in, and the poorly-outfitted Afghans fought tooth and nail for almost a decade. However, it was Reagan's full commitment and aid to Afghanistan that caused the Soviets to weaken and eventually retreat. America's financial support, training and logistics caused the Soviet's first humiliating defeat, being a major turning point in the Cold War.

Reagan's immense military buildup, aid to oppressed nations, covert PSYOPs (psychological operations, which intimidated the Soviets), and his open remarks of securing peace through strength by taking any military steps necessary (including nuclear) to secure democracy had taken its toll on the Soviets. However, it simultaneously gave some people the impression that Reagan was a warmonger. Reagan had consistently exhibited a militant mindset over the previous decades when he chastised the Eisenhower, Johnson, and Nixon administrations for not being aggressive enough with the Soviets. His impatience with Johnson grew to outrage, citing that the soldiers were not receiving the support or supplies they needed to secure a victory. Reagan also despised Johnson's passive speech whereby he assured the North Vietnamese that America would not use nuclear capabilities.

Despite his zeal, we should not take Reagan's warring "nuclear" words as evil intent. Reagan was simply deft enough to realize that in war you never comfort or embolden your enemy by limiting your arsenal or rhetoric. This would be like a boxer saying that he'll tie both hands behind his back and, in the case of Vietnam, America's bloody face revealed the outcome; hence, why he criticized Johnson. In regards to his critics, however, Reagan knew who the warmongers truly were, for the Soviets were wreaking havoc in third world nations all across the globe. Hence, Reagan's militant words and actions were designed to end aggression with strength.

Taking this firm policy with him into the Oval Office, Reagan gave the Soviets no quarter. The former Soviet Ambassador, Anatoly Dobrynin, aptly offered testimony that confirmed Reagan's firm stance against communism. Dobrynin later revealed that whenever they tried to make a diplomatic maneuver to soften his position or even break his will, Reagan remained impervious, and resolutely stood his ground. Reagan received a great deal of opposition from his own advisors, as well as European allies, yet he never wavered. The payoff was the demise and implosion of the Soviet Union, as it shattered into shards of satellite nations. So, perhaps it is very fitting that in 1964, Ronald Reagan had prophetically revived FDR's famous words, for he truly made that *rendezvous with destiny* and led America to victory.

A strong anti-war sentiment runs through many *modern day* liberals who abhor fighting. They believe weapons are the archaic tools of the past, and that the pen is the sole instrument of peace. This is a very idealistic and alluring reverie; however, that peaceful dream does not always exist in the real and restless world. Warmongers have always been a part of world history, and the day that Americans, Iranians, North Koreans, Soviets, Chinese, Christians, Jews, Muslims, Hindus, etc., can all think alike is either a dream or a reality for a very distant and divine future.

In a similar fashion, people who pride themselves on their sophisticated intellect, while deriding others as primordial warmongers, unfortunately cannot comprehend that the whole world does not share their sensible beliefs or ideology, and this is their perpetual blunder. In this regard, they habitually render themselves as Athenians, who perpetually fall victim to the warmongering Spartans, by continually failing to realize that some foes are savage aggressors and require force.

Therefore, "warmonger" and "aggressive defender of peace" carry two different meanings, and sometimes the latter is necessary. Huge military expenditures like those of Ronald Reagan, or even George W. Bush, are often required and always meet with strong opposition. The more liberal factions tend to criticize these huge budgets as wasting valuable funds that could be used to enhance the quality of life rather than destroy it. However, this is a short-term viewpoint that sounds logical and righteous on the outset, but when placed within the context of their volatile times, its flaws are revealed.

When an aggressive rival threatens a nation, logic dictates that defense spending will hopefully preserve life during and after the conflict. Greater arms and strength are the most outward and visible signs of this investment; however, quite often, what remains overlooked is the advent of spin-offs. Military R&D (research and development) has proven to be a major contributor to the broad spectrum of advances that have impacted the modern world. All these technologies eventually overflow into the public sector. They advance commercial aviation, space exploration, computer technologies (that profoundly impact businesses and education), medicine, and many other tangential industries that all significantly enhance society. Therefore, many of the positive benefits that society reaps are primarily due to these new technologies, which were initially discovered through an adequately funded military. These advances cannot be ignored, and many statistics indicate that those who lambaste defense spending as pure madness or a waste of valuable resources rarely, if ever, add these long-term benefits into the equation. Out of any horrible situation, there is often a silver lining. And in this case, beyond winning a victory in war to preserve a nation, there are many spin-offs that add to that positive end goal.

Interestingly enough, hindsight reveals that this spin-off effect has been around for countless centuries. The Romans built roads initially to increase the mobility of their army, yet they quickly adapted them to handle trade and commerce. Additionally, necessities on the battlefield spurred the invention of movable bridges, or the fashioning of bronze and iron for weapons, which later transformed into textiles, surgical tools, building materials, and other useable devices. Therefore, we can see that projects originally designed for the destructive insanity of warfare, often produce the most productive and rational spin-offs.

The hydrogen bomb is a prime example of how the science used to create the most destructive force known to mankind, was likewise used to produce a highly efficient energy source. Nuclear power plants have become major power sources throughout Europe and Asia. Furthermore, the positive uses of hydrogen have not yet been fully explored or revealed, as continued research heightens the possibilities.

As for the advancement of weaponry itself, the stealth bomber or sophisticated smart bomb may seem like expensive gadgets to kill humans, but these high-tech instruments actually reduce fatalities. During WW I, WW II, and Vietnam, ghastly weapons like mustered gas, aimless V1 and V2 rockets, or the highly-flammable napalm or Agent Orange herbicide killed, not only millions of soldiers, but innocent civilians in appalling numbers. Throughout history, evil leaders and their lethal armies have been like a recurring virus that has continually plagued world history, and this virus shows no signs of ever stopping; henceforth, if new weapons can target these militant germs exclusively, without collateral damage, then that's a sound investment and a worthwhile goal.

Such rationalizations may seem ludicrous to some that deem war and military spending as being futile, yet it is uncontestable that military R&D has benefits that exceed the initial objective of survival. Again, this does not condone war, but simply finds a silver lining in hell's inexorable shroud. If good and evil must inevitably collide, good *must* prevail.

Hence, Ronald Reagan, even with his undefined religion, clearly demonstrated his deep spiritual belief in good and evil. Living his life with these clearly defined lines, Reagan was able to focus on and achieve his objectives, regardless of the errors he made along the way. Therefore, in conclusion, Ronald Reagan did prove to be an exceptionally strong leader.

However, regarding Reagan's successful military operation in Afghanistan, one of the unforeseen side effects of this victory was that this also gave radical Muslims confidence in their Jihadist movement, especially when they saw the Soviets retreat. This garnered a new perspective, for if a small defiant third-world nation could unite to repel and defeat a world superpower, so could they. Osama bin Laden would remember this incident very well in the decades ahead. However, the reality remains that beyond able leaders and manpower, a successful operation demands huge financial resources and a network of strong allies. This was something Osama had only dreamt of previously, but that he now could put into practice.

OSAMA BIN LADEN: *Islamic Jihad and American Weakness*

Osama bin Laden was born on March 10, 1957, in Saudi Arabia, into a family of enormous wealth and privilege. He grew that fortune into an immense underground machine for funding and training terrorist guerillas. Additionally, Osama made connections with rogue states that were eager to sponsor his waves of terror. During the Clinton administration, Osama was well known by intelligence agencies as being a primary threat. Yet, even after the first bombing attack on the World Trade Center in 1993, Clinton remained ambivalent. In fact, Clinton didn't even bother to visit the bombsite or attempt to console the victims. Further still, the Clinton administration was plagued with officials such as Janet Reno, Jamie Gorelick, Vice President Al Gore and Mary Ryan who all eroded national security.

Bill Clinton appointed Mary Ryan as Assistant Secretary of State, and she established what became known as Visa Express. This policy authorized ten Saudi travel agencies to handle interviews, screenings, and to even fill out visa forms, whereby the U.S. consular office only needed to stamp and mail the visas to these unknown Arab applicants. This thoughtless policy was directly responsible for allowing the 9-11 terrorists free access to the United States for many years before the attack to train, surveil, and then finally execute their deadly plan. Fortunately, the Bush Administration shut down the Ryan-Clinton visa policy several months after the 9-11 attacks. However, the mounting inactions of Bill Clinton were emboldening the watchful Jihadist leader.

After the 9-11 tragedy, directed by Osama bin Laden, President Bush's swift retaliation found America directly reentering Afghanistan with a full air and ground assault. In time, many high-ranking al-Qaeda terrorists were eventually caught or killed. However, leftist liberals, who preferred accusing Bush of conspiracy theories when we entered Iraq, often ignored these positive accomplishments. American operations continue to sever al-Qaeda's financial support from its network of rogue states, but with a lack of full commitment from the Iraqi people, a successful conclusion remains questionable.

Although there has always been grave unrest in the Middle East, and covert American involvement since the 1950s, these recent Jihadist events appeared to accelerate after Reagan's communist victory. They began to metastasize during the administration of George H.W. Bush, yet without major incident. These were primarily the networking and training years of Osama bin Laden. Although Osama is still suspected of having been in contact with Saddam Hussein, no connection was made during the Bush senior administration.

However, when Saddam Hussein attacked his tiny oil-rich neighbor of Kuwait in January of 1991, Bush senior initiated the Gulf War with Desert Storm. The mission commenced with a series of strategic air attacks and a ground force that within four weeks forced Saddam's troops to retreat. Osama bin Laden's intense anti-American hatred grew, as he loathed how American infidels interfered with Muslim nations, which included maintaining army bases throughout Saudi Arabia to protect their oil interests. However, the full-blown cancer of Osama's terrorist organization truly metastasized under the eight year, double term, of Bill Clinton. Hence, Bill Clinton would personify American weakness.

BILL CLINTON:
Dismantler of State Security + Moral Vacuum = Disasters

Bill Clinton took office on January 20, 1993, and a month later, on February 26, the first World Trade Center bombing occurred. Naturally, the planning for this operation occurred before his taking office, but the response of a new leader was about to be tested. When government agents captured the Muslim terrorists, they were tried in civil court, despite their suspicions that the kingpin of the operation, Ramzi Yousef, had affiliations with al-Qaeda. President Mubarak of Egypt even rushed to visit Clinton to warn him of this new global "phenomenon" of Islamic extremism, which demanded a military not civil response. Yet Clinton remained more than civil, he remained inert. Thus sending a clear message to the terrorists, particularly Osama, who now lauded "taking the fight to America."

Months later, on October 3, 1993, the Black Hawk down incident occurred in Somalia, where an American task force of two helicopters was shot down. Clinton had ordered the mission a go, but when it horrifically ended in failure, with eighteen American soldiers dead, Clinton quickly blamed General Garrison, and sheepishly ordered a full evacuation. Once again, the terrorists got the message they had anticipated, loud and clear.

A year later, on April 6, 1994, an airplane carrying President Habyarimana of Rwanda was shot down, and a tyrannical militia group immediately rounded up the prevailing Tutsis, and began killing them en masse. Clinton and the United Nations turned a blind eye, and one of the worst atrocities in history occurred, as almost a million people were brutally slaughtered in a three-month period. The eyes of Osama and the terrorists, however, took heed.

In January of 1998, accusations surfaced that Clinton had sexual relations with White House intern, Monica Lewinsky, and the press began their rigorous coverage of the tawdry affair. Other allegations against Clinton were mounting and in May, a scandal in the White House Travel office triggered an FBI investigation. At the same moment (May, 1998), a most revealing broadcast aired, which many Americans took little notice of, yet would have immense repercussions in the near future. ABC News reporter, John Miller, had an exclusive interview with the CIA's most monitored terrorist kingpin, Osama bin Laden.

In this landmark interview, Osama clearly mentioned that America's weak leadership and fear of losing soldiers in battle was now evident; this gave Osama and his Jihadist guerillas not only confidence, but also deadly motivation. In essence, Clinton's ambivalence toward the World Trade Center bombing, his retreats in Beirut and Somalia, his blind eye to the mass genocide in Rwanda, and his mounting scandals which triggered impeachment, sent a clear signal, one that Clinton had no idea he was transmitting to our new and most feared enemy, an enemy who was now emboldened to step-up and intensify their terrorist operations.

On October 12, 2000, the navy destroyer *USS Cole* was attacked by two of Osama's al-Qaeda suicide bombers, killing seventeen American sailors. Meanwhile, Clinton, once again, sent another clear message to the terrorists by ignoring this direct and hostile declaration of war. However, Clinton did manage to lie to a grand jury about his sexual relations with Monica Lewinsky. Also mounting, were more sex scandals with six other women, in addition to other investigations, including the famous Whitewater scandal involving illegal real estate transactions, and impeachment proceedings. Added to the Clinton baggage were alleged illegal campaign contributions by a foreign nation, namely the Peoples

Republic of China, and separate legal cases resulting in Clinton's being disbarred from using his Arkansas law license and fined $25,000. Additionally, Clinton was suspended from the high court, thus prompting the evasive president to resign from the Supreme Court bar. Sadly, most leftists have chosen to ignore or forget these criminal and immoral acts.

More damaging than Clinton's self-destruction, however, is that after only six months in office, Clinton dispensed with CIA briefings, and slowly dismantled state security. With Reagan ending the Cold War, Clinton believed the world no longer posed a threat, as such, he assumed that federal agents were expendable, since satellite intelligence appeared to be sufficient. When incidents arose with Saddam Hussein, Clinton and staff froze with anxiety. As James Simon Jr. of the CIA said, "They had fifth or sixth thoughts about almost everything." Then when Clinton did make a decision, it always fell short or failed. As CIA station chief, David Manners, said, "Under Clinton, the White House wanted to appear to be doing something without doing something. It was a joke!"

Likewise, Ramzi Yousef, who masterminded and successfully bombed the World Trade Center in 1993, managed to escape the United States and fled to Pakistan. Yousef's string of devious plots included the assassinations of President Clinton and Pope John Paul II, bombing Jewish communities in New York City, and a sophisticated plan to hijack several planes in the Philippines to use them as bombs. This diabolical scheme was fortunately thwarted, but was the evil template for the 9-11 attacks. The U.S. government posted a $2 million reward on Yousef, and his disloyal coconspirator turned him in. Yousef was duly sentenced to life in prison without parole. Yet, a full investigation was never conducted at that time to find the full extent of Yousef's ties to al-Qaeda. Further still, even though a few in the CIA began connecting some of the dots, and even surmised the feasibility of the hijacking scheme, Clinton was uninterested. Unfortunately, all was neglected under an administration that cut intelligence and defense funding, manpower, and daily CIA briefings that drastically crippled national security, while simultaneously being barraged by investigations, and even impeachment proceedings.

Sadly enough, because the economy was in a boom cycle, the nation unwittingly became financially fat and content, not to mention blind to

Clinton's political ineptitude. Moreover, they became immorally accepting of his perpetual sins. Americans were making money and living the good life, so anything Clinton did, they figured, couldn't be that bad.

Some have blamed George Bush (who was only in office eight months) for the 9-11 tragedy. Despite these allegations, Bush inherited a Clintonian government that had no infrastructure for gathering or analyzing human intelligence, revolving-door visa and airport policies, and had made devastating decisions for eight years that emboldened Osama bin Laden. This immense breakdown in national security had all transpired under Clinton's inept and scandalous administration.

However, beyond Clinton's damaging cutbacks, oversights, reticence or ambivalence, which in turn encouraged and invited terrorism, are other egregious acts, which some call traitorous, yet I deem as more ineptitude.

Clinton hadn't the slightest interest in or understanding of foreign affairs, at least not in the realm of military politics. With a predisposition toward financial interests, particularly for his elitist crowd of supporters, such as Don Tyson, the poultry mogul from Arkansas, all of Clinton's foreign policies revolved around his being Mr. Appeasement. Basically, he exchanged security for sales. Defense and national security reporter, Bill Gertz, aptly summed up Bill Clinton, when he said; "His flower-child 'can't we all just get along' approach to global power politics has left the nation weakened and vulnerable in a dangerous and hostile world."

Quite naïvely, Clinton redirected $80 billion of the defense budget toward the economy. This did make many Americans rich, especially his ultra-rich lobbying friends who also showered Clinton with gratitude. The downside to this seemingly euphoric economic boom was that Clinton's main talent for spin had to work overtime to pull the rich wool over his satiated sheep's eyes. For unbeknownst to the American lambs was the fact that Clinton's foreign policies were feeding the communist wolves.

Firstly, the Soviets were given hundreds of millions of U.S. dollars by Clinton to supposedly disarm their nuclear missiles. However, not only was that money dishonorably redirected into new weapons development, such as the SS-27 missile or their new models of nuclear submarines, but it also helped to fund the largest strategic underground bunker ever built. Called Yamantau Mountain, translated as Evil Mountain, this gargantuan subterranean command center is as large as Washington DC, and is located on the distant outskirts of Moscow. Naturally, Evil Mountain's purpose is not for peacemaking, but rather to shelter warmongers; namely all high-ranking Soviet officials and scientists in the event of nuclear war.

Unfortunately, Clinton was the first American president to preside over a world where America was the lone superpower. This great opportunity to dismantle Russia's nuclear weapons and aid them with democratic initiatives and trade networks that would allow Russia to export goods, akin to post war Japan, could have truly built a friendly and productive Russian ally. However, Clinton's rich friends, such as Don Tyson, who was only looking to reap the benefits of feeding the jobless Russians, managed to secure the one-way deal. Russia's inability to make democracy work has forced them to fall back on the only thing they truly know how to do, and that is to prepare for war. Furthermore, not only did Clinton never receive reports on Russian missile reductions or an accounting of where the hundreds of millions of U.S. dollars went, but he also turned a blind eye as the Russians sold missiles and launchers to America's enemies. Hence, Clinton had mindlessly (others say traitorously) funded and revitalized America's old enemy, who in turn continues to proliferate nuclear and conventional weaponry to a host of enemy states.

However, Russia wasn't the only nation that Clinton emboldened. On March 8, 1996, China set off an unprecedented series of war exercises that entailed bombing areas north and south of Taiwan for over two weeks. U.S. military officials obviously perceived this as a prelude to a full invasion of Taiwan and, as such, sent two U.S. aircraft carriers as a sign of strength. Chinese officials took umbrage at the move; yet despite China's aggressive threats, Clinton made another one of his patently inept post-Cold War maneuvers. The generous peace-loving Americans would openly offer all U.S. technologies to communist China. The Red Chinese lunged at the golden opportunity, receiving new high-tech computers (which they never had before), military weapons, and cutting-edge satellites from Hughes Electronics and Loral Space & Communications. Regrettably, China even sold some of these technologies to North Korea.

Henceforth, the litany of grievances against Bill Clinton includes numerous legal investigations, such as Whitewater, Travelgate and

Filegate; his consistently adulterous escapades with Monica Lewinsky, Paula Jones, Jennifer Flowers and four other women; his defiant perjury to a grand jury and the entire United States; his jeopardizing national security by dismantling the CIA, which lost a quarter of its agents and whose warnings Clinton rebuffed; his broken visa and airport policies that invited terrorists; his giving Russia hundreds of millions of dollars to deactivate their missiles, which instead went toward building new weapons and a nuclear bunker; his open exchange program whereby China received satellite and nuclear technologies, which they also sold to North Korea; pardons for Puerto Rican FALN terrorists; and finally, his consistent inability to respond to foreign emergencies, genocides, terrorist attacks, or even explosive declarations of war against the United States.

Despite these devastating flaws, Clinton has the miraculous ability to maintain that he was a world champion. In his Chris Wallace interview, Clinton forcefully snapped, projecting himself as the fearless crusader who tried everything in his power to kill Osama bin Laden, but was thwarted by the CIA. The fact that Clinton hamstrung the CIA, who repeatedly urged aggressive action in Afghanistan to no avail, and—as records indicate—were clearly ordered *not* to kill Osama, makes Clinton's claim either deceitful or delusional, neither of which can exonerate his actions.

Naturally, Clinton did achieve positive goals while in office, and even more so after leaving office, with his humanitarian aid projects which are commendable, yet Clinton and his followers remain blind to the fact that he was the prime *(not sole)* reason why Osama's vile plans and public declarations escalated. Osama's TV interview was documented proof from the evil horse's mouth, yet it was foolishly ignored. However, the bombings of the American warship *USS Cole* and the Twin Towers in 1993 cannot be ignored. Clinton's weaknesses also explain why the Rwanda genocide reached fulfillment, why helping Somalia failed, why Russia and China have become greater threats, and why Osama's operations of terror escalated to the point of successfully executing the 9-11 tragedy.

Henceforth, despite Bill Clinton's victories of advocating gays in the military, cutting the deficit, and aiding an already booming economy, the litanies of severe damages, which exceed those herein, brand Clinton as a very weak president. Beyond these facts or any American's viewpoint, either pro or con, the most important verdict was by Osama bin Laden, who publicly called Clinton and his administration *weak*. That astute and damning judgment unfortunately had immense ramifications for America. Nevertheless, Clinton managed to avoid impeachment and, true to form, left the cigar-stained Oval Office holding his mendacious head up high.

Before concluding this examination of Clinton, a special postscript is required to address Clinton's breakdown in morals, and the nation's apathetic acceptance. Personal character has always been one of America's prime measuring sticks for electing and assessing its leaders. However, an interesting feature about *modern* Democrats is that with Clinton's full-blown and internationally-embarrassing sex scandals, they find no problem in dismissing these immoral and adulterous affairs and, furthermore, claim that they have little to do with running the office of the presidency. However, a Republican like Rudy Giuliani, for example, is badgered about his multiple marriages. It was acceptable that Clinton could perform lewd adulterous activities right in the Oval Office, which clearly interfered with operations, opened the leader to blackmail, and cost taxpayers millions in impeachment proceedings, yet a Republican cannot get married more than once. This is clearly a deplorable double standard.

Oddly, Richard Nixon, in his twilight years, denounced how Clinton evaded the draft, admitted taking drugs, and engaged in immoral sexcapades that even the American public seemed to accept, yet if he or any other president of yesteryear were caught (literally with their pants down), they would have been immediately impeached. Nixon blamed the liberal media and Hollywood for barraging the American public with sexual innuendos and blatant permissiveness that conditioned this breakdown and passive acceptance. And while that is certainly a primary reason for the decay of morals in America, in this particular instance, the fact that some get a free pass (like Clinton) and some do not (like Giuliani) points to only one thing— a distinctly political double standard.

The issue of whether or not the sexual activities of an individual have any effect on political proficiency has long been a subject of debate with no clear answer. However, history abounds with leaders who did have adulterous affairs or numerous marriages, yet they somehow managed to lead with lucidity and success. However, others, like Clinton, disrupted government, crippled his own ability to administrate, and cost a nation investigation and trial expenses. In the end, moralists can condemn or absolve Clinton of his sins as they see fit, but no one can exonerate one person who is rapaciously adulterous, and condemn another who has been married more than once, without being hard-pressed to defend that stance on truly just and righteous grounds. Alas, bias sadly prevails.

We conclude the Clinton examination with CIA Director George Tenet's testimony that a PDB briefing was submitted to Clinton on December of 1998, entitled,

"BIN LADEN PREPARING TO HIJACK U.S. AIRCRAFT AND OTHER ATTACKS."

Despite this shocking warning, and urgent requests by the CIA for funding, Clinton did *nothing*. Tenet aptly summed up Clinton's concern for national security, when he said, "By the mid- to late-1990s American intelligence was in Chapter 11." Thus, shamefully ensuring 9-11.

GEORGE W. BUSH: *Prejudged by Speech and Academic Grades* | UNDERSTANDING ISLAM | *Religious Cowboy vs. Religious Extremists*

With George W. Bush recently out of office, it would be negligent to say that we can complete a full evaluation at this time. Furthermore, all thorough and fair judgments of presidents must be conducted years later, as repercussions materialize that either benefit or plague their successors. Added to this is the fact that America, presently, is still engaged in the Iraq War. Hence, we can only comment on what has transpired, and offer conjecture about the ramifications of future actions.

George W. Bush slid into office with a controversial vote that had Al Gore screaming for a recount, along with half the nation being filled with apprehension. Unlike Richard Nixon, who gracefully walked away from Kennedy's tampering, for he didn't wish to subject the nation to a political circus, Al Gore wielded his megaphone and cried for a recount, costing taxpayers millions in the process. Regardless, Bush entered office.

Right from the outset, Bush was ridiculed about his ineptitude at public speaking and appearing to be uneducated and even dim-witted. First, Bush's grades were higher than his future opponent's was, namely

John Kerry, and second, not all leaders are proficient at public speaking, or need to be. The important issue is whether or not they can get the job done. Hence, this merits a critical review of the past.

The Roman Emperor Claudius was viewed by most as being feeble-minded, since he talked with a lisp, walked with a limp, was timid, and as such, appeared unmanly. Claudius was even the rightful heir to the throne, yet he was intentionally overlooked, and his nephew, Caligula, was instated. This was clearly because Caligula was articulate, able-minded, and certainly more popular. That mistake cost the empire dearly.

Caligula soon revealed his notorious depravity, which triggered his assassination, resulting in thirty stab wounds. Meanwhile, his uncle, Claudius, feared for his own life and hid in the palace, for he rightfully assumed he was next. However, his rich bloodline to Julius and Augustus saved his frail neck. To the shock of many, Claudius rose to be an extremely able leader, despite his mumbled speech and odd quirks. Claudius became a great builder, and constructed one of the grandest seaports of antiquity, the Portus Augusti, as well as several aqueducts and many other excavation projects to aid agriculture. Additionally, Claudius successfully conquered Britain where his far greater ancestor, Julius Caesar, failed; hence, this must serve as a lesson for all those who judge a man by his outer appearance or speech alone, for as we know, we should not judge a book by its cover.

In a more modern sense, President Gerald Ford was often ridiculed for being clumsy and apparently dim-witted; however, even the highly critical intellectual, Henry Kissinger, praised Ford's abilities, and viewed him as an effective administrator. This raises that other prevalent oddity of how most people judge a person's effectiveness or leadership skills entirely by their academic certificate.

Many people have criticized Ronald Reagan for being a simpleminded actor, while many others forget that FDR's grades were often only average, yet both men became supreme world leaders. In fact, professors from Harvard, MIT, Columbia University, as well as Arthur Schlesinger and Henry Kissinger all offered their high-minded views that criticized Reagan's foreign policy, yet everything Reagan predicted and implemented proved successful. Therefore, all these so-called brilliant minds, were simply wrong. Likewise, we must never forget that Thomas Edison and Henry Ford both had no formal education whatsoever, and their impact on American society, and the entire world for that matter, has exceeded astronomical.

Conversely, the brilliant-minded James Madison has long been hailed as one of America's finest theoreticians who significantly shaped our *Constitution* yet, as president, his ineffective delegations and strategies, which directly incited the War of 1812, enabled the British to easily penetrate and burn the nation's capital.

Even Bill Gates stated that when looking to hire effective administrators, Microsoft soon realized that people with intelligence alone did not make the best managers. Some people may be better thinkers, making them great legislators like Madison, while others are better leaders and administrators, like Washington. In fact, Madison was Washington's ghostwriter for many transactions, including Washington's inaugural address. Meanwhile, many others have several degrees from a variety of top-notch colleges, yet they remain idle encyclopedias who can only reiterate the wealth of knowledge they ingest. In essence, they are certified professors of parroting. Therefore, a flashy academic certificate is by no means the measuring stick for success.

In similar fashion, many are dazzled by Al Gore, who scored a 1355 on his SAT and graduated from Harvard. However, when Gore was vice president under Clinton, he was put in charge of airline security. This was because of Ramzi Yousef's attempt to use several commercial airliners as bombs in the Philippines. Luckily, Yousef's plans were thwarted, but as we now know, that plan would later become the blueprint for the attacks on 9-11. In addition to Gore's blindness to this shockingly unique and ominous tactical strategy, he enacted anti-profiling measures, because he was concerned about the civil liberties of Middle Eastern and Asian Muslims. A year later, the FAA prohibited the FBI from screening commercial airline databases, thus effectively eliminating all security. Hence, a Harvard education did not serve Al Gore too well or, more importantly, our country's safety.

With all the books being published, and so much knowledge at our fingertips, many people still haven't learned how to measure a person's abilities. Edison was quoted as saying, with regard to his own inventions, "Its sale is proof of utility, and utility is success." In this regard, I state, "*Academic knowledge is useless, unless it's effectively utilized.*" Or in a more measured vein, "*The measure of brilliance is in its utility.*"

Hence, George W. Bush is not without flaws, in fact, he has many, but he shouldn't be judged by his inarticulate speech or academic record.

Nevertheless, George W. Bush entered office in January 2001 with a collapsed intelligence network, while a violent Jihadist tsunami was ominously mounting. After almost two decades of escalating storm activity, due to the free reign granted it by Clinton and his administration, the world was about to witness the most wicked waves of Jihad.

Bush had been in office just over a month when the Taliban bombed and destroyed two huge Buddha statues that were carved into the side of a mountain in Afghanistan. These religious statues were built in the sixth century; however, when the Muslims conquered Afghanistan in the twelfth century, Buddhists slowly emigrated, so that by 2001 their population vanished. Muslim leaders had made a statement only two years previous, claiming that they would not destroy the statues, as they appeared to be valuable sources for generating tourist dollars. However, with the rising influence of the Taliban, decisions were made to destroy all religious idols in Afghanistan. The reason was that they were constructed by the infidels for a false god, and only Allah was worthy of worship. After their sacrilegious bombing, they were publicly quoted as being proud of their religious act of destruction and their servitude to Allah.

Yet, the true tsunami that would crash upon American shores was yet to come. Four months later, the devastating horror of the Twin Towers being bombarded and turned to rubble by two hi-jacked airplanes shocked a nation and the world. Added to this notorious act was the partial destruction of the Pentagon by a second hi-jacked plane, and a third crashed plane that attempted to bomb the White House or Capitol Building, which was heroically thwarted by American passengers. Osama bin Laden had finally achieved what had been carefully conceived and planned for over four years.

As mentioned earlier, the decisions of presidents sometimes have repercussions that surface years later and, in this instance, Clinton, more than any other president, is most responsible for this attack. This is not to say that Clinton is the root cause of Osama's Jihadist movement, but no president did as much as Clinton to encourage or even aid Osama, as outlined previously. Additionally, Clinton enacted policies that treated terrorists like U.S. citizens. Not only were these militant rebels tried in civil court, but their testimonies were protected. What became known as *the stovepipe*, hot incriminating evidence could not be exchanged between intelligence communities. Hence, CIA, FBI, or police officers violating Clinton's federal mandate, which was enforced by Jamie Gorelick of the DOJ, would be fired and face criminal prosecution.

Basically, under Clinton, foreign terrorist murderers had better rights and protection than the American officers attempting to enforce the law, or the federal agents looking to prevent terrorist attacks against the United States.

It is common knowledge that many presidents inherit the burden of their predecessors, as Bill Clinton did from George Bush senior, and George Bush junior did from Bill Clinton, yet how a reigning president reacts to those problems is the crucial element that matters most. Clinton clearly failed to respond with effective leadership, force, or even the ability to create the appropriate infrastructure, and here is where George W. Bush must be given credit for the firm actions he instinctively took.

The tragedy of 9-11 was immensely devastating to Americans; yet, there is a far greater tragedy, which even dwarfs 9-11, and that tragedy is that many Americans have already forgotten 9-11. The reason for this is twofold: First, is because Bush managed to keep our country free of any terrorist activities since 9-11, and this has made many feel that the threat no longer exists, hence, they dropped their guard. Second, the strong propaganda campaign by the Democrats and the leftist media, have slammed Bush for the war, and for supposedly knowing of the attack beforehand, as if he wanted New York and DC bombed. Yet, they have no real solutions, just political rhetoric that Bush was wrong and that America should withdraw its troops. Interestingly enough, they refer to Iraq being another Vietnam, yet here they choose to repeat the same blunder of withdrawal and defeat, not to mention welcoming another devastating dive in America's credibility worldwide as a superpower.

The effect of Democrats being so heatedly against Bush, and the entire Republican Party for that matter, sent a clear signal of disunity, and now with the new Obama administration, with its many polar objectives and plans for cutting back intelligence and military spending, America's lack of vision is evident. This signal has already been clearly received by the terrorists who have come to rely upon this weakness, as they patiently await their moment to, once again, exact atrocities upon our fortress, which shall be conveniently stripped of its ramparts and soldiers.

By drawing parallels in history and, in particular, America to its Roman model, we can compare Carthage to the Soviet Union and Rome to America. Once the Romans finally defeated their ultimate rival, they, too, became the sole superpower of their day. However, defeating their seemingly ultimate rival did not end other conflicts, for conflicts of beliefs, whether political, cultural, or religious always divide mankind and show no signs of ever changing, at least not to the point of a singular and harmonious global mindset. Then, as now, we cannot change the hearts and minds of unyielding religious fanatics; we can only deal with them.

However, Rome's success over Carthage was due not only to Scipio's great abilities as a general to defeat Hannibal, but also to Rome's solidarity and goal of unconditional victory. This is why the defeat of Carthage was complete and enduring. Yet it was only one of many engagements with other rivals over Rome's long tenure of being the ultimate empire.

The Romans sense of unity was so strong when threatened that they even devised the temporary position of dictator to handle these perilous eruptions. Complete faith was entrusted to one man to handle such situations who, in turn, had complete authority in all decisions pertaining to war and state security. This was deemed necessary due to the blatant reality that large governing bodies, such as their Republic, could not make quick and effective decisions in matters of war. This is also why Lincoln, FDR and others needed to curtail laws and liberties to achieve their goals. Nowadays, with the mixed signals in Washington that are spreading across the nation, a divided America places us in harm's way, and directly into the explosive crosshairs of the terrorists.

Despite the conspiracy theorists, most Americans would agree that the initial response in Afghanistan was justified, and that the new president was unshaken, firm in his resolve, and in a word, valiant. The glowing spotlight of respect, however, started to wane when Bush switched his attention to the Iraqi dictator, Saddam Hussein. This issue divided the Democrats from Republicans but, more importantly, with the liberal media's amplification, it divided a whole nation. This issue exceeds Bush's objectives—whether being genuinely for national security or a personal vendetta, which Democrats have derided either way—and into a moral realm that many liberal Democrats unwittingly overlook.

Liberals rightfully take great pride in humanitarian issues to help the needy, save the poor, aid those stricken with disease, and save the oppressed. However, the fact that Saddam Hussein murdered hundreds of thousands of his own people, innocent people who were killed in cold blood and many brutally tortured, this quite remarkably does not disturb them. Or does it? We must ask why is this so?

Is it that they are callous, self-serving hypocrites who speak about good deeds, but don't deliver? Naturally, some are, just like some of their rightwing counterparts, however, some are not. With their huge programs of goodwill, such as food aid, financial aid, and medical aid to poverty-stricken third-world nations, we must realize that a compassion for foreigners in dire need is something they have consistently shown, even if plagued with graft. This raises another possibility, namely that giving aid to a weak and broken nation, which accepts aid willingly, makes it easy for the benefactor to administer aid. The keyword here is *easy*.

However, when a foreign nation is in a state of civil unrest or outright war, this instantly flashes two red lights to some liberals. One stating *"Not easy!"* and the other *"Find an excuse!"* Therefore, the excuses that some liberals offer for the Iraqi War seem to suggest cowardice or apathy. Securing peace in the Middle East would ease relations and end Jihadist retaliations. As the sole superpower, which still must confront an unstable Russia, China, Iran, North Korea, Pakistan and Jihadists, it is up to Americans to not only aid the Iraqis in quelling their radical leaders, but also secure our own nation from the vengeful terrorist attacks that will most assuredly return if America turns a blind eye.

The stakes are high, especially when dealing with a country that has been groomed for centuries to suppress women (even mutilating or killing them for minor disobedience), or has been perpetually oppressed by religious dictators who have destroyed educational facilities, legitimate economic networks, and enact violence under the banner of Islam. Leftists moan about a Republican agenda for oil, or a Bush agenda of personal revenge, or an unjust attack on a nation not fully proven to contain weapons of mass destruction, yet all these issues should evaporate under the glowing agenda of helping the Iraqis to overthrow their radical leaders, and thus secure our own nation's safety, regardless of not being easy.

The post World War II Marshall Plan in Germany took ten years to affect change. However, that was with a Westernized nation that had even been more advance pre-war than the Allied nations. So its revival was swift. In contrast, Eastern nations, with alien traditions and religions, which include the Jihadists' brainwashing of youths, have a much longer history of abuse and violence. This requires a completely new educational infrastructure that will literally take generations to affect change, requiring extensive rehabilitation, including the need for minors to be educated with wholesome information, not hatred.

It will take time, money and patience, and this is understandably humiliating to Americans. But the options are to walk away, leaving innocent Muslims to suffer and radicals to fester, and in turn launch future attacks on American soil, or step in and deal with the situation to eradicate, or at least subdue, the toxins so that a more harmonious relationship can be achieved.

As Americans, we cannot ignore the deadly backlash of a strong resurgence of terrorism against the United States if we decide to walk away, especially with our porous borders. This crucial issue should make all Americans see the necessity of this endeavor, even if they reject the utopian idealism or benevolence of such a task, because America's security depends upon a continued effort in the Middle East until some degree of stability is achieved. Terrorist attacks have consistently occurred in England, Spain, France and elsewhere, yet, once again, because America has avoided another catastrophe, many believe the war against terrorism is no longer relevant.

It is also emblematic how history repeats itself, just like the American isolationists back in the 1930s, who inertly slept while toxic evil spread. Great nations and their leaders must be benevolent, and even attempt peaceful negotiations, but they must also realize that militant regimes or terrorists that continually expand their evil networks, cannot be controlled with prayer, a blind eye, or a civilized slap on the wrist.

Many left-wing intellectuals feel that war is not the solution. Moreover, they denounced supporters of the Iraqi War as being dumb like President Bush. Yet, if they feel intelligence rules such decisions, it's interesting that the ultra-savant of our age, Albert Einstein, was also a pacifist, until he realized that war was the only solution to end Hitler's madness. Intelligence thrives on idealism, but must succumb to realism when dealing with an un-idealistic regime. As the adage goes, desperate times require desperate measures. Hussein may have been a minor version of Hitler, but a brutal murderer just the same. Therefore, the Iraqi War, if executed properly, could offer both the Iraqis and the USA relative peace.

America's War on Terror is so significant that it naturally exceeds this examination on President Bush. This explosive event shifted our attention away from a world that was briefly free of the Soviet Cold War to the horrors of innocent civilians being unjustly massacred by a cowardly band of religious fanatics. Therefore, before returning to Bush it is imperative to take a side step to address the religion of Islam.

Understanding Islam

Catholics, Protestants, Baptists, and the entire spectrum of Christian sects, as well as the root Jewish faith, all have a similar religious tradition. That the United States is overwhelmingly a Christian nation, which naturally is familiar with its Jewish roots, leaves most Americans somewhat acquainted with the Jewish religion; however, the vast majority is totally in the dark about the extreme minority of Muslims in America and their Islamic religion.

Many pacifists speak about Americans being snobbish or even condescending toward alien cultures and religions that apparently seem inferior. This is especially true for most superpowers of their day that innately evolve into believing that they are superior to all others. Hence, the ability to accurately assess one's enemy truly becomes a crucial and serious obligation. However, these pacifists arrive at the wrong conclusion, for their remedy is to be tolerant and peaceful with radical Muslims, and this crucial point needs clarification.

I fully believe that most Americans do not fully understand their current enemy. Most Americans rightfully believe that Muslims throughout America are peaceful practitioners of an unfamiliar religion. In addition to this tolerance and respect is the fact that crimes by Muslim-Americans have never been an issue to cause alarm; hence, most Americans have no cause to believe that Islam is a violent religion. Most believe that radical Muslims have manipulated the faith to their own evil intent. This, however, is where the slide into ignorance begins.

Although some Muslim leaders in America appeared in the media to allay fears after the 9-11 tragedy, especially with the soothing testimony that their religion is a peaceful sister religion to Judaism and Christianity, this is not true. The religions may be relatives, but they are very distant and, as will be shown, even deadly relatives. Therefore, it becomes necessary to examine the sacred book of Islam directly to avoid hearsay, fabrication, misrepresentation, or outright lies.

The Muslims' sacred book is called the Koran, and in the following section, we shall briefly examine the religion and use direct quotes from the Koran, as not to mince words. The intent is to truthfully tell Americans what exactly is contained in the Koran, so Americans can make educated rebuttals to any Muslim or uninformed American that claims otherwise.

As mentioned, contrary to what Americans have been told by the media, the Muslim religion has many significant differences right from its very core. The core begins with its founder Muhammad. Muhammad was a merchant who at the age of forty began receiving revelations from God, via the angel, Gabriel, in AD 610. Building a strong following, Muhammad became the leader of his tribe, which soon became entangled with neighboring tribes vying for greater control and territory. Built upon and following the Judaic religion, Muhammad was hailed as a prophet by his men, but not by the Jewish community or Christians. Many regional battles ensued as Muhammad vied for supremacy. By AD 630, Muhammad overtook the large city of Mecca and he demanded submission from all his new captives. *Islam* in Arabic means *submission*.

Hence, a whole religion emerged upon the dictates of Muhammad, who demanded complete submission.

Muhammad constructed his new religion by divine revelation and military engagements to win territory, and then indoctrinated his conquered subjects. The Qur'an, or Koran as we know it, was the Islamic bible that was written after Muhammad's death by his followers who, like the Christian apostles, recollected his words and deeds. Therefore, the Koran does not contain any direct writings by Muhammad himself.

However, unlike the Jesus account, they did not hail Muhammad as their God, but only as the last prophet. Also emanating from Adam, the Muslim branch or bloodline allegedly began with Abraham's illegitimate son, Ishmael. Nevertheless, the reason for Muhammad's mission on earth was to rectify the corrupt deviations made to the religion by false Jewish and Christian prophets. This includes Jesus, who is not viewed as the Son of God or the Lord God in any sense, but rather as a false prophet.

Despite sharing a similar Judaic root, the militant birth of this new Islamic sect stands in direct contrast to the peaceful mission of Jesus. As such, this militancy seems odd to most Christians. However, where the Christians have been lambasted for their militant Crusades during the Middle Ages it must be understood that the term Holy War, or Jihad, was inaugurated by Muhammad almost five hundred years before the Crusades. Hence, Islam was born by Jihad, while Christianity was not. Most importantly, Muslims do not recognize Jesus as divine.

"They are surely infidels who say: "God is the Christ, son of Mary."

"There is no God but Allah, and Muhammad is His prophet."

These powerful words were also etched into Islamic tradition beyond just appearing in the Koran. In AD 690, the Muslim king Abd al-Malik sacked Jerusalem and built the famous Dome of the Rock shrine. This was built right over the hallowed spot where God instructed Abraham to sacrifice Isaac. As far as some Jews are concerned, this shrine is probably looked upon as Doom of the Rock.

However, beyond merely appropriating this sacred ground, the Muslims then inscribed on the shrine itself, words that denounce the Holy Trinity. The inscription states, *"God cannot be divided and can only be one God, and far be it from His glory that He should have a son."*

Hence, the Muslims desecrated a Judaic holy ground, and then blatantly annulled Jesus, and the entire Christian faith, all in one fell swoop. Beyond this devastating deed are the Islamic commandments, which again are contained directly in the Koran, telling Muslims how to handle infidels, namely all peoples who fail to submit to Allah.

"Remember thy Lord inspired the angels with this message: I am with you. Give firmness to the Believers. I will instill terror into the hearts of the Unbelievers. Smite ye above their necks and smite all their finger tips off them."

Smiting above their necks remains in practice today, as Jihadist Muslims often slit their victims' throats—the gruesome decapitation of American journalist Daniel Pearl is only one example. Naturally, this is profoundly shocking to Christian and Jewish Americans who never realized what the Koran actually endorses, especially one claimed to be a friendly sister religion. Meanwhile Muslims defend their religion as being peaceful, and the oddity is that the large majority is. Their obvious rebuttal is that even the Christian and Jewish faiths are tainted with blood, jealousy, and revenge.

Did not the Jewish God smite the Egyptians, thus allowing Moses his Exodus? Moreover, the Israelites were then instructed by God to attack and conquer the Canaanites to found Jerusalem and acquire the Holy Land. Likewise, did not the Jewish God take revenge upon the entire world when He summoned the great Flood, only offering safe passage to Noah, his family, and diverse cargo? And did not the Christians engage in the bloody Crusades for centuries, or enact the brutal Inquisition as well as other horrors upon their own brethren? After all, the Inquisition ruthlessly slaughtered and expelled the Muslims out of Spain.

Therefore, it becomes necessary to put all these issues in context and not jump to the conclusion that every practitioner of these three similar, yet very conflicting religions practice every word committed to scripture. Over the course of many centuries both Jewish and Christian faiths, in general, have focused more on living a good life according to scripture rather than the warring directives that God gave to his chosen people in the Old Testament. Few Christians today contemplate the disturbing issue that God not only instructed his chosen people to commit war but also engaged in wrathful destruction Himself. Many also view the Christian

Crusaders, Inquisitors, or the Puritans who purged the Native Americans as following their own doctrines, for these particular acts were not clearly dictated in the Bible. Therefore, for modern Christians, who focus on the loving words of Jesus, these aggressive and lethal directives in the Koran do come as a chilling surprise, and it does make it difficult for Christians to understand such a faith, particularly one claiming to be a sister religion.

Unfortunately, most pacifists and most secularists simply do not understand how intensely devout most Muslims are in their beliefs. This may seem like trivial ancient drivel to them, with their lax interpretation of their religion or blank slate of atheism, but this ancient mindset is the Muslims' very life, soul, and primary mission. Moreover, the radical Muslims who feel biblically instructed to execute this religious Jihad, which is against all infidels, remain before the rest of the world's population as a major threat.

This threat extends beyond our borders, such as the growing Muslim communities throughout Europe. Illegally infiltrating various free nations, they drain the financial resources of their liberal hosts' weak policies. Some Muslims in Europe have become far more antagonistic and disruptive in recent years as they riot and carry banners that proclaim the fall of all infidels, the rise of Islam, and an end to all democratic nations.

At a more serious and frightening level, the true masterminds of mass destruction operate below the radar. Many respectable journalists and high-ranking U.S. officials, including former CIA Director George Tenet, have made clear how Pakistani physicist, Dr. A.Q. Khan, and Sultan Bashirrudan Mahmood, among others, have been aiding al-Qaeda in their efforts to obtain weapons of mass destruction. Mahmood was the former director of Pakistan's Atomic Energy Commission and has since led the private organization Umma Tameer-e-Nau (UTN), which supposedly extends social aid and welfare programs; however, many on the executive board are former Pakistani nuclear scientists and the UTN doubles as a trafficker of nuclear materials and technologies.

Mahmood also happens to be an expert in chemical warfare and had even concocted a plot to detonate a cyanide explosion in New York City's subways, yet his plan was called off by Osama's second in command, Ayman al-Zawahiri, who said he had an even better plan in mind. Ever since Al-Zawahiri made that chilling statement, George Tenet has been plagued with the thought of what that better plan was, and worse yet, is that plan still on the drawing board waiting to be unleashed. This brings us to nuclear capabilities.

Dr. A.Q. Khan is the man who developed Pakistan's atomic bomb decades ago, and has clandestinely been providing plans and materials to China, North Korea, and Iran ever since. Added to his dark client list was Osama bin Laden. Dr. Khan's meetings with bin Laden and the terrorist's request for nuclear capabilities have been clearly documented. These clear and present dangers prompted President Bush to immediately dispatch CIA Director George Tenet to visit Pakistan's President Musharraf directly after 9-11. After some initial finger-pointing at the Russians, and their "loose nukes", which were—and still remain—a critical problem, Musharraf agreed to follow Tenet's outline of the steps needed to surveil and prevent Osama bin Laden from gaining nuclear capabilities.

As such, it is shameful that so many Americans never truly listened to or truly comprehended Osama's own words about al-Qaeda's terror attacks. The Islamic warlord said the war is between those of the faith and those outside the faith, between those who submit to the believer's law, and those infidels who do not. Americans *are* those infidels.

Henceforth, the peaceful Islamic community has a huge responsibility to step forward and be equally proactive. They must publicly denounce all radical extremists, as well as actively educate their entire Muslim community that those violent passages in the Koran need not be taken literally. The situation is nearing critical mass, as a full-blown religious conflict of global proportions is on the verge of erupting.

Sadly, this is not the case, as Muslim leaders primarily chastise Christian and Jewish Americans for racial profiling and slandering their religion. It is imperative that peaceful Muslims around the world take responsibility, and openly condemn radical Muslims to not only show good faith to its religious neighbors, but to also deter young, corruptible minds from joining this evil band of terrorists. With the large influx of Muslims entering the Western hemisphere, by the millions up in Canada, and by the millions down in Central and South America, the United States needs to be vigilant to protect itself from radical Islamic insurgents who are easily crossing its porous borders.

In addition to America's pathetically open borders is the screening that is crucial at airports. Among a litany of remedies, America needs to install a biometric system whereby requiring travelers to swipe their finger across a sensor or have a retina scan to gain access. As such, their complete identity would be available for monitoring, and people without them would be detained for screening. This system would be similar to an EZPass and would actually speed up passenger lines at terminals, and provide better security.

This returns us to President Bush, who may be applauded for his strong stance against terrorism, yet strongly condemned for his weak stance on securing the borders. This lack of vigilance was in stark contrast to his resolve to end terror, and only seems to validate Bush's elitist economic agenda. Naturally, big business continues to sway and control many aspects of politics, as Enron, Halliburton, the Carlyle Group, Bilderberg Group, and even drug trafficking all warrant further investigations. However, the border/immigration issue made Bush's reticence unforgivable, while men like New York Congressman Pete King and Hazelton, Pennsylvania Mayor Lou Barletta should be applauded.

The lobbying muscle of big business, and the growing power of the CIA under Bush also caused much concern. As more details are uncovered, more explanations are required from the extremely powerful Bush family, as well as their inner circle of power-lords who brokered with foreign leaders and secretive eco-political agendas. Nevertheless, Bush finished his second term without proving that border control was something that he took seriously, and this remains a serious dark mark.

At certain critical moments in history, uncustomary actions and remedies were made that may appear like false solutions. Hadrian built his wall to keep the barbaric tribes to the north from swarming down and wreaking havoc. From a modern perspective, we can look back on Hadrian's Wall, the Berlin Wall, or even the Great Wall of China and see these devices as broken and useless. However, in their day they served a very real and vital purpose until the climate of conditions changed.

Hence, constructing walls around our borders may appear useless, or even anti-democratic in nature, yet America is a sovereign nation that does not and cannot provide its own rich cornucopia of gifts of freedom and prosperity to the entire world. The world needs to emulate America if they wish to achieve the same bounty, and indeed much of the modern world is doing just that. With China reaping a tremendous amount of wealth and prosperity from American intervention, as well as a collection of other nations mirroring our capitalistic model, America must be mindful of its actions. It cannot be expected to take on the burden of millions of illegal immigrants with an unstable economy that is now in competition with a global market that dwarfs us in size; doing so would never allow America to maintain stability or its lead. Moreover, if Americans intend to remain in the forefront, we must be vigilant and fight for our nation's sovereignty, economy, and, in a word, self-preservation.

However, President Bush was not only criticized for failing to recognize the severity of America's weak borders, but also for engaging in the Iraqi War, due to his family's vendetta against Saddam and interest in oil. The Bush family has a long connection to the oil industry, as does Vice President Dick Cheney. As the president of Halliburton, Dick Cheney undoubtedly shares a common interest in the Middle East. Furthermore, a caustic allegation by Mike Ruppert states that Dick Cheney not only overrode Bush by directing national security during 9-11, but also intentionally tied up fighter jets in training exercises during the attacks.

However, Ruppert's compelling evidence does have gaping holes and relies upon misinterpreting evidence. He purports that Cheney, with malicious intent, engaged war games to delay a U.S. response to the 9-11 attacks. Testimonies of phone calls between the vice president and then New York City Mayor, Rudy Giuliani, appeared to have time discrepancies that Ruppert asserts showed Giuliani committing perjury, and in collusion with Cheney to delay a response. That Giuliani was in the building next to the tower that was struck, and being told that another plane was on its way would make Giuliani either an extremely fanatical rebel in this evil conspiracy or a total fool; in either case, akin to a deranged Jihadist that welcomed death. The horror of both towers eventually imploding and Giuliani's genuine and highly admirable leadership captured on live TV, makes Ruppert's assertions all the more outlandish and deplorable, especially when we consider how Giuliani *(see page 715)* cleaned up New York City and also brought down the Mafia. As FBI Director Louis Freeh said, "Rudy was not only a brilliant lawyer and U.S. attorney, but he epitomized for me the highest principles of public service." With Giuliani's long and honorable career of enforcing U.S. law, restoring integrity and rooting out corruption, Ruppert's vile claims not only fly in the face of reason, but also shamefully slander a true American hero.

Mike Ruppert is certainly well educated, principled, and had practical experience in the L.A. Police Department. Yet his resignation, due to being approached by CIA agents to engage in illegal drug operations, which might be credible, has made Ruppert overzealous in indicting any and all government officials. Henceforth, these biting allegations can only be deemed malicious or misinterpreted conjecture.

On the other hand, the deep religious resolve of George W. Bush certainly indicated a sincere desire to eradicate what he saw as an evil threat to America; hence, it seems plausible that any personal gain stood behind that wall of faith.

Personal greed, however, does blatantly fall in the lap of some of America's allies. The truth is that French President Jacques Chirac and Saddam Hussein had a multi-billion dollar business alliance since the 1970s. France was exchanging weapons technology for oil, as a result, when America launched its Iraqi War, France's condemnations against America, for being a warmonger, was based solely upon Chirac's losing his financial investment and France's valuable oil resources. Likewise, the Germans have done more than their share in supplying weapons and technology, as have the economically broken Soviet blocks. Yet, some Americans bought into the accusations that America was unjust for invading Iraq, and that our intentions were purely for oil. However, the reality is that these European nations had the audacity to badmouth America for what they in large measure bred, for Saddam would never have been as powerful and threatening without their continued support over many decades, despite America's interest in oil.

The interest in oil has long been a priority to all world leaders, and very few realize that the quest for oil domination started with the German

Kaiser during World War I. The Kaiser recognized his country's future need for oil and that prompted him to build a railroad from Berlin to Baghdad. This also explains why England and France both took a stake in colonizing northern Africa and the Middle East. Additionally, this was also the prime reason why Hitler invaded Russia. Historians have long since pondered Hitler's apparent reckless and illogical second front, yet Hitler needed oil to fuel his war machine. Added to this was the Bolshevik movement, with its Jewish sympathies as outlined by Vladimir Lenin. Lenin had launched the ruthless rebellion that effectively toppled the Russian monarchy. Hence, in Hitler's paranoid mind, he had a threatening Jewish precedent to confront, and a legitimate need for oil.

Beyond President Bush's interest in oil, Bush had also been criticized for his tax breaks that not only aided the middle and lower classes, but also offered immense returns for corporate moguls. When one considers how the estimated $720 million in tax rebates that CEOs in companies such as Enron and General Electric received, the words injustice and investigate, among many others, spring to mind.

Interestingly, President Bush was also tagged as a dictator. Most curious, however, were the accusations by Nancy Pelosi and Hillary Clinton, who both claimed that Bush abused his authority by waging war. However, these politicians seem to forget that even Lincoln was criticized as being a dictator in his day. Whether they forgot or intentionally overlooked how Lincoln seized control of the U.S. government remains anybody's guess. However, it appears that since Lincoln ended the Civil War and emancipated the slaves, they readily dismissed Lincoln's daring and unconstitutional moments. As such, them calling Bush a dictator should likewise be dismissed, especially when we view the following.

Naturally, we never wish to condone executive decisions that would jeopardize America, but the bottom line is that when the nation is at risk, firm commands and timing are crucial for success, and this is why Lincoln did what he had to. However, Bush did receive authorization from Congress to enter Iraq. At the time, not only was the United States Congress in unison, but the United Nations and America's allies all concurred that Saddam Hussein had weapons of mass destruction. In addition, and most importantly, by Saddam's refusal of seventeen UN resolutions, he unquestionably signed his own death warrant.

Oddly enough, the fact that American troops managed to kill Abu Musab al-Zarqawi in Iraq, who was a lead operative for Osama bin Laden's al-Qaeda network, never manages to make these cynics connect the dots that Saddam very likely sponsored al-Qaeda. Instead, they still moan that Saddam and Iraq were innocent victims of a Bush agenda.

This leaves us with George W. Bush teetering in the balance as to his strengths and weaknesses as president, at least at this particular moment in time. Bush made some valiantly good and deplorably bad decisions, however the scale presently leans toward bad. Regardless, what seems certain is that Bush was guided by something more than self-interest or his family's Iraqi revenge, which some have accused him of, for his religious convictions drove him forward in the face of adversity and stern condemnation. This driving force has reappeared over the course of history to propel many leaders to great heights, and after reviewing the warring words in the Koran that radicals acted upon, Bush's agenda aligned with survival, as its core mission was to disarm a deadly foe. Hence, at least in this regard, George W. Bush was a religious cowboy in the best sense.

Moreover, upon reviewing the past we can see this more clearly. The intent is not only to understand leaders and how they think and act, but also to better guide us in recognizing and backing a leader who will make tough decisions today for a better world tomorrow. Naturally, better has different meanings to different people, but better here refers to a world in harmony with America's core values and traditions, and, of equal importance, one that is tolerant of other nations. However, those other nations *must* be tolerant and non-threatening to our culture, otherwise, survival instincts *must* prevail. And at least in this single regard, George W. Bush honorably stepped up to the plate. Just how well the country fares with its new Obama administration remains to be seen. Bush's full evaluation likewise remains to be seen, which will occur several years from now once all the details of military initiatives, covert operations, secret alliances, and economic effects are fully revealed and analyzed.

The Impetus for Great Leadership & Closing Commentary for Americans

Reagan styled himself a mystic who believed that a divine plan guided his actions, just like Constantine, and many other great leaders who affected major change in world history. And even though Augustus, Titus, Elizabeth, Washington, Churchill, or Gandhi all had varying motivational beliefs, and did make errors, they each rose to a higher ideal, other than egocentric glory or greed to benefit mankind. The list of history's influential minds naturally exceeds political leaders to include religious leaders such as Moses, Jesus, Buddha and Mohammad, as well as all those who serve as sublime role models in a plethora of fields. Perhaps most notably missing is the medical field, which is of major importance yet, as noted, a project of this magnitude required omissions.

We have also seen how mankind has repeatedly corrupted many inherently good seats of power, be they in government or religion. However, excluding those who used religion as a shackle to oppress their flock, it is noted that a firm belief in a higher divinity that propels one's heart, mind, and spirit to engage in righteous endeavors, and achieve them recurs throughout Western history. It is also unfortunately common that religious fanatics will rise to intolerantly use that statement for their own exclusive sect. But it is crucial to note that this divine influence held true for pagans who believed in many gods, as well as the monotheists who believed in one God. To deny the achievements of the polytheist pagans is as wrong as denying the achievements of the monotheists.

Divine inspiration has more often than not been the driving impetus in the creation of worthy enterprises, noble causes, and grand deeds that have enhanced civilization. Regardless of how misdirected (or even blasphemous, like the self-centered, self-deified pharaohs who built huge mausoleums only for themselves), the many noble enterprises of the Egyptians, Greeks, and Romans, among others, in advancing engineering and progress, or creating magnificent edifices to honor their gods, have by far towered over and dwarfed all the tribal hordes elsewhere in the world that never rose beyond their basic modes of existence. Whether they were godless savages or simply worshiped nature, their eyes and aspirations remained downward upon the Earth and never rose heavenward, even if the true Creator is unknown. As such, their cult-like ethos either persisted marginally in a pathetic state or decayed and completely vanished.

Likewise, even the egotistical creations of dictators such as Stalin's massive empire, have not only crumbled, but his name has been scratched off Stalingrad to form modern-day Volgograd. In the same fashion, Nero was forced to commit suicide, while his ostentatious golden house was destroyed. Pope Boniface VII, after murdering his predecessor and then later fleeing the Vatican with all its treasures, was likewise murdered and rightfully declared an antipope. England's King George III, after tyrannically oppressing the American colonists, lost his New World kingdom and his sanity, being locked inside Windsor Castle for the last nine years of his life (quite fittingly, New Yorkers pulled down his statue and then melted it to make bullets).

Napoleon rose like a savior, yet turned tyrant and was effectively defeated and exiled in disgrace. Mussolini's selfish delusions of grandeur mirrored Nero's as he was shot and then hung upside down on meat hooks. Hitler's demonic war machine and death camps were victoriously crushed, as the deranged dictator who hated all but his own exclusive Aryan race was forced to shoot himself. Then with sighs of relief his savage swastikas were ripped off every building. Meanwhile Saddam's feeble Nazi emulation resulted in his capture, demise, and execution, while his vainglorious statue and billboards were likewise pulled down. Hence, evil rulers of both secular and religious realms have consistently been stripped of any achievements, and justly maligned by history.

Yet those motivated by a purely altruistic ideal to benefit mankind have illuminated the timeline of history. They shine like an infinite line of torches with their unique flares of achievement and inspiration that bathe future generations. They stand as beacons, as calls to humanity, to pause, contemplate, and then actively emulate. And while America may be one of the youngest nations on earth, it has unequivocally proven that it indeed does have a *rendezvous with destiny*. Whether that mission is pre-designed by God, achieved by his free-willed mortals, or by those who believe in an unknown Creator, one thing remains certain, the lofty destination remains the same.

As we ponder the American spirit, we must realize that although the majority of these prominent figures shared a common belief, it was not a singular or monolithic belief. Even the founding fathers and our entire budding nation were a religious tapestry of separate strands as Puritans, Quakers, Anglicans, Catholics, Presbyterians, Huguenots, Episcopalians, Congregationalists, Jews, Freemasons and even Deists composed this rich fabric. And they often did not see eye to eye. Hence, God clearly existed, but different doorways were used to access his or its divine wisdom.

When composing the *Declaration of Independence*, the founding fathers did not refer specifically to the Christian Jesus, Judaic Yahweh, or any other God. Beyond these initial authors, a long succession of presidents, including such icons as Andrew Jackson, Abraham Lincoln, and Ulysses Grant, all stood firmly against legislation to incorporate only Jesus into our nation's *Constitution* or *Bill of Rights*. This is because such an act would be against the freedom of religion concept first posited by Constantine in his Edict of Milan, and firmly established by the founding fathers. For as we know, early colonial America was not just Protestant, it was a superfluity of religious sects.

As such, we must bear in mind that James Madison loathed witnessing the intolerance practiced by many of these sects, as he firmly believed that liberty inspired genius, while religious fanaticism shackled and debilitated the mind. He believed it made their congregations unfit for any noble enterprise. Upon examining these sects and history, when the church lost its way and seized total power, Madison said, *"What have been its fruits? More or less in all places, pride and indolence in the clergy, ignorance and servility in the laity; in both, superstition, bigotry and persecution."*

As the prime author of the *United States Constitution*, Madison made sure that this crucial document remained largely secular in tone and temperament, and distinctly separate from the *Declaration of Independence*, thus making four direct, yet intentionally obscure, references to a "Creator," "the supreme judge of the world," "Nature's God," and *"divine providence."*

Likewise, Thomas Jefferson lamented how his home colony of Virginia Puritans persecuted Quakers, Presbyterians, and all others who did not conform to their strict dogmatic dictates. Their intolerance even included the death penalty for nonconformity. Jefferson deeply admired the words of Jesus, and even extracted them from the Bible, but loathed the radical clergymen who fabricated dogma. He called the clergy mystery mongers, false prophets, pseudo-Christians and the like, for he knew history and mankind very well. In that vein, Jefferson said, *"My religious reading has long been confined to the moral branch of religion, which is the same in all religions; while in that branch which consists of dogmas, all differ."*

For Jefferson, dogmas inherently caused rifts and intense conflict, whereas morality is universal and instills harmony. This logical assessment, however, did not resonate with some of his peers, who unwittingly confirmed Jefferson's belief by angrily calling him a Deist or a Unitarian. Some, like Hamilton in the heat of political campaigning, even called Jefferson an atheist, which he wasn't.

Hence, the fledgling nation that sought liberty, God's protection, and religious freedom was far from united in godly spirit, or their belief of whom or what exactly constituted God. Jefferson perceptively summed up his thoughts about religion by stating that mankind, since the beginning of time, has been fighting, torturing, and killing one another for abstract beliefs that are completely beyond the comprehension of human thought.

Jefferson's astute statement warrants consideration. Although men have fought bitterly for their exclusive set of beliefs, as if they emphatically knew the divine order and truth of the universe, this realm of God, we must come to realize, is as abstract and diffuse as the sublime heavens above. Since the dawn of creation, man has looked up and marveled at the cosmos, believing somehow that beyond our limited senses, which are like a single droplet of water in the oceans of knowledge, that something magnificent must be the ultimate source and grand architect. Regardless of what names man has ignorantly conjured over countless millennia, the only truly apt one is simply *God*.

Since the dawn of Western civilization, man has bowed to the Sun, Ra, Yahweh, Zeus, Apollo, Jupiter, Jesus, or Allah, yet no single humanly created piece of scripture or practiced dogma can or should be imposed upon all, for it always forms a sacred straitjacket. History proves that freedom of religion proved gainful for the Romans, at least when practiced, as well as for its distant heir, the United States. History also shows that Rome's downhill progression, although caused by a myriad of reasons, including a new capital in the East, invasions, non-assimilating immigrants, or even pestilence, may have initially begun with imperial corruption, but it did not fully begin to spiral downward until Christianity became the state's helmsman. This was due to its passivity and trusting goodwill, which neglected defense, and its arrogance, which omnipotently sought to control every person's earthly estate and spiritual domain. Once in the hands of a dogmatic clergy, the church oppressively constricted the life and spirit of its flock, which was forced to obey and attain salvation only through its small Roman Catholic doorway to heaven. The Dark Ages and Middle Ages were the culmination of their dogmatic efforts. Their suppressive censorship and mounting greed eventually caused millions to flee and seek other Christian doorways during the Reformation, and even they, too, fell victim to the same fanatical disease, as Puritans in the New World persecuted and burned fellow Christians as heretics.

Since the beginning of Christianity, men have ambitiously sought positions of power within the religious realm, and with this power came new creeds, and with these new creeds came conflict, and with this conflict came war or inquisitions. As Thomas Jefferson aptly said, *"There would never have been an infidel if there had never been a priest."*

However, the glorious power of God stridently prevails, for history also clearly shows that purely secular states without morals have only fallen into chaos, unchecked madness, or eventual ruin. The colossal stockpile of the world's history books are weighted heavily with pages of godless greed, war, and self-interest. The lesson learned by America's founding fathers was that religion was crucial, yet church and state needed to remain separate.

If we view these two opposing sides as oil and vinegar, we instantly see that they do not mix, and perhaps never molecularly will, however, when mixed properly they do make a magnificent salad. This appetizing concept our founders astutely ingested, and this unique recipe is America's marvelous heirloom. However, the fanatical factions that habitually arise on either side of the divide need to be routinely checked in order to create a state that is stable and balanced.

In assessing the long history of either side of this political/religious divide, another concern also becomes clear. Mankind has habitually tried to simplify the complex mysteries of life by categorizing issues into basic dualities, such as black and white, good and bad, right and wrong, light and dark, night and day, war and peace, democracy or dictatorship, republican or democrat, gnostic or agnostic, righteous or evil, religious or secular, to make these complexities easier for themselves and the masses to comprehend. Yet this innate flaw persistently overlooks that sprawling gray area, which provides food for thought and, at times, even the best solution, as extremes often perpetuate conflict, for they inevitably trample on someone else's intransigent beliefs, not to mention sometimes being simply wrong. Hence, this is why America avoided becoming a polar extreme, as it sits wisely in that gray, middle ground, neither secular nor theocratic. However, much remains unresolved.

Righteousness is not as simple as discerning right from wrong, for we have seen how mankind has faltered even under its supposedly best solutions to foster righteousness with theocratic and democratic regimes. Interpretations of the Old and New Testaments, the spectrum of sacred scriptures, the *Declaration of Independence*, the *Constitution*, or the *Bill of Rights* have and continue to be open to new revelations, and never shall be finite sources that define a single irrefutable answer to each and every uncertainty in life. Knowing this truth, however, should not instill pessimism. On the contrary, mankind must continue to pursue that utopian goal with righteousness as our motive to propel our endeavors, even if never fully attaining that glorious state of utopia, for that ultimate state of perfection ultimately resides with God alone. Not to try, however, ensures failure or the inevitable conquest by those with opposing and aberrant views who do apply unyielding effort.

In a world with consistently recurring empires of evil, from the barbarians right up to the Fascists, Nazis, Communists, and now Islamic terrorists, the perpetual prescription for survival has always been to righteously confront, challenge, and collapse contagions, for turning a deaf ear, blind eye, or complacent heart and mind has always proved fatal. Just as diseases need to be combated with surgical removals or vaccines, human nature has been infected with evil souls, which even the Bible mentions are part of our existence. Pacifists need to understand this simple human, and even biblical fact. In this challenge throughout history, nations have fought for their own ideologies or faiths, yet only one country has consistently fought for others, at least others who share that magnanimous endeavor of ensuring liberty for each and every individual, in both the secular and religious realms, and that nation is America.

It is easy to bemoan our flaws or listen to feeble foreigners jealously lambaste the titan, for this will always be a part of our existence, as it was and still is for the Romans. But this nation's heritage radiates with luminous souls that are staggering in stature and blinding in brilliance, so much so that it dwarfs even the pride we devout descendants can muster in trying to convey this miracle called America.

With Columbus courageously unlocking the door to the Western hemisphere, our European ancestors braved the turbulent Atlantic to escape the status quo and ventured into uncharted territory to craft a better world. Hence, the grand stage was set. Even as a fledgling British colony, John Winthrop first envisioned this budding nation as that shining city on the hill that would serve as a beacon for all the world to see and aspire to. Thomas Paine's fiery words sparked George Washington and our luminous assemblage of founding fathers to take arms to fight and secure that budding city. Taking pen in hand, Thomas Jefferson, with the aid of Madison, Adams, Hamilton, Franklin and others, profoundly etched a *Declaration* that exceeded the state and bordered upon biblical. This milestone would be symbolically sealed with the deaths of both Thomas Jefferson and John Adams, who died fifty years later, and only four hours apart from each other on that most legendary day, the fourth of July.

Many tenants of the elected presidential office followed, each fanning the radiant flames of providence, as James Monroe secured the sovereignty of the Western Hemisphere with his bold Doctrine. James Polk secured the largest expansion of territory for the growing nation with the Oregon Territory. Lincoln stitched together a nation torn by racism and soaked in blood. Theodore Roosevelt grabbed the loose reins of a sauntering nation, instilled strength while busting up oppressive monopolies, and then galloped valiantly into the twentieth century. Woodrow Wilson engaged Germany for the first showdown and declared it "a war to end all wars", as he idyllically envisioned a peaceful League of Nations. Franklin D. Roosevelt, despite being crippled, gallantly marched through four unprecedented terms to battle the nation's worst depression. Then despite a nation's cry for isolationism, he was clairvoyant enough to see how the golden flames of democracy were dying under a despotic black cloud, and bravely confronted the most horrific cast of evil spirits to ever scourge the earth. With a resounding victory, he rescued not only America, but the entire free world. John Kennedy's gift for oration and charisma sold a nation on Eisenhower's space race, while von Braun's dream of landing a man on the moon yielded Neil Armstrong's historic lunar landing, thus opening the gates of modern technology and the computerized world. Ronald Reagan restored a failing nation's pride, and against popular opinion he vigorously out-maneuvered and strategically forced the dismantling of the Soviet Union, thus relegating it to the *"ash heap of history."* And while George W. Bush incites much opposition and scorn, the history books of our great grandchildren will more likely than not be written in English, not Arabic. It will most likely credit Bush with being the unwelcome hero, with a large degree of flaws, who resolutely confronted and defended America and Western civilization against its most underrated and misunderstood foe.

This misunderstanding is due to the Islamic terrorists' profoundly disturbing credo, which comes from their Koran and calls for the targeting and killing of all infidels of Allah, regardless of age, sex, or civilian status. And although a part of the Islamic community are peace-loving Muslims who do not practice those passages, and independently deserve our continued fellowship, compassion, and understanding, this lethal credo *is* embraced and enforced by Muslim radicals, and they *will* continue their bloodthirsty Jihad at all costs.

One must also comprehend their new tactical mode of operation, for distant confrontations in remote battlefields are no longer the theaters of war, as restaurants, shopping malls, office buildings, airports, railway stations and even mosques, churches, temples and shrines are the new and vulnerable targets. Nothing is sacred or safe from these ruthless and relentless zealots who have a complete disregard for the sanctity of human life. Where our old Russian enemy shared our love of life and fear of death, our new radical-Islamic enemy only embraces *death*, be it their own *in martyrdom*, or that of their hated enemies *in Jihad*. And it is this archaic yet very lethal religious credo—which fuels its warriors with fervent faith and triggers their deadly attacks—that is lost on most Americans today. Americans' "Isolationist Fever" prevents them from comprehending this harsh and deadly reality which, if left unchecked, would leave America's future as a big IF.

Meanwhile, those who are seriously acquainted with history and religion will lucidly perceive the age-old dynamics at hand, and will rally to preserve our productive way of life and rich culture, for a passive America can indeed become another Athens. Ronald Reagan clearly understood this dynamic, as he would not permit the Soviets to resurrect the Spartan legacy.

This also brings to mind the words of the ultimate defender of our American republic, Franklin D. Roosevelt, who said, *"We do not retreat. We are not content to stand still. As Americans, we go forward, in the service of our country, by the will of God."*

Moreover, we must pause to recognize the harsh reality that if FDR had failed to act as he did, by slyly prodding Americans into battle, the outcome would have been catastrophic. The Allies would have lost, and Nazi Germany would have advanced into the Western hemisphere. The sobering thought remains that if America had jumped to the aid of their European allies sooner, as FDR would have liked, millions of lives could have been spared, and the holocaust might have been averted, or at least minimized.

Moreover, although some today deride Machiavelli's coldhearted logic, his sound advice is timelessly succinct, for he said, *"One should never allow disorders to develop in order to avoid a war, for war is not avoided, but only deferred to your disadvantage."*

FDR's great cousin, President Theodore Roosevelt, also knew better, and stated, *"The pacifist is surely a traitor to his country and to humanity as is the most brutal wrongdoer."*

In essence, passivity costs lives.

Americans, in our finest hour, have historically overcome adversity through heroics, for our nation was forged in heroic blood, knowing full well that anything worth fighting for always requires sacrifices. Patrick Henry's cry *"Give me liberty or give me death,"* or Nathan Hale's last words on the gallows, *"I only regret that I have but one life to lose for my country,"* may seem like melodramatic lines out of a modern day movie, yet they, and countless others, meant every searing and fatal word, for they truly knew what they stood to lose.

Henceforth, being an American begets great pride, for despite our nation's obvious flaws (including the corrosive effects of outsourcing to China and India, or illegal immigration that demands firm action from *we the people* to pressure our leaders to effectively secure our nation's borders as well as protect our financial solvency, core values, language, and legal integrity), this country stands alone and remains radiantly unique. America offers what no other country on Earth ever granted, and is the glorious offspring of an immensely rich heritage. It has encapsulated the best principles and practices of the best civilizations that the Western world had to offer. In gathering and solidifying those various flames of inspiration, America's united torch burns with a fervid intensity unrivalled by any other mortal manifestation.

Beyond the noble dreams of our ancestors who first envisioned America as that *"city upon a hill"*, this volatile nation and its rich culture have been more than just a luminous beacon of intangible light to inspire others, instead, it has actually transformed and enhanced vast expanses of the globe. American technology, engineering, science, medicine, entertainment, literature, and, more importantly, good will, permeate global communities, many of which became kindred souls. Although some may mock America's inevitable facets of corruption or excessive liberties, which most certainly need correction, the reality is known that the young wayward protégé has become the highly developed and most benevolent maven. The once rough and unpolished stone has indeed become the glittering gem.

America has uplifted and supported more nations than any other, and has magnanimously offered aid and its precious root of *Republicanism* to friends suffering from oppression, for liberty stands on the high altar of America's providential shrine. As Americans, we are born and blessed with this divine gift, yet many of our innocent brethren remain shackled in vacuous deserts. Therefore, as the world's new leader, it is incumbent upon us to irrigate these toxic wastelands with liberty so that the roots of republicanism may grow. At the same time, if our efforts in the Middle East prove useless, due to a half-hearted campaign or the failure of the friendly native factions to establish their own government and effective police and military forces to suppress the radicals and be self-sufficient, then we must alter our plans accordingly. For no endeavor should ever burden us to the point of making our nation weak and vulnerable. Yet, it is crucial to at least make the attempt to secure world peace and mandatory to quell our foes that aim their aggression at our citizens or upon our shores…and never sacrifice our high ideals.

As Eisenhower wisely said, *"A people that values its privileges above its principles soon loses both."*

As Americans, we must summon the brave and courageous spirit of the great souls before us to ensure that America remains the pinnacle of humanity's earthly endeavors, as well as the ultimate beacon and active defender of freedom, compassion, progress, and hope. With God's grace, and my fervent wishes, may all Americans come to realize that our nation is one to be deeply cherished, vigorously sustained, and heavily applauded, as we sail upon *the winds of time*.

The Winds of Time

EPILOGUE

The fascinating story of Western civilization is fundamental for all westerners, particularly Americans, to understand our place in this glorious, yet precarious timeline. It has inspired aspects of this book, which hopefully will agitate thought and prompt awareness, as America's survival depends upon sound knowledge and proactive vigilance. I hope it rekindles the true American spirit to stand up and fight for our way of life, for the aberrant options and dire consequences would be devastating for civilization. One of the seeds for this magnum opus appeared many years earlier, on October 22, 1999, with the creation of a short poem bearing the same title. Hence, it seems appropriate to let one of the kernels of inspiration that helped ignite this work also conclude it.

THE WINDS OF TIME

Mystical winds sweep across a magnificent sphere
As countless millenniums swirl into a nebulous void
Mutations of civilizations flow precariously in the squall
As weathered masses acquiesce to inevitable forces

Amid the current, Jupiter rises, only to succumb to Jesus
The almighty eagle soars on high, only to falter to the gale
Endless crusades sweep the Holy Land under banners of God
While in the womb of faith, bigotry and violence flourish

Imperial trophies are worn with pride, then wilt with pestilence
As limestone and marble steadily decay under mistral moons
Hannibal, Hitler, and Hussein permeate the primordial core
As a technological facade conceals then reveals the virus within

Yet amid malignant gravity, strident will and solid virtue arises
Able to rekindle hope, and kinetically ignite creative wonders
For the FDRs, in all forms, who energize and revitalize
The Da Vincis, Liszts, Dantes, Elizabeths, Edisons or Einsteins

Their influential tempest of genius empowers cerebral circuitry
The ultimate upgrade to quench and quell man's flaws and fears
With resolve, we must actively engage the whirlwinds of wisdom
As we sail the new millennium upon the mystical winds of time.

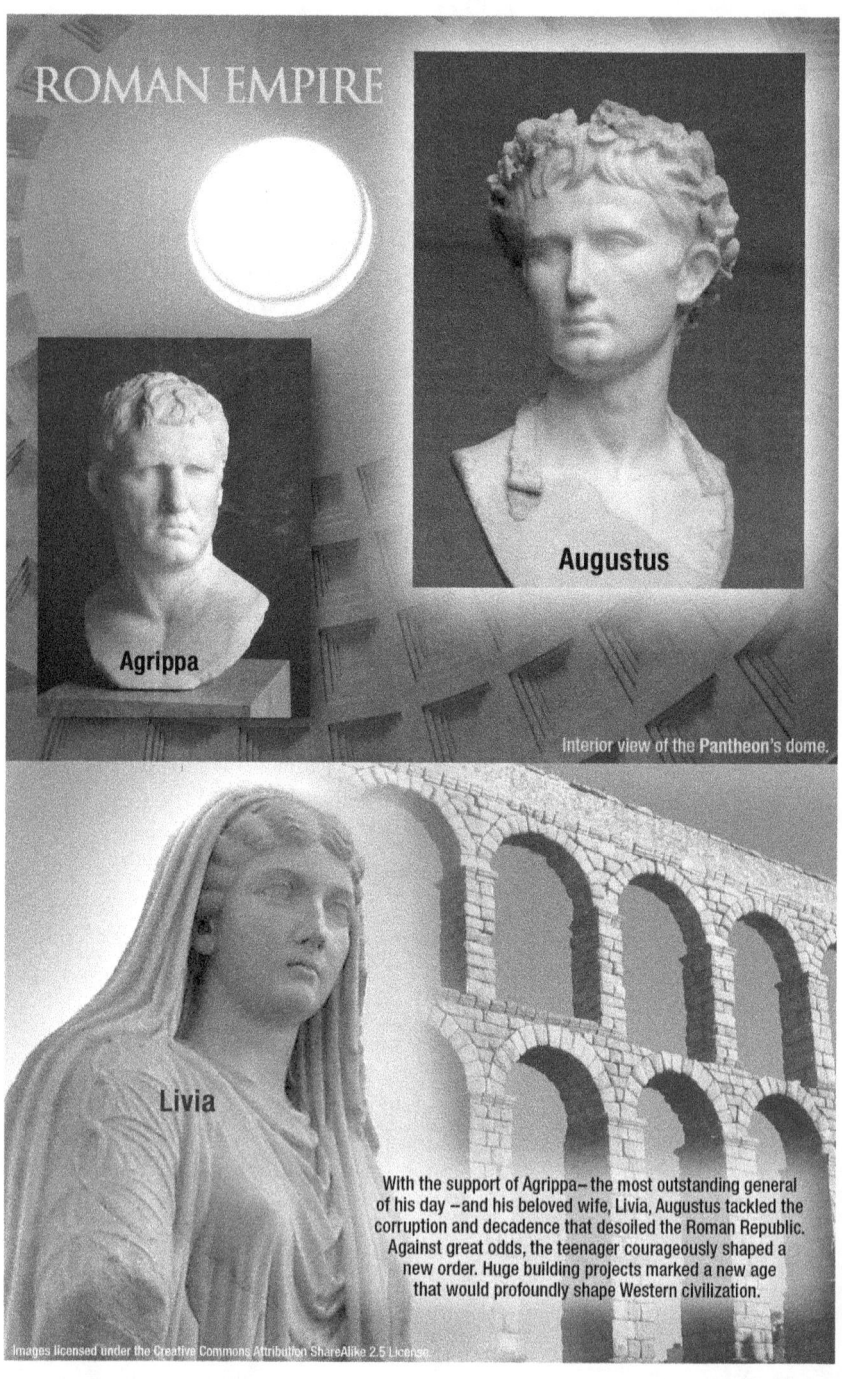

ROMAN EMPIRE

Agrippa

Augustus

Interior view of the **Pantheon's** dome.

Livia

With the support of Agrippa—the most outstanding general of his day—and his beloved wife, Livia, Augustus tackled the corruption and decadence that desoiled the Roman Republic. Against great odds, the teenager courageously shaped a new order. Huge building projects marked a new age that would profoundly shape Western civilization.

Images licensed under the Creative Commons Attribution ShareAlike 2.5 License.

Photos/Illustrations

Constantine the Great
(Head from a once colossal statue.)
Constantine's influence on Western civilization defies calculation and was equally colossal.
Photo courtesy of Creative Commons

Replica of the Greek **Parthenon** built in Nashville, Tennessee.
Photo by Ryan Kaldari

Trajan's Column
Photo by Matthias Kabel
Trajan's triumphal column depicts his victory in the Dacian Wars.

Pantheon *Painting by Giovanni Paolo Panini*
Built in AD116 by Hadrian, the Pantheon was the world's first domed building. It still stands, still baffles engineers, and was the template for all domed buildings.

Head from a statue of **Roman emperor Diocletian**
Photo by Giovanni Dall'Orto

Close up of the **Arch of Titus** depicting the Roman victory over the Jewish Revolt
Photo by Hebrew Wikipedia

Close up of relief on Trajan's Column.

St. Jerome *by Da Vinci.* Jerome translated the Bible into Latin.

Hadrian's Wall was an effective solution for centuries. *Photo by Mark A. Wilson*

Jesus

Jesus has been interpreted by many artists throughout history, from a humble shepherd to even a pagan-like warrior. His divinity has even been amplified in a surrealist vision by this author.

Jesus as a shepherd boy.

Jesus represented as Apollo.

Crucifixion *by Albrecht Altdorfer.*

6th century mosaic in Ravenna, Italy.

Divine Crucifixion *by Rich DiSilvio*

Photos/Illustrations

Pope Julius II, by *Raphael Sanzio*
The warrior pope and ultimate patron of the arts who tore down St.Peter's basilica, built by Constantine, to construct the gargantuan marvel we know today.

Pope Alexander VI
The Borgia pope who put even the most unscrupulous emperors to shame.

Cesare Borgia
Duke and ruthless son of Pope Alexander VI.

Catherine de Medici
by *François Clouet.*
Strategically exported by the mighty Medici family to France, Catherine gave birth to three future kings of France.

Martin Luther
by *Lucas Cranach*
The German monk irrevocably tore apart Christianity by defying Rome.

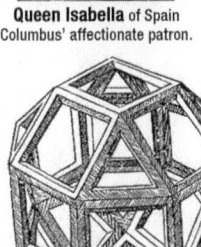

Queen Isabella of Spain Columbus' affectionate patron.

Niccolo Machiavelli - Brilliant political analyst and author of *The Prince*

Leonardo da Vinci's polyhedron published in Pacioli's *De Divina Proportione*

Filippo Brunelleschi's pioneering and influential dome

Galileo Galilei by *Cristiano Banti*
Galileo "The Father of Science" facing the Roman Catholic Inquisition.

Cosimo de Medici
by *Jacopo Pontormo*
Cosimo and his father Giovanni di Bicci were the key patrons and founders of the Renaissance movement.

Michelangelo's **David.** Photo by David Gaya

The **HERCULEAN ART** of Michelangelo
The *Enigmatic Realism* of Leonardo

Leonardo's *Virgin and St. Anne* and *Mona Lisa* display his soft realism as compared to Michelangelo's obsession with Herculean masculinity, as his painting of *Eve* and statue of *Night* (at bottom) both indicate.

Photos/Illustrations

Raphael's *School of Athens*: Raphael studied Leonardo's work and here displays his mastery of form and perspective. He honored Leonardo by using his likeness for Plato (center left) who is speaking with Aristotle. He used Michelangelo's likeness for Heraclitus (gloomily sitting in the foreground).

Leonardo Da Vinci's Ringed Fortress

Leonardo's radical fortress design was conceived for Cesare Borgia to replace the medieval La Rocca fortress. His sleek futuristic profile would deflect cannon fire and allow 360° vision. But, his clever concept was never built.

Illustrations of Leonardo's design by Rich DiSilvio

Christopher Columbus
The titanic and courageous explorer that opened the doors to a New World.

Sultan Mehmet II conquered Constantinople in 1453 causing a sea of explorers to find new ways to travel to the East.

Duke Ludovico Sforza
Patron to Leonardo and Bramante, yet instigator of the Italian wars.

Giovanni da Verrazzano
Forgotten hero who was the first to explore the North American Continent from South Carolina up to Newfoundland. His discoveries fell to later explorers, such as Raleigh, Smith & Henry Hudson.

Hernán Cortés takes Mexico by wiping out the brutal Aztecs.

PHOTOS/ILLUSTRATIONS

The Empires of England & Spain

King Henry VIII
by *Hans Holbein*
The Vatican's refusal to grant Henry an annulment caused the tyrant king to abandon Catholicism, thus forcing all of England to become Protestants.

Captain John Smith

Queen Elizabeth of England
Strong-willed ruler that by luck defeated King Philip's superior Spanish Armada, and made England a world leader.

Sir Walter Raleigh
Adventurer who initiated England's true thirst for exploration by naming his newly-founded colony "Virginia" in honor of his virgin queen.

William Shakespeare
The most revered and influential writer in the English language.

King Ferdinand of Spain
The founder of the great Spanish Empire. A long line of offspring would rule his empire and his daughter Catherine was the first wife of King Henry VIII of England.

Tomb of Sir Isaac Newton in Westminster Abbey

King Philip II of Spain
Distant relative and heir of King Ferdinand and Queen Isabella. Philip's loss to England marked the end of the Spanish Empire.

PHOTOS/ILLUSTRATIONS

Voltaire French Enlightenment philosopher and one of the leaders of the secular movement.

Napoleon Bonaparte
The Italian born French general-turned-dictator who modeled his regime upon the Roman Empire. His many successes, however, ended in failure, thus being exiled on the island of Saint Helena.

Charles Darwin
Darwin caused titanic waves in the both the scientific and religious communities with his theory of evolution.

John Locke
English philosopher whose ideas mirrored those of the Roman Statesman Cicero, both men having a huge influence on the Founding Fathers of the USA.

Adolf Hitler utilized the Roman eagle to great effect in building, and imprinting upon his people, a strong iconic vision of his Third Reich.
Photo: German Bundesarchives. Creative Commons

Guglielmo Marconi
Italian inventor and titan who gave the world wireless communications.

Josef Stalin The Soviet dictator who killed more people than Hitler yet slyly managed to conceal his atrocities from the free world, until recently.

Richard Wagner *by Rich DiSilvio*
The influential German composer (Hitler's idol) in front of his custom-built Festspielhaus, featuring symbols from his operas; *The Ring, Tristan un Isolde* and *Lohengrin*.

Hermann Göring
(SA Commander in Chief - 1920s)
Photo from German Bundesarchives
Creative Commons license.

Woodrow Wilson: Idealist

A young and restless **Teddy Roosevelt**

Henry Ford, **Thomas Edison**, and **Harvey Firestone**
Three fathers of modernity.

First successful flight of the Wright Flyer, by the Wright brothers.

Manfred von Richthofen
WWI's Red Baron

Heinrich Himmler: Unstable Reichsführer-SS

Fritz Haber
Father of chemical warfare in WWI. His Zyklon-B was used by Hitler.

Photos/Illustrations

Winston Churchill Titanic figure for Allied Forces during WWII.
Imperial War Museum Collection

Franklin D. Roosevelt Only four-term president, provocative New Deal administrator during the Depression, and wily WWII leader. Ultimately the savior of Western civilization.

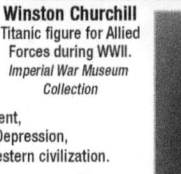

George Westinghouse
Photo by Joseph G. Gessford
Honest pioneer in AC electric power.

Albert Einstein Brilliant physicist whose theories allowed others to invent the atomic bomb.

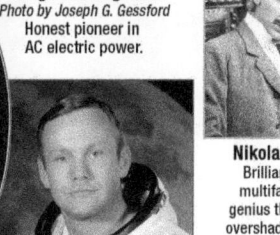

Enrico Fermi Italian physicist who migrated to America and was crucial in developing the atomic bomb.

Nikola Tesla Brilliant and multifaceted genius that was overshadowed by Thomas Edison.

John Pierpont Morgan Monopolizing tycoon that ruthlessly dominated numerous industries and significantly shaped American capitalism.

Neil Armstrong First man to walk on the moon.

Condoleezza Rice Intelligent Secretary of State. Rice, along with Obama and millions of other successful blacks, dispels the hype of suppression.

Rudy Giuliani Titanic Mayor of New York City who combated the Mafia and effectively restored New York.

Ronald Reagan Titan who fulfilled his life-long goal of collapsing the USSR via strategy and strength.

Wernher von Braun Brilliant Nazi German scientist who was recruited by the Americans, thus becoming the mastermind of NASA who successfully landed man on the moon.

ACKNOWLEDGEMENTS

With deep gratitude I would like to thank all the truly great characters of history, for without them this book would have been rather pithy, and the world rather paltry. These great men and women shaped our world and often remain ignored, unsung, and some even unknown, yet their contributions have enabled us to live in a modern world, which too many today take for granted in our fast-paced, cyber-electronic age.

Along with the titans, or even the Satans who spurred the benevolent to rise up and conquer evil, were the many historians that took the time to record these amazing events. For without the voices of Tacitus, Livy, Suetonius, Eusebius, the apostles and a universal chorus of many others the word and even the notion of "history" would be a total enigma. Additionally, I must thank all the many contemporary historians, theologians and authors that were an endless font of knowledge and inspiration. Unfortunately, the topic I have chosen is so infinitely broad that I must apologize for all the many great figures of history that I could not squeeze into the petite binder of this book.

Of course, I literally could never have written this book without my dear, yet sadly departed, mother, Marian Milo DiSilvio. Her love and guidance defies words and happily resides in beautiful memories. Then there are my dear three brothers, and my good friends, like Z Hufnagel, Steve Labriola, Ben Furman, Steve Kaiser, Claudio Crivici, Ted Rosen and Jim Barnum who offered encouragement, enthusiasm, and advice during my five-year adventure. Their advocacy is deeply appreciated. Special thanks goes to my inimitable father-in-law, John Smith, for his wealth of knowledge and treasured companionship.

Finally, *and certainly first in my heart*, are my wife Eileen, three daughters and son who make life worth living. Truth be told, my children planted the seed of inspiration for this grand endeavor. As a father, I felt as though there never was enough time to convey all the things I wished my children to learn before leaving the nest, and although this book certainly doesn't address all those concerns, it does offer a respectable amount of material to digest. May they and all others walk away with at least one new great thought, kernel of inspiration, or hopefully a deeply passionate craving to do something kinetic to make this world an even better place to live.

BIBLIOGRAPHY

The following is a partial but primary list of the books that have been crucial in this endeavor. I am indebted to all the authors for the wealth of knowledge I've acquired, even those with aberrant viewpoints. In essence, they have turned this writer into a detective, thus leading to further investigations and new perspectives that in the end proved very rewarding. Additionally, connecting the dots that others have missed is like finding gold, and hopefully there are enough gilded gems herein to keep many minds very busy. However, over a 100 ample sources of inspiration are listed for the eagerly ambitious and mildly curious. Enjoy!

1. A SHORT HISTORY OF BYZANTIUM – John Julius Norwich
2. ABUSE OF POWER: THE NEW NIXON TAPES – Stanley Kutler
3. AL QUR'ĀN – *Translated by* Ahmed Ali
4. ALBERT EINSTEIN AND THE FRONTIERS OF SCIENCE – Jeremy Bernstein
5. ALEXANDER HAMILTON – Ron Chernow
6. AMERICA IN BLACK AND WHITE – Stephan & Abigail Thernstrom
7. AMERICAN DYNASTY: *Aristocracy, Fortune, and the Politics of Deceit in the House of Bush* - Kevin Phillips
8. AMERICAN GOSPEL – Jon Meacham
9. AMERICAN MACHIAVELLI: ALEXANDER HAMILTON – John Lamberton Harper
10. AMERIGO – Felipe Fernandez-Armesto
11. ANCIENT GREECE: *From Prehistoric to Hellenistic Times* – Thomas R. Martin
12. ANCIENT ROME – Nigel Rodgers
13. ANDREW JACKSON AND HIS INDIAN WARS – Robert V. Remini
14. ARE WE ROME? *The Fall of an Empire and the Fate of America* – Cullen Murphy
15. AT THE CENTER OF THE STORM: *My years at the CIA* – George Tenet
16. AUGUSTINE: *A New Biography* – James O'Donnell
17. AUGUSTUS: *The Life of Rome's First Emperor* – Anthony Everitt
18. AUGUSTUS CAESAR: *Architect of Empire* – Monroe Stearns
19. BACKING HITLER – Robert Gellately
20. BECAUSE HE COULD: *Bill Clinton* – Dick Morris and Eileen McGann
21. BETRAYAL: *How the Clinton Administration Undermined American Security* – Bill Gertz
22. BEYOND BELIEF: *The Secret Gospels of Thomas* – Elaine Pagels
23. BILL CLINTON: *Mastering the Presidency* – Nigel Hamilton
24. BRUNELLESCHI'S DOME – Ross King
25. CALIGULA: *The Corruption of Power* – Anthony A. Barrett
26. CHRISTOPHER COLUMBUS: *The Four Voyages* – *Translated by* J.M. Cohen
27. CHRONICLE OF THE ROMAN EMPERORS – Chris Scarre

28. CHRONICLE OF THE ROMAN REPUBLIC – Philip Matyszak
29. CIVILIZATION: *A New History of the Western World* – Roger Osborne
30. CONSTANTINE AND THE BISHOPS – H.A. Drake
31. CONSTANTINE'S SWORD – James Carroll
32. DANTE: *The Poet, the Political Thinker, the Man* – Barbara Reynolds
33. DESCARTES: *The Life and Times of a Genius* – A.C. Grayling
34. EDISON: *Inventing the Century* – Neil Baldwin
35. EINSTEIN IN AMERICA – Jamie Sayen
36. ENRICO FERMI: Physicist – Emilio Segre
37. FAITH & THE PRESIDENCY – Gary Scott Smith
38. FALLEN FOUNDER: *The Life of Aaron Burr* – Nancy Isenberg
39. FDR – Jean Edward Smith
40. FDR AND HIS ENEMIES – Albert Fried
41. FORTUNE IS A RIVER – Roger D. Masters
42. FRANKLIN AND WINSTON – Jon Meacham
43. FREUD: *Darkness in the midst of vision* – Louis Breger
44. FREUD: *Inventor of the Modern Mind* – Peter D. Kramer
45. GALILEO'S DAUGHTER – Dava Sobel
46. GOD AGAINST GODS: *The History of the War between Monotheism and Polytheism* – Jonathan Kirsch
47. GOD CHOSE TO SAVE – Joseph Bianchi
48. HADRIAN – Stewart Perowne
49. HIS EXCELLENCY: GEORGE WASHINGTON– Joseph J. Ellis
50. HITLER'S SECOND BOOK – Gerhard L. Weinberg
51. HITLER'S VIENNA: *A Dictator's Apprentiship* – Brigitte Hamann
52. HOW THE CATHOLIC CHURCH BUILT WESTERN CIVILIZATION – Thomas E. Woods Jr.
53. IKE: *An American Hero* – Michael Korda
54. JAMES K. POLK – John Seigenthaler
55. JAMES MADISON – Garry Willis
56. JOSEPH MCCARTHY: *Reexamining the life and legacy of America's most hated Senator* – Arthur Herman
57. JOURNEY OF THE JIHADIST: *Inside Muslim Militancy* – Fawaz A. Gerges
58. KING JAMES *version of the* BIBLE
59. KISSINGER: *A Biography* – Walter Isaacson
60. LOST CHRISTIANITIES: *The Battles for Scripture and the Faiths We Never Knew* – Bart D. Ehrman
61. MEDICI MONEY – Tim Parks
62. MR. LINCOLN GOES TO WAR – William Marvel
63. MURDER AT GOLGOTHA: *Revisiting the Most Famous Crime Scene in History* – Ian Wilson
64. NICCOLO MACHIAVELLI *THE PRINCE AND OTHER WRITINGS* – *Translated by* Wayne A. Rebhorn
65. NIKOLA TESLA: *A Spark of Genius* – Carol Dommermuth-Costa
66. NIXON IN WINTER – Monica Crowley
67. NIXON: *Ruin and Recovery 1973 – 1990* – Stephen E. Ambrose
68. PRESIDENT NIXON: *Alone in the White House* – Richard Reeves

69. REAGAN'S WAR: *The Epic Story of His Struggle and Final Triumph over Communism* – Peter Schweizer
70. ROMAN REALITIES – Finley Hooper
71. SAILING FROM BYZANTIUM: *How a Lost Empire Shaped the World* – Colin Wells
72. SAINT PETER – Michael Grant
73. SAVING THE JEWS: *FDR and the Holocaust* – Robert N. Rosen
74. SHADOW WAR: *The Untold Story of How America Is Winning the War on Terror* – Richard Miniter
75. SIGNOR MARCONI'S MAGIC BOX – Gavin Weightman
76. SONS & BROTHERS: *The days of Jack and Bobby Kennedy* – Richard D. Mahoney
77. SPARKS OF GENIUS – Robert and Michele Root-Bernstein
78. SPREZZATURA – Peter D'Epiro & Mary Desmond Pinkowish
79. STALIN: *Triumph & Tragedy* – Dmitri Volkogonov
80. TESLA: *Man Out Of Time* – Margaret Cheney
81. THE AMERICANIZATION OF BENJAMIN FRANKLIN – Gordon S. Wood
82. THE ANNALS OF IMPERIAL ROME – Tacitus– *Translated by* Michael Grant
83. THE ARCHAEOLOGY OF THE ROMAN ECONOMY – Kevin Greene
84. THE BROTHER OF JESUS– Hershel Shanks & Ben Witherington III
85. THE CIA AT WAR: *Inside the Secret Campaign against Terror* – Ronald Kessler
86. THE CLOSING OF THE WESTERN MIND – Charles Freeman
87. THE DARK SIDE OF CAMELOT – Seymour M. Hersh
88. THE DECLINE AND FALL OF THE ROMAN EMPIRE – Edward Gibbon
89. THE DEVIL'S DISCIPLES: *Hitler's Inner Circle* – Anthony Read
90. THE EVOLUTION-CREATION STRUGGLE – Michael Ruse
91. THE FIRST AMERICAN: *Ben Franklin* – H.W. Brands
92. THE FOURTH CRUSADE – Jonathan Phillips
93. THE GREEK ACHIEVEMENT – Charles Freeman
94. THE LIFE & TIMES OF CONSTANTINE THE GREAT – D.G. Kousoulas
95. THE LOST GOSPEL: *Quest for the Gospel of Judas Iscariot* – Herbert Krosney
96. THE NAG HAMMADI LIBRARY: *The definitive translation* – James Robinson
97. THE RENAISSANCE – Michel Pierre
98. THE ROMAN EMPERORS – Michael Grant
99. THE STORY OF THOUGHT – Bryan Magee
100. THE TWELVE CAESARS – Suetonius– *Translated by* Robert Graves
101. THE VICTORY OF REASON: *How Christianity Led to Freedom, Capitalism and Western Success* - Rodney Stark
102. THE WARS OF THE JEWS – Flavius Josephus
103. WHAT WOULD THE FOUNDERS DO? – Richard Brookhiser
104. WHILE EUROPE SLEPT: *How Radical Islam is Destroying the West from Within* – Bruce Bawer
105. WHY THE JEWS REJECTED JESUS– David Klinghoffer
106. WINNING THE FUTURE – Newt Gingrich
107. WOMEN OF ANCIENT ROME – Don Nardo

INDEX

A

Acheson, Dean, 591, 604
ACLU, 492-493, 610
Adams, John, 69, 214, 421-422, 436, 438-441, 444, 461-462, 472-474, 696
Adams, John Quincy, 214, 457, 615
Adams, Samuel, 421-422, 427, 466
Agricola, 190
Agrippa, 31-32, 64, 66, 73-77, 81-84
Akhenaten, 131, 132
Alaric (Visigoth king), 203
Alberti, Leon Battista, 322, 336
Albizzi family, 333-334
Alexander the Great, 14, 42, 92, 93, 318, 486
Alexander, Bishop, 218, 222-223, 228, 231
Alighieri, Dante, 63, 108, 293-302, 304-306, 309, 318, 322, 473
Allah, 130, 270, 674, 681-682, 693, 697
al-Zarqawi, Musab, 689
al-Zawahiri, Ayman, 683
Ananus, High Priest, 141, 150
Anthony, Susan B., 621
Antiochus, King, 120
Antony, Mark, 39, 62, 67-80, 83
Anubis, 80
Apuleius, 15
Aquinas, St. Thomas, 254-255, 305, 382
Archimedes, 46
Aristarchus, 46, 318
Aristotle, 15, 23, 44, 46, 105, 270-272, 304, 309, 315, 318, 337, 380-382, 386-387, 493, 573
Arius, 218, 221-224, 226-228, 231
Armat, Thomas, 562
Armstrong, Neil, 697
Athanasius, 221-222, 224, 227-228, 231
Atomic Pile, 572
Attila the Hun, 237
Augustine, St., 102, 203, 221, 255, 256, 274
Augustus, 25, 28-41, 55, 63, 81, 83-92, 98-112, 121-122, 125, 138, 150, 167, 178, 187, 195, 214, 225, 233, 236, 300, 318, 350, 375, 432, 646, 672, 690

Aurelian, Emperor, 203
Aurelius, Marcus, 202
auto-da-fé, 372
Ayres, William, 318

B

Bacon, Francis, 378
Bajazet, Sultan, 402
Bar Kochbah, Simon, 198
Barberini, Cardinal, 383, 385
Barlaam of Calabria, 338
Baroncelli, 414
Battle of Anghiari by Da Vinci, 396
Beatrice (Dante's muse), 298, 301-302
Beethoven, Ludwig von, 424
Begin, Menachem, 549
Bell, Alexander Graham, 496, 500, 563
Ben-Gurion, David, 616
Bentson, Lloyd, 170
Berardi, Gianotto, 357, 364-365
Beria, Lavrenty, 484
Bernhardt, Sarah, 559-560
Bernini, Gian Lorenzo, 322, 383
Bernoulli, Daniel, 396
Bessarion, Cardinal John, 342-343, 345
Big Bang theory, 291
Biltmore Declaration, 128
bin Laden, Osama, 270, 480, 603, 662-665, 667, 669-670, 674, 684, 689
Blumrich, Josef, 265
Boccaccio, Giovanni, 305, 322
Boleyn, Anne, 375
Bonaparte, Charles Joseph, 584
Bonaparte, Napoleon, 74, 424, 437, 438, 445, 447, 486, 521, 561, 584, 691
Bonfire of the Vanities, 416
Book of Ezekiel, 263, 264
Boone, Daniel, 95
Borgia, Cesare, 311, 317, 390-395, 397-400, 403-405, 407
Borgia, Lucretia, 398, 399
Borglum, Gutzon, 446
Boscovich, Rudjer, 574
Boston Tea Party, 421, 434
Botticelli, 322, 364, 414, 416
Boudica (warrior queen), 189, 197

Braddock, General, 431, 432, 433
Bramante, Donato, 196, 269, 322, 393, 405
Brezhnev, Leonid, 641, 656
Brown, Dan, 283
Brown, Robert, 579
Brunelleschi, Filippo, 196, 266-267, 311, 318-319, 321-322, 332, 336, 344, 346-349
Bruni, Leonardo, 338
Bruno, Giordano, 344
Brutus, Lucius Iunius, 41, 54
Brutus, Marcus Iunius, 34, 42, 63, 68, 296
Bryan, William Jennings, 492
Buckley, William F., 641
Burr, Aaron, 441, 454, 460-461, 463, 464-466
Bush, George H.W., 610, 634, 664
Bush, George W., 214, 611, 660, 663, 667, 671, 674-675, 677, 679, 684-689, 697
Butler Law, 492-493

C

Cabot, John, 322, 419
Caecina, 180
Caepionis, Servilia, 63
Caesar, Julia, 64
Caesar, Julius, 13-15, 28-29, 33-34, 36-38, 42, 60-69, 71-72, 74, 79, 80-82, 84, 91, 99, 108-110, 117, 189, 296, 300-301, 318, 375, 377, 399, 405, 439, 513, 672
Caesar, Render to, 151, 153
Caesarion, 74, 79-80
Caiaphas, 157-162, 164-165
Caligula, Emperor, 86, 111-112, 121-122, 672
Callender, James, 460, 461, 462
Calvin, John, 106, 239, 322, 411-412
Canaanites, 98, 127, 682
Caonabo (Taino chief), 352-353
Capone, Al, 590
Caracalla, Emperor, 202
Carroll, Bishop John, 104
Carter, Jimmy, 609, 645, 655-659, 669
Cassius, 63, 68, 296
Castro, Fidel, 588-590, 592-594, 649, 650, 654, 656
Catherine of Aragon, 375
Cato, 56, 108, 340

Cavalcanti, Guido, 300, 301
Chamberlain, Houston Stewart, 524
Chamberlain, Neville, 526
Charlemagne, 220, 286, 301, 306
Charles V, King, 374, 411
Charles VIII, King, 400-403, 416
Charles IX, King, 330, 385
Chávez, Hugo, 649
Chirac, Jacques, 687
Churchill, Ward, 318
Churchill, Winston, 283, 318, 502, 528-541, 544-548, 550-553, 690
Cicero, 23-24, 46, 69-71, 96, 301, 338, 340-341, 442, 478, 645
Cincinnatus, 23, 33, 104, 435, 455
Claudius Gothicus, Emperor, 203, 214, 215
Claudius, Emperor, 111-112, 122, 190, 195, 203, 214-215, 672
Cleisthenes, 43, 48
Cleopatra, 14, 72, 74-80
Cleveland, Grover, 568
Clinton, Bill, 462, 610, 617, 663-671, 673-675, 688
Clinton, George, 456-457, 459, 463, 466
Code of Hammurabi, 24
Columbus, Christopher, 97, 318, 322, 350-371, 374, 388-389, 418-419, 448, 568, 572, 657, 696
Commodus, Emperor, 29, 202
Common Sense by Thomas Paine, 422
Constantine, 204-212, 214-235, 237, 239, 241-244, 248-249, 253-255, 268, 275-280, 282-288, 292, 300, 305, 318, 326, 337, 393, 405, 410, 690, 692
Constantius, Emperor, 211-212, 214
Copernicus, 272, 322, 381, 388, 486
Cosby, Bill, 628-629
Council of Nicaea, 218, 228, 232, 234
Crockett, Davy, 119
Curatores viarum, 88

D

Da Gama, Vasco, 322
Da Vinci Code, 283
Da Vinci, Leonardo, 248, 268, 310-315, 317-322, 348-349, 380, 387, 391-396, 401, 414
Dali, Salvador, 489
Darlan, Jean-Francois, 550-551

INDEX 725

Darrow, Clarence, 492-493
Darwin, Charles, 36, 476-478, 486, 489-490, 492-497, 524
de Bobadilla, Francisco, 357
de Hojeda, Alonso, 354, 357
de Jumonville, Monsieur, 429-431
de Las Casas, Bartolomé, 353, 355-356
de Ovando, Nicolás, 357, 359, 361
Dela Porta, 196, 349
del Virgilio, Giovanni, 294-295, 299, 306
Democritus, 97
Demosthenes, 57
Descartes, René, 321, 384, 385
Diem, Ngo Dinh, 647
Dinwiddie, Gov. Robert, 427, 429
Dio, Cassius, 203
Diocletian, Emperor, 18, 40, 60, 86, 131, 204-205, 207-208, 210-214, 220, 225, 240
Djem, 402
Dobrynin, Anatoly, 592, 660
Donatello, 316, 322, 332
Donation of Constantine, 285, 287, 343
Donatists, 218-219, 221, 224, 228, 232
Donatus, Magnus, 219-221
Douglas, Frederick, 628
Douglas, Helen, 632
Drake, Francis, 376
Drusilla, Livia, 32, 55, 73, 100
Dumas, Alexander, 505

E

Edict of Milan, 216-217, 234, 278, 692
Edison, Thomas, 318, 371, 559-566, 568-571, 673-674
Ehrlichman, John, 634
Eichmann, Adolf, 514
Eiffel, Gustave, 504
Eight Symphony by Shostakovich, 483
Einstein, Albert, 128, 273, 290, 292, 380, 531-532, 545, 574-580, 603, 679
Eisenhower, Dwight, 20, 82, 85, 539, 547, 550-551, 581, 588, 597, 599, 632, 653, 659, 697, 700
Eleazar, 116
Eliezer, Rabbi Israel ben, 515
Eliot, T.S., 296, 302
Elizabeth, Queen, 69, 82, 375, 376, 377, 378, 419, 690
Emmerich, Anne Catherine, 162-163

En-lai, Chou, 637, 639, 640
Erasmus, 282
Ericsson, Leif, 370
Eroica Symphony by Beethoven, 424
Euclid, 46, 271, 273, 318
Eusebius, 178, 206, 208, 219, 248, 282, 702
Ezekiel, 263-265

F

Faraday, Michael, 574
Farnese, Giulia (Pope Alexander's mistress), 402
Fausta (Constantine's wife), 215-216, 276
Felix (Roman procurator), 141, 181
Ferdinand, King, 350, 353, 355-357, 363, 365, 368, 370-375, 405
Fermi, Enrico, 531-532, 571-573, 576, 580
Festus (Roman procurator), 141, 182
Fibonacci, Leonardo, 307
Five Solas, 412
Fonseca, Bishop, 353, 356-357, 361, 363-364, 370, 372
Ford, Henry, 318, 504, 562, 570, 673
Fort Duquesne, 428-430, 432
Fort Necessity, 430-431
Francis I, King, 311, 317, 419
Francis II, King, 330
Francis of Assisi, Saint, 295
Franco, Francisco, 512, 551
Franklin, Ben, 23, 103-104, 420, 425, 440, 466, 467-474, 480, 696
Freeh, Louis, 687
Freud, Sigmund, 379, 478, 485-487, 489, 497
Frisch, Otto Robert, 532
Froebel, Friedrich, 578
Frugardi, Roger, 331
Fust, Johann, 345

G

Galerius, Emperor, 212-214, 240
Galilei, Galileo, 240, 273, 344, 380-388, 475, 478, 493-494, 573
Galton, Francis, 496
Gage, General Thomas, 421
Gates, Bill, 673
Gates, Sir Thomas, 376, 377
Gatling, Richard, 312

George III, King, 434, 439, 691
Ghiberti, Lorenzo, 346-348
Giancana, Sammy, 585, 589
Gibson, Mel, 159, 162-164, 166
Gingrich, Newt, 611, 617
Giotto, 266, 267, 322
Giuliani, Rudy, 670, 686-687
Gobineau, Arthur de, 495
Goebbels, Joseph, 514, 523
Goldzier, Hans, 525
Gorbachev, Mikhail, 541, 599, 601-602
Gore, Al, 663, 671, 673
Gorelick, Jamie, 663, 675
Göring, Hermann, 512, 514, 517, 522
Grant, Ulysses S., 214, 692
Greene, Kevin, 194
Groves, General Leslie, 532
Gruet, Jacques, 411
Guacanagari, 352
Guernica, 511-512
Guernica by Picasso, 512
Gutenberg, Johann, 318, 345, 346, 371

H

Haber, Fritz, 545-546
Hadrian, Emperor, 126-127, 187-190, 194-199, 201-203, 325, 327, 400, 485, 685
Haldeman, Bob, 634
Hale, Nathan, 699
Halloween, 410
Hamilton, Alexander, 23-24, 37, 434, 437-438, 440-441, 443, 445, 448-450, 452-467, 693, 696
Hancock, John, 421, 466
Hanfstaengl, Ernst, 522-523
Hanisch, Reinhold, 507
Harrison, Benjamin, 214
Hawking, Stephen, 553
Hedley, William, 504
Hegel, Georg, 106, 480
Helena (Constantine's mother), 210-211
Hendrix, Jimi, 628
Henry III, King, 330
Henry IV, King, 384-385
Henry VIII, King, 322, 372, 375, 418
Henry, Patrick, 421, 466, 699
Herod Antipas, 144, 147
Herod, King, 75, 114, 126-127, 144, 234
Herodias, 144

Hertz, Heinrich, 502-503
Hess, Rudolf, 519
Himmler, Heinrich, 514, 523, 526, 604
Hirohito, 548, 552, 556
Hirtius and Pansa, 68, 70
Hiss, Alger, 598, 605, 631
Hitler, Adolf, 53, 267-268, 270, 312, 337, 484, 495-496, 503, 505-527, 529, 531-532, 536-537, 539, 541-552, 556-557, 575-577, 580-582, 605, 615, 618, 625, 679, 688, 691
Hoffa, Jimmy, 589, 594
Holbein, Hans, 322
Homer, 15, 45, 271, 297-298, 306, 337, 368
Homo habilis, 491-492
Hoover, Herbert, 542
Hoover, J. Edgar, 584-585, 604, 610
Hopkins, Harry, 530-532, 605
Horace, 107, 301
Hörbiger, Hans, 525
Houdini, Harry, 500
Hudson, Henry, 419
Hughes, David, 502-503
Hume, David, 255, 478, 494
Hunt, Howard, 650
Hussein, Saddam, 35, 527, 664, 666, 677, 679, 687-689, 691
Huxley, Thomas Henry, 490, 495
Hylacomylus, 367-368

I

Irenaeus, 182-186, 222, 226, 243-248, 261
Isabella, Queen, 350, 371-373, 374
Ishii, Shiro, 549
Ivan the Great, 345
Ivan the Terrible, 345

J

Jackson, Andrew, 94, 557, 692
Jackson, Jesse, 620-622, 624
James (Jesus' brother), 139, 140, 142
James I, King, 419
James, William, 488
Jay Treaty, 424, 460
Jefferson, Thomas, 23-24, 93, 100-103, 105, 196, 216, 289, 422, 425-427, 438-447, 456, 459, 461-466, 557, 612, 614-615, 636, 652, 692-694, 696

INDEX

Jerome, St., 69, 282
Jesus, 26, 63, 96, 103, 105, 126, 130, 133-140, 142-174, 176-185, 203, 206, 208, 209, 211-223, 225-229, 232-233, 238, 241, 243-262, 269, 278, 280-281, 283, 288-289, 291-292, 296, 314, 329, 336, 406, 425-427, 444, 456, 509-510, 520, 681-683, 690, 692-693
John the Baptist, 143-145, 147
Johnson, Lyndon B., 585-586, 596-597, 612, 617, 623, 650, 653-654, 656, 659
Jones, Rev. Jim, 289
Jones, Paula, 669
Jonson, Ben, 377
Josef, Emperor Franz, 515, 520
Josephus, 116, 119-120, 122-124, 149, 165
Judas, 63, 155-157, 159, 164-165, 171, 175, 177, 183-185, 244, 251, 296, 300
Julian the Apostate, 235
Jupiter (planet), 381
Jupiter (Roman god), 24-26, 126, 219, 325, 693
Justinian, Emperor, 24, 237-238, 302, 304, 340

K

Kant, Immanuel, 318
Keith, Sir William, 468-469
Kemmler, William, 566
Kennedy, Jackie, 588, 593-595
Kennedy, John, 170, 426, 583, 584, 585, 586, 587, 588, 589, 590, 591, 592, 593, 595, 596, 597, 598, 623, 630, 633, 635, 647, 650, 653, 654, 697
Kennedy, Joseph, 531, 542, 585-586
Kennedy, Robert, 588-594
Khan, A.Q., 683-684
Khomeini, Ayatollah, 480, 657
Khrushchev, Nikita, 589-590, 592, 597, 633, 639
King, Pete, 685
King Jr., Martin Luther, 584, 612, 617, 619-620, 629
Kissinger, Henry, 608, 634-636, 638-648, 651, 654-655, 672

L

La Rocca Fortress, 317, 391
Landels, J.G., 191-192
Last Supper by Da Vinci, 268, 311, 313, 321, 330, 390, 393
Lenin, Vladimir, 480-482, 536, 600, 688
Leo III, Byzantine Emperor, 241
Lepidus (Roman triumvir), 71, 74
Lewinsky, Monica, 665, 669
Lewis and Clark, 446
Lewis, C.S., 260
Licinius, Emperor, 216-217
Lincoln, Abraham, 103, 446, 542, 554-557, 612, 615, 652, 676, 688, 692, 696
Lindberg, Charles, 542
Lippi, Filippino, 315
Liszt, Franz, 507-508, 511
Livy, 108, 340-341, 408, 702
Locke, John, 23-24, 216, 442
Longfellow, Henry Wadsworth, 306
Louis XII, King, 401, 403
Louis XVI, King, 422
Louisiana Purchase, 445
Lucretia (wife of Collatinus), 54-55
Ludendorff, Erich, 518
Ludwig II, King, 511
Lueger, Karl, 525
Luther, Martin, 106, 239, 258, 322, 372, 409-412, 417, 508, 517, 519, 520
Lyell, Charles, 476-477

M

MacArthur, General Douglas, 544, 578, 606
Maccabees, 121
Machiavelli, Niccolo, 37, 103, 277, 288, 317, 322, 341, 391-392, 394-395, 407-409, 416, 479, 489, 551, 633, 698
Madison, James, 23, 214, 216, 436, 440, 445-448, 454-459, 466, 557, 673, 692, 696
Maecenas, 64, 66, 72, 107
Magna Carta, 328
Magritte, René, 489
Mahler, Gustav, 516

Mahmood, Sultan Bashirrudan, 683
Manhattan Project, 532, 551, 572-573, 577
Marcello, Carlos, 594
Marcionites, 185
Marconi, Guglielmo, 499-503
Margaret of Valois, 385
Marshall, General George, 534, 551
Martin, Dean, 587
Martines, Fernão, 350
Marx, Karl, 478-480, 485, 497, 521, 646
Mary of England, Queen, 375
Mary of Scotland, Queen, 375
Mason, George, 434, 442, 466
Massacio, 152
Maxentius, Emperor, 206-207, 210, 215
Maximian, Emperor, 212, 214-215
Maximinus Thrax, Emperor, 202
Maxwell, James Clerk, 575
McCarthy, Joseph, 598-599, 602-604, 606-607, 610, 612
Medici, Catherine de, 330, 385
Medici, Cosimo de, 152, 333-337, 341, 343
Medici, Giovanni di Bicci, 332
Medici, Giuliano de, 315, 413-414
Medici, Giulio de, 341
Medici, Lorenzo de, 311, 343, 413-415
Medici, Lorenzo II de, 330
Mehmet II, Sultan, 152, 350
Mein Kampf by Adolf Hitler, 510, 515, 517, 518-519, 526, 548
Meir, Golda (Israeli prime minister), 549
Melville, Herman, 247
Mendez, Diego, 359, 361-362
Mengele, Dr. Josef, 615
Michelangelo, 196, 268-269, 313, 315, 316, 319, 321-322, 330, 335, 344, 346, 349, 406, 414, 416
Mitchell, R.J., 502
Mithras, 211, 240, 250
Monroe, James, 424, 445, 454, 458, 460-463, 466, 557, 696
Monroe, Marilyn, 586, 587
Montesinos, Father, 373
Montesquieu, 23
Montgomery, General, 544, 552-553
Moore, Gordon, 268
Morgan, J.P., 560, 563-566, 571
Morgenthau Jr., Henry, 549
Morris, Gouverneur, 423-424, 460, 466

Morse, Samuel F.B., 563
Moses, 98, 127, 140, 153, 172, 179, 181, 206, 208, 248, 520, 613, 682, 690
Mott, Lucretia, 622
Moynihan, Daniel Patrick, 608
Mozart, Wolfgang, 389, 579
Mubarak, Egyptian president, 664
Muhammad, 166, 241, 292, 340, 680, 681
Mussolini, Benito, 527, 548, 572, 691

N

Nefertiti, Queen, 131
Negroponte, John, 648
Nero, Emperor, 53, 86, 90, 104, 111-113, 116, 118, 121-122, 131, 149-150, 167, 182, 186, 189-190, 213, 318, 691
Newton, Sir Isaac, 273, 384, 475, 478, 573-575
Nicholas, Saint, 283
Nietzsche, Friedrich, 524
Nixon, Richard, 598, 607-608, 630-641, 643, 645, 646, 648-650, 652, 654-656, 659, 670-671

O

Odoacer, King, 236, 237
Oedipus Rex by Sophocles, 49, 486
Oppenheimer, Robert, 532, 572, 577, 580
Orosius, 203
Osborne, Roger, 87, 319, 322
Oswald, Lee Harvey, 593-595
Outb, Sayyid, 479, 480
Ovid, 107, 301

P

Pacioli, Luca, 322
Pagels, Elaine, 250
Paine, Thomas, 251-252, 422-426, 442, 460, 466, 470, 696
Palladio, Andrea, 442
Palmer, Mitchell, 603-604
Pantheon, 19, 195-198, 237, 243, 325, 326, 346-347, 383, 405, 442
Patton, General, 82, 547, 552

Paul, Saint, 105, 139-142, 171, 174, 176-182, 206, 208, 220, 229-230, 244, 254, 279, 296, 305, 613
Pax Romana, 91
Pazzi family, 344, 413-414
Peculium, 23
Pepin, King, 285, 286
Pestalozzi, Johann, 578
Peter, Saint, 105, 137, 139-142, 145, 151-152, 168, 171, 175, 177-181, 197, 232, 252, 261, 285
Petrarca, 69, 296, 322, 338
Philip II, King, 374-376
Philo of Alexandria, 165
Picasso, Pablo, 192, 512
Pilate, Pontius, 147, 157-161, 165
Pistoia, Cino da, 302, 304
Planck, Max, 545, 580
Plato, 15, 44, 48-49, 59, 105-106, 255, 270-271, 274, 315, 337, 341, 386, 387, 407
Pliny the Elder, 187
Pliny the Younger, 187
Plutarch, 485
Pocahontas, 376
Polk, James, 91, 557, 696
Pollack, Jackson, 248
Polo, Marco, 350
Polybius, 43
Pompey the Great, 13-14, 62, 72
Pompey, Sextus, 72-74
Pompilius, King Numa, 125
Pope Alexander VI, 364, 372, 390, 391, 397-400, 402-404, 406-407, 416
Pope Boniface VIII, 241, 299
Pope Calixtus III, 397
Pope Clement V, 397
Pope Clement VII, 330, 341, 409
Pope Eugenius IV, 333, 337, 342
Pope Innocent III, 134, 397, 398
Pope Innocent VIII, 402
Pope Julius II, 268-269, 313, 322, 393, 398, 402, 404-406
Pope Leo III, 286
Pope Leo X, 311, 313, 330, 406, 409, 410, 411, 417
Pope Leo XI, 330
Pope Nicholas V, 343
Pope Paul III, 613
Pope Pius II, 397
Pope Sixtus IV, 372, 398, 406, 412-413
Pope Urban II, 207
Pope Urban VIII, 383
Pope, John Russell, 197

Powell, Colin, 623, 628
Prokofiev, Sergei, 483
Ptolemy (Roman Astronomer), 270, 271, 382, 386, 493
Ptolemy XIII, King, 13-14
Ptolemy XIV, King, 14
Puccini, Giacomo, 516
Pythagoras, 386

Q

Quantum theory, 545, 580
Quintilian, 186-187

R

Ra (Egyptian Sun god), 131, 225, 693
Rachmaninoff, Sergei, 483
Raleigh, Sir Walter, 376, 419
Raphael, 315, 322, 335
Redick, J.J., 628
Read, Deborah, 468
Reagan, Ronald, 485, 540, 542, 599-602, 607, 608-612, 618, 636, 641, 645, 658-660, 662-663, 666, 672, 690, 697-698
Reno, Janet, 663
Revere, Paul, 421
Riccardi family, 307, 344, 413
Rice, Condoleezza, 623, 628
Richthofen, Manfred von, 512, 517
Richthofen, Wolfram von, 512
Rienzi, 508-510, 523
Röhm, Ernst, 521-522
Roldan, Francisco, 353
Rommel, Erwin, 534, 552
Romulus, 27, 41, 107, 125, 236
Romulus Augustus, Emperor, 236
Roosevelt, Eleanor, 541
Roosevelt, Franklin D., 129, 214, 436, 446, 526, 528-558, 562, 572, 577, 604-605, 660, 676, 697, 698
Roosevelt, Theodore, 155, 214, 312, 458, 496, 499, 500, 501, 504, 540, 657, 696, 698
Rosenberg, Julius & Ethel, 606
Rosselli, Johnny, 585, 589-590, 593-594
Ruby, Jack, 594
Rucellai, Giovanni, 336
Rüdin, Ernst, 496, 525
Rwanda, 615, 665, 669
Ryan, Mary, 663

S

Sacco and Vanzetti, 604
Sadducees, 147-148, 157-158, 161, 164
Salome, 144
SALT, 608, 641, 643-644, 655
Sanger, Margaret, 496
Sappho, 57
Savonarola, Girolamo, 415-417
Scheidemann, Philipp, 518
Schönerer, Georg von, 525
Schopenhauer, Arthur, 105
Scipio, Publius, 42, 676
Society of Cincinnati, 23
Scopes, John, 492, 493
Scribonia, 72-73
Segrè, Emilio, 573
Seneca, 23, 96, 104, 318, 338, 340
Septimius Severus, Emperor, 202
Sforza, Duke Ludovico, 313, 317, 392-393, 401, 403
Shakespeare, William, 377-378, 380, 593
Sharpton, Al, 620, 622
Shepard, Alan, 597
Shostakovich, Dimitri, 482-483
Shriver, Sargent, 617, 623
Silva, Flavius, 115
Sinatra, Frank, 587
Smith, Adam, 23
Smith, Captain John, 376, 378, 419
Smith, Clark Ashton, 296
Smith, Gerard, 641
Socrates, 44, 105
Soderini, Piero, 367
Sol Invictus, 209-211, 215, 218, 250, 278
Solomon, King, 126
Sophocles, 45, 49, 473
Sorrell, Herb, 600
Spitz, Mark, 627
S.P.Q.R., 47
Stalin, Josef, 479, 481-485, 526-527, 536-540, 548, 553, 604-606, 608, 610, 691
Stanton, Elizabeth, 621
Stamp Act, 421
Stark, Rodney, 86-88, 191-194, 319, 322
Stephen, Bishop, 285-286
Stephenson, George, 504
Stevens, John Frank, 504
Stravinsky, Igor, 483

Suetonius, 39, 55, 110, 150, 702
Sulla, Lucius, 61
Swan, Joseph, 560
Swaggart, Rev. Jimmy, 289, 630
Szilard, Leo, 531, 545, 576, 577

T

Tacitus, 180, 186, 190, 340, 520, 702
Taiping Heavenly Kingdom, 329
Taliban, 674
Tanacharison, 428, 429
Tarquin the Proud, 41
Teller, Edward, 545, 577, 580
Tenet, George, 671, 684
Tesla, Nikola, 502, 563, 565, 567-571
Thatcher, Margaret, 609
Theodosian Code, 284
Theodosius I, Emperor, 235
Thieu, Nguyen Van, 647, 648
Thmermospheria festival, 57
Tho, Le Duc, 647, 648
Thomson, Elihu, 564-565
Tiberius, Emperor, 32-33, 40, 55, 111, 112, 150, 157, 160-161
Titus, Emperor, 112-118, 120-124, 126, 167, 186, 198-199, 230, 690
Tojo, Hideki, 591
Torquemada, Tomás de, 372
Torrijos, Omar, 657
Toscanelli, Paolo, 349, 350
Trafficante, Santos, 594
Trajan, Emperor, 186-187, 197, 439, 485
Trotsky, Alexander, 481, 537
Truman, Harry, 577-578, 581, 604-607, 639, 653
Tse-tung, Mao, 606, 639, 640, 645
Tut, King, 131-132
Twain, Mark, 378-379, 565, 569
Twelve Tables, 24, 58, 105, 251

V

Valentinians, 185
Valla, Lorenzo, 343
Van Gogh, Vincent, 390
Vanderbilts, 560
Venus de Milo, 54
Verdi, Giuseppe, 516
Verrazzano, Giovanni da, 97, 322, 419
Verrocchio, Andrea del, 310, 316, 318, 322, 346, 349, 414

Versailles Treaty, 505, 522
Vespasian, Emperor, 112-114, 116, 118-120, 122, 149-150, 167-168, 186, 190, 195, 199
Vespucci, Amerigo, 365-369, 371, 394
Vestal Virgins, 27, 75, 125
Victoria, Queen, 198
Vigiles Urbani (Roman police), 85
Virgil, 25-26, 51, 107-108, 194, 297, 298, 300-301, 338, 368
Virgilio, Giovanni del, 294-295, 299, 306
Volkogonov, Dimitri, 485
Volta, Alessandro, 561
Voltaire, 472-473, 478, 494-495
von Braun, Wernher, 268, 580-582, 596, 598, 697
von Däniken, Erich, 264-265
von List, Guido, 525

W

Wagner, Richard, 507-511, 516-517, 524
Wagner, Winifred, 510
Wallace, Alfred Russel, 477-478
Wallace, Chris, 669
Wallace, Henry, 604
Wallace, William, 561
Walter, Bruno, 516
Washington, George, 23-24, 33, 93, 102, 214, 271, 420, 422-424, 426-440, 447-448, 451-455, 459-460, 464, 466, 474, 555, 557, 673, 690, 696

Wedgwood, Emma, 477
Welles, Orson, 319, 599
Wells, H.G., 495, 496
Westinghouse, George, 565-567, 571
Whitman, Walt, 379
Wigner, Eugene, 576-577
Wilson, Woodrow, 496, 541, 554, 608, 696
Winfrey, Oprah, 628
Wise, Rabbi Stephen, 549
Wood, Ralph, 194
World Ice Theory, 524, 525
Wright brothers, 312

X

Xiaoping, Deng, 657
Xiuquan, Hong, 329

Y

Yahweh, 118-120, 130, 146, 178, 256, 692-693
Yamantau Mountain, 667
Yeshu, 138
Young, Thomas, 575
Yousef, Ramzi, 664, 666, 673

Z

Zakkai, Yohanan ben, 120, 124
Zeno, Emperor, 236
Zinoviev and Kamenev, 481-482

www.ingramcontent.com/pod-product-compliance
Lightning Source LLC
Chambersburg PA
CBHW021823090426
42811CB00032B/1996/J